D1603062

The Wayward Welfare State

The ★★★★★★★★★★★★★★★★★★★★★★★★★★★★★ Wayward Welfare State

Roger A. Freeman

Hoover Institution Press
Stanford University, Stanford, California

*The Hoover Institution on War, Revolution and Peace, founded at
Stanford University in 1919 by the late President Herbert Hoover,
is an interdisciplinary research center for advanced study on
domestic and international affairs in the twentieth century. The views
expressed in its publications are entirely those of the authors
and do not necessarily reflect the views of the staff, officers,
or Board of Overseers of the Hoover Institution.*

Hoover Press Publication 249

© 1981 by the Board of Trustees of the
  Leland Stanford Junior University
All rights reserved
International Standard Book Number: 8-8179-7491-1
Library of Congress Catalog Card Number: 81-81170
Printed in the United States of America

Second printing, 1982

To President Ronald W. Reagan

★★★★★★★★★★

Contents

List of Figures   ix
List of Tables in Text   xi
List of Tables in Appendix   xv
Preface   xvii
Technical Notes on Statistics   xxiii

1. *The Public Payroll:* Government as a Trough   *1*
The Expanding Bureaucracy   *2*
Productivity in Government   *12*
Governmental Pay   *33*
Government Pensions   *41*
Unionization in the Public Service   *46*

2. *Public Revenues:* Government as a Siphon   *55*
Taxation in a Federal System of Government   *62*
The American Tax System   *67*
Many Unhappy Returns: The Personal Income Tax   *74*
The Corporation Profits Tax   *95*
Consumption Taxes   *102*
The Social Security Tax   *106*
The Property Tax   *112*

3. *Public Expenditures:* Government as a Well   *122*
Upward Trends   *124*
A Declining Share for National Defense   *126*
A Shift from the Purchase of Goods and Services
    to Transfer Payments   *127*
Explosion in Spending for Domestic Purposes   *128*
A Policy Reversal in the Late 1970s?   *132*

Reordering National Priorities—Guns vs. Butter 134
How Much Defense Do We Need? 141
Military Manpower on the Downgrade 148
A Shift in the Military Balance: Can It Be Reversed? 149
Can the Budget Be Controlled? 151
Attempts at Budget Reform 157
Reforming the Congressional Budget Process 162

4. The Promise and the Harvest of the Welfare State 167
Federal Aid to State and Local Governments 169
The Input and the Output of the Welfare State 177
The Income and the Outcome of Education 181
The Alchemists in Our Public Schools 200
Income Support and the War on Poverty 209
Welfare's Snakepit—Aid to Dependent Children 215
How Secure Is Social Security? 232
Unemployment Compensation and the Unemployment Rate 245
Medical Services and Health 260
Crime Without Punishment 274
Housing Blight, City Plight and the Evanescence of
    Urban Revitalization 289
Civil Rights and Civil Wrongs: The Minorities Problem 318

5. Issues and Prospects 360
A Built-in Growth Trend? 364
The Protagonists of Governmental Expansion 373
The Failure of the Great Society and the Rise
    of the Neoconservatives 379
Redistributing Income 382
The War on Poverty and Other Great Society Escapades 393
Concentration of Power and Loss of Freedom 399
Judicial Supremacy vs. Government by the People 407
Two Decades to the Millenium? Prophecies, Projects
    and Prospects 417
Trends and Prospects 421
Twilight of the Welfare State? 434

Appendix 439
Notes 477
Index 505

★★★★★★★★

Figures

Chapter 1:   *The Public Payroll*

  1. Governmental Employment, by Function   10
  2. Increase in Governmental Employment, Domestic Functions   11
  3. Growth Rate in Patients and Employees of Hospitals   24
  4. Growth Rates in Salaries, Selected Categories   36
  5. Grade Creep Among Federal General Schedule Employees   40

Chapter 2:   *Public Revenues*

  6. Current Government Receipts and Expenditures in OECD
     Countries   61
  7. Governmental Revenues in the United States   63
  8. Sources of Governmental Revenues in the United States   67
  9. Types of Taxes Used in the USA and in OECD Countries   69
 10. Nontaxable Personal Income Tax Returns (as percent of all
     nontaxable returns)   79
 11. Nontaxable Personal Income Tax Returns (as percent of all
     returns in income bracket)   80
 12. Federal Personal Income Tax (percentage shares by income
     bracket)   80
 13. Federal Personal Income Tax (effective tax rate)   81
 14. Shares òf National Income   98
 15. Shares of Personal Income   99
 16. Social Security Tax on Employee, Selected Earnings Levels   109

Chapter 3: *Public Expenditures*

17. The Governmental Expenditure Dollar   126

Chapter 4: *The Promise and the Harvest of the Welfare State*

18. Rate of Increase in Public and Private (Personal) Consumption   169

★★★★★★★★★★★★★★★★★

Tables in Text

Chapter 1: *The Public Payroll*

Increase in Governmental Employment by Function, 1952 to 1978 (Federal, State, Local) 9

Enrollment and Employment in Public Education, 1952 and 1978 21

Average Daily Census and Personnel in Hospitals, 1952 and 1978 23

Growth in Average Life Expectancy Between 1949–51 and 1977, in Years 25

Number of Persons Surviving to Age 65 for Every One Thousand Born, 1949–51 and 1977 25

Wages and Salaries per Full-time Employee in Selected Categories in 1952 and 1978, in *Constant* 1978 Dollars 35

Average GS Grade in Selected Federal Agencies, 1952 and 1978 39

Chapter 2: *Public Revenues*

Growth of Governmental Revenues in Twenty-year Periods, as a Percentage of GNP, 1913 to 1978 56

Governmental Debt, 1952 and 1978 57

Types of Taxes as a Percentage of Total Taxation in OECD Member Countries in the Average of 1975–1977 68

Types of Taxes as a Percentage of Gross Domestic Product in OECD Member Countries in the Average of 1975–1977 68

Governmental Revenues, 1952–1978 74

Nontaxable Income Tax Returns by Income Brackets, 1977   78

Nontaxable Income Tax Returns as a Percentage
of All Returns, 1978   78

Shares of the Federal Income Tax by Major Income Brackets, 1977   82

Breakdown by Income Size of the Difference Between Adjusted
Gross Income and Taxable Income, 1977   87

Shares of National Income, 1952 and 1978   96

Shares of Corporation Income, 1952 and 1978   97

Shares of Personal Income, 1952 and 1978   97

Federal Revenues from Consumption Taxes, 1952 and 1978   103

Consumption Tax Revenues of State and Local Governments,
1978   105

Social Security Tax Increase on Employees at Selected Earnings
Levels under the 1977 Social Security Amendments   108

Property Taxes and National Tangible Wealth, 1902 and 1975   115

Effective Property Tax Rates on Single-Family Houses in Cities,
100,000 and over, 1976   119

Distribution of Property Tax Receipts Among Governments, 1978 120

Chapter 3: *Public Expenditures*

Governmental Expenditures (Federal, State, Local) in Percent of
GNP, 1902 to 1978   125

Governmental Expenditures (Federal, State, Local) by Function,
1952 and 1978   127

Types of Government Expenditures (Federal, State, Local), 1952
and 1978   128

Governmental Expenditures (Federal, State, Local) for Domestic
Purposes in 1952 and 1978   129

Allocation of Federal Expenditures Between "Traditional" and
Other Functions, Fiscal Years 1902, 1952 and 1978   132

Federal Expenditures by Major Functions, Fiscal Years 1969, 1975
and 1981   133

Change in Shares of Federal Expenditures by Major Functions,
Fiscal Years 1969, 1975 and 1981   134

National Defense Outlays, FY 1969 to 1983   135

Summary of Department of Defense Programs, 1969 and 1981   137

Uncontrollable Expenditure Items in FY 1971 and FY 1981   156

Chapter 4: *The Promise and the Harvest of the Welfare State*

Federal, State and Local Expenditures for Domestic Purposes, 1952 and 1978   168

Governmental Expenditures for Domestic Purposes, by Level of Government, 1952 and 1978   170

Federal Grants to State and Local Governments, by Major Functions, FY 1981   175

Selected Data on Public Education in 1952 and 1978   182

Estimated Lifetime Earnings from Age 18 to Death, 1972   190

SAT Scores and Parental Income, 1978–79   199

Income Support by Federal, State and Local Governments, 1952 and 1978   211

Population Under 18 Years in the Population and on AFDC, 1952 and 1978   218

Monthly Average OASDI Cash Benefits, 1940 to 1980   237

Examples of Monthly Cash Benefits Awards Under the Social Security Act   240

Average Overtime Hours   252

National Health Expenditures, 1952–1978   262

Consumer Price Index for Medical Care and Other Items   265

Expenditures for Police Protection (Federal, State, Local), 1952 to 1978   280

Additional Housing Units for Low-Income Families, U.S. Budget FY 1981   302

Median Money Income of Families by Ethnic Categories in Selected Years 1947 to 1978 in *Constant* (1978) dollars   322

Chapter 5: *Issues and Prospects*

Growth of Federal Outlays for Domestic Functions During Presidential Terms, 1952–78   368

Growth of Federal Nondefense Expenditures During Presidential Terms, 1960 to 1980   368

Governmental Nondefense Expenditures and Personal Consumption Expenditures 1929, 1952 and 1978   376

Distribution of Families, According to Money Income, 1955 and
1979, in *Constant* 1979 Dollars   387

Inflation Rate by Presidential Terms, 1952 to 1980   428

Gross National Product in *Constant* (1972) Dollars, Selected Years
1929–1979   433

★★★★★★★★★★★★★★★★★★★★★★★★★

Tables in Appendix

1. Governmental Revenues in the United States, 1902–1978 (by Level of Government)   440

2. Government Employment and Population, 1870–1978   441

3. Governmental Employment, Private Employment, and Population, 1952 and 1978   442

4. Governmental Expenditures in the United States, 1902–1978   443

5. Federal Expenditures, 1902–1978   444

6. Average Annual Earnings per Full-time Employee by Industry in Current and Constant Dollars, 1952 and 1978   445

7a. Governmental Employment by Level of Government, 1952–1978   446

7b. Governmental Employment by Level of Government, 1952–1978 (per 1000 Population)   448

8a. Governmental Employment by Function, 1952–1978   449

8b. Governmental Employment by Function, 1952–1978 (per 1000 Population)   451

9. Average Number of Full-time and Part-time Employees by Industry, 1952 and 1978   453

10. Comparison of Federal Salary Ranges Under the General Schedule, 1952 and 1978   454

11. Comparison of Federal Employee Average Salaries by General-Schedule Grades, 1952 and 1978   455

12. Grade Distribution by Major Groups of Federal General-Schedule Employees, 1952 and 1978   455

13. Public Employee Compensation and Retirement Benefits in 1952, 1968, and 1978   456

14. Governmental Revenues and Expenditures as a Percentage of Gross National Product, Net National Product, National Income, and Personal Income, 1952 and 1978   457

15. Current Government Receipts in OECD Member Countries in 1978 (As a Percentage of Gross Domestic Product)   458

16. Governmental Revenue From Own Sources, 1952 and 1978   459

17. Individual Taxes as a Percentage of GDP at Market Prices in OECD Member Countries (Average 1975–1977)   461

18. Individual Taxes as a Percentage of Total Taxation in OECD Member Countries (Average 1975–1977)   462

19a. Adjusted Gross Income, Taxable Income, and Effective Tax Rates on Federal Income Tax Returns, 1977   464

19b. Shares of Income and of Income Tax by Income Bracket on Federal Income Tax Returns, 1977   465

20. Current Government Expenditures in OECD Member Countries, 1978 (as a Percentage of Gross Domestic Product)   465

21. Federal Expenditures, 1952 and 1978   466

22. State and Local Expenditures, 1952 and 1978   468

23. Governmental Expenditures in the United States, 1952 and 1978   470

24. Federal Expenditures, 1952–1978   472

25. Governmental Expenditures in the United States, 1952–1978 (Federal, State, Local)   474

26. Public and Private Consumption, 1952 and 1978   476

★★★★★★★★

Preface

Government is not the solution to our problem; government is the problem. . . .

It is my intention to curb the size and influence of the federal establishment. . . .

President Ronald W. Reagan
Inaugural address, January 20, 1981

★ The term *welfare state* has in recent years acquired a negative, almost pejorative, connotation. For generations the dream of the future of the political left, the welfare state was first carried into reality by the political right. Otto von Bismarck established compulsory social insurance in the 1880s—to take the wind out of the sails of the socialists—and Winston Churchill during World War II commissioned Sir William Beveridge to design the first "cradle to grave" security plan, probably for reasons similar to Bismarck's. It seems an irony that both, Bismarck and Churchill, were driven from office not too long after they became patrons of the welfare state. For most of the past century, it was the political left which fought and bled for, established and expanded the major programs which constitute the building blocks of the welfare state. Its ideas were adopted and instituted in most industrial nations within half a century; over the succeeding fifty years they were also embraced by most of the less developed countries, in principle, if not always in economic reality.

It was its triumph of being nearly universally welcomed, adopted, and enormously expanded that made the welfare state a victim of its own success, brought about its troubles, its loss of luster and, through attitudinal and political changes in some Western countries, its fall from grace.

The exuberance of the 1960s in the United States visualized a multiplication and intensification of social programs as a certain and effective cure for nearly all social ills. It set out to attain the millennium well before the millennial year 2000. But it soon tripped along the rocky road. Initial enthusiasm promoted programs founded on noble but vastly exaggerated hopes and on ignorance or disregard of the reality of human nature. Unrealistic expectations were bound to be disappointed and by their failure generated unfavorable to hostile reactions. The welfare state was led astray by splendid intentions and daydreams which turned it into the *wayward welfare state,*[1] as I called it some years ago and now chose as the title of this volume.

The idea for this book originated in the mid-1960s. I had then been studying governmental problems such as taxes, education, welfare, the military, intergovernmental relations, and dealing with them, in the White House and at a governor's office, for about fifteen years. My responsibilities required me to focus on the broad aspects, on budget and economic policies, on priorities in resource allocation, on the potentials and consequences of major programs. After extensively writing in several of those fields, I decided to prepare a comprehensive treatment of public affairs.

I presented a paper "The Service State at the Midcentury" to the annual conference of the American Society for Public Administration (ASPA) in 1965 and subsequently rewrote it for the *National Review* (September 21, 1965). Early in 1966, I restructured and expanded the ASPA paper, at Seymour Harris' invitation, into a speech "Big Government—Friend or Foe?" which I delivered at the San Diego Open Forum. For that widely reprinted speech, the Freedoms Foundation at Valley Forge accorded me its George Washington Honor Medal Award as "an outstanding accomplishment in helping to achieve a better understanding of the American Way of Life." I prepared a new version of the theme in 1970 as keynote address for the annual conference of the Governmental Research Association. It was reprinted several times and earned a George Washington Honor Medal Award from the Freedoms Foundation for a summary in *The New York Times* of December 4, 1971.

I then received several suggestions to turn the paper into a comprehensive research project on "The Growth of American Government." Under that heading it was approved by the Hoover Institution on War, Revolution and Peace and occupied much of my time for several years. Urgent requests for special studies, reports, analyses, articles and speeches of current topical interest and periods of public service interfered and delayed completion.

The Growth of American Government was published by the Hoover Institution in 1975, was widely reviewed and received the Governmental Research Association's *Most Distinguished Research Award* for 1975.

The size of government and its rate of growth had not been much in the forefront of public interest prior to 1975 but were then beginning to attract increasing attention. After *Newsweek* filled the cover of its December 15, 1975, issue with the picture of a grotesquely bloated Uncle Sam, under the caption BIG GOVERNMENT, other media followed with extensive coverage and *Big Government* became a focal subject of the 1976 presidential campaign. It has remained in the center of interest ever since, with attitudes toward it, positive or negative, often serving as the dividing line between the ideological and political right and left.

Governmental expansion did not, as it sometimes seems, originate in the 1960s or 1950s, nor in the Great Depression of the 1930s. Scope and magnitude of governmental programs have been growing for a much longer time, as Solomon Fabricant so effectively demonstrated in *The Trend of Government Activity in the United States Since 1900*, a comprehensive analysis of the vast expansion in the size and function of government during the first half of the twentieth century.[2] His study was based on data from 1900 to 1949. M. Slade Kendrick, in *A Century and a Half of Federal Expenditures*, carried federal expenditure data historically back to 1789 and forward to 1952.[3] Fabricant as well as Kendrick found and reported a consistent upward trend in public spending and concluded that it would continue as far as one could see ahead.

The Growth of American Government is a critical analysis of governmental activities in the years 1952 to 1972, a period that covered developments from the later stages of the Korean War to the later stages of the Vietnam War.

After reprinting the volume several times, the Hoover Institution asked me in 1979 to bring the book up-to-date. I soon realized that a mere updating would not do. Too much happened in the intervening six years, in terms of programs, political changes, research studies and public attitudes. Moreover, I felt that several subjects now required a more thorough explanation and discussion than I had prepared in 1974. Above all, several issues that then seemed less important, and were barely mentioned, have since acquired great significance. New chapters and sections had to be written. In other words, this is an entirely new book, in title as well as substance. Its basic thesis has not changed but as the new title indicates, its emphasis has shifted further from a consideration of the magnitude of government to a critical review of the nature and consequences of its activities.

The charitable approach of the welfare state—the idea that government should help the less fortunate among its citizens cope with some of the major hazards of life, which demonstrably they cannot meet by alternative means without such aid—has been generally accepted. It is no longer controversial. Nor would anyone in a position of responsibility, now or in the foreseeable future, want to dismantle our social security system and its major components—or could if he tried. The system needs reform, not repeal. What is at issue is not the welfare state as such but the *wayward* welfare state.

In program after program, assistance to individuals who for manifest and tangible reasons were faced with insuperable problems, turned out to be the proverbial camel's nose in the tent. Definitions of need were broadened so as to include vastly larger numbers, to add political support to that of an initially narrow group of eligible recipients. Benefits were adjusted to attract a less than poorest-of-the-poor clientele. To labor at arduous or menial jobs became less necessary or urgent for unskilled persons of low-productive and therefore low-earning capacity. With the work ethic but a faint memory of bygone days, social problems multiplied exponentially—from family breakup to evasion of support responsibility and to all types of violent and property crime.

Increasingly, the welfare state shaped its tax and spending policies to pursue egalitarian ideas and made redistribution of income—from those who earn it to those who yearn it—its foremost goal. To punish effort and success and reward indolence and failure, even if not so intended, takes an inevitable toll on the growth potential of a dynamic economy. Other indirect effects of the wayward welfare state may have no less serious—and possibly more ominous—consequences. Ever more generous social benefits pushed government outlays up faster than the prevailing rate of economic growth. Between 1952 and 1978 aggregate governmental expenditures multiplied sevenfold, Gross National Product (GNP) sixfold. Inflation, caused by excessive public spending and resulting huge budgetary deficits meanwhile cut the purchasing power of the 1978 dollar to 40 cents of the 1952 dollar (by 1981 to 29 cents). Expressed in *constant* (price-adjusted) dollars, government expenditures multiplied 3.0 fold between 1952 and 1978, GNP 2.3 fold.

But this tells only part of the story. The federal government—disregarding for the moment state and local government outlays—expended in the early 1950s four times as much for national defense as for domestic services and benefits. In the late 1970s it was spending nearly three times as much for domestic functions as for defense. The share of national defense dropped from 49% of all governmental outlays (federal, state, local) in 1952 to 16% in 1978. The share of domestic outlays meanwhile doubled, from 38% to 76%.

Reduction to one-third of their former share in national resources has had a devastating impact on the ability of our Armed Forces to deal with emergencies, on their readiness to cope with broader challenges that may arise on short notice or none. America's military strength fell from unquestioned superiority a quarter century ago to a condition where in many or most respects it is inferior to the power the Soviet Union can array against us.

What did we get in return for a perilous weakening of our national security? A sixfold increase (*constant* dollars) in governmental spending for domestic functions between 1952 and 1978. That means that a population, 39% larger than it was a quarter century earlier, consumed 498% more in outlays for welfare, income maintenance, education, medical care and a myriad of other domestic services.

The past few decades have seen a drastic change in the nature of American government. Public opinion polls and elections suggest that a majority of the American people no longer favor the trends outlined above—if it ever did. There seems to be a broad national consensus that our defense capability needs to be significantly strengthened and the expansion of other major public programs restrained. The adjustment process will not be easy and may be painful. Expectations may change from the "soaring sixties" a couple of decades ago to the "sobering eighties." Whether the changes outlined above will actually take place within the critical next decade or two no one can foretell. I hope that this book may contribute to a better understanding of what has been happening in and to the United States over the past quarter century—and what could or may happen if we refuse to learn from the lessons of the past.

I am deeply grateful to W. Glenn Campbell, director of the Hoover Institution, for his interest in and unstinted support of the project, to Dennis L. Bark, deputy director, for guiding the manuscript through the publications department, to Richard T. Burress, associate director and chairman of the publications committee, and to those of my Hoover colleagues who reviewed chapters or sections of the manuscript and were helpful in offering suggestions, giving me advice and commenting on my ideas and their presentation. This includes especially Martin Anderson, Michael Block, Rita Ricardo-Campbell, Paul Hanna, Robert Hessen, Sidney Hook, Richard Muth, Fred Nold, Alvin Rabushka, Dan Throop Smith and Thomas Sowell. Benyam Mulugeta assisted me by extensive library research, statistical work and in many other ways, through much of the time this book was in preparation. Anna Boberg did most of the typing and proofing with her usual speed, precision, as well as library work, except for two months of world travel during which time Linda Sandham filled her place. Maria Jedd prepared the graphs with understanding and technical skill.

I owe thanks to all of them. Responsibility for the facts I present and for the opinion I express remains, of course, exclusively my own.

Stanford, California   Roger A. Freeman

★★★

Technical Notes on Statistics

★ Statistics on governmental revenues, expenditures and employment are prepared periodically by several departments of the federal government which use different concepts and definitions. The statistics therefore differ from each other and reviewers have to exert great care not to compare data from different sources or sometimes even from the same sources published in earlier or later years. For several decades the most widely used source of federal financial data was the *administrative budget*. But as the use of trust funds and the volume of their transactions grew, the administrative budget (which excludes trust fund operations) reflected a shrinking share of total federal transactions. So a second measure came into broader use, *cash payments to the public*, more commonly called the *cash-consolidated budget*. In fiscal year (FY) 1940 the difference between the adminisrative and the cash-consolidated budget amounted to only $0.5 billion, but in FY 1967 it totaled $29.4 billion: the administrative budget showed expenditures of $125.7 billion, the cash-consolidated budget of $155.1 billion. United States Treasury accounts reported outlays of $158.4 billion, the United States Bureau of the Census of $166.8 billion. The federal sector of the National Income and Product Accounts (NIPA) showed in 1967 the same total as the cash-consolidated budget: $155.1 billion. But that was a mere coincidence; in the preceding year the NIPA figure was $5.5 billion smaller, in the succeeding year $4.9 billion smaller than the cash-consolidated budget.

In 1968 a new concept was introduced, the *unified budget*, which differs from all the other measures and has been used as the standard presentation of the United States budget ever since 1969. Preparation of the administrative budget and the cash-consolidated budget were discontinued and data are not available for years after 1968. The unified budget was computed back (by function) only to 1959. Therefore, it is impossible to make historical comparisons with years prior to 1959 or subsequent to 1969 using some of the major budgetary yardsticks.

The tendency to "debudget" transactions, which reduced the comprehensiveness and impaired the usefulness of the administrative budget from the 1940s on and led to its replacement by the unified budget in 1968, has since affected the unified budget. Several operations are carried on through the "off-budget" Federal Financing Bank. That includes federal off-budget entities and designated activities of on-budget federal agencies. *Off-budget* are the Rural Electrification and Telephone Revolving Fund, certificates of the Farmers Home Administration, lending for low-rent public housing, the Student Loan Marketing Association, the U.S. Railway Association (Amtrak), the Postal Service Fund (but postal subsidies are included in the budget), etc. Off-budget expenditures were estimated at $16.8 billion for FY 1980, not counting government-sponsored enterprises at $16.4 billion. The Board of Governors of the Federal Reserve System is not included in the budget nor are the federal reserve banks which are regarded as privately owned though they carry out federal functions and are clothed with governmental authority. Great caution must therefore be exercised in making historical comparisons of federal expenditure data.

Unified budget data are presented in the president's budget, submitted to Congress in late January or early February, with final figures for the preceding fiscal year, estimates for the current fiscal year, the president's recommendations for the succeeding fiscal year, and projections for the two fiscal years after that. Thus the U.S. Budget for FY 1981 released on January 28, 1980, displayed final data for FY 1979, estimates for FY 1980, recommendations and estimates for FY 1981, and projections for FYs 1982 and 1983. But no comparisons can be made of those figures with U.S. budget data for years prior to 1959, nor are state and local fiscal data available consonant with the unified budget.

Bureau of the Census concepts have remained unchanged and statistics have been published annually since 1952; data are also available for selected years back to 1902. Not only are these statistics internally consistent, but they also are the most comprehensive data, and offer comparable information for state and local governments. The Bureau of the Census reports are the only source of comparable financial statistics for each state and major city and for other major units of local government. Bureau of the Census reports offer very valuable data, but are long in preparation. The report, *Governmental Finances in 1977/78*, was released in February 1980.

The Social and Economics Statistics Administration (SESA) of the

United States Department of Commerce publishes each year, in its *Survey of Current Business*, the National Income and Product Accounts (NIPA), which contains revenue and functional expenditure data on a *calendar* year basis for the federal government and a combined total for all state and local governments. (Consistent state-by-state, city, county, and other local government financial statistics can be found only in reports of the Bureau of the Census.)

SESA financial statistics are available back to 1952 and are published annually in July for the preceding calendar year.[1] They are very useful for historical comparisons, as far as they go. There are conceptual and magnitudinal differences between SESA, unified budget and Census and caution must be used in making comparisons. For example, federal expenditures for the four fiscal years 1975 through 1978 totaled $1,546 billion in the unified budget, $1,623 billion according to SESA, $1,644 billion according to Census. Four-year totals from SESA were 5.0% higher than from the unified budget which varied from 9.4% in one year to 2.0% in another. Census prepared the most comprehensive tabulation which was 1.3% higher than SESA for the four-year total, varying from plus 4.2% in one year to minus 4.3% in another. Long-range comparisons reflect roughly parallel trends.

Employment statistics from SESA, the U.S. Bureau of Labor Statistics and the U.S. Bureau of the Census are not directly comparable with each other; historical and other comparisons should be made only with data from the same source and within the same series. It should be kept in mind that employment and most economic statistics are retroactively revised by the originating departments at unspecified intervals and that older sources do not always tie in with current series.

Many of the statistical tables and historical comparisons in this volume are based on the period 1952 to 1978. The year 1978 was chosen because it was the most recent year for which comprehensive financial data were available during preparation of the tables; it still was, in December 1980. Wherever relevant and available, data for 1979 or 1980 were used to bring information as closely up-to-date as possible.

The choice of 1952 as a starting year of the twenty-six year period was governed partially by technical factors: it is the earliest year for which governmental financial data are available from the national income accounts. Also, it made consistent decennial series possible because censuses of government were taken in each year ending with 2 (except in 1913 instead of 1912). Such information is therefore available from census sources only for years ending in 2, prior to the initiation of *annual* census surveys in 1952.

It is of concern that 1952 was in some respects not a "normal" year.

Neither were 1932 nor 1942. For that matter, it is difficult or impossible to define and identify a year that is "normal" in all or most respects and to prepare a time series with steady intervals. 1952 coincided with the later stages of the Korean war, following unilateral U.S. disarmament in 1947–1950. But the possible military challenges with which the United States may be faced in the 1980s, the armed might that could threaten the nation in the years ahead, is far greater than it was in 1952.

The fact that we selected 1952 as the starting year for some of the basic statistical tables does not imply that it should be regarded as a standard or norm, for defense or domestic expenditures. No year establishes a standard for the future because conditions and requirements differ from year to year and must be individually evaluated. Comparisons between 1952 and 1978 merely portray changes that took place over the most recent quarter century—or, to be exact, twenty-six year period—for which sufficient statistical data were available.

Financial comparisons over long periods of time have become misleading in recent years if totals are expressed in current dollars. The 1978 dollar buys only what 40 cents bought in 1952; the 1980 dollar buys only the equivalent of 32 cents in 1952. For meaningful comparisons therefore dollars must be converted into *constant*, i.e., price-adjusted dollars.

Some economists prefer the *implicit price deflator for GNP* which is available for a number of several separate categories. But the use of more than one conversion factor, useful though it can be for specific purposes, is confusing to the public. The 151-page rules of the Financial Accounting Standards Board for the inflation adjustment of corporate financial data, announced in October 1979, have generated widespread controversy among experts and for some may have confused the picture more than clarified.

The index most widely used for inflation adjustments is the Consumer Price Index (CPI) monthly computed by the Bureau of Labor Statistics. The CPI has shortcomings, as has every other conceivable index. For general purposes and wide acceptance CPI beats all alternatives. That it is criticized by recipients of escalated income as too low, and by payers as too high is not surprising.

The use of the CPI for the escalation of wages (in collective bargaining and the U.S. Civil Service), social benefits, rents, retirement annuities, child-support payments, food stamps, and for dozens of other purposes has become so widespread that the CPI has been almost universally accepted as a measure of inflation. Above all, the public understands what the CPI means.

Wherever it seemed advisable to present historical comparisons on a *constant* dollar basis, the CPI was used in this volume for the necessary adjustment of current dollar totals.

There is no uniform fiscal year in the United States; in fact, it is less uniform now than it was five years ago. The United States government from its founding to 1976 used a fiscal year beginning July 1. So do most—but not all states, school districts and many other local governments. But many cities use a calendar year for their accounting and financial reporting. Congressional budget reform changed the beginning of the federal fiscal year from July 1 to October 1 from 1976 on, in what proved to be a vain attempt to make the federal budget process more rational and effective.

In relating financial data based on a fiscal year to Gross National Product (GNP) which is reported by calendar years, we tried to compute GNP for the appropriate fiscal year by averaging calendar quarters, when available, or the two years involved for the period before quarterly economic data became available. The Office of Management and Budget has recently been computing a fiscal-year GNP, based on the October to September fiscal year established in 1977.

Calendar year financial totals were related to calendar year GNP in this book.

1 ★★★★★★★★★★★★★★★★★★★★★

The Public Payroll
Government as a Trough

★ On the face of it, the role of government in employment has remained remarkably stable over the past quarter century—contrary to a widely held belief that public payrolls—the government bureaucracy—expanded disproportionally during that period. Here is the record:

Governments (federal, state, local) accounted for 18.9% of *all* employment in the United States in 1952 and for 19.1% in 1978. In terms of payroll, that is the amount of wages paid, government's role inched up from 18.0% to 19.8% of the U.S. total.[1] Government's wage bill meanwhile went from $33 billion to $218 billion which, in *constant* dollars, means an increase of 166% compared with a wage bill increase of 137% in private business. Slightly more rapid growth in the government wage cost consisted of two factors:

a) Employment, expressed in terms of full-time equivalent employees, grew 56.6% in government, 54.5% in the private sector.

b) Average wage per full-time employee grew (in *constant* dollars) 70% in government, 55% in private business. This means that the government worker was 6% behind his colleague in private employment in 1952, 4% ahead of him in 1978. In the latter year the government worker averaged $13,758, the privately employed worker $13,263.

On first glance it thus appears that government employment and private employment moved at almost parallel rates in the past quarter century with a slight improvement in public compensation. But, as so often, the overall total serves more to hide the crucial facts than to disclose them. Overall governmental employment growth of 56.5% consisted of a 37% *cut* in national defense manpower (41% percent in the Armed Forces and 27 percent in the Department of Defense) and a 154% increase in nondefense jobs. This means that the number of persons administering domestic *public* functions grew nearly three times faster than the number of people producing *private* goods and services. Most of the growth in domestic functions was offset by cuts in manpower for national defense so that the share of government in total employment remained almost stable.

The Expanding Bureaucracy

There is one person working for government for every 4.5 employees in private industry producing the multitude of goods and services needed, used and consumed by 226 million Americans or exported. The 18 million persons drawing their wages from public sources and their families possess a significant voting power, which they use to exercise influence on hiring and pay decisions by the legislative and executive branches of the governments they serve. It is becoming increasingly difficult for officials in either branch of government to vote against higher pay for public workers. This was clearly shown by the ease with which Congress in September 1974 overrode President Ford's decision to postpone federal pay hikes for three months. It was again demonstrated in August 1979 when President Carter, after proposing a 5.5% federal pay boost in his 1980 budget—and vowing to stay with it as part of his anti-inflation program—was pressured into accepting a 7% federal pay hike at an additional cost of about $1 billion.

With about one person in every four in the United States now obtaining most of his or her livelihood through workless pay from one or several social welfare programs, it is evident that taxpayers are confronted by a powerful voting bloc with a direct and vital stake in pushing government services to ever higher levels. To be sure, a coalition of government workers and welfare recipients does not, as a rule, command a voting majority, except in some of our urban communities. But those groups tend to be better organized than the general taxpaying public and with the help of ideological allies they often succeed in electing to office candidates who will fight for their economic interest by expanding redistributive government programs.

Most Americans, if asked where the greatest increase in governmental employment has taken place, will probably reply "in the federal government." In fact, the whole debate about soaring public payrolls has been carried on largely in terms of the national government. In his widely quoted *Fortune* (May 7, 1979) article "Why Bureaucracy Keeps Growing," Tom Alexander and the experts he quoted focused exclusively on the federal bureaucracy. But this is not where disproportionate growth has taken place.

Between 1952 and 1978 federal civilian employment increased by 12% while the U.S. population grew 39%. *This means that the number of federal civilian employees per 1,000 population declined from 16.4 in 1952 to 13.2 in 1978. What did grow enormously was state and local government employment—from 4.5 million to 12.7 million which amounts to an increase of 182 percent.* For whatever reason, however, public attention seems to concentrate more on the 350,000 boost in federal payroll than on the 8.2 million jump in state and local government jobholders.

This modest increase in federal employment over the past quarter century—actually a decline in relative terms—stands in strong contrast to developments in the first half of the twentieth century when federal employment multiplied ten times while the United States population merely doubled. That strong concentration of public interest on the federal payroll was a powerful factor in keeping the federal payroll low. Presidents and members of Congress repeatedly urged and exercised restraint in hiring and then pointed with pride at their achievement in keeping federal employment under tight control.[2] Every president since Eisenhower has imposed ceilings on federal employment.

The size of the government bureaucracy has always been politically a most sensitive issue in the United States. It goes back to grievances in the Declaration of Independence that King George III had "erected a multitude of new offices, and sent . . . swarms of officers to harass our people and eat out their substance."

Similar charges are still frequently being levied—most commonly by conservatives or by the party out of power—because they seem to feel that there is a direct relationship between the size of the federal bureaucracy and the power it exercises. Eugene C. Pulliam, publisher of several major newspapers, began his oft-copied speech, "Will the Federal Bureaucracy Destroy Individual Freedom in America?," as follows: "The most serious threat to freedom in America today—including freedom of the press—comes from a Federal bureaucracy which seems determined to gain control over every facet of American life."[3] The Republican Coordinating Committee preambled its *Declaration on Economy and Efficiency in Government* in January 1967 (when the Republican party was out of office) thus: "The Federal Government has become a bureaucratic jungle, rampant with overlapping, duplication and waste. A major carefully planned effort to review Executive branch programs and their administration is urgently needed. Such a study must be followed up by an active program to press for meaningful reorganization and reform."

Politically conscious presidents have always been very much aware of the traditional American dislike for a large bureaucracy. In his first budget message in January 1964, President Johnson wrote:

> Although both our population and our economy are growing and placing greater demands upon the Government for services of every kind, I believe the time has come to get our work done by improving the efficiency and productivity of our Federal work force, rather than by adding to its numbers.
>
> This budget proposes a reduction in Federal employment in 1965— from 2,512,400 to 2,511,200 civilian employees—and I have directed the heads of all departments and agencies to work toward reducing employment still further. This reversal in the trend of Federal employment results from a rigorous appraisal of personnel needs, determined measures to increase employee productivity and efficiency, and the curtailment of lower priority work. It will be accomplished despite large and unavoidable increases in workloads.

One year later President Johnson's budget message declared:

> The result of such efforts has been and will continue to be a reduction in the size of the Federal work force relative to the work being accomplished. The effectiveness of these controls may be seen in the fact that had Federal employment kept its 1955 relationship to total population, Federal employees would have totalled 2,747,000 on June 30, 1964, more than 275,000 above the actual number as of that date.

President Johnson's statements were correct. The number of federal civilian employees per 1000 population had declined from 14.3 in 1955 to 13.2 in 1964 and stood at 13.3 in 1965. But at that point the trend was reversed. In 1966 there were 14.6 federal civilian employees per 1000 population, in 1967 15.0, in 1968 14.9 Not surprisingly, there was no further reference to federal work force reductions in President Johnson's budget messages after 1965. In the second half of the 1960s federal civilian employment rose from 2.5 million to 3 million. Part of this was due to additions in the Department of Defense, related to stepped-up action in Vietnam—something President Johnson had not foreseen in 1964–65 when he proposed "a substantial reduction in total civilian employment in the Executive Branch" and directed agency heads to make strenuous efforts to cut staffs and set agency ceilings. But much of the growth originated in new and enlarged social programs which President Johnson succeeded in pushing through Congress (a policy of "guns *and* butter").[4]

Disturbed by a 400,000 jump in federal civilian employment between 1965 and 1967, Congress directed government agencies in 1968 (in a bill imposing a 10 percent income tax surcharge) to fill no more than three of every four vacancies in permanent jobs until employment was reduced to the level of June 30, 1966. These and similar attempts were continued by the Nixon administration and the federal civilian payroll dropped 200,000 between 1969 and 1972. But all of this came from cuts in the Department of Defense while other (civilian) departments' staffs slowly crept up throughout the 1970s. Altogether, Department of Defense employment was cut 385,000 between 1969 and 1978 while the other agencies added 304,000.

In his 1976 campaign President Carter promised that he would as his "first piece of legislation" send to Congress a proposal to reduce the number of federal agencies from 1900 to no more than 200 "with a great savings in tax money."

As Governor of Georgia Mr. Carter had reduced the number of state agencies from 300 to 22 and then claimed that he had cut administrative costs by 50%. But the number of Georgia state employees and the size of expenditures went up during his administration. Georgia State Auditor Ernest Davis could find no administrative savings by the Carter administration. The agencies that were abolished were those which had been dormant for years, while the rest of the administrative reorganization consisted of mergers which saved little.

It was clear to all familiar with the Washington scene that there never was a chance to cut the number of federal agencies substantially, let alone from 1900 to 200, and that even if such an approach were attempted it was not likely to save much money. Federal organizations tend to be "immortal" and few federal programs ever are permitted to expire without being replaced by some other, and usually more expensive program.[5]

In 1977 President Carter won approval from Congress for a four-year renewal of the *Reorganization Act of 1949* which Congress had permitted to lapse during Mr. Nixon's incumbency. It gave the President authority to reorganize executive agencies, subject to Congressional veto. Mr. Carter used that authority sparingly and did little to reduce the number of federal agencies. He split the near-century-old Civil Service Commission into two offices and created two new cabinet departments (Energy and Education).

Mr. Carter apparently realized not long after he became President the political impossibility of drastically cutting the number of federal agencies. In sending his proposal on civil service reform to Congress on March 2,

1978, he called it "the centerpiece of governmental reorganization during my term in office." It contained little related to agency consolidation and the campaign promise was never mentioned again.

In the *Civil Service Reform Act of 1978* Congress limited the number of jobholders in the executive branch (excepting the Postal Service) at the end of fiscal years 1979, 1980 and 1981 to the actual level on September 30, 1977, giving the President authority to raise the ceiling by the percentage of U.S. population growth. Population has been rising at about 0.8% annually in recent years which would restrict growth in the job rolls to about 17,000 a year. The President on October 25, 1978, ordered an immediate limitation on federal hiring to half of the vacancies occurring after that date. On the whole, Mr. Carter, as some of his predecessors, kept federal civilian employment stable or barely rising. However, employment ceilings led to an expanded use of consultants.[6]

Unfortunately, those widely publicized efforts by several presidents and the Congress to put restraints on expansion in the governmental bureaucracy were more cosmetic than real. They were accompanied by simultaneous actions which drove state and local government employment to dizzy heights.

Most of the social programs enacted or enlarged in recent decades— and in fact most domestic functions of government with a few exceptions such as the postal service and social security—are administered through state and local governments. That helps to maintain the myth of continued respect for state autonomy and local home rule while hiding the federal takeover and control of virtually all governmental programs in the United States.

Federal aid to state and local governments soared from $2.6 billion in 1952 to $79 billion in 1978—estimated at $96 billion in the 1981 budget—and the number of such programs, most of them federally controlled to minute detail, jumped from a few dozen to about 500. But the persons who administer those programs—save for the top command—are statistically classified as "state and local government employees" and therefore excluded from statistics of federal employment.

What this all means is that the Washington mirror fight about controlling the size of the governmental bureaucracy is a fraud and deception. It is being won largely by the statistical trick of omitting most of those who for all practical purposes are federal employees.

National Journal (May 5, 1979) estimated "Uncle Sam's Army of Invisible Employees" at 8 million, or about three times the size of *direct* federal employment.

U.S. News & World Report (February 18, 1980) also estimated "U.S. Government's 'Invisible Workers'" at 8 million: five million in jobs created in state and local governments by federal funds and three to four million hired through private contractors. Former HEW Secretary Joseph Califano told Congress that while his department carried a payroll of 145,000 in 1978 it actually supported another 656,700 in state and local governments, 121,100 at universities and research institutions and 202,800 with private contractors and others. Consultants and part-time workers are being used to an increasing extent to circumvent official employment ceilings.

At the top level, in Congress and the presidency, the use of such statistical tricks is sometimes not quite as easy. That is why Congress wisely exempted itself from job limitations and ceilings. Its staff quadrupled—from 5,000 to 20,000 over the past quarter century. To accommodate that work force the Senate is, at this writing, constructing its third office building and the House is planning to add a fourth to its existing three huge office complexes. That Congress is now enacting fewer laws than it did two to three decades ago will by some be regarded as a manifestation of Parkinson's Law. Others may count the enactment of fewer laws an unmixed blessing.

The White House has long engaged in various devices to make its staff appear smaller than it is. Extensive "detailing" of persons on the payroll of other federal agencies was supposed to have been eliminated years ago but was going on through the 1970s. Congress was told in 1979 that the White House staff had been reduced by 134 persons. But at least half of them were simply shifted to a newly established Office of Administration, doing what they had been doing right along.

In August 1978 Congress passed a bill limiting the number of top-level White House staff—at almost twice the number then occupying such positions. The fact is that the number and scope of federal activities and programs have tremendously expanded and, with numerous other proposals in the hopper and promised to special constituencies by their sponsors, the workload of Congress and the presidency is growing—and so is the staff necessary to cope with it, openly or in disguise.

There are several reasons for faster job growth at the state and local level. For one, state and local expenditures multiplied 12 times between 1952 and 1978, federal outlays only 6.5 times. Also, federal activities have shifted increasingly from performing services to distributing money. Federal transfer payments—that is payments to individuals for income support—jumped from $37 billion in 1969 to $232 billion in 1981. Federal payments to state and local governments went from $20 billion in 1969 to $95 billion in 1981. These two items alone now account for half the U.S. budget. At the federal level this is personnelwise an efficient operation, largely the preparation and mailing of checks totaling over $300 billion.

State and local activities require far more "groundwork," dealing with individuals.

Had the purpose of Congress and the President on restraining governmental employment been to save money, their concern and their actions would have had to include not only federal but also state and local positions, which are at least partially paid from federal funds. Federal payments to state and local governments totaled $95 billion in 1981, approximately equal to the entire federal payroll of $91 billion. They accounted for about one-fourth of all state and local revenues. Moreover, state and local taxes are paid by American taxpayers just as federal taxes are. But congressional action has for some years been deliberately boosting the size of state and local government payrolls even beyond enacting social programs. Those employment programs generally aim at providing jobs for low-skilled persons who cannot find jobs in the market because the wages they would have to be paid are higher than the value of their work. Also, their earning capacity often does not equal potential income from welfare.

A few small federal programs to boost state and local government employment were begun in the 1960s but when Congress enacted the *Comprehensive Manpower Act of 1970*, President Nixon vetoed it, commenting that WPA type programs were not the answer to unemployment. Less than a year later, however, Mr. Nixon yielded and signed the *Emergency Employment Act of 1971*, the largest government employment program since the 1930s. It was scheduled to expire in two years and Mr. Nixon wanted to let it lapse. However, Congress insisted on the *Comprehensive Employment and Training Act of 1973* (CETA) which the president finally signed. An enlargement by Congress in 1975 was vetoed by President Ford.

CETA was extended in 1978 for another four years at an annual cost of about $4 billion not counting over $2 billion youth employment programs which were extended in 1977.

Here is the result of a policy of restraining hiring at the federal level while promoting it in state and local government:

Federal civilian employment remained perfectly stable: 2,881,000 in 1970; 2,888,000 in 1978, an increase of only 7,000 jobs in eight years. State and local government payrolls meanwhile jumped from 8,582,000 in 1970 to 10,724,000, an increase of 2,142,000, for an annual average of 274,000.[7] About two-fifths of the state and local job growth was in education. The number of jobholders in public education increased by almost one million, or 22 percent, between 1970 and 1978 although student enrollment did not increase at all.

The growth of public employment can be understood more clearly by dividing employment along functional lines rather than by level of government. A functional breakdown in Table 8a shows that governmental employment between 1952 and 1978 jumped by 7,051,000—which consisted of a reduction of 1,830,000 (= 37%) in national defense and an increase of 8,881,000 (= 154%) in domestic fields. The rate of growth over the 26-year period was: in education 250%, in health and hospitals 168%, in police protection 171%, in all other fields combined 91%.

INCREASE IN GOVERNMENTAL EMPLOYMENT BY FUNCTION, 1952 TO 1978
(FEDERAL, STATE, LOCAL)

	Increase in Thousands	Increase in Percent	Distribution of Increase in Domestic Functions Percent
Total	+ 7,051	+ 66%	
National Defense	−1,830	− 37	
Armed Forces	−1,475	− 41	
Department of Defense and International Relations	− 355	− 26	
Domestic Functions	+ 8,881	+ 154	100.0%
Education	+ 4,702	+ 250	52.9
Health and Hospitals	+ 990	+ 168	11.2
Police Protection	+ 435	+ 171	4.9
Highways	+ 128	+ 28	1.4
Postal Service	+ 125	+ 24	1.4
Natural Resources	+ 223	+ 76	2.5
All Other	+ 2,278	+ 130	25.7

SOURCE: Table 8a.

Well over one-half of the increase in governmental employment between 1952 and 1978 was accounted for by education, 69% of the total by the three services that were most loudly claimed to suffer from personnel shortages: education, health and hospitals and police protection. These are also the functions which recorded by far the highest *rates* of increase. In each of these fields, the growth in the size of the staff greatly exceeded the growth rate in the size of the clientele (students, patients, etc.). Obviously

FIGURE 1.

GOVERNMENTAL EMPLOYMENT, BY FUNCTION

1952 to 1978

per 1000 population

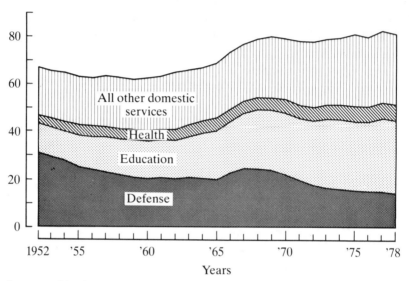

Source: table 8b

they were not fields on which official efforts to restrain public payrolls focused.

It is clear that the real growth in government employment over the past quarter century was not due to the addition of an extraordinary number of federal bureaucrats in Washington but to the growing number of "street-level bureaucrats" in state and local governments in social and other domestic services, particularly education, health and hospitals, and police. This is why determined and repeated efforts to cut the public payroll through administrative reorganization—thereby saving taxes—have not been very successful. Structural reshuffling or consolidation of agencies may at times be advisable. But it is not likely to make a major impact on the size of the public payroll, which is set largely by the nature and scope of domestic public programs.

This was pointed out well by Rowland Egger three decades ago:

> The attempt to sell administrative reorganization legislation on the basis of tax reduction, however honorable the motives and however laudable

FIGURE 2.

INCREASE IN GOVERNMENTAL EMPLOYMENT, DOMESTIC FUNCTIONS
1952 to 1978
Total increase: 8,881,000

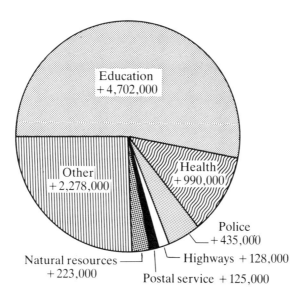

the hopes of those who support administrative reorganization for this
reason, is a snare and a delusion. . . . Administrative reorganization per se
has never saved large sums of money. . . . The plain fact is that the only
way to save significant sums of money in the federal establishment is to
eliminate activities and reduce the scale of operations. . . . There is no
royal road, no painless way, to governmental economy.[8]

*In other words, if taxpayers' money is to be saved by limits on governmental
employment, it will have to be done largely by restraint on public programs
and their nature, scope, and intensity. Congressional and presidential ceilings on
federal employment may be good publicity stunts but they yield few benefits to
taxpayers unless accompanied by tight ceilings on state and local government
employment—which are unlikely without restraints on the programs themselves.* This does not mean that the growth in administrative costs could
not be slowed down by increased efficiency, by efforts to increase governmental productivity.

Productivity in Government

The concept of productivity has long been established in economic activities. It expresses the ratio of input to related output, in other words, the ratio of resources used to goods and services produced. The value of the input can usually be determined because most of its ingredients must be paid for. The output of private business is sold in the market at a price acceptable to buyer and seller and its value can also be determined. But how do we value the type of output that is not sold? Most public services are not sold to individual consumers at a price but "given away." That is why national economic accounting generally values government services—the government "product"—at its cost, that is, wages paid and goods purchased.[9] Therefore, input equals output. This means that while productivity and its changes in time can be measured in private business, there is no such overall measurement for government.

Productivity in the private business sector grew at an average annual 2.4% rate between 1952 and 1978, slightly faster in the 1950s and 1960s, somewhat more slowly in the 1970s. Output per man-hour increased 85% between 1952 and 1978 in the private sector.

Has government productivity also grown, and if so, how much? Nobody knows. No gauge has yet been found by which we can measure the value of the services which government performs for the public. Therefore, there is no overall measurement of government productivity or its changes over time. That does not mean that there is no way by which productivity in governmental functions can be evaluated or its progress or lack thereof ascertained. But it is a very laborious process of studying each service to arrive at valid or even tentative findings.

There have been sporadic efforts over the years to develop yardsticks of productivity in government. Many of them were undertaken for the purpose of developing impartial aids to executive and legislative decision making on governmental spending proposals, the setting of authorizations and appropriations for specific programs. Some of these efforts were motivated by a wish either to justify or to criticize existing or desired levels of appropriations for public services.

At a Symposium on Productivity in Government at Wingspread, Wisconsin, May 15–16, 1972, cosponsored by The Johnson Foundation and the University of Wisconsin Graduate School of Business, diverse views were aired: "There is a widespread feeling that government—from the little neighborhood school to the most sprawling federal agency—is doing too many things too poorly at too high a price."[10] Charges were levied at waste, mismanagement, bureaucratic empire building, and archaic civil service rules that cripple efficiency.[11] Other participants, however, "warned that over-zealous pursuit of economy and efficiency could endanger some of the nobler purposes of government—such as enhancing justice and equity." It was said that "when efficiency increases, social goals may suffer."

A follow-up conference, five years later, showed some activity but little progress.[12] Papers for that symposium demonstrated "that advances indeed have occurred. But the general tone is somber and guarded for a number of reasons." Jesse Burkhead and Patrick J. Hennigan of Syracuse University summarized:[13]

> In the 1972 *Public Administration Review* symposium on government productivity, Edward K. Hamilton commented that: "The public is now assailed by more irrelevant facts, half facts, and non-facts on this subject than on any issue in public affairs." It would be comforting to report that in the intervening five years issues have been clarified, concepts uniformly defined, academics and practitioners have come to agreement, and productivity improvements have been registered in federal, state, and local governments. Unfortunately, the entire subject seems to be in greater and greater disarray.

Early in the 1960s the Bureau of the Budget tried to explore the potential for constructing overall productivity indexes in five major governmental agencies, but the undertaking gradually fizzled out. Nor has PPBS, the Planning, Programming, Budgeting System, which for many years was hailed as the bright hope of bringing greater rationality, efficiency and more sophisticated decision making on public spending, produced the promised and expected results. Many of its former spokesmen and supporters have become thoroughly disillusioned.

Ratios of work load to staff are available or can be prepared in many fields of activity and often may give at least a rough indication of productivity trends over time. But the quality of the service is far harder to measure and such evaluations are frequently influenced by the commentator's friendly or critical attitude toward the goals, means or methods of the program under review. Therefore, many evaluations in terms of approaching or reaching program goals are based on general observations, are subjective, and often highly controversial.

In 1970 Senator William Proxmire, as chairman of the Joint Economic Committee of Congress, asked the U.S. Comptroller General to have prepared a comprehensive evaluation of the possibilities for measuring productivity in the federal sector of the economy. The report, dated August 4, 1972, stated that while many agencies were making use of work measurement data there was little use of overall productivity measures.[14]

A survey of seventeen federal agencies found related activities in 114 organizational units covering about half the work force. It concluded that techniques have been developed by which productivity trends could be measured covering between 55 and 60 percent of the federal civilian employees. The study group found that in the participating public services—numerically dominated by the postal service—productivity had increased 3.4 percent in the four-year period 1967–1971. As usual in reports of this type the group suggested that further efforts and studies be undertaken.

In a follow-up report submitted December 17–18, 1973, the Comptroller General, as chairman of the study group, told the congressional committee that the survey now covered 187 organizational elements in forty-five agencies with 1.7 million man-years of employment. A six-year sample (1967–1972) "showed annual rates of productivity improvement which varied from 1.1 percent to 2.8 percent with an average annual gain of 1.7 percent."[15] They found that mechanization was the dominant factor behind productivity gains in industrial and manufacturing operations and that computerization of clerical operations had a major impact.

A subsequent survey covering about 1.7 million man-years or 61 percent of the employment in the federal civilian government in 200 units spanned the fiscal years 1967–1973. It reported an average annual productivity gain of 1.6 percent, which within sixteen functional groups ranged from −2.4 percent (for standard printing) to +5.8 percent (for power and general support activities).[16] The postal service averaged an annual gain of 1.3 percent, agriculture and natural resources 2.0 percent, while medical services showed a decline of 0.7 percent. This compares with a productivity gain of 3.1 percent in the entire private economy, 5.8 percent in farming, 2.6 percent in nonfarming.

The Joint Financial Management Improvement Program, an interagency task force headed by the General Accounting Office, reported in 1976 that the measured portion of the federal work force improved its productivity by an average of 1.3 percent between 1967 and 1975. Although federal budget instructions call for productivity data in agency budget justifications, the actual use in the budget process has been spotty.

In 1970 the President established a National Commission on Productivity, which was renamed National Commission on Productivity and Work Quality in 1974 and was succeeded under a 1975 act of Congress by a National Center for Productivity and Quality of Working Life. Despite this evident high-level interest in productivity, progress has been disappointing. A conclusion at the November 1976 Symposium on Productivity in Government was that "the National Center for Productivity and Quality of Working Life has not lived up to the high hopes that many had for it when it was organized."[17]

Congressional hearings on productivity in the federal sector were held in February and March 1978.[18] The U.S. Comptroller General, the Executive Director of the Congressional Budget Committee and others testified extensively on the extent and use of productivity measurements, their validity and usefulness, and incentives for cooperation to managers and employees and their unions. Though the sentiment expressed generally favored productivity studies, it became apparent that this is a very complicated and difficult as well as controversial subject which requires custom-tailored approaches to most of the hundreds of federal agencies and that we are still a long ways from a meaningful overall yardstick. Encouraging as these efforts may be, they are only preliminary steps toward a comprehensive measurement of productivity in government.

Work-load data and their relationship to manpower and expenditures have been used for many years in the budgetary process, by administrative departments to justify their appropriation requests and by the Budget Office and congressional committees to evaluate these requests. Work-load data—the ratio of work units to employees—are of course not a definite measure of productivity without much additional information. A tax collection agency, for example, could reduce its staff to just a few clerks who deposit the checks which arrive in the mails but engage in no enforcement activities. It would show an extremely high ratio of tax returns to staff—and a very low administrative cost when related to receipts. But this would not be an efficient method of tax collection, of getting as nearly as possible all the money that taxpayers owe under the law. Nor would a welfare agency be efficient which accepted claims without investigation of entitlement and paid claims indefinitely without periodic checkups.

Here are work-load and background data on a few departments (from the *U.S. Budget, Statistical Abstract* and departmental reports):

Postal employment grew by one-fourth over the past quarter century while the volume of mail nearly doubled. More specifically, the number of items handled grew from 50 billion to 97 billion between 1952 and 1978 (= +94%) while the staff increased from 525,000 to 650,000 (= +24%). This means that the number of mail pieces per employee went up from 95,000 in 1952 to 149,000 in 1978 (= +57%). Improvement was gradual but not at an even pace. Between 1952 and 1960 the number of pieces handled by the average employee grew from 95,000 to 112,000; in the succeeding decade they barely moved—inching up from 112,000 to 117,000. In 1970 the Postal Reorganization Act transformed the cabinet-level Post Office Department into the U.S. Postal Service, a semi-independent division of the Executive Branch. Within a few years the Postal Service installed about $1.2 billion worth of machinery, mechanized procedures and boosted the mail volume per employee from 117,000 in

1970 to 149,000 in 1978. Is this a satisfactory result, an adequate return on the investment? More thorough studies would be required to yield a firm answer. The Postal Service claims that its delivery has improved, that 95% of the scheduled overnight delivery mail now arrives on time, compared with 90% a few years back. However, complaints about slow service seem to be as frequent and as vocal as ever.

The Postal Service is highly unionized and raised its compensation faster than the rest of the federal establishment.[19] It also boosted rates—first-class letters from 6 cents to 15 cents between 1968 and 1978—a 150% boost in a period when the Consumer Price Index climbed 88%. As a result, postal operations were in the black in FY 1979 for the first time after more than three decades of deficits. This may have been a short-lived improvement. More deficits may be in the offing, as more efficient private services make inroads on the postal monopoly.

Under the reorganization act, the Postal Service is to be largely financed from user charges, with the federal subsidy constituting payment for federal mail carried for free or at reduced rates and certain liabilities of the former Post Office Department.

Postal reorganization had intended to reduce political influence and place postal operations on a more businesslike basis. However, politically determined tightening regulations on hiring and promotion worked in the direction of making postal operations less efficient. The Postal Service enjoys a monopoly in first-class mail but competes with private operators for merchandise shipments. Its parcel rates tend to be higher than those of the United Parcel Service. In all likelihood the Postal Service will continue to need sizable federal subsidies most of the time in years to come in spite of boosts in postal rates in 1981 and planned for 1982.

Veterans Administration staff expanded 31 percent between 1952 and 1978 (from 175,000 to 229,000) while the number of living veterans grew 56 percent (from 19.3 million to 30 million). Recipients of pensions and compensation grew 58 percent (from 3.1 to 4.9 million). The number of cases per VA employee thus rose from 17.7 to 21.4.

The Veterans Administration work-load potential is bound to grow as the veterans of WWII, Korea and Vietnam age. In 1978 there were in addition to 30 million living veterans, 23 million spouses, 36 million other dependents, aside from 4 million survivors of deceased veterans for a total of 93 million, equal to 43 percent of the U.S. population.

Agriculture Department employment went up 64 percent between 1952 and 1978, from 78,000 to 128,000. The department's wide-flung and diversified activities consume about 1.5 percent of all federal expenditures, but the budgets of its more than 100 divisions fill 11 percent of the big budget book (appendix)—135 out of 1188 pages. Still—less than one-fourth of those divisions display work-load data. This may be explained by the nature of their programs, but it also means that an evaluation of departmental employment trends must be related more to general background data. The 64 percent jump in Agriculture Department employment was accompanied by a *decline* in the farm population of 64 percent, from 21.7 to 7.8 million persons, and the number of farms fell to one-half, from 5.2 to 2.7 million.

Superficially this might suggest the type of inverse relationship in agriculture that C. Northcote Parkinson reported about the number of ships in the Royal Navy and the size of the Admiralty staff. But the more significant fact may well be that output per man-hour on farms multiplied more than four times between 1952 and 1978. This means that farmers with half the manpower they had a quarter century ago, working one-third as many hours, produced half again as much in crops and livestock. The American agricultural productivity record is widely admired and envied, unequaled elsewhere in the world and—in terms of improvement over time—far ahead of other industries. Some of the department's divisions —Agricultural Research, Extension and Soil Conservation Services—can legitimately claim some of the credit for this achievement.

But to keep things in proper perspective. All agricultural research and services of the Department of Agriculture consumed less than one-fifth of its total budget in FY 1977 and 1978. More than four-fifths was allocated to the support of farm prices and incomes. That is an item which highly fluctuates from year to year and jumped from an average of less than $1 billion in the early 1950s to $6.6 billion in 1978.

How much of an achievement is it to boost farm prices at a time when soaring food prices account for a good share of double-digit inflation? Did sharply increased spending for support of farm prices and income help to increase productivity in the farm sector, or in the U.S. economy as a whole? In summary, while some of the jobs added in the Agriculture Department contributed toward greater productivity on U.S. farms, many of the other new positions may not have done so.

The *Internal Revenue Service* staff grew 45% between 1952 and 1978 (from 56,309 to 81,505), almost as fast as the number of tax returns filed which went up 54% (from 89 to 137 million). Thus the number of tax returns per IRS employee barely rose from 1580 in 1952 to 1606 in 1978—during a period of the most intensive mechanization and computerization. Audits meanwhile declined from 4.4 to 2.3 million (from 4.9% to 1.7% of all returns), but some of the other work-load data cannot be compared because of changes in IRS reporting methods during the 1970s.

The number of returns audited has declined but those returns now are more likely to show sizable tax deficiencies because of the introduction of more sophisticated methods of selecting returns for audit. Among the more than hundred million tax returns, the machines spot those containing items which do not appear "normal." A return is far more likely to be selected for audit if it exceeds in some respect the norms established by TCMP, the taxpayer compliance measurement program, and if the aggregate points exceed the cutoff score of DIF, the discriminant functions system. So the auditing staff now drills fewer dry holes and is able to concentrate its time and energy on the returns most likely to yield significant amounts of additional revenue. Between 1968, the year before DIF was introduced, and 1978, the number of individual returns whose examinations resulted in no tax change dropped from 43% to 24%.

Also, only a small percentage of information returns, form 1099, used to be collated with tax returns. This is still true of 1099s coming in on paper strips. Fifteen percent of them were matched against the master file in 1978. But more than 55 percent of the 484 million information returns in 1978 were submitted on magnetic tape and all of those were collated with tax returns. IRS planned to collate 400 million out of a total of 500 million information returns in 1980.

Additional tax and penalties recommended after examination totaled $6.8 billion in 1978, equal to 1.7% of all internal revenue collected. That manifests a very high degree of taxpayer compliance but it does not mean that 98.3% of the revenue would have come in without enforcement. It is public awareness of strict enforcement—and occasional free publicity about someone going to jail for tax fraud—that puts fear in taxpayers' hearts.

Additional assessments in 1952 amounted to $1.8 billion, or 2.8% of all internal revenue collected. The drop in additional audit revenue from 2.8% in 1952 to 1.7% in 1978 could mean that audits are now less productive because they are less thorough. It could also mean that taxpayer compliance has improved. But prevailing evidence suggests that tax evasion has been increasing.

An IRS task force, for the first time, conducted a study of unreported income and estimated that between $75 and $100 billion in legal income had not been reported for 1976 and $25–35 billion in illegal income, for a total of $100–135 billion equal to 9.3% to 12.6% of all reported income.[20]

More thorough studies of the review and auditing process, and of gaps through which income escapes unreported and undiscovered, will be required to form a judgment whether enforcement has become stricter over the past quarter century, despite the lower number and percentage of audits or whether it grew more productive because of more effective procedures.

That the civil service grade average in IRS jumped from GS 6.1 to GS 8.8 may suggest that a staff of higher competency was active in 1978 compared with 1952. But it could merely manifest a grade "creep," a relaxation of grading and promotional standards in the service as a means of raising salaries beyond step advancement and congressional approval of salary boosts.

The four departments mentioned are among the most amenable to productivity measurement in the federal establishment and they account for more than half of all federal *non*defense employment. But all federal nondefense employment accounts for only 13% of the total governmental (federal-state-local) nondefense payroll. Eighty-seven percent of all government nondefense employment is state and local. Even more significant: ninety-three percent of the 1952 to 1978 *increase* in governmental nondefense employment occurred in the state and local field.

In other words, whatever has happened in federal nondefense employment or may happen in the future, can have only a minor impact on productivity in the government sector. By far the dominant factor in determining overall governmental productivity is set by developments in state and local government. Of the total increase in governmental nondefense employment between 1952 and 1978 of 8,881,000 only 660,000 is accounted for by federal departments. Simultaneously, 8,221,000 persons were added to state and local payrolls.

Although 93 percent of the growth in governmental nondefense employment took place at state and local levels, most public and academic concern about a growing bureaucracy focused on the federal level and attention centered on productivity of federal agencies. The few articles and reports dealing with productivity in state and local governments expressed valid thoughts but did not get down to brass tacks.[21]

Several state governors, such as Patrick J. Lucey of Wisconsin and Daniel J. Evans of Washington—not to forget Governor Jimmy Carter of Georgia in 1972–74—and municipal officials in Dallas; Detroit; Milwaukee; Nassau County, N.Y.; New York City; Palo Alto, California; Phoenix, Arizona; Tacoma, Washington, and others have tried in recent years to improve productivity in their respective administrations with varying and uncertain results.

One reason for the lack of success has been the strongly hostile attitude of public employee organizations toward improved productivity, because it usually means fewer jobs. The head of the American Federation of State, County and Municipal Employees, AFL-CIO explained:

> Productivity then, as now, was mostly a word hurled against municipal employees as an attack by people who really didn't then and don't today understand anything about the process of motivation and gratification in the work place to achieve real productivity. . . . They start not with the

goal of how to improve productivity but how to screw the worker and the unions as much as they can. They are dealing in politics first and productivity as a political issue. . . .[22]

In December 1978 the U.S. Comptroller General submitted a report to Congress, *State and Local Productivity Improvement: What is the Federal Role?* The report found that "state and local government productivity is lower than it could be." It assessed the federal role: ". . . the major federal impact on state and local productivity itself is achieved through the grants system. At this point, the structure and strictures of the grants system exert a primarily negative impact on productivity." The report recommends: "The Congress should institute fundamental changes in the grants system by removing negative barriers retarding state and local government productivity and by incorporating positive incentives to reward improved productivity in existing and future grant programs where appropriate." This, unfortunately, is too general. The report does not specify what could or should be done concretely to boost productivity and largely restricts itself to suggesting that efforts at the federal level to help state and local governments improve productivity should be better organized. The fears of the General Accounting Office "that federal involvement in this crucial area could dissipate" may well be justified. At this point prospects for effective action do not look promising.

The potentially most fertile fields for improvement in state and local government productivity are the programs which account for most of the staff increases over the past quarter century: education, health and hospitals, and police. *The table on p. 9 shows that education alone accounts for more than half of the total rise in nondefense employment—4.7 million out of 8.8 million. The aggregate of education, health and hospitals and police accounts for well over two-thirds. Strong action must be taken in those fields—or the subject of boosting governmental productivity will remain a purely academic and unproductive exercise.*

Between 1952 and 1978 enrollment in public education (higher and lower) less than doubled while employment more than tripled. There was one employee for every 14.8 students in 1952, one for every 8.0 in 1978. In the public elementary and secondary schools, which account for 83% of all public education, there was one member of the instructional staff (teacher or other professional) for every 35.6 pupils in 1900, one for every 26.2 in 1952 and one for every 18.7 in 1978.[23]

If we define productivity as the relationship between resources used and results achieved, then trends in public education and in the American economy have been running in opposite directions. While in the private business sector—industry, trade, agriculture, etc.—productivity nearly

ENROLLMENT AND EMPLOYMENT IN PUBLIC EDUCATION, 1952 AND 1978

	1952	1978	Percent Increase or Decrease
Students	27,862,000	52,818,000	+90%
Employees	1,884,000	6,586,000	+250
Employee-Student Ratio	1:14.8	1:8.0	−46

SOURCES: Enrollment, 1952: U.S. Office of Education, *Statistical Summary of Education, 1951–1952* (Washington, D.C., 1955.) Enrollment, 1978 (Fall 1977): National Center for Education Statistics, *Digest of Education Statistics* (Washington, D.C., 1979); Employment: see Table 8a.

doubled between 1952 and 1978 (*increase 85%*),[24] it dropped to half (*decrease 46%*) in public education (see preceding table).

The negative trend in educational productivity was strong during the past quarter century but has been apparent for longer, at least back to the turn of the twentieth century. Many members of the educational establishment regard this as a most desirable method of upgrading the educational quality of the schools. That a union such as the National Education Association or the American Federation of Teachers, AFL-CIO, should favor smaller classes and thereby the employment of more teachers is understandable and requires no explanation. That educational leaders echo that demand is harder to understand. Voluminous research going back over several decades has failed to show a positive correlation between class size or teacher-pupil ratio and the students' learning on measurable skills and knowledge. The *Encyclopedia of Educational Research* summarized as early as 1950 over 200 research studies of class size and pupil achievement: "On the whole, the statistical findings definitely favor large classes at every level of instruction except kindergarten." Nor could the massive survey of American schools by James Coleman in 1966 find a correlation between class size and pupils' learning.[25] Restudies of the Coleman report strongly confirmed those findings. A survey of New York City's public schools in 1967–68 showed a consistent negative correlation between small classes and achievements in reading and arithmetic.[26] A recent study sponsored by the National Academy of Education confirmed that "there is no consistent relationship between cognitive achievement and class size. In fact, more often than not, any effect of class size or teacher-student ratio is found to be absent."[27]

While the teacher-student ratio was cut almost in half and spending for public education multiplied beyond the wildest dreams of a quarter century ago, the quality of education, the skills and knowledge acquired by students have consistently and precipitously dropped. There had been complaints two to three decades ago about inadequately prepared high school and college graduates, about failures from the grade schools on up—when George Iddings Bell, Arthur Bestor, Mortimer Smith, Hyman Rickover, Rudolf Flesch were leading critics. But what then seemed a slide on a downward slope has since turned into a steep fall.

There is no comprehensive national measurement of the skills and knowledge of students. The Scholastic Aptitude Test (SAT) by the College Entrance Examination Board is the closest thing to a national yardstick. Scores on verbal tests have consistently fallen, from 478 in 1963 to 424 in 1980, scores on mathematics tests from 502 to 466. Hundreds of studies in individual school systems and states show an equally dismal record of a strong downward trend in scores on national tests of basic skills and knowledge.

To be sure, national educational tests have been criticized sharply in recent years as being unfair to some groups. In fact, there is a strong drive to discontinue and suppress all educational tests because of their "built-in bias." Those charges would warrant far greater credibility if the critics would devote their time and efforts toward devising "unbiased" tests of general validity instead of merely showing a negative attitude toward current tests. To be sure, test critics tried to devise better tests decades ago, again and again. But the results of those tests did not differ significantly from the established IQ and achievement tests. We must then conclude that the critics are not just opposed to currently used national tests but to tests as such because they are unwilling to accept impartial and objective measurements which disprove their favorite prejudices. They follow the principle: If you don't like the heat, throw out the thermometer.

Controversies over educational quality caused the Education Commission of the States, an organization of governors, legislators and educators to set up in 1969 a *National Assessment of Educational Progress* (NAEP). Its first report, in 1974, showed a decline in about every knowledge and skill area in the sciences tested and subsequent results have been no better. After spending $55 million in federal funds and involving 810,000 students over the past ten years NAEP results indicate clearly that public high schools and their students are in real trouble.

As shown earlier, productivity in public education—as measured by the student-staff ratio—dropped by almost half over the past quarter century, while productivity in the private economy nearly doubled. A judgment based on quantitative measurements might have to be modified if there were evidence that quality has improved. There is no such evidence. Quite the contrary, all signs point to a consistently falling quality of education. There must be something terribly wrong with the methods used by schools in recent decades to produce such results. Nor is it any wonder that some of the nation's largest school systems are in financial trouble because they built up a completely unrealistic structure which the public is not willing to bear indefinitely in the absence of positive results.

What may be wrong with the schools and what can be done about it will be discussed later, in the section on educational expenditures. These conclusions may be drawn: *By far the most significant item in governmental productivity is the ratio of staff to students in education. If for whatever reason we cannot take the bull by the horns and carry the battle in a field which accounts for over half the increase in the public payroll over the past quarter century, then we might as well give up talking about improving productivity in government.*

Next to education, health and hospitals recorded the greatest employment increase over the past quarter century. In hospitals the average daily census of patients dropped between 1952 and 1978 by one-fifth while full-time personnel almost tripled. There was on the average less than one employee—0.84 to be exact—for every patient in 1952, while in 1978 there were 3.04 employees per patient.

AVERAGE DAILY CENSUS AND PERSONNEL IN HOSPITALS, 1952 AND 1978

	Average daily patient census*	Full-time personnel	Employees per patient
1952	1,336,000	1,119,000	0.84
1978	1,078,000	3,280,000	3.04
Percentage change	−19%	+193%	+262%

SOURCES: American Hospital Association, *Statistical Guides, 1952* (Chicago, 1953); and idem, *Hospital Statistics, 1979 edition* (Chicago, 1980).
*The average number of inpatients receiving care each day during a twelve-month period. Excludes newborns.

Manpower input per patient tripled because hospitals were more amply staffed and personnel hours were shortened. Much of it is due to greater specialization, and the extended use of technicians to relieve physicians of duties that can be performed by less highly qualified professions. Medical gadgetry has multiplied and each hospital seems to be ambitious to have every conceivable type of equipment that any other hospital has. Some feel that surgery is being used excessively. The enormous growth of malpractice suits—and the outsized amounts awarded by some juries—have

FIGURE 3.

GROWTH RATE IN PATIENTS AND EMPLOYEES OF HOSPITALS

1952 to 1978

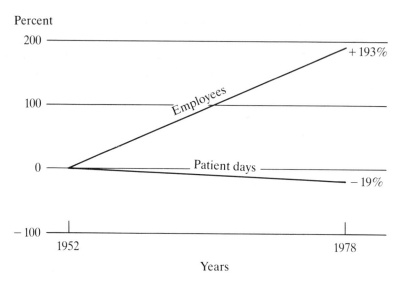

Years

caused doctors and hospitals to have every diagnosis and other details, etc. checked and rechecked and additional tests performed, more to protect themselves than the patient.

Last but not least: hospital income multiplied—especially from government and from insurance. *The public was and is apparently willing to tolerate spiraling costs for what it hopes will be better medical care, if the bill seems to be paid by someone else.* That means more personnel of all types, as long as the money to pay their wages is available, thanks to government.

Has this improved the quality of health care? By all signs it has. The U.S. death rate hovered around 9.5 per thousand from the early 1950s for nearly two decades but then shrank to 8.9 by 1980. Life expectancies gained substantially in every category. The number of persons surviving to age 65 per thousand births increased significantly—and as shown in the table on p. 25—much more for blacks than for whites. Expectancy for blacks, is, however, still shorter than for whites.

The infant death rate (per 1,000 live births) dropped from 23.6 in 1955 to 12.3 in 1977 for whites and from 42.8 in 1955 to 21.7 in 1977 for blacks.

The average length of patient hospital stay declined from 10.6 days in

Growth in Average Life Expectancy between 1949–51 and 1977, in Years

| | White | | Black | |
---	male	female	male	female
at birth	+ 3.7	+ 5.7	+ 5.7	+ 10.4
at age 20	2.4	4.5	3.5	8.4
at age 40	2.2	4.2	2.9	6.9
at age 65	1.1	3.4	1.2	3.3

Sources: U.S. National Center for Health Statistics, *U.S. Life Tables and Actuarial Tables, 1949–51* (Washington, D.C., 1979); and idem, *Vital Statistics of the United States, 1977* (Washington, D.C., 1979).

Number of Persons Surviving to Age 65 for Every One Thousand Born, 1949–51 and 1977

White	
males increased from 635 to 707	+ 11%
females increased from 768 to 838	+ 9%
Black	
males increased from 452 to 558	+ 23%
females increased from 524 to 727	+ 39%

Sources: As above.

1950 to 8.3 days in 1977, which could be due as much to the tremendous rise in hospital costs and better general living conditions at home as to improved hospital care.

The incidence of many major illnesses has been sharply cut—particularly of polio, tuberculosis, brucellosis, diphtheria, measles, whooping cough, typhoid, encephalitis, tetanus. But it has increased in gonorrhea, diabetes and strep throat. There has been a shift in death causes from cardiovascular diseases to malignancies which is a grim reminder that methods to deal effectively and decisively with carcinoma have yet to be discovered.

On the whole, it seems that the health of the American people improved significantly over the past quarter century. A number of factors contributed toward that advance for which hospital care undoubtedly can claim a share of the credit. We may conclude that the decline of manpower productivity in hospitals was probably not as great as staff/patient ratios would suggest.

The third largest increase in public employment was in police protection, from 254,000 in 1952 to 689,000 in 1978. That 171 percent rate of growth is second only to education (+250%) and occurred during a period when U.S. population went up 39 percent. There were 1.6 police employees per thousand population in 1952, 3.2 in 1978 (Tables 8a and 8b). So there were in 1978 just twice as many persons working in police protection—as related to the population—as there had been in 1952.

We might then expect that with a doubled protection for the people, crime would have diminished. That, however, is not what happened: according to the FBIs *Uniform Crime Reports* there were in 1957 (earliest year available) 1,422,000 crimes known to police to have been committed. In 1978 the FBI reported a total of 11,141,300.[28] That would suggest a 1957 to 1978 growth of 657%. However, because of changes in reporting procedure the rate of growth may be estimated at 441 percent.

No one has suggested that there is a relationship between the increase in police and the increase in crime. It is conceivable that crimes might have multiplied eight or ten times—instead of only five times—had police manpower been kept stable instead of nearly tripling. But the record provides no prima facie evidence of the effectiveness of adding numbers to police forces—if crimes can quintuple while the staff nearly triples. The fault could lie in the methods applied by the police—under restrictions imposed on it by the judiciary and sometimes by the executive and legislative branches. The evidence at hand does not suggest that ballooning the police force is an effective or promising way of stemming the growth of crime.

Highway department staffs expanded from 460,000 in 1952 to 588,000 in 1978. That increase of 28 percent was substantially slower than growth in population of 39 percent, in registered motor vehicles of 180 percent (from 53 to 149 million), and in miles traveled of 200 percent (from 512 to 1,535 billion miles).

However, highway construction meanwhile sagged. In 1952, 22,147 miles were completed on the federal-aid highway system; construction then climbed to a new high of 32,633 in 1959—after the interstate highway system was authorized in 1956—but fell back to about 11,000 miles in the later 1960s and has run below 10,000 miles a year ever since 1973. So we have here a group of departments whose staffs increased and whose work load expanded in some respects while their most important output—new roads—shrank.

The redeeming—and overriding—fact is that the traffic fatality rate dropped from 7.4 deaths per 100 million miles in 1952 to 3.3 in 1978. Only a small part of the reduction can be credited to the imposition of a 55 mile limit in 1974. The fatality rate had already dropped sharply, from 7.4 in 1952 to 4.1 in 1973, although the average vehicle speed meanwhile rose from 49.5 miles per hour in 1952 to 65.0 in 1973.

Had the 1952 fatality rate remained unchanged, there would have been 116,400 deaths on the nation's roads in 1978, more than twice the actual number of 51,900. A savings of 64,500 lives a year, not to mention lower injury and economic loss ratios, is certainly a spectacular achievement over a quarter century. Extensive construction of modern automobile (limited access) roads was probably the most important factor, with vehicle re-design for greater safety second. But education and stricter law enforce-ment—in which highway departments played a significant role—helped greatly to improve driving habits and thereby to reduce a major cause of accidents. Improper driving was involved in 73% of the fatal accidents in 1978 and in 83% of *all* vehicle accidents. So, while the picture is mixed, it appears that increased investment in manpower may have paid off in contributing to greater highway safety.

These data on manpower productivity trends in those four large cate-gories of public nondefense employment—education, hospitals, police protection, and highways—are, as mentioned earlier, very crude measures that permit at best only generalized and tentative judgments. With more determined efforts practitioners could have developed far more refined and reliable methods for the evaluation of productivity trends in those four and other domestic services. Even in the area of defense some progress could be made on ascertaining trends in input-output relationships although there are definite limits to it. Only "the battle is the payoff," and though it can be simulated in maneuvers it cannot quite be equaled. A major mistake could mean ultimate disaster.

But productivity measurements, an indispensable tool in private in-dustry, often are a two-edged sword in governmental activities. They may at times serve to support the demands of administrators and interest groups for increased appropriations and manpower. But more often they may offer little encouragement for program and staff expansion and even discredit them or throw doubt on their advisability. Practitioners in the various functional areas therefore tend to use only selected data—those that support their requests—and they neglect or omit others that would provide a more balanced picture. If progress is to be made in evaluating productivity in government it will have to be achieved by researchers with no organiza-tional, political, or ideological ties, or commitments to the programs and goals under review. They must be generalists who are not awed by the expertise of the specialists nor swayed by their claims.

We must recognize that, in contrast to private industry, where competition and the profit goal impose pressure for greater efficiency and a natural and generally reliable gauge of productivity, governmental programs have built-in counterproductive trends. It is a natural tendency for a public employee to want to handle fewer cases—pupils, tax returns, welfare families, crimes—in the belief that he could do a better job if he had a smaller work load, and most certainly have an easier life. For the supervisor there is a definite gain in stature, position—and even grade—by having a larger number of subordinates. This and the ideological commitments to the program goals and methods of their professional fraternities provide a powerful and well-nigh irresistible incentive for empire building.

Only elected chief executives are aware of the political attractiveness and profitability of a reduction in public bureaucracy and they will try to achieve it, whether in fact or, more often, through somewhat slanted presentations or claims.

Like President Johnson, President Nixon claimed that he had reduced federal employment. His 1975 budget message said that "the decline in total federal civilian employment since January 1969 has been substantial. The overall reduction in the executive branch from January 1969 through June 30, 1973, was 226,264 or 7.7 percent."[29] What Mr. Nixon did not mention is that this staff reduction was composed of a 278,338 cut in the Department of Defense and an increase of 52,074 in the domestic service departments. Nor did he say that state and local government payrolls jumped by about 1.6 million, helped by a boost in federal aid to state and local governments from $22.6 to $44.1 billion between FY 1970 and 1974.

It is evident from the record that reduction in the size of the bureaucracy was more apparent than real, more facade than substance. The size of the federal payroll was increased inconspicuously by shifting most of the increase to a category that was statistically not classified "federal" and the rest was offset by hiding it behind a reduction in defense manpower.

The power of the central bureaucracy over the state and local apparatus in each functional area continued to grow apace in keeping with the expansion of federally financed programs and the imposition of detailed controls. *Horizontal* or "layer-cake" government of three levels of government—federal-state-local—was converted to a chain of command from Washington to Podunk, to a *vertical* functional autocracy.

Efficiency of the public bureaucracy and productivity in governmental programs have long been viewed with suspicion by the general public, which in turn led to sporadic studies of administrative effectiveness by presidents or the Congress and attempts to limit the size and growth of the public payroll.

In his budget for FY 1981, President Carter stressed the tight controls he had imposed on federal employment. He added a 25-page section,

"Improving the Efficiency of the Federal Government" (Special Analyses, pp. 339–63) which described his efforts to raise productivity in the federal service.

The report recognized at the outset that the basic cause of the problem is governmental growth. "In the last two decades, there has been a dramatic expansion of the role of government in American life." The report goes on to cite inadequate motivation of the federal work force, excessive regulation, red tape, etc. as contributing to inefficiency. It claims that "productivity of the federal work force has grown in a relatively constant rate over the past ten years" but wisely refrains from saying what that rate might be nor offers any evidence.

Civil Service reform, proposed by President Carter and enacted in 1978, which authorized bonuses for improved performance to senior federal executives was praised as a promising tool as was a reorganization of personnel procedures regarding grievances, charges, etc. which was more structural than substantive.

The report then claimed that "the project has resulted in more effective coordination among agencies involved in national security planning and decision-making, particularly in preparing staff work for the President, developing defense policy, programs and budgets, and preparing for potential crisis." Presidential foresight and U.S. government preparedness and action in some of the recent crises in Asia and Africa inspire little confidence in the efficacy of that project.

As may be expected in such a report, there is reference to a reduction of paperwork. The Federal Commission on Federal Paperwork in its final summary report in 1977 estimated the cost of federal paperwork at more than $100 billion a year—resting half on government and half on industry and the public—of which it believed about $10 billion to be unnecessary. This means that 90 percent of the current paperwork is necessary to meet governmental objectives. With numerous proposals for new or expanded programs pending in Congress, expectation of tangible relief from the burden of paperwork should be modest. Late in 1980 Congress passed the Paperwork Reduction Act, which called for a cut in federal paperwork by one-fourth within three years. The prospects for reaching that goal must be viewed with skepticism.

Paperwork is immense because the requirements of federal programs demand it. There has been talk about simplifying the tax laws but the Internal Revenue Code has become enormously more complicated in the past dozen years by the addition of thousands of pages of amendments. A radical way to simplify the tax law would be to abolish all or most deductions, exemptions, exclusions and credits and to change from a graduated rate structure to a flat rate. That would abolish thousands of jobs in the

Internal Revenue Service and in the legal and accounting professions. It would, of course, be a major policy change which does not have a chance in a million in the Congress.

Similarly, procedures for the dozens of millions of persons and firms which receive payments from the federal government could be simplified. But the cutting of paperwork could prove a costly experiment if it affected the maintenance of proper controls over the spending of over $600 billion a year, if it interfered with the minimization of error, waste and fraud as with thorough pre- and post-audits.

Federal aid to state and local governments is now divided into a nightmare of 492 programs totaling $78 billion in FY 1978, estimated at $95 billion in FY 1981. It could be simplified by consolidating them into one fiscal grant with spending decisions left to state and local governments. That would leave the president and the Congress free to concentrate their time and efforts on the subjects which only they can decide, especially national security and foreign affairs. But here again, there is no chance that Congress would adopt such a plan.

Greater governmental productivity is not an idea that is apt to arouse enthusiasm among bureaucrats whose dedication and allegiance to expanding the services they perform or oversee far exceeds their belief in the concept of governmental economy or frugality.

The outright hostility that the educational establishment showed in the spring of 1970 toward a presidential proposal suggesting the concept of accountability in education was rather typical of an attitude that pervades much of the public service. But in view of the tremendous absolute and relative growth in governmental nondefense employment in recent decades the time may well have come to undertake a comprehensive study of productivity in the governmental service. At this time there appears to be at least good reason for doubt that manpower productivity in the public sector has risen comparable to the progress in private industry—if it has risen at all and not possibly declined.

In a review of academic studies of governmental bureaucracy in the *Public Administration Review* (March–April 1974), Kenneth F. Warren concludes: "The authors' consensus, with Mainzer dissenting, is that American bureaucracy is guilty of the gross mismanagement of the public interest. The real accountability crisis is that even if our bureaucrats act inefficiently and against our interests, as is too often the case, we cannot realistically hope for administrative abuses to be checked by the present 'watchdog' system."

In an earlier volume, *Democracy and the Public Service*,[30] Frederick C. Mosher found that professionalism in governmental bureaucracy and the power of the civil service pose a distinct threat to democratic control, that is, they are self-serving rather than serving the public interest. Sharp criticism came from Richard S. Rosenbloom in the *Harvard Business Review* (September–October 1973): "The largest employer group in the United States has shown the least concern for worker productivity. This seems absurd in a society that prides itself on management and efficiency, but the fact appears to be indisputable. . . . Not only is productivity in these groups lagging, but little is being done about it." Rosenbloom adds, "One is less surprised at the absence of evident productivity growth in government when it is recognized that none of the major forces operating in the private sector applies in government."

In its self-image the governmental bureaucracy constitutes a group of dedicated public servants who labor diligently, efficiently, and untiringly at low pay to provide better service to the people of the United States. They continue to do so despite the criticism and open hostility often shown to them by some officials in the executive and legislative branches, by political appointees or opponents, by the media and, frequently, by an ill-informed and ungrateful public. On the other hand it is apparently true that "complaints keep cropping up that a caste of career public servants—enjoying locked-in job tenure under civil service—is trying to run the country, without much regard for policies laid down by elected officials."[31]

About a century ago the establishment of the federal civil service aimed to abolish the spoils system and replace it by the merit principle—impartial competitive examinations and evaluations for hiring and promotion based on individual qualification. It has helped greatly to attract qualified persons to government employment, to reduce the role of patronage and political pressure and to raise federal service to high levels of competency. Unfortunately, procedural growth has also helped to protect the inefficient, by making it more difficult if not impossible to remove them. There also have been other inroads such as veterans preference, union rules, political factors and, until about four decades ago, discrimination against nonwhites and sometimes against women.

Selection and promotion by competitive examination was firmly established as the cornerstone of federal personnel administration until, in the 1960s and 1970s, a new goal, racial or ethnic representation, was granted priority over individual merit. The Ramspeck Act in 1940 outlawed discrimination in both employment and promotion and this principle was reconfirmed, strengthened, extended and tightened in subsequent statutes and executive orders. Employment action "*without regard* to race, color, religion, sex or national origin" seemed firmly anchored. When demands arose for racially preferential hiring to achieve proportional representation, Congress proscribed such action in the Civil Rights Act of 1964, Section 703(j), the Dirksen-Mansfield compromise, which reads:

> Nothing contained in this title shall be interpreted to require any
> employer . . . to grant preferential treatment to any individual or to any
> group because of race, color, religion, sex, or national origin of such
> individual or group on account of an imbalance which may exist with
> respect to the total number or percentage of persons of any race, color,
> religion, sex, or national origin employed by any employer. . . .

It is a supreme irony that federal authorities have been and are demanding
hiring and promotional goals based on racial representation which in most
cases cannot be accomplished without granting specific preferences and
that they are doing so under the title of "equal opportunity"—the exact
reverse of what is to be done under the program—using the euphemism of
"affirmative action."

To be sure, minorities are not underrepresented in federal employment; they inched up from 19.4 percent in 1970 to 21.6 percent in 1977.
But they are overrepresented in the lower ranks—29.3 percent in GS 1 to
4—and underrepresented in the higher positions—6.1 percent in GS 14 to
18. This is true in every federal department, including the White House,
Department of Justice and the Supreme Court. Minorities account for 25.2
percent of postal employment—but for only 10.2 percent at level 20 and up
in the postal field service. Congress, wisely, exempted itself from this and
most other regulations applicable to all other branches and agencies of the
federal government and is looking on impassively while affirmative action is
imposed on all other employers, public and private.

Thus there is incessant pressure on federal departments for promotion
or hiring to higher positions of minorities—as there has been on private
employers throughout the country ever since the Civil Rights Act of 1964
outlawed it. In a perversion of language, preference is granted to members
of some groups, on the pretense that by giving such unequal treatment, the
agency is carrying out the *equal* rights clause of the Constitution. Because
the Civil Service Commission turned out to be not sufficiently flexible and
so devoted by long tradition to the principle of judging by individual merit
without regard to race, etc., it was deprived of jurisdiction over so-called
equal employment programs which were transferred to the Equal Opportunities Commission by Reorganization Plan No. 1 of 1978.

To settle pending litigation, the Department of Justice proposed early
in January 1981 to scrap the Professional and Administrative Career
Examination, the most important civil service test, because some minorities
had performed poorly on it. The government undertook to guarantee that a
certain number of black and Hispanic candidates would pass and get
high-level civil service jobs.

The extent to which the weakening of the principle of selection of the best-qualified individual on a competitive basis has lowered the effectiveness of the federal personnel system within the past two decades is presently unknown. But there is no doubt that an increasing shift toward promoting not the most highly qualified candidate but the one with the right group membership will have a detrimental impact on the federal service and on public administration in general.

Governmental Pay

In February 1962 President Kennedy recommended to Congress that federal pay rates be made comparable with prevailing private enterprise salaries for the same levels of work as determined by painstaking statistical surveys and careful job comparisons. Congress adopted this rule eight months later in the *Federal Salary Reform Act of 1962* and subsequently reaffirmed the principle in the *Federal Pay Comparability Act of 1970*. Each year the Bureau of Labor Statistics makes an extensive survey of professional, administrative, technical, and clerical salaries in private enterprise and the President adjusts federal pay rates accordingly. He may propose an alternative to the comparability adjustment which takes effect unless overruled by either House of Congress. For example, the 1978 comparability study suggested an increase of 8.4% from October 1978 on, which President Carter capped at 5.5 percent with a savings of $700 million. The 1979 study proposed a 10.5 percent raise which the President tried to cap at 5.5 percent. Under congressional pressure, however, he upped this to 7 percent, effective in October 1979, which added nearly $1 billion, pushing the cost of the pay hike to $4 billion.

Despite the announced intent of the 1962 salary reform to maintain comparability between federal offices and private industry, federal wages climbed more rapidly. In 1964 a federal civilian employee averaged $1864 more than a jobholder in private industry; in 1978 he averaged $5685 more. In price-adjusted dollars the federal worker's compensation rose 20 percent, the private industry worker's 12 percent. In 1964 the federal employee earned 33 percent more than the private industry worker; in 1978, 43 percent more. That continued a trend of faster wage growth at the federal level prior to 1963. (An interesting sidelight is that per capita income is higher in the District of Columbia than in any state except Alaska where prices and wages are higher than in the contiguous states because of higher transportation costs.)

The announced goal of salary reform, to keep salaries in the federal civil service comparable to those in private business, was not quite achieved. A Civil Service Commission official explained:

The government has become increasingly responsible for complex large programs with far-reaching national and international implications. . . . Private industry, of course, has no comparable program-management responsibility.[32]

Official surveys comparing federal and private salaries are not as precise as they appear or as would be desirable. It is one thing to establish wage standards for stenographers and other routine clerical workers, for craftsmen and other blue-collar workers, and for general technicians. It is something else to compare technical specialists with diverse skills in certain industries with those in governmental services. The higher the occupational level, the more difficult it is to compare knowledge, expertise, or responsibility, especially when dealing with positions that call for decision making or policy formulation. Although the annual surveys, which cover over 3,000 firms employing about one-fourth of the relevant labor market, are conducted by trained specialists of the Bureau of Labor Statistics and audited by the General Accounting Office, they leave considerable leeway for judgment; comparisons between jobs are sometimes tenuous.[33] Nor is there a provision for adjustment by location, though wage levels differ among the various locations and regions of the United States and between major metropolitan centers and rural areas.

Salaries are set at a level intended to attract able and competent persons to the federal service. Government, in establishing a "prevailing wage," wishes to compete with private firms for the most qualified employees. In drawing conclusions from "prevailing wage" reports we probably should keep in mind that the surveys are undertaken and supervised by federal employees whose own pay is directly affected by their findings regarding the relative job classifications and level of federal and private pay. As the country's biggest employer with a $78 billion payroll in 1978, the federal government exercises substantial market power and therefore makes an impact on what it is trying to survey. Also, as a monopoly, the federal government is not as dependent as most private businesses on cost factors and competitors, domestic or foreign, in setting wage rates.

State and local government jobs are not included in the annual surveys,[34] yet the federal government often competes with—and sometimes outbids—state, city, or county governments or schools for specialists in the numerous social services provided by government. Nor do the surveys take into consideration the extent of fringe benefits—which now average more than one-fourth of the monetary compensation—the higher prestige and power vested in the federal service, and last but not least, the greater job security and tenure.

Overall salary comparisons between government and private employers over the 1952–78 period are given on page one. However, compensation levels and rates of change vary substantially among levels of government and types of functions and the several categories should be considered individually.

Here are the most significant facts:

WAGES AND SALARIES PER FULL-TIME EMPLOYEE
IN SELECTED CATEGORIES IN 1952 AND 1978
in *Constant* 1978 dollars

	1952	1978	Increase percent
Federal civilian	$10,329	$18,948	+83%
Federal military	7,106	11,588	+63
State and local governments			
Education	7,789	13,392	+72
Other functions	7,659	12,512	+63
Private industry	8,578	13,263	+55

SOURCES (and further details): Table 6.

Average federal civilian pay almost doubled, in *constant* dollars, and also improved more than any other governmental category, and more than private industries or any major category of private industry (see Table 6).

The averages are of course affected by the "job mix." If proportionately more positions are added in the top skill and pay levels, the average will move up. Was this true in the federal civilian service more than in state and local governments, in the military, and in private industry? To judge by civil service grades, federal workers certainly moved up steeply. But this is not a valid yardstick, as will be discussed later in this section. There is no evidence that the qualifications of federal civilian workers have risen faster than those of all other employees. It is a more likely assumption that federal bureaucrats in Washington are more politically sophisticated and successful in influencing Congress to raise their compensation than any other major category of employees. Most members of Congress depend for their own success on the cooperation and assistance of federal agencies and officials and can ill afford to antagonize them.

In *constant* 1978 dollars the federal civilian worker was in 1952 $2539 ahead of a state and local employee in education and in 1978 by $5550. He was ahead of other state and local employees by $2669 in 1952 and by $6436 in 1978. And he was ahead of workers in private industries by $1750 in 1952, by $5685 in 1978. The federal civilian worker averaged in 1952

FIGURE 4.
GROWTH RATES IN SALARIES, SELECTED CATEGORIES
1952 to 1978
in _constant_ dollars

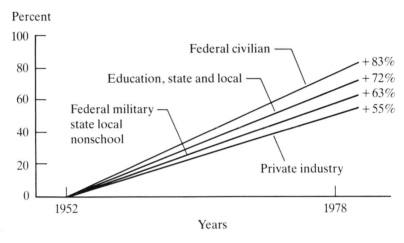

120 percent of his counterpart in private industry; in 1978 he averaged 143 percent.

Total compensation consists of more than wage and salary payments; it includes so-called fringe benefits—pensions, medical programs, vacations, other time off, etc. A recent study by the Congressional Budget Office arrived at these conclusions:

> Altogether, GS employees now receive more compensation in the form of fringe benefits than they would if the common practices of the private sector were adopted. Adopting private sector practices would reduce the annual cost to the government by the equivalent of some $637 million.[35]

Federal civilian pay is governed by several compensation systems:

General schedule	55%	(typically white collar)
Federal wage system	18	(typically blue collar)
Postal pay plans	23	
Other systems	4	
	100%	(as of September 30, 1978)

The Armed Services have their own pay scale.

General Schedule—for short GS—accounts for more than half the federal civilian employment and is the most amenable to analysis. GS consists of 18 grades—"normal" grades 1 to 15 and "super" grades 16 to 18. Grades are divided into ten steps each.

Between 1952 and 1961 GS salaries were raised three times, but since the passage of the Federal Salary Reform Act in 1962 they have been boosted every year. Table 10 shows maximum and minimum rates of the General Schedule in 1952 and in 1978 with increases, computed in *constant* (1978) dollars rising from 16 percent in the lowest grade, GS 1 (now little used), to a maximum of 64 percent in the highest "normal" grade, GS 15. Boosts in the "super" grades, GS 16 to 18, amounted only to between 31 and 51 percent because the basic rate for GS employees is limited to the lowest rank (level V) of the Executive Schedule. That ceiling was raised from $39,600 to $47,500 in February 1977, and to $50,112 in October 1979.

Prior to the 1962 salary reform it had been customary to boost wages in the lower brackets proportionately more than in the higher ranks, in keeping with egalitarian trends which influence public policy decisions. As a result, routine clerical skills gradually became overpaid in the federal service when compared with equivalent positions in private industry while higher skills became underpaid. The annual comparison surveys reversed that trend and led to sharper boosts, in amount as well as percentagewise, for higher ranks. But Congress decided that there was a limit to this un-egalitarian policy when top salaries in the General Schedule started to exceed the lowest level of the executive schedule, which sets compensation for policymaking executives, appointed by the President. Congress several times considered lifting salaries in the executive schedule for the senior executive service and, last but not least, for itself. But on weighing political repercussions it discarded the idea, for the time being. It could, of course, have boosted all pay but its own. But that might have removed the justification and diminished prospects for future congressional salary raises. The executive schedule is as follows:

	Type of Position	February 1977 to September 1979	From October 1979 on
Level I	Secretaries of executive departments	$66,000	$69,630
II	Secretaries of military departments Heads of major independent agencies	57,500	60,662

III	Under secretaries of executive departments Chairmen of boards and commissions	52,500	55,387
IV	Assistant secretaries and general counsels of executive departments Undersecretaries and assistant secretaries of military departments Members of boards and commissions	50,000	52,750
V	Heads of some major bureaus, General counsels of military departments	47,500	50,112

Nearly all members of the senior executive service created by the 1978 civil service reform, though divided into 6 ranks, are now paid $50,112. Since 1977 the top seven civil service grades have been limited to the same $50,112 maximum salary. The issue here is not sympathy for bureaucrats or a living wage. But this "pay compression" has led to an exodus and brain drain of the most talented experts who leave for better paid positions outside government.

Salaries of selected high federal officials were as follows:

	1952	1978	From October 1979 on	Percent Increase 1952 to 1978 in *constant* dollars
President	$100,000	$200,000	$200,000	− 19%
Member of Congress	12,500	57,500	60,663	+ 87
Member of Cabinet	22,500	66,000	69,630	+ 19
Associate Justice of the Supreme Court	25,000	72,000	81,288	+ 17

While Congress obviously took better care of itself than of the presidency in setting base pay and also provided generous perquisites for its members, it permitted the fringe benefits of the White House to go far beyond its own.

Actual salaries in the various grades of GS increased between nothing (zero percent) and 56 percent in *constant* dollars, but the overall average of all GS salaries increased 72 percent between 1952 and 1978 (Table 11). This means, of course, that there has been a general upward shift in grades, usually referred to as "grade creep." It is illustrated in Table 12. The number of employees in GS 1 to 3 dropped by two-thirds while GS 11–12 jobs increased by 281 percent (nearly quadrupled), GS 13 to 15 jumped 501 percent and the supergrades 754 percent. Had grading standards remained stable this would suggest that the number of top qualified persons multiplied 8-1/2 times and the total number of GS employees only 1.5 times. This, putting it mildly, is not a very persuasive proposition. The median GS grade, that is, the point at which there are as many employees above as below, moved from 3.9 in 1952 to 6.8 in 1978. The arithmetic mean rose from 6.4 to 8.1 in 1978.

The average GS grade increased among agencies as follows:

AVERAGE GS GRADE IN SELECTED FEDERAL AGENCIES, 1952 AND 1978

	1952	1978	Increase
Internal Revenue Service	6.1	8.5	2.4
Forest Service	6.3	8.3	2.0
Food and Drug Administration	7.7	9.5	1.8
Federal Highway Administration	7.3	10.1	2.8
Civil Service Commission	5.8	7.9	2.1
Veterans Administration	4.1	6.2	2.1
Social Security Administration	4.3	7.5	3.2

SOURCES: *The Budget of the United States Government, FY 1954*; and idem, *FY 1980*, Appendix.

Some explain the grade creep as a process of upgrading the quality of the federal service: persons of greater competence are being hired and more employees are being promoted on individual merit. To induce technical specialists and outstanding administrators and executives to leave their present jobs and accept federal appointments they must be offered higher salaries, which, in the civil service, means higher grades.

This is probably true—in some cases. But the nature of much or most of the grade creep is a disguised salary increase in excess of the raises authorized by the Congress. It is also affected by the expansion of federal domestic programs from $13 billion in 1952 to $281 billion in 1978. A substantial share of the grade creep is due to *affirmative action*. Efforts have

FIGURE 5.
GRADE CREEP AMONG FEDERAL GENERAL SCHEDULE EMPLOYEES
1952 to 1978

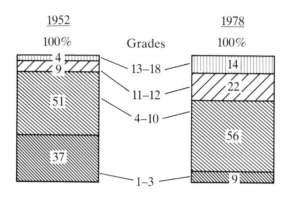

Source: table 12

been consistent throughout the federal establishment to promote members of minorities out of the lowest grades—which explains their shrinkage to one-third their former size; also, to promote as many as possible to the higher ranks of the civil service, as well as to hire minorities at elevated GS grades.

Overall it appears that employee compensation has been increased more substantially in the federal service than in private industry. This is also true, to a lesser degree, in state and city governments and in the largest local government service, the public schools. It is well known that except in the case of rare and unusual specialties the number of applicants for civil service jobs usually exceeds the number of openings particularly at lower and medium occupational levels and that there is intense competition for vacancies among applicants who commonly use all the political and other pull they can muster. By all appearances, governmental openings are usually regarded as highly desirable by numerous jobseekers.

Municipal workers have not been doing too poorly. The Urban Institute computed wages and salaries, retirement and other benefits in New York City in 1979 on an hourly basis at an average of $17.14 for police officers, $16.13 for fire fighters, $14.56 for refuse collectors, $11.73 for bus operators, $7.99 for stenographers. Based on a 40-hour week, counting no overtime, that would amount to: $35,651 for a police officer, $33,550 for a fire fighter, $30,285 for a refuse collector, $24,398 for a bus operator and $16,619 for a stenographer. In Los Angeles those amounts would be respectively: $34,590, $25,251, $24,944, $21,923 and $15,662.[36]

Government Pensions

Employees who devote their working life to governmental service are entitled to receive adequate pensions after they have retired. The certainty of those annuities in addition to job tenure during good behavior gives them a proper feeling of stability and security during their active career. The question is: How much is fair to the government worker and to the taxpayer who foots the bill?

Every comparative survey in recent years has indicated that the public employee is ahead of the average worker in private industry with regard to supplemental compensation, particularly retirement pay. A Twentieth Century Fund study concluded: "The benefit levels of the public plans are, as of January 1, 1972, approximately double those prevailing in private industry."[37] A U.S. House Education and Labor Committee Task Force found in 1978 that "Generally, the benefit levels and benefit provisions of public employee retirement systems compare favorably with those found under private sector pension systems."[38] The report estimated that about half the state and local government employees retiring after 30 years at age 65 will more than replace their preretirement net income and that about one-eighth of them will be at least one-fourth better off than before retirement. On the other hand, there are some public workers who are pensionwise worse off than their counterparts in the private sector.

Retirement pay has been climbing much faster than wages at all levels of government. Between 1952 and 1978 employee retirement payments jumped from $1.2 billion to $30.9 billion. This means that public employee pensions multiplied eleven times (+ 984%) in *constant* dollars while salaries and wages multiplied 2.7 times (+ 169%).

A review of developments over the past ten years may be more enlightening in understanding current trends and their implications for the future. Table 13 shows that in the federal civil service, pensions grew four times faster than wages. Civil service retirement payments jumped from 12 percent of salaries in 1968 to 29 percent in 1978. *If federal civil service salaries and pensions were to continue growing at their 1968 to 1978 respective rates, retirement pay would amount to more than half the payroll by 1988 and exceed it in the early 1990s.* This is very unlikely to happen—although a few cities may face such a situation soon unless they do something about it. It is also inconceivable that federal pensions will continue to increase in relation to salaries at the rate at which they have been growing in the past ten years.

At state and local government levels retirement pay also grew faster than salaries and wages but at a more moderate rate than in the federal government. But this is somewhat deceptive because state and local government employees were not covered by federal social security in 1952 and were only then given the option to join. About 70% of state and local

government employees now participate in the social security system. Social
security benefits, however, are not included in Table 13.

These are the major public employee retirement systems:

At the federal level 97.5% of the participants are covered by the Civil
Service Retirement System (2.7 million active members) or the Military
Retirement System (2.1 million active members). The remaining 2.5%
belong to 67 small plans—for the judiciary, foreign service, Congress, etc.
There exist, according to the 1977 Census of Governments, 3075 public
retirement systems of state and local governments with 11 million members. However, 94% of the employees are in the 172 largest systems with
5,000 or more members. Seventy-one percent of the state and local systems are very small and account in the aggregate for only one-half of one
percent of the total coverage.

Federal civil service employees have 7% of their salary withheld,
military uniformed personnel contribute nothing, while state and local
government employees pay typically between five and six percent. Most
private pension plans call for no employee contributions because they
would be "tax-inefficient." An employer can deduct his employee pension
plan payments when reporting income for tax purposes, but an employee
cannot, save in exceptional cases. The worker will have to pay income tax
on his employer-financed pension—but only years later when he receives
the benefits. His tax rate may then be much lower because social security benefits, which probably account for a material share of his income,
are tax exempt.

Historically, it was intended that retirement contributions be shared
equally between employer and employee. This is still true for social
security where each party paid 6.05 percent of the gross wage in 1978, 6.13
in 1979 and 1980, 6.65 percent in 1981, with the rate scheduled to rise
eventually to 7.65 percent in 1990. Social security now covers 90 percent
of the labor force, including virtually all private employees. In 1952 the
federal government gave state and local government employees an option
to acquire social security coverage. About 70 percent of state and local
workers now belong to the social security system, paying contributions to
two systems and receiving two benefits upon retirement, usually under a
coordinated schedule. A few of them net more when retired than while
they were working.

State and local systems tend to do well for long-term employees who
spend their entire working life in them and retire after 30 or more years.
Senior civil servants who have mastered the art of survival through successive administrations generally know what they want, have a pervasive
influence on legislators and executives and are able to shape the benefit

formulas in their favor. Employees who stay only for a few years, and leave either because of their own volition and career plans or due to changes in the political atmosphere, do poorly. Often they are lucky to get back their own contributions.

Federal civil servants are not eligible for social security but almost half of them manage to acquire coverage by working in nonfederal jobs either before or after their federal employment. They may retire from their federal jobs at age 55 after 30 years which enables them to build up a respectable wage base in social security over their remaining working years. Because of the redistributive factor in social security which bestows proportionately far higher benefits on workers with low wage credits, persons who work only for a limited number of years and at modest wages can earn disproportionate social security benefits. Some federal employees acquire social security credits by moonlighting or otherwise working part-time at private jobs.

On the average state and local governments contribute to retirement 2.4 times as much, and the federal government 3.6 times as much, as their respective employees. Thus, public employees do better contributionwise than the one-half of private employees who are covered only by social security (of which they pay half). They may be worse off than some other private employees who enjoy pensions which are entirely employer-financed—as are federal military pensions.

Virtually all public pension systems provide post-retirement cost of living adjustments, federal systems twice a year. Many private systems do, but not all. But since private jobs are covered by social security, which adjusts benefits annually by the Cost of Living Index, those pensioners have at least part of their income increased as prices go up.

On the whole, government employees have been able to improve their compensation more substantially than their counterparts in the private economy in recent decades. Much of the financial gain of government workers is not revealed in official wage statistics and comparison studies because it is hidden in pension rights that are payable years or decades later.

Congress and presidents prefer to grant federal employees more substantial pension boosts than salary raises because higher current pay cannot easily be disguised, would show up quickly in the budget, and may produce bigger deficits. Improved retirement pay is expressed in intricate formulas whose meaning and cost will not be known for a long time.

At state and local levels, governors and mayors—and legislators—when confronted with insistent demands for major salary raises sometimes face the agonizing alternative of a tax boost or a paralyzing strike. One way out of this politically perilous squeeze is to offer a more generous pension hike payable in a distant future. They are thereby not just postponing the day of reckoning but usually avoiding it forever. No one will figure out ten or twenty years later that the cause of the jump in the budget was that old pension boost. By that time the executive who had made the decision will no longer be in office, the pension claims will be a firm legal and inescapable obligation, and the resulting tax boost will be an "uncontrollable" item or "just one of those things." It has been said that "politicians can win friends with current generosity while deferring costs to the future."[39]

Public employees and their organizations often find liberal pension offerings to be an attractive compromise solution by which they can obtain more in future benefits than they could by alternative immediate salary raises. Resulting savings to the recipient employee also weigh heavily in favor of such deferred compensation. Legislators, at federal, state and local levels, have the final say on employee benefits and usually are conscious of the fact that their own pensions cannot be too far out of line with those of the employees of their respective governments.

The public is almost always unaware of the huge pension commitments that are being piled up, and learns of them far too late to do anything about them. Because pension boosts create a sizable long-range obligation for the taxpayers, former Mayor Frank P. Zeidler of Milwaukee suggested that they ought to be subjected to a referendum, just as bond issues usually are.[40] This could offer at least some safeguard for the taxpaying public at state and local levels though it is constitutionally not now available at the federal level.

In the aggregate, the finances of state and local retirement systems appear to be solid. Their receipts totaled $28 billion in 1978—up 48% in three years—their benefit payments only $11 billion, which left $17 billion or nearly two-thirds of the receipt for the reserves. The systems held $162 billion in assets in 1979—up from $18.5 billion in 1960—over four-fifths of it in nongovernmental securities. But this is no unmixed blessing. Nearly half the systems' assets consisted of corporate bonds—and the market price of first-rate (AAA) corporate bonds dropped 40% between 1978 and early 1981, because of soaring interest rates.

Some local retirement systems are overextended and pension rolls have become a grave problem in New York City and several other municipalities which have a hard time avoiding bankruptcy. Pensions are time bombs ticking in many local treasuries, with cotton wool in the ears being the only apparent defense preparation of responsible local officials and communities. State and local retirement benefits have grown from 4.4 cents for every dollar in wages in 1952, to 5.8 cents in 1968, to 7.8 cents in 1978, and are still heading up. Only one-fifth of the systems' receipts come from employee contributions, less than one-third from interest earnings and about one-half from government funds. This raises the question whether taxpayers will be willing indefinitely to keep boosting their contributions to public employee pensions, that exceed the benefits which those tax-payers can expect from their own retirement plans. Prospects at the federal level are no less troublesome.[41] Only about half the civil service retirement contingent liabilities estimated at $100 billion are funded (in federal securities) and none of the military retirement is funded toward an estimated $200 billion obligation. Military pensions equaled 3 cents per dollar wages in 1952, 11 cents in 1968 and were estimated at 43 cents for every payroll dollar in the President's budget for 1981. How much farther can this go?

This brings up some fundamental questions. Federal civil and military retirement systems were initiated at a time before social security came in and were then fully justified. So were many state and local retirement systems. But over the past half century social security has become a universal system, covering 90 percent of the labor force with government employees remaining the only major exception to compulsory participation. Even so, state and local government employees began coming in 30 years ago, with about 70% of them now covered. Military personnel have been getting social security benefits for over 20 years, and about half the federal civil servants have acquired social security benefits on their own by taking jobs in private business. In many cases but not all social security coverage is coordinated (or integrated) with state and local retirement systems.

Has the time come to make federal social security truly universal by including public employees and leaving federal, state and local governments free to grant supplemental and coordinated retirement benefits for their employees? About half of all employees in the private sector, usually those working for large companies, now enjoy such supplemental coverage. To unravel the diverse and complicated obligations of over 3,000 governmental systems and to coordinate them with social security will be no easy task. It may take years to accomplish. But, the sooner it is begun—or at least a plan developed toward that end—the sooner it can be operating. Is there a good reason why the public's servants should permanently be separated from the old-age security used for other workers? The main reason is the strong opposition of public employee organizations which know that their members do better if they are not treated as all other members of the labor force are.

The generosity of social security and other public retirement systems—and, in fact, of some corporate plans—raises serious doubts whether they will prove financially feasible in the long run, in view of apparent demographic trends. A crisis could develop within a few decades or sooner. It could at least be delayed by more cautious policies regarding government pensions.

Unionization in the Public Service

How can we explain the more rapid rise of salaries and fringe benefits in the public sector despite its slower growth in productivity? Why are public employees now overcompensated compared to private sector workers although their productivity has increased less—and in the biggest growth industry, education, has shown a strongly negative trend?

The answer suggested by the record: rapid unionization in the public sector over the past twenty years. It can best be measured by the number of strikes. Strikes against government have always been illegal—and still are prohibited in all but a few jurisdictions. But strikes are a union's most potent weapon and the extent of their use is a good yardstick of union power. There were just a few sporadic strikes in the public service prior to 1960. Between 1960 and 1965 work stoppages at all levels of government averaged 34 annually with a loss of 64,000 workdays. In 1966 and 1967 strikes averaged 162 per year and the idle days 853,000. Between 1968 and 1977 strikes against governments averaged 377 annually with 1,684,000 days lost; 1980 could establish a new record with over 2.5 million workdays lost. In the private sector meanwhile the number of work stoppages in the late 1970s did not materially exceed those in the early 1950s.

What happened in the first half of the 1960s to change the picture so radically? The turning point was President Kennedy's Executive Order 10988 of January 17, 1962, which sanctioned unions, collective bargaining, and exclusive representation, soon supplemented by dues checkoff. Its crucial features were not the voluntary provisions but the compulsory rules which were subsequently tightened. Though it directly applied only to the federal service, it set the pattern for public employment at all levels of government. Most states adopted public bargaining laws. Executive Order 10988 became the *Magna Carta* of unionism in the public service just as the *National Labor Relations Act* (Wagner Act) of 1935 did in the private sector.

President Nixon expanded the unionizing provisions in October 1969 by Executive Order 11491 which still governs union recognition in the federal government. Strikes continued to be forbidden but events soon manifested that no one dared enforce the law and the severe penalties it imposed.

New York City's twelve-day subway strike early in 1966, which the Transit Workers Union won unconditionally, set an example and the postal strike in March 1970, the most extensive strike against government in U.S. history, completed the process of governmental surrender. President Nixon, at first, attempted to uphold the law, obtained court injunctions and even moved a few token federal troops—unarmed and in fatigues, not battle dress—into some New York post offices where they were soon replaced by reserves and national guard. But within a few days the executive branch instead of invoking the law began bargaining with the representatives of the illegal wildcat strikers and conceded virtually all economic and other retroactive and prospective demands. Congress quickly capitulated and extended the salary raises to the entire federal establishment, civil and military. Court injunctions against the postal strikers were never enforced and none of the penalties, mandatory under the law, was imposed. As a final irony, the new contract retained the strike prohibition which had just been demonstrated to be a sham, intended to fool the public.

In the private sector union participation reached its highest level in the 1930s and 1940s but dropped from one-third of all employment to one-fourth over the past quarter century. Total union membership slid from 33.2% of nonagricultural employment in 1955 to 28.4% in 1965, to 27.5% in 1970 and to 24.5% in 1976. For private employment it may now be estimated between 22% and 23%, and in relation to the total labor force, below 20%.

Historically, unions played almost no role in public employment up to the 1950s. There was virtually no collective bargaining; work stoppages were extremely rare and risky, affected few workers and usually produced very little for those who participated in them. To be sure, there were some early examples such as the craftsmen in some naval shipyards in the 1830s and letter carrier associations in the 1890s. Postal unions came into being after the enactment of the Lloyd–La Follette Act of 1912. But those were sporadic developments with no broad impact.

Over the past fifteen years, while unions *relatively* declined in the private sector, they expanded phenomenally in the public sector. The U.S. Civil Service Commission reported that in 1978 88% of the postal employees were covered by exclusive union recognition, 62% in the Department of Defense and 56% of the other civilian employees, for an overall total of 1.8 million persons or 65% of executive branch employment.[42] Strong efforts have been under way for the past few years to unionize the armed forces.

A 1976 survey by the Departments of Commerce and Labor reported that 50% of the full-time employees of state and local governments were organized.[43] The Bureau of the Census placed state and local unionization in 1977 at 48%.[44] Fire fighters are most highly unionized at 73%, teachers 64%, police 53% and most other groups in the 40s or 30s. This includes well over 600 associations which prefer to label themselves "professional" although they perform the functions of a labor union in all or most respects. The largest are the National Education Association (NEA) with 1.8 million members and the American Nurses Association with over 200,000 members. Their policies and activities have become virtually indistinguishable over the past fifteen to twenty years from those of unions although they prefer to remain outside the AFL-CIO.[45]

A study of the record suggests that the growth of unionization in the public service in the 1960s and 1970s should not have been unexpected or difficult to understand: it proved the most effective weapon in the hands of public employees to advance their financial well-being relative to workers in private industry and to the general economy. In the late 1950s less than a million public employees belonged to labor unions and somewhat over a million were members of quasi-union associations. In 1978 organized public workers totaled at least 6.5 million.

The recently acquired wallop of federal employee unions was well demonstrated when President Ford recommended that a 5.5% increase in federal salaries be postponed from October 1, 1974, to January 1, 1975. The Senate voted nearly two to one (64:35) on September 1974 to approve a resolution overriding the presidential request. President Carter insisted for the first eight months of 1979 to hold a federal wage boost to 5.5% as part of his anti-inflation program. But on August 31 he agreed to up this to 7% in view of the overwhelming determination of Congress to yield to federal union demands.

Public school teaching offers a good illustration of what has been happening in public unionization. The dominant organization is the more than a century old National Education Association (NEA) which does not label itself a labor union although it has long lobbied with Congress and state legislatures for federal and state aid, its local groups present demands to school boards and, in recent years, have been negotiating with them. The American Federation of Teachers, AFL-CIO, though it grew rapidly to a half million members, is still far smaller and influential only in New York City and a few other cities.

In 1960 there was not a single collective bargaining contract in existence for teachers in public education; by 1970 there were 3522 contracts in districts with 1,000 pupils or more, and almost all personnel were covered by exclusive bargaining agreements in the country's large school systems. Not only had collective bargaining become the rule, it covered far more than salaries and other benefits and extended to the number of positions, class size and numerous other policy subjects that used to be regarded as the exclusive prerogative of management, that is, boards of education and top administrators.[46] One result was the far more rapid increase in the number of teachers than in the number of pupils in the years when enrollment was growing, and a determined resistance to reduction in the number of teaching positions in recent years when enrollment has been shrinking (see p. 21).

Between 1960–1961 and 1969–1970 the number of teacher strikes jumped from 3 to 180 a year. There was an annual average of three teacher strikes in the school years 1960–1961 to 1962–1963, with 10,300 participants and 13,500 man-days lost. In the annual average of the school years 1967–1968 to 1969–1970, there were 142 teacher strikes, with 102,500 participants and 1,270,000 man-days lost.[47] Only one-fourth of the strikes were called by teacher unions, about two-thirds by "professional organizations." Teachers' strikes fluctuated at approximately their 1970 level for nearly a decade but a new record of 215 teacher strikes was reported during the first six months of the 1979–80 school year.[48]

The NEA has become a major partisan-political force, endorsing candidates for Congress since 1970—310 individuals in 48 states in 1974 and 349 in 49 states in 1976.[49] In return for proposing the establishment of a U.S. Department of Education, Jimmy Carter was endorsed by the NEA in 1976 and was endorsed by it again in 1980 for having accomplished this longtime NEA goal.

Developments in other governmental fields paralleled those in education: unionization, an insignificant factor prior to 1960, was a dominant fact of life by 1970. Increase in influence far exceeded numerical expansion of membership. Much of the change came about by the growth in political power exercised by the nationally organized labor movement. Though less than one-fourth of the workers in private industry are unionized, their political impact on nearly half the members of both houses of Congress and on the executive branch, as well as on their counterparts at state and municipal levels, has become decisive.[50] In times of a labor crisis, when crucial decisions had to be made, few chief executives or legislative bodies dared to go against organized labor. Regardless of considerations of the economic or financial impact, the weight of government has almost always come down on the side of labor when the alternative meant open warfare. This was particularly evident when the operation of vital public functions was at stake.

To be sure, civil service strikes are just as illegal at federal, state, and local levels of government today as they were 60 years ago when Calvin Coolidge was put on the road to the presidency for firing striking Boston policemen in 1919 with the famous statement that "there is no right to strike against the public safety by anybody, anywhere, any time."[51]

When he supported the Wagner Act as a charter of freedom for workers generally, Franklin D. Roosevelt said:

A strike of public employees manifests nothing less than an intent on their part to prevent or obstruct the operations of government until their demands are satisfied. Such action, looking toward the paralysis of government by those who have sworn to support it, is unthinkable and intolerable.[52]

Yet there are now about 400 public workers' strikes every year. Many of them cut off vital public services without which people cannot live in today's cities. But rare is the president, governor, or mayor nowadays who has the courage to fire and replace striking public employees though the laws permit or even mandate it. Most of the mere handful of private employers who within the past ten to twenty years attempted to fire and replace striking employees failed, due largely to the force of government thrown decisively on the scales in favor of organized labor.

These events merely proved that there is no policy but unconditional—or at best qualified—surrender to firm demands of organized labor in today's reality and that continued resistance for the purpose of upholding a principle has become quixotic besides being ruinously expensive. If unions and management were treated equally, that is, if they were subjected to the same prohibitions against collusion in restraint of trade, market forces could well provide the balance between the opposing interests. But efforts in that direction appear beyond hope at this time. The presidents, governors, and mayors who refused to try to break a strike of public employees and gave in to their demands may have assessed the relative power and political facts of life more realistically than those who counseled or attempted resistance.

The courts also have come a long way since Judge T. Alan Goldsborough in December 1946 sentenced the United Mine Workers Union to a fine of $3.5 million and John L. Lewis to $10,000 for disobeying an order to postpone strike action. The conviction was upheld 7 to 2 by the United States Supreme Court because "the course taken by the union carried with it such a serious threat to orderly constitutional government, and to the economic and social welfare of the nation, that a fine of substantial size is required in order to emphasize the gravity of the offense of which the union was found guilty."[53] Although a court may occasionally still slap a mild fine on a union for disobeying an order, nothing like the United Mine Workers' case has happened since nor, in all likelihood, could happen in the political atmosphere that pervades all three branches of American government at the start of the 1980s. A District of Columbia superior court imposed fines and jail sentences against leaders of the striking Washington teachers in September 1972—but vacated them on the following day. When a state superior court ordered a picketing ban in a San Francisco municipal strike in 1974, the mayor refused to enforce it because he "would not act as a strike breaker."[54]

To be sure, we still read from time to time that a mayor or school board fired and replaced strikers and asked a court to impose statutory penalties. The United States Supreme Court's *Mackay Doctrine*[55]—which states that employers may permanently replace economic strikers—is still valid law after four decades though it has been substantially narrowed. Some judges still uphold the discharge of illegal strikers.[56] But the political cost of winning in court prevents most elective officials from following that course.

New York City set the pattern for many other cities and for much of the country with a "nonstop crisis" since the mid-1960s, of slowdowns, strikes, strike threats, and sabotage by teachers, subway workers, nurses, doctors, policemen, firemen, garbage men, welfare workers, and others. To be sure, New York state had a strict law against strikes of public employees, the Condon-Wadlin Act. It was never enforced because officials deemed it to be too severe and punitive. So, after a twelve-day subway strike in 1966, the governor of New York sponsored a repeal of the draconic law and its replacement by the more lenient Taylor Act. But in February 1968, when New York City's mayor tried to hold firm against striking garbage workers, the governor intervened. Instead of carrying out the mandate of the Taylor Act or calling out the National Guard as the mayor had requested, the governor within one day capitulated to the demands of the strike leaders. He had acted similarly a few years earlier in a New York City teachers' strike. His surrender to the garbage workers' "blackmail" (as Mayor John Lindsay called it) so enraged the American public that it may have cost Governor Rockefeller the presidential nomination which, instead, went to Richard Nixon who had declared: "Breaking the law of the state must not be rewarded."

New York's garbage strike gave public employees and their unions an object lesson which they learned well and which has been repeated many times since: strikes against government, can be undertaken with impunity. When postal workers struck in 1970, the president did not invoke Public Law 330 of 1955 which makes striking against the government a felony punishable by fine and imprisonment and provides that anyone thus striking could no longer hold federal employment. Quite the contrary, the postal strikers got their juiciest contract ever. Such unlawful strikes pay off in fat wage agreements because public officials lack the courage—and probably the political strength—to uphold the public interest against the self-interest and demands of the "street bureaucracy." Nothing succeeds like success.

It should have come as no surprise when New York City's public servants in 1971 locked a dozen bridges in uncrossable positions in New York City, thereby stopping traffic, letting tons of waste pile up, turning the city into a pestilential garbage dump, letting huge amounts of raw sewage spew into metropolitan waterways, closing the schools, cutting off school lunches, and sabotaging New York City's citizens in dozens of other ways. They knew they could do it without punishment and they did it, time and again—at a handsome profit to themselves. When the city of Memphis tried to hold out against a strike of its garbage workers—and against demonstrations during which Dr. Martin Luther King was to lead a protest march but was assassinated—it was forced by the federal government to back down.

New York City's transit workers struck again, in open defiance of court orders, for 11 days, in April 1980. The workers had earned an average of $18,000 p.a., demanded a 25% two-year boost, the deficit-ridden N.Y. Transit Authority offered 12%, and both parties settled for 17% and a cost of living increase. New York City's mayor called the settlement outrageous. He knew well that it would encourage the other city unions to settle for no less. Aside from the inconvenience and harassment to millions of residents, the economic cost of the strike far exceeded one billion dollars and pushed the city, which had been hovering on the brink of bankruptcy, closer to the abyss.

There is a difference between striking against an individual business and striking against government. If clerks walk out on Macy's, customers can shop at Gimbel's and hundreds of other stores. If the union strikes General Motors, would-be customers can buy a Ford or Chrysler, not to mention an imported brand. But the public has no such choice in vital public service areas in which government exercises a monopoly. There is no readily available alternative to fire fighters, police, postmen, prison guards or hospital attendants. Citizens must be able to rely on elected public officials who have sworn to uphold the law. But there is ample evidence that too many of those officials are unwilling to enforce the law or unable to stand up against pressure or blackmail.

Some have concluded "that it is impossible to establish collective bargaining in the public sector in precisely the form that it has developed in the private sector."[57] When the Research and Policy Committee of the Committee for Economic Development attempted to devise a compromise solution, it provoked sharp dissents from advocates as well as opponents of collective bargaining in government.[58]

Some believe that binding arbitration offers a way out when the parties are unable to arrive at a compromise agreement. But others feel that compulsory arbitration amounts to illegal delegation of constitutional powers and "taxation without representation." Some state supreme courts have upheld compulsory arbitration, some have declared it unconstitutional and others have deadlocked on it.[59]

After the postal strike of 1970 Congress decided to shift the painful responsibility of setting postal pay to an independent postal corporation under collective bargaining. Here is the digest of a report by the Comptroller General in February 1979:

> Since the Postal Service Reorganization Act of 1970, postal employees whose pay is determined through collective bargaining have received higher wage increases than other Federal employees and employees in some parts of the private sector. For example, average salary for postal employees has increased from $7,594 in fiscal year 1970 to $14,747 in fiscal year 1977 (94 percent). In contrast, the average basic pay for Federal white-collar employees increased only 47 percent during the same period. Postal employees also receive certain benefits—health and life insurance—at less cost than other Federal employees.
>
> The major causes for the increase in Postal Service bargaining employees salary have been rapid in-grade advancements and substantial increases in the pay schedules. Since the Reorganization Act, postal employees are able to advance to the maximum salary in their respective grades within 8 years, compared to 21 years before reorganization. In contrast, it takes 18 years for Federal white-collar employees and 6 years for Federal blue-collar employees to advance as far.
>
> In addition, certain other postal employees—first-line supervisors, secretaries, and clerical employees—have received higher pay increases because of their direct relationship to employees covered by collective bargaining.
>
> Some postal employees in professional and management positions, however, are not involved in such a work relationship and have not received higher pay increases. More of these postal employees are now attempting to organize.
>
> Also, Postal Service employees' real compensation—an index for comparison of wage increases with inflation—has exceeded that of other Government civilian employees and private sector employees.[60]

No comment seems necessary. The Comptroller General recommended that Congress consider "budgetary controls or constraints similar to those that exist for bargaining groups in the private sector and at other levels of government."

Have constraints at other levels of government proven more effective? It hardly seems so. In 1979 employees of San Francisco's Bay Area Rapid

Transit system crippled operations because they were dissatisfied with an average annual pay, including overtime, of $25,100 or a train operator's regular pay of $21,900. Chicago's bus and train drivers called a strike to protest their average annual $23,932 pay and District of Columbia teachers struck against an average of $21,500 salary for about 170 workdays a year of 6.5 hours each. (That equals about half the annual hours on a forty-hour week basis.)

Wage setting has greater financial impact on local government than on federal and state governments. Personnel compensation accounts for only between one-fourth and one-fifth of all expenditures in federal and state governments, because huge transfer payments (welfare) and aid to lower levels of government consume the major share of the budget. But in local governments, employees account on the average for over one-half of total outlays and in some cities and school districts for close to three-fourths. Local governments which still retain part of the welfare responsibility are federally and state reimbursed for a sizable share of those outlays. But much of their personnel costs rests on their own resources.

A major cause of New York City's bankruptcy in 1975—from which it was saved by last-minute congressional action—was brought about by the willingness of city politicians to buy peace from its unions, during or under the threat of a strike, with exorbitant wages, pensions, other benefits and the hiring and keeping on the payroll of large numbers of unnecessary employees. Between 1960 and 1970, while population was stable, "full-time employment in the City government rose 43% and civil service union membership increased almost fourfold. By 1970 roughly three-quarters of the city's workers were union members, compared to approximately one-third in 1960, and over 90 percent of the city's employees were represented by a civil service union for collective bargaining purposes."[61]

The financial "plight of the cities" and the "financial squeeze on the schools" are largely the result of pressure by employee unions which elective officials felt they could not resist without jeopardizing their own political survival. Insulation of public employees from much or all of the impact of runaway inflation and the costs of those pay and pension boosts at a time of growing taxpayer resistance or revolt may bring those issues to a head in the early to mid-1980s.

2 ★★★★★★★★★★★★★★★★★★★★★★★

Public Revenues
Government as a Siphon

★ When someone remarked that death and taxes are the two inescapable evils, Mark Twain dryly commented: "But death doesn't get worse every time the legislature meets." The history of taxation suggests that his point was well taken: Taxes *have* been increasing for as long as our records go back, and possibly for longer. Has the rate of their growth been accelerating? That depends, as it so often does in statistics, on how we measure it.

The sum of all governmental receipts (federal, state, local) in the United States jumped from $100 billion in 1952 to $732 billion in 1978, an increase of $632 billion or 632 percent, which is a new record high. If we convert the 1952 figure into 1978 dollars by the use of the Consumers Price Index (CPI), the growth rate does not look as outrageous—"only" 197 percent. That is not quite as bad, considering that Gross National Product (GNP) meanwhile grew 134 percent. As a percentage of GNP, taxes grew more slowly between 1952 and 1978 than they had in preceding time periods of equal length—for whatever comfort that may give us. Growth rates are bound to decelerate as the total moves closer to 100 percent.

But taxes did go up, consistently, spectacularly and painfully, in the twentieth century. Governmental revenues multiplied 57 times between 1902 and 1978 in *constant* dollars, while GNP multiplied less than twelvefold. This means that during this century government intake has multiplied four and a half times faster than production and income, from 8.2% of GNP in 1902 to 36.5% in 1978 (Table 1). That may explain the taxpayers' groans which have been growing louder over the years.

GROWTH OF GOVERNMENTAL REVENUES IN TWENTY-YEAR PERIODS,
AS A PERCENTAGE OF GNP 1913 TO 1978

Fiscal Year	Governmental Revenues as a Percentage of GNP	Percentage Points Increase over Preceding Period 20-year rate	Percentage Increase
1913*	8.2%		
1932	15.3	7.1%	89.0%
1952	29.6	14.3	93.5
1972	34.4	4.8	16.2
1978	36.5	7.0	20.4

SOURCE: Table 1.

*The decennial census of governments, usually conducted in years ending with 2, was taken in 1913 instead of in 1912.

Public revenues did not rise at a constant rate. In the first decade of the twentieth century they moved up parallel to the national economy. In each of the two succeeding twenty-year periods they nearly doubled *as a percentage of GNP*. Over the past 26 years government receipts have been growing only moderately faster than GNP. Reasons for these varying growth rates are easy to see. Each of the first two twenty-year periods (1913 to 1932 and 1932 to 1952) saw a world war during which income taxes were boosted drastically and never brought back to prewar levels. After World War I federal tax rates were cut moderately, after World War II only slightly—mostly for cosmetic reasons to partially offset inflationary impacts. Federal receipts did not increase between 1952 and 1978 as a percentage of GNP. Most of the enormous growth in federal domestic programs during the postwar period was financed by slashing outlays for national defense to less than half their former share. State and local governments meanwhile boosted taxes to nearly twice their previous share of GNP.

In FY 1978 aggregate receipts of all governments equaled 36.5% of GNP, 45.3% of National Income, and 45.2% of Personal Income (Table 14). If trends of the past 26 years were to continue, governmental revenues would run at 44% of GNP and at 55% of National Income by the end of this century.

Governmental revenues in FY 1978 amounted to $3347 per capita or $13,388 for a family of four. Is that burden too heavy to bear for the individual taxpayer with an average per capita income of $7856 in 1978? Is government levying too much in taxes to maintain adequate and stable growth in the nation's economy?

By some measurements government is not levying enough. Federal revenues fell short of meeting expenditures in twenty-two of the past twenty-six years, receipts equaled only 92.2% of outgo, with 7.8% of expenditures deficit financed. Financial adequacy has been deteriorating. Federal budget receipts covered 97.1% of outgo between FY 1952 and 1960, 95.7% between 1961 and 1970 and 90.1% between 1971 and 1980. Deficits during those three periods totaled $20 billion, $60 billion and $371 billion respectively though there were no wars in the 1970s.

What caused deficits to multiply in the 1970s? During the 1950s and 1960s most of the buildup in social programs could be covered by shifting the flow of funds from the military to domestic fields. But that well ran dry in the 1970s when Americans became increasingly aware of the need and the cost of preparedness in a hostile world. To meet, at least in part, their promises and commitments, but unwilling to face their constituents with commensurate tax boosts, political leaders in the executive and legislative branches of the federal government chose the seemingly easier course of budgetary deficits.

State and local governments did financially better in covering their current outlays, according to their published reports. But they charged most of their capital outlays to the future, thereby multiplying their indebtedness nearly tenfold and raising it from 8.9% of GNP to 14.0%. The

GOVERNMENTAL DEBT, 1952 AND 1978

	Total	Federal	State-Local	Total	Federal	State-Local
	in billions of dollars			in percent of GNP		
1952	$ 289	$ 259	$ 30	85.3%	76.4%	8.9%
1978	1,061	780	280	52.9	38.9	14.0
Increase in percent (current $)	267%	201%	832%			
Increase in percent (*constant $*)	49%	23%	279%			

SOURCES: U.S. Bureau of the Census, *Historical Statistics on Governmental Finances and Employment*, 1967 Census of Governments, 1969; *Governmental Finances in 1977–78*, 1980.

federal government, which includes capital outlays in the regular budget, tripled its debt—but halved it as a percentage of GNP from 76% to 39%.

Should the federal government follow the state and local procedure of not including capital projects in its regular budget? That would reduce or wipe out most deficits and has repeatedly been suggested. Private business firms do not show capital outlays as current expenditures. In fact, they are not permitted to do so under the Internal Revenue Code and Securities and Exchange Commission rules. But they do make allowance for depreciation in their current accounts, a practice unknown to governmental budgeting and accounting. Even more significant is that federal public works construction is a continuing, and usually growing, activity, year after year, with no letup and it should therefore be financed on a current basis as a regular and recurring expenditure. This is also true, if sometimes to a lesser degree, at the state level and even at municipal and county levels. Accounts of state and local government expenditures understate true costs by not making adequate allowance for the depreciation of facilities which someday will have to be replaced.

Governmental debt is shown as having declined from 85% of GNP in 1952 to 53% in 1978. This is technically correct but misleading. It does not count numerous contingent obligations arising from social security, pensions, guarantees and other commitments, that total several trillions of dollars, far exceeding GNP.

Do the American people feel that their taxes are too high? Answers to opinion polls give no clear-cut answer and are sometimes contradictory. The Roper organization asked in May and July 1978 and May 1979 whether respondents thought that four different taxes (federal income, state income, property and social security) were excessively high, somewhat high, about right, or extremely low. Not surprisingly, only between 1% and 2% found taxes extremely low. The rest was about evenly divided between the other three choices. In other words, only about one-third found taxes extremely high.

When asked about the most important thing that needs to be done by government, those polled ranked lowering income taxes only tenth among 15 choices in 1978 and seventh in 1979. Remedial action on inflation, energy and crime rated far higher than cutting taxes. Asked whether they were satisfied with the taxes they personally paid, 52% responded negatively but as many individuals were satisfied as were angry—24% each.

When the Harris poll asked in September 1979 whether the public wanted a federal income tax cut "which might be inflationary," the response was 48 to 47 percent. *Newsweek* had the Gallup organization conduct a poll in February 1980 on whether the respondent would be more or less likely to vote for a candidate who advocated a cut in the individual income tax: 73% favored the candidate with a cut and 14% did not.

In the end, of course, the ballot box is the only meaningful poll. Citizens cannot vote directly on federal taxes but they can and do contact and influence members of Congress on issues up for decision. It is significant that Congress has for many decades raised taxes (besides social security contributions) only in an emergency such as World War I, World War II, Korea and Vietnam. The oil windfall profits tax could be the first exception—unless we regard it as an aspect of the energy emergency. It is also not a tax that an ordinary citizen pays directly. Federal revenues remained stable at 21.2% of GNP in 1952 and 21.4% in 1978.

There have been numerous tax boosts at the state level—the Advisory Commission on Intergovernmental Relations [ACIR] counted 50 new major taxes enacted and 468 tax increases enacted by state legislatures between 1959 and 1971—aside from thousands of tax increases by cities, counties and school districts. Many of those actions had to be voted on by the taxpayers and most of them, at state and local levels, were subject to referendum. The taxpayers approved or acquiesced in most of those boosts, as is evidenced by the jump in state and local government revenues from $28 billion in 1952 to $302 billion in 1978, from 8.4% of GNP to 15.1%. This would not have been possible had there been a strong antitax sentiment prevalent among the American public.

A change in attitude seems to have occurred in the late 1970s. The election of the only candidate among 14 competitors in his party to announce opposition to "big government," Jimmy Carter suggests that the atmosphere was turning less friendly toward taxes.

State executives and legislators sensed this trend; taxes were slightly reduced in 1973 and 1974 and again at the 1978 and 1979 state legislative sessions—contrary to a strong long-term trend of raising taxes. A taxpayers' revolt which manifested itself by the adoption of California propositions, #13 in 1978, #4 in 1979, and several similar measures in other states, indicated a swing in voters' sentiments against taxes. Voters cut taxes where constitutionally they could act directly, at state and local levels.

Tax cuts by direct legislation in a number of states could indicate a long-lived national trend which might also make its impact felt on the federal scene. Developments in 1980 however suggested that the 1978 tax revolt may have been an evanescent development.

There are large economic and ideological segments in the population which hold that government is not taxing enough—at least not groups other than their own—and that, as a result, many vital public services are being starved, inflicting suffering on the poor, while better-off consumers luxuriate. According to this view, the consumer is allowed to keep more of his earnings than he knows how to spend or invest wisely. The protagonist of those who hold that government is not taxing enough is John Kenneth Galbraith who broke new ground in 1958 with his book *The Affluent Society*. The ensuing controversy will be discussed on pp. 374–75.

Compared with other industrial countries, the American tax burden appears to be moderate. According to reports of the *Organization for Economic Development and Cooperation* (OECD), the United States was in 1978 17th among 22 countries, ranked by governmental receipts as a percentage of gross domestic product (Table 15). At 32.0 percent, the United States ranks below the average of 39.3% for all OECD member countries, far behind Sweden with 60.9%, and Netherlands with 54.0% or Germany, Austria, Great Britain and France which were shown between 43.5% and 40.6%.

Only five countries—Greece, Portugal, Turkey, Spain and Japan—showed up lower than the United States. It may be significant that the tax burden rose by 4.7% of gross domestic product in the average of the OECD countries between 1972 and 1978, and only 0.5% in the United States.

Though much improved in recent years, international economic and fiscal comparisons are still somewhat tenuous and the figures cited above may be imprecise. Also, some transfer programs such as Blue Cross–Blue Shield which are classified private in the United States though they are under government control, are governmentally operated in most of Europe. But the fact that the total tax load in most leading industrial countries is heavier than in the United States has long been known and appears to be well established.

Many of the countries with a heavier tax burden have long experienced and continue to enjoy respectable economic growth rates, often doing much better than the United States. Though it stands to reason that heavy taxes act as a depressant on economic growth, because they reduce the capital available for private industrial investment and expansion, the available data supply no proof that high taxes *necessarily* mean slow economic growth. One tentative conclusion we might draw is that the magnitude of taxes, important though it is, may not be as significant an adverse factor in economic expansion as is widely assumed. The *composition* of the tax structure, the type and nature of the major taxes—and possibly the use to which public funds are put—may have a greater impact on a nation's economy than the size of the aggregate. How *much* a country taxes its citizens may not be as important as *how* it taxes them.

FIGURE 6.

CURRENT GOVERNMENT RECEIPTS AND EXPENDITURES IN OECD COUNTRIES
1978
as a percentage of gross national product

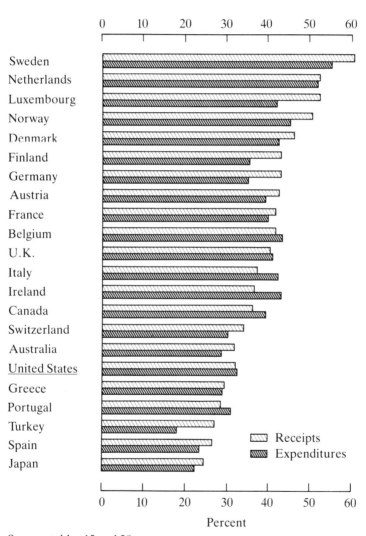

Source: tables 15 and 20

Incentives—or disincentives such as taxes—are affected not as much by an overall tax burden rate as by marginal rates. Decisions on action that may lead to added earnings are governed by an individual's top rate, not by his or the country's average tax rate.

Taxation in a Federal System of Government

Federal and state governments exercise separate and independent taxing powers under the United States Constitution and state constitutions, whereas local governments, as subdivisions of the state, possess only such taxing powers as the state may delegate. For much of the time prior to World War II (except for the period of World War I), state and local governments combined collected about twice as much each year as the federal treasury. In 1941, federal receipts exceeded state-local receipts for the first time, and they have remained larger ever since.

In the early postwar period the federal treasury took in, on the average, about twice as much each year as the aggregate of state and local governments. But state and local finances were coming up faster than federal, the ratio between them changed to 1:1.5 and has in recent years slid even lower. In historical perspective, the relative position of federal and state-local treasuries was reversed between pre–World War II and post–World War II years. This seemed to confirm the widely held belief that the federal government has a much stronger taxing capacity than the states, that its relative strength is growing. It led to suggestions that the national government should make an increasing share of its abundance available to "hard-pressed' state and local governments. Further proof appeared to be adduced by the fact that between 1902 and 1978 state and local government revenues (from their own sources) multiplied 38 times (in *constant* dollars), federal revenues 86 times—more than twice as fast (Table 1).

But some developments cast doubt on the belief in the federal government's growing fiscal power. For one, income fell short of outgo in 22 of the past 26 years and covered only ninety percent of expenditures in the decade of the 1970s, as mentioned earlier. Moreover, between 1952 and 1978 federal revenues increased 143%, state-local revenues 332% in *constant* dollars. Consequently, the state-local share of total governmental revenues, which had fallen to a low of 20.6% in 1944, increased to 28.4% in 1952 and to 41.3% in 1978. While federal receipts simultaneously remained virtually stable at 21.2% and 21.4% of GNP, state-local receipts jumped from 8.4% of GNP to 15.1%.

Historical analysis back to 1902 shows that state-local revenues always grew faster than federal revenues except during wartime. Between 1902 and 1916, as well as between 1945 and 1978 state-local revenues increased several times faster than federal revenues; between 1920 and 1940 federal receipts declined while state-local receipts more than doubled. In each of those periods federal revenues grew more slowly than GNP, state-local revenues substantially faster.

It was only during wartime that state and local fiscal growth came to a virtual standstill while federal revenues skyrocketed. During both World War I and World War II, federal receipts multiplied approximately seven times within four to five years while state-local income, intended to support domestic services, simultaneously advanced only moderately.

In the immediate postwar period, when the state-local share of governmental revenues had shrunk to one-fifth of the total, some economic and political experts concluded that the fiscal powers of state-local governments had become insufficient to meet contemporary requirements and had about reached their practical limit. The view became more widely accepted that the federal government would have to assume most of the revenue-raising responsibilities and either render more aid to the other governments or take over the operation of major domestic programs. Federal aid to states did, in fact, increase sharply in the immediate postwar period.

FIGURE 7.

GOVERNMENTAL REVENUES IN THE UNITED STATES

1952 and 1978

by level of government

as a percentage of gross national product

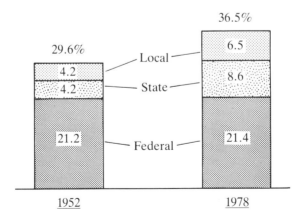

Source: table 16

In the late 1940s members of Congress, under the leadership of Senator Robert Taft, became concerned that the multiplying flow of funds from the U.S. Treasury to state treasuries was altering the traditional balance in our federal system. They feared that this shift, if permitted to continue, would concentrate power and responsibility in Washington, converting the states into subordinate provinces.

Congress in 1953 established a Commission on Intergovernmental Relations—composed of members of Congress, state and local officials, and private citizens appointed by President Eisenhower, for the purpose of recommending policies to preserve the role of the states as partners with the national government.

The Commission and its successors produced many volumes of research and recommendations but failed in the task which their originators had hoped they would accomplish: to help reverse the centralizing trend. The drive for ever increasing federal money to state and local governments continued. The funds multiplied from $2.5 billion in 1952 to $78 billion in 1978, estimated in the President's 1981 budget to rise to $112 billion by 1983.

State and local governments meanwhile steeply expanded their own revenues, from $28 to $302 billion. This, however, was taken not as a proof of their fiscal strength but as an indication that by that extraordinary effort they had exhausted their capacity and would henceforth have to depend increasingly on the federal treasury. If state-local governments had not increased their receipts so spectacularly in the postwar period this would of course have been taken as proof that they were unable to do so and that recourse to the federal treasury was the only answer. This seems to be a "heads I win, tails you lose" proposition. The underlying issue appears to be not so much whether state-local governments *are able* to raise larger funds but whether it is *desirable* that they do so.

The assertion of inadequate state-local fiscal capacity and of greater federal fiscal capacity which has been advanced innumerable times to justify demands for more federal money is unsubstantiated. Virtually all income, wealth and transactions which can be taxed by the national government are located within the borders of the 50 states and subject to their jurisdiction. Taxing powers are constitutionally as wide for the states as they are for the federal government—in some respects even wider—subject only to such limitations as the citizens of each state decide to place upon their own governments. Local taxing powers are as broad as the voters in each state and their elected representatives deem wise to confer upon city and county councils and school boards.

It has been asserted that competition among states for industrial development constrains them to keep taxes too low. Even if this were true—and the record of state-local taxes multiplying over the past quarter century suggests that it is not—what would be wrong with that? What keeps private business from charging excessive prices is competition, which is just as sound to maintain between states and communities as between retail shops. States and stores offer certain benefits, facilities and services—and charge a price for them. This leaves the decision to would-be customers. It is competition that impels retail stores to charge the lowest possible price for merchandise and give the customers the most for their money. That principle should work equally well to maintain competition between state and local areas.

Two factors combine to increase fiscal centralization. The spending-to-tax relation is close at the state level but more distant and impersonal at the federal level. Appropriation of funds for public purposes is closely related to the need to levy and possibly raise taxes at the local level. A member of Congress, however, who sponsors or votes for a program is under no obligation to vote for the tax boost it may eventually require. A governor or mayor or other local official cannot as easily avoid that onerous duty. He craves the praise and support he expects to get for initiating or expanding a program but hates to incur the political penalty of being blamed for higher taxes. Budgetary deficits have become a matter of federal routine in recent decades—they are illegal or held intolerable at state and local levels. The other factor that generates frequent preference for federal over state-local financing is the heavier federal use of income taxes at the federal level which will be discussed later in this chapter.

Over the centuries imaginative minds have invented and ambitious legislatures enacted a great number and diversity of taxes. In a society where demand for public services is low, the revenue needs of government can be met from just one or a few sources. But as governmental activities expand and fiscal requirements multiply, a variety of methods must be employed to exact huge sums from a reluctant public. Attractive as the proposition of a single tax—the "ideal" tax—may be, it becomes unrealistic when government claims 20 or 30 percent or more of GNP. At that level even confiscatory rates of a tax would not suffice; they would become self-defeating. Hence dozens of taxes have had to be conceived and imposed to conceal their total from the taxpayer and to make the bite less painful and less destructive.

How are taxes allocated among the several levels of government in the United States? There is probably no more appealing idea in the field of intergovernmental tax relations than the concept of a clean separation of sources, with each government assigned certain taxes for its exclusive use. If that is not how the system now operates then it is not for the want of trying. But it never worked for very long, in the United States or anywhere else. Long ago, Germany, Switzerland, Canada, and several other countries allocated indirect taxes to the central government and direct taxes to states, cantons, or provinces. So, incidentally, did the United States for the first 120 years of its existence. But to public officials, as to human beings in general, the other fellow's grass always looks greener. So in the United States and in other federal countries, central governments gradually ventured into direct taxes, while state and local governments adopted a widening range of excise and sales taxes. Eventually everybody was working both sides of almost every street. Three levels of government levy income taxes in the United States, three levels consumption taxes, two levels property and estate taxes.

Recommendations and attempts to reduce or eliminate tax overlapping have consistently failed. Government leaders are always on the prowl for more rather than fewer sources and are unwilling to give up what they have. The chance for tax separation or even a significant cutback in tax overlapping is slim indeed. Fortunately, tax overlapping is not as pervasive as a mere listing would make it appear. Analysis shows that there still is a distinct pattern of tax concentration at each level of government. The federal government collected 85 percent of all income taxes in 1978—down from 96 percent in 1952—local governments collected 96 percent of all property taxes in 1978—unchanged from 1952. The most significant change took place in consumption taxes, with the state share jumping from 37 percent in 1952 to 63 percent in 1978. Moreover, the 27 percent share of consumption taxes claimed by the federal government in 1978 consisted mostly of customs duties and excises on liquor, tobacco, and motor fuel. All of these, except motor fuel, have historically been prime federal tax sources. In fact, they accounted for most federal revenues from 1789 to 1913, except during the Civil War. General retail sales taxes are levied only at state and local levels, with the states' share increasing from 78 percent in 1952 to 85 percent in 1978. A strengthened role of the states in income as well as sales taxation has been an important change in the past twenty years.

The dependence of each level of government on a particular type of taxation follows an identical pattern. Using the Bureau of the Census definition of taxes—which excludes social security contributions, as did the administrative budget that was in use through 1968—the federal government derived 82 percent of its *tax* revenues from income taxes in 1952 and 88 percent in 1978, states obtained 58 percent of their taxes from consumption taxes in 1952 and 57 percent in 1978, local government obtained 87 percent of their tax revenues from property taxes in 1952 and 78 percent in 1978. It is evident that the picture has remained virtually unchanged over the past quarter century. What really counts in the end, as far as the taxpayer is concerned, is the aggregate "mix" of all types of taxes imposed upon him by all levels of government. That sets the nature of the tax system.

FIGURE 8.

<small>SOURCES OF GOVERNMENTAL REVENUES IN THE UNITED STATES</small>

1952 and 1978

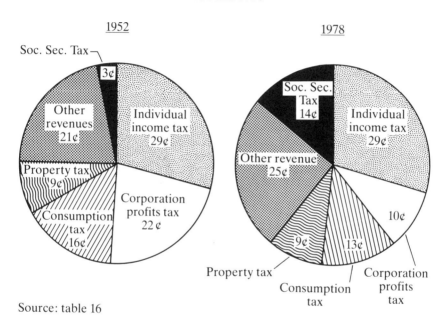

Source: table 16

The American Tax System

For reasons not immediately apparent to the untrained eye, the multitude of uncoordinated and overlapping taxes that Americans are called upon to pay to their federal, state, and local governments is called our *tax system*.

The American tax system is like no other in the world. Most other countries balance their taxes on personal income and on consumption, with slightly more weight on one side or the other. The United States is the only industrial country whose national government levies no broad-based major consumption tax. Instead it leans more heavily on the income tax.

Here is a comparison between the United States and the OECD countries by types of taxes used:

TYPES OF TAXES AS A PERCENTAGE OF TOTAL TAXATION
IN OECD MEMBER COUNTRIES IN THE AVERAGE OF 1975–1977

	Average of All OECD Member Countries		United States
	Mean	Median	
Taxes on goods and services	28.1%	26.0%	15.7%
Taxes on incomes and profits	37.1	39.0	44.0
Households	29.5	30.5	33.2
Corporations	7.1	5.6	10.8
Social security	26.3	27.8	24.6
Other taxes	9.7	7.1	15.7

TYPES OF TAXES AS A PERCENTAGE OF GROSS DOMESTIC PRODUCT
IN OECD MEMBER COUNTRIES IN THE AVERAGE OF 1975–1977

	Average of All OECD Member Countries		United States
	Mean	Median	
Taxes on goods and services	9.9%	9.7%	4.7%
Taxes on incomes and profits	13.4	13.4	13.2
Households	10.8	11.1	9.9
Corporations	2.5	2.0	3.3
Social security	9.2	8.3	7.4
Other taxes	3.1	2.5	4.6

Does not add to total because data for some countries are not available.
SOURCES: Tables 17 and 18.

The United States adopted a personal income tax in 1913, much later than most European countries. After a deceptively easy start, it soon proceeded to levy it with a vengeance and has been doing so ever since. Not so much because an income tax was judged to be the most powerful method of raising funds to support government. Large sums could have been raised with less economic distortion by following the principle of neutrality in taxation by also using taxes which leave taxpayers in the same *relative* position after taxes which they were in before.

A "progressive" income tax was preferred as the most effective tax

FIGURE 9.

Types of Taxes Used in the USA and in OECD Countries

1975 through 1977

as a percentage of all taxes

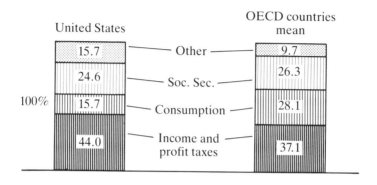

Source: tables 17 and 18

method of narrowing economic differences among individuals for an approach toward the ideal of an egalitarian society. It is a powerful instrument for redistributing income from those who produce more to those who produce less.

During the congressional debate in 1913, the proponents assured their colleagues that the proposed 1% to 7% rate certainly would never be raised as high as 10%. Yet within five years it was boosted to a temporary top rate of 77% and, after a postwar reduction some years later, to an all-time high of 94% in 1944. In 1965 the highest rate was lowered to 70% which is still very effective in cutting off the top—especially when we consider progressive estate taxes as well as state income taxes. General consumption taxes and other taxes, more proportionate to income—and thus of no use in helping to redistribute income—were held unacceptable and so remain to this day.

Another use of the income tax achieved prominence in the post–World War II period: economic stabilization. Experience with New Deal policies in the 1930s had disillusioned economists and politicians about the effectiveness or, at least about the adequacy, of enlarged public spending to stimulate and produce economic growth and stability. But the focus was still on maintaining and promoting aggregate demand and if a counter-cyclical policy could not be fully assured by spending policies, then it would have to be accomplished by fine-tuning the economy through manipulating taxes, and, when deemed desirable, resulting budgetary deficits.

Economic fluctuations remained within tolerable levels in the decades following World War II for which incumbent administrations and Congresses and their economists claimed no little credit. If we consider how often and how far those economists were off in their forecasts, we may feel some doubt on just how much praise the fine-tuners deserve.

Those who believed in the management of aggregate demand as the most effective instrument toward keeping economic trends on a steady upward course also used their influence toward keeping wage rates rising rapidly. They saw to it that the weight of government power was placed on the scale of labor union demands which, counting votes, seemed the politically wise course anyway. Only years later was it realized that boosting wages in excess of increased productivity rates inevitably drives up prices.

How can productivity be improved? Most effectively by providing incentives for investment in technological advance. That was the message that Walter Heller, then chairman of the Council of Economic Advisers, brought back from Europe to President Kennedy. Congress approved a 7% investment credit in 1962, boosted it to 10% in 1975. The stimulative effect of investment credits, however, is diminished by inadequate depreciation rates, by capital gains taxation which at times of inflation amounts to part-confiscation and by other tax changes aimed at maintaining the effectiveness of redistributive taxation.

Only in recent years has it become more widely recognized that the channeling of too many resources into consumption and government does not leave enough funds for capital formation for industry and that this, more than any other *single* factor is responsible for unsatisfactory performance of our economy.

Federal Reserve Board Chairman G. William Miller well expressed this conclusion in a speech to the National Press Club on June 7, 1978:

> It is time for us to take new directions to help shape a stronger America and a better world.
>
> One such new direction would involve a conscious shift in the philosophy for a U.S. economic policy from demand or consumption management to supply or investment management. . . .
>
> During the last decade, it has become apparent that government spending does not always produce results—economically or socially—and may not be the most effective way of reaching our desired objectives. . . .

Mr. Miller named a balanced budget with full employment and a reduction in the percentage of GNP taken by the federal government as his first two points. He continued:

Third, should be a policy to achieve a substantial increase in business fixed investment. The United States has been neglecting its capital base: the issue of investment for the future. . . .

We are falling behind other principal nations. Japan spends 15 percent of its GNP for capital investment; Germany 21 percent; United States 8 or 9. Over the decades we are falling behind in our productive capacity, our efficiency, our productivity and our technology.

One technique in stimulating more capital investment would be a substantial liberalization of depreciation guidelines so that the cash flow from risky investments would justify the investment.

President Carter's 1978 tax reform proposals to Congress, however, were populist redistributive and hostile toward business. A few months after Mr. Miller's speech President Carter appointed him Secretary of the Treasury. But he did not develop Treasury initiatives to carry out the ideas which Mr. Miller expressed so well in June 1978.

Mr. Miller's predecessor as Federal Reserve chairman, Arthur F. Burns, voiced similar thoughts succinctly a few months earlier (October 26, 1977) at Gonzaga University. Mr. Burns' main theme was:

the fact that the profits being earned by American business are at an unsatisfactory level.

Mr. Burns criticized Treasury depreciation rules which caused "a huge understatement of costs" and overstatement of profits. "These raw profit figures are misleading and they should never be taken at face value." He estimated that "the level of corporate profits was overstated in 1976 by about $30 billion, and that this resulted in an overpayment of some 10 to 12 billion dollars in income taxes." Mr. Burns predicted that "unless the willingness of businessmen to invest in new plant and equipment increases decisively, the expansion of economic activity now under way will continue to lack balance. . . . Historically, there has been an impressively close correlation between the rate of return on stockholders' equity and the rate of real investment."

Savings, the main source of investment funds, have been slim in the United States compared with other industrial nations and slipped to new lows in the late 1970s. This is not hard to understand in view of the hostile policy toward business profits and property income in U.S. tax policy. While Japan, France, West Germany and Britain boasted of 13.7% to 25.0% rates in aftertax personal savings, the U.S. rate which averaged 6.4% between 1952 and 1977 dropped to 5.2% in 1978 and was even lower in 1981.[1]

Stanford economics professor (and Hoover Institution senior fellow) Michael J. Boskin pointed out that "the most important long-run structural problem with the U.S. economy is that we undersave." He added that "current U.S. tax policy is preventing the nation from accumulating enough capital."[2]

Why has there been no action to alleviate punitive taxation of profits and of business in general? Because it would run counter to the populist income-redistributive policies which dominated American politics and the Congress for so long. All of President Carter's tax proposals, from his 1976 campaign on, focused on reducing or eliminating taxes of persons in low income brackets while tightening rules and raising taxes for persons in higher brackets and in business. Until this type of tax policy is changed, prospects for economic improvements will remain dim. Tax and spending policies which redistribute income from high earners—who would save part of it—to low or no-income earners—who will quickly spend the money— are largely responsible for inflationary trends and declining productivity.

Only in the late 1970s did statements which suggest a better understanding of economic facts and a friendly attitude toward policies which could lead to economic improvement come forth from congressional leaders. The chairmen of the two tax-writing committees in the 96th Congress were among them. Chairman Al Ullman of the House Ways and Means Committee stated, "Over the years we have come to over-rely on income-type taxes and underrely on consumption-type taxes. If we're going to improve capital formation—and increase productivity— we need to restructure our taxation of savings and business income."[3] Mr. Ullman added, "All taxes are ultimately paid by the consumer. We're kidding ourselves if we think otherwise. But there would be no inflationary impact if a Value Added Tax were used to offset other taxes, like the Social Security payroll tax or corporate taxes." When asked about closing loopholes, he replied: "We've been through ten years of very dedicated, tough reform of tax shelters. It became obvious last year that perhaps we moved too far. We were tightening up the tax system to the point where people had little incentive to invest."

Senate Finance Committee Chairman Russell B. Long spoke in similar terms in March 1980:

> It means that tax cuts are going to have to be geared to increasing productivity, or to incentives to produce or save. . . . I'd like to see further reductions in the effective capital-gains tax rate from the present 28 percent to, say, 21 percent. It would make money for the government, and it would be anti-inflationary.
>
> People I talk to in the Senate, especially on the Finance Committee,

feel that any tax cuts should encourage production. They find a lot of appeal for suggestions to shorten the depreciation period for business equipment and things of that sort. . . . Someday we're going to consider substituting a value-added tax for at least part of the Social Security Tax.[4]

Another type of tax which has recently been considered as possible partial or full replacement for income taxes (personal and corporate), besides the value-added tax, is an expenditures tax. Hoover Institution Senior Research Fellow Dan Throop Smith—who served as Deputy to the Secretary of the Treasury for Tax Policy throughout the Eisenhower administration—pointed out in testimony before the Senate Finance Committee on June 14, 1977:

> Our tax system conspicuously discriminates against capital and income from capital. Income which is the only source of new savings and capital is first taxed. Then the income from capital is also taxed. This is double taxation of the most fundamental sort. The most complete relief would involve a shift from income taxation to the sort of cash flow or expenditure tax which is so well analyzed in the recent Treasury publication *Blueprints for Basic Tax Reform.*[5]

The mentioned publication prepared under the direction of Treasury Secretary William E. Simon discussed two possible alternatives to the present tax structure: a) to make the personal income tax more comprehensive by eliminating many exclusions and deductions—and then lower the tax rate—and to integrate personal and corporate taxes; b) to replace the personal income tax with an expenditure or "cash flow" tax. It would be simpler than the income tax, would encourage savings and discourage spending, thus exerting an anti-inflationary impact, and could be graduated, just as the income tax is. It would also seem fair to tax persons not on their contribution to the economy (as expressed by their earnings) but on their withdrawals or consumption of the products of others. An individual would then be taxed on his income minus his savings—in other words, on what he spends. He would thus be taxed not on what he puts into the economy, as he is now, but on what he takes out of the economy.

Chances for such reform do not appear promising at this time. This leaves us with the problem of our counterproductive tax system, dominated by the income tax. The *relative* role of the personal income tax in the U.S. tax picture did not change much between 1952 and 1978, as the table below shows. The corporation profits tax, however, dropped sharply, partly because an excess profits tax imposed between 1950 and 1953 to help finance the Korean War expired, but largely because of the declining role of corporate profits. That phenomenon is discussed further in the section on the corporation tax. The most significant change, however, over the past quarter century was the steep rise of the social security tax which in *constant* dollars multiplied twelve times. The other taxes more or less held their own, though in the aggregate, the revenues of federal, state and local government tripled, in *constant* dollars, and their "burden" rose from 29.6% of GNP to 36.6%.

The remaining sections of this chapter deal with the major types of taxes—personal income, corporation profits, consumption, social security and property.

GOVERNMENTAL REVENUES, 1952–1978

Fiscal Year	1952 (in millions)	Percent	1978 (in millions)	Percent	Percent Increase	Percent Increase *Constant* $
All revenues	$100,245	100.0%	$731,736	100.0%	630%	197%
Taxes	$79,067	78.9%	$468,161	64.0%	492%	141%
Income	50,983	50.9	284,854	38.9	459	127
Individual	28,919	28.9	214,164	29.3	641	201
Corporation	22,064	22.0	70,690	9.7	220	30
Consumption	15,689	15.7	93,049	12.7	493	141
Property	8,652	8.6	66,422	9.1	668	212
Other	3,743	3.7	23,836	3.3	537	159
Social Security contributions	3,547	3.5	104,502	14.3	2846	1099
Other revenue	17,631	17.6	159,073	21.7	802	267

SOURCE: Table 16.

Many Unhappy Returns: The Personal Income Tax

"The federal taxing process has produced a magnificent tax system which compares favorably in its structure and administration with any in the world." This paean by Roy Blough who had helped to shape the system while working in the United States Treasury and on the Council of Economic Advisers[6] was paralleled in President Kennedy's 1962 tax message: "This message recognizes the basic soundness of our tax structure."

Some years later, in his first presidential campaign, and on subsequent occasions, Jimmy Carter denounced the present tax structure as "a disgrace to the human race" and a "disgrace to the country." "It's just a welfare program for the rich."

All these three statements were meant to refer primarily to the income tax. Roy Blough and President Kennedy praised the tax structure because the graduated income tax plays a more prominent role in the U.S. than it does in other countries and its "progressive features" effectively redistribute income down, from the rich to the poor. Also, because the United States, in contrast to other industrial countries, deliberately eschews the imposition of a national general consumption tax because such a tax is regarded to be regressive and would not help to redistribute income. Mr. Carter, however, denounced the tax system because in his opinion it lets rich people off too cheaply.

The basic sentiment in all these statements, contradictory as they seem, is thus the same: the criterion for judging a tax structure is performance of the prime task it is intended for—to take money from those who earn or have more and give it to those who have less. Messrs. Blough and Kennedy thought that the income tax did its intended job well, Mr. Carter that it did not do enough of it.

Positions in the tax controversy hinge on whether one feels that individual income should be determined by a person's contribution to the economy, according to the judgment of the market, or whether society should, by the political process, overrule the rewards and punishments of the market. In a broader sense then, this is part of a class struggle, of societal sectors fighting each other for a bigger slice of the pie. An exception are persons who cross over to the other side—in either direction—because their ideological concepts are not those of their economic class or because their political instincts or personal ambitions tell them that this will be more rewarding.

The ideological-political debate over the fairness of tax policy—whether it should help to approach egalitarian ideals or whether it should accept market decisions as basically just—is carried on in terms of arguments over the size of the tax contribution which each economic bracket should be required to make and what magnitudes or types of income should be freed from taxation by general or special provisions in the tax code. I shall examine the facts on the proper tax base and the exemptions therefrom later in this chapter.

Other considerations focus largely on the impact of a tax on economic trends, on its potentially repressive or incentive influence on the economy. To be sure, taxation is by nature repressive on income and economic growth, but it can be endowed with incentive qualities by making certain aspects less repressive than others. This, in today's language, is frequently called a loophole, a term commonly applied to a provision in the tax law which the commentator deems beneficial not to him but to others or to economic sectors other than those to which he belongs or is in sympathy with.

A tax such as the graduated income tax whose marginal rates rise sharply as income grows, acts as a deterrent to increased or maximum effort, to expansion, to new ventures. The more successful those activities turn out to be, the smaller a share of the return is the taxpayer able to keep. A graduated income tax is comparable to a graduated highway speeding fine which rises with the number of miles the driving speed exceeds the legal limit. Such a graduated fine is intended to deter people from speeding and is effective in keeping most automobilists from reckless driving. The progressive income tax has rightly been called a penalty for "reckless thriving." Many of the "loopholes" aim to reduce the economic speeding fine and thereby lower the disincentive for economic effort.

Despite tax disincentives, the *work ethic* though weakened still survives. In a Roper survey in January 1978 respondents were asked whether they agreed with the statement that people should place more emphasis on working hard and doing a good job than on what gives them personal satisfaction and pleasure. Nearly two-thirds—62%—answered in the affirmative, with positive replies inversely related to age. What gives cause for concern is the distribution by education. Among those who had completed only grade school, 79% voted for hard work, among the high school graduates 62%. But college graduates were about evenly split (52:48) between those who favored hard work and those who preferred personal satisfaction and pleasure. It really should not be surprising that college graduates find personal pleasure more attractive than hard work. They have, on the average, higher earnings from which government takes a much larger slice than of the wages of less highly educated persons. So they keep only a smaller share. But it raises grave questions about the future of a nation whose elite is evenly divided in its preference for pursuing more pleasure or engaging in hard work.

One of the often cited advantages of the income tax is its elasticity: its yield increases with economic growth, but at a faster rate, and decreases— also at a faster rate—during an economic decline. Thereby the tax tends to counteract economic fluctuations and serves as an automatic stabilizer. The precise relationship between economic growth and tax receipts depends on the rate of inflation and various other factors. A few years ago the Advisory Commission on Intergovernmental Relations (ACIR) estimated that federal income tax yields grow 75 percent faster than GNP, consumption tax yields at the same pace as the GNP, and property tax yields grow only at 75 percent of GNP (i.e., 25 percent more slowly). This makes the income tax politically very attractive. In periods of growth and inflation, the income tax brings in greatly enlarged amounts without the need to raise rates. Sales and property tax receipts increase more slowly and can be made more productive only by tax boosts—a politically distasteful and risky process.

The system works splendidly for the government whose revenues rise at a much faster rate than the economy, without a rate boost. It doesn't work so well for the taxpayer who is being pushed into higher tax brackets, year after year, even if his real income is growing much less, not at all, or is declining. So the burden of his income tax is getting heavier although the *appearance* of no tax boost is preserved. Congress was able to reduce the income tax several times—once in the 1950s, twice in the 1960s, four times in the 1970s—and gain all the political glory from cutting taxes while the burden of the tax actually grew heavier. That system is hard to beat.

The inflation-generated discrepancy between the growth rates of income and of income taxes could of course be corrected by indexing tax brackets—just as many wages and social benefits were indexed in the 1970s. Six states have recently indexed their income taxes. But this is not likely to happen at the federal level, at least not soon. The current method of *seeming* to cut the income tax while actually *increasing* its load is too attractive and rewarding for members of Congress.

Who Pays Income Taxes and Who Doesn't?

For at least a decade, stories have appeared from time to time in news media—and even a few books were written—asserting that rich people get away with paying no taxes by courtesy of certain intricacies of the tax code. Working people in middle and lower income brackets who cannot escape, have to pay the taxes which the wealthy manage to avoid. Most of these stories are fictitious or untrue. Some are deliberate distortions, others naive repetitions of what the author read or heard somewhere and regarded as a sensational scoop he could not miss. If man bites dog, that's news.

To be sure, we all have seen advertisements offering fabulous tax shelters that promise to save a taxpayer huge amounts. But these schemes generally have a price, carry a risk or are marginally or outright illegal. Some people are emotionally so charged against taxes that they will deliberately manage to have less income, incur sizable losses, take high chances, or settle where otherwise they wouldn't live, because they derive compensatory satisfaction from beating the tax collector. There *are* ways of arranging one's affairs in a manner that can reduce tax liability, but claims that the Internal Revenue Code or the IRS permit wealthy persons to get away with paying no taxes on a high income are a myth.

In the tax year 1977, 22 million income tax returns, one-fourth of all returns, were reported to be nontaxable, besides about twenty million, more or less, other adult persons who filed no income tax returns. We have only sketchy information about the latter group, and I shall discuss it later. But we have detailed information from the Internal Revenue Service about the nontaxable returns. By income brackets they are distributed as follows:

NONTAXABLE INCOME TAX RETURNS BY INCOME BRACKETS, 1977

	Number of Nontaxable Returns	
All *non*taxable Returns	22,143,519	100.0%
Adjusted Gross Income (AGI) under $5,000	18,271,382	82.5
$5,000 to under $10,000	3,416,152	15.4
$10,000 to under $30,000	427,269	1.9
$30,000 and over	28,716	.1[7]

If we relate the nontaxable returns in each bracket to the number of *all* returns in that bracket, the picture is as follows:

NONTAXABLE INCOME TAX RETURNS AS A PERCENTAGE OF ALL RETURNS, 1977

All nontaxable returns (as a percent of *all* returns filed)	25.6%
Adjusted Gross Income (AGI) under $5,000 nontaxable	78.6%
$5,000 to under $10,000	17.7
$10,000 to under $30,000	1.1
$30,000 and up	.5

In the $200,000 and up AGI bracket, 0.08% of all returns—one in 1231—was not taxable.

It is apparent that almost all of the nontaxable returns are in the lowest brackets—as they should be. But why are there 28,716 nontaxable returns in the $30,000-and-up AGI brackets? Because the tax law considers an infinite number of situations, of special burdens, ranging from taxes paid to state and local governments or foreign governments to interest payments and casualty losses. Also, because in some instances the government tries to encourage certain economic activities such as investment in new plants and equipment or creation of new jobs and, as an incentive, makes the tax burden therefore less repressive.

Are the Rich Paying Too Little?

If the rich do pay taxes, as the record indicates, surely they don't pay enough! At least, that is what we would conclude from reading repetitive

FIGURE 10.

NONTAXABLE PERSONAL INCOME TAX RETURNS

1977

by gross income brackets

as percent of all nontaxable returns

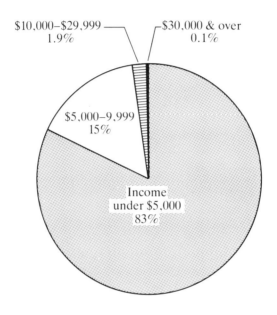

$10,000–$29,999 — 1.9%

$30,000 & over 0.1%

$5,000–9,999 15%

Income under $5,000 83%

Source: same as table 19

newspaper and magazine articles and listening to popular commentators who commiserate with the middle income group for being overburdened. The charge may be correct; the middle class may taxwise be overburdened, but certainly not compared with persons in higher brackets.

This is clearly demonstrated in the table below. The middle income group, defined as taxpayers with a gross income between $10,000 and $30,000 filed in 1977 44 percent of all returns, reported 58 percent of all income and paid 51 percent of the income tax. So it is slightly ahead of the game.

Persons with an income under $10,000 accounted for 49 percent of all returns, 17 percent of all income, but only 6 percent of the tax. Taxpayers with an income of $30,000 or more accounted for 7 percent of the returns, 26 percent of all income, but 43 percent of the tax liability. In other words, the income tax is *progressive*; it takes proportionately more from persons in

FIGURE 11.
NONTAXABLE PERSONAL INCOME TAX RETURNS
1977
by gross income brackets
as percent of all returns in income bracket

78.6%

17.7%

1.1%

0.5%

Under $5,000 $5,000 to $9,999 $10,000 to $29,999 $30,000 and over

Source: same as table 19

FIGURE 12.
FEDERAL PERSONAL INCOME TAX
1977
percentage shares by income bracket

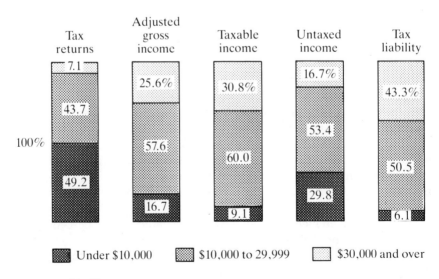

Tax returns	Adjusted gross income	Taxable income	Untaxed income	Tax liability
7.1	25.6%	30.8%	16.7%	43.3%
43.7	57.6	60.0	53.4	50.5
49.2	16.7	9.1	29.8	6.1

100%

■ Under $10,000   ▨ $10,000 to 29,999   ☐ $30,000 and over

Source: table 19a

the high brackets and less from those in the low brackets—notwithstanding statistical acrobatics that try to prove that 3 is more than 5.

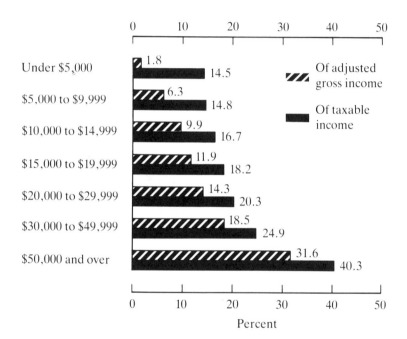

FIGURE 13.
FEDERAL PERSONAL INCOME TAX
1977
effective tax rate

The middle class, which earns more than half of all income, inevitably pays about half the tax. The oft-repeated charge that middle income groups bear a disproportionate share of the federal income tax has of course an undeniable political appeal. Everybody likes to feel sorry for himself and, after all, the tax *does* take a big slice out of a wage earner's salary. But the charge of relative overburden has no basis in fact.

The top 12% of all taxpayers (AGI $25,000 and up) pay more than half the tax (55%), the lowest 49% pay only 6% of the tax. The tax rate on the first group averages 21.1%, on the second group 4.7%. The middle income group ($10,000–$30,000) with a 12.1% tax rate is still taxed somewhat below the national average of 13.8%.

Political officeholders and office seekers are not unaware of the fact that under this system about half of all taxpayers—the 49% under $10,000

SHARES OF THE FEDERAL INCOME TAX BY MAJOR INCOME BRACKETS, 1977

AGI Bracket	Tax Returns	Share of AGI	Share of Tax Liability	Effective Average Tax Rate
Total	100%	100%	100%	13.8%
Under $10,000	49	17	6	4.7
$10,000 to under $30,000	44	58	51	12.1
$30,000 and over	7	26	43	23.5
Exhibit:				
$25,000 and over	12%	36%	55%	21.1%

SOURCES: Tables 19 and 19a.

AGI—pay an average tax rate of 4.7% while the seven percent of tax-payers in the top group ($30,000-and-up AGI) pay a rate of 23.5%. Vote-wise, that amounts to a ratio of one to seven—or if we compare the under $10,000 group with those over $50,000 income—a ratio of one to thirty-one. When a member of Congress, or a candidate, is called upon to take a stand on a tax issue, or to vote, with whom will he side? With the 49 percent of his constituents or with the 7 percent—or, with the 1.6% with an AGI of $50,000 and more?

The economic and political disequilibrium is actually much worse than those figures suggest. More than $150 billion in social security, unem-ployment and other transfer payments need not be reported on tax returns and are omitted from the cited statistics. Therefore, far more money and somewhat higher incomes than the tables above would indicate are untaxed.

The threshold income for the filing of an income tax return was:

	1977	1980		1977	1980
	Under 65 Years			65 years and over	
Single	$2950	$3300		$3700	$4300
Couple	4700	5400		6200	7400

On top of this, individuals and couples may receive sizable income which need not be reported on income tax returns and is tax-free. It averaged:

	1977	1980	
Social security, retired worker	$2916	$4083	(October)
Social Security, retired worker's spouse	1477	2057	(October)
Unemployment benefits	4097	5135	(July)
Aid to Families with Dependent Children	3000	3253	(June)

SOURCE: *Social Security Bulletin*, February 1981.

This means that a couple over 65 with an income of $7400 plus average social security retirement checks of $6140 ($4083 and $2057) for a total income of $13,540, not counting medical and other in-kind benefits, did not have to file a tax return for 1980.

Twenty-three million income tax returns reported an income of less than $5,000 for 1977. But the Census survey of money income in 1977 showed only 12.5 million households with an income under $5,000.[8] Nontaxable government income security payments probably accounted for most of the 11.5 million gap (not counting nonfilers) aside from differential underreporting of income for income tax purposes and for the Census.

In addition to 22 million nontaxable returns—which since 6.6 million of them are joint returns represent 29 million men and women—there are about twenty million persons in the population who file no income tax return. Most of them do so lawfully: they have an income which, not counting tax-free transfer payments, is below the taxable limit or not much above it. They pay no tax—but they can vote. In all likelihood they will vote for their own economic benefit for candidates who advocate the imposition of heavier taxes on persons in higher income brackets with which to finance more generous social benefits for persons in low economic brackets.

Many voters in the middle income group may vote similarly. When they look upwards, at persons above them on the income scale, they feel envy; when they look down at those poorer than themselves, they feel compassion. Result: they are likely to favor tax—and spending—policies that grow increasingly more progressive (income redistributive).

Some of the progression is achieved by a rate scale which since 1965 has been graduated from 14% to 70%. But more of the progression comes from leaving carefully selected types of income untaxed.

Income data used in the tables and discussion above—adjusted gross income (AGI)—were taken from IRS statistics of personal income tax returns. They excluded in 1977 $376 billion of personal income—as defined by the national income accounts—which need not be reported on tax returns and are tax free. This, more than any other factor, accounts for the progressivity of the income tax.

Who Benefits from Those Infamous Loopholes?

The Internal Revenue Code proclaims its intent to tax "all income from whatever source derived." But then it undercuts that sweeping statement by allowing a myriad of exclusions, exemptions, deductions and credits, now commonly called loopholes.[9]

Loopholes in the tax code through which huge amounts of income escape scot-free have been a subject of lively controversy for about a quarter century. Judging from a review of the nation's press, radio, and television networks and the utterances of public officials, political parties, and large organizations, there appears to be a widespread consensus that tax loopholes ought to be closed or at least sharply tightened. The tax-writing committees of both houses of Congress have held extensive hearings that produced strong statements and voluminous documentation—although sometimes conflicting testimony—on just which types of currently tax-free income ought to be subject to taxation.

In view of this public sentiment it is not surprising that Congress has taken action repeatedly to close tax loopholes: it passed six tax-reform acts within 10 years—in 1969, 1971, 1976, 1977, and 1978—all overtly aimed at capturing some of the untaxed income. Surprisingly, though, every time Congress has enacted a tax-reform bill, the amount of untaxed income was larger afterwards than it had been before. And the percentage of personal income exempted from the federal income tax as well as the number of Americans paying no income tax has substantially increased.

The difference between *total* personal income—according to national income accounts—and the *taxable* income that is reported on individual income tax returns totaled $357 billion in 1969, equal to 47.9% of all personal income. Three years later, thanks to the *Tax Reform Act of 1969*, that difference had grown to $495 billion, equal to 52.1% of all personal income.[10] The percentage zigzagged in subsequent years, pushed up by inflation, pushed down by more doses of "tax reform." By 1977 the difference between personal income and taxable income—the untaxed income—totaled $800 billion. It may be estimated at well over a trillion dollars in 1979—courtesy of "reforms" in the *Revenue Act of 1978*—out of $1.9 trillion personal income.

To be sure, Congress meanwhile tightened several minor loopholes, mostly in the high brackets, and imposed a new "minimum" tax on so-called tax preferences. But it more than offset those efforts by opening or widening other loopholes with an impact largely in the lower and middle brackets. This suggests that the "close-the-loopholes" drive aims not so much at capturing tax-free income as to shift the burden from some economic groups to others. The real purpose of these actions, further eroding the base and structure of the income tax—ironically called "tax reform"—is to make the income tax more income redistributive than it already is. In plain words: to soak the rich.

Taxpayers have long complained that property and sales taxes allow many exemptions that erode the tax base, thereby cutting the revenues of schools, cities, and states, and giving unfair advantage to some citizens over others. But exemptions in property and sales taxes amount to between one-fourth and one-third of their respective tax bases. In the federal income tax they total more than half the base, and the income tax has become "the leakiest tax in town."

All *personal* income in 1977, according to national income accounts, totaled	$1532 billion	100.0%
Taxable income, as reported on personal income tax returns for that year amounted to	731 billion[11]	47.7
Which leaves an untaxed income of	$ 801 billion	52.3%

There are, however, about $110 billion which the tax code treats as taxable income which the national income accounts do not regard or treat as personal income. These are mostly employees' and self-employed persons' social insurance contributions, capital gains and capital consumption adjustments. If we relate taxable income of $731 billion to personal income of $1642 billion ($1532 billion plus $110 billion) we arrive at the conclusion that about 55% of personal income escaped federal taxation in 1977.

We could cut our current rates in half—from a scale of 14 percent to 70 percent to a scale from 7 percent to 35 percent—and get more revenue than we do now by repealing all exemptions, exclusions, deductions and credits, and subjecting *all* personal income to the tax. Or, alternatively, a flat rate of 10 percent on *all* personal income would produce an equal amount of revenue and greatly simplify the tax. Why is this not done? Because eliminating all "loopholes" would cause a major shift in the tax burden from the higher to the lower income brackets. That would be politically unacceptable to Congress. And, of course, simplifying the tax would deprive tens of thousands of accountants, lawyers, tax advisers, and revenue agents of their jobs because most people could then prepare their own returns.

This may sound strange because we have been told hundreds of times over a quarter century that huge tax loopholes benefit mostly the rich, enabling them to avoid paying taxes—or at least a fair share of the taxes—while offering no such escape hatch to persons in the low brackets. Such assertions pervert the truth. The fact is that most untaxed personal income accrues to those in the middle and lower brackets, and only a small share to persons in the top brackets.

Let me demonstrate this in specific terms. A direct comparison by income size brackets between personal income and taxable income is statistically impossible because the Department of Commerce quit in 1964 computing personal income by size brackets.

So we have to follow a more complicated procedure, an analysis in two steps, if we want to find out how the $800 billion of tax-free income in 1977 was divided among the various economic brackets. First we compare adjusted gross income (AGI) with taxable income (TI)—a difference of $424 billion—and then we compare adjusted gross income (AGI) with personal income (PI)—a difference of $376 billion. The first part is readily available, the second part more intricate.

Personal income means all income as defined and computed by national income accounts. Adjusted gross income means gross income as defined by the tax code—omitting most government transfer payments—minus various adjustments such as moving expenses, employee business expenses, alimony payments, payments to an IRA or Keogh plan, etc. Taxable income is the final net income to which the tax rates are applied to determine tax liability.

The $424 billion difference between adjusted gross income and taxable income consisted of two major components: 161 billion for personal exemptions (at $750 per person)[12] and $263 billion in deductions. Under 1977 code revisions, three-fourths of the 1977 deductions was for "zero bracket amounts," a flat amount based on marital status ($2200 single person, $3200 joint returns).[13]

This means that about 85% of the $424 billion is deducted on a per person basis so that taxpayers in higher brackets deduct a much smaller percentage of their income than those in the lower brackets. That is evident in the following table.

The table on p. 87 shows that 83 percent of the difference between AGI and TI—untaxed income—goes to taxpayers in the under $30,000 brackets. Only 6 percent redounds to taxpayers with an income of $50,000 or more. Furthermore, two-thirds of all income under $10,000 is thus freed from taxation while in the $50,000-and-up range only one-fifth is tax-free. Even if all AGI in the top brackets were taxed away by government, it would make little difference to total revenues or to persons in the low and middle brackets.

That still leaves the question: Who gets the other $376 billion in untaxed income, the difference between personal income and adjusted gross income? The U.S. government unfortunately prepares no data that would enable us to break down this amount by income brackets. But we can identify the items which compose those $376 billion—generally types of income that under the Internal Revenue Code need not be reported on income tax returns: government income maintenance programs such as

BREAKDOWN BY INCOME SIZE OF THE DIFFERENCE BETWEEN
ADJUSTED GROSS INCOME AND TAXABLE INCOME, 1977

AGI size bracket	Adjusted Gross Income (AGI)	Taxable Income (TI)	Difference between AGI and TI (untaxed income)	Percent of total	Untaxed income as percent of AGI
			Billions of Dollars		
Total	$1,155.7	$731.4	$424.3	100.0	36.7
Under $10,000	193.7	67.2	126.5	29.8	65.3
$10,000 to under $30,000	665.8	438.9	226.9	53.5	34.1
$30,000 to under $50,000	173.5	129.0	44.5	10.5	25.6
$50,000 and over	122.7	96.3	26.4	6.2	21.5

SOURCE: *Statistics of Income, 1977 (Preliminary) Individual Income Tax Returns*, Internal Revenue Service (6–79).

social security, unemployment compensation, public assistance, supplemental security income, veterans benefits, etc., $160 billion; untaxed labor income (employer contributions to pension and welfare funds, nontaxable income in kind, etc.), $92 billion; nontaxable food and fiber produced and consumed on farms, nontaxable military pay allowances, income below taxable levels on which no return needs to be filed; income that is not reported,[14] $124 billion.

Most of the above-mentioned types of income—social welfare payments, labor income, income in kind—go to persons in the low brackets, some to those closer to the middle; very little goes to high-income taxpayers.

In summary: In both analyses above—between AGI and TI and between TI and PI—most of the tax-free income, which in the aggregate amounted to $800 billion in 1977, was found to accrue to persons with a below-average income. Upper-bracket taxpayers received less than ten percent of the total. But claims that tax loopholes primarily benefit the rich are still being repeated and even widely believed, despite conclusive evidence to the contrary.[15]

The Myth of the Rich Nontaxpayers

Though the largest share of the untaxed income goes to low and middle brackets, political attention focuses mainly on the relatively small amounts of untaxed income in the high brackets. President Carter stated on March 6, 1977:

> During the campaign and in my acceptance speech . . . I said that I thought that the income tax system of this country was a disgrace. I haven't changed my opinion about that. . . . Before the end of September we will propose basic reforms in income tax structure . . .
>
> We anticipate in September eliminating a great number of the loopholes that benefit the rich and the powerful and the savings that are derived from that will be passed on to the low and middle income families.

Mr. Carter never submitted proposals to eliminate "a great number of the loopholes that benefit the rich and the powerful." In fact, his recommendations on January 21, 1978, were relatively moderate, presumably because a closer study of the facts convinced him that certain proposals he had advanced earlier would be unacceptable to Congress. They would, if enacted, have had disastrous economic consequences. But the myth survives that the "rich and powerful" escape taxation, wholly or partially, because it is deliberately nurtured for political reasons.

For many years the most articulate spokesman for this theory was Stanley Surrey, who served as Assistant Secretary of the Treasury for Tax Policy from 1961 to 1969. But none of the presidents he served would submit Mr. Surrey's recommendations to Congress. Neither would the succeeding president. But, by a quirk of history, an event that occurred two days before Mr. Nixon's inauguration, made that approach to tax reform a major congressional topic in his first presidential year.

On January 17, 1969, Joseph Barr, who then served as interim Secretary of the Treasury (for 31 days), told the House Ways and Means Committee—two days before he had to leave office—that the country faced a taxpayer revolt,

> not because of the level or amount of the taxes they must pay but because certain provisions of the tax law unfairly lighten the burden of others who can afford to pay. People are concerned and indeed angered about the high-income recipients who pay little or no federal income taxes. For example, the extreme cases are 155 tax returns in 1967 with adjusted gross income above $200,000 on which no federal income taxes were paid, including 21 with incomes above $1,000,000.

That sensational charge—that the very rich escape paying income taxes—emanating from the Secretary of the Treasury caused a national stir. There was no taxpayers' revolt brewing *before* Mr. Barr exploded his bomb. But one surely was in the making afterwards. It prodded Congress into frantic action and produced within a few months probably the worst piece of tax legislation up to that time—the *Tax Reform Act of 1969*, which soon became affectionately known as the Lawyers and Accountants Full Employment Act of 1969.

To be sure, most of the 155 tax returns with a $200,000-and-up adjusted gross income reporting no tax liability in 1967, which Mr. Barr cited, represented persons who were rich mainly because of the Internal Revenue Code's reporting requirements. They did not have a high income that year in a meaningful sense of the word.

The 1969 Tax Reform Act imposed a 10% minimum tax on what it called "tax preferences." Subsequent amendments tightened the tax and raised its rate to 15%. Together with other action this helped to reduce the number of nontaxable returns with an AGI of $200,000 or more to 43 over the succeeding ten years. It helped to make about 100 or more persons in high AGI brackets pay at least *some* income tax. It did, however, not catch the huge amounts of income which allegedly escaped tax-free in the top brackets. The minimum tax accounted in 1977 for less than five percent of the total income tax paid in the brackets from $200,000 AGI up. What the 1969 Tax Reform Act did very effectively is liberate billions of formerly taxable income in the lower brackets and free millions of income recipients from having to bear any share in the income tax burden.

While little purpose would be served in now analyzing the 155 tax-free returns which Mr. Barr cited in 1969, it is useful to examine tax-free returns reporting high AGI in the latest year for which the necessary data are available.

According to preliminary IRS statistics, there were in 1978 69,039 returns with an AGI of $200,000 or more, of which 68,958, or 99.9%, were taxable; 81 returns were not taxable. Let us now put first the taxable and then the nontaxable returns under the microscope.[16]

The 68,958 taxable returns reported an average AGI of		$369,192
Less: exemptions		2,642
Less: itemized deductions		
medical	$ 759	
state and local		
taxes	26,212	
charitable		
contributions	24,821	

interest	15,627	
miscellaneous	6,381	
Total		73,800
Plus: adjustments		3,224
Taxable Income		$295,974
Total Income Tax		$161,599

This means that those 68,958 top-bracket taxpayers paid taxes that equaled 43.8% of their AGI and 54.5% of their taxable income. The comparable rates for income tax returns with an AGI under $200,000 were: 14.6% of AGI and 17.6% of taxable income. In other words, the highest income group bore in proportion to income about three times as high a tax burden as the rest of the taxpayers.

That still leaves us with the question: How did the other recipients of an income of $200,000 or more manage to avoid income taxes? In 1978 there were 81 nontaxable returns—out of a total of 69,039 returns with a $200,000-and-up income. Seventy-one of these showed an income between $200,000 and $500,000, ten above $500,000. Thus there was one nontaxable return for every 852 taxable returns; slightly over one-tenth of one percent of all returns in that bracket was nontaxable. That is somewhat less than disturbing, but we still are entitled to an answer to the question why they were.

The 81 returns reported, on the average, a taxable income of $203,311 and a tax liability before credits of $98,062, which corresponds to a tax rate of 48.2%. But they did, in the end, not owe taxes because they had earned tax credits that offset their total tax liability. About 70% of the credits were for income taxes paid to foreign countries. The IRS has published no breakdown for the remaining 30%. But in all likelihood it was similar to 1977 data when 22% were accounted for by new job credits (hiring of disadvantaged persons), 7% by investment credits and 1% by general and other credits. It is evident that within this tiny group many derived most of their income from sources in foreign countries. Under local laws they had to pay income taxes to those countries on their local earnings. To impose American income taxes on top of foreign levies would make it economically impossible for Americans to conduct business beyond our borders. That is why the Internal Revenue Code grants a credit for foreign income taxes, regardless of whether the recipient lives there or here. So, on 70% of the income, foreign governments had a legitimate prior claim. As for the other 30%, it is possible to disagree on the need or justification of new job credits or investment credits. But that is an entirely different issue from the one we are examining here: whether and why persons with a high AGI may owe no taxes to the federal government. That question has been satisfactorily answered.

This should end once and for all the myth that rich people pay no income tax. It does, however, not settle the problem of huge amounts of income evading taxes.

In July 1979 the General Accounting Office published a report *Who's Not Filing Income Tax Returns* in which it estimated that five to six million income earners avoid filing tax returns each year, depriving the Treasury of an estimated $2 billion annually. Most nonfilers were found to be low-income persons. Many of them were occasional or part-time workers or illegal aliens. Only 5 percent of the nonfilers were estimated to make $20,000 or more, much of it from illegal activities. GAO blamed IRS for much of the gap because it concentrated its enforcement on nonfilers with large tax liabilities, disdaining to go after "small fry."

The Internal Revenue Service conducted in 1978–79, for the first time, an investigation of unreported income and came up with disturbing findings.[17] It estimated that in 1976 between $100 and $135 billion income went unreported, three-fourths of it from legal sources and the remainder from criminal activities. One-third of the total was believed to be attributable to nonfilers, the rest to persons who reported only part of their income. The tax loss was placed between $19 and $26 billion a year.

The greatest amount of unreported legal income was attributed to self-employed persons, ranging from lawyers to peddlers, the next highest share to wages and salaries, mostly of casual employees in small establishments or working for private persons. Illegal income came mostly from drugs and gambling. While the IRS indicated that it was planning countersteps, it did not hold out great hope of being able to reach much of the unreported income with the means at its command. IRS cannot audit returns that are never filed. Earlier the IRS had estimated from its Taxpayer Compliance Measurement Program (TCMP-surveys) that 93% of the taxpayers reported all their income and taxes.

Others have come up with far bigger estimates of unreported income, going as high as $200 to $400 billion and more.[18]

This repeats a lesson which Americans learned—or should have learned—from prohibition: a law which a large segment of the population regards as unjust, as an oppressive interference in their lives and with their rights, is difficult or impossible to enforce adequately, especially when transgression offers high rewards. Some of the states have found out that alcohol or tobacco tax rates that far exceed those of their neighbors are widely evaded by smuggling. Many Americans feel that taxes are too heavy and unfair. They believe that they have a valid grievance, that government is cheating them in several ways, particularly through inflation, and they strike back where they can—by underpaying taxes—with no qualms.

The drive for tax reform over the past quarter century has not helped to lift the standing or acceptance of the income tax. While Congress closed a few loopholes on one end, it widened many at the other end and freed millions of additional persons from having to pay any tax. So, an increasing number of people take the law into their own hands and rationalize tax evasion.

How can one have respect for a law which taxes single persons up to 20% more than it taxes married persons on the same income, while simultaneously taxing *some* married couples—in upper-middle income brackets with each spouse having about the same income—up to 19% more than if they were not married?

Congress has been aware of this "marriage tax" for some and "singles tax" for others for a decade now, but has done nothing to correct the inequity. Prospects for putting the income tax on a basis where *all* personal income would be taxed and taxed alike still appear dim.

The movement to close loopholes aims only at repealing certain types of alleviative provisions but is deliberately blind to others. To validate its claims its supporters manipulate income data in an attempt to show that the income tax is not as progressive as it appears to be. A carefully chosen selection of nontaxed items are now called "tax expenditures," a term which suggests that government has a prior claim to all income and generously allows the earner to keep some of it.

Under mandate of the 1974 Budget and Accounting Act, tax expenditures are now tabulated in each year's federal budget. Many of the amounts shown are fictitious, being based on the assumption that a taxpayer would not alter his activities if taxes thereon were sharply boosted. Though the budget specifically warns against trying to add the estimates for various "tax expenditures"—because they are interdependent—some commentators have undertaken to total them and arrived at $114 billion tax expenditures in 1977, projected at $269 billion in 1984. But these are purely hypothetical exercises of no practical value.

To be sure, tax differentials—or "loopholes"—were put in the law not by accident, oversight, or inadvertence, or to protect the rich from having to pay their fair share of taxation. They were inserted, almost always after extensive public hearings by the two tax-writing committees of Congress, to achieve one or both of the following objectives:

1. To provide greater equity, horizontal or vertical, among taxpayers and different types and magnitudes of income by taking into account differing circumstances and offering relief for hardships;

2. To provide incentives to taxpayers to engage in or enlarge activities that are held to be desirable as a matter of public policy. This is done by offering rewards to some and imposing penalties on others.

This should not be interpreted as justifying most of the tax alleviative provisions or advocating their continuation. It only aims to explain that most of those rules are not the result of sinister machinations of lobbyists for moneyed interests who either bribed lawmakers or pulled the wool over the eyes of unsuspecting congressmen and the public. No public laws are subjected to more painstaking and detailed congressional study, to more thorough debates, year after year, than the tax laws.

Most of the "middle class" deductions such as for state and local taxes and interest paid, for medical costs and casualty losses, as well as joint returns, have proven impervious to repeated attacks over the past two decades. So have deductions for educational, charitable and religious contributions. To turn those deductions into direct governmental subsidies—as Stanley Surrey and others have suggested—would sound the death knell to most voluntary activities. Some would be abandoned, and donations for religious purposes could for constitutional reasons not be replaced by government subsidies. To substitute federal appropriations for donations to private education or charity would subject those activities to governmental control and, for all practical purposes, terminate them. It would extinguish much of the freedom that is still left to Americans after the vast expansion of governmental regulation and authority in recent decades. The most beneficial action that could be taken at this time would be to convert some of those deductions into tax credits.

One of the most frequently attacked "loopholes" is the taxing of long-term capital gains at half the normal tax rate. That provision was sharply cut in 1969 and President Carter promised repeatedly to delete it altogether and tax capital gains as ordinary income. He tried but failed.

It may well be asked: why should money made from money be taxed more lightly than money made from working? That rhetorical question sounds persuasive but is misleading.

Suppose someone bought a house ten years ago for $20,000 and now sells it for $50,000. Should he have to pay income tax on his $30,000 gain? That gain is obviously fictitious because he would have to pay at least $50,000 to buy another, equivalent house. Congress recognized this and exempted such gains on the sale of owner-occupied homes. But it did not exempt it on the sale or rollover of other types of investment. That might be explained as a political expediency—we just need to compare the number of homeowners and the number (and income brackets) of persons who have and switch other types of large investments.

To tax as current income the paper gain on long-term capital transactions, particularly at times of rapid inflation, amounts to part confiscation. That is why other countries do not tax capital gains (Germany, Japan, Netherlands, Australia, Italy, etc.) or tax them at lower than normal income tax rates. This also accounts for the higher rates of capital formation, nonresidential investment and productivity growth which those countries have been enjoying, compared with the United States.

When the United States, between 1918 and 1921, tried to tax capital gains as ordinary income, investors ceased to sell assets with gains. They sold mostly assets with losses so that the U.S. Treasury had a net revenue loss. That might happen again if normal tax rates were applied to capital gains. Investments would be "frozen" which could well be the most effective way to assure stagnation in the national economy. Claims in the tax expenditures statement that federal revenues could have been boosted $18.5 billion in 1977 by fully taxing capital gains are fictitious.

When Congress turned around and considered easing capital gains taxation in 1978 (Steiger Amendment), Mr. Carter denounced it as "a plan that provides huge windfalls for millionaires and two bits for the average American." But Congress enacted the plan in November 1978. A Treasury study late in 1980 reported that nearly all the predicted revenue loss from the cut in the top capital gains rate from 49% to 28% was offset in 1979 by stepped-up capital gains, taxes on which totaled $2.5 billion instead of the $900 million the Treasury had predicted.

Consideration of national economic impact, however, does not diminish the drive to free additional millions—or dozens of millions—of persons from the income tax. It enlarges the number of persons who clamor for ever greater government benefits and services, knowing that they do not have to contribute toward them. The division among the American people—between those who pay to support the government and those who are supported by it—may have ominous long-range implications. An increasing irresponsibility of voting—*of representation without taxation*—poses a grave threat to the preservation of free government in the United States. But it does make for a more equal distribution of aftertax income than if income depended mostly on individual effort and success.

There have been suggestions for replacing the personal income tax, at least partially, by other forms of taxation, particularly a broad-based consumption tax. Because a retail sales tax is the mainstay of most states, federal plans focus more on a value-added tax (VAT) which in recent decades has become the prevailing tax in European countries, gradually eliminating turnover and sales taxes. Another possibility is an expenditure or cash-flow tax, mentioned earlier in this chapter. No discussion of the income tax would be complete without mention of the use of that tax by the states. Expansion of personal income taxation was particularly strong at the state level where collections multiplied 32 times between 1952 and 1978 (from $913 million to $29.1 billion) while federal income tax receipts multiplied eight times, and personal income 6.4 times. This means that the *burden* of state income taxes went up fivefold.

Most state income taxes were adopted in the 1930s, a few in earlier years; by 1937 there were thirty-one states levying a personal income tax. But when federal income tax rates, soon after, soared to unprecedented levels, states sought greener pastures and no state enacted a new income tax between 1938 and 1960. But then increasing fiscal pressure became irresistible. Forty-one states now levy a personal income tax and another three states tax some or all investment income only. Most states meanwhile raised their rates once or several times or tightened the tax in other ways. A few states conferred the right to levy an income tax on cities and other local governments.

In 1973–74 the upward trend in state income taxation was slightly reversed and this was even more pronounced in 1978 and 1979. The tax revolt that blew out of California in 1978 with the adoption of proposition 13, may have caused some state legislators to try to forestall more drastic action by their constituents.

In California very little relief was provided on the income tax and collections soared. Between 1967 and 1978 state income tax receipts in California jumped from $500 million to $4.6 billion, which in *constant* dollars means a 375% rise while personal income went up only 45%. The ratio between state income taxes and personal income multiplied more than threefold in the short span of eleven years (0.7% in 1967, 2.3% in 1978). This propelled a constitutional initiative onto the June 1980 ballot that proposed to cut state income taxes in half. It proved too much for Californians, who had cut their property taxes in half two years earlier and limited state and local spending by a constitutional initiative in November 1979. Voters were afraid that another sharp tax reduction might adversely affect vital public services and turned thumbs down on what had come to be called "Jaws II."

The Corporation Profits Tax

In contrast to virtually all other major taxes which expanded heavily over the past quarter century, government revenues from corporation profits taxes, federal and state, have relatively declined. Profits taxes accounted for 22% of all governmental revenues in 1952, for a mere 10% in

1978 (Table 16). If we take just the federal tax, which accounts for 85% of aggregate federal-state corporation taxes, receipts fell from 6.3% of Gross National Product to 3.0%. In 1952 the federal personal income tax yielded 32% more than the corporate tax; in 1978 it produced 202% more, or three times as much.

Why has the corporation tax turned from a major to a minor revenue producer?

Have slick lobbyists succeeded in persuading Congress to shift the burden of taxation from business to individuals, from the owners to the workingman? It hardly seems so: for thirty years the corporation tax has consistently exceeded the dividends which the companies paid to their shareholders. If the government is getting relatively less from corporations, so too are their owners.

Three factors are mainly responsible for the decline of the corporation tax since 1952.

1. A temporary excess profits tax, imposed in 1950 to help finance the Korean War, expired in 1954. But it accounted only for 8% of the corporation tax in 1952, so it was not a major factor.

2. The tax rate on most corporate income was reduced from 52% to 48%. There goes four points, or another 8 percent.

3. The most important cause for the decline of the corporation tax was a significant shift in income shares over the past quarter century from ownership to labor. It is shown in three tables, in terms of National Income, Corporate Income and Personal Income.

SHARES OF NATIONAL INCOME, 1952 AND 1978

| | 1952 | 1978 | 1952 | 1978 | Increase | Decrease |
	Billions of Dollars		in percent of National Income		between 1952 and 1978	
Total	$285.8	$1,724.3	100.0%	100.0%		
Proprietors	42.9	116.8	15.0	6.8		−8.2%
Corporation profits	35.4	167.7	12.4	9.7		−2.7
Rental income	8.8	25.9	3.1	1.5		−1.6
Net interest	3.0	109.5	1.0	6.4	+5.4%	
All ownership	$ 90.1	$ 419.9	31.5%	24.4%		−7.1%
Employee compensation	$195.7	$1,304.5	68.5%	75.6%	+7.1%	

SHARES OF CORPORATION INCOME, 1952 AND 1978

	1952	1978	1952	1978	Increase Decrease between 1952 and 1978
	Billions of Dollars		in percent of Corporate Income		
Total	$156.0	$1,051.3	100.0%	100.0%	
Pretax profits*	32.8	166.4	21.0	15.8	−5.2%
Employee compensation	123.2	884.9	79.0	84.2	+5.2%

*Including: interest, inventory valuation adjustment, capital consumption adjustment.

SHARES OF PERSONAL INCOME, 1952 AND 1978

	1952	1978	1952	1978	Increase Decrease between 1952 and 1978
	Billions of Dollars		in percent of Personal Income		
Total	$270.4	$1,717.4	100.0%	100.0%	
Proprietors	42.9	116.8	15.9	6.8	−9.1%
Dividends	8.5	47.2	3.1	2.7	− .4
Rental income	8.8	25.9	3.3	1.5	−1.8
Personal interest	10.3	163.3	3.8	9.5	+5.7%
Total ownership	$ 70.5	$ 353.2	26.1%	20.6%	−5.5%
Wages and salaries	$185.4	$1,103.3	68.6%	64.2%	−4.4%
Other labor income	5.2	106.5	1.9	6.2	+4.3%
Transfer payments	13.1	224.1	4.8	13.0	+8.2
less: Social insurance contributions	3.8	69.6	1.4	4.1	−2.7
Total labor and transfer	$199.9	$1,364.3	73.9%	79.4%	+5.5%

SOURCES: *The National Income and Products Accounts of the United States, 1929–1974*, A Supplement to the *Survey of Current Business*, 1979; *Survey of Current Business*, July 1979; and *Economic Indicators*, September 1979.

It is apparent that in these three national summaries the share of employee compensation, including perquisites and transfer payments (which almost entirely go to the labor sector), has increased by 5.2 to 7.1

percentage points of total income while the share of ownership commensurately shrank. The only property income that advanced was from interest received, due to rising interest rates and increased consumer borrowing.

The American public is entirely unaware of this shift in the slicing of the national pie and goes on believing that business reaps enormous and ever expanding profits. It could hardly believe anything else from daily reading of our newspapers and magazines and listening to radio-TV. A 1976 survey of the Opinion Research Corporation showed that Americans believe that the average manufacturer keeps 29 cents of every sales dollar. An August 1979 survey by the same firm revealed that the public thinks that aftertax profits total 32 cents per sales dollar. The fact is, according to the Federal Trade Commission, that manufacturers earn, after taxes, 5.4 cents per sales dollar.

Does the average American think that profits are six times higher than they really are because he is so poorly educated? In all likelihood he gets

FIGURE 14.

SHARES OF NATIONAL INCOME

1952 and 1978

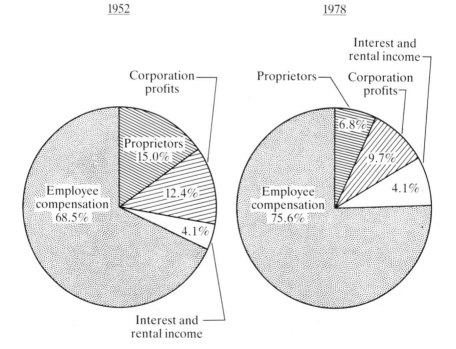

FIGURE 15.
SHARES OF PERSONAL INCOME
1952 and 1978

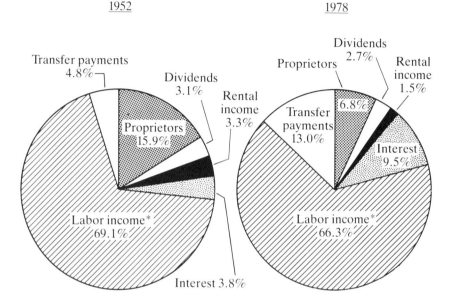

1952

1978

*Minus social security contributions

his information from the daily or weekly media. Is it purely accidental that there are so many stories about huge and growing business profits, and far less about the much larger number of companies which struggle desperately to make ends meet? Is there system in that madness—or misinformation?

If corporations actually were reaping high profits, investors would fall all over themselves to get part of the action by buying common shares. But just between 1970 and 1977 corporate stocks dropped from 38% to 21% of financial assets.

A final judgment of the profitability of corporations is expressed by the valuation of the stock market. It is where people put their money, not just their mouths. And they have not been putting their money into corporate ownership.

Stock prices blossomed in the 1950s but stagnated through the 1960s and 1970s. The Dow Jones index (30 leading industrials on the New York Stock Exchange) stood at 911 in 1965 and again in July 1980. Since the dollar meanwhile lost 62 percent of its value (the reciprocal of CPI growth from 94.5 in 1965 to 248 in July 1980), the owner of an average common share lost nearly two-thirds of the value of his investment. In *constant* dollars the value of an average common share dropped from $1.00 to 38 cents. This, more than any other single fact, demonstrates the poor profitability of American corporate business.

The fact is that corporate profits are too low to attract sufficient investment capital—and the investment rate is substantially less in the United States than in other industrial countries (see section on the *American Tax System*, p. 71). Low profits and inadequate business investments also relate to low productivity growth. The President's *Economic Report, January 1980* (p. 85), shows that annual growth in GNP per employed worker averaged 1.9% in the United States compared with rates in other major industrial countries from 2.4% to 8.7% between 1963 and 1973; it fell in the United States to virtually zero between 1973 and 1978, and turned negative in 1979 and 1980 though other countries still produced respectable rates.

The corporation tax—and the general treatment of private enterprise by government—have substantially contributed to this sad state of American business.

The Internal Revenue Code forces companies to report and pay taxes on fictitious profits. It mandates depreciation based on historical values—which may be only a fraction of current or replacement values—and taxes phantom inventory gains from inflation. The Bureau of Economic Analysis in the U.S. Department of Commerce estimated that 1979 profits reported by corporations under established IRS rules should be adjusted downward by $58.6 billion to offset inadequate capital consumption allowances and inflation-boosted inventory valuations.[19]

To restore "truth in corporate reporting" the *Financial Accounting Standards Board*, a nongovernmental organization, issued new rules in October 1979. Large corporations (assets of $1 billion or more) must now present *inflation-adjusted* data in their annual reports to stockholders, in addition to their established financial accounting which they must keep to meet Internal Revenue Service requirements.

Only a few decades ago many believed the corporation tax to be a good tax. *Fortune* wrote in 1959: "The corporate income tax is undoubtedly the most efficient system for collecting federal revenues yet devised by a frequently ingenious Congress. Indeed, it may be the simplest mechanism ever developed by a modern state for exacting vast sums of money from an economy."[20] Would any economic journal so write today?

It is true that the corporate tax is for the government the least expensive tax to collect. Most of it comes in big chunks, most of the work is done by the taxpayer, and audits are facilitated by strict rules of the SEC and the accounting profession. The broad popularity of the corporate tax may be attributed to a general belief that it is borne by the corporation, that is, by the stockholders. It stands to reason that the more heavily government taxes business, the more generously it can afford to treat individuals and the working man or woman.

There is just one nagging uncertainty: who really pays the corporation profits tax? The stockholders by lower dividends and values, the employees by lower wages, or the consumers by higher prices?

Economists, as so often, disagree among themselves. There probably is no single or simple answer that holds true for all industries, all corporations, at all times. The weight of evidence suggests, however, that in the long run a major part of the corporate profits tax, or possibly all, is shifted forward in the price. The corporate tax rate varied from 11.0 to 13.5 percent in 1925–1929 and the net (aftertax) earnings of leading manufacturing corporations averaged 11.0 percent of new worth. In 1970–72 when the rate stood at 48 percent, the net return still averaged 11.0 percent. This suggests that all of the increase in the tax rate from 11.0–13.5 percent to 48.0% was shifted to the consumers. In 1975–1978 earnings averaged 14.6 percent—probably because firms tried to compensate for the unrealistic accounting methods they were forced to observe.[21]

Even so, evidence on whether the corporation tax is borne by the stockholder, the employee or the consumer is not conclusive. But regardless of who eventually pays it, the corporation tax has a harmful impact on the economy; it punishes the efficient producer (by holding an umbrella over the inefficient one), thereby restricts industrial expansion, penalizes capital formation and adversely affects American competitiveness in international trade.[22] It is in economic terms the most detrimental tax in our system though politically immensely appealing.

A fierce, dedicated and well-organized antibusiness, anti–free market, pro-redistribution and pro–government control campaign has made "profit" a dirty word and given the American public distorted notions about corporations.[23] Too often it sees them as monstrous multibillion Molochs which reap huge profits from a naive and exploited consumer public.

It is true that there *are* some big corporations—one in a thousand has assets of $250 million or more. They grew big because customers found that they get more for their money from them, and that it is to their own advantage to deal with those companies. But out of 2.1 million active corporations in 1976, only 1.3% had assets of $10 million or more, 93% had assets of less than $1 million.[24]

To be sure, two thousand big corporations—with assets of $250 million or more each—account for about two-thirds of the assets, profits and taxes of all two million corporations in the country. But they are not running the government nor the economy—Kenneth Galbraith, Ralph Nader, et al. to the contrary notwithstanding. In fact, the government is controlling corporate business and its policies more tightly than is good for the country and it is taking more money from the corporations than their owners get.

Thirty-nine percent of all active corporations reported a net loss in 1976, reminding us that ours is a *profit and loss system*. Most corporations, of course, manage to have a net profit, without which they will go broke, sooner or later. Most corporations do not reap excessive profits, judging by the apparent disinclination of Americans to buy and hold shares in them and by their low value in the stock market. Common stocks are probably the only commodity which one still can buy at approximately mid-1960s prices.

Some day the drive to replace the corporation tax, partially or wholly, with a value-added tax or integrate it with the personal income tax may succeed. What has kept it alive so long is the myth that it comes out of the pockets of big business and its wealthy stockholders. At the rate at which employee pension funds are expanding their holdings of corporate shares, working people will increasingly come to realize that they pay the corporation profits tax, one way or the other, as employees, as consumers or as owners.

Consumption Taxes

Taxes on consumption—which by definition include customs duties—provided more than half the support of the United States government for the first 125 years of its existence. Imposition of income taxes started a downward trend in the role of consumption levies which has continued for over six decades. Between 1952 and 1978 they dropped from 13% of all federal revenues to 6%. Consumption taxes now contribute a smaller share of public revenues in the United States than in any other industrial country except Japan. While other OECD countries raise about as much through consumption taxes as through the personal income tax, our federal, state and local treasuries net from consumption taxes less than half as much as from the personal income tax. We are now the only industrial country which does not levy a broad-based national consumption tax. American consumption taxation consists mainly of retail sales taxes levied by 45 states, customs duties and a few federal excises.

American failure to utilize the potential of consumption taxes was not accidental but springs from a deliberate decision of the Roosevelt administration, on ideological and political grounds, not to use a sales tax in the financing of World War II. That policy resulted in the paying of a far smaller share of the cost of the war from current taxation than in other countries and in the accumulation of a huge national debt. It also reduced consumption taxes from 37% of U.S. Treasury receipts in 1936 to 15% in 1946.

Objections to consumption taxes relate to their regressivity: they equal a higher percentage of the income of persons at the lowest income levels—who usually spend all receipts immediately on consumption goods—than of the income of the rich who save part of theirs. In the absence of a national general consumption tax no conclusive and universally applicable finding on regressivity of consumption taxes can be made. Some state sales taxes, particularly those that exempt food bought in grocery stores, are proportionate to income through much of the middle-income range and regressive only at both ends of the scale. Some sales taxes are more regressive. Opposition to consumption taxes is based not just on their regressivity but on the fact they are not, as a rule, progressive, that is, they do not shift income from the higher to the lower brackets.

Some sales taxes tend to offset, to a small extent, the sharp progressivity of the graduated income tax. This is held to be their fundamental fault. Neutrality in taxation has become a cardinal sin. Those who view redistribution of income to be government's primary task, condemn a tax that does not add to progression and is proportionate or even regressive as distinctly evil. Those who believe that all citizens who have the right to vote on public issues—directly or by choosing representatives—ought to bear part of the burden, favor consumption taxes as a necessary part of the overall tax system. They do not deem it necessarily wrong to base taxes not on a person's contribution to society (as expressed in earnings) but on his consumption of the products of other people's labor.

FEDERAL REVENUES FROM CONSUMPTION TAXES, 1952 AND 1978

	1952	1978
	millions of dollars	
Total	$9,332	$25,453
Customs duties	532	6,823
Motor fuel taxes	720	5,083
Alcohol taxes	2,549	5,594
Tobacco taxes	1,565	2,451
Other excises	3,966	5,502

SOURCES: *Historical Statistics on Governmental Finances & Employment*, U.S. Bureau of the Census, 1977 Census of Government, 1979; and idem, *Governmental Finances in 1977–78*, 1980.

Between 1952 and 1978 federal consumption tax receipts increased from $9.3 billion to $25.5 billion, but dropped from 2.8% to 1.3% of GNP. Throughout the XIX century and the early part of the XX century customs collections accounted for about half or more of all U.S. Treasury receipts. In 1952 they equaled 0.7% of federal revenues, in 1978 1.6%. That rise was due to import growth and higher rates.

Historically, the size of customs duties was aimed less at producing the most revenue than at building tariff walls high enough to protect domestic industries, or to accomplish regulatory purposes. Average customs rates inched up from 4.9% in 1952 to 5.9% in 1972, then, because of multiplying crude oil bills, dropped to 3.9% in 1978.

The United States has until recently been much more self-contained and less dependent on imports than most other industrial countries. Foreign trade does not play as big a role here as it does in Europe. Still, merchandise imports grew from 3.1% of GNP in 1952 to 4.8% in 1972. Until a few years ago, the U.S. produced domestically all or most of the crude oil it consumed but, in the 1960s, started to become increasingly dependent on imports. When OPEC quintupled crude oil prices in the 1970s, imports jumped to 8.3% of GNP in 1978. Replacement of imported oil by domestic raw materials—coal, nuclear, shale oil, tar sands, solar—has made but slow progress despite the pressure of high prices and heavy government levies.

Alcohol and tobacco tax rates are related to volume and not to the amount of the bill. Revenues, therefore, do not go up with prices. Expressed in *constant* dollars tax receipts declined over the past quarter century.

A haphazard assortment of federal excises was built up over time, such as taxes on furs, jewelry, luggage, toilet preparations, sporting goods, music instruments, matches, film, light bulbs, admissions and stamp taxes and dozens of others. They were repealed within recent memory to no one's regret. Federal excises remain on alcohol and tobacco, on motor fuel and other highway-use related items and on telephone and transportation.

Motor fuel tax rates also are related to volume and not to price. Federal gasoline taxes were boosted from 2 to 4 cents a gallon in 1955 and other highway user taxes raised or imposed for the declared purpose of financing the interstate highway system and certain other roads. Long-standing efforts to divert highway user tax receipts to other uses such as urban rapid transit began to succeed in recent years. Motor fuel tax revenues were rising rapidly, as gasoline consumption more than doubled (+ 127%) between 1952 and 1972. When energy conservation for reduced dependence on oil imports became the motto of the 1970s, gasoline consumption flattened out. It has barely inched upwards since 1973. With a tax rate unrelated to prices, highway user tax receipts have been stagnating, with a devastating impact on highways whose construction and maintenance costs soared faster than ever. Expressed as a percentage of the price of gasoline, federal and state taxes have shrunk to a fraction of what they were ten years ago. The gap between highway needs and highway user tax receipts is becoming increasingly grave, threatening a crisis in the years ahead.

State and local governments play a much greater role in the consumption tax field than the national government.

CONSUMPTION TAX REVENUES OF STATE AND LOCAL GOVERNMENTS, 1978

	Million	
Total	$67,596	
General sales and gross receipts taxes	41,473	
Selective sales and excise taxes	26,123	
Taxes on motor fuel		$9,598
Taxes on alcohol		2,424
Taxes on tobacco		3,785
Taxes on public utilities		4,676
Other taxes		5,640

SOURCE: *Governmental Finances in 1977–78*, U.S. Bureau of the Census, 1980.

About 60 percent of state and local consumption taxes are collected as general retail sales and gross receipts taxes by states and by some cities, counties and other local governments. Forty-five states now levy retail sales taxes—up from 31 states in 1952. Tax rates which typically ran at 2 percent in 1952 now average about twice as high, ranging from 2% in Oklahoma to 7% in Connecticut, with the majority of states at 3% and 4%. Those rates are far lower than the 12% to 20% consumption tax rates charged in almost all European countries.

In 1972 and 1976 the Advisory Commission on Intergovernmental Relations had a nationwide opinion survey conducted by the Opinion Research Corporation on the question: "Suppose your state government must raise taxes substantially; which of these would be the best way to do it—state income tax, state sales tax, or state property tax?"

Responses showed a state sales tax with 45 to 46% as the first choice, with the state income tax second at 25%, and the property tax, last. The sales tax led substantially in every category—sex, age, education, occupation, location, income, race, etc.

Between 1952 and 1978 state personal income tax collections had multiplied in *constant* dollars 13 times, state sales tax collections 6.4 times. If state officials accept the results of this opinion survey as a true reflection of their constituents' wishes, they might place greater emphasis on sales taxes than on income taxes in years to come.

At the national level suggestions to levy a general consumption tax have always met with a negative response. President Nixon considered in 1969–70 proposing a value-added tax (VAT) but finally decided that only a Democrat could afford to recommend the imposition of a sales tax—just as only a Republican could afford to grant de facto recognition to the People's Republic of China. Within the past few years the sentiment in Congress for a VAT has become more friendly and in 1980 the chairmen of the tax-writing committees of both Houses favored it—as part and offset of a reduction in income taxes (corporate and/or personal) and social security taxes. At this point, the prospects for such a proposal to succeed appear slim unless a financial emergency—which sooner or later is likely to arise—helps overcome objections to the imposition of a "sales tax."

Norman Ture, who in 1981 was appointed Undersecretary of the Treasury for Tax Policy, pointed out that "as a substitute for part or all of the existing income taxes, the advantages of the VAT would be substantial. It would result in significant reductions in the cost of work relative to leisure and of savings relative to consumption." But he also warned that "the added revenues projected with the tax substitution might, before too long, become extremely tempting as a means of financing considerably higher levels of government spending." VAT could become "an engine for inflating government demands on the nation's production resources . . . a formidable device for expanding the public sector while shrinking the private market's influence on the allocation of production capability."[25] That warning, derived from a long and intimate acquaintance with Congress, its strength and weaknesses, needs to be heeded.

The Social Security Tax

Over the past quarter century the rate of the social security tax (FICA-tax)[26] multiplied fourfold, covered earnings (the maximum wage up to which the tax is levied) multiplied fivefold, and collections multiplied thirtyfold. Expressed in *constant* dollars, tax receipts multiplied twelvefold and they quintupled as a percentage of Gross National Product, from 1.1% to 5.2%. Thus, by any conceivable yardstick the FICA-tax grew faster than any other type of tax between 1952 and 1978. In 1952 FICA-tax collections equaled 13% of the federal personal income tax, in 1978 58%, and they were still gaining fast. We have reached a stage where a majority of workers pays a bigger social security tax than income tax, or will be doing so shortly.

But even that was not enough to satisfy our voracious social security system. When social security seemed to be at the point of running out of money Congress passed the biggest tax boost in U.S. peacetime history, effective in 1979, which was estimated to bring in another $227 billion over the ensuing decade. This may tide social security over a few years, but will not cover benefit commitments for long. Congress has a choice of: a) boosting the tax again, b) adding another tax source, or c) making a U-turn on its half-century-old policy of liberalizing social security benefits at frequent intervals. Benefit restraint may be the best solution.

Social security has come to play an increasingly important role in the redistribution of income from higher to lower brackets. That may sound strange because we have heard the social security tax criticized and condemned as a regressive tax. That claim reminds me of the sportswriter who reported that the Cincinnati Reds got ten runs without bothering to point out that the Dodgers got twelve to win the game.

Viewed in isolation, the social security tax appears to be regressive because it does not tax earnings above a certain level, $17,700 in 1978. Thus Joe Smith who is making $17,700 had $1,071—6.05% of his gross wages—withheld. George Brown with a $50,000 salary also had $1,071 withheld, which however equals only 2.1% of his salary.

That would be regressive were it not for the fact that social security *benefits* cut off at the same level as *taxes*. This would make the system neutral if benefits were not weighed heavily in favor of low-wage workers. As of 1980, retirement benefits equaled 90% of the first $194 average indexed monthly earnings (AIME), 32% of the next $977 and 15% of all taxable earnings over $1171. So the employee in the low brackets gets six times as much in proportion to his contribution as his coworker in the high brackets.

Moreover, an "earned income credit," authorized in 1975, increased and made permanent in 1978, relieves some "low-income" persons (up to about $15,600) from having to pay the entire or even any social security tax. Withheld amounts may be offset by a credit on the income tax which is paid to persons who owe no income tax by the U.S. Treasury.[27]

Were it not for the skewed benefit formula and the earned income credit, it might be held that the upper taxability limit on the social security tax serves as a counterpart to the lower taxability limit on the income tax. As it is the advantages are all on the side of low-income earners.

The social security tax has been reshaped increasingly to multiply the burden of persons with higher earnings. While the tax rate has remained uniform for all brackets and still is equally divided between employer and employee (because Congress in 1977 rejected President Carter's proposals which would have shifted more than half to the employer),[28] the upper limit of taxability was lifted several times, with a "progressive" effect.

In 1952, worker A with $3600 earnings (the taxable maximum) paid a tax of $54. In 1978 he paid, on the same earnings, $218—four times as much. Worker B with $17,700 earnings paid in 1952 also $54, but in 1978 he paid $1,071—twenty times as much. An increase in earnings would still have left a big difference in the rate of tax boost between workers A and B.

Between 1965 and 1978 the social security tax was boosted 61 percent for workers with earnings of $4800 or less, 515 percent for workers at the upper taxable limit. But social security benefits were increased proportionately more for persons in the lower brackets.

When it became obvious in the mid-1970s that the system's income would have to be augmented, the OASDI fund trustees recommended in 1976 an "appropriate increase in tax rates." President Ford so proposed but Congress did not act. President Carter made it clear in 1977 that he did not want an across-the-board tax boost but intended to place the entire additional burden on business and on employees in the higher brackets—which the trustees had recommended against. Congress yielded to the president, at least in part. As a result, social security taxes will go up little over the next decade for workers with below-average earnings; they will by 1986 double at the $30,000 level and more than triple at $47,700.

The social security changes which took effect in 1979 amount to a major step in eroding the concept of an earnings- and contributions-related

SOCIAL SECURITY TAX INCREASE ON EMPLOYEES AT SELECTED
EARNINGS LEVELS UNDER THE 1977 SOCIAL SECURITY AMENDMENTS

Annual Earnings	SS Tax 1978	SS Tax 1986	Increase in SS Tax Dollars	Increase in SS Tax Percentage	Tax Increase as Percentage of Earnings
$10,000	$605	$715	$110	+ 18%	1.1%
$20,000	1071	1430	359	+ 34	1.8
$30,000	1071	2145	1074	+100	3.6
$47,700*	1071	3411	2340	+217	4.9

*Estimate.

FIGURE 16.
SOCIAL SECURITY TAX ON EMPLOYEE, SELECTED EARNINGS LEVELS
1978 and 1987

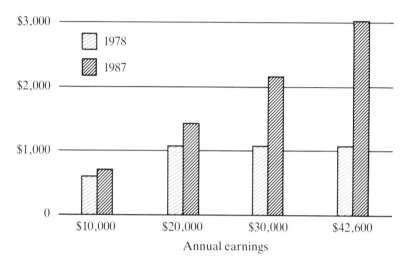

Annual earnings

Source: 1977 Social Security Amendments

insurance system, with at least a semblance of individual equity, and in converting it into a welfare system aimed at "social adequacy."

When social security was first proposed in the mid-1930s, it was described and sold to the American public as an insurance plan, comparable in many ways to private pensions or annuities. The employee would pay monthly premiums over his working life (equally matched by his employing firm) and he would be able to draw on the accumulated fund plus interest in his retirement years. That is how many or most persons now paying contributions regard it, a view that is officially encouraged because it makes withholding and even tax boosts much more acceptable to the worker. Everybody seems to be paying for his own retirement—at least in theory.

One thought behind the principle of having the system financed from a special tax paid equally by employers and employees (though economically borne entirely by the employee) was not only to give participants a feeling of ownership and security but also to create a built-in automatic restraint against organized excessive demands for higher benefits.

The idea of an actuarially sound fund—similar to private pension funds—soon proved to be impractical. Contributions would have had to rise to intolerable levels and would have drawn astronomic amounts out of the economy.

To be sure, social security cannot help but be an adverse factor in savings and capital formation, and thus in regard to productivity and economic growth.[29] But there is a significant difference between the impact of a fully funded and a pay-as-you-go system. A small reserve, equaling one to four years benefits, to offset fluctuations in income and outgo, appears to be a reasonable compromise.

Also, investment of funds which by now would total between three and five trillion dollars would have presented a vexing problem. To put it into American industry would have amounted to a gradual takeover of American business by government, something the American public would be strongly opposed to. What alternative is there? To print and keep in the fund government bonds for trillions of dollars would have added nothing to the existing government commitment or to financial security for the potential beneficiaries.

Pay-as-you-go means that each succeeding generation pays for the support of its elders. It is actually inevitable that the working generation produces the goods and services which the retired generation needs and consumes. The rest is "bookkeeping." Throughout human history support of the aged was provided mostly within a family, community or tribe. Beginning in the late XIX century, it became a societal task, organized by the national government. But it still means that the new generation provides sustenance for the old. Pay-as-you-go came about not by intent but by the natural workings of economic and political forces. It did not operate as smoothly as it could and should have because of Congress' apparent inability to resist demands for ever more generous benefits.

The Old Age and Survivors Insurance Trust Fund equaled four years benefit payments in 1955 and one year in 1970. In 1971 the Advisory Council on Social Security recommended the maintenance of a one-year level. Within two years the fund began to fall short, equaled eight months disbursements in 1975 and a mere four months by the end of 1978. That is why Congress found itself impelled to enact a major tax boost. It had been pressured for many years to use "general revenue funds" for social security purposes. But the U.S. budget was consistently in a heavy deficit condition so that no funds were available from it. To appropriate general budget funds for social security, as President Carter recommended in 1977, would have produced even bigger budget deficits.

Congress has so far rejected such proposals. It may at some point consider imposing a value-added tax, to supplement—and partially substitute for—the social security tax, on the assumption that the latter tax has reached its maximum tolerable level. Compared with other OECD countries, social security taxation is not high in the United States. In 1975–77 it averaged 7.4% of gross domestic product in the U.S.—compared with a median of 8.3% and a mean of 9.2% of all OECD countries (Table 17). Nor are our payroll tax rates for old age, survivors, and disability insurance (*ex*cluding medical insurance) high compared with other industrial countries. They stood as of January 1, 1979, as follows:

U.S.A.	10.16% of payroll
Germany	18.0
France	12.9
Austria	19.5
Netherlands	28.2
Italy	23.76
Japan	9.1
Switzerland	9.4

SOURCE: *Social Security Bulletin*, August 1979.

The American public ranked the social security tax as "most fair" (24%) followed by the sales tax (19%), state income tax (17%), federal income tax (13%) and the property tax (10%), in a 1978 CBS News poll. That certainly does not suggest that the social security tax ought to be supplemented or partially replaced by general revenues which come largely from the income tax.

Under current law the social security tax (*in*cluding Medicare) is scheduled to rise from 6.15% in 1980 to 7.15% in 1986, on the employee as well as on the employer, while the taxable earnings limit will climb from $25,900 in 1980 to $42,600 by 1987. Thus the maximum aggregate tax on employee and employer will double, from $3186 in 1980 to $6092 by 1987.

Not long after enacting steep social security tax boosts to take effect from 1979 on, Congress considered reducing some of the exorbitant increases. But by 1980 it had become apparent that the scheduled rates would not bring in sufficient revenue to finance current benefit levels. Moreover, demographic changes will occur in future decades, especially when members of the postwar baby boom will begin to retire around the year 2010 and be succeeded by a much smaller working generation.

Restraint is likely to be the motto of social security from now on, not only in the United States but also in other countries.

Social Security Commissioner Stanford G. Ross in a 1979 article "Social Security: A Worldwide Issue" wrote:

The new economic and social forces at work today clearly have brought to an end the long period of expansion of social security programs. Social security systems are now entering a difficult period of painful adjustments in which finances and benefits will have to be closely scrutinized and carefully balanced. The optimistic expansionist philosophy that underlay social security planning ever since World War II has now changed to one of guarded hope that the best of the past can be preserved while the considerable needs of the future are addressed.[30]

The Property Tax

No tax has been as bitterly maligned and assailed as the property tax: by the taxpayers because it is too big and rises too fast and by the school and other spending forces because it is too little and rises too slowly; by some because it is restricted and by others because the restrictions are not tight enough; by some because assessments are too low and by others because they are too high. The real curse of the property tax which primarily accounts for its unpopularity is that, in contrast to almost all other taxes, it is not hidden but out in the open, clearly labeled by purpose. What is more, it identifies the official who is doing the taxing. Such relationships are veiled or obscured for sales and income taxes, particularly at the federal level. The trouble with the property tax is that the taxpayer knows that he is paying it, what he is paying for, and who is taxing him.[31]

Nor is there a tax whose decline and fall has been predicted more often or with greater assurance. Half a century ago the standard textbook on the property tax said: "If any tax could have been eliminated by adverse criticism, the general property tax should have been eliminated long ago. . . ."[32] Twenty-five years later an eminent economist predicted: "Glancing ahead now, over the next two decades, I would expect to see the property tax all but wither away. Further relative decline is a foregone conclusion, but I would go beyond this and predict that in absolute terms property taxation is headed for oblivion."[33] As it happened, between 1954—the latest year for which statistical data were available at the time these words were spoken (at the 1956 National Tax Conference)—and 1978, property tax collections jumped from $10 to $66 billion. Withering away indeed!! Year after year, however, articles are published under titles such as "The Trouble with Property Taxes"[34] or "What's Wrong With the Property Tax?"[35]

Despite its unpopularity the property tax kept growing at an amazing pace. Between 1952 and 1978 property tax collections tripled in *constant* dollars—as did the aggregate of all other public revenues such as income and sales taxes—and rose from 2.6% to 3.3% of GNP. This is surprising because no other tax is as restricted as the property tax by various intricate constitutional and statutory limitations in most states, none is as dependent for rate boosts on the taxpayers' approval at the ballot box. In hundreds of local elections, the voters, although grumbling, regularly approve property tax increases on their homes. Most state governors called for property tax relief in their "state of the state" messages year after year and some was granted.

When the citizens of California, Michigan, Colorado, and Oregon had an opportunity at the November 1972 elections to vote for proposals to abolish or further restrict the use of property taxes, they defeated those proposals overwhelmingly. Maybe they realized—better than politicians were willing to admit—that the size of their total tax bill is set more by the magnitude of public expenditures than by the form in which taxes are levied. Perhaps they were also aware of the dependence of home rule and local autonomy—whatever vestige there is of it—and of decentralized decision making on an independent local source of taxation and that there is no adequate local substitute for property taxes.

Suddenly, in June 1978, the oft-predicted property taxpayers' revolt erupted when the citizens of California with a two-thirds majority adopted proposition 13, which cut property taxes in half. Only a decade earlier they had rejected a proposal that would have limited property taxes to *two* percent of current market value. Why did they change their minds and now decide to cut property taxes to *one* percent of current value?[36]

Property tax collections in California had in the interim risen no faster than personal income in the state and more slowly than income taxes. Several substantial property tax relief measures were enacted and took effect during the decade. Was there a substantive reason for the reversal of the 1968 vote or was it simply a change of mind on the part of the electorate?

A material shift did take place during the 1970s when some of the weight of property taxes shifted from business to residential property. Business property, especially of public utilities assessed by the state rather than by locally elected assessors, had long been appraised at higher ratios to current value than homes. That is politically understandable. But the discrepancy was narrowed because of demands for constitutionally mandated uniformity. Also railroad property, once a major item in property values became a minor factor. But the major force was the steep rise in home prices which exceeded general inflation rates as well as price trends in commercial and industrial real estate. That difference made itself felt through tax assessors' periodic reappraisals.

As long as public utilities—gas, electric power, telephone, pipeline companies, etc.—were able to shift their disproportionate property taxes to consumers through higher rates, no one got too excited although there were battles at state regulatory commission meetings. But homeowners did get excited when tax bills on their own homes soared—and they acted.

However, the main force behind #13 may have been a growing public sentiment that government and its demands had grown too fast and too far. So the citizens decided to send a message which its representatives could not ignore: through a constitutional amendment intended to cut government off at the pocket (at least in part). From all appearances—and some polls—the voters had not intended to cut the support of the recipients of property tax funds: school districts, counties and cities and their services, education, police, fire, sanitation, etc. Taxpayers wanted to get at that amorphous thing "big government and bureaucracy" and they struck out at what was within reach, the property tax.

During the #13 campaign organized opponents had predicted dire consequences if the proposition were passed. Vital services would be eliminated or cut, tens or hundreds of thousands of public employees dismissed. Supporters of #13 forecast sizable reductions in public spending. But all that happened after the proposition won was that the promised cut in half of property taxes took place. Most of the local funds were soon replaced by the state of California which at the time enjoyed a $5 billion surplus in its treasury because the income tax and other taxes had proven more productive than the governor and the legislature had estimated. With 1978 a gubernatorial election year in California, there is little doubt but that income tax rates would have been cut in 1979 had #13 not been voted in.[37]

The passage of #13 did not bring large reductions in governmental staffs or services nor even in public spending as a forthcoming volume *The Tax Revolt* by Hoover Institution researchers Alvin Rabushka and Pauline Ryan documents. It did result in a substantial transfer of the support of schools and other services from the local to the state level and in a corresponding upward shift in policy direction and control to the state bureaucracy.

Proposition 13 was, above all, a symbol. It told officeholders in California and throughout the nation that taxpayers wanted a change in direction, from a growing to a shrinking government. It was so interpreted in many other states where measures to restrain taxing and spending were adopted, though most of them were far milder than #13. Congress heard the message too and its attitude toward taxes and expenditures underwent a change in 1979, as became evident after the submission of the President's budget in January 1980. Whether this really means a reversal in the long-range trend toward an ever-growing government remains to be seen.

It is still too early to know what impact the passage of Proposition 13 and similar measures in other states will have on the future of the property tax. Up to the beginning of the twentieth century and for about three decades after (except in wartime), property tax collections accounted for nearly as much as all other taxes, federal, state and local combined. Since the mid-1950s property taxes have been contributing between 9% and 11% of all public revenues. Most of the change occurred between 1932 and 1944 when, under the impact of the depression and World War II, property taxes dropped from 43.6% to 7.1% of all public revenues, due largely to the spectacular expansion of the income tax and the "freezing" of the property tax. After the war, property taxes recovered but never regained their former role. The burden of the property tax at 3.3% of GNP in 1978 is virtually unchanged from 3.4% of GNP in 1902. The aggregate of all other governmental revenues meanwhile soared from 4.8% to 33.2% of GNP.

As a percentage of total national wealth, property taxes have increased by about one-fourth since the turn of the century.

PROPERTY TAXES AND NATIONAL TANGIBLE WEALTH, 1902 AND 1975

	National Tangible Wealth (in billions)	Property Tax Collections (in millions)	Property Taxes as a Percentage of National Tangible Wealth
1902	$ 95	$ 706	0.74%
1975	5,588	51,491	.92

SOURCES: National wealth for 1902: Raymond W. Goldsmith, Dorothy S. Brady, and Horst Menderhausen, *A Study of Savings in the United States* (Princeton, N.J.: Princeton University Press, 1956), vol. 3, table W-1 (pt. 2), p. 14.

National wealth for 1975: U.S. Department of Commerce, *Statistical Abstract of the United States*, 1979, p. 472.

Property taxes: *Historical Statistics on Governmental Finances and Employment*, 1977 Census of Governments, 1979.

The tripling (in *constant* dollars) of property tax collections between 1952 and 1978 represented a catch-up process to make up, at least in part, for the lag during the preceding 20 years. Between 1932 and 1952 property taxes fell from 6.7% to 2.6% of GNP; they climbed to 3.3% of GNP by 1978. It does not appear likely that they will rise higher.

Most of the $58 billion increase in property taxes between 1952 and

1978 was levied on newly created or increased values. New construction in that period totaled $4.6 trillion (in *constant* 1978 dollars), of which $3.3 trillion was private construction: $1.8 trillion residential, $1 trillion commercial and industrial, and $0.5 trillion vacant lots, farms, etc.[38] A property tax of 1.7%—the current effective rate—on $3.3 trillion of new private structures alone (not counting the land) would amount to $56 billion in taxes. This, of course, does not take into account either the value of structures destroyed or abandoned or depreciation. But destruction and depreciation were largely offset by a simultaneous rise in values. The composite construction cost index increased 195% between 1952 and 1978, while the Consumers Price Index went up only 146%.[39] That pushed up the value of existing buildings; older houses did not lose in value but often sold for more than they had cost ten or twenty years before. Land and acreage costs multiplied even faster than construction costs. Moreover, privately held real estate was helped through various public improvements such as roads, street lighting, bridges, sewers, schools, hospitals, etc. New public construction totaled $1.3 trillion (in *constant* 1978 dollars) between 1952 and 1978. It was generally not taxable, but helped to raise values of adjoining private real estate.

No charge is levied more frequently against the property tax than that it singles out the homeowner and places a discriminatory and intolerably heavy burden on him. On closer analysis that charge makes no sense whatsoever. All United States residents, and all taxpayers, are either homeowners or renters. Would it be fairer to place a larger share of the load on the renters? They pay a proportionate share anyway: landlords recoup the net cost of property taxes and other costs, plus a profit, through rents. Currently 65 percent of all occupied dwellings are inhabited by their owners, 35 percent are rented. Families living in their own home had in 1978 an income 80 percent higher than that of renting families. The growing popularity of condominiums may be attributed largely to the tax advantages they offer (comparable to homeowning) to persons who prefer smaller dwellings (apartments) to houses.

Some economists have developed a theory according to which the residential property tax does not rest on the user but falls on capital and is either less regressive than widely assumed or may even be progressive.[40] It is doubtful, however, that this theory will be generally accepted.

Property taxes now account for 9 percent of all governmental revenues. About 55 percent of all property taxes is derived from residential property and 84 percent of that from single-family homes. This means that homeowners contribute about half of all property tax collections, which accounts for a mere 4.2 percent of all governmental revenues in the United

States. Since homeowners as a group are economically somewhat better situated than renters, they account for at least 70 percent of all income received in the country, though they equal only about 65 percent of the population. In all likelihood they contribute directly or indirectly at least 70 percent of all public revenues. This means that the homeowner pays about 6 percent of his total tax burden through the property tax, 94 percent directly or indirectly through other taxes and in other ways.

Why then is the property tax so unpopular? Because it is the only tax of which the average homeowner and taxpayer is painfully aware because he has to pay it directly to a tax collection agency. Most of the income tax is deducted from his pay before he ever sees it, sales taxes are collected in small amounts on purchases, and business taxes are, when shifted forward, included in the price of goods and services and thereby hidden. Both the visibility of the property tax and the need to actually pay it over at a particular time in a sizable amount are primarily responsible for the general aversion to this type of tax.

A public opinion poll, conducted by the Gallup Organization shortly after the proposition 13 vote showed the property tax clearly to be the most unpopular tax. Forty-five percent of the respondents strongly favored (and only 15% strongly opposed) a cut even if it meant a reduction in local services or an increase in other taxes. Respondents rated sales taxes (43%) and income taxes (36%) as the fairest taxes to finance state and local services; only 10% gave a nod to the property tax. Asked: "Of the different taxes you pay, which do you most object to?" thirty-one percent picked the property tax, an equal number the income tax, 16% the sales tax. However, when asked "which level of government gives you the most value for your tax dollar?" 35% designated local government, 23% state government, only 22% the federal government.[41]

What this adds up to is that the public, according to this poll, prefers local government but actively dislikes the property tax. That is also evident in a public opinion poll by the Opinion Research Corporation nearly a year after the #13 vote. Identical polls in prior years had consistently judged the property tax to be the least fair tax. But its unpopularity declined from being rated the worst tax by 45% in 1972 to 27% in May 1979. What may be equally significant, the share of the American public rating the federal income tax to be the "least fair" tax went up from 19% in 1972, to 37% in 1979. In May 1979 the federal income tax, for the first time, outranked the property tax as the "least fair" tax.[42]

Another oft-repeated charge is that property taxes not only allow too many exemptions which erode the tax base but also are regressive because they place a heavier burden on residences and low-priced homes than on commercial property and high-priced homes. It is true that there are many exemptions in the property tax for veterans, public, educational, and charitable properties, etc. In the national average about one-fourth of all real estate is thus left tax free. But we should remember that the federal income tax reaches less than half of all personal income (see p. 84). By comparison with the federal income tax, therefore, the property tax looks quite good with regard to its tax base and exemptions.

Assertions that residences are assessed at higher ratios to their market value than commercial or industrial properties are conclusively refuted in the property value reports of the quinquennial surveys of the U.S. Bureau of the Census. The 1977 Census showed an average assessment-sales ratio of 32.5% for single-family homes and 35.7% for commercial and industrial property.[43] The ratio was lower for acreage (land) which was on the average assessed at 21.1% of sales value.

Nor is there evidence in the 1977 housing survey that low-priced homes are taxed at higher ratios to value than high-priced homes.[44] Real estate taxes averaged 1.3% to 1.5% of value in all value brackets from $10,000 on up. It was somewhat higher for the 4% of all housing units with below $10,000 value, possibly so because many of those houses were in a state of neglect and had lost value since their last assessment.[45] Real estate taxes averaged 1.4% of value in the survey, rising from 1.2% for families with income under $3,000 to 1.6% for families with an income of $35,000 or more.

There sometimes is a problem with families which occupy more living space than they can afford, that is, space whose value is disproportionate to their current income. In the 1977 housing survey the median home value to income ratio stood at 1:5.0 at income below $5,000, gradually declining to a ratio of 1:1.5 at $35,000 income or more. This is part of a broader problem of individuals and families who try to live beyond their means. In the case of earned income this amounts to people aiming to consume more than they produce. Particularly in the case of some elderly homeowners, that raises problems which have been turned into a political issue with emotional connotations. It can, and in some states is, effectively resolved by deferring some of the taxes for the period of the aged person's occupancy. Many states have adopted "circuit breakers," which forgive rather than postpone the taxes. This helps the person's heirs to inherit a bigger estate and appears to be an unnecessarily generous remedy.

In 1976 effective property tax rates on single-family nonfarm homes averaged 1.7% of current market (sales) value, varying from less than one percent in some parts of the south to 4% and more in a few northern states. The distribution among cities of 100,000 population or more was:

EFFECTIVE PROPERTY TAX RATES ON SINGLE-FAMILY HOUSES IN CITIES,
100,000 AND OVER, 1976

Effective property tax rate	Number of Cities	Percent of Cities
Total	144	100%
Less than 1%	16	11
1.0 to 1.4%	45	31
1.5 to 2.4%	57	40
2.5 to 3.4%	18	13
3.5% and up	8	5

Here are rates for a few large cities:

Montgomery, Ala.	0.28%
New Orleans, La.	.52
Honolulu, Hawaii	.56
Seattle, Wash.	.88
Salt Lake City, Utah	.91
Kansas City, Mo.	1.19
Cincinnati, Ohio	1.22
Washington, D.C.	1.24
San Francisco, Cal.	1.35
Minneapolis, Minn.	2.06
Philadelphia, Pa.	2.12
New York City, N.Y.	2.21
Los Angeles, Cal.	2.24
Hartford, Ct.	3.20
Detroit, Mich.	3.47
Newark, N.J.	4.30
Boston, Mass.	4.68
Jersey City, N.J.	4.94

SOURCE: *Taxable Property Values and Assessment/Sales Price Ratios,* 1977 Census of Governments, U.S. Bureau of the Census.

Differences in the property tax burden are extremely wide. This is the result of our system of leaving decisions on the scope and intensity of public services to each state—except for services which are mandated by national legislation or rules—and inside states to communities—within the limits of

local autonomy granted by the state. Even more so, it shows the freedom
the citizens of each state have—and within narrower ranges, also of communities—to decide how they want to be taxed. Some rely mainly on sales
taxes, others on income taxes and still others on property taxes. This is
an expression and manifestation of the principle of home rule which,
though sharply cut back in recent decades, still prevails in many parts of the
United States.

Nearly all property tax proceeds—96 percent—go to local governments
and they account for more than half—58 percent—of all revenues local governments raise under their own power. For school districts property taxes
represent 84 percent of all local funds, not counting state and federal aid.

DISTRIBUTION OF PROPERTY TAX RECEIPTS AMONG GOVERNMENTS, 1978

Type of Government	Amount millions	Share of Total	Property taxes as percent of all revenues from own sources
Total	$ 66,422	100.0%	22.0%
State governments	2,364	3.6	1.4
Local governments:	64,058	96.4	57.9
School districts	28,183	42.4	83.8
Counties	14,017	21.1	55.7
Municipalities	16,293	24.5	41.1
Townships	4,065	6.1	79.8
Special districts	1,500	2.3	20.9

SOURCE: *Governmental Finances in 1977–78*, U.S. Bureau of the Census, 1980.

Without the property tax, school districts and many other local governments would be unable to raise a significant share of their fiscal needs
from their own constituents. In the absence of an adequate replacement
they would have to depend largely or wholly on grants from their parent
governments. As we have seen in the United States and throughout the
world, this would mean that those governments would exercise the right
parents commonly exercise as long as they provide their offspring's sustenance: the right to rule. The claim to decision making on one's affairs, to
whatever extent of independence, hinges on one's willingness and ability to
raise one's own support. That is true of individuals as well as of states and
communities. In other words: the cause of local government in the United
States, of local autonomy and home rule, stands and falls on the maintenance of a viable property tax.

At a time when governmental revenues and expenditures equal about 45 percent of national or personal income, there is nothing wrong with raising 4.5 percent of the total support by a tax which is levied in proportion to the consumption of living space.

Homeowners are certainly not singled out for extra burdens. In fact, they obtain benefits under provisions of the Internal Revenue Code that are denied to renters. The deduction for income tax purposes of mortgage interest and real estate taxes and the nontaxability of imputed income from owner-occupied homes offset a substantial part of the home property tax bill. The renter, who pays for these items in his rental, is granted no such benefits and is at a serious disadvantage. On balance, the homeowner does taxwise much better than the renter. If there is tax discrimination, then it is *for* and *not against* the homeowner. This explains the remarkable growth of condominiums in recent years—with the main development yet to come.

It is, however, true that the federal income tax deduction of real estate taxes (and other state and local taxes) introduces an element of regressivity: a person in the top bracket offsets 70 percent of his deductible items in his tax liability, a person in the lowest bracket only 14 percent. What this amounts to is that state and local taxes are really not as regressive by their own characteristics—if at all—as by their treatment in the federal income tax. This could be corrected by shifting from deductions from AGI to credits against tax liability.

Many of the deficiencies or inequities in the property tax are the result of inadequate or faulty administration. Assessments are frequently made at a fraction of the value mandated by state constitutions and statutes, often at one-third or one-fifth of current market value. This leads to great unevenness—but strangely enough the courts, when called upon to provide redress, have shown reluctance to order administrators to set values as provided by law. At least some progress has been made in providing greater horizontal equity, as the narrowing *coefficient of dispersion* of assessed values in the quinquennial surveys of the Bureau of the Census indicated for some years. More recently, discrepancies have widened, largely because inflation progressed at a rapid pace with which local assessors, on a multiyear schedule of reappraisal, could not keep up.

A widespread and detrimental practice, however, is the undervaluation of land versus improvements. If anything, there ought to be greater emphasis on land values than on improvements. This could have a most wholesome impact on urban and suburban areas in curbing decay and encouraging sound development.

Though in ill repute, the property tax is an essential and important part of our tax system, indispensable if some semblance of meaningful local government is to be preserved.

3 ★★★★★★★★★★★★★★★★★★★★★

Public Expenditures
Government as a Well

In FY 1978 federal, state and local governments in the United States expended $745 billion which means that, expressed in *constant* dollars, their spending had tripled since 1952.[1] The national government, which until the 1930s accounted for about one-third of all public outlays, has in recent decades been responsible for about two-thirds, with the remaining one-third split almost evenly between states and local governments.

Public spending has been setting a new record nearly every year since the founding of the republic, multiplying 59-fold, in *constant* dollars, since the turn of the twentieth century. It equaled 8.0% of Gross National Product in 1902, 37.2% in 1978 (Table 4). This means that government outlays have grown almost five times faster than the nation's income and product. Omitting the cost of wars and national defense, we find that all other government expenditures, mostly for domestic services, grew between 1952 and 1978 by 498 percent, personal consumption expenditures only 153% (in *constant* dollars) (Table 26). In other words, over the past quarter century government's "living standards" expanded more than three times faster than those of the average American family. This suggests that the growth of public spending is attributable less to the high cost of living than to the cost of high living.

How can we explain this much more rapid improvement of living standards for American government than for the American people themselves? Since in a democracy action by government is somehow related to and dependent on the consent of the governed, we may ask: what caused the American people to consent to raise their government's standards three times faster than their own?

The seeds of this expansion were planted in the 1930s when the depression and the New Deal created the ideological basis therefor, the political alliances and the legal structures. But an adequate financial base was then lacking. Such a base was produced in the 1940s by the tremendous war-caused growth of taxes which were afterwards only slightly reduced. After the war ended governmental programs began to expand by utilizing the huge additional funds. That this could be done without boosting taxes, in fact while even reducing rates, made the raising of the needed revenues painless and politically acceptable. The American people had by then become accustomed to bearing a heavy tax burden ("an old tax is a good tax"). However, a problem could have arisen from the nature of our tax structure.

In the United States, and in some other countries, public expenditures as well as taxes are intended not only to finance public services, but also, in the process, to narrow economic differences among segments of the population. That presents no problem in a society whose income distribution is shaped like a pyramid: there are ample votes at the bottom likely to favor redistribution. It does present a problem in a society like ours, whose income distribution is shaped more like a pear: sufficient votes for strong income redistribution might not be easy to find without winning the consent of the biggest group, the one in the center of the income scale. Its approval could be gained by giving it the impression that it can thereby receive more than it is giving.

Thus some or much of the tax burden must be hidden—e.g., by taxes on business which are shifted in the price of goods and services—to keep persons in the middle from knowing how much they pay (though, like everybody else, they will always feel that they are paying too much). That is also the reason why expenditures—which to meet their redistributive goals would need to go only to persons low on the income scale—must be expanded to include a sufficient number of individuals (and votes) at and above the center of the income scale. In contrast to *taxes* on the center group which must in part be hidden, *expenditures* for that group must be made very visible to it.

As a result of thus expanding the number of recipients, the magnitude of public expenditures will far exceed what would be needed for redistribution only to those at the low end. The middle group must be given the impression that it gets sizable benefits, presumably paid for by those above them on the income scale. While persons in the upper brackets will be taxed more heavily, the added proceeds are not sufficient to help those at the bottom *and* benefit the multitude in the middle. There simply is not sufficient income at the top. Thus persons in the middle of the scale must be *taxed in unobtrusive ways* while granted *obtrusive benefits*.

So, from robbing Peter to pay Paul we shifted to robbing Peter to pay

Peter. To maintain a middle-class illusion of receiving worthwhile benefits without knowing the cost to themselves is, at least in part, the secret of the success of the welfare state in the past quarter century. The question is whether the process can go on forever, whether public spending and taxing can continue to grow indefinitely, in absolute as well as in relative terms.

The foremost aim of the modern welfare state is not just a shift of activities from the private to the public sector, thereby expanding government services and expenditures. Taxing and spending are largely techniques to accomplish income redistribution. But income redistribution cannot be made increasingly powerful without the support of a large group which economically has little or nothing to gain from it, because it is right in the middle between the rich and the poor.

Will the middle class become increasingly aware of the price it is paying in personal freedom for sending its earnings on an expensive round trip? Will it eventually see through the facade of governmental munificence and rise in a tax revolt? There have been occasional manifestations of a brewing tax revolt, most recently in the late 1970s, but they seldom went very far nor lasted very long. In the end they usually fizzled. But hope springs eternal.

Upward Trends

Public spending did not rise at a constant pace. Wars, political and economic upheavals and fluctuations, here and abroad, and other events, speeded up or slowed down the *rate* of growth. But spending never receded to its prior level after an upswing. The secular trend points strongly upwards, temporary deviations notwithstanding.

When we look at the dollar amounts (Table 4) it appears that most of the increase in government expenditures took place in recent years. For example, the increase between 1932 and 1942 amounted to $33 billion, between 1962 and 1972 to $223 billion. But to let it go at that would give a distorted picture. To see developments in proper perspective we must view trends in *relative* terms and express magnitudes in percent of national economic totals.

The sharp increase between 1913 and 1922 shows the continued fiscal effect of World War I, while the rise to 1932 may be explained by the steep fall of GNP to the depth of the depression. Then comes the jump due to World War II and the ensuing drop to 1952. Since 1952 growth has been proceeding at a less hectic but still very substantial rate which, if continued, would bring public expenditures to 50% of GNP by the year 2030.

GOVERNMENTAL EXPENDITURES (FEDERAL, STATE, LOCAL)
IN PERCENT OF GNP, 1902 TO 1978

Fiscal Year	Expenditures As a Percent of GNP	Increase or Decrease As a Percent of GNP	Increase or Decrease As a Percent of the Rate
1902	8.0%		
1913	8.8	+ 0.8%	+10%
1922	12.8	+ 4.0	+45
1932	18.5	+ 5.7	+45
1942	32.2	+13.7	+74
1952	29.5	− 2.7	− 8
1962	32.3	+ 2.8	+ 9
1972	35.9	+ 3.6	+11
1978	37.2	+ 2.0 (decennial rate)	+ 5 (decennial rate)

SOURCE: Table 4.

Expressed as a percentage of national income or personal income, public expenditures equaled 45.8% in 1978 and will, if they progress at the rate of recent decades, reach 50% by the end of the 1980s.

International comparisons of governmental expenditures are imprecise despite substantial progress achieved in accounting and statistical methods by the economics divisions of the United Nations and the OECD within the past two decades. The latest comparison by OECD (Table 20) ranked the United States 15th among 22 countries. Current government expenditures, expressed as a percentage of gross domestic product, were reported at 32.6% for the United States, compared with a mean of 37.4% and a median of 40.1% for 22 industrial countries. Most of the leading countries spent proportionally more than the U.S.: Germany 41.3%, France 40.4%, United Kingdom 41.5%. Sweden ranked tops with 55.6% followed by Netherlands at 52.3%. Switzerland at 30.4%, and Japan at 22.3% were lower than U.S.

In evaluating these data we should remember that most free world nations, especially European countries, Japan, Canada, etc., devote a smaller share of their resources to national defense than does the United States—because they depend on the United States to come to their aid if attacked by the Soviet Union, or another major aggressor. This means that many of those countries, and particularly the leading industrial noncommunist nations, allocate a larger share of their national product—and of

FIGURE 17.
THE GOVERNMENTAL EXPENDITURE DOLLAR
1952 and 1978

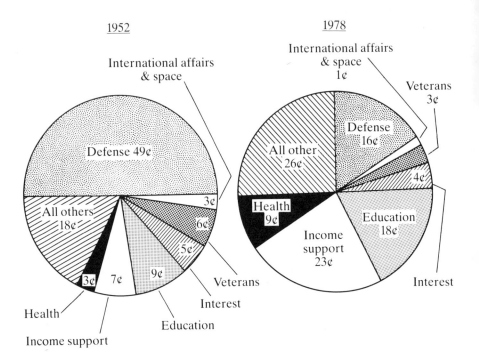

Source: table 23

their public expenditures—to the support of domestic services than the United States.

There is no adequate statistical basis at this time for a more specific comparison between the United States and other countries of non-war-connected expenditures. Although the United Nations publishes in its annual *Statistical Yearbook* public revenue and expenditure reports from many countries, they do not, in most cases, include governments below the national level (state, province, municipalities, etc.) and their comparability with United States statistics is very doubtful because of differences in comprehensiveness and definitions.

A Declining Share for National Defense

Any meaningful analysis of public expenditures must distinguish between outlays for military and for domestic functions.

As the table below shows, defense lost two-thirds of its share of the public dollar over the past quarter century, while the share of domestic functions doubled. As a percentage of GNP, defense fell from 13 to 5 percent, and domestic functions jumped from 10 percent to 25 percent.

GOVERNMENTAL EXPENDITURES (FEDERAL, STATE, LOCAL)
BY FUNCTION, 1952 AND 1978

	Expenditures billions		Percent increase in	Percent of Total Expenditures		Percent of GNP	
	1952	1978	*constant* $	1952	1978	1952	1978
Total	$93.9	$686.0	+ 197%	100.0%	100.0%	27.0%	32.2%
National defense	46.2	109.0	− 4	49.2	15.9	13.3	5.1
Other national security[a]	.7.9	29.2	+ 50	8.4	4.3	2.3	1.4
Interest paid	4.5	27.7	+ 153	4.8	4.0	1.3	1.3
Domestic functions	35.4	520.2	+ 498	37.7	75.8	10.2	24.5

SOURCE: Table 23.
[a]International affairs, space research and technology, veterans services and benefits.

Historically, War and Navy Department expenditures were relatively small before World War I, averaging approximately one percent of GNP. After a short-lived jump in World War I—to a maximum of 11 percent in FY 1919—they dropped back to around one percent of GNP in the 1920s and 1930s. World War II lifted military spending to a new height of 38 percent of GNP in FY 1945, with a subsequent fall to 5 percent in FY 1948. This was followed in June 1950 by the invasion of South Korea by North Korean forces—probably not entirely unrelated to U.S. unpreparedness. American intervention pushed the cost of national defense up to 13 percent in FY 1952. During the ensuing cold war decades, our opponents multiplied their arms spending while U.S. defense spending gradually slid to 5 percent of GNP by the end of the 1970s.[2]

A Shift from the Purchase of Goods and Services to Transfer Payments

The table below shows that while employee compensation and interest payments retained their relative roles in total government expenditures, a drastic shift from "purchase of goods and services" to "transfer payments" took place. Transfer payments are payments for which government gets no material return. Their purpose is to provide income to individuals such as social security benefits, unemployment compensation, public assistance, retirement annuities, etc.

TYPES OF GOVERNMENT EXPENDITURES (FEDERAL, STATE, LOCAL), 1952 AND 1978

| | 1952 | 1978 | Percentage Increase in | Percentage Share of Total Expenditures | |
	millions		*Constant $*	1952	1978
Total	$93,887	$685,985	197%	100%	100%
Employee compensation	31,161	229,577	200	33	33
Purchase of other goods and services	44,421	206,015	89	47	30
Transfer payments	14,191	218,673	527	15	32
Net interest	4,470	27,744	153	5	4
Other	356	3,976			1

SOURCES: *The National Income and Product Accounts of the United States, 1929–1974*, Statistical Tables, A Supplement to the *Survey of Current Business*, U.S. Department of Commerce, 1977, and *Survey of Current Business*, July 1979.

The share of purchase of goods and services (other than employee compensation) declined by 17 percentage points, the exact number by which transfer payments increased. This signifies a change in the main task of government from providing services to redistributing income; in other words, *from the service state to the welfare state.*

Explosion in Spending for Domestic Purposes

Governmental expenditures for domestic purposes grew steadily during the first half of the twentieth century, approximately doubling their share of GNP. Then they virtually exploded. Outlays for domestic services (federal, state, local) jumped from 38% of total governmental expenditures in 1952 to 76% in 1978.

Most of the growth occurred in three functional areas: income support (public welfare, unemployment compensation, social security); health and hospitals; education.

GOVERNMENTAL EXPENDITURES (FEDERAL, STATE, LOCAL)
FOR DOMESTIC PURPOSES IN 1952 AND 1978

	1952	1978	Percentage Increase in *constant* $ 1952–1978	Percent of GNP 1952	1978
	billions				
Total	$35.4	$520.2	+498%	10.2%	24.5%
Income support	6.3	156.8	919	1.8	7.4
Health and hospitals	2.6	59.6	838	.7	2.8
Education	8.4	120.8	487	2.4	5.7
Other social services[a]	.9	13.9	553	.3	.7
Other	17.3	169.1	298	5.0	7.9

SOURCE: Table 23.

[a]Housing, community development, labor.

In the three above-mentioned areas—income support, health, education—expenditures in *constant* dollars multiplied eight times, in the aggregate of all other domestic functions, four times—in a quarter century during which population increased only 39%, personal consumption 153%. Developments in these three areas will probably in the future, as they have for some time, determine the trend in government spending for domestic purposes.

It is ironic that in each of the three fields which advanced most rapidly over the past quarter century, huge new federal programs were repeatedly urged upon Congress but failed of adoption. In 1969 President Nixon proposed the Family Assistance Plan, a form of guaranteed annual income, which would have doubled the number of public assistance recipients immediately. The bill passed the House of Representatives twice but failed in the Senate. President Carter recommended a similar plan in 1977 which also managed to get through the House but died in the Senate. He tried again in 1979 with no better luck.

Comprehensive national health insurance plans were advanced repeatedly by the White House and by members of Congress which would have added multibillion-dollar amounts to the budget. They will undoubtedly be pushed again.

A drive for a program of general federal support of the public schools has long been active. Several such bills passed one house or the other a century ago. But although that campaign was periodically renewed, extended to colleges, and pursued by larger organized forces and probably with firmer determination and effort than most similar movements, it failed every time.

Had the proposed major health, education and welfare bills been enacted, public spending for domestic purposes would probably have climbed even faster than the exorbitant rate of recent decades. Most of those campaigns are still being actively pursued and one or several of them could some day succeed.

Developments over the past quarter century can be brought into even sharper focus by an analysis of *federal* expenditures. In 1952 the federal government spent for domestic purposes $12.6 billion, in 1978 $286.9 billion, or 22 times as much (Table 21). This means that the annual increase over that 26-year period averaged $10.5 billion which is almost as much as the magnitude which total expenditures had reached in 1952—163 years after the inception of the republic. Let me repeat that: the *annual* increase between 1952 and 1978 almost equaled the *total* growth between 1789 and 1952!

Domestic services accounted for 18% of all federal spending in 1952, for 62 percent in 1978. As a percentage of GNP, federal domestic expenditures jumped from 3.6% to 13.5%. Where did those enormous funds, equal to 10% of GNP, come from? Not from boosting taxes: federal revenues remained virtually steady at 21.2% of GNP in 1952 and 21.4% in 1978.

Most of the funds that made it possible to multiply federal domestic spending ninefold in *constant* dollars and fourfold as a percentage of GNP came from slashing national security. While the budget share of domestic outlays jumped 44% (from 18% to 62%) the national security share dropped by 46%, from 76% of the budget to 30%. While domestic outlays *increased* by 10% of GNP, national security *declined* by 9% of GNP.

Whenever defense funds could not be cut enough to meet social program demands, the remainder was "raised" by resort to deficit financing. The federal budget went from a surplus of $49 million in 1952 to a deficit of $49 billion in 1978.[3] Small wonder that the inflation rate which stayed within a one to two percent annual range from 1952 to 1965 soared to two-digit levels in the 1970s.

That the nature of the federal government underwent a significant change between 1952 and 1978 is apparent from the allocation of its resources (see table, p. 132). In 1902 87% of federal expenditures went for what may be called the "traditional" federal functions: national defense, international relations, post office, veterans services and benefits, interest on the general debt, financial administration and general control. All other activities accounted for a mere 13% of the budget. Half a century later, after two world wars, the Great Depression and the New Deal the share of those "other" (nontraditional) outlays had grown moderately to 19%. By 1978, however, those "other" = *nontraditional* outlays accounted for 60%, the major share of the federal budget. Most of those services, largely in the social welfare field, had been either insignificant or nonexistent prior to 1952. In other words, until a quarter century ago, the dominant functions of the federal government were—national defense, foreign relations and related programs, ministerial services such as the post office and general and financial administration—as they had been for 163 years. Those activities consumed in 1952 more than four-fifths of federal financial resources.

Between 1952 and 1978 the federal government came to play not only a much bigger role than ever before but also a different role. Social services and income redistribution, previously nonexistent or of minor significance, became major and controlling elements in the budget and thereby a prime function of the federal government. It is most remarkable that such a fundamental change, from concepts that prevailed from the inception of the republic on for well over a century and a half could have been brought about without amending the U.S. Constitution. To be sure, some amendments such as the sixteenth (income tax) and the seventeenth (direct election of senators) had contributed toward that end. Few, if any, of the legislators who voted those amendments into law suspected or could have imagined the drastic changes they would bring about in the nature and activities of the U.S. government and in American society. Not until many years later would their impact be fully recognized and felt.

In the final analysis, the change in the focus of federal activities was brought about by statutory and appropriative action of Congress, largely on the initiative of incumbent presidents. It was aided by the Supreme Court's reinterpretation of several provisions of the Constitution, particularly with regard to the substantive meaning of the welfare clause (Art. 1, Sec. 8) and the equal rights clause (Amend. 14, Sec. 1), and by the deactivation of the tenth amendment (powers not delegated to the United States nor prohibited to the states are reserved to the states or to the people).

Someone reading our leading newspapers and journals about public expenditure trends or reviewing hundreds of speeches on that subject in and out of Congress could easily reach the conclusion that the 1950s to 1970s were characterized by an enormous increase in military spending, financed by cutting domestic services and starving social welfare programs. But the record shows that just the opposite took place.

Interestingly enough this was particularly true during the 1970s when three presidents with proclaimed dedication to governmental frugality and fiscal restraint held office. This brings to mind a recent study, sponsored by

ALLOCATION OF FEDERAL EXPENDITURES BETWEEN "TRADITIONAL"
AND OTHER FUNCTIONS, FISCAL YEARS 1902, 1952 and 1978

	1902 (in millions)	Percent	1952 (in millions)	Percent	1978 (in millions)	Percent
Traditional functions:						
National defense and international relations	$165		$48,187		$114,811	
Veterans benefits and services	141		2,428		19,691	
Interest on general debt	29		4,262		39,330	
Post office	126		2,612		15,271	
General control and financial administration	34		608		4,365	
Total	495	87%	58,097	81%	193,468	40%
All other expenditures	77	13	13,471	19	285,829	60
Total expenditures	$572	100%	$71,568	100%	$479,297	100%

SOURCES: U.S. Bureau of the Census, *Historical Statistics on Governmental Finances and Employment*, 1977 Census of Governments, 1979; and idem, *Governmental Finances in 1977–78*, 1980.

the U.S. Advisory Commission on Intergovernmental Relations, which concluded that federal growth should be attributed mostly to Congress and not to incumbent presidents. It "revealed a surprising amount of congressional activism" together with a "surprising lack of presidential importance in the policy process."[4]

A Policy Reversal in the Late 1970s?

Official pronouncements and media reports in the late 1970s suggested that decisive changes were taking place in the allocation of federal funds: the share of defense was being materially increased while restraints were being placed on social programs. The succeeding two tables show federal spending in 1969, 1975 and as proposed for FY 1981 in the President's budget, submitted in January 1980. They indicate no increase in defense or decrease on the domestic side.

Trends as depicted in the table below are unequivocal. While it had taken 180 years—from 1789 to 1969—for federal expenditures for domestic

FEDERAL EXPENDITURES BY MAJOR FUNCTIONS,
FISCAL YEARS 1969, 1975 AND 1981*

	1969	1975 billions	1981*
Total	$184.5	$326.2	$615.8
National security	89.0	96.5	162.3
National defense	80.2	85.6	146.2
International affairs	3.8	6.9	9.6
Science, space, technology	5.0	4.0	6.4
Interest	15.8	30.9	67.2
Veterans benefits and services	7.6	16.6	21.7
All other (domestic functions)	72.1	182.2	364.5

SOURCE: *The Budget of the United States Government, Fiscal Year 1977*; idem, *Fiscal Year 1981.*

*1981 data are estimates in the President's Budget for FY 1981.

purposes to reach a level of $72 billion, it required only another twelve years to add $300 billion more. If outlays for military and domestic functions are related to budget totals or to GNP—as they are in the table below—they indicate a continued strong shift between 1969 and 1981 in the direction of domestic programs.

In *constant* dollars—following computations in the FY 1981 budget (p. 613)—federal expenditures grew 29 percent between 1969 and 1981. But this composite result consisted of a *decline* in national defense outlays of 18 percent and a 104 percent *increase* on the domestic side. What the tables on pp. 133 and 134 also demonstrate is a substantial slowing down of the trend toward domestic spending between 1975 and 1981.

The table on p. 135 shows defense spending, year by year from 1969 to presidential proposals in the FY 1981 budget. The GNP share of defense reached its lowest level at 5.1% in 1978 and 1979; it will, by these projections, come up to 5.3% in 1981, then remain even. As a share of the U.S. budget, defense reached a low of 23.3% in 1978, inched up to 23.8% in 1979, and down again to 23.1% in 1980. Under President Carter's proposed program it may be up to 23.7% in 1981—which still is the lowest figure except for 1978 and 1980.

Claims by President Carter to the contrary notwithstanding, a genuine reversal in the shift from defense to domestic programs, which has dominated U.S. fiscal policy since 1952, had yet to take place when he left office.

CHANGE IN SHARES OF FEDERAL EXPENDITURES BY MAJOR FUNCTIONS,
FISCAL YEARS 1969, 1975 AND 1981*

	As a percentage of total federal expenditures			As a percentage of Gross National Product		
	1969	1975	1981*	1969	1975	1981*
Total	100.0%	100.0%	100.0%	20.4%	22.4%	22.3%
National security	48.2	29.6	26.3	9.8	6.6	5.9
National defense	43.5	26.2	23.7	8.9	5.9	5.3
International affairs	2.1	2.1	1.6	0.4	0.5	0.3
Science, space, technology	2.7	1.2	1.0	0.6	0.3	0.2
Interest	8.6	9.5	10.9	1.7	2.1	2.4
Veterans benefits and services	4.1	5.1	3.5	0.8	1.1	0.8
All other (domestic)	39.1	55.9	59.2	8.0	12.5	13.2

SOURCE: *The Budget of the United States Government Fiscal Year 1977*, idem, *1981*.

*1981 data are estimates in the President's Budget for FY 1981.

Reordering National Priorities—Guns vs. Butter

The battle cry to "Reorder National Priorities" meant for many years one thing: demand for a shift in federal funds from national security to social programs. Hundreds of organizations with an economic, political or ideological interest in promoting particular domestic programs have long been fighting in Washington for a bigger share of the taxpayer's dollar. Gradually many of them came to realize that by competing with each other they were "eating each other's bread" and that they could do better by uniting in a drive to get more from where most of the money went: national defense. For many years military appropriations totaled more than the federal funds allocated to domestic services. So—why not work a gold mine instead of laboring in a stone quarry?

Historically, domestic public functions were held to be in the realm of the states and communities while the national government—founded to unite the colonies in a common defense against the king's armies to win and keep the independence they had proclaimed—would do only what the states could not do if each acted separately. The traditional concept of a limited federal government of specified delegated powers eroded in the early part of the XIX century and became a pure facade when in the

NATIONAL DEFENSE OUTLAYS, FY 1969 TO 1983*

Fiscal Year	Billions of dollars	Billions of 1972 dollars	Percent of all federal expenditures	Percent of Gross National Product
1969	$79.4	$97.9	43.0%	8.8%
1970	78.6	90.3	40.0	8.2
1971	75.8	81.2	35.9	7.4
1972	76.6	76.6	33.0	6.9
1973	74.5	70.0	30.1	6.0
1974	77.8	67.9	28.9	5.7
1975	85.6	67.2	26.2	5.9
1976	89.4	65.6	24.4	5.5
1977	97.5	66.5	24.2	5.3
1978	105.2	66.6	23.3	5.1
1979	117.7	69.3	23.8	5.1
1980E	130.4	70.7	23.1	5.2
1981E	146.2	73.2	23.7	5.3
1982E	165.5	76.6	24.1	5.3
1983E	185.9	80.0	24.0	5.3

SOURCE: *The Budget of the United States Government, FY 1979, 1981.*
*1980–83 estimates

aftermath of World War II the rapid dismantling of defense made large resources available and whetted the appetite for more.

While the struggle for greater funds for the various services continued in state capitals, county seats and cities, the main effort of special interest groups for a bigger slice of the public pie was nationally organized and shifted to Washington. The demands of organized leaders went in many directions but they knew that the more they could cut from the military budget, the more they would be able to get for their own ends. Various alliances and coalitions were founded with the common objective of reducing allocations to defense.

The National Urban Coalition's *Counterbudget* proposed a cut in the president's defense budget for FY 1975 of $37 billion, with a boost in domestic outlays of $70 billion.[5] The organization pursued identical aims in its congressional testimony on national priorities in the 1980 budget.[6] A more forceful case was made at the same hearings by former Congresswoman Patsy Mink as president of Americans for Democratic Action. Mrs. Mink complained that "the President's budget favors weapons over people," "Carter offers catchy phrases: 'Increased efficiencies,' 'cost savings,' 'elimination of waste and fraud' and 'targeting' of federal funds to those most in need. . . ." "The military budget is one of the most wasteful and inefficient portions of the federal budget." "Human needs programs [are being] sacrificed for austerity policy."

Hundreds of statements of this type complaining about governmental preference for defense at the expense of the needy, underprivileged, and minorities were made from the 1950s through the 1970s. The president of the National Urban League, Vernon Jordan, wrote in 1978: "But the New Negativism's attack on taxes is an attack on government's ability to meet social needs. 'Trimming the fat' and charges of 'waste' seem only to apply to social programs, and not to the swollen military budget."[7]

The primary goal of other groups has been not so much to obtain federal funds for their own programs as to cut defense for other reasons. The most prominent members of the "antidefense lobby" descend from the anti-Vietnam movement of the 1960s and tend to have far-left connections or lean toward radical or terrorist objectives.[8]

Some defense critics alleged that the military establishment has grown too big for the job at hand and that conventional forces should be cut by 40 percent, strategic forces by 90%, and research and development expenditures by 60 percent.[9] Another critic cited economic reasons, charging that "the huge, wasteful military colossus, along with the staggering deficits that have accompanied it, was the single most important inflationary factor in our society."[10] The *New York Times* editorially attacked Mr. Carter's FY 1980 budget as austerity for civilians and liberality for defense.[11]

The table below shows what actually did happen to the various segments of our defense program between 1969 and 1981.

The declines shown on p. 137—such as 48% in strategic forces, 28 percent in general purpose forces—understate the case. As weapons systems become more sophisticated, item prices multiply far faster than the growth of the Consumer Price Index, which was used in this, as in other tables, to convert current dollars into *constant* dollars. For example, the cost of an XM1 tank is three times the price of an M60 tank, the cost of an F14, eight times the price of an F4. Also, conversion from 1979 to 1981 was done by using estimates in the FY 1981 budget: a 10.4% increase in 1980 and an 8.6% growth to 1981. The inflation rate was 12.4% in 1980—and is running at similar rates in 1981. This means that the rates of program decline will be larger than the table indicates.

The long-range discrepancy between the rise in the general price level and the cost of weapons systems is enormous. The CPI multiplied five times between World War II and 1981. The cost of an aircraft carrier meanwhile jumped from $55 million to $2.5 billion, of an attack submarine from $5 million to over $300 million, of an advanced bomber from $218,000 to $100 million, of a fighter plane from $54,000 to $19 million.

SUMMARY OF DEPARTMENT OF DEFENSE PROGRAMS, 1969 AND 1981*

	1969	1981	Increase or decrease in percent (in *constant* [1981] dollars) 1969 to 1981
	(in billions of dollars)		
Total	$78.7	$158.2	−24%
Strategic forces	8.6	11.7	−48
General purpose forces	30.7	58.3	−28
Intelligence and communications	5.8	10.6	−32
Research and development	4.7	14.1	+13
Central supply and maintenance	9.4	15.6	−37
Training, medical, personnel activities	12.4	32.9	0
All other	7.1	15.0	−20

SOURCE : *The Budget of the United States Government*, FY, 1971, 1981.

*This table was renamed NATIONAL NEEDS: DEFENSE, MILITARY in the 1979 ff budgets. Data for 1981 are estimates from the President's Budget for 1981.

The declines in defense spending reflect in part the impact that anti-defense forces made on Congress. This raises the question: How does Congress arrive at its decisions on the defense budget?

In the Brookings Institution's *Setting National Priorities: The 1973 Budget* the authors suggested that "defense spending for the most part has not been subject to partisan politics. . . . Of the four general considerations affecting the defense budget, domestic factors are quantitatively the least important. . . ."[12] The authors admit though that "the pressure of competing domestic requirements now exercises greater restraint on increases in defense spending than at any time since the end of the Second World War."[13]

That partisan politics is not a major factor in setting defense policies is partially true because the division is not drawn strictly between the political parties but along ideological lines which sometimes cross party boundaries. But domestic and political considerations became main factors in setting the size of the defense budget. There simply is no way in which some of the favorite schemes for expanding domestic benefits could have been financed except by cutting it out of the hide of the military.

In 1968 Brookings Institution President Kermit Gordon ventured the hypothesis that social program policy depended on defense budget decisions: "It is quite possible that the decisions of the new administration and the new Congress on the post-Vietnam defense budget will be the most important factor in determining the scale on which the nation attacks its internal social problems."[14] But a closer look at how policy decisions are made at the top level suggests that cause and effect relationships are the exact reverse.

Congressman Lee Aspin, author of an amendment cutting defense procurement appropriations adopted by the House on July 31, 1973, said that it was necessary to convince his colleagues "that you've got to cut the defense budget if you want sufficient money for your own programs." This is not a new approach. Two decades ago Samuel P. Huntington of the Institute of War and Peace Studies at Columbia University wrote in a carefully documented study of postwar budget policy formation:

> In both the Truman Administration before the Korean War and in the Eisenhower Administration after the war, the tendency was:
> 1. to estimate the revenues of the government or total expenditures possible within the existing debt limit;
> 2. to deduct from this figure the estimated cost of domestic programs and foreign aid; and
> 3. to allocate the remainder to the military.[15]

This finding may have been true at the time when balanced budgets were the rule and the size of the federal debt had barely changed since the close of World War II. But the federal debt was raised by $700 billion over the past two decades (which in turn pushed inflation to double-digit rates). For many years the restraining influence on the budget of prospective revenues has been considerably weakened by a readiness to recommend and approve ever higher debt ceilings. But even so, there is a limit, economic or political, to how much the debt ceiling can in peacetime be boosted in any one year.

When Huntington wrote his report, congressional sentiment still seemed to favor national security. In the early 1960s Congress raised defense appropriations above the president's request almost every year. But then the mood of the country and of the Congress changed when the dilatory conduct and inconclusive outcome of the long-drawn-out Vietnam war divided the American people and generated widespread frustration and negative feelings toward the military establishment. From the later 1960s through most of the 1970s Congress reduced the president's defense budget year after year.

By the mid-1970s evidence that the Soviets were in the process of overtaking the United States in military power or had already done so became available and finally overwhelming. President Ford proposed a few increases in defense appropriations but found Congress not very receptive.

In the 1976 presidential campaign Mr. Carter repeatedly advocated a $5 to $7 billion cut in defense appropriations. He proceeded to redeem his promise after entering the White House. In testimony before the Senate Armed Services Committee in October 1979, former Secretary of Defense Donald H. Rumsfeld computed that the shortfall in defense budget authority totaled $38.6 billion in the first three budgets of the Carter administration and would total $84 billion by 1982 if current plans were carried out.

President Carter canceled the B-1 bomber, shelved the neutron bomb, delayed production of the new land-based MX mobile missile and the Tomahawk Cruise missile, slowed development of the Trident missile submarine, sharply cut the naval shipbuilding program, and vetoed the construction of a large (Nimitz class) nuclear aircraft carrier—while proposing numerous sizable expansions of social programs. As late as May 25, 1978, Mr. Carter declared defense a primary target for FY 1980 budget cuts.

Gradually, in the second half of the 1970s the mood of the American public began to change. A Harris poll in 1971 reported that 49 percent of the respondents favored a decrease in defense spending while only 11% opposed it. A similar Harris poll in July 1978 disclosed a 50:36 opposition to higher military outlays, but a poll in September-October 1979 showed that 60% favored higher defense spending while only 9% preferred lower defense spending.

That was *after* President Carter had asked Congress for a 3% annual increase in defense authority, a plan subsequently upped to 5 percent.

Congress and the President were quite aware of the changed climate. As a result, national security outlays which had dropped 3.2% of GNP between 1969 and 1975, lost only 0.7% between 1975 and 1981. Domestic functions which had gained 4.4% of GNP between 1969 and 1975, inched up only 0.7% between 1975 and 1981 (see Table, p. 134.) Are we again "reordering national priorities"—but now in the other direction?

Clearly, the defense-to-social-program shift lost its momentum. But—has it been reversed, as some claim—or is it in the process of being reversed? There was no sign of a willingness to restrain social programs early in 1980 but a sense for enlarged defense spending developed as the year wore on. In late August a military authorization bill that substantially exceeded President Carter's recommendations zipped through the Senate by a 78 to 2 vote and by 360 to 49 through the House. But where are the funds to come from for a stronger defense?

Growth is built into the domestic programs and is likely to absorb most if not all of the revenue increase from economic growth and inflation. That, at least, has been the experience over many years. Large deficits were the rule through the 1970s but became objectionable under anti-inflationary policies toward the end of the decade. Major tax boosts, besides those already enacted, are unlikely. In fact, the pressure appears to be growing for tax relief. For more than two decades the defense budget was quarried to amplify the social budget. Has the time come to feed the defense budget from the social budget? There simply is no other source. But there still is great reluctance to cut heavily into social programs. The reworking of the 1981 budget by President Carter and in Congress showed clearly that though budgetary acrobatics may be used to present a balanced budget, no serious attempts were being made to come to grips with the mushroom growth of social transfer and service programs. It still seemed politically difficult to take the bull by the horns. Without a firm resolve to deal with the growth in domestic programs, prospects for returning defense spending to high levels of earlier years remain in doubt.

The enormity of the change that took place is not widely enough realized. The federal government spent in 1952 four times as much on defense as on domestic services. By 1969 domestic outlays exceeded defense, for the first time. In 1978 domestic spending amounted to nearly three times as much as the military budget (Table 23).

To reverse such a powerful trend would require an even stronger counterforce. Where is it to be found? A *Newsweek* poll (3/3/80) in February 1980 asked, "Would you be more or less likely to vote for a candidate who took the following positions?" "Favors large increase in defense spending" returned an affirmative vote of 64 to 20. The only stronger vote in that poll (73:14) was on "favors a tax cut for individuals." So where is the money going to come from? I have yet to see a poll which suggests that the public favors cutbacks or even restraints on social programs, except in public welfare (public assistance). As a rule there are more votes in favor of expansion than reduction of spending in most public opinion polls. This makes it difficult to be confident about the prospects of reversing the 1952–78 trend of shifting funds from military to domestic functions.

In an article "National Defense is Affordable"[16] Paul McCracken, former chairman of the Council of Economic Advisers, suggested that we can afford to raise defense spending by 17% annually which, over the next five years, would double the total. It would then (1985) equal 8.6% of GNP—as it averaged in the 1957 to 1965 period. That seems plausible. However, in a letter to the editor, Edwin Dale of the *New York Times* replied that Mr. McCracken "neglected to mention an uncomfortable fact." In the early 1960s federal spending on transfer payments averaged only 4.3% of GNP. In 1979–81 it is running at 9.1%. Mr Dale added: "Anyone who believes that these domestic outlays can be significantly reduced is whistling in the dark."[17] Could he be right?

The late Air Marshal Sir John Slessor once said:

> It is customary in democratic countries to deplore expenditures on armaments as conflicting with the requirements of the social services. There is a tendency to forget that the most important social service that a government can provide for its people is to keep them alive and free.[18]

That leaves us with the question, "How much defense do we need?"

How Much Defense Do We Need?

At the start of the 1980s the federal government is allocating a smaller share of its financial resources to national defense than it did at any time in its history, save in the 1870s to 1890s. In no year since 1941 has the United States devoted a smaller percentage of its national product to defense, had a smaller segment of its labor force in military uniform or in defense-related work than it had at the close of the 1970s.

Does the decision so to allocate our resources express a belief of the American people that they and their country are now more secure, less subject to a challenge, provocation, blackmail or attack from abroad than at any time since before World War II? If so, is this based on the knowledge that our position in the world is more powerful and our military might greater than anybody else's, that we are so invincible that no potential aggressor would dare assail or defy us? If not, if we recognize that all preceding questions must be answered with a resounding no and if we accept the fact that the United States now finds itself in greater peril than ever before, then we must ask the simple question—why? Why have we let our supremacy, unquestioned a few decades ago, slip away? How did we come to our present sad state? Is it because we lacked the necessary resources or because we devoted those resources to other ends?

The answer to the last question is obvious. We have the resources but we decided to allocate them to other purposes. This reminds me of a famous saying by Somerset Maugham:

> If a nation values anything more than freedom, it will lose its freedom; and the irony of it is that if it is comfort or money that it values more, it will lose that too.[19]

As was shown earlier in this chapter, military outlays of the United States declined over the past quarter century from 13 percent of GNP in 1952 to 5 percent in 1978 to 1980. The magnitude of spending may not be a sufficient yardstick of military capability. On the whole, however, we must assume those whom we elect to the presidency and to Congress and their appointees in the Pentagon and the Armed Forces to be competent to make cost-efficient choices: to get for whatever sums available "the most bang for the buck."

Inevitably there are and always will be differences among experts, but how can we find persons better qualified to make the critical defense budget decisions than by electing candidates to office who will identify and appoint them? The selection they make will have to be in terms of weapons systems, but dollars are the only common denominator for an overall determination of needs.

The 1981 defense budget stated the basic national security objectives of the United States well: "To provide for its physical security as a free nation; to maintain its fundamental institutions and values; and to advance and protect U.S. interests in the world. To achieve these objectives we must be able to deter attacks on the United States, our allies and friends; to prevent others from imposing their political will on the United States by military means; to influence international affairs from a position of recognized strength; and to fight successfully when necessary." Implementation, unfortunately, fell far short of these promises.

The goal of defense policy is plain: We must at all times exceed the strength of hostile forces that may confront us. This means that we must be stronger than the Soviet Union—the only country which for as far as we can see ahead could be a serious military adversary and—together with our allies in NATO—we must be stronger than the Warsaw Pact nations.

Until just a few years ago we militarily exceeded anything the Soviets could muster. We no longer do. Experts disagree only on one issue: some believe that the Soviet Union has already attained military supremacy while the optimists feel that the Russians have achieved equality with the United States but will, given current trends, achieve supremacy within a few years, say in 1985.

U.S. armed forces are undermanned and underequipped, in quality even more than in quantity, to a point where their ability to defend the nation and its vital interests is in grave doubt. The Soviets have been outspending us in arms outlays for over a decade, and the global balance of military power has been shifting toward them. Odds now appear to favor the USSR in a war with the United States. Much of our Navy is unseaworthy, much of the Air Force not ready to fly combat missions and the Army, in the words of its chief of staff, is "hollow."

Since we cannot do much about the speed of the Soviet buildup, we can influence the outcome only by decisions on our own spending. Those decisions and their consequences may well prove to be irreversible. Therefore, the critical question is very simple: Do we want Soviet supremacy or do we not? And, if we don't, are we willing to do whatever needs to be done to prevent our becoming the underdog?

At congressional hearings on the FY 1980 budget, General David C. Jones, Chairman of the Joint Chiefs of Staff, said that the Soviets are not an economic superpower nor a technological superpower. "The only aspect of power that gives them a superpower status is military capability, and I believe that that is the reason they have imposed such sacrifices on their people and put such a great priority on the military."[20]

It may help us to understand the decline of American military power if we trace it back historically to the end of World War II when the United States reached its apex. Euphoria over the splendid victory was quickly followed by drastic disarmament. Samuel Huntington described events as follows:

> In 1946, the President informed the Secretaries of War and the Navy that the armed services could have one-third of the total budget for FY 1948 after fixed charges had been met. "It was here," Walter Mills points out, "that President Truman for the first time laid down the arithmetical formula that he was to adopt toward the military budget in the ensuing two years."[21]

Defense outlays fell precipitously, to about five percent of GNP in 1948, a level so low that it was not touched again for thirty years. That rapid dismantling of America's military might have helped encourage the North Koreans to attack their neighbors to the south in 1950, which in turn led to U.S. intervention. The military budget was then pushed to over thirteen percent of GNP in 1952, from which level it has been declining ever since.

To justify defense cutbacks, the American people deceived themselves with hopes that the Soviets would follow suit, and that strategic arms limitation agreements would make huge outlays unnecessary. Détente turned out to be an officially created illusion. At congressional hearings in February 1980 Defense Secretary Harold Brown described his eventual disappointment: "We build, they build; we cut, they build." For many years Americans were encouraged by their highest officials in the belief that they could avoid paying the price of national security. Only toward the end of the 1970s did more people come to realize that we shall have to pay the full price of defense, whether we want to or not, either in advance in the form of greater resources for the military or afterwards, by defeat at the hands of our adversaries.

In the late 1950s attention focused on arms control and disarmament with ensuing discussion on how the government could best spend the funds that would result from defense cuts. I then warned, in a presentation at a 1962 conference on national security, that we should also think of "how to increase funds for national security" because, "unfortunately, the threat of war is likely to hang over us as long as the Communist forces control some of the major countries. They will never *voluntarily* recede from their goal of world domination."[22]

In his inaugural address, President John F. Kennedy uttered inspiring words:

> Let every nation know, whether it wishes us well or ill, that we shall pay any price, bear any burden, meet any hardship, support any friend, oppose any foe, to assure the survival and the success of liberty.

President Kennedy acted courageously when in October 1962 he issued an ultimatum to the Kremlin to turn back its missile-loaded naval ships then steaming toward Cuba. Analysts of the Joint Chiefs estimated at the time that if a nuclear war were to ensue the Soviet Union would suffer ten times as much damage as the United States, that Russian military analysts would probably present their government with a similar estimate and that the Soviet leaders would probably decide to yield to the ultimatum—as in fact they did.

During the Eisenhower years the defense budget had remained almost steady at or slightly below ten percent of GNP. It also seemed stable between 1962 and 1965, at $48–$52 billion, but the percentage of GNP fell from 9.0 percent to 7.2 percent. The Vietnam war raised that level temporarily to 9.5% in 1968. Defense again declined, to 8.2% of GNP by 1970, then gradually skidding to about five percent by the end of the 1970s. (Data from the FY 1981 U.S. Budget.)

A large literature has developed on defense policy and budgets in the three decades since the founding of the Department of Defense in 1947.

Lawrence J. Korb of the Naval War College wrote an excellent summary of the process and politics of the defense budget, 1947–77.[23] Korb divided the time into three segments: the Truman-Eisenhower period, the McNamara period and the post-1968 period. At first, presidential ceilings for defense were set by arithmetic formulas—one-third of the budget under Truman, ten percent of GNP under Eisenhower. The McNamara era—which Hanson Baldwin, the *New York Times'* military editor called "The McNamara Monarchy"[24]—was characterized by a complete centralization of decision making, to the detail, in the person of the Secretary of Defense, whom the Bureau of the Budget did not dare touch and even President Johnson did not overrule. Introduction of PPBS (planning, programming, budgeting system) [25] and emphasis on cost-effectiveness analysis successfully concealed the fact that decision making in the Department of Defense became more intuitively guided, politics-conscious and personally directed than ever before. Military input was supremely disregarded while Mr. McNamara flaunted his disinterest in the opinions of the Joint Chiefs of Staff. To illustrate the point—and subsequent developments—I want to quote from what I wrote in 1965:

> Air Force leaders are deeply troubled by the decline in our bomber power. The B-47s are being phased out and the lives of the ten-year-old B-52 (modified) and B-58 are being stretched out for up to another ten years. They are to serve as our only bombers into the early or even mid-1970s. Responsible military experts have repeatedly demanded a more advanced "follow-on" bomber such as a supersonic plane with high and low altitude penetration capability or a missile-carrying strike plane (AMSA). But they have been unable to persuade Mr. McNamara that manned bombers are needed at all. [26]

I underestimated the amazing survival capacity of the B-52. President Carter in 1977 vetoed construction of its intended successor, the B-1. The B-52s, already a quarter century old, will have to serve, with some modernization, as our manned bombers well into the 1980s.

The Soviets took the lesson of President Kennedy's 1962 ultimatum to heart. I was told in the Kremlin in 1964 that they would do everything in their power to prevent a repeat of their humiliation. The USSR has since been engaged in a rapid armament program that boosted defense outlays by 4–5% annually—which amounts to a doubling of the total in 15 to 18 years.

The United States responded by cutting its defense budget from nine percent of GNP in the early 1960s to five percent at the close of the 1970s.

Budgetary processes became more decentralized in the Department of Defense after 1968 but expenditure ceilings were no less governed by political and economic considerations than before. Even the decentralization was reversed in 1978 and decision again concentrated in the office of the Secretary of Defense, as Lawrence Korb reported. [27]

The often mentioned *Arms Race* between the U.S.A. and the USSR never took place. They raced but we slowed down. The U.S. Arms Control and Disarmament Agency reported in October 1979 that, expressed in *constant* dollars, military expenditures had *risen* by 31 percent between 1968 and 1977 in the Soviet Union, *declined* by 26 percent in the

United States.[28] How can this be called a race? The same report also estimated that USSR accounted in 1977 for close to one-third of world defense expenditures, U.S.A. for less than one-fourth—down from nearly two-fifths in 1968.

All comparisons between American and Russian defense outlays are, at best, tentative. When Soviet Finance Minister Vasily Garbuzov in November 1979 presented the 1980 budget, he said that military spending would amount to the equivalent of about $26 billion or 6 percent of the total budget of $435 billion. Of course, this is wholly meaningless. Most Soviet military outlays are hidden in other parts of the budget and the pricing of weapons systems is arbitrary.

But even true costs, converted from rubles into dollars, would not give us a valid comparison of relative strength. Sixty cents of every Pentagon dollar goes to personnel, only 30 kopeks of every military ruble. The Soviet Union pays its conscripts meager pocket money—about $10 a month to a recruit. But that does not mean that a Soviet soldier is less combat effective than an American.

The Central Intelligence Agency has for some years attempted to price Soviet defense outlays in dollars so as to find out what it would cost to duplicate the Soviet defense establishment in the United States.[29] This is what it reported:

In terms of the total defense budget the USSR caught up with the U.S.A. in 1971 and exceeded it by 45 percent in 1978. The Soviet Union allocated in 1978 three times as much as the U.S. to strategic forces and about 35 percent more to general purpose forces. The Soviets exceeded the U.S. in military investment by 65 percent, in operating costs by 25 percent.

In terms of manpower, Soviet forces are now twice as large (4.4 million vs. 2.1 million), although the USSR population is only 20 percent bigger than ours. Over the past decade Soviet armed forces *increased* by more than half a million while U.S. armed forces *shrank* by 1.5 million.

The above-cited data from the mentioned CIA report constitute *input* and do not necessarily represent equivalent *combat effectiveness*. Only "the battle is the payoff." But that may be too late to find out—certainly too late to do something about it.

The "gap" between a 5 percent of GNP defense investment by the U.S. and a 13 percent investment from a 40 percent smaller GNP by the Soviets is reflected in the size of their respective weapon systems: In strategic arms the USSR is far ahead in number and throw weight of intercontinental ballistic missiles (ICBMs) and substantially ahead in the number of submarines and submarine-launched ballistic missiles (SLBMs), while the U.S. is ahead in the number of long-range bombers—antiquated as most of them now are despite several modernizations. We also have more strategic nuclear warheads.

The Soviets are far stronger in general purpose forces—the U.S. Defense Intelligence Agency has described the Soviet Army as "the most powerful land army in the world." The Russians have four to five times as many tanks, four times as much artillery and are outproducing us two to one or more in combat planes and helicopters. They have more navy ships though we still lead in total displacement. We are far ahead in aircraft carriers (13:3) though the number of ours was cut to almost half over the past dozen years, to a level that is inadequate for the vast ocean areas they are supposed to cover. The dispatch of carrier task forces to the Indian Ocean in early 1980 left the Atlantic and the Pacific with inadequate naval presence because less than half of our carriers are ready for sea duty at any particular time.

For many years the Soviets have been outspending and outbuilding us in tanks, guns, airplanes, nuclear missiles and navy ships. The outcome of these trends, unless soon reversed, is foreseeable and inevitable.

Five-year plans in the FY 1981 budget for the new ICBM mobile MX missile, cruise missile, Trident submarine, XM1 (Abrams) tank, global rapid deployment force and CX transport plane, construction of 97 new naval ships, etc. will help. But they will not enable us to catch up with what the Russians are doing. Quantities of new systems and old, now deployed, authorized and funded at the close of 1980 were insufficient throughout our arms inventory.

Defense critics have long alleged that we already have too much of everything, especially strategic weapons, that we possess an "overkill" capacity which could destroy the people and facilities in the Soviet Union several times over.

Even if this were true, the fact remains that the Soviet Union has more of almost everything we have or, according to more optimistic appraisals, at least as much as we have but is accumulating weapons faster. There is nothing we can do to stop them. They have given us ample evidence that they don't stop even if we do.

We can either continue our partial unilateral disarmament of recent decades or try hard and fast to grow stronger.

To continue our inadequate defense preparations for a few more years would almost inescapably result in a manifest and overwhelming Soviet superiority and in subjugation of the United States. An adequate rearmament program now could at least give us a chance for survival as an independent nation.

Military Manpower on the Downgrade

For several years after the Army shifted from conscription to an all-volunteer force in 1973, the Armed Services were able to meet their recruitment goals. But this was no longer true by the end of the 1970s when each branch fell short, the Army by 10% in 1979. Together with numerical deficiencies in the Reserves and the National Guard, the gap has assumed perilous dimensions. In past conflicts the United States always had ample time between the outbreak of war and participation in actual combat in which to mobilize, train and deploy its forces. The next war could be won or lost in the first few days or even hours. It will require instant readiness.

Recent recruiting scandals suggest that accession goals were reached or approached only by excessive pressure and sometimes by questionable methods. Thus even some of the former enthusiasts of an all-volunteer system are no longer so certain that this first attempt by a world power to maintain adequate strength without conscription has proven as successful as they had hoped.

But the greatest concern is not over numbers but about the caliber of recruits. Many able youths who would have volunteered—as a preferable alternative to being drafted—now choose civilian careers. Recruiting came closer to reaching goals in 1980 than it had in 1979 by lowering require-ments and accepting a larger proportion of non-high-school graduates. This continued a trend of lowered quality in military personnel. The Department of Defense annual report for FY 1981 revealed that Army personnel in the two upper categories of mental capacity (I and II) declined from 34% of the total force in 1972 to 20% in 1979, and simultaneously grew in the two lower categories (III and IV) from 66% to 79%. This means that four-fifths of the service accessions are in the lower half of the mental capacity scale. A similar trend was reported in the Navy, Marine Corps and Air Force. Increasingly, the Armed Forces seem to attract young men who are unable to land jobs in the open market and join the services as long as standards are low enough to accommodate them. Thus the military no longer represents a cross section of the American people. Can the people have confidence in such a force?

This is a delicate and controversial subject. Congressman Les Aspin (D-Wisc.) proposed in February 1980 that the military services should *lower* their intelligence standards for recruits, and quit establishing "un-realistically low quotas for personnel in mental category IV" (the lowest). Mr. Aspin is known as a longtime opponent to U.S. military preparedness.

Inadequate compensation is causing a serious shortage of trained technicians and engineers who find out that they can get better paid jobs in industry after a few years of training in the services. Retention is dropping, e.g., in the Navy and Marine Corps by one-third between 1973 and 1979, because fewer of the more experienced specialists reenlist.

The Armed Forces are "bleeding dry" of competent manpower needed for combat readiness. Maintenance is suffering and some of the ships, airplanes and weapons systems are marginally ready or plainly not ready. The breakdown of three out of eight helicopters on the attempted Iran hostage rescue raid, and the failure of the mission before even meeting an adversary, raises many questions which at present remain unanswered. The Army reported a shortage of 46,000 noncommissioned officers, the Navy of 20,000 petty officers, early in 1980.

Ethnic minorities accounted for 41% of Army personnel in 1979 and also for disproportionate shares in the other branches. This raises the specter, if trends of recent years continue, of two ethnic minorities someday constituting a majority of the United States Army.

Serious shortages exist in the officers corps. Pilots are leaving in droves and there are not enough physicians. As shown in Table 6, average pay rose between 1952 and 1978, in *constant* dollars, by 85% in the federal civilian establishment and by only 63% in the military. This was still ahead of the growth of 55% in private industry. But 1978 pay averaged less in the military than in most major industries. The "pay squeeze" has caused a heavy talent drain which can be stopped by raising the levels of compensation. That may be a very expensive move because compensation accounts for well over half of the defense budget dollar. Melvin Laird, who served as secretary of defense when conscription was abolished, recently pointed at the most urgent defense need in a monograph, titled *People, Not Hardware: The Highest Defense Priority*.[30]

A Shift in the Military Balance: Can It be Reversed?

In the Hoover Institution's symposium *The United States in the 1980s*, Fred Charles Iklé and Edward Teller voiced their concern about the shift in the military balance to the Soviet Union and other geopolitical changes and over the grave threat they pose to the survival of the United States as a free nation.[31] Both painted frightening but starkly realistic scenarios and offered keen analyses and alternative strategies and weapons systems potentials. In this book I do not aim to lay out a rearmament program. I only want to document and emphasize the urgent need for it and discuss its fiscal requirements and ways to meet them.

How much defense is enough? Enough for a credible deterrence and to make the price for attacking the United States or jeopardizing its vital interests anywhere in the world intolerably high. Any country that may want to risk a confrontation with us must be made to realize that we have the will and the wherewithal to assure our eventual victory.

When Japan attacked the United States in 1941, we had one to two years leeway to build up our forces to an adequate size. There is no such grace period in the last fifth of the twentieth century. The job must be done now or never. In view of the relentless buildup of hostile military power in the USSR we can do no less than our best.

What does this require? Wayne Schroeder was undoubtedly right when he wrote in December 1979: "A five percent real growth in defense spending will not begin to make up for the severe shortfall and stretchout problems that are facing the U.S. defense planners at the present time."[32] Former Army Chief of Staff General Maxwell D. Taylor estimated in 1978 that about eight percent of GNP over several years might do.[33] What we have since learned—e.g., from admissions that our intelligence services had greatly underestimated the rate of Russian arms buildup—suggests that we should allocate between eight and ten percent of GNP to the defense budget, as quickly as this can physically be done and keep it so indefinitely. That was the level of military outlays through much of the 1950s and 1960s, at times of balanced budgets and inflation rates below two percent per annum.

Can this now be done fiscally? Allocations to defense probably cannot be raised from five percent to eight or ten percent of GNP while governments spend 32 percent of GNP for *non*defense purposes—17 percent at the federal level, 15 percent at the state-local level. To boost the tax level by another five percent of GNP by, for example, the imposition of a value-added tax does not seem a likely alternative. Adoption of such a tax has been considered as an offset to desired commensurate cuts in income and social security taxes. Prospects for levying it on top of current taxes—save in case of a warlike emergency—appear doubtful, though a combination of restraint on domestic spending and addition of a low-rate value-added tax might at some time offer a politically feasible compromise.

In any case, there is no chance that under budgetary and fiscal policies that prevailed until 1980 our defenses can be brought to an adequate level—a level that will either prevent an attack on the United States and its lifelines or, failing to do so, assure the defeat of any power that would subject us to its will.

What this requires is a *Reordering of National Priorities*, a reversal of the trends that have governed budget policy for about a quarter century. That is a *political* problem. The president and the Congress cannot afford to take the necessary actions without the implicit consent of the American people. Of course, our highest officials can take leadership in publicly advocating and fighting for such goals. That requires a president and a

Congress who are dedicated to those ideas—elected to office by a majority of Americans who believe that national defense has a first and overriding priority over all other claims. Within the next few years, the American people will have to make decisions that may irrevocably decide the fate of their country, the nation and the free world for many generations.

Can the Budget Be Controlled?

As the decade of the 1970s drew to an end the need for tighter control of the federal budget seemed to gain wider attention in Congress and support among the American public. During the 1970s, revenues fell about ten percent short of meeting federal expenditures, and related problems, particularly inflation rates climbing steeply at double-digit levels, were causing concern. The concept of a balanced budget which had long been paid mere lip service, with a slight undertone of polite contempt for a relic that should have been retired, gained renewed respect, even with some nostalgia for the years when federal budgets *were* balanced and price rises seldom exceeded two percent.

While the proposition that budget deficits are not the only cause of inflation, and possibly not even the leading one, was broadly accepted, it was also increasingly acknowledged that inflation could probably not be ended nor even sharply cut *without* determined efforts to bring the budget into balance. But that was easier said than done.

For two decades or more, military outlays were the first area to be mentioned when the discusion turned to the goal of narrowing budgetary deficits or financing new projects. But by 1980 defense accounted for less than a fourth of the federal budget. Even more important, the shift in the military balance from the United States to the USSR and the existence or prospect of Soviet military superiority, vetoed considerations of further cutbacks in the defense area. That still left about three-fourths of the budget to work on, namely spending for domestic services.

There is a curious ambivalence in the American attitude toward governmental spending. The public harbors a generalized preference for keeping public budgets low while it cheers officeholders and office seekers who promise to increase funds for their favorite programs. This often causes political leaders to assume a paradoxical position of advocating restraint in general while pushing for enlarged appropriations for popular public programs.

When in national opinion polls respondents are asked which of a list of public services they would like to have cut or expanded, a majority usually favors expansion. In a Gallup poll for *Newsweek* in June 1978 which asked whether spending for nine services ranging from schools to police and welfare was too much or too little, 16 percent replied in the aggregate that it was too much, 26 percent that it was too little, and 45 percent that it was just about right. In other words, 16 percent might agree to a cut, 71 percent would not.

This is like asking children whether they want candy.

A poll of this type is of little value unless it asks the respondent not only whether he wants more service but also whether and how he is willing to pay for it from his own pocket. If the question leaves the implication that "the government" or other economic sectors would bear the cost, the answers have no validity. Who would reject something that might be available for free?

What the public always demands—and politicians promise with elaborate articulation—is the elimination of waste, fraud, inefficiency, duplication and excessive bureaucratic overhead. While efforts in that direction are essential, long experience with "reorganization" should teach us not to get our expectations up too high. Most of the cost of government is in the program itself, not in the overhead.

Every president in recent memory ran for office on a platform of governmental austerity and, during his incumbency, described his budget recommendations as frugal and lean. Each president seemed to feel sincerely that his budget was tight. He had been resisting pressures from many sides for larger funds, had experienced the budget process largely as a strenuous exercise in saying *NO* to persuasive and powerful forces. He probably felt that his negative responses may have lost him the support of numerous individuals and organizations who felt that they did not get as much as they were entitled to.

Franklin Delano Roosevelt campaigned in 1932 by denouncing President Herbert Hoover for his "reckless and extravagant" deficit spending and asserted that federal expenditures could be cut twenty percent. The record has it that this is not exactly what happened in the Roosevelt administration: federal expenditures more than doubled between 1932 and 1940.

In President Eisenhower's first two years, expenditures did, in fact, decline by $9 billion. This turned out to be the result of a $10 billion cut in defense and a $1 billion increase in the rest of the budget. To have kept nondefense outlays virtually stable for two years reveals an extraordinary effort of that administration, compared with its successors. There were no more overall budget reductions in the succeeding twenty-five years.

President Kennedy, who as a young congressman had warned in strong terms of the dangers of an expanding state, promised as president to build a *New Frontier*. Frontier building turned out to be expensive.

In his first budget message in January 1964, President Johnson pointed out with pride that his recommendation "calls for a reduction from the preceding year in total administration budget expenditures" and was "only the second budget in nine years to do so." That year, as all succeeding ones, ended with a sizable increase. The *Great Society* did not come for free.

President Nixon entered office with an announced dedication to governmental austerity and recommended a $2.4 billion reduction in the FY 1970 budget prepared by his predecessor. But when final accounts were in, outlays in FY 1970 were $1.3 billion higher than President Johnson had originally recommended. Subsequent year-to-year increases were far higher.

To be sure: there is ample evidence that the White House in the Nixon-Ford years exerted strenuous efforts to stem the tide of federal outlays and to resist pressures for an even faster growth. The loud and consistent outcries of special interest groups in and out of Congress about the "miserly" level of the president's programmatic and budgetary recommendations suggest that his aims were usually on the frugal side. In most of the president's constant battles with Congress over spending, he was on the side of lower expenditures except on national defense. Spending ceilings he recommended were either not adopted or shot full of holes so that they were largely ineffective. Appropriations he regarded to be excessive were prominent among President Nixon's about forty vetoes, only five of which were overridden by Congress.

The practice of impounding funds, that is, not spending moneys appropriated by Congress, was used occasionally by earlier presidents but not as extensively as by President Nixon, whose impoundments in his first term have been estimated at $40 billion.

The president's legal power to impound funds was questioned and a dozen lawsuits were filed in federal courts, with most decisions going against the administration. Thus impoundment often delayed but did not prevent the spending of the controversial amounts. During the Watergate years the president's power was sharply reduced, and his influence on Congress and on public opinion sharply diminished, with Congress assuming control. In 1974 Congress ended, for all practical purposes, the practice of impoundment.

In terms of budget policy, President Ford continued his predecessor's approach, with a modest impact on congressional decisions.

In his first presidential campaign Mr. Carter ran against big government in Washington and promised to shrink it, if given a chance. He was the only one among 14 presidential candidates in his party to do so and he won. But among his first actions after entering office was a boost in his predecessor's budget, succeeded by substantial increases in annual budget projections.

The tenor of Mr. Carter's pronouncements, however, remained restraint on spending. He called his 1980 budget "lean and austere" and wrote in the accompanying message that "we must reduce the growth of total federal spending. . . ."

A review of federal budgets, going back several decades, shows that actual expenditures went up steeply, under Republican and Democratic administrations, at comparable rates of growth. The distinction was, as a keen observer wrote, that Democratic presidents stimulate spending while Republicans try to hold it back; Democrats try to hide increases while Republicans disguise cutbacks.[34] Or, as Samuel M. Cohn, who in three decades in pivotal positions in the Bureau of the Budget came to be known as "Mr. Budget," remarked: "They are both spenders. But somehow I seem to have the impression that the Democrats enjoyed it more."[35] That jibes with the public's impression as a November 1979 poll by Market Opinion Research suggested which asked which party would do a better job of controlling government spending: 39% of respondents picked the Republicans, 22 percent the Democrats.[36]

Democratic as well as Republican executives like to call their budgets lean, tight, austere. If presidents attempted to slow spending growth, or at least tried to give the public the impression that they did, why did budgets keep soaring to astronomical heights? Was it because the presidency, particularly in the post-Watergate atmosphere, came to play only a minor role in the shaping of budgetary decisions, with the real power assumed and exercised by Congress? Was it the Congress rather than the president who should get the credit or blame for the spending growth? Probably so, but even the budget and appropriations committees of Congress have only limited say on the budget.

The fact is, that only a minor part of the budget is subject to control by the congressional and presidential budget process. Most of the large federal programs are "open-ended" and expenditures are controlled by formulas in law authorizing a program and are thus exempt from the normal budget process. The president and the fiscal committees of Congress simply place estimates of a program's cost in the budget. If actual outlays exceed estimates, as they usually do, supplemental appropriations must be passed by the Congress. In fact, certain items do not require annual appropriations. In other words, the elaborate budget process from the Office of Management and Budget to the president and to the budget and appropriations committees of both Houses plays only a minor role in determining the size of federal spending.

In the FY 1981 budget which totaled $616 billion, no less than $472 billion was designated "uncontrollable." This means that expenditures amounting to nearly half a trillion dollars and accounting for more than three-fourths of the total budget are barely affected by budgetary decisions of the president or Congress. They are placed in the budget mainly for information purposes and grow under their own rules. That means that much of the budgetary process is a sham—because most of the decisions were made before the process even started.

The trend is toward more "uncontrollable" spending. Two-thirds of expenditures were uncontrollable in FY 1971. Uncontrollables exceeded three-fourths of the budget in FY 1981.

Equally significant is that 88 percent of nondefense expenditures are uncontrollable, but 63% of defense expenditures are controllable.

To put it in other terms: 88 percent of the noncontrollable items are in nondefense, only 12% in defense. This explains why during the 1970s attempts to reduce deficits usually focused on defense. Most spending for domestic purposes is determined by substantive law and not subject to decisions relating to the annual budget.

The table below shows uncontrollable items in the FY 1971 and FY 1981 budgets.

Most of the "uncontrollable items"—aside from interest on the debt and prior-year contracts—are social welfare payments whose entitlements are set by law, either as payments to individuals directly or as reimbursements to states for payments they made or services they rendered or for payments to vendors.

It is apparent in the table (p. 156) that the uncontrollable items in nondefense *increased* at a much faster rate than the controllable items. In the case of defense, the controllable items *declined* far more than the uncontrollable items. In other words, the policy of exempting certain items from annual budget control has proven eminently successful for the benefited functions. The controllable items, on the other hand, got the short end of the deal.

Subsidy programs are an example of "uncontrollable" items. They may involve no or small payments to start or for several years. But irrevocable federal commitments for housing extend for periods from 15 to 30 years. The average federal cost, as of 1981, was estimated at $160,200 per unit in subsidized public housing, at $203,700 for Indian housing over a 30-year period. That is more than many middle-class families who must pay apartment rentals from their own earnings can afford. Homeownership subsidies reduce mortgage interest to the benefited families to 4% per annum—a subject of envy to families who must pay rates three or four times as high from their own pockets. Of course, much of what recipients of those subsidies do pay for housing, whether rented or owned, comes from social welfare programs anyway.

Many federal loan and guarantee programs do not go through the budget process at all. At the end of FY 1981 there are estimated to be $176 billion in direct loans outstanding, of which more than half are off-budget;

UNCONTROLLABLE EXPENDITURE ITEMS IN FY 1971 AND FY 1981

| | 1971 | 1981 | Percentage increase in |
| | | | |
	billions		*constant* dollars
Nondefense			
Social security and railroad retirement	$ 37.1	$142.1	
Medical care	11.2	53.9	
Cash, food and housing assistance	10.1	39.8	
Unemployment compensation	6.2	18.7	
Federal employee retirement and insurance	6.8	25.2	
Net interest	14.8	54.8	
General revenue sharing	—	6.9	
Prior year contracts	19.1	60.8	
Other	10.5	15.1	
Total nondefense, uncontrollable	$115.8	$417.3	+ 59%
Total nondefense, controllable	22.4	58.5	+ 16
Total nondefense outlays	$138.2	$475.8	+ 52%
Defense			
Prior year contracts	$ 21.1	$ 40.6	
Military retirement	3.4	13.7	
Total defense, uncontrollable	$ 24.5	$ 54.3	− 2%
Total defense, controllable	51.3	91.8	−21
	$ 75.8	$146.1	−15%
Summary			
Uncontrollable items: Total	$140.3	$471.6	+ 49%
Nondefense	115.8	417.3	+ 59
Defense	24.5	54.3	− 2
Controllable items	$ 73.7	$150.3	−10%
Nondefense	22.4	58.5	+ 16
Defense	51.3	91.8	−21

SOURCE: *The Budget of the United States Government, Fiscal Year 1981.*

another $253 billion in loan guarantees are off-budget. Most loan guarantees will result in no federal cost except in case of default. But if there is default, the federal commitment must be redeemed. The estimate for new direct loan obligations in FY 1981 totals $61 billion—almost half off-budget—and $81 billion in new loan guarantee commitments, for a total of $142 billion.

For many years, the administrative budget presented an adequate picture of federal fiscal operations. But from the 1940s on a growing number of activities were excluded from the administrative budget. When they accounted for more than one-fourth of all federal outlays, efforts were made to change to comprehensive accounting. The unified budget was thus established in 1969, intended to include all federal fiscal activities.

In 1971 the first exception was made and as of FY 1981 an estimated $18 billion of outlays are excluded from the unified budget. The largest of them is the Federal Financing Bank, which finances activities of several federal agencies; others include the Postal Service Fund and the Rural Telephone Bank. The Import-Export Bank was exempted in 1971 but returned to the budget in 1976. Operations of the Board of Governors of the Federal Reserve System, the country's central monetary authority, are not shown anywhere in the budget, nor subject to outside control.

Several attempts were made over the years to attain more effective control of the budget by improving procedures. Here are some of the recent efforts.

Attempts at Budget Reform

Efforts to improve the review of spending proposals and to bring about a better understanding of the return on investment in public programs gained momentum about three decades ago when a change from line-item budgets (by items of expenditure) to program or performance budgets (by purpose or goal of expenditure) was suggested. Commercial business can measure the effectiveness of its investments and return thereon by an objective and conclusive yardstick: profits. No such all-inclusive or ultimate gauge is available for governmental outlays. But approaches can be developed along similar lines by relating input to output, holding the magnitude of the resources employed against the product, and comparing the hopes and promises of the sponsors with the tangible results.

The Planning, Programming, and Budgeting System

Program or performance budgeting was much talked about when it gradually developed into the Planning, Programming, and Budgeting System (PPBS)—particularly at state and municipal levels, and gained wide acceptance, among theoreticians more than among practitioners, among academicians writing about it or acting as consultants more than among responsible officials or politicians. It gained ascendancy in the early

1960s when Robert McNamara and his whiz kids—who had come from big business corporations and think tanks—introduced in the Department of Defense cost-effectiveness as the guiding principle by which to make rational choices among expensive weapons systems. On August 25, 1965, President Johnson ordered the heads of all federal departments and agencies to establish PPBS and asked them to "begin at once to develop plans for the creation of your program and planning staffs." His budget director, Charles L. Schultze, expressed confidence that "it will provide the information and the analyses needed by government managers as the basis for an improved ability to make rational choices among the alternatives offered."[37] A new era in which scientific methods would supplant instinct, guessing, and political horse trading in the formation of public programs and budgets seemed to dawn. Top executives would now be able to measure government output and allocate public funds accordingly.

Seldom has an idea gone so fast from Great White Hope to disillusion and abandonment. In but a few years from its inception PPBS had a great future behind it. Why did PPBS fail? Because the output of many major public programs is not as objectively measurable as industrial and commercial goods and cannot be adequately gauged by slide rule or computer. It often depends on imponderables and, above all, on human judgment, which in turn is governed by a person's set of values and political ideology. This is why PPBS, initially hailed as a breakthrough in the decision-making process, could not even penetrate major decision making in the Department of Defense where it had the widest acceptance and its strongest supporters at the top.

When PPBS was first proposed, conservatives, who generally like a cost-accounting, productivity-measurement, profit-and-loss statement approach, were somewhat apprehensive that PPBS would be turned by the administrators into a more sophisticated means of justifying ever larger spending for social purposes. Liberals viewed PPBS as a new method of documenting what they had known by instinct right along: that expanded or multiplied public spending for social purposes would yield high returns in education, welfare activities and social work, community development, health, and similar "investments in people." But after a few years of PPBS its input-output and cost-benefit studies were unable to deliver positive proof of the effectiveness of such programs, findings frequently were inconclusive or showed negative results, and outcomes often seemed to suggest that the programs did not or could not deliver on the promises of their sponsors. Thus liberals soon became disillusioned and concluded that rhetoric and appeals to compassion and envy were still more effective tools to accomplish their aims than such cumbersome and insipid analyses.

Top administrators, policymakers, and special interest groups commonly viewed PPBS not as a means of obtaining answers to policy questions but as a method of providing proof to support policies in keeping with their leanings and goals. When little "helpful" material was forthcoming, liberals became disenchanted; so did conservatives who rarely bother to wade through voluminous records for evidence that might help their case.

Zero-Base Budgeting

It has long been customary in governmental budgeting to carry last year's base over to the following year as a matter of routine and then prepare a justification for desired additional appropriations. In 1969, Arthur F. Burns, who as counselor to the president then headed the White House Office for Domestic Programs and Policies, proposed—based on an earlier idea by Aaron Wildavsky—that each department should have to justify not only the increments it wanted but its entire appropriation request. By starting from scratch—the zero base—existing programs would have to be re-evaluated each year to prove that they merited continued existence.

Concern over the added work load stopped progress in 1969. But a few years later Governor Jimmy Carter invited Peter Pyhrr, who had instituted zero-base budgeting (ZBB) at Texas Instruments, to help him prepare the Georgia state budget for 1973 on the same principle. Accounts differ on whether it produced any savings.

A few weeks after assuming office, President Carter issued in February 1977 instructions to heads of departments and agencies to develop a zero-base system with the help of the Office of Management and Budget. The idea of requiring a re-examination of the worth of existing programs before approving any funds for them is attractive but is not easily applied in the federal system. Three-fourths of the outlays are "uncontrollable" by the budget process, as was explained in the preceding section. What point is there in having to present an elaborate justification each year for, say, the Internal Revenue Service, the FBI, the State Department or the continuation of social security? Is that not like reinventing the wheel as an annual routine? Added paperwork and administrative time are tremendous.

Under presidential orders the zero-base system was introduced in the various agencies and has resulted in some managerial efficiencies. Neither those savings nor the incremental costs of the system can easily be ascertained.

In his FY 1979 budget message President Carter said:

As I promised during my campaign, zero-base budgeting systems have been applied throughout the federal government. This budget is the product of a comprehensive zero-base review of all federal programs, both existing and new. In reviewing each agency's proposals I have used zero-base budget alternatives and an agency's rankings to compare and evaluate the many requests competing for resources.

However, Allen Schick of the Urban Institute slightly differed:

The first president to promise a zero-base budget has delivered the most incremental financial statement. . . . The fiscal 1979 budget . . . hardly terminates or curtails anything of significance, continues most spending at inflationary levels, and offers few program initiatives. . . . Virtually every function, subfunction, and major program is funded at or slightly above its current service level. . . . The fiscal 1979 budget comes out just about where disembodied incrementalism would tend to.[38]

In his FY 1980 and FY 1981 budgets President Carter again praised ZBB highly as having helped "get the best government possible for the resources we can afford."

The jury on the tangible achievements of ZBB is still out. Nor does anybody need to keep his breath waiting for the verdict.

Sunset Laws

Since 1976 numerous sunset laws have been introduced in every session of Congress, several of them with widespread support. Sponsorship ranged from Senators Goldwater and Helms to Senators McGovern and Kennedy. President Carter endorsed sunsetting in his 1976 campaign and later as part of his anti-inflation program. What the bills propose is that all federal programs automatically expire after four or five or six years unless Congress specifically reauthorizes them, forcing Congress to investigate the need and justification for each of thousands of federal agencies and programs periodically.

The idea of a sunset law is most appealing. It would help clean out the deadwood and keep alive only programs which are proving their worth. Sunsetting would be a "self-destruct unless resurrected" technique for old programs and new. It would end the "old agencies never die; they don't even fade away."

Conservatives hoped that some of the "giveaway programs" would be allowed to lapse, while liberals expected that sunsetting would help wipe out their most disfavored "tax expenditures." Which is exactly what put both groups on the alert and shaded their initial enthusiasm for sunsetting. Who wants to hoist his own petard? Members of Congress also had second thoughts about the enormous work load sunsetting would place on committees which are now struggling desperately to keep up with pending "must" legislation.

Almost half the states have adopted some form of sunset legislation, usually with limited application. Their experience "has shattered any notion that the technique is a panacea for bureaucratic sprawl. In those states only a handful of obscure agencies have actually been dissolved. . . . State legislators are demonstrating that they can easily spend more money evaluating agencies than they save as a result of such reviews."[39] Pioneering states have learned, and Congress will find out if it ever puts some form of sunset law on the statute books, that only small agencies with a few diminutive programs will be scratched. Agencies and programs with a sizable clientele swing enough power to survive all onslaughts.

Many of the federal programs enacted in recent decades carry expiration dates of two, three, four or more years. Those clauses were attached to the bills in order to overcome resistance of opponents and facilitate passage. They fooled no one because both sides knew that they were but a sham and that renewal would come as a matter of course—possibly after a *pro forma* objection for the record—no matter how ineffective or wasteful the program had proven to be. Once a program has acquired a large clientele with a vested interest, it has become indestructible. It is a rare special interest group indeed that forgets to cover its Achilles' heel.

Few federal programs are allowed to expire at the end of their designated term unless they are replaced with a new and bigger one—as happened with the discredited urban renewal program in 1974. Repeated experience with attempts to terminate programs, which have outlived their intended purpose or demonstrably failed to live up to their promise, convey an unequivocal lesson. Opponents to a particular program, who were unable to beat it in the Congress when it was up for approval, may hope that sunsetting will help them to kill it later. But they are in for a disappointment because sunsetting as such will not change the determination or relative voting strength of the program's supporters.

Robert D. Behn described events at a committee hearing on Senator Muskie's sunset bill:

> Although everyone applauded the neutrality of the sunset concept and praised the virtues of terminating useless programs, no one suggested a single program that might just possibly be a candidate for termination. To do so would have destroyed the wonderful, warm consensus that permeated the committee room. Every witness, liberal or conservative, had an opportunity to oppose waste and inefficiency without making any enemies. What could have been more rewarding?[40]

Once a program has acquired a large enough group with a special interest in its continuance, it is virtually impossible to kill. Every president from Eisenhower to Carter recommended repeal of part of the federally impacted areas program but Congress extended it every time. Large programs which have for years been unable to deliver on their sponsors' promises, such as the law enforcement assistance program or the compensatory education programs under Title I of the Elementary and Secondary Education Act of 1965, were extended by Congress time after time because the flow of federal money to recipients throughout the country had built up an invincible political force. Pork barrel politics still rule and will not be changed by the adoption of a sunset law.

Sunset laws and zero-base budgeting are well intended but pathetically inadequate to fulfill the hopes which their protagonists hold out. They are mechanical gimmicks which, when up against the reality of political power, are bound to fail. They are no substitutes for having more votes than a program's promoters.

There is nothing wrong with sunset or zero-base budgeting laws, except that they don't work. They do not bring the hoped for and promised results. And for "no return" the added work load and its cost are too high.

Reforming the Congressional Budget Process

Many members of Congress became increasingly dissatisfied in the early 1970s with the existing budget process. They felt that the system did not enable them to evaluate the president's budget adequately and that they had to depend too much on the judgment of the chief executive, who belonged to the opposite political party, and on reports by his Office of Management and Budget. Appropriation requests and recommendations were reviewed by Congress on a piecemeal basis, usually in thirteen separate bills. They were amended up or down and seldom passed until well into the fiscal year, whose spending they were supposed to control.

The early 1970s, of course, were the Watergate years, when the legislative branch was eager to seize a unique opportunity of wresting as much power as possible from a weakened executive branch, at a time when public opinion would condone and even support such a move. Liberals who for four decades had pushed for an increasing shift in authority from a "foot-dragging" congress to a "progressive" presidency, found it easy to reverse themselves in view of the existing political coloration of the White House. So Congress voted itself a legislative budget, independent of the Executive Office of the President. At no time did Congress seriously consider what would otherwise seem to be a natural step in a move to tighten the budget: giving the president the right of item veto which many governors possess. In fact, it virtually eliminated presidential impoundments.

The new plan established a budget committee in each House and a Congressional Budget Office (CBO) to undertake the necessary research and investigations. Their combined staffs totaled less than those of the Office of Management and Budget. But, they could also call on the large manpower of other congressional agencies, such as the Legislative Reference Service and the General Accounting Office.

CBO's staff was to be selected on a nonpartisan basis and indeed turned out to be as nonpartisan as could normally be expected of appointments by a president pro tem of the Senate and a Speaker of the House who belonged to the same political party. Professional staffs of the Senate and House budget committees, however, were politically divided between majority and minority under established formulas.

The start of the fiscal year was postponed from July 1 to October 1 in order to give Congress more time to complete its work prior to the beginning of the new fiscal year. A rigid time schedule was established for the entire process. Budget submission by the president was left unchanged—fifteen days after Congress reconvenes in January. Subsequent consideration by the two committees was to result in a tentative budget with priorities and targets (*not* ceilings) for budget authority, outlays and deficit (or surplus) to be adopted by a *first concurrent resolution* of both Houses by May 15. All congressional action on the budget was to be completed by September 25, six days before the beginning of the new fiscal year.

The Congressional Budget and Impoundment Control Act of 1974 was passed almost unanimously—75:0 in the Senate, 401:6 in the House. Budget reform was among the last bills signed into law by President Nixon before his resignation and was put into practice in 1975. Considering the wide disagreements within Congress over some of the substantive issues, this vote proves the irresistible charm of an attractive label such as *reform* in a field in which the public had long been demanding improvement.

It was hoped at the time that it would prove to be the type of reform that the public expected. It turned out to be largely a procedural revision without much effect on the outcome. To be sure, procedure sometimes can beat substance. But the same persons, the members of Congress, holding personal convictions, continued to make the decisions and worked their will, despite procedural obstacles. The final battle on major controversies is in the end almost always fought out and decided on the basic ideological-political *substantive* issues, at least in the legislative-executive arenas.

Subsequent evaluation of budget reform was well expressed in the title of an article in the *National Journal* on September 29, 1979, captioned,

"The Congressional Budget Process—Is It Worth All the Headaches?" The honeymoon of what five years earlier had been greeted as "the most important budget reform since the establishment of the national budget in 1921" was over.

In this book's predecessor, *The Growth of American Government*, at a time when the ink was barely dry on the new bill, I wrote (pp. 131–32):

> Whether this new budgetary procedure will provide a tighter or more effective control is, to say the least, questionable. It leaves undisturbed the fact that the major items of expenditure for domestic purposes are set by program legislation and immune to budgetary review. Nor does the new law help to resolve the basic conflicts between the forces that want higher spending and those that want less spending; those conflicts are ideological and political, not procedural. The new procedure may help each side to bolster its arguments with more background data. This budget reform is, however, likely to accomplish its real purpose: to shift more power from the White House to the Congress ("the spirit of '74").

When the budget reform was under consideration, Congress had long been unhappy about estimates by the president's Office of Management and Budget which turned out to be wide of the mark. Annual budget projections between 1954 and 1973 added up to a 20-year deficit of $65 billion. When the record was in, deficits totaled $157 billion and gross national debt had jumped $182 billion.[41] Revenues had been overestimated, outlays underestimated.

Accuracy of forecasts did, at first, seem to improve. But luck did not hold out. The FY 1980 deficit was placed at $23 billion in the May 1979 concurrent resolution, looked like $30 billion late in 1979, and eventually came in at $60 billion. Spending totaled $580 billion instead of the $532 billion in the first budget resolution.

Unexpectedly high back-to-back deficits reached magnitudes unprecedented in peacetime. That the five fiscal years after the establishment of the new budget process (1976 to 1980) wound up with an aggregate deficit of $260 billion was not necessarily the fault of CBO or the two budget committees. It might have happened anyway. But it did not noticeably enhance their standing.

Congressional budget procedures do occasionally help to prevent higher spending, as Rep. Corman learned when he tried to boost from $57 to $141 million funds for services to children who otherwise would be placed into foster homes. It was turned down, on procedural grounds. Mr. Corman recognized that it might have been defeated anyway, but "it wouldn't have been as easy." "The whole budget process," Mr. Corman commented, "is an extra layer of legislative process that has not served any good purpose. If it would disappear tomorrow, I'd be delighted."[42]

In the earlier mentioned *National Journal* article of September 29, 1979, Richard E. Cohen reported:

> Many congressional insiders say that if Congress could take a secret vote on the budget act's future, it would dismantle it. Nearly all sides concede, however, that public demands for congressional budget tightening make it politically impractical to support a frontal attack on the 1974 statute.

In other words, the public's belief that the congressional budget process tightens the budget must not be undermined. The fact is that the act has made little if any impact on major budget decisions. It has given some of those decisions a more respectable background, a more sophisticated justification.

The CBO's top staff members, as Eugene McAllister in 1979 pointed out, "possess a strong bias in favor of increased government spending."[43] To be sure, CBO reports have generally avoided policy recommendations. What they have failed to do is what the public and many members of Congress had hoped they would do (and others hoped they would *not* do): investigate the effectiveness of spending programs in achieving the goals for which they were established. Congressional disenchantment is due in part to the added work load for its members but mostly to the sad fact that budget decisions would not have been much different under the old system.

The 1974 congressional budget reform tried to discourage entitlements because they diminish annual congressional control over spending. But the percentage of the budget designated "uncontrollable" *increased* over the past five years. So did off-budget outlays, so did long-range commitments, so did loan guarantees, so did the multibillion-dollar obligations of the trust funds, so did, in consequence of all this, the rate of inflation.

Budget reform authorized a process called reconciliation. If it became apparent that spending targets would be exceeded because of entitlements in the basic legislation, Congress could instruct the proper committees to prepare statutory revisions to produce the necessary changes. Reconciliation has been used only once.

The budget process can be made effective not by devising new procedures but probably only by changes in the membership of the budget committees and of both houses of Congress. The budget will be balanced when that is accorded top priority by the Congress or when it is forced upon Congress by a failproof constitutional amendment.

Federal revenues rose from 18.5% of GNP in FY 1976 to 20.8% in

1980 and are estimated to climb to 22.7% in 1983, as estimated in the budget for FY 1981. A proposal by Senators Roth and Domenici and 27 other senators on December 5, 1979, would have gradually eased the federal tax burden to 19.5% by 1983. It failed when the chairman of the Budget Committee pointed out that this would conflict with budget act procedures. Senator Jepsen commented in December 1979 that this "confirms the view that many people now have, that the purpose of the budget act is to justify high levels of spending and frustrate efforts to cut taxes. Every time we try to do something for the American taxpayer, it is the Budget Committee which raises an objection. But it appears to me that very little of the same effort goes into cutting spending."[44]

To "establish national priorities" was a declared purpose of the 1974 budget act. But it has established no priorities, or changed existing priorities. The basic issue is and will remain: guns versus butter or national defense versus social welfare. Whether or how much the congressional budget process has contributed toward moderating the growth in the rate of social spending in the second half of the 1970s is debatable. A changed sentiment in the Congress, in keeping with the mood of the country, is a more likely cause.

By the end of 1980 there had been no "reordering of national priorities" by Congress. Nor, if such a reordering does take place, is there reason to expect that it will be due to the 1974 budget reform rather than to the November 1980 elections.

For five years in a row Congress did not pass the necessary appropriation measures until well into the new fiscal year and had to resort to stopgap funding to keep government operations from having to close down. In 1980 Congress did not meet a single deadline set in the budget reform act and did not pass even one of the appropriation bills for fiscal year 1981 by September 30, the end of fiscal year 1980. For the first time since 1974—prior to the budget reform act—Congress was forced to reconvene after election day for a lame-duck session to pass some "must" money bills.

President Carter's budget for fiscal year 1981, submitted in January 1980, estimated a deficit of $16 billion. By mid-June—four weeks after the deadline—Congress, after going through the ritual ordained by the budget reform act, passed a budget resolution which called for the first balanced budget in 11 years. It was, as everyone concerned knew, a sham, produced by fiscal acrobatics. Congress' second budget resolution a few months later projected a $27 billion deficit. In early 1981 President Carter placed the fiscal 1981 deficit at $55 billion, among widespread expectations that it would in the end be bigger. It is now manifest that the budget reform of 1974 has failed to impose fiscal discipline or fiscal restraint and, for all practical purposes, turned into a useless exercise.

4 ★★★★★★★★★★★★★★★★★★★★★★★★★★★★★★★★★

The Promise and the Harvest
of the Welfare State

Federal, state and local governments spent in 1978 $520 billion for domestic purposes, six times as much in *constant* dollars as they did in 1952. Population meanwhile grew by only 39%, Gross National Product (GNP) by 135%. Domestic functions doubled their share of total government expenditures—from 38% in 1952 to 76% in 1978—in the past quarter century, and more than doubled their percentage of GNP, pushing it from 10% to 25% (Table 23).

Public outlays are spread over dozens of activities and many hundreds of programs, but nearly two-thirds of the total money is allocated to but three functions: health, education and welfare. Spending in those three areas multiplied eightfold in *constant* dollars between 1952 and 1978, the aggregate of all other services fourfold. Therefore, the story of governmental growth in the past quarter century can be told largely in terms of what happened in health, education and welfare. I propose to do so in this chapter with sidelights on some of the other fields.

The table on p. 168 gives a perspective of past trends and of outlays in 1978.

It is evident that while education and general administration approximately maintained their share of total outlays, income support and medical programs enlarged their slice of the taxpayer's dollar substantially. The percentage going to the other services was correspondingly reduced, with highways the main losers.

Compared with the spectacular domestic expenditure growth over the past quarter century, shown in the table, federal projections for the

FEDERAL, STATE AND LOCAL EXPENDITURES FOR DOMESTIC PURPOSES,
1952 AND 1978

	1952	1978	1952	1978	Increase in
	billions		Percent		*constant* dollars
Total	$ 35.4	$520.2	100.0%	100.0%	+498%
Income support (social security, public welfare, unemployment compensation, etc.)	6.3	156.8	17.8	30.1	+919
Education	8.4	120.8	23.7	23.2	+487
Health, hospitals, medical insurance	2.6	59.6	7.3	11.5	+838
Transportation (highways, transit, railroads, air)	5.7	35.6	16.1	6.8	+154
Fire, police, corrections	2.0	23.6	5.6	4.5	+382
Conservation, natural resources, agriculture	3.3	24.4	9.3	4.7	+201
Utilities and sanitation	1.0	10.5	2.8	2.0	+320
General administration	4.4	66.6	12.4	12.8	+517
Other	1.7	22.3	4.8	4.3	+431

SOURCE: Same as Table 23.

next five years appear quite modest. The president's budget for FY 1981 projected nondefense outlays to grow an aggregate of 8% (in *constant* dollars) between 1978 and 1983, the Congressional Budget Office estimated the 5-year growth (1979 to 1984) at 11%. This suggests that almost no expansion of domestic services is planned for the next five years, which represents a remarkable change from developments in the past decade or quarter century.

The federal government which played a minor role in domestic public services up to the early 1950s has since become a dominant factor.

According to the table on p. 170, the federal share of domestic expenditures has risen from 36% to 55%. But this far understates the role which the national government has played in this development. A critical factor in the vast expansion of public services was the dramatic growth in federal payments to the states.

FIGURE 18.
RATE OF INCREASE IN PUBLIC AND PRIVATE (PERSONAL) CONSUMPTION
1952 to 1978
in *constant* dollars

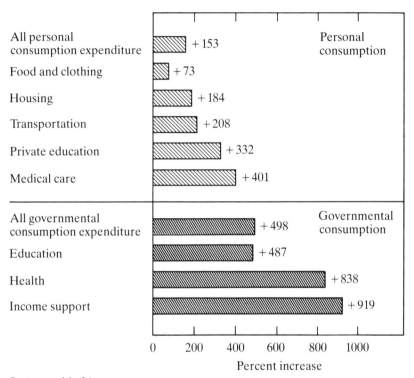

Source: table 26

Federal Aid to State and Local Governments

Federal financial assistance to state and local governments was insignificant prior to the 1930s and remained below $1 billion until 1946. It exceeded $2 billion in 1950, reached $7 billion in 1960, $23 billion in 1970 and is estimated at $96 billion in FY 1981. But the *amount* of the grants, the cash flow from the federal treasury to state capitals, counties and cities, may in historical perspective be less significant than the growth in the *number* of federal aid programs from barely a dozen after the war to a hundred in the late 1950s, to over 200 by 1964, to 400 in the late 1960s and to about

GOVERNMENTAL EXPENDITURES FOR DOMESTIC PURPOSES,
BY LEVEL OF GOVERNMENT, 1952 AND 1978

	1952		1978	Increase in *constant* $ percent
		billions		
Total	$ 35.4		$ 520.2	+498%
Federal government	12.7		286.9	+822
State and local governments	$ 25.2		$309.7	
less federal grants	− 2.5		− 76.4	
from *own* sources		22.7	233.3	+318

SOURCE: Same as Table 23.

500 by the end of the 1970s. Federal aid programs now cover and control virtually every function of state and local governments, and distinctly affect even programs not directly benefited; they encompass numerous activities that but a few years ago were largely or wholly in the private sphere.

A "fiscal mismatch" is sometimes cited as creating the financial need for expanded federal aid. State and local governments, it is said, are constitutionally and traditionally responsible for most of the domestic public services, their requirements are multiplying, but the national government has preempted the most lucrative revenue sources.

That sounds persuasive. But if financial need really were the principal justification for federal aid, it could be met by a monetary grant to each state. To substitute one monetary grant for hundreds of programmatic grants would greatly simplify the system and produce large administrative savings. I proposed to the congressional Joint Economic Committee in 1957 that the federal government should "leave programmatic decisions on the volume and type of local services and construction to states and communities, and render financial support through nonearmarked, unconditional grants or tax sharing."[1] Within a few years the *Heller plan*—named after its author, Walter W. Heller, who later became chairman of the Council of Economic Advisers under Presidents Kennedy and Johnson—also proposed purely *fiscal* grants to the states. It attracted broad attention but brought no action.

State and local finances could also have been strengthened by authorizing federal income tax credits for state and local taxes—instead of mere deductions—and by reducing the federal tax burden whose weight is the main obstacle to state fiscal expansion.

Had the true purpose of the federal aid drive been to provide financial assistance to where it might be needed most urgently, then it could have been proposed to aid low-income areas—whether states, counties, cities or school districts—without sending millions in federal funds to the most affluent states and communities. But no such proposal was ever seriously made or considered by Congress. Federal aid goes to rich states and poor.

State and local revenues have consistently been rising at a faster rate than federal since the end of World War II. Between 1952 and 1978 the receipts of state and local governments *from their own sources* jumped from $28 billion to $302 billion, an increase of 345% in *constant* dollars, compared with a 151% rise in federal revenues (see Table 16).

The claim of state fiscal inadequacy is hard to substantiate. Virtually all resources available to the national gonverment are located within the 50 states and subject to their taxing power. What may be strained and close to exhaustion is not the fiscal capacity of the states but the willingness of their citizens to tax themselves more heavily for the support of programs whose desirability, methods or positive results they may deem questionable.

The federal government forbids the states to direct or influence welfare recipients on how they ought to spend their monthly benefits. It is very careful about suggesting to foreign governments on how to spend U.S. grants, for fear of offending sensitive feelings. But it shows no reluctance to condition and control aid to the states to a minute detail. The elected governments of American states or cities apparently cannot be trusted to use U.S. funds as wisely as foreign governments or welfare recipients.

Federal departments, and their constituent client groups, are strongly opposed to nonearmarked, unconditional federal grants and similar forms of financial assistance to the states. They aim to expand their control of activities, not to hand it over to the states. It has long become manifest that demands for federal grants were and are primarily not intended to provide money to help the states perform their functions but to tighten federal control over public services. The purpose of piling hundreds of "categorical" federal aid programs on top of each other has been to have programs operated under federal rules—drafted by special interest groups and professional bureaucrats—whether state and communities regard such programs necessary and desirable or not.

Taxpayers probably are more careful in approving expansion of public services if they know that the cost will come from their own pockets. They will be more amenable if told that they can get facilities and services for 50 cents or less on the dollar through federal aid. If taxes are hidden or seemingly borne by others—by the federal government in Washington or by other economic groups—even extravagant services become desirable. Whether a service or a good is worth the cost can be adequately judged only if the persons making the decision know that they must foot the whole bill.

That is why a welfare state is almost always created, controlled and largely financed "from the top," that is, by a national government. To have domestic public services concentrated in and run by the national government is not as easy a proposition to implement in the United States as it is in Europe. European countries were created and ruled "from the top" ever since kings subdued feudal fiefdoms. The principle of national primacy remained there after parliaments came in and even when republics replaced some of the monarchies.

But our federal system was created "from the bottom" up, when the 13 colonies formed the United States government to perform specified "delegated" functions. The American system was founded on a concept of a dispersal rather than concentration of power, a system of checks and balances, with authority assigned to several branches and levels of government so that no one segment should gain power over the others.

Because of the strong tradition of local autonomy and home rule, it would have been extremely difficult, if not impossible, for the United States government simply to take over most of the domestic services and to turn the states into subordinate divisions. Even in the exigency of the 1930s many of the emergency programs were carried on through state and local governments. After the war, the creation of dozens and eventually hundreds of conditional federal grant programs was the technique by which national power was imposed on states and communities. It accomplished what otherwise or outside the United States might have required a coup d'état or a revolution.

How was it possible to raise federal grants from less than $1 billion in 1946 to nearly $100 billion in 1981, from a handful to five hundred? Several forces combined to propel federal grants to the states to dizzying heights. National organizations, each with an interest in promoting one or several social or other domestic services, found out that it is much harder to wrest enlarged appropriations from 50 state legislatures and hundreds of city councils than from Congress. State and local officials commonly must accept personal responsibility for the tax boosts they may have to propose to finance new or expanded programs. Members of Congress do not. Moreover, Congress for some years was in the fortunate position of being able to reduce taxes—from wartime record levels—and increase appropriations at the same time. Special interest groups traded with members of

Congress political support and campaign contributions in return for votes for their favorite grant programs.

The technique of using federal grants to states in place of direct federal service operation has a charm of its own: millions of employees hired to execute new and vastly enlarged old programs were added to state and local payrolls and this did not swell the ranks of federal civil servants. That enabled every president and member of Congress to boast that he had kept the number of federal bureaucrats down to an austere no-growth minimum (see pp. 4–28). Federal aid seems in many ways the answer to a maiden's prayer. Members of Congress who vote for the programs can claim credit in their districts for having brought home the bacon. State and local officials become heroes for helping to provide large local benefits at little or no local cost, above all, no tax boost.

Earlier generations of responsible state or city officials might have felt qualms about taking, let alone asking for, federal handouts. New crops of governors and mayors show no reluctance about lobbying for federal funds on almost any terms—hat in one hand, begging cup in the other ("in times like these we must rise above principles"). They generally hold the taxes available to them, especially the property tax, to be of an undesirable type while "the taxes that somebody else levies and I spend are of course the most desirable type." Mayors, county and city officials and their administrative department heads have found Washington to be a far lusher hunting ground than their state capitol.

Federal aid programs help weld professionals in each of the various public functions at federal, state and local levels into a solid fraternity, strong enough and ready to fight off the savages outside, who do not understand the importance of each particular service nor appreciate the magnitude of its financial needs. The professional bureaucracy can now write its own rules, and prevail against its nominal bosses at every level of government. Representative government survived mostly in high school textbooks.

Soon after federal grants began their meteoric rise, growing concern led in August 1948 to a conference of representatives of Congress and the Governors' Conference which felt that "the pleasure of spending public monies should be connected to the pain of raising them." It recommended that aid should be cut 20% in 1950. Amounts actually were one-third larger in FY 1950 and kept climbing. President Eisenhower in March 1953 called upon Congress to have the problem investigated. The law creating a study commission outlined the felt need for the undertaking "because the activity of the federal government has been extended into many fields which, under our constitutional system, may be the primary interest and obligation of the several states. . . ." In his 1954 budget message Mr. Eisenhower said: "This budget marks the beginning of a movement to shift to state and local governments and to private enterprise federal activities which can be more appropriately and more efficiently carried on in that way."

It did not work out that way. The Commission on Intergovernmental Relations prepared large amounts of valuable research but rendered an ambivalent report after its membership changed as a result of the 1954 congressional elections. It left no imprint on the course of events. Its opponents charged the commission with trying to turn back the clock of history and the news media ignored it. During its short life and in the thereafter, the commission managed to attain a degree of anonymity which the CIA envied and has been trying to equal ever since.

During the mid-sixties the number of federal grant programs doubled under the impact of President Johnson's *Creative Federalism*, a euphemism for unlimited expansion of federal aid to states. This was done although Mr. Johnson recognized resulting chaos in a congressional message in March 1967:

> There are today a very large number of individual grant-in-aid programs, each with its own set of special requirements, separate authorizations and appropriations, cost-sharing ratios, allocation formulas, administrative arrangements, and financial procedures. This proliferation increases red-tape and causes delay. It places extra burdens on State and local officials. It hinders their comprehensive planning . . . fundamental re-structuring of our grant-in-aid programs is essential.

Even so, President Johnson in pursuit of the lofty goals of his Great Society continued pushing for more and larger grant programs. States and cities were seldom mentioned without prefacing them with "hard pressed," a custom which his successors continued. Which raises the question: hard pressed by whom? By their constituents who demand expanded services? If so, all they have to do is pay for what they desire. But, if it is not worth their own money—why should it be worth someone else's?

A movement started in the late 1960s to bring order into the chaos of federal grants which then numbered about 400. In 1967 the Republican National Committee set up a task force which I chaired. We recommended that the approximately 400 aid programs be consolidated into a small number of block grants by major functions and that revenue sharing and other fiscal means be employed instead of building up the grant system.[2]

In 1972 President Nixon proposed revenue sharing, largely as a substitute for categorical grants. Congress approved revenue sharing *on top of the categorical grants*, with no consolidation. The number of federal aid programs continued to proliferate to 492 in 1979.

The FY 1981 budget estimated outlays for federal grants to state and local governments at $96.3 billion, budgetary authority at $119.8 billion. The largest budget authority, because of its long-range nature, was for subsidized housing where FY 1981 outlays were estimated at $3.6 billion, obligational authority at $20 billion.

FEDERAL GRANTS TO STATE AND LOCAL GOVERNMENTS,
BY MAJOR FUNCTIONS, FY 1981

		Billions
Total		$96.3
Education	$7.7	
Social services	5.8	
Employment and training	9.7	23.2
Income support, public assistance, housing assistance		20.3
Medicaid and other health services		17.8
Urban and rural development		6.3
Urban mass transit		3.3
Highways, airports, railroads		9.0
Sewage treatment plants and other environmental programs		5.0
Other categorical programs		2.0
Revenue sharing and other fiscal grants		9.4

SOURCE: *Budget of the United States Government, Special Analyses, FY 1981.*

Revenue sharing had been enacted by Congress in 1972 with great reluctance and only after a coalition of state and local governments mounted a forceful campaign. But Congress never warmed up to the program and when it came up for renewal in 1976 one Congressman said that if a secret vote were held, revenue sharing would be voted down in both Houses by at least two to one. But the state-local alliance succeeded in securing another 4-year lease on life for revenue sharing until the end of FY 1980.

In 1979 the foes of revenue sharing adopted a new strategy: divide and conquer. They focused their attack on the states, leaving local governments alone, for the time being. The states, they said, are financially better off than the federal government, some of them have surpluses while the national budget is running a deficit, and many states have been cutting taxes. Why should they get subsidies from a federal government which is desperately trying to balance its budget?[3] (Here goes the fiscal capacity argument which I discussed earlier.)

What may be decisive: there are only 50 states but there are 39,000 localities, with several officials each, which receive revenue sharing. They are anxious to save their own skin and will not lift a finger for the states.

In the 1980 drive to balance the federal budget a search was on for large expenditure items with a small clientele, for items that could be cut without much political damage. Revenue sharing for the states seemed an ideal candidate: the 50 governors never swung much weight in Congress and did less so in 1980 than ever before. Moreover, they had led the charge for a balanced federal budget. To abolish revenue sharing for states seemed to Congress a made-to-order opportunity to get back at the governors and give them a dose of their own medicine.

The states are already being bypassed in a number of grant programs that go directly to local governments. Congress, after extended negotiations between the two Houses in the 1980 lame-duck session, decided to skip state revenue sharing in fiscal year 1981, but to resume it on a more restricted basis from 1982 on. Thus the states avoided disaster but they were badly bruised. Their standing and influence had suffered.

To what outcome do apparent trends point? I referred to this in concluding an address "Federal Grants and the Decline of the Federal System" at the 1965 *National Tax Conference*:

> At the General Assembly of the States in December 1948 Roscoe Drummond said, "The issue has been foreclosed by events. The federal system no longer exists. The trend toward centralized federal government is overwhelming, inevitable, irreversible, and to a degree, irresponsible. It is a part of American life." He added that the federal system can no more be restored than an apple pie can be put back on the apple tree. Some state officials felt at the time like replying with Mark Twain's famous telegram to a newspaper, "Notice of my death greatly exaggerated." But Mr. Drummond was at most slightly premature. In July 1965, David Brinkley, speaking to the assembled students of the University of Ohio said: "The decline and fall of the 50 state governments will be completed within our lifetime. The movement of political power from state capitols to Washington is inevitable and unstoppable whether we like it or not."[4]

Developments and events in the years since Messrs. Drummond and Brinkley made their quoted statements have done nothing to contradict them but added weight to the predictions. In terms of policy formation and major decisions, the federal system of government has, for all practical purposes, been abolished in the United States. Only some traditional forms and rituals are still being observed.

It has well been said that states' rights were first thought out, then fought out, and finally bought out.

The demise of the federal system was brought about largely by the growth and proliferation of federal grants which were used as an instrument to establish the welfare state in America. Whether categorical grants can be consolidated and replaced by fiscal remedies to the extent necessary, is doubtful.

One question remains: How beneficial have the programs and activities of the welfare state proven to the American people?

The Input and the Output of the Welfare State

In trying to arrive at decisions about future investments on how to allocate available resources among numerous alternatives, we are normally guided by experience on the returns we received from past ventures, or returns others received from comparable actions. For a meaningful appraisal that will help us to choose wisely we must relate input to output, compare earnings rates and try to project or speculate on the extent or manner in which future forces and conditions may differ from the past.

Input can usually be ascertained, though there are some costs that may not be known for a long time. But, by and large we can arrive at a valid estimate of cost in terms of money and human and material resources of the various enterprises we embarked on. Output can also be determined if the desired return can be clearly defined and measured. In most business activities the desired return is the highest attainable earnings rate on the investment. But government action seldom aims at monetary returns. Its goals are manifold and often difficult or impossible to quantify and to measure. Moreover, there are wide divergencies of opinion on the desirability of goals, on priorities and on the degree of achievement. While some societal goals are universally agreed on to be desirable, many others are not and success or failure often is in the beholder's eye.

Political association or ideology or self-interest—of the individual or of the group of which he is a member or with which he is allied—often overrules all other considerations. Comparing a program's results with its sponsors' promises may seem a proper evaluation. But there are examples of programs that produced well but were slimmed down, while there are many cases of programs which fell far short of promised results but were substantially expanded. A program's enthusiasts will usually contend that there is nothing wrong with it that could not be corrected by doubling or tripling its appropriations and giving it more time. In comparing the visible or tangible results of public programs with their fate at the hands of governing bodies, it is sometimes hard not to turn cynical, not to despair about the usefulness of research, of trying to relate output to input, comparing results with goals and purposes. But there is no alternative to trusting that in the long run informed intelligent action and sound judgment will prevail and that they are at least influenced, if not fully determined, by the findings of factual investigations.

It has been said that free government rests on the belief that the people are capable of judging vital public issues. If they were not, there would be little purpose in holding elections, in voting for representatives or on ballot issues. Elections would merely be haphazard popularity contests, unrelated to reason. So, there does not seem to be an acceptable alternative to acting AS IF each person voted intelligently, using the best information at his command, in the common interest. We must try to gather the most pertinent data on the performance of governmental programs in the hope that our labor will exert a proper impact on the public and its representatives in making crucial decisions on government policy.

I intend to present my findings on the results of governmental programs with the data I was able to obtain. Enormous amounts of information have been produced in recent years, but they often do not include the crucial or vital facts we need. But usually there is more than one way to skin a cat. As a rule, we can obtain alternative data that will give us, if not certainty, at least a high degree of probability that we are on the right track. In this case—as usually in life—we cannot wait until all the relevant information is in. By that time, if ever, the time for decision may have passed. We must judge and act on the facts we have, in the hope that we are at least close enough to the truth to allow us confidence in the outcome.

As was shown earlier, government spending for domestic purposes multiplied about six times in *constant* dollars and two and a half times as a percentage of Gross National Product over the past quarter century. That is a rate of growth which is not only unprecedented but also incapable of being repeated. It reveals an enormous enthusiasm and unbounded optimism which prevailed at least in the early part of the period. It was expressed with supreme exuberance in President Lyndon Johnson's vision of a Great Society on June 26, 1964:

> We stand at the edge of the greatest era in the life of any nation. For the first time in world history, we have the abundance and the ability to free every man from hopeless want, and to free every person to find fulfill-

ment in the works of his mind or the labor of his hands.

Even the greatest of all past civilizations existed on the exploitation of the misery of the many.

This nation, this people, this generation, has man's first chance to create a Great Society: a society of success without squalor, beauty without barrenness, works of genius without the wretchedness of poverty. We can open the doors of learning. We can open the doors of fruitful labor and rewarding leisure, of open opportunity and close community—not just to the privileged few, but to everyone.[5]

As it turned out, the United States stood, in 1964, not at the edge of its greatest and happiest experience but of probably its worst—a time of worsening tensions within and without—of the Vietnam war and its abject failure, civil violence, a decline of economic and military strength, its power and security, of its spirit and determination, of its standing among nations, and of the admiration and respect in which much or most of the world used to hold America.

Not that all of this should or could be blamed on the Great Society. All of it could be the product of a change in the attitude, mentality, mood prevalent among the American people in the 1960s and 1970s—what President Carter referred to as a malaise. Certainly the enthusiasm of the early 1960s has turned into disillusionment, frustration, alienation, cynicism of the late 1970s. Many scholars who until fifteen or twenty years ago wrote in glowing colors about the promise of the new social programs have become more cautious, many have been turned off and are sadder—and more than a few seem to have become wiser.

We cannot know now whether the negative mood of the American people will change in the 1980s, or ever. But we can explore the impact of the programs of the Great Society, the trends that led up to it and its consequences.

Its largest programs and steepest expansion were in the fields of income support (social welfare), education and health as the table on p. 168 shows.

More generous income support for a widening number of persons certainly has sharply reduced the incidence of poverty. Some observers hold that poverty has for all practical purposes been wiped out. But to make a large and growing segment of the population dependent for its sustenance on government has its price. Incentives for self-support and for economic expansion have been sharply weakened and social ills of many kinds have been multiplying, not accidentally so. Expenditures and manpower for law enforcement have been going up and so has the incidence of crime—at approximately the same rate.

Educational spending has soared and the number of graduates increased, as has the number of years which our young people spend in school. But—are their skills, knowledge, understanding commensurately improving? Or, are they going down, as they seem to? Are schools effectively serving their purpose of teaching young students better to cope with the challenges of life? If so, why does so large a number seem unable to cope? Are we barking up the wrong tree?

Government intervenes in many areas with the best of intentions, bent on solving a problem, helping to meet a need. It so did in health care but wound up pouring in so much money that it drove medical costs out of proportion. That forced millions of people who otherwise could have taken care of their needs, to seek help from government, in a never ending spiral. Housing offers a close parallel. Government funds multiplied effective housing demand which, in turn, pushed up construction costs beyond the reach of middle-class households. Affected families then claimed government assistance, were found eligible, which expanded demand further . . . and so on. Government intervention in the field of energy aggravated rather than solved a problem that could have been taken care of by the working of market forces.

Government's attempted solutions often fail because of a wrong diagnosis of the nature and cause of the problem and then lead to the wrong therapy. Usually the medicine that government prescribes and administers is the infusion of more money—which like a narcotic may make some of the patients feel good but makes the ill virtually incurable. To be sure, correct therapy sometimes calls for more money. But unless something is done about the root causes, desired and hoped-for improvements won't occur. Diagnosis often is wrong not because of inability to identify the nature and cause of the problem but because of unwillingness to accept them because they are not what the investigator feels they should be.

It is part of the philosophy of the welfare state that all shortcomings in human beings or conditions are the fault of society and environment. The egalitarian ideology which has for so long dominated social research tries to bring everybody up to average. It seems that in a country as rich and powerful as ours, everybody ought to be above the average. The fact is that in terms of every ability or personal trait, just as many are and must be below the average as are above it. That is what makes it an average. And just as many individuals are substantially *above* the average, many others must be substantially *below* it.

Social programs of the welfare state tried their best to raise everybody to the average. When education, training and related programs proved to be largely ineffective, the next best approach was to redistribute income to a level *as if* everybody's productivity had been raised to the average. Also, to broaden the basis of political support, programs had to be expanded upward to include a sufficient number of potential beneficiaries.

The trouble with this approach is that it can never solve the problem at hand, that, like narcotics it requires ever larger doses, that it does not quench the thirst but whets it for more of the same. That is why welfare state programs kept growing and never seemed to get closer to their ultimate goal.

The Income and the Outcome of Education

Education is America's largest and most ebullient growth industry, involving in 1978 30 percent of our total population, mostly on a full-time basis—59 million as students, 6.6 million as employees. Educational institutions in the United States expend 7.5% of the Gross National Product compared with about 4.1% in the Soviet Union. This is the reverse of military allocations where the shares of GNP run at 5% for the U.S.A. and 13% for the USSR.

In the United States, as throughout the world, most of education is government operated. Ninety percent of the students at the elementary-secondary level and 78 percent of students in higher education are enrolled at governmental institutions, mostly local or state. In contrast to the major role of the national government in most other countries, only 10 percent of the funds for public education in the United States comes from the federal government. Education is the largest item in state-local government finance. But even in the aggregate of federal, state and local governments, education has always been among the largest items, at times exceeded by defense spending, in recent years by outlays for income support (welfare).

Input and Output of Public Schools and Colleges

To understand the current condition and prospects of education, it is necessary to know what happened in the field, in quantitative terms, over the past quarter century.

The following table shows that the schools almost doubled their manpower in proportion to enrollment and more than tripled the cost per student in *constant* dollars. The number of employees in public education per 100 students increased 84%—from 6.8 to 12.5—which corresponds to a *decline* in productivity of 46% while, over the same period, productivity in the private American economy *increased* 85%. In no way can this be explained as being justified by or as having resulted in a corresponding improvement of quality in the output. Available evidence points at a simultaneous *decline* in quality, as will be shown later in this chapter.

SELECTED DATA ON PUBLIC EDUCATION IN 1952 AND 1978

	1952	1978	Increase in percent (amounts in *constant* dollars)
Government expenditure for education (millions)	$ 8,374	$120,823	+487%
Government expenditure for education (% of GNP)	2.4%	5.7%	
Enrollment in public education (thousands)	27,862	52,818	+ 90
Enrollment in public education percent of U.S. population	17.8%	24.2%	
Employees in public education (thousands)	1,884	6,586	+250
Employees in public education percent of employment in U.S. Total	3.0%	6.8%	
Ratio of employees to students	1:14.8	1:8.0	− 46
Employees per 100 students	6.8	12.5	+ 84
Average annual earnings per full-time employee			
in state and local education	$ 3,169	$ 13,392	+ 72
in all government	3,269	13,758	+ 70
in private industry	3,490	13,263	+ 55
Average cost per student	$ 301	$ 2,288	+219

SOURCES: Tables 6, 8a, and 23. Also: U.S. Office of Education, *Statistical Summary of Education, 1951–52,* 1955; and National Center for Education Statistics, *Digest of Education Statistics, 1979,* 1979.

Summary data on public education are affected by the relatively steeper expansion in more expensive postsecondary schools. If we view only the public elementary and secondary schools—using the official reports cited above—we find that between 1952 and 1978 the ratio of instructional staff to average daily attendance (ADA) declined from 1:23.0 to 1:16.2 or by about one-third. That means that the average teacher now faces 6.8 *fewer* pupils than he or she did a quarter century ago. Cost per pupil in ADA exactly tripled in *constant* dollars. The only other segment of the U.S. labor force which in proportion to product ballooned at a comparable rate is hospital workers (see p. 23).

The number of employees in public education climbed from 1.9 million in 1952 to 6.6 million in 1978. The 4.7 million increase accounted for over half of the total growth in governmental employment (federal, state, local) of 7 million between 1952 and 1978 (see p. 9).

It is amazing that schools were able to obtain the funds to expand their staffs so much faster than enrollment, at a time when American schools experienced the most rapid enrollment growth ever. Birthrates soared after World War II and dire predictions were voiced that the schools would be unable to cope with the "tidal wave of babies," that they would not be able to increase the number of teachers and classrooms proportionate to pupils. As it turned out, the schools outdid the baby boom so effectively that teacher-pupil ratios sharply declined.

In the early 1950s the National Education Association (NEA) and its allies strongly asserted that state and local governments would be financially unable to support an expansion of staff and facilities sufficient to keep up with the rate of attendance growth. Therefore, the federal government would have to assume responsibility for a large share of school support. NEA had been demanding federal money for nearly a hundred years but in 1950 seemed to have a more fact-based case.

Congress held hearings on proposals for federal aid to education every year at which chamber of horrors scenarios were painted about the impoverished condition of the schools, and the exhausted fiscal capacity of states, cities and school districts from which only the national treasury could rescue them.

I testified at many of those hearings, often as the principal witness in opposition to the pending bills, assuring the committees that states and communities could and would provide adequate financial support. Most other witnesses, largely employees of school systems, strongly backed federal aid plans, but Congress never approved a bill providing general support of schools or colleges. In the early 1980s state and local governments still raise 90% of the support of public education under their own power, as they have for a long time. They not only kept funds up with enrollment growth but enabled schools to triple spending per pupil (*constant* dollars).

In his first education message in 1961 President John Kennedy declared that 600,000 classrooms should be built during the 1960s to take care of all needs, and that state and local governments would be unable to meet that goal unaided. He proposed federal aid to school construction—which

Congress never enacted. But state and local governments built 700,000 classrooms during the 1960s—without a federal construction aid program. By 1970 there were five children less per classroom than there had been in the early 1950s. That was done in a period when enrollment almost doubled.

A dozen years after the war the baby boom ended, and the number of births began to decline. By the late 1960s school enrollment started to fall—but the number of teachers kept going up. Between the school years 1968/69 and 1978/79 public school attendance dropped 5% but instructional staff increased 14%. Consequently the number of pupils per instructional staff member—teachers, aides and other professionals—fell from 19.2 in 1969 to 16.0 in 1979 (data from the NEA report, *Estimates of School Statistics, 1978–79*). The average teacher now faces 3.2 *fewer* pupils than he or she did ten years earlier. The cost per pupil in ADA meanwhile rose another 42% in *constant* dollars.

But the NEA, on March 3, 1979, asked the U.S. Senate Budget Committee to lift the federal share of educational spending from the current 10% to 40% by 1982 and to 50% by 1985 (an amount of $50 billion or more). It attempted to justify that claim: "Reports from all parts of the country speak of the squeeze on the escalating needs and problems of the public schools, on the one hand, and the contracting resources for meeting those needs on the other."[6]

Many school systems are hard pressed for money and some, such as those in Chicago, Boston and Cleveland, were reported to be near bankruptcy. Considering the enormous increases they enjoyed in their revenues, year after year, far in excess of enrollment growth, such a condition can only be the result of utter irresponsibility in fiscal management.

The NEA's push for more federal funds is understandable because its local affiliates find it increasingly difficult to prove genuine need to their communities and state legislatures. Federal money for the schools means more jobs for teachers at higher salaries. NEA wants to reduce teacher-pupil ratios even further because that would generate more job openings and more dues-paying members for NEA. Such a demand is natural for the country's second largest labor union. While teachers are speaking for teachers and not for children, the public increasingly seems to feel that the schools ought to be run for the benefit of children and not of teachers.

Federal aid equaled about 4% of school revenues between 1952 and 1964, most of it as compensation in "federally impacted" areas where federal land pays no property taxes. Congress rejected all broad school support proposals in the 1950s and 1960s until, in 1965, President Johnson was able to squeeze through Congress a proposal for aid to "disadvantaged" children. It raised federal aid to 10% of school finances, where, despite the addition of several dozen smaller programs, it has remained ever since.

In the second half of the 1970s a surplus of teachers and classrooms developed because widespread publicity about a teacher shortage had induced hundreds of thousands of young men and women to seek a teaching career. Unfortunately, they had to learn the hard way that job openings were not increasing as fast as they used to. Prospects for landing a teaching job will remain poor, at least through the 1980s. The classroom shortage, widely publicized in the 1950s and 1960s, has now given way to "for sale" or "for lease" signs on numerous school buildings throughout the nation. This suggests that it may sometimes be expensive to believe in and act on one's own propaganda. Some school districts, however, are earning handsome profits from selling surplus real estate.

A shortage of teachers and classrooms used to be the main problem about which school administrators complained prior to about 1970. Now they complain about a shortage of students. The solution to both problems is supposed to be more money. Is this really the core problem and would it cure what really ails the schools?

About three-fourths of current school expenditures go for salaries and wages. Therefore, the lowering of teacher-pupil ratios was a major factor in soaring per pupil expenditures. They might have been justifiable if there had been proof that children learn more in smaller classes. But evidence is conclusive—and was known *before* the period now under review—that, within reasonable limits, class size is irrelevant to educational progress.

The 1950 edition of the *Encyclopedia of Educational Research* reviewed several hundred research studies on class size and pupil achievement undertaken in the preceding half century, during which the teacher-pupil ratio had declined from 1:35.6 in 1900 to 1:26.1 in 1950.[7]

The *Encyclopedia* found that 40% of the research reports favored large classes, 22% small classes. Of the more scientifically controlled studies, 50% favored large classes, 21% small classes. It summarized (p. 212):

> On the whole, the statistical findings definitely favor large classes at every level of instruction except the kindergarten. . . . The general trend of evidence places the burden of proof squarely upon the proponents of small classes.

Numerous studies attempted to prove that there is a positive correlation between small classes and students' learning but they failed. When James S. Coleman, under the auspices of the U.S. Office of Education, embarked upon the most extensive survey of American schools ever undertaken, (*Equality of Educational Opportunity*, 1966), he expected that it would demonstrate a resources-results relationship. But when it was completed he reported with undisguised surprise that "the evidence revealed that within broad geographic regions, and for each racial and ethnic group, the physical and economic resources going into a school have very little relationship to the achievements coming out of it."[8] Christopher Jencks, in summarizing the ensuing national debate, concluded: "Variations in schools' fiscal and human resources have very little effect on student achievement—probably even less than the Coleman report implied."[9]

In a report of a committee of the National Academy of Education in 1979 Lawrence J. Lau of Stanford University reviewed relevant research findings and concluded that "there is no consistent relationship between cognitive achievement and class size. In fact, more often than not, any effect of class size or teacher-student ratio is found to be absent."[10] He noted that "there is no consistent relationship between cognitive achievement and various dimensions of teacher quality." Lau's first point was that achievements are highly correlated to each student's individual background.

The organized public school profession had long held it to be an axiom that quality of education is proportionate to the number, pay and qualification of teachers and that dollars expenditure per pupil in ADA is the best yardstick of educational quality.

Paul R. Mort of Teachers College, Columbia University, wrote in a symposium volume by the National Conference of Professors of Educational Administration:

> Every empirical study of the relationship between expenditure level and quality of education adds its bit to the presumption that the relationship is strong. . . .
>
> The presumptive relationship appears to hold through all levels of expenditure as yet experienced in public education, from the lowest . . . to the highest. . . . There is presumptive evidence that even the highest expenditure public schools do not begin to approach the point, if there is one, where the relationship drops off. . . . The presumptive relationship is an accelerating one. . . .[11]

That was written in 1952. At the NEA's 1970 *National Conference on School Finance*, at a time when evidence to the contrary was already overwhelming, it was still asserted that "research over the past 30 years has shown that student achievement is closely related to teachers' salaries, the amount of money spent on each student, adequate staffing and class size."[12]

This emanated, understandably, from the NEA Legislative Commission, whose principal assignment is to lobby in Congress for federal aid to the schools.

But, in school systems from which necessary data are available, income and outcome have been moving in opposite directions. The country's largest school system, New York City's, offers a devastating example of the futility of infusing huge amounts of money. "Our schools are the most lushly funded school system in the country," boasted Mayor John Lindsay in 1969, adding that "it has the best teacher-pupil ratio of any city—not just some but any city in the country."[13] But his advisory panel had reminded him in November 1967: "The New York City school system, which once ranked at the summit of American public education, is caught in a spiral of decline."

Here is what happened in New York City schools between 1952 and 1978: enrollment (ADA) increased 11%, instructional staff 61%, the staff-pupil ratio dropped from 23.8 to 16.4. Achievement scores in reading, mathematics, and other subjects were consistently at or *above* national norms in the early 1950s and just as consistently and substantially *below* national norms in 1978.[14]

If we measure educational attainment by years of attendance, our schools have made progress. A person 25 to 29 years old in 1950 averaged 12.0 years of schooling completed, in 1978 12.9 years. In 1950, 53% of persons 25 to 29 years old had completed 4 years of high school, in 1978 85%. The number of young people graduating from public high schools increased by 168% between 1952 and 1978, of persons graduating from public 4-year colleges 181%. That sounds impressive. But what does it mean? Thirty percent of students who entered 5th grade in 1924 eventually graduated from high school, 58% of those who entered in 1950, and 74% of those who entered in 1969. That does not mean that more than twice as high a proportion of students now acquire the knowledge and skills thought to be associated with secondary school graduation.

For many years public schools have been trying to keep all young people in attendance for twelve years, whether they participate or learn or not, whether they are capable of absorbing a secondary education or not, and finally give them a diploma that certifies nothing but twelve years of residence. What does a comparison of the number or percentage of high school graduates mean when we know that for some years schools have been awarding diplomas to students who can barely read, to some who can't even read their own diploma? The recent "competency test" drive has advanced but gingerly. Public high schools would not dare to require 12th-grade performance for a high school diploma. Usually they settle for 8th-grade basic skills, in some cases for less.

In 1975 full-time school enrollment of 15- to 19-year-olds equaled 72% of the age group in the United States, between 41% and 51% in France, Germany, Italy and Britain, according to OECD reports. But the graduate of a European secondary school is about two years ahead of his counterpart in the United States.

In the 20 to 24 age group, 24% are enrolled in the United States, compared with 9 to 12% in the major European countries. But the European will, on the average, complete his doctorate several years before his American counterpart, which makes its acquisition far less costly and enables him to begin practicing his profession much earlier and for more years.

So, if we want to learn what the American people receive in return for tripling over the past quarter century the amount expended on the education of a student, we must find out not only how many attended and for how many years, or how many graduated, but how much they learned. This is not as easy to ascertain. But it seems essential to know.

Is Educational Quality Declining?

Dissatisfaction with the schools is neither a recent nor a surprising phenomenon. Parents tend to expect their children to perform better in school than they actually do. Some parents may be deceiving themselves about their own achievements when they were young, and are thus more likely to blame the schools rather than lack of ability or drive of their offspring. Employers, disappointed with job applicants' skills and knowledge, are also wont to attribute deficiencies to the schools applicants attended. But dissatisfaction with educational results among the American people is too deep, too widespread and too long lasting to be explained away easily. Where there is so much smoke there must be a fire.

Within a few years after World War II, a wave of books appeared, sharply critical of public school results, authored by Arthur Bestor, George Iddings Bell, Hyman S. Rickover, John Keats, Mortimer Smith, James D. Koerner, Albert Lynd, and many others. Some of them such as Rudolf Flesch's *Why Johnny Can't Read* became best-sellers. More recent examples are Frank Armbruster's *Our Children's Crippled Future* and Paul Copperman's *The Literary Hoax*. Copperman charged that "for the first time in the history of our country, the education skills of one generation will not surpass, will not equal, will not even approach those of their parents." Leading national magazines periodically feature articles whose titles and content refer in stark terms to educational failure of our schools.[15]

The frequency and wide audience of these books, articles and other media programs reflect a belief among the American public that schools do not educate children as they should—nor as they used to. In earlier decades critics of educational achievement often blamed shortcomings on inadequate financing of the schools. But the record of multiplying funds over the past quarter century makes such charges senseless. More and more people are asking: why are we getting less education for more money? When the Roper Organization in a national opinion poll in March 1978 listed a number of current developments and asked which of them "posed a serious threat," *decline in quality of education* was checked by 33% of respondents, a rating exceeded only by *rapid depletion of natural resources* (44%).

There is no comprehensive national measurement of skills and knowledge of students and graduates which would amount to a historical record, depict historical trends or report relative nationwide standings. President Johnson's last secretary of HEW, Wilbur Cohen, criticized in 1967 "the voluminous, yet unsuitable data now available for assessing the products of our education." He complained that "practically none of it measures the output of our educational system in terms that really matter—that is in terms of what students have learned." He added that it is an "incredible fact that the nation has, year after year, been spending billions of dollars on an enterprise without a realistic accounting of that investment."

The nearest thing to a national achievement report is the scholastic aptitude test (SAT) of the College Entrance Examination Board (CEEB). Scores have steadily declined. Verbal scores fell from 466 in 1967 to 424 in 1980, mathematics scores from 492 in 1967 to 466 in 1980. The one million students who took the SAT tests in 1979 account for two-thirds of high school graduates who went directly to college and they were representative of the upper layer of their classes. If all three million high school seniors had taken the test, their verbal scores would have averaged 368, their mathematical scores 402, according to CEEB estimates.[16] Test scores correlate well with the students' self-reported class ranks and probably are a fairly accurate evaluation of their achievements and a good predictor of their prospects.

There has been much speculation about the cause of the continued decline in SAT scores. In 1977 a CEEB panel found that the inclusion of many less qualified students who in earlier years might not have applied to colleges was no longer a significant cause in the 1970s. Nor was a sometimes alleged cultural bias. The group regarded a lowering of educational standards in the high schools as the major identifiable cause.

The National Assessment of Educational Progress reported after a decade of surveying that results since 1969 clearly indicate that the nation's high schools and their students are in real trouble. In mathematics, writing, science, social studies, achievements have been declining, particularly at ages 13 to 17. A special task force of the National Academy of Education which the assistant secretary for education of the Department of HEW established, reported in March 1978 (*Improving Educational Achievement*) that the decline in writing skills and SAT scores was due to four changes in school practices, which relate to less rigorous educational standards and confusion about methods.

While annual Roper polls indicate that the public's rating of the schools' performance has been declining for twenty years, some hold that the much higher earnings of persons with more education prove that, on the whole, our educational institutions are performing their duties well. A Census study in 1972 estimated the lifetime earnings of men with different levels of education as follows:

ESTIMATED LIFETIME EARNINGS FROM AGE 18 TO DEATH, 1972

Schooling completed	Lifetime income
Less than 8 years	$280,000
8 years	344,000
1–3 years high school	389,000
4 years high school	479,000
1–3 years college	543,000
4 or more years college	758,000

SOURCE: U.S. Bureau of the Census, *Current Population Reports*, Series P-60, #92.

This suggests—and has widely been interpreted as meaning—that a person can add $135,000 to his lifetime income by attending high school for 4 years (instead of quitting after 8 years of grade school) and another $279,000 by attending college. But that is unmitigated nonsense. There is no proof that higher income is the *result* of the additional years of schooling. More likely both, the length of schooling and the level of income, reflect the intelligence, persistence, and personal drive of the individual.

It is unlikely that the approximately 350,000 young people who now quit high school before completing 11th grade could add $90,000 to their lifetime income by staying for another year. Nor could they add $369,000 by adding four years of college. Most of them drop out because they are unable to assimilate a 10th- or 11th-grade curriculum. How would they cope with a college education—even if some institutions were willing to admit them and give them a degree after 4 years? Would an empty degree boost their earnings by hundreds of thousands of dollars? Most of the dropouts might need some additional training to enable them to earn their sustenance in a competitive world. Unfortunately, few American high schools provide the type of training the dropouts need, which is why they quit.

Surveys relating educational attainment to income go back to the 1950 Census, have spawned a sizable literature and have now become an annual affair. They show that in 1978 a man with 4 years of high school had an annual median income of $16,396, with 4 years of college of $22,095. But they also show that the ratio between earnings of a high school graduate and a college graduate has gradually narrowed from 1:1.50 in 1967 to 1:1.35 in 1978.[17]

This could mean that the supply of college graduates has increased faster than the number of college-level job openings. It could also be a reflection of the lowering of college admission and graduation standards and an observed decline in the knowledge and occupational skills of college graduates. In any case, the evidence from a broad array of sources appears conclusive that the skills and knowledge of students and graduates of public schools and colleges has been declining while the resources for public educational institutions have been multiplying. The question is WHY?

Less Education for More Money

Unhappiness about the appalling discrepancy between increasing funds and decreasing achievements in public education has been growing. While decline is particularly obvious in the essential tools of learning, the three R's, it extends far beyond the basic skills to most fields of knowledge in the physical as well as the social sciences.

Some regard this as the natural consequence of a governmentally imposed monopoly operation that is protected from competition, and not subjected to the discipline of the market. A far greater variety of instructional methods, they feel, could be tested if diverse types of schools trying to outdo each other were available. Schools might upgrade their offerings if the public had a genuine choice among them, unaffected by the heavy economic penalty for attendance at nonpublic institutions. The cost of sending one's child to a private school, except a parochial school, is too high for most parents. They cannot afford to pay for education twice. If the cost differential were narrowed or eliminated, public and private schools could freely compete with each other and those operating the most effective educational program would attract most students. The best would win in an open race.

This could be accomplished by governmental vouchers that parents would use in paying tuition at a private school or by income tax credits for tuition payments. Public school forces have been fighting such plans bitterly. They suspect that without a sizable cost differential, many or most able children would be sent to private schools with high standards while public schools would be left with a disproportionate number of pupils who cannot pass admissions tests or live up to the requirements of private schools. And if public schools also raised their standards, how would less able children fare? Common schools, attended by all or most young people—90% at the present time—are regarded an essential preparation for life in a free and democratic society by spokesmen for the public schools. Those schools would undoubtedly lose a substantial number of students if alternatives were made less expensive than they now are. Measures to bring private school attendance within the reach of middle-class families would end the dominant position of the public school system—an outcome that some would view as a major disaster, others as liberation from a heavy yoke.

Absence of competition may explain why public schools can continue to pursue ineffective methods but it does not identify the particular instructional practice responsible for poor educational results. Moreover, governmental schools are the rule in most European countries where they do not seem to have produced the dismally low achievements typical of American public schools. Therefore, it is not government operation per se that produces bad results.

Some language arts experts attribute the failure in reading and writing to a shift, a few decades ago, from the phonetic method to "look-see." Outside the United States, the phonetic method of learning to read still prevails. Rudolf Flesch and other authors and the Reading Reform Foundation have made a good case for this explanation. Some observers blame the so-called "new math" for an appalling low in arithmetic skills, for seemingly valid reasons.

But educational deficiencies extend to levels above and beyond the basic skills. Many critics trace the downward trend to a softening of the curriculum, to a lowering or abandonment of standards of grading, promotion, discipline, graduation requirements, to a general permissiveness in public schools and an easing or neglect of admission standards in colleges. An analysis of the courses taken by students, of the hours devoted to solid subjects and to "breeze" classes, of the time spent on activities of a playlike character and in front of TV screens goes a long way in explaining low achievement levels. A study by the National Center for Education Statistics reported that the percentage of seniors who spent at least five hours per week on homework dropped from 36% in 1972 to 25% in 1980. But 33% of the 1980 seniors got all A's and B's, compared with only 29% in 1972.

Like most adults young people follow the path of least resistance—and find out what minimum effort they can get by with and still "pass."

Goldbricking is not restricted to schools and is widely practiced in today's society.

Public schools did not lower or abandon standards and "hard content" because their administrators prefer mediocrity and would not love to attain or maintain excellence. But they know that a sizable segment of their student body would fail if faced with higher standards, and teachers, administrators, and boards would be blamed not only by the parents of the failing students—which is excusable—but also by legislative bodies, news media, taxpayers, and the public at large—which is inexcusable.

Accountability in education is an eminently sound concept. President Nixon proposed it in the early 1970s with little lasting effect. Most people, unfortunately, misunderstand accountability as meaning that the schools and their staffs should be held responsible for every student's performance or failure. The schools, in self-defense, retreat to the lowest common denominator, that is, to standards and practices by which everybody—or almost everybody—can pass. Students' deficiencies in skills and knowledge are widely held to represent a failure of the school rather than of the student—although differences *within* each school are far wider than *among* schools or between students' scores today compared with scores years or decades earlier. Even schools and classes with low average scores usually contain some students who do well.

Half a century ago, high schools could maintain an intellectually rigorous curriculum because only the top 30% to 50% in ability, of the age group, enrolled in or finished high school. For some years now *all* children have been expected to complete high school. This forces administrators to downgrade the curriculum to a point where pupils of limited endowment can be pushed through the 12th grade.

What happened to the high schools three to five decades ago was subsequently done or is being attempted in colleges through "open enrollment" in different forms. The Consortium for Financing Higher Education, an association of private colleges, revealed that 430 applicants with verbal SAT scores between 750 and 800 were rejected in the fall of 1978, while 5531 students with verbal SATs between 500 and 550 were admitted. If that occurs at some of the nation's most selective institutions, what is happening at the general run of colleges?

Many college freshman classes have for years been swamped with students who lack the necessary capacity or preparation to absorb an academic curriculum. About one-fourth of the freshmen now require remedial instruction, and many drop out before graduation. It ought to be obvious—but seemingly is not—that a university is not the best place to provide a high school education. Why do postsecondary schools admit applicants who are marginal or unqualified? Public colleges accept them because greater enrollment helps them to justify bigger appropriation requests to state legislatures. Private colleges take them because tuitions provide much or most of their income and they feel that they cannot afford to leave seats empty in their enlarged plants.

In a mad rush for unlimited growth, higher educational institutions succeeded in tripling enrollment and the number of new degrees in the course of the 1960s and 1970s and expanded beyond need. Two to three times as high a proportion of our young people now attend postsecondary schools as do their counterparts in leading European countries. This does not mean that relatively more Americans are academically qualified or that we need so many more college graduates than Great Britain, France, Germany or the Soviet Union. Many of our college graduates now hold non–college level positions and others are desperately looking for jobs.

It means that Europeans learn in secondary school—in gymnasium, lycée, realschule—much or most what Americans do not face until their college days, in the liberal arts, the sciences and the humanities. In the language fields Europeans learn in secondary (middle) schools more than most Americans in their postsecondary years.

Behind the lowering of academic standards in our postsecondary schools lies the egalitarian spirit which holds that if some go to college, all should go or at least be entitled to go in a system of "open enrollment." In our eagerness to make everybody fit for college, we have made college fit everybody. Sometime in the 1950s, Father Gannon, president of Fordham University, asked: "Are we going to get fewer sheep just by handing out more sheepskins?"

Our practices have lowered the value of a college degree just as earlier we have made a high school diploma nearly meaningless. Europeans enter a university for professional or graduate study. Most of our students are not ready for such study until about four years later. Consequently, Americans enter a professional career and gainful activity several years later than Europeans. This would not be the case if talented Americans were challenged to the level of their capacity during their years of attendance at the lower schools. In a mad rush for the elusive goal of equality, American educational institutions have neglected the pursuit of excellence, at an enormous cost to their students, donors, and to the taxpayers.

It is irresponsible to encourage young people of limited intellectual endowment or drive to spend years in a futile attempt to obtain what they are promised would be a passport to a well-paid and guaranteed employment and higher socioeconomic status. It wastes scarce resources—faculty, facilities, student aid. For a far lower investment in time and money many of the students could have been prepared for intellectually less demanding occupations in which the number of openings will continue to be high—such as for competent mechanics, technicians and numerous other skills in a wide variety of fields.

In the 1960s President Milton Eisenhower of Johns Hopkins University proposed that a hundred universities should raise their admission requirements in order to force high schools to lift their curriculum and graduation standards. The plan attracted little attention in higher education and much derision among high school systems, whose managers were under pressure to find methods of getting every student through to graduation. A more than minimal dropout rate or nongraduation percentage is nowadays regarded as a failure of the particular high school and its administrators.

The report of the National Academy of Education mentioned earlier (*Improving Educational Achievement*, 1978) opposed statewide minimum competency standards because "it will create more social problems than it can conceivably solve." It strongly recommended against creation of "national tests"—mandatory or voluntary. A most ludicrous undertaking is the "competency tests" which are now administered in some states. Students are supposed to pass a test which generally is at the eighth grade level—lower at each school's discretion—for which they are granted a high school (= 12th grade) diploma. That is like granting an M.D. or bar examination passage for mastering a freshman curriculum. Why should students not be given an eighth grade diploma for passing an eighth grade test?

Any test, any examination, any standard, no matter how designed, aims to separate the wheat from the chaff, the qualified from the unqualified, which means that some will pass and some will fail. The war against tests is widely presented as a fight against improperly devised tests, which are charged with being culturally biased or aimed at eliminating some groups of students. If this charge were sincere, opponents of current tests would long ago have developed alternative tests that are fair to all and impartially measure capacity, skills, knowledge and performance of applicants. Some, in fact, tried decades ago. The Davis-Eels games (1953) and similar tests were designed as culturally unbiased. Unfortunately, their results barely differed from those of traditional tests, which caused those emotionally unable to accept the results to oppose all testing.

The war against tests is directed not at their alleged inadequacy or unreliability but at the principle of testing, of evaluating, of grading as such. The NEA, Ralph Nader's groups and others are campaigning with some success to have standardized testing abolished in the public schools and everywhere else. They don't want objective measurements whose results

Reprinted with courtesy of *The Saturday Evening Post.*

contradict and disprove dearly held beliefs—just like the overweight woman in the cartoon pictured shooting her bathroom scale.

All human traits are distributed on a curve of some shape. If there were no tests, there still would be 10% at the upper end and 10% at the lower end of the scale. But it might not be so obvious. So—if you don't like the heat, throw out the thermometer.

Objective measurements of human capacities are anathema to the egalitarian principle, the "spirit of the welfare state," which has come to dominate not only our schools but our whole society. The egalitarian trend which resents and penalizes excellence, hard work and success and aims at equalization, characterizes philosophical attitudes which have been in ascendancy for several decades and have been carried out in many forms of legislation, regulation, and practices. Erosion of standards is not limited to schools. It mirrors a trend toward forcing everybody into a uniform mold—in what may well be called *Operation Procrustes.*

In Greek mythology the Eleusian robber Procrustes adjusted travelers to the length of his bed—by stretching them or chopping off their feet. Our public schools are trying to adjust children to a rigid structure instead of building one that is flexible enough to accommodate children of widely varying capacities. We start all children at age 6 in grade school, promote them one grade each year through high school, and give them a diploma after twelve years. We know that some children are ready to learn before the age of six and some later, that some can absorb a 12th-grade curriculum long before they turn 17 and others will never be able to master it, that some need and can absorb an academic education and others can at best acquire simple skills.

But to admit this and adjust schools and progress through them to the widely varying capacities of children would be contrary to egalitarian principles, might give some children an inferiority complex—as if they didn't know anyway—offend some parents and antagonize politically powerful groups. Above all, we are told—it would be "undemocratic."

How do schools cope with the wide range of ability among pupils? Until a few decades ago they would retain a student in grade if he had not absorbed the prescribed curriculum and acquired the necessary skills. In 1950 21.6% of 12-year-olds were below their "modal grade" because they had been held back one or more years, 26.4% of the 15-year-olds. But around that time the schools discovered the secret of perpetual promotion. So most public schools gradually shifted to automatic promotion and by 1976 only 7.5% of the 12-year-olds and 9.6% of the 15-year-olds were below modal grade. The number of 8- to 13-year-olds two or more years behind was down to 1.9% in 1977, of 14- to 17-year-olds to 3.5%.[18]

Automatic promotion created insuperable problems for the schools. How can a teacher do justice to all of his pupils if they are several grades apart in their skill level? How can he do justice to *any* of them? An 8th-grade class may hold pupils who read and write at 4th- or 5th-grade level and others who perform at 10th-grade level. If you tried to produce a Rolls-Royce and an MG in the same shop, you'd get lousy MGs at a higher than Rolls-Royce price.

That's exactly what happened in the schools. They attempted to cope with the situation they had created and lowered class sizes because teachers complained that they could not teach in one room 30 or 25 children whose skill levels were 4 to 6 grades or more apart. The trouble is that no class size is small enough to teach children effectively if they are so dissimilar. Lowering teacher-pupil ratios turned out to be an extremely expensive process with appalling educational results. Able children were not challenged and took it easy, and those of limited capacity dropped out or goofed off—instead of acquiring minimum occupational skills.

Some schools tried to cope by offering diversified curricula by operating three or four separate "tracks" or "streams," according to pupils' ability and interest. But the dominant egalitarian forces frowned on tracking because it identified pupils by mental group. Some courts even declared it unconstitutional. The more optional courses were offered, the more children picked the easy ones. The fact is that a complicated patchwork cannot adequately substitute for a well thought out system that permits each pupil to develop his talents and ambitions to their fullest.

Secondary schools outside the United States maintain a dual or multiple system. Children apply for and are aptitude-tested for several types of academic or nonacademic and vocational schools, in which they can expect a curriculum consonant with their individual capacity.

That enables Europeans to obtain their liberal education in secondary school, enter professional school at a university at age 18 and go on to acquire a doctor's degree at an age at which most American students get a B.A. or M.A.

No country outside the United States attempts to keep all children up to age 18 in the same type of school, nor promotes them automatically every year. Their educators know that a unitary secondary school with annual promotion cannot work; if any further evidence was required to prove the point, the American public school has provided it over the past few decades.

Retention in grade cannot adequately solve the problem. To hold a child back for one year may help in many cases, but retention for several years creates more problems than it solves. Only the maintenance of several parallel curricula designed for a range of mental abilities can give all or most children the type of education they need and can absorb.

The Coleman report and several subsequent studies found no relation between the magnitude of input (resources) and the learning of students. The only substantial and persistent correlation with educational achievements was the home background of children as defined by their parents' socioeconomic standing. This has caused some researchers to suspect that low educational achievements are caused by parental poverty. The lack of books in the home, the absence of a type model to imitate, and deprivation by deficient nutrition are being cited most frequently as effects of poverty in the home and as causing low educational achievements. The argument sounds persuasive but has a serious flaw.

If home surroundings were the prime cause of educational retardation, then we would expect the impact gradually to decline the longer a child remains in school. Home was the only environment it knew when it entered school. But as the years went by, the influence of home will be increasingly diluted by the impact of school. Environmental factors might then be divided between home and school. The fact, however, is that retardation typically *grows*, for example, from an initial 6–9 months at age 6 to about 2 to 3 years at age 17 or 18. In 1950, before automatic promotion became a universal practice, the percentage of children in submodal grades grew from 6.6% at age 8, to 15.7% at age 10, to 21.6% at age 14. Above age 14 the percentage declined because lagging children would drop out. This suggests that each individual may have an inherent limit to intellectual growth and maturity which some reach at an earlier age than others. Reaching that limit can be accelerated by intense instructional methods, but the effect is likely to be temporary. The limit can be stretched somewhat by great efforts, but not much. It has been said that you can lead a horse to the trough but you can't make him drink. That seems to be equally true of children in education.

Some declare it undemocratic to hold back some children or to assign them to different schools with lower educational standards. Fact is that there is a strong correlation between the learning of parents and of children and between parental income and educational achievement. For example, the percentage of children enrolled two or more years below modal grade is inversely related to parental income: among 14- to 17-year-olds it equaled 8.8% of all children at a family income below $5,000, slowly decreasing to 1.2% at an income of $15,000 or more in 1977. Among 8- to 13-year-olds it declined from 4.1% at family income under $5,000 to 0.8% at $15,000 and more.[19]

Scores on SAT tests are perfectly correlated with family income:

SAT Scores and Parental Income, 1978–79

Median income	Average SAT score
$14,900	below 350
19,200	350–399
20,700	400–449
21,800	450–499
23,200	500–549
24,500	550–599
25,800	600–649
28,300	650 or over

Source: *National College-Bound Seniors*, 1979, College Entrance Examination Board, p. 16.

Students who take SAT tests have been exposed to books and schools long enough to be little affected by the number of books in their home—a dozen years earlier. Why are children of high-achieving parents more often than not high achievers in education and the children of low-achieving parents low achievers? Some observers argue that high or low educational performance of children is caused by the wealth or poverty of their parents. That amounts to standing causal relationships and logic on their heads. Is rain due to people opening their umbrellas? Are big feet the result of wearing big shoes? Why should we be surprised when the scores of children on the educational tests of school more often than not parallel their parents' scores on the economic tests of life? Recent agricultural research findings suggest the probability that apple trees tend to bear more apples than plums.

We can now see more clearly why income and outcome in American public education have been moving in opposite directions. American public schools have been unwilling to accept certain facts of life, refused to act *with* rather than *against* nature. Dominated by egalitarian ideas, they have been trying to force all children into an identical mold, in supreme disregard of inherent differences. This has imposed a tremendous cost—in money and in poor results.

If American education diversified its schools and curricula to accommodate the widely differing abilities and aspirations of children, the now negative ratio between income and outgo could become positive *after* the necessary reforms have been carried out. At least one-third of the staff of public educational institutions would become redundant if children were able to attend schools and classes that are designed to fit their individual capacities more closely. Student achievements, instead of sliding downhill, could rise and approach those of European students who have a choice of schools according to their individual needs.

Economic interests of powerful groups will not be easy to overcome. It may take another Theseus to slay this Procrustes. Moreover, belief in the magic quality of the educational dollar, especially if it is of federal provenance, dies hard.

But to continue current practices and methods is self-destructive for American education and, in the long run, for the nation. No single governmental program demonstrates more clearly and conclusively the futility and waste of year after year pouring multibillion-dollar amounts into activities which have proven and continue to prove to be incapable of reaching, or even making progress toward, hoped-for and promised results as compensatory education for so-called disadvantaged children. The story is told in the following section.

The Alchemists in Our Public Schools[20]

For nearly two thousand years some of the most brilliant and erudite minds of their time devoted untiring efforts and their wealthy sponsor's money to a task which, as we have since learned, is not within man's power:

to convert common metals into gold by removing their impurities: Why did the alchemists—who were scholars—and their backers—who were men of affairs—remain impervious for so long to ample evidence of the futility of their search? Their stubborn refusal to draw from their defeats the lesson that there is no shortcut to *Eldorado* suggests a deep emotional need to believe that there is. So they persuaded themselves, and others, that what *ought to be* possible, *was* in fact possible.

A modern parallel to that triumph of emotion over reason appeared on the scene in the mid-1960s: a large number of knowledgeable and dedicated men and women asserted, insisted and tried to prove that there is a shortcut by which poverty can be wiped out quickly and painlessly—without the price of blood and sweat and tears that nations paid which over several centuries became the world's wealthiest.

That new elixir of life, a contemporary counterpart of the philosophers' stone, our latter-day alchemists believe to be *education*. Some hold that the survival of poverty in the midst of plenty is a paradox that needs to be promptly corrected. Poverty in the midst of plenty is a paradox to the same extent to which shade is a paradox when the sun shines: if there were no sun, there would be no shade.

If Americans were not so rich—family income averaged $19,684 in 1979—a cash income of $7,450 for a family of four would not be regarded to mean poverty. To most of the globe's inhabitants, an income of that size still represents a wealth they can never hope to achieve for themselves. But in the U.S. of 1980 it is labeled poverty. There were in 1977, according to Bureau of the Census estimates, some 25 million persons (5.3 million families and 5.2 million unrelated individuals) below an income which is officially defined as the poverty line. Their poverty was attributed to deficiencies in their education. If that deficiency could be offset by "compensatory education" they would be able to earn an income above the poverty line, their children would grow up in nonpoor homes and poverty would be wiped out in the United States. At least, so the theory went.

In the exuberance of the mid-1960s, added investment in the education of children of poor parents seemed to be the perfect and complete answer to ending poverty forever. Experience with compensatory education over the succeeding ten to fifteen years has made many of the early enthusiasts sadder and it has made some of them wiser—though not necessarily all of them.

Henry J. Aaron, the Carter administration's assistant secretary of HEW for planning and evaluation (formerly a Brookings Institution fellow), superbly illuminated the change in public attitude by prefacing the chapter on "Education and Jobs" in his book *Politics and the Professors: The Great Society in Perspective*[21] with two quotations, eleven years apart, which are hereby repeated:

With respect to the distribution of personal income . . . changes in the
investment in human capital are the basic factors reducing the inequality
in the distribution of personal income. . . . Modifications in income
transfers, in progressive taxation, and in the distribution of privately
owned wealth are relatively weak factors in altering the distribution of
personal income.—Theodore W. Schultz, "Reflections on Investment in
Man," *Journal of Political Economy*, vol. 70 (October 1962, supplement),
p. 2.

I do not know anyone who contends that education reform is a more
effective way to reduce the inequality of income than giving the poor
more money.—Alice M. Rivlin, "Forensic Social Science," *Harvard
Educational Review*, vol. 43 (February 1973), p. 65.

Some scholars seem to have learned from experience with compensatory
education that "investment in human capital," like any other investment
or seed, can come a cropper, if planted in arid soil. So, if poverty is defined in terms of cash income and if the government's policy is to abolish
poverty, handing out enough money still appears to be the direct way to
accomplish that end. That is what the Great Society and its successors have
been doing at an increasing scale ever since, thereby approaching their
splendid goal as efficiently as a dog turning in a circle to catch his tail.

Not that the spectacular failure of compensatory education had kept
Congress from extending the program six times since 1965 and multiplying its authorized funding sixfold. Compensatory education became what
may well be the outstanding boondoggle of the century. I testified against
the pending bills at the original House and Senate hearings and subsequently described their passage. The story may be well worth telling.[22]

The National Education Association has attempted for well over a
century to persuade Congress into authorizing broad federal support of the
public schools but failed consistently until the 1960s. After resounding
electoral triumph in 1964, President Lyndon Johnson realized that tying
education to his Great Society program could give him a striking success in
an endeavor in which his predecessors up to and including John Kennedy
had failed. Administration economists viewed the problem of poverty as an
economic condition with an educational solution. Through compensatory
education lagging school pupils could be turned into skilled and productive
members of the work force, thereby solving several problems with one
blow. Holding out the hope of thus reducing welfare outlays, this approach
found a more favorable reception than federal school aid proposals had
in earlier years. Even so, it took all of President Johnson's power, then at
its peak, and much arm-twisting, to railroad the bill through a reluctant
Congress.

No one, at the time, paid attention to the consistent failure in the late 1950s and early 1960s of several compensatory education projects such as "New Horizons" in New York, "Bannecker" in St. Louis, "Madison" in Syracuse, in Berkeley and in other cities. They seemed irrelevant.

The passing of the *Elementary and Secondary Education Act of 1965* (ESEA) was widely hailed as the beginning of a new era. Every year since 1965, ESEA has been supporting projects in about 14,000 school systems, involving 7 to 9 million children with an aggregate cost which by now exceeds $30 billion. It created jobs for hundreds of thousands of teachers and other school personnel and succeeded in many ways but one: it failed to raise the educational achievement level of "educationally disadvantaged" or "deprived" children, which had been the program's prime purpose and promise. The law's focal part, Title I, authorizes programs for disadvantaged children, a newly coined euphemism for pupils who lag behind their classmates and modal grade in educational achievement. On the assumption that all children of low-income parents are behind educationally, and that all lagging children come from low-income homes, the law distributes federal funds by the number of poor families. According to the law's preamble, it aims to aid "areas with concentrations of children from low-income families." But funds are distributed to nearly 90% of all school systems and to 95% of all counties. If that is concentration, then we may wonder what a wide dispersal would look like.

In the year following the passage of ESEA, the Coleman report (see pp. 185–86) was published which revealed that "the physical and economic resources going into a school had very little relationship to the achievements coming out of it." Then HEW reported that "about three-fourths of the disadvantaged pupils attend schools that enroll a relatively small proportion of disadvantaged pupils."[23]

This and the disclosure that achievement differences are wider within than among schools suggest that whatever the schools do or not do could not be the cause of the children's poor performance. Otherwise, all or most children attending the same school would be similarly affected.

The U.S. Civil Rights Commission found in 1967 that "none of the [compensatory education] programs appear to have raised significantly the achievement of participating pupils" (*Racial Isolation in the Public Schools*, p. 138).

In 1968 the assistant secretary of HEW for planning and evaluation, Alice Rivlin, disclosed to a congressional group that "federal funds so far have failed to stop the downward spiral of poor children's achievements."[24] HEW tried to keep a straight face when its Advisory Council on the Education of Disadvantaged Children opined in 1969:

Comparatively modest as the financing and scope of Title I are, however,

we believe that this single piece of legislation overshadows all other
federal aid-to-education laws in importance, for it strikes one of the
earliest and potentially most effective blows at the self-perpetuating cycle
of poverty in the United States.[25]

Soon, reports from all over the country were reiterating the absence of
positive results of Title I programs. President Nixon summarized the
program's failure in his Message on Education Reform of March 3, 1970:

> *. . . the best available evidence indicates that most of the compensatory edu-*
> *cation programs have not measurably helped poor children catch up.* [Em-
> phasis added.] Recent findings on the two largest such programs are
> particularly disturbing. We now spend more than $1 billion a year for
> educational programs under Title I of the Elementary and Secondary
> Education Act. Most of these have stressed the teaching of reading, but
> before-and-after tests suggest that only 19 percent of the children in such
> programs improve their reading significantly; 13 percent appear to fall
> behind more than expected; and more than two-thirds of the children
> remain unaffected—that is, they continue to fall behind. In our Headstart
> Program where so much hope is invested, we find that youngsters en-
> rolled only for the summer achieve almost no gains, and the gains of those
> in the program for a full year are soon matched by their non-Headstart
> classmates from similar poor backgrounds.

Two years after President Nixon's Education Reform Message,
Newsweek conducted a survey of the new programs in school districts
throughout the country and reported on April 3, 1972, that "despite the
expenditure of billions of federal dollars in the nation's largest school
systems, compensatory education—designed to offset the cultural disad-
vantages of ghetto children—has been widely judged a failure." The article
mentioned that "as recently as the mid-1950s big city schools were almost
universally regarded as centers of academic excellence in the U.S."
Achievements in those same school systems from New York City to San
Francisco are now at the bottom of all schools, and slipping further year
after year. What has changed? Billions of federal, state, and local dollars
have been added, per student costs have been mounting, but the type of
children who attend those schools has changed. There is now ample
experience to show that differences in pupils' traits cannot be offset by any
amount of money. It is the children more than the schools that determine
the educational outcome.

New York City's *More Effective Schools* (MES) project of 21 schools, aided under Title I of ESEA, spent twice as much per pupil as other New York Schools but reported lower test scores in the three R's.

Students in the 30 elementary schools in New York City with a per pupil expenditure in 1967–1968 of $1,100 or more (their average was $1,330) scored half a year or more *lower* on reading and arithmetic tests in fifth and sixth grades than students in the 101 elementary schools with an expenditure below $600 (average $551). The teacher-pupil ratio in the MES schools averaged 1:12.3, in the high-achieving schools, 1:25.9. The 62 Oakland elementary schools showed a clear inverse relationship between the staffing level and reading, arithmetic and language scores.[26]

In 1976, when compensatory education programs under ESEA had been operating for a decade, the Comptroller General of the United States submitted to Congress a report which concluded that only one out of ten local educational agencies having measurable goals was achieving them.[27] Also: "Most Title I students were (1) not reading at levels sufficient for them to begin to close the gap between their reading level and the national norm, (2) widening the gap in reading levels, or (3) not retaining Title I gains after they left."

HEW turned to SRI (formerly Stanford Research Institute) for a review of the many evaluation reports of Title I. SRI drafted a report: "We have no evidence that at the end of the sixth grade, Title I students are better off than eligible students who have not participated. . . . Therefore, we must face the disturbing proposition that something is wrong with the program itself. . . ." SRI's final report was noncommittal: "Without multiyear evaluations we cannot conclusively assess the impact of Title I."[28]

When compensatory education programs were unable to report positive results, John Coleman came up with a brilliant idea which was carried into practice by the Office of Economic Opportunity (OEO) in 1969–71: *Performance contracting.* The project turned the task of raising the educational level of the students over to private contractors who were to be paid on a sliding scale, according to progress as measured on standard achievement tests. "We'll educate your kids—or your money back." In most cases payment was to be made only for a student who gained one school year of growth between the fall pretest and the spring posttest. The OEO staff "saw great promise in performance contracting as a means to help poor children achieve the same results from classroom effort now achieved by nonpoor students."[29] OEO, contractors, and the schools "really believed that the lagging pupils were disadvantaged only in their prior experience; that the public schools were terribly ineffective teachers; and that the application of the usual psychological principles would cause extraordinary leaps in achievement."[30]

The project involved 18 cities and 23,000 students. Results were devastating: there was no detectable effect of the experiment. The OEO reported: "In half of the 10 cases there was no difference between the gains of the experimental and control groups. In four of the cases there was a difference of as much as two-tenths of a grade level. These overall differences are so slight that we can conclude that performance contracting was no more effective in either reading or math than the traditional classroom methods of instruction."[31] OEO abandoned the project forthwith. Even the contractors lost their enthusiasm—and their money; most went out of business.

Some observers contended that the age of 5 or 6 is too late to undo the damage which disadvantaged children suffer from an injurious home environment. So, preschool enrollment was extended downward and expanded. Attendance by 3-and 4-year-olds rose from 20% in 1970 to 34% in 1978. When that did not produce significant results, demands arose that the rehabilitation process should be started earlier, at age two or even at birth. But the record of adopted children and of siblings separated since birth offer little proof of a strong influence of the foster home. This and other evidence suggest that intervention at birth may come about nine months late.

In an extensive review of studies and reports on Title I of ESEA and Headstart programs, the assistant secretary of HEW for planning and evaluation, Henry J. Aaron, found:

> These evaluations almost universally reported negligible effects or improvements that faded away after the treatment was stopped. Children in schools aided under Title I remained behind norms for children of the same age or fell further behind. Headstart seemed to produce small improvements in reading readiness, but no improvements beyond the first grade could be discovered. . . .[32]

Mr. Aaron concluded sadly that faith and beliefs, not research, had been the basis for the programs' commitment to social reform. The evanescence of the temporary gains, reported in some projects, suggests that while water can be pumped uphill, it will not continue or even remain uphill when the pumping stops.

The overwhelming evidence of the ineffectiveness of compensatory education shook the confidence of many scholars—educators, economists, sociologists, political scientists—in the power of education, the unlimited malleability of the human mind, the ultimate perfectibility of man and, in a few extreme cases, even in the omnipotence of the federal dollar. Some now seem more willing to admit than they were before that there is a law of diminishing returns in social programs and that increased input does not yield greater output from a certain point on—a point that was reached in most American public schools long ago. A few are not as certain as they used to be that all "investment in human capital" is necessarily productive and they might even concede that investment of any type has a better chance of proving fruitful if placed where the prospects of a proper return are highest, not where they are lowest.

Congress, typically, seemed far less haunted by self-doubt about the wisdom of the action taken than the academic community. To be sure, reports on the effects of ESEA and its Title I went to Congress by the hundreds. What did Congress do about them? Why—it extended the program six times, the last time in 1978 for five years and it multiplied authorized funds sixfold, as I mentioned earlier. Needless to say, there was little reference in congressional debates to any spectacular advances in basic skills and knowledge among the many millions of participating students in 15 years of operation, nor to high wages Title I alumni were able to earn subsequently by virtue of their educational progress. There just did not seem to be much to brag about.

Congressional debates at renewal time focused mainly on just one subject: how to split the billions of federal money among the 50 states, nearly 3,000 counties and 13,000 school systems, all of which were hungrily waiting for the manna from heaven. The lofty promises of 1965 produced a plain pork barrel operation. So, while President Kennedy's education bill had failed in the House 160:242, and ESEA in 1965 passed 263:153, the 1974 extension sailed through 380:26. Who would want to shoot Santa Claus?

The 1965 bill originally allocated the funds according to the number of low-income parents. That had some logic: parents who were unsuccessful in life have a good chance of procreating children with low achievements in school—and later in life. Special attention and programs in school will at least make them feel better. Many members of Congress then still believed that the program might help the children succeed educationally and occupationally. However, given the income distribution among the states, allocation by low income would have channeled most of the money to the South. But most of the votes in the House of Representatives are in the North and among the high-income states. The 14 highest per-capita-income states control 53% of the votes in the House.

So the Pucinski amendment was added: Not only low-income people were to be counted but also the number of AFDC (Aid to Families with Dependent Children) cases. In many northern states AFDC benefits exceed the income limits of ESEA. Counting AFDC gave the richer states additional money. In the beginning, AFDC accounted for 10% of all eligible cases. But with growing affluence and higher welfare benefits, the AFDC share grew to 53% in 1974.

At that point "the South rose again," under the leadership of the committee chairman, one of the shrewdest Southern politicians. He succeeded in getting a reduction, for allocation purposes, of the AFDC count to two-thirds of the AFDC cases through the committee, the House and the Senate. That boosted allocation to the sunbelt states substantially, at least for a few years. Northerners soon realized that they had been had and in 1978 restored the 100% counting of AFDC cases in the allocation formula.[33] What decides in the end still is the number of votes and members of Congress can forget only at their peril that what counts with their organized constituents is, who brings home the bacon. Charity begins at home.

Consequently, ESEA and compensatory education are still going strong and growing bigger. The "disadvantaged" children are as disadvantaged and illiterate as they ever were, and the number of persons below the poverty line has not receded for over a dozen years although government income support meanwhile soared. There is no evidence that Title I has helped significantly to raise earnings for ESEA graduates. It did so for the teachers and aides to whom it gave jobs that were better paid than the wages they could have earned elsewhere.

Youth unemployment is as high as ever—at 20.1% among males and 15.5% among females 16 to 21 years old, in January 1981; it ran in the 30% to over 40% range among minority youngsters—despite several huge vocational training programs. Early in 1980 President Carter proposed another "$6 billion program designed to teach poor youths the three R's so they can get a job."

Despite the appalling experience with ESEA, Mr. Carter proposed

> to establish a grant program to support special supplementary education programs in school districts with high concentrations of poor and unemployed youth. The new program will help needy junior and senior high school students learn the basic academic and employment skills necessary for them to graduate from high school and obtain jobs. . . . Such a joint effort will help assure that disadvantaged students receive the basic skills and work experience needed for a full productive and rewarding life.[34]

That sounds like a carbon copy of Mr. Johnson's plea fifteen years earlier. Where had Mr. Carter been all those years? Why can't those youths—at least those among them who possess an adequate mental capacity—learn the three R's in the regular grade schools? Why should anybody who has not learned the three R's be admitted to a high school? Public schools have failed because they have been trying to educate all youngsters from the lowest IQ to the highest in the same school and in the same classroom. That just cannot be done. The low-IQ kids can't learn that way and the gifted ones squander precious years unnecessarily.

Does that make American public schools more democratic? I do not believe so. It does make schools more egalitarian, and it certainly makes them ineffective and wasteful. This is a shame in a nation that believes itself to be the leader of the free world and is, according to the U.S. Budget, in 1981 spending $200 billion on educational activities.

Income Support and the War on Poverty

Every president from Franklin Roosevelt to Jimmy Carter has declared elimination of poverty in America one of his primary and most cherished goals. Poverty has indeed declined substantially since the 1930s and especially in the past quarter century, as measured by every known yardstick—whether we use the official poverty index or make some of the proposed adjustments in it. Several keen observers of the scene have suggested that, for all practical purposes, poverty has been wiped out in the United States with, at worst, a few small pockets still hanging on a short while longer.

Does this mean that those presidents and the actions they recommended and carried out have been successful? Yes and No. Poverty certainly has disappeared as a mass phenomenon and given way to a society with widely dispersed affluence. But this was not accomplished in the ways and by the means emphasized by recent presidents. Each of them proposed that poor people should be made or helped to become self-supporting, by various governmental services—education, occupational training, various types of youth and other employment projects, incentives and subsidies to the individuals and their potential employers—and thereby become less dependent on public support. All of our recent presidents expressed the hope that reliance on the dole would shrink and gradually fade away.

But the record of the past quarter century shows that efforts to shift millions of people "from welfare to workfare" have largely failed, some of them spectacularly so. Welfare rolls have ballooned and give no sign of "withering away." The incidence of poverty was reduced to a fraction of its former size, mostly by an unprecedented expansion of governmental income support programs, in cash and in kind, which continue to expand.

The *War on Poverty* has been won, as Martin Anderson, Senior Fellow at the Hoover Institution, proved conclusively in his excellent book in 1978.[35] But it was not won by the approach or strategy by which the War on Poverty and similar drives were sold to the Congress and the American people. Many, and possibly most, of those who played influential or decisive roles in the formation of the welfare state sincerely believed at the time that reduction of poverty by a shift "from welfare to workfare" could be achieved by the measures they advocated and put into practice. Many others knew or soon learned that this could not be done and aimed to achieve their goals by redistribution of income. They succeeded, at least in part, and created a *New Leisure Class.*

Redistribution of income—from those who have more to those who have less—toward a more equal condition, closer to an egalitarian ideal, is at the very heart of the welfare state. Some of its protagonists appear more eager to make the rich poor than to make the poor rich because, judging from the nature of their appeals to the public, they seem to be driven by envy-caused resentment of the successful more than by charity for the poor.

Income redistribution is being sought and accomplished by tax and expenditure policies. On the expenditure side, it is most effectively carried out by income support of individuals, which has become the biggest and fastest growing item of government outlays. In official documents *income support* is usually referred to as *income maintenance*, an incorrect designation because those payments seldom aim to "maintain" income at a pre-existing level. They either provide *less* income than the recipient had before—as, for example, in unemployment and old age benefits—or provide *more* income than he or she had before—as is often true in public assistance and other antipoverty programs.

Income support accounts for the major part of what in national income accounting is called *transfer payments.* It is workless pay—payments to persons for which they render no current services. Transfer payments increased over the past quarter century from 4.8% of all personal income to 13.0% which of course means a commensurate shrinkage in the net income share of the economically active population, whether from work or ownership (see pp. 97–98). Since transfer payments create effective demand without increasing the supply of goods and services, they have a strong inflationary impact. Some of the transfer payments such as public employee pensions and veterans benefits may be regarded as deferred compensation for services. The remainder are government payments, in cash or kind, for the purpose of providing income support; they accounted for 48% of transfer payments in 1952 for 70% in 1978.

Income support, shown in the table below, multiplied tenfold in *constant* dollars between 1952 and 1978, growing from 6.7% of total government expenditures to 22.9%, from 1.8% of GNP to 7.4%. This does not include certain in-kind programs such as medical and housing services and subsidies. Defense spending equaled 7.4 times income support outlays in 1952; in 1978, income support totaled nearly half again as much as the cost of defense.

INCOME SUPPORT BY FEDERAL, STATE AND LOCAL GOVERNMENTS, 1952 AND 1978

	1952	1978	Percentage increase in *constant* $
	in millions of $		
Total	$6,262	$156,803	+ 919%
Old Age, Survivors and Disability Insurance	2,240	92,523	+ 1579
Public assistance and related welfare	2,954	54,999	+ 657
Unemployment compensation	1,068	9,281	+ 254

SOURCE: Table 23 and sources listed there.

Did the economic conditions or employment situation of the American people deteriorate so badly in the past quarter century to necessitate such a spectacular growth in governmental support of individual incomes? The unemployment rate increased—from 3.0% to 6.0% of the civilian labor force. But this was due partially to a 4.7 percentage point growth in labor force participation (from 59.0% to 63.7% of the noninstitutional population, 16 years and over). While U.S. population increased 39%, civilian employment expanded 57%.

For every employed person there were in 1952 1.6 nonemployed persons in the population, most of them not in the labor force (too old, too young or other reasons); in 1978 each employed person had to support only 1.3 nonworking persons which amounts to a substantial easing of the burden. Per capita GNP meanwhile increased from $3843 to $6401 in *constant* 1972 dollars, a 67% growth.

The ratio between the productive age groups (18–64) and the rest of the population was almost the same in 1950 (1.55:1) and in 1978 (1.50:1). The ratio had slipped sharply from 1.55 persons in the productive ages for everyone in the under 18 or over 64-years-old group to a low of 1.23 to 1 in 1960, slightly improved to 1.28 to 1 in 1970, and showed a substantial growth to 1.50 to 1 in 1978. With a higher ratio between productive and nonproductive age groups, the ratio of persons dependent on government support might have been expected to decline. But it rose substantially.

In other words: demographic changes offer no explanation for the growth in government income support. While the number of old persons (65 years and over) grew as a percentage of the population, from 8.1% in 1950 to 11.0% in 1978, the percentage of young persons (under 18) fell from 31.0% to 29.0%. In the aggregate both groups increased insignificantly, from 39.2% of the total population in 1950 to 40.0% in 1978.

If neither demographic nor economic trends were responsible for the rapid growth in governmental income support, what was it caused by? A good part of the growth was undoubtedly brought about by the maturing of the social security system. It was in its adolescence, barely 16 years old in 1952, but a generation older and in the prime of life—though not necessarily at its apex—in 1978. Few retired persons had accumulated sizable credits in the early 1950s, but millions were retiring with substantial benefits toward the end of the 1970s. Far larger numbers are looking forward to retiring in the 1980s, 1990s, and beyond, at still higher annuities.

No one knows how many persons now draw income support from government. Most recipients participate in several of the many cash and in-kind programs simultaneously and the extent of the overlap is not known. We may estimate that more than one-fourth of the U.S. population is now involved. A staff member of the Congressional Budget Office came up some years ago with an estimate of one-fifth of the U.S. population receiving governmental income support. But that seems to me too low, at this time.

Most of the tenfold growth (in *constant* dollars) of government income support payments can be traced to a congressional policy of liberalization, which opened the rolls to additional millions of more or less deserving persons and boosted their benefits at frequent intervals, usually in years that were even-numbered or divisible by four. Congressional decisions were influenced by official reports that the extent of poverty has not been shrinking for many years and has remained relatively steady at around 24 to 25 millions persons and between 11 and 12 percent of the U.S. population since the later 1960s, despite sharply rising infusions of public funds. That seemed to call for stronger efforts to alleviate the plight of the needy.

That those estimates are seriously flawed and misleading was pointed out by several analysts who, however, seem to have made no impact on the powers that be. Opposing forces have a vital interest in *not* letting it be known widely how small the residual incidence of poverty has become.

For many years no breakdown of personal income statistics by size brackets has been available. The Department of Commerce discontinued such reports in 1964 because it doubted its ability to prepare them with sufficient accuracy with the means at hand. My subsequent efforts to have appropriations for that purpose authorized failed, although the required sums were tiny compared with the $1 billion cost of the decennial census in 1980.

Annual sample surveys of the Bureau of the Census are now the only source of income size data. They suffer from serious underreporting and fall about $300 to $400 billion short of personal income according to national income accounts. The Census surveys report only money (cash) income and omit income-in-kind—food stamps, housing assistance, medical benefits, child nutrition (e.g., school lunches), child care, etc., which account for a sizable share of income at the lower end of the income scale. This makes personal income in those brackets appear to be lower than it actually is. In-kind income has been growing faster than cash income over the past 10 or 20 years so that comparisons of cash income alone give a distorted picture.

Many persons only *seem* to be poor; some incur losses which give them a low or no income in a particular year that is not representative of their true economic bracket, some may have had little income because they began or ended their earning career during that year, some may have taken time off for leisure, travel, study, going back to school—paying current outlays from savings or their earnings of earlier years. A growing number of young people leave their parents' home of their own volition to set up a separate household—which makes them poor. If they move in with others to whom they are not related, each of them may be labeled poor although their *aggregate* household income may be above the poverty line.

What this all amounts to is that a large number of persons and families are reported to have a money income below the official poverty level in a particular year but may not be poor in any meaningful sense of the word.

In this book's predecessor, written in 1974, I made an educated guess that proper adjustments would reduce the poverty rate from an officially reported 11.7% in 1972 to 6.7%. Subsequent estimates have arrived at similar results. The Congressional Budget Office came up with a 6.4% poverty rate in 1977, compared with an official rate of 11.6%. A Brookings Institution report in 1976 estimated the poverty rate at 5%.

Morton Paglin, in a thorough study of low-level income, estimated that in 1976 3.6% of the population—7.8 million persons—had income below the official poverty threshold—compared with 12.3% according to the Census survey.[36] Census had estimated the "poverty gap"—the amount of money necessary to raise the incomes of all poor persons up to the poverty threshold—at $16.1 billion in 1975. Paglin placed it at $4.1 billion—a small amount considering the size of our total welfare bill.

Poverty has been defined in terms of an annual income for a family of specified size. For a nonfarm family of four—most commonly used as an example—the poverty threshold was at $3317 in 1966, at $6662 in 1978, at $7450 in 1979, and at $8400 in 1981. The official poverty formula was prepared in the early 1960s by Olly Orshansky of the Department of HEW, using nutritional and other requirements. Inevitably though, it is related to current concepts of poverty and average standards of living. A 4-person family with an income of $8,400 would be regarded as very affluent by most of the world's population, the great majority of which has only a fraction of that amount to live on. Its equivalent at the turn of the century (converted by the price index) would have labeled most Americans in 1900 as poor.

Until early in the twentieth century, poverty relief was a responsibility of voluntary charity, secular or religious, and of local communities. State assistance developed slowly from about 1911 on.

Prior to the 1930s, outlays for public welfare—virtually all state and local—were insignificant, averaging less than 1.5% of all government spending. At the end of the 1970s they accounted for one-fourth of the total outlays of federal, state and local governments.

The big turn came with the passage of the Social Security Act of 1935. The system's architects did a magnificent job that has stood the test of time well. It would still serve its intended purpose adequately if it had not subsequently been perverted and so badly abused by its managers that it needs, and has needed for some time, a thorough restructuring, lest it inflict ever greater damage on society and the body politic.

As formed in 1935 the social welfare system consisted of three major parts:

a) federal programs of social insurance against economic deprivation resulting from such hazards of life as old age, death of the breadwinner, temporary joblessness. Disability and some medical services were subsequently added.

b) federal-state-local programs offered public assistance in case of need due to clearly identifiable and verifiable causes which resulted in a person's inability to earn his and his family's support. It was intended to be a *temporary* bridge until social insurance coverage became comprehensive and universal.

c) state-local "general assistance" programs for residual cases of need, resulting from an infinite variety of individual deficiencies which could not be nationally categorized through uniform rules and therefore were to remain a state-local responsibility.

The social insurance systems have on the whole been working well for nearly half a century and are no longer controversial. Some of them have been overloaded beyond their bearing capacity and will have to undergo reasonable slimming operations to avoid more serious trouble later on. But no responsible person would now want to alter their basic structure—nor could if he wanted to. Not that we might not be able to design a better system if we started from scratch. But that is now purely academic. Future changes will focus on details, important details to be sure, but not on fundamentals.

With the maturing of social insurance, which has for many years covered over 90% of the civilian labor force—counting government retirement systems about 96%—the time came to terminate the public assistance programs which had been intended to be temporary.

Testifying at U.S. Senate hearings on welfare reform, on January 27, 1972, I recommended to shift Old Age Assistance (OAA), Aid to the Blind (AB), Aid to the Totally and Permanently Disabled (ATPD) and Aid to Families with Dependent Children (AFDC) for widows and orphans and for families of disabled fathers to national social insurance.[37]

Congress assumed federal responsibility for public assistance to the aged, blind and disabled effective in 1974. It did not blanket them into social security however—because some felt that this might jeopardize the integrity of the contributor-financed insurance system—and established a new federal program of supplemental security income (SSI) with federally mandated contributions by states that had established benefits at levels in excess of the federal standard. It is a complicated system, requiring a means test, with currently 4 million recipients at an annual cost of over $7 billion. The number of aged on the program has been declining very slowly while the number of disabled persons has sharply increased due to an easing of eligibility practices.

Congress did not act on AFDC, the nation's largest, most costly and most controversial cash assistance program. Presidents Nixon and Carter tried to replace AFDC with a program of guaranteed annual income. Their proposals were considered in the 91st, 92d, 95th, and 96th Congresses but failed to pass. AFDC remains the outstanding example of mismanagement in public welfare.

Welfare's Snakepit—Aid to Dependent Children

During the extensive congressional debates leading to the passage of the Social Security Act of 1935 its Title IV on Aid to Dependent Children (ADC) was barely mentioned. ADC had been recommended by President Roosevelt's Committee on Economic Security as an expansion, with federal assistance, of the widows' pension programs which all but two of the states had been operating for years. Supplementation of mothers' pensions, as the program was sometimes called, with federal funds was so noncontroversial that only a few words, praising the idea, were spoken in the House of Representatives, by Rep. Dr. Sirovich. They bear repeating:

> Death through the loss of the breadwinner has broken many a home. For centuries the widows, orphans and dependent children have cried aloud for help and assistance in their tragic periods of economic insecurity. In the past the only recourse for orphaned children was the poorhouse, almshouse, and the orphan asylum. . . . [*Congressional Record*, April 16, 1935, p. 5786.]

Forty-two years later President Carter tried to abolish and replace ADC, denouncing it in his congressional message on August 6, 1977, in withering terms:

> The welfare system is anti-work, anti-family, inequitable in its treatment of the poor and wasteful of the taxpayers' dollars. . . . It provides incentives for family breakup. In most cases two-parent families are not eligible for cash assistance and, therefore, a working father often can increase his family's income by leaving home . . . it discourages work. . . .

That this could be said of a plan instituted to provide financial assistance to widows and orphans, demonstrates how the splendid intentions of its originators had been prostituted to serve purposes they would have despised and rejected. For more than two decades now, ADC has not only been the most controversial public assistance program, it has come to epitomize everything that has gone wrong with welfare and turned it into a cancerous growth, not just because of its cost but because of its destructive impact on society. It has managed to arouse the ire of the ideological and political left as well as the right and continues to exist only because the two sides have been unable to agree on an acceptable replacement. Numerous attempts at improving the program by patching it up made it worse and overall reform failed every time it was proposed, because the ideological chasm—and vested interests—prevented a compromise.

E. Uhr of the University of Wisconsin's Institute for Research on Poverty recently described some of ADC's shortcomings:

> This system for providing support for children in one-parent families does not do what it was intended to do: namely furnish a reasonable

standard of living for children in a household headed by a single parent. And it does do a number of things that were not the intent of those who framed it, such as encourage the dissolution of families, aid and abet those who wish to evade economic responsibility for their children, discourage single custodial parents (in more than nine cases out of ten, women) from seeking employment, and enforce the collection of child support more stringently for those least able to pay.[38]

From its origin and for a long time after, ADC was regarded to be an interim program to bridge the time until social security coverage became universal. Testified federal security commissioner Arthur J. Altmeyer in February 1947:

> So, if we had the coverage of the old-age and survivors insurance system which include the whole working population—farmers and farm laborers particularly—we would find that our old-age assistance rolls and our aid-to-dependent-children rolls would decline rapidly [House Appropriations Committee hearings, *Labor—Federal Security Appropriations Bill*, 1948, p. 603].

Old-age assistance rolls gradually declined, though very slowly after the federal takeover by federal SSI (supplemental security income) in 1974.

There were in 1947, 1,060,000 children on ADC, largely orphans and children of disabled fathers, and in 1950, when extensions of social security coverage were enacted, 1,661,000.

In 1977, at the time of the last ADC survey, there were close to 200,000 children on ADC rolls whose father had died, 450,000 whose father was disabled, 380,000 whose father was unemployed. That seems to bear out Mr. Altmeyer's prediction in 1947, that the rolls would decline.

But the number of recipients of ADC—which by then had been renamed AFDC (Aid to Families with Dependent Children)—totaled more than 10 million in 1978. Children whose father was dead, disabled or unemployed were then largely supported by old age and survivors insurance and unemployment insurance. Most of the children in that situation had moved off the ADC rolls in the early 1950s. But another group of children moved in for whom ADC had not been intended nor designed when the program was approved by Congress in 1935.

In 1978, 85% of the children on AFDC were on the rolls because their parents would not support them. Nor did they have to, because ADC had been turned into a convenient alternative for fathers who do not want to pay for their children and for mothers who have little incentive to go to work as long as the presence of children gives them a meal ticket that compares favorably with what most of them could earn by the sweat of their brow.

Between 1952 and 1978

the number of children under 18 in the U.S.A. increased	26%
the number of children on AFDC increased	383%
the number of adults on AFDC increased	530%

POPULATION UNDER 18 YEARS IN THE POPULATION AND ON AFDC, 1952 AND 1978

	Population under 18 years	Children on AFDC	Percent
1952	50,271,000	1,495,000	3.0%
1978	63,376,000	7,226,000	11.4%

SOURCES: *Historical Statistics of the United States, Colonial Times to 1970*, U.S. Bureau of the Census, 1975; *Statistical Abstract of the United States, 1979*, U.S. Bureau of the Census; and *Social Security Bulletin*, Department of HEW, December 1979.

In 1952 there was one child on ADC for every 33.6 children under 18 in the population, in 1978 there was one child on AFDC for 8.8 children under 18, although employment, incomes and economic well-being had simultaneously substantially improved. About 6.5 million children were on AFDC in 1977 whose fathers were reported to be "absent." One-fourth of the parents were divorced, nearly one-third of the fathers had left without a divorce and two-fifths of the fathers had never been married to the mother and had "moved out."

About half a million adults were on ADC rolls in 1952, 3.3 million in 1978. But the number of adult beneficiaries was actually much larger. A woman on AFDC with a sizable government check coming in regularly every month is highly regarded and sought after in her circles. Many a father leaves his family—thus making it eligible for AFDC—to move in with another AFDC mother for whose children he is not responsible and then lives off her AFDC check plus whatever else he makes. That leaves everybody better off financially—except the taxpayer. No attempt has been made by welfare agencies to ascertain the extent of this musical chairs operation.

The congressional Joint Economic Committee had a nationwide study conducted by its staff in 1974 which concluded that AFDC and related welfare programs encourage family breakup and childbearing and offer a disincentive to work. Here are some of the report's findings:

Does Welfare Encourage Family Breakup?

This analysis found sizable financial incentives for family-splitting; the amounts generally exceed the extra costs of maintaining separate households. Weighted by AFDC caseload, the county figures revealed these national income differentials:

If an unemployed father deserted, the average gain in cash and food benefits varied from $1,004 for the one-child families to $1,318 for families with three children, a gain of about one-third in family income;

If the deserting father worked full time at $2 an hour, the average gain ranged from $1,806 to $2,358, a gain of nearly one-half in family income;

Adding in housing benefits raised these averages by as much as $400; and

If medicaid were counted, many of the female-headed families would become newly eligible for free health care after the fathers left home, adding another several hundred dollars to the gain from splitting.

Since the above figures are national averages, the family-splitting incentive in specific situations can be lower, or it can run much higher. . . .

Does Welfare Encourage Motherhood?

The county data show a sizable financial incentive for a woman to have her first child in order to receive AFDC and medicaid benefits. The gain, both relatively and absolutely, declines for subsequent children, although the childbearing incentive for a middle-aged woman whose youngest child is age 18 or over is the same as that for a woman having her first child. The county data, when weighted for AFDC caseload size, show the following:

An unemployed, childless woman can almost double her benefits with an additional $1,159 in cash and food benefits by having her first child;

Adding in the value of public housing raises her gain to $1,447 on average, and medicaid would add nearly $400 more based on the cost of the care provided;

If this woman has a second child, the average gain in cash and food benefits is $756, an increase in income of 31 percent; and

The average gain for having a third child is $628, which is a 20 percent rise in cash and food benefits. . . .

How Much Incentive Is There to Work?

Since welfare benefits must be reduced in some way when recipients go to work, the return from working is measured by subtracting from wages the taxes paid, the expenses incurred because of work, and the welfare benefits lost. It has long been argued that this net gain from working is quite small and is, therefore, a factor in recipients' decisions about whether to work or how much to work.

The belief that work disincentives are high is supported by this study. Weighted by the AFDC caseload distribution, the county data show the following:

Due to the way income is counted, AFDC and food stamp benefits do not decline very rapidly as earnings rise, but net income left after work expenses for working mothers on AFDC and food stamps averages as little as 20 cents per dollar earned;

For such women who live in public housing, the average gain drops to as low as 11 cents for some cases;

For cases ineligible for regular AFDC benefits, other benefit losses, coupled with taxes and work expenses, hold down the net return from each dollar earned. Average gains run around 30 cents for singles and couples, 33 cents for two-parent families on AFDC-UF [unemployed fathers], and 50 cents for two-parent families in non-UF States; and

Fathers on AFDC-UF who go to work full time at the old ($1.60) or new ($2.00) minimum wage face net losses in discretionary income, because the AFDC benefits lost generally exceed the smaller net wage. A man with a wife and three children who finds a full-time job at $1.60 an hour has an after-tax income of $3,034, but loses AFDC-UF benefits of $3,840 a year in San Francisco and $3,588 in Portland, Ore.

The most striking of these findings is that low-wage workers now excluded from AFDC still may face high disincentives to work due to the combination of taxes, work expenses, and benefits lost from GA [general assistance], food, and housing programs. In fact, taxes alone averaged 14 percent of wages for single people earning $4,000 a year, and 10 percent for couples with no children.[39]

The abandonment of parental responsibility for children, beginning in the 1950s, is a phenomenon without parallel or precedence. "Throughout most of history," Daniel P. Moynihan wrote, "a man who deserted his children pretty much ensured that they would starve, or near to it, if he was not brought back, and that he would be horsewhipped if he were." Earlier he said: "The poor of the United States today enjoy a quite unprecedented de facto freedom to abandon their children in the certain knowledge that society will care for them and, what is more, in a state such as New York, to care for them by quite decent standards."[40] Welfare and food stamp benefits for a family of four averaged $544 a month in New York in 1979. Distribution among all states was as follows:

$500 and up	11 states
$400 to $500	23 states
$295 to $400	16 states

Mississippi with $295 was the lowest state, Hawaii with $657 the highest.

An AFDC mother, whether married to her child's father or not, whether she had agreed to the separation or divorce—or had demanded it—or not, often prefers getting a dependable monthly check from AFDC than having to wait, often in vain, for a smaller check from the children's father. In many cases she is now getting more money from the government than she was ever able to get out of him. Why should she help to locate, apprehend and prosecute him? It is a lot easier and less trouble to get money from AFDC than from a recalcitrant man with low earning capacity.

It has correctly been said that putting a father in jail does not give his family much money. But making nonsupport a federal offense and imposing a prison sentence on nonsupporting fathers, suspended during "good behavior," might work wonders—even on fathers who have not yet been found or are now only *thinking* about playing a game of musical chairs.

It is undoubtedly true that many men, particularly those with low occupational skills, have difficulty landing and keeping a job. But individual efforts play a significant role. That is why, in November 1980, married men, 20 to 64 years old, with spouse present, had an unemployment rate of 3.9%; divorced, separated, widowed or single men a rate of 10.9%.

Welfare agencies and social workers also contribute to parental desertion. They feel that their loyalty belongs to the needy family, not to the taxpayer. They show little sympathy with efforts to reduce public assistance rolls. An HEW official and leader in the social work profession wrote in 1962: "Caseworkers who are caught up in the child's need, or what they regard as the mother's best interests, on occasion advise women to get rid of their men."[41]

It seems that for families in the lower half of the socioeconomic scale, family breakup usually leads to AFDC dependency. For almost half of all fathers, family breakup may mean liberation from having to devote a sizable share of their earnings to the support of their families. While male-headed families grew 20% between 1960 and 1978, female-headed families grew 83%. Women now head a fourth of all households.

Under the original ADC concept which focused primarily on children of deceased or disabled fathers, most of today's AFDC cases would have had to seek relief through the general assistance program (GA). That was indeed the case in the early years, but admission practices changed decisively in the 1950s. Welfare applicants never liked GA—if there was an alternative—because its benefits are austere and intended to be temporary. AFDC grants are more generous, can go on forever and, what weighs heavily with welfare departments, they are partially or largely paid from federal funds, while GA outlays must be paid entirely from state and local taxes.

For obvious reasons, state officials prefer welfare recipients to be on AFDC rather than GA. The federal government reimburses states for 50% to 83% of their AFDC outlays, with no upper limit. Spending 17-cent dollars—or up to 50-cent dollars—locally (with the rest coming from the federal treasury) is popular and may be politically rewarding. At the federal level, AFDC is one of the "uncontrollable" items in the U.S. Budget and not limited by prior congressional appropriations. That makes everybody happy—except officials responsible for federal fiscal operations.

From Welfare to Workfare?

Multiplying AFDC costs generated growing concern in Congress and the White House and spawned thoughts of trying to get people to work so as to "get them off the rolls." Most of those ideas were not exactly novel and dated back four centuries to the Elizabethan poor laws and beyond.

Franklin Roosevelt wrote to Col. Edward M. House in November 1934, while social security was being readied: "What I am seeking is the abolition of relief altogether. I cannot say so out loud yet, but I hope to be able to substitute work for relief." The president warned in his 1935 State of the Union message that "continued dependence on relief induces a spiritual and moral disintegration fundamentally destructive to the national fibre" and declared: "The federal government must and shall quit this business of relief." On signing the 1935 Social Security Act he verbalized a vision: "I can now see the end of public assistance in America." That suggests, with the benefit of hindsight, that FDR must have been able to see much farther ahead than we can now, nearly half a century later. It would be a rash man indeed who would today dare predict the end of public assistance in America.

When public assistance rolls expanded through the 1950s into the 1960s, President Kennedy submitted to Congress early in 1962 proposals intended to reverse the trend. On signing on July 26, 1962, a bill "shifting the emphasis of the nation's welfare program for the needy from the dole to rehabilitation," the president said that it "makes possible the most far-reaching revision of the public welfare program since it was enacted in 1935. This measure embodies a new approach—stressing services in addition to support, rehabilitation instead of relief, and training for useful work instead of prolonged dependency. . . . Our objective is to prevent or reduce dependency and to encourage self-care and self-support—to maintain family life where it is adequate and to restore it where it is deficient."

Shortly after, on September 21, 1962, I addressed the National Legislative Conference of the Council of State Governments and predicted that ADC rolls which were then approaching 3 million "may exceed 4 million by 1970, and could run close to 5 million, if present trends continue."[42] I was way off. AFDC rolls ran close to 10 million in 1970. This was the harvest of some of the "reforms" inflicted upon welfare during the 1960s.

Soon after President Kennedy's recommendations were put into effect, President Johnson, in his first State of the Union address, declared an *unconditional War on Poverty*—which meant more welfare "reforms." On signing the *Economic Opportunity Act of 1964*, President Johnson issued a statement:

> We are not content to accept the endless growth of relief or welfare rolls. We want to offer the forgotten fifth of our people opportunity and not doles. This is what this measure does for our times. . . .
>
> *The days of the dole in our country are numbered.* I firmly believe that as of this moment a new day of opportunity is dawning and a new era of progress is opening for us all. [Emphasis supplied.]

The similarity of this statement to Franklin Roosevelt's in 1934 is no more surprising than the fact that nothing had been learned from the experience of the intervening thirty years. Over two million recipients were added to AFDC rolls during Mr. Johnson's incumbency. The rolls more than tripled in the 1960s and their growth rate showed no sign of slowing down.

On August 11, 1969, President Nixon presented new proposals and declared in a message:

> The present welfare system has failed us—it has fostered family breakup, has provided very little help in many states, and has even deepened dependency by all too often making it more attractive to go on welfare than go to work.
>
> I propose a new approach that will make it more attractive to go to

work than to go on welfare, and will establish a nationwide minimum payment to dependent families with children. . . .

This would be total welfare reform—the transformation of a system frozen in failure and frustration into a system that would work and would encourage people to work. . . .

For the first time, the more than 2 million families who make up the working poor would be helped toward self-sufficiency and away from future welfare dependency.

For the first time, training and work opportunity with effective incentives would be given millions of families who would otherwise be locked into a welfare system for generations. . . .

For the first time, every dependent family in America would be encouraged to stay together, free from economic pressure to split apart.

When the 91st and 92d Congress failed to pass Mr. Nixon's proposals, President Carter prepared a similar plan and stated in his accompanying message of August 6, 1977:

As I pledged during my campaign for the presidency, I am asking the Congress to abolish our existing welfare system, and replace it with a job-oriented program for those able to work and a simplified, uniform, equitable cash assistance program for those in need who are unable to work. . . .

This new program will accomplish the following:

Dramatically reduce reliance on welfare payments. . . .

Ensure that work will always be more profitable than welfare. . . .

. . . combine effective work requirements and strong work incentives with improved private sector placement services and create up to 1.4 million public service jobs. . . .

Mr. Carter's proposals were not adopted by the 95th Congress and, when resubmitted in a scaled-down version, fared no better in the 96th Congress.

Welfare Reform—for Better or for Worse?

Numerous sincere efforts by presidents from Franklin Roosevelt to Jimmy Carter to shift *from welfare to workfare*, as John Kennedy expressed it, went to naught. Some of the policies and practices that were adopted turned out to have counterproductive consequences and other proposals were rejected by Congress because they would have had effects that were worse—some of them far worse—than AFDC they were intended to replace.

One example of a "reform" that was carried out: In February 1961 President Kennedy recommended that needy children of unemployed fathers (UF) should be included in ADC so as to make it unnecessary for their fathers to abscond (AFDC-UF). The idea was quickly approved by Congress and 26 states adopted the AFDC-UF program. The results between 1960 and 1971:

> In the 26 states in which children of unemployed fathers were eligible (not counting the children on the rolls for reasons of father's unemployment):
> the rolls increased by 3,107,000 children or 229%
>
> In the 24 states which had *not* adopted AFDC-UF:
> the rolls increased by 1,354,000 children or 133%.

Evidence suggests that fathers left their families in larger numbers at an accelerated rate in the states where unemployment made their families eligible for AFDC. Why? Because desertion often is more lucrative than nondesertion, even with AFDC-UF.

The outstanding example of proposals that were not adopted are the guaranteed income plans by Presidents Nixon and Carter. Lyndon Johnson rejected the idea though it was strongly suggested to him, but Richard Nixon was persuaded by Daniel P. Moynihan, who then coordinated urban affairs at the White House, to adopt it. It would, Nixon was told, win him wide public support and favorable editorials in the liberal press, as, in fact, it did—temporarily. Together with some of my colleagues on the White House domestic staff, I opposed the idea but was overruled. The president recommended the "Family Assistance Plan" (FAP) to Congress in August 1969.

The House passed FAP in the 91st and 92d Congress. When the bill was under consideration in the Senate Finance Committee, I was invited to testify which I did on January 27, 1972.[43] (I had meanwhile returned to Stanford.) News media were confidently predicting at the time that FAP would be on the statute books by spring. As it happened, the bill was dead by April.

I told the committee my reasons for opposing a guaranteed annual income. Proof of need that stems from objectively determinable and verifiable causes, which are not readily subject to manipulation, such as old age, disability, death or incapacity of the breadwinner, should continue to be a requirement for federal income support:

> A national system of public assistance that disregards the causes of dependence and offers benefits comparable to low-skill wages is bound to grow without limit. It is a permanent and irresistible invitation to abuse

and ruin. In most AFDC cases the cause of need is not economic but social and requires individual consideration and judgment which are impossible under a national uniform program.

Persons with a low productive capacity can, by doing the type of work they are capable of, seldom net more from working than they can from public welfare benefits. That has been proven true under AFDC. A guaranteed annual income would extend the option of workless pay to far larger numbers. It would abolish, at one blow, labor supply for low-skilled work. The need for that labor would then have to be met increasingly, as it already is in part, by the importation of foreign workers, mostly from countries to our south, to whom even our lowest wage rates and benefits appear to be wealth and prosperity.

The proponents of a guaranteed annual income denied that it would have work-disincentive effects and asserted that, above all, it would end the family-disruptive impact of AFDC. They were in for a rude shock. A massive multiyear social experiment was undertaken to disprove the assertion that a guaranteed annual income would produce negative results. When the findings of the Seattle-Denver project were in—after the Nixon and Carter proposals had already been buried—they showed that marital breakups multiplied and work effort diminished under a guaranteed annual income plan. Both men and women worked substantially fewer hours. So the research project backfired on its sponsors with a vengeance, as did the Coleman report on equality of opportunity in education (see pp. 185–86).

Some of the keenest and most knowledgeable minds in the field have devoted an extraordinary amount of time and effort to devise a formula for guaranteed annual income that would meet three essential requirements: to furnish a minimum adequate subsistence, keep cost at a politically tolerable level and provide sufficient incentive to work. My colleague—at the Hoover Institution and on the White House staff—Martin Anderson, has analyzed this problem probably more thoroughly than anybody else. He concluded:

It is impossible to change any of these three main variables without affecting the others. . . .

When any two of the three basic elements of radical welfare reform are set at politically acceptable levels, the remaining element becomes unacceptable. . . .

There is no way to achieve all the politically necessary conditions for radical welfare reform at the same time.[44]

An essential and prominently featured part of the many attempts at welfare reform in recent decades has been dozens of manpower programs, piled on top of each other. Most of them provide occupational training for welfare recipients, require registration for job openings, acceptance of "suitable" jobs, distribute subsidies to workers and employers. Some of the programs created millions of governmental jobs, usually at state and local levels, so that federal employment could be kept low (which is politically more desirable).

After a decade of experience with a large number of manpower programs, the congressional Joint Economic Committee had its staff examine the better and more recent studies "for particular insights into the impact of training on low income and disadvantaged persons."

The report found:

> Manpower programs have been oversold in the past, fostering the illusion that they would (1) eliminate unemployment. . . . (2) mitigate the severity of the inflation-unemployment trade-off by increasing the productivity and the occupational and geographic mobility of the low-income population, and (3) reduce the duration of unemployment experienced by those displaced by automation.

In the five programs examined (Manpower Development and Training Act [MDTA], Neighborhood Youth Corps [NYC], Job Corps [JC], Job Opportunities in the Business Sector [JOBS], and the Work Incentive Program [WIN], the "evidence was mixed . . . the caliber of research is extremely poor . . . conclusions are not encouraging . . . it is precarious to generalize findings. . . . Some training programs are expensive and the costs exceed the benefits. . . ."[45]

It concluded: "The robust expenditures for research and evaluation of training programs ($179.4 million from fiscal 1962 through 1972) are a disturbing contrast to the anemic set of conclusive and reliable findings."

What this all means—if we remove the Washington gobbledygook—is that the programs failed and that even expensive evaluation attempts were unable to identify positive results for the many billions of expenditure. But . . . the programs were expanded, new ones added—and more were being proposed in 1980.

Why does it seem so impossible to shift from *welfare* to *workfare*? Because available jobs call for skills welfare recipients do not possess? If so, why did occupational training of "hard-to-place" people prove so ineffective? Do people lack occupational skills necessarily only because there were few books in their parents' home, or the building they attended school in was too old, or their school classes did not have the desired color mix?

Are there no unskilled or low-skilled jobs available? Why has the number of domestic service workers steadily declined, from several million to less than a million in the 1970s? Not because there are no jobs but because most people won't take them. In 1976 59% of all domestic service workers were 50 years or over and 75% were 40 or over. Why? Because it is not easy to qualify oneself for AFDC at an advanced age. At a child-bearing age there are options which are far more attractive than domestic service and similar "menial" jobs. Illegitimate births jumped from 4% of all births in 1950 to 16% in 1977. We send more of our young women—and men—through college than any other country. But then we force our university-educated women and men for the rest of their lives to spend uncounted hours on cleaning and similar low-skilled work instead of de-voting more time to professional or other high-skill activities—and we force them to pay taxes to keep others in leisure.

How do the five to eight million "undocumented" aliens, who are estimated to be in the United States illegally, support themselves? The answer to that is evident: By working, because Americans won't take the type of jobs with which Chicanos earn their bread. That's why the United States does not enforce its immigration laws and pays welfare and un-employment benefits to millions of Americans.

At a congressional hearing a senator asked me: "Don't you agree that most people would rather work than take welfare?" to which I replied: "Yes, Senator, I believe that most people prefer to work. In fact, most people *do* work to support themselves and their families. Only a small minority does not. Most people do not commit burglary, robbery or murder, and would not do so even if committing such felonies would not put them into prison." But some people *do* commit robbery, burglary or murder despite the risk. That is why we have to enforce the law against those who would not abide by essential standards of conduct unless threat-ened with dire consequences.

Persons with low earning capacity have little to gain by working—as long as we are willing to supply them with sustenance for which they do not have to work. That is why I believe that everybody who claims public benefits—except those who are physically or mentally totally incapacited (and are covered by disability or similar programs)—should be required to work. Their output may be worth little. But persons who are willing to work several hours each day can thereby prove the legitimacy of their need. We would then need no means tests—which are loathed by all, open to widespread fraud and very costly to administer.

We forget too easily that the *work ethic*, though now widely recog-nized in the United States, is a concept that dates back only a few centu-ries—according to Max Weber, to the time of the Reformation. Working by "the sweat of one's brow" was imposed on mankind as *punishment* for disobeying God's command, in the Book of Genesis, it was not instituted as a desirable way to live. A world in which daily toil is not required is generally called *Paradise*. Small wonder that many people in this world regard work as a curse, a hated necessity that should be avoided whenever possible. Of course, mankind could not survive unless most people worked. Therefore work is required, even in a welfare state.

A work requirement for persons able to work, if strictly enforced rather than purely on paper, can have a distinct impact on a welfare program. When Governor Reagan of California established a work requirement for AFDC in 1971—and had enough political pull in Washington to get a temporary exemption from the general ban on work relief—results were remarkable: ADFC rolls dropped by 342,000 between March 1971 and June 1974. The number of recipients *declined* by 21% in California and *nationally increased by 6%* in the same time period. As Reagan's welfare administrator, Charles D. Hobbs, described the reform, it made welfare "an unattractive alternative to work for able-bodied recipients."[46]

Lower benefits also make welfare less attractive. The nationwide rapid increase in AFDC rolls, described earlier, slowed down to a crawl in the 1970s and finally turned negative: the number of recipients *declined* by 760,000 between December 1975 and May 1980. Why? Because AFDC benefits—in contrast to social security—are not indexed to prices and the average AFDC grant per family declined in *constant* dollars 14% over the same period. That is why some of the "marginal" AFDC recipients (or potentials) no longer found welfare sufficiently lucrative and chose the otherwise less desirable alternative of working.

Nowadays we would not describe this phenomenon in the terms which the commissioners of the English Poor Laws of 1834 used nearly a century and a half ago: "Every penny bestowed that tends to render the condition of the pauper more eligible than that of the independent labourer outside is a bounty on indolence and vice." But human response to economic alternatives does not seem to have changed much. Unfortunately it is still necessary to make life on the dole "uncomfortable."

One study found that female AFDC recipients are less likely to remarry than other women, which may be due to a cool evaluation of relative economic advantages.[47]

On last count 93% of AFDC children lived with their mothers. It may thus be worthwhile to review the female employment situation. The labor force participation rate of women has steadily grown for decades, from 34.8% of the female population 16 years and over in 1952, to 51.9% in January 1981. Men's labor force participation rate meanwhile declined from 87.2% to 77.6%. Most persons not in the labor force, are in the under-22 group and completing their education or in the 65-and-over group and beyond normal working years.

In March 1979, the latest month for which these data are available, the majority of American women with children under 18 were in the labor force.

The following percentages of women were in the labor force:

49.4% of married women whose husband was present

58.8% of married women whose husband was absent

74.0% of divorced women

61.6% of women with children 6 to 17 years

45.5% of women with children under 6

Among women who *headed* a household (no husband present)

48.8% of women with no children under 18 (up from 45.8% in 1970)

56.1% of women with children under 6 (up from 46.9% in 1970)

71.6% of women with children 6 to 17 (up from 67.0% in 1970).[48]

In 1970 55% of women who headed a household and had children under 18 were members of the labor force; by 1979, participation had gone up to 62%. In other words, nearly two-thirds of the women who maintain a family and have children, work. Why does the other one-third not work?

Some of them are in comfortable economic circumstances and prefer other activities or leisure. But the majority are women with low occupational skills who are making the rational economic choice of not working or seeking a job which would yield them little more, if any, than they are getting from government without working.

As divorce laws and court practices have developed in recent years, "increasingly housewives are assigned no more than temporary maintenance payments to tide them over until they get an education or a job."[49] Nowadays, most divorcees within a reasonable time after the breakup provide their own support and part of their children's by working. Why should those of low skills and drive be kept at leisure indefinitely at taxpayers' expense while much work they could do remains undone or must be performed by persons with higher skills and potential who are already on full-time jobs?

The men and women on welfare certainly are not to be blamed for being "on the dole." It is our representatives in Congress who are responsible for the perversity of skilled working persons having to spend many hours on simple menial tasks, while unskilled people are kept in idleness. Federal officials are responsible for permitting millions of illegal immigrants to occupy jobs that should be available to Americans—who at present, understandably, prefer workless pay to stoop labor. Does someone who has no skill that would justify more than minimum subsistence wages for dirty work have an inherent claim of being supported at leisure by the taxes of hardworking people?

The Soviet Union follows more reasonable principles in giving no welfare payments to able-bodied persons. Anybody who cannot find a job on his own is entitled to being assigned work by a labor exchange at a pay of 70 rubles (about $100) a month. This is why streets and subways and other places are sparklingly clean in Russian cities, in stark contrast to the filthy condition of American cities. It also is why most persons in the Soviet Union prefer to find a job rather than be assigned minimum-level work. Female labor force participation in the Soviet Union is even higher than in the United States. Which causes some, but not insuperable, problems with children.

The claim that children need their mothers at all times is a myth that should have been buried decades ago. In a feature article on "The Superwoman Squeeze" *Newsweek* (May 19, 1980) summed it up: "Most child experts seem to agree with Cornell University psychologist Urie Bronfenbrenner 'that there is no hard evidence that day care has a negative effect.'"

Does day care necessarily have to be found in government day care centers where highly trained and well-paid specialists babysit so that unskilled mothers can work at low-paying jobs? Is there any reason why a woman while babysitting with her own children cannot supervise the children of other mothers in the hours during which the mothers are at work? This could be that woman's job for which she is entitled to be compensated.

How can the problem posed by AFDC be resolved? Certainly not by replacing AFDC with a guaranteed annual income program.

1. Both parents, if able-bodied, should be held responsible for the support of their children. Government may have to intervene if a minority of parents will not or cannot fulfill their natural duty. Government may have to support some children or contribute to their support, just as in the case of parentless children it has to make alternative arrangements.

Parents who claim to be unable to find a job or to support their children, will have to perform government-assigned work, with most of their compensation, except for a truly austere minimum, withheld to pay for the cost of maintaining their children. Failure to support should be made a federal offense for both parents.

2. Decisions on whether parents should be required to work—or be partially or wholly exempted because of personal impairment—should be

made locally. The necessary judgment in each individual case cannot be exercised under a national program with uniform standards. The citizens of each community should be able to set the standards by which they wish to support their needy neighbors. Sound judgment on any kind of public expenditure can be arrived at only if the same group of officials is responsible for decisions on spending and on raising the necessary funds by taxation. This does not rule out federal financial assistance, provided that it is allocated by objective formulas that consider population size and economic condition. It cannot be done fairly, as AFDC has taught us, by reimbursing local expenditures through open-ended federal appropriations. This plan is fully consonant with the design of the architects of our welfare structure in 1934–35. The system could be as sound today as it seemed nearly half a century ago.

Is it politically possible? AFDC certainly has lost much support and numerous public opinions polls identify welfare as the respondents' first choice for government expenditure cutbacks. That Congress has withstood pressure to tie AFDC benefits to the Consumers Price Index—as it has most other programs—is a clear sign of a change of sentiment there. Attitudes toward welfare spending at the top levels of government are not what they were a decade or two ago. Whether that makes a return to the principles of the economic security plan of 1935 possible, remains to be seen.

How Secure Is Social Security?

Compared with storm-tossed, turmoil-embroiled public welfare, social security towers like an island surrounded by surf which is trying to gnaw at its base. As social security approaches its fiftieth anniversary in the United States—and its hundredth in major European countries—it has become one of the most successful governmental institutions, firmly rooted in the conscience of the public, certain to survive in its major aspects for as far ahead as we can see. Nine out of ten workers now contribute toward it, one in seven Americans is getting monthly benefits and the rest are looking forward—eagerly or with mixed feelings—to the day when they will be getting their regular retirement checks.

This wide sharing of the current load among almost all income earners—with half of it disguised as a tax on business—combined with a relative concentration of its emoluments on a far smaller group, enabled the system to be increasingly generous toward recipients without becoming overly burdensome on its contributors. Social security contributions have been growing at a faster rate than other taxes and now account for over one-fourth of federal budget receipts. Though a majority of Americans probably pay more in social security taxes than in income taxes, there have been fewer outcries about the burden of social security taxes than about income or property taxes.

The statute that limits outgo to income has kept the system in balance and restrained Congress' ingrained proclivity toward liberalized spending from exceeding its willingness to accept political responsibility for boosting taxes. Repeated suggestions to tap the general budget for social security purposes have failed. The absence of spending restraints on the U.S. budget has permitted the buildup of deficits in general federal operations to a public debt which is now approaching $1 trillion. Social security by comparison appears better managed and protected against financial excess or adventurism. Occasional shrill publicity that the social security system is moving toward bankruptcy because it has built up four or five trillion dollars in obligations which are backed by no solid assets, is more alarmist than alarming. There is no sensible way in which reserve funds of that magnitude could have been accumulated or invested.

While the United States government let the dollar's value slide to sixteen cents over the past four decades with little more than oratorical counteraction, no Congress and no president could politically survive if they let social security go bankrupt. It seems that wide sections of the public are more concerned about keeping the safety and value of social security than about keeping the value of the dollar, although Americans have huge amounts of dollar assets whose value continues to shrink. Maybe it is simply that they don't know how to stop inflation but do know how to keep social security solvent.

The system's security rests on the confidence of the American people, on the certainty that the economically active population will in the future, as it has in the past, provide the necessary funds. The working generation knows that it has to go on supporting its elders and will not abandon them. It prefers to do this through a universal system and will not go back to the former way of each child or set of children paying individually for the sustenance of their own parents whose working years have ended. Above all, members of the working generation prefer to believe that by having a goodly share of their current earnings withheld, they are providing security for their own old age.

The belief that each worker is saving for his later years by social security contributions is one of the myths we live by. Wage deductions are not individual savings, accumulating with interest to be drawn on in later years. They are intergenerational transfer payments by which, in a pay-as-you-go system, the young generation provides for its aged parents' needs. The working generation, of course, hopes and confidently expects that its own children will do likewise when the time comes. That children take care of their aged parents has been a precept of mankind from times immemorial. Current OASI pensioners receive several times as much as a straight annuity of their contributions including interest would yield—according to one estimate they now get, on the average, about five times as much. This obviously cannot continue forever and a sustainable balance between contributions and benefits will gradually have to develop.

Why should these intergovernmental transfers be made by governmental compulsion, some ask, why through a social security system that is full of inequities and waste? Why not let it be done voluntarily, as each family chooses to do in its own way?

What would happen in the absence of compulsion? Most earners would make provisions for their own old age by savings and investments, while they still can. But many would not—whether because they are improvident, or meet with misfortune of one kind or another, or never earn much to save by their own will. Today's society will not let them—or their surviving dependents—starve. Why then should the provident, who save for their own old age, also have to pay for others who are improvident? There is no way in which those who lack the necessary self-discipline can be forced to make provisions for their old age during their active years, except by governmental compulsion. Universal coverage is therefore a necessity.

Social security outlays are governed by eligibility and benefit provisions in the law and not subject to annual appropriations. This means that they are not controlled by the federal budget process. Therefore, costs must be carefully watched and projected for years—and decades—in advance, so that warning signals are flashed early enough to permit the adoption of corrective measures, on the expenditure as well as on the revenue side.

When it became obvious in the mid-1970s that projected revenues were running short of requirements, Congress passed a bill in December 1977 boosting social security taxes by $227 billion over the succeeding 10-year period. This was thought to be sufficient to meet needs to the end of the century. But reports soon indicated that spending was outrunning projections. The trust fund of old age and survivors insurance (OASI) dropped from $40 billion in 1975 to $31 billion in 1978, then fell to $24.6 billion in September 1980, equal to two and a half months benefits. At that rate the fund would run dry sometime in 1982 or 1983 and be unable to meet its obligations. This cannot be allowed to happen. Either revenues must be increased—by again raising social security taxes or by creating new sources—or by reducing benefits. To reverse the trend of evermore generous benefits will not be easy.

Outlays are controlled by various factors, the broadest of which are demographic and labor force trends. Between 1978 and the turn of the century the 65-and-over population is expected to grow by one-third, the working-age population by only one-fifth. Labor force participation rates have been rising for women but declining for men, with no sign, so far, of a change. The social security tax rate is scheduled to rise from 13.3% (for employer and employee combined) in 1981 to 15.3% in 1990 and then remain even. That will not be enough, from present indications. At least 16.0% may be required before the year 2000, and substantially more a few years after.

From about 2010 on, the age cohort of the postwar baby boom—birth years 1945 to the 1960s—will turn 65 and swell the aged population by more than one-half over the succeeding fifteen years. While there were about three contributors to one beneficiary in 1980, there will be only two contributors for each retired beneficiary by the year 2025. This means that, other circumstances even, each contributor's load will go up by about one-half. The tax rate would have to double, from 13.3% in 1981 to about 24% or more of gross wages in 2025. This is heavy but not necessarily unbearable. In some European countries, social security tax rates are already close to the 25% level. The time when social security taxes may require about one-fourth of a worker's wage in the United States is still about three decades ahead, with more moderate increases sufficient in the meantime. But a drastic tax boost will be required around the year 2010, unless eligibility and benefits are adjusted downward or new taxes employed for social security purposes. With income taxes already overburdened—unable to raise enough revenue for current budget purposes—and widespread demands for income tax cuts, a value-added tax (VAT) is the most likely candidate.

The use of a new tax source would weaken or eliminate restraint and fiscal discipline, which the architects of our social security system wisely built into its structure. Also, there is no evidence, to my knowledge, that the American public is more willing to accept the imposition of a value-added tax than a boost in social security taxes. It may thus be advisable to explore possibilities of staying *within* projected revenues of social security taxes, at rates which workers are willing to pay. It could be accomplished by controlling the number of beneficiaries and the size of benefits.

A long period of steady expansion of social security benefits appears to be coming to an end, not only in the United States but also in Europe. "Social security systems are now entering a difficult period of painful adjustments in which finances and benefits will have to be closely scrutinized and carefully balanced," wrote social security commissioner Stanford G. Ross in a worldwide review in 1979 (see pp. 111–12).

Social security's benefit structure is very complicated because it is intended to serve several disparate purposes. Primarily, the benefits are intergenerational transfer payments from the working to the no-longer-working population (and its dependents and survivors) to the tune of over $100 billion a year, equal to more than 5% of all personal income. System spokesmen try to stress contributions-related benefits, so as to assure contributors of *individual equity*. That helps to boost wide acceptance and support.

Another aspect is *social adequacy*, that is, payment of an existence minimum to persons who for whatever reason did not acquire sufficient credits for a comfortable level of benefits. It has become the dominant factor.

Benefits are computed (as of 1981) as 90% of the monthly earnings base up to $211, 32% of the next $1068 and 15% of all taxable earnings beyond. That is an extremely "progressive," and income-redistributive formula. Persons at low earnings levels get six times as much, in relation to the taxes they paid, as do persons in high brackets. No insurance system could so operate, without compulsion.

In an excellent discussion of social security issues Stanford economics professor Michael Boskin proposed to gradually separate the transfer and annuity goals—or the insurance and welfare aspects of the benefit structure.[50] James M. Buchanan, economics professor at Virginia Polytechnic Institute suggested this some years earlier.[51] That would greatly clarify and simplify the system. The welfare part could then be taken care of through the supplemental security income (SSI) program while social security could be largely or wholly contributions-related. But this proposal will certainly run into heavy opposition from those who prefer the welfare part of a social program to be hidden from sight by combining it with benefits which accrue to the middle class.

At this time, very few persons know much if anything about the skewed benefit formula. Most workers believe—and prefer to believe—that they are getting benefits in proportion to their contributions. If the welfare part of social security were separated from the insurance part, for example through SSI, low-income earners might find it more difficult to be as generously supported as they are through social security.

Monthly social security benefits have multiplied two-and-a-half-fold in *constant* dollars since 1940, as the table below shows.

Congress raised benefits at frequent intervals, preferably in even-numbered years, yielding to insistent complaints about economic hardships of the aged population. The assertion that all, or most, aged persons live in poverty and misery was demonstrated to be a myth by Alvin Rabushka and Bruce Jacobs in *Old Folks at Home*.[52] But millions of older men and women undoubtedly have a hard time getting by, especially in inflationary times.

MONTHLY AVERAGE OASDI CASH BENEFITS, 1940 TO 1980

Year	Retired workers	Widows	Children	Retired workers	Widows	Children
	current dollars			*constant* 1978 dollars		
1940	22.60	20.28	12.22	105.09	94.30	56.89
1950	43.86	36.54	28.43	118.86	99.02	77.05
1960	74.04	57.68	51.37	162.89	126.90	113.01
1970	118.10	101.71	82.23	198.41	170.87	138.15
1978	263.19	238.84	182.12	263.19	238.84	182.12
1979	294.27	266.87	205.53	264.55	239.92	184.77
August 1980	339.30	307.08	237.63	265.67	240.44	186.06
Increase in Percent	+1401%	+1414%	+1845%	+153%	+155%	+222%

SOURCE: *Social Security Bulletin*, January 1981.

By their growing numbers and effective organization they exert a powerful influence on Congress and succeeded in having social security benefits annually adjusted by the consumer price index (CPI), beginning in 1975.

Whether or not the tying of social security benefits to the CPI exaggerates necessary living cost adjustments is controversial. Some hold that most aged persons are not directly affected by the extraordinary rise in the prices of homes and mortgages, and that CPI therefore *over*states the inflationary impact on retired people. But the American Association of Retired Persons asserts that the CPI *under*states the rising costs of "food, shelter, fuel and medical care" on which the elderly spend most of their money.

The question is whether we can continue to insulate a sizable segment of the population from the impact of inflation. Indexing is of course very popular with its direct beneficiaries but it is inevitably done at the expense of those whose income is not indexed. Moreover, the more indexing we do for *some* people, the more we assure the perpetuation of high-rate inflation for *all*. Consideration is now being given to limiting cost-of-living increases for social security to between 75% and 85% of the CPI.

Average weekly earnings (wages) in the private nonagricultural economy increased between 1973 and 1980 by 61% in *current* dollars; but in *constant* dollars, adjusted for prices, they *declined* by 13% (from $109 to $95 in 1967 dollars). This is due, to some extent, to the fact that productivity in the American economy slowed down to a standstill in the mid-1970s and turned negative at the end of the 1970s. Can we afford much longer to raise social security benefits while working incomes do not go up or even decline? Will the working population stand for it, will it tolerate higher taxes to make social security more generous? The maximum social security tax soared from $60 in 1949 to $3950 in 1981 and is estimated to hit $10,200 by 1990 (aggregate of employer and employee contribution). Even that amount will not be enough to cover costs projected for 1990.

Higher social security benefits lead to a more rapid expansion in the number of beneficiaries. Over the past two decades a combination of statutory and automatic increases lifted scheduled benefits between 1959 and 1978 by 164%.[53] This is substantially faster than the CPI which grew only 124%. Simultaneously, but not coincidentally, the number of workers receiving monthly benefits grew 128% (8.1 million in 1960, 18.4 million in 1978), while the U.S. population, 65-and-over, increased only 44% (16.7 to 24.1 million).

This happened between 1950 and 1980:

U.S. population 65-and-over doubled (12.4 to 25.0 million)

Social security recipients multiplied ninefold (3.5 to 30 million)

Cash benefit payments from the OASI trust fund multiplied 138-fold ($727 million to $101 billion)

Converted into *constant* dollars, benefit payments multiplied 41-fold.

Part of the growth expresses the maturing of the social security system and the extension of its coverage to near universality. But a sizable share of the expansion is due to improved benefits which made receipt of social security more attractive than work to several million men in their sixties and seventies. Nearly half of all men 65-and-over were working in 1950; this shrank to less than one-fifth by 1980. These are the labor force participation rates of men 65-and-over:

1950	45.8%
1960	33.1
1970	26.8
1980	19.0

In the 55-to-64 age group men's labor force participation rate remained steady at 87% between 1950 and 1960. But after retirement benefits were made available at age 62, the rate fell to 83% in 1970 and to 72% in 1980.

Labor force participation remained almost stable in the 1970s for men in their main working years; but it dropped nearly 8 percentage points for the 65-and-over group and 11 percentage points for the 55-to-64 year group.

The unemployment rate in November 1980 stood at 5.9% for men 20 to 64 years old, at 3.1% for men 65 years-and-over. Unemployment was at 12.4% for men 20 to 24 years, at 3.3% for men 60 to 64 years old. This suggests that most men in their 60s and older who are not at work are not looking very hard for jobs either. Retirement (and disability) benefits look so much better to many of them than jobs.[54] Matter of fact—they were *intended* to look better.

Social security has a deliberately built-in antiwork bias. When established in the 1930s social security was supposed to motivate older persons to retire from the labor force in order to create openings for young people who were unemployed or graduating from school. Married women were to be discouraged from competing with men-breadwinners in the job market. There did not seem to be enough jobs for all.

But the American economy of the 1980s and in the succeeding half century and beyond, needs more workers, not fewer. We must try to raise the ratio between the working and the nonworking population. Men and women in their sixties and seventies should be encouraged and induced to continue in productive pursuits as long as they can. This means that the incentive structure of social security benefits must be changed and, in some respects, reversed.

In 1978 Congress outlawed mandatory retirement of employees prior to age 70. That seemed a step in the right direction. Unfortunately, Congress did not get around to taking the next and more important step: to make retirement less attractive than work by changing the benefit structure.

A few figures may illustrate trends over the past 3 decades:

The number of retirement benefit recipients, 65-and-over, as a percentage of all insured workers in that age group, increased from 59% in 1950 to 94% in 1977. For men 65 to 69 the percentage increased from 44% in 1950 to 88% in 1977 for women 65 to 69 from 46% to 86%. There are not many people left, 65-and-over, who do not claim social security benefits.

What is equally significant: more than half of the workers no longer wait until age 65 to collect retirement benefits: half the men and nearly two-thirds of the women who demanded and were awarded social security in 1976 were 62 to 64 years old. Their benefits are *permanently* reduced by up to 20%. The percentage of workers retiring with reduced benefits—because of early retirement—grew from 21.5% of all new recipients in 1962 to 57.5% in 1977—although by waiting till age 65 they could have received substantially higher checks for the rest of their lives.

We may conclude therefrom that current benefits are so generous that even after a one-fifth cut for early retirement they still prove irresistible to more than half of all eligible workers. This is not necessarily true for high-skill professionals. But persons with a low earning potential—or an intense desire for leisure ("work interferes with my fishing") now retire as soon as they are able to get social security benefits. Many do so for good reasons, as the table below illustrates:

Examples of Monthly Cash Benefit Awards
under the Social Security Act
Benefits effective June 1980

| | Average monthly earnings base | | | | |
	$200	$400	$650	$900	$1475
Retired worker, claiming benefits at 65, alone	280	422	599	695	874
Retired worker, claiming benefits at 65 with spouse	419	633	898	1043	1310
Widowed mother with 2 children	419	770	1047	1216	1529

Source: *Social Security Bulletin*, November 1980.

Benefits shown in the table were raised by 11% in June 1981. This means that workers with a low income base can now get retirement benefits which are substantially higher than their average monthly earnings were. Workers in higher earning brackets may not be able to do quite as well. But they can get checks which compare not unfavorably with their former take-home pay—that is wages after withheld income and social security taxes and other deductions. Which may be a major reason why the labor force participation rate of males, 16 years and older, dropped from 87% in 1950 to 78% in 1980—and is still heading down.

Retirement might not be a preferred choice for many were it not for earnings limitations (retirement test). A social security recipient is subject to a 50% tax (withholding from benefits) on earnings beyond a certain limit which in 1981 stood at $5500 for a person 65 to 71 years old. Fifty percent is the highest federal income tax rate on *earnings*. A single person reaches the 50% rate of the income tax law at a taxable income of $41,500. But a social security recipient was in 1981 subject to a 50% tax rate on his earnings over $5500. Many or most persons are unwilling to settle for netting only half the wages they earn. Those in lower wage brackets usually decide against working. Which is exactly what the social security law intended forty years ago. The question is whether this still is a wise public policy in the 1980s. The retirement test is widely held to be unfair. Why should a worker not get his social security benefits from age 65 on, whether he works or not, after having paid contributions all of his working life? Why should he be penalized for working?

Abolishing the earnings test would be a politically popular move, but it would also be expensive and require a boost in the social security tax rate. Social security, after all, is *not* insurance against living beyond the age of 65. It is earning replacement, intended to be insurance against losing one's livelihood for reasons of age or disability.

It is of course possible to devise insurance that bestows unconditional annuities from age 65 on. Premiums based on actuarial tables would be high but economically justifiable. However, social security is not simply insurance. It is also a welfare program with a strong bias toward low-income recipients. This makes unconditional annuities and a continued raising of the exempt amount prohibitively expensive. The repeal of the earnings test at age 72 was costly. So will be the scheduled reduction in 1982 of the age limit to 70. But potential beneficiaries are far more numerous below the age of 70 than above. That is why repeal of the retirement test would aggravate the core problem of the social security system. Therefore we must devise other ways to induce workers to keep working for several more years after they have become eligible for old age benefits.

Under current law a claimant suffers a 0.555% reduction in his benefits for every month he starts receiving checks prior to reaching age 65. That amounts to a 20% cut for collecting benefits from age 62 on which apparently is not enough of a cut. Earlier cited data suggest that current reductions have proven ineffective in deterring most workers from applying for early retirement. A gradual doubling of the current rate over a period of years might possibly do the trick. The adequacy and appropriateness of that level could be reevaluated at periodic intervals, and adjusted if necessary.

Some object to heavier reductions for early retirement. Older persons, they say, cannot find jobs in today's labor markets, especially if they have no advanced skills. Why should the least able be penalized? The fact is that unemployment rates are much lower at higher ages than at the prime of life, as mentioned earlier. Many older persons could find jobs if they tried harder and were less choosy about the type of job and the rate of pay. As long as minimum wages are higher than some workers' productivity and permit no exceptions, many eligibles find it hard to get hired. With old age benefits more attractive why should should they try?

It has appropriately been said:

> It isn't surprising that older workers react to such powerful antiwork incentives by leaving their jobs. Our social security system, in effect, levies a special tax on work as we get older, a tax that has become increasingly significant as benefits paid through the system have increased.[55]

Workers could be induced to work beyond their retirement eligibility age by higher benefits for their remaining years. A 1% bonus for each year's delay in claiming benefits, under current law, is ridiculously low. Even a boost to 3%—in the 1977 amendments for persons born after 1917—is not enough. The social security tax which they must pay, if working, is rather sizable (6.65% in 1981). Considering that most older persons will derive no benefit from paying contributions, because their wages at that point may be no higher than their accumulated earnings base, it might be advisable to free aged employees and their employers from social security tax liability.

In a private insurance plan a person in his sixties or seventies who postpones the receipt of annuities and continues to pay premiums would get between 10% and 20% higher annuities for each year's delay. Many workers would forgo social security retirement for several years if they could thereby materially increase benefits in their later years, after they have retired.

The most powerful means of controlling the cost of social security could be a raise in the eligibility age. In 1975 the Advisory Council on Social Security proposed that the age be increased from 65 to 68 and that early retirement be correspondingly advanced from age 62 to 65. This would of course have to be phased in over a number of years. All workers still could choose to receive benefits from age 65 on—at a reduced rate; no new claims under 65 could be approved. With the evident and growing popularity of early retirement, such a change will be extremely difficult to get through Congress. The political power of older persons' organizations should not be underrated. But considering demographic and economic trends, the change may someday become inevitable. The sooner the phase-in can be started, the easier it will be to do it at a slow pace.

In 1979 the Advisory Council on Social Security proposed that one-half of social security benefits be subjected to income taxation. This would seem fair. Recipients paid income tax on the amounts that were withheld from their wages, but not on the matching funds paid by their employers. Nongovernmental pensions are being taxed to the extent to which contributions (and taxes on that income) were not paid by the beneficiary. Most European countries tax social security benefits. The tax exemption of social security benefits was not granted by Congress. That "loophole" was created by an Internal Revenue Service ruling in 1941. A reversal now however would not be possible without congressional approval.

There will of course be strong objections to taxing social security benefits—which go to 35 million recipients—because it would "tax those least able to afford it". But that charge is unfounded. Aged persons who have no income besides social security will generally not be taxable. An aged couple with an income under $7400 is presently not taxable. If half the benefits were made taxable, only persons with income besides social security would become subject to income taxation. They generally are not those "least able to afford it."

In a system that redistributes over a hundred billion dollars of income each year, taking from some and giving to others, and tries to accomplish several diverse and often conflicting objectives, the existence of hundreds of controversies, of disagreements on what is "fair," is inevitable. What some call an inequity is to others a provision essential to economic justice. One man's meat is another man's poison. More appropriately in this case: a man's meat may be a woman's poison. Or, a working woman's meat may be a nonworking woman's poison. And so on. . . indefinitely. . . .

One of the most frequently cited inequities is the fact that a working wife, though she may have paid social security taxes for many years, derives no benefits from them if her accumulated credit does not exceed half of her husband's. If social security followed insurance principles it would pay each worker according to his or her own contribution. A worker could then make additional contributions to cover his nonworking wife and other dependents (a method used in some medical insurance programs). To meet standards of social adequacy, spouses and children are now automatically covered without an extra premium. To add earned benefits for working wives would be an expensive burden for the system.

My colleague Rita Ricardo-Campbell, who chaired the 1975 Advisory Council on Social Security's subcommittee on the treatment of men and women has over the years repeatedly pointed at the inequity in benefits between working and nonworking women. She proposed in what the Department of HEW labeled the "Campbell Plan" to phase out over 30-year and 50-year periods retired spouse and surviving spouse benefits.[56] With more than half of all women in the labor force at a point of time, and 90% of women with 10 years or more of covered employment, a shift to full recognition of their contributions is certainly overdue. But exactly how this should be accomplished has proven so controversial that very little has been done to grant women benefits as workers rather than as spouses.

Men complain that a unisex benefit schedule places them at a disadvantage, since women live about 5 or 6 years longer than men—a substantial share of the retirement years—women get *in toto* much higher benefits than men though their *monthly* benefits may be identical.

The 1972 amendments granted divorced women 100% benefits after a marriage that had lasted 20 years (reduced to 10 years by the 1977 amendments). Therefore several 100% benefits may now be paid for just one credit and one contribution—to the worker, his last spouse (and possibly later widow) and to one or several divorced wives. The added beneficiaries do not complain, of course. But adding more beneficiaries increases the burden on the system.

The last large group of workers not included in social security coverage are public employees although many of them have acquired credits in the system by temporary or part-time private employment. The time has come where federal, state and local employees should be integrated into the social security system—as discussed on pp. 43–45.

A discussion of some of the many "inequities" in social security would exceed the frame of this book. The emphasis here is on social security's main problem: keeping the social security system solvent at tolerable tax rates by controlling benefits. Some of the current provisions are counterproductive because they reward retirement and penalize productive work. This needs to be corrected.

Disability Insurance

When Congress added disability to old age and survivors insurance in 1956 it thought that it had so tightly restricted eligibility for access to the rolls that only a limited number of persons would qualify for the program. A claimant had to be unable by reason of an impairment to do his previous or customary work, and his impairment had to be so severe that he would be unable to engage in substantial gainful employment. But disability insurance (DI) turned into a virtual runaway program. The number of workers on DI exceeded 1 million in 1966, 2 million in 1973 and 2.8 million in 1977. The growth rate then seemed to slow down. Including dependents there are now 4.8 million beneficiaries. The amount of benefits reached $1 billion in 1962, $3 billion in 1971 and $15 billion in 1980. Outlays are estimated at $17.4 billion in the U.S. budget for FY 1981. To keep the trust fund from going broke, Congress in December 1977 boosted the DI tax rate—initially at 0.5% of taxable wages in 1956—from 1.15% to 1.65% and scheduled it to rise to 2.2% by 1990.

What caused this rapid growth? DI repeated an experience of several other welfare programs in social security and public assistance. No definition of eligibility can effectively restrain access to the rolls when economic incentives make receipt of benefits attractive. Claimants will find ways to make themselves eligible and manage to stay on, frustrating all efforts to rehabilitate them. Getting and keeping a job calls for a deliberate and sustained effort even under good circumstances and even more so for disadvantaged persons.

Studies conducted by the Social Security Administration show that earnings replacement rates rose from 51% to 59% between 1969 and 1975. "One-fourth of those entitled in 1969 had replacement rates of at least 80 percent of their previous earnings, but by 1975 this proportion had increased to 31 percent. In fact, one-fourth of the newly entitled received more in benefits than they earned while working."[57]

Occupational disability can often not be as clearly proved and documented or disproved, as for example age or the breadwinner's death which control access to other benefit programs. Workers with marginal earning capacity qualify themselves by mental and emotional problems that make it difficult for them to compete for jobs in a cold and hostile world.

With major medical advances in recent years one would expect that proper treatment could ease or remove many disabilities. In fact many handicapped persons with the requisite social security credits, never apply for disability benefits and make their way by their own efforts. But once on the DI program only about 10% are rehabilitated. Many DI recipients also receive benefits from other welfare programs. About half the persons on supplemental security income (SSI) are disabled. In a recent study of men 45 to 54 years old, Harvard economist Jonathan Leonard suggested that higher benefits cause men to drop out of the labor force and become DI beneficiaries.

The number of DI beneficiaries has been projected to double to 10 million by the end of the century or before. As of now, restraint on the level of benefits seems to be the only method by which the program's expansion could be halted. In June 1980 Congress authorized mild restraints on DI awards and reduced some of the work disincentives. How effective the new law will be remains to be seen.

Unemployment Compensation and the Unemployment Rate

The specter of unemployment and resulting deprivation and misery haunted workers and their families as an ever present danger for uncounted generations. It no longer does. Unemployment, to be sure, has not been wiped out, despite efforts and promises of our political leaders. Though several huge federal programs were enacted to bring it down, and federal fiscal and monetary policies were focused on the same objectives, the official unemployment rate averaged substantially higher in the 1970s than it had in the 1960s, 1950s, or 1940s. But its sting has been effectively softened by unemployment insurance which now covers 97% of all working persons, tides them over layoffs and bridges the income loss between jobs.

To many skilled or professional workers, accustomed to relatively high wages, unemployment may still mean temporary hardship because their benefits equal less than 50%, 40% or even less than 30% of their prior net earnings. That is why not many of them are on the rolls and few for long. But to millions of others who lack higher skills or drive, unemployment compensation, at 60% or more of their prior take-home pay, has become a frequent and not too uncomfortable alternative—and option—to the necessity of having to labor at menial and cumbersome jobs to make just a few dollars more than they can get tax free (plus food stamps) while at leisure. That may explain, at least in part, the seemingly paradoxical fact that while the employment rate (related to population) has risen substantially in recent decades, so has the official unemployment rate. It is now widely agreed among economists who have studied the subject that the easy availability and generosity of unemployment compensation play a major role in the growth and high level of unemployment.

It was certainly not so intended or envisaged when, in 1935, President Franklin D. Roosevelt, recommended to Congress, as part of this social security program, the establishment of a system of unemployment insurance through a joint federal-state program. Following the example of European industrial nations, it aimed at aiding workers with a firm attachment to the labor force, by partial wage replacement during temporary periods of involuntary unemployment. Congress enacted the plan, and the system has now been operating for nearly half a century. The funds are raised by a tax on employers, based on their payroll and channeled through trust funds, separate from the general funds of state governments. States were given considerable discretion in setting standards.

Definitions and objectives of the programs have remained the same but practices underwent significant changes and led to a generosity and abuses which eventually got the system into serious financial difficulties.

In the mid-1970s, when for the first time since the 1930s the country went through a sharp recession, half the states' unemployment trust funds went broke. The balance in those funds dropped from an aggregate of $10.6 billion in 1974 to $3.4 billion in 1976. However, benefit checks continued to go out to claimants because the federal government advanced

$5.6 billion to states, assumed half the cost of extended unemployment compensation, and the federal unemployment trust funds borrowed $8 billion from the U.S. Treasury although the budget itself was in a heavy deficit position. The advances to state and federal unemployment trust funds were supposed to be repaid quickly. But by 1980 most of those loans were still outstanding and prospects for repayment remained hazy.

Main debtors are not the low-income states but industrial, high-income states such as Pennsylvania, Illinois, Connecticut, New Jersey, Massachusetts, and New York. Those states in which labor unions pack a political punch pay high benefits but are less eager to boost tax rates for fear of impairing their competitive attractiveness for investment and industrial location and expansion. As an alternative to tightening their loose benefit practices, those states have been pleading for federal forgiveness of their accumulated debts. However, other states which raise the funds needed to meet their unemployment compensation outlays from their own industries, are understandably opposed to also paying for the extravagant spending of their neighbors and competitors. Congress has so far refused to write off the debts nor has done much to enforce collection. States generally impose a tax on wages up to $6000 per annum (higher in a few states) at rates which averaged about 1.5% of taxable wages for many years but were boosted during the 1970s, reaching an average of 2.8% in 1977. In some states the tax now exceeds 6%. This is on top of a 0.7% federal tax. After 1976 rate boosts helped to build up state trust funds to a $8.5 billion balance by the end of 1978. High unemployment in 1980 and 1981 threatened a new crisis.

During the 1970s an average of 2 million workers were getting benefits; in 1980, 3.4 million; with 4.1 million estimated during 1981. Unemployment outlays averaged $10.3 billion annually in the 1970s, amounted to $16.2 billion in 1980 and are estimated at $23.5 billion in 1981. There could be trouble ahead.

To examine the financial health of the unemployment system, the President and Congress in 1976 appointed a National Commission on Unemployment Compensation.

In its interim report in November 1978 the commission painted a somber picture of large deficit operations during the 1970s and for the future and concluded "that the financial integrity of the unemployment system as it has functioned for forty-one years is now in question." Recommendations in the final report in July 1980, if carried out, would substantially liberalize benefits and seek a solution to the financial problem by raising taxes and tapping the federal Treasury for even larger amounts, despite the U.S. budget's heavy deficit condition which the commission regarded as none of its concerns.

Unemployment increased by over 20 percent in 1980 and continued at a high rate in 1981. This put a further squeeze on already overburdened trust funds and is likely to lead to federal action. Congress may boost unemployment taxes, draw upon other sources, and also restrain the generosity of unemployment benefits. The last will politically not be easy at a time when unemployment is projected to be high, which is when Congress in the past usually liberalized and expanded benefits. On the other hand, there is little steam behind a tightening of benefits at a time when unemployment and financial pressures are low. The early 1980s will in all likelihood see some changes in unemployment insurance. Organized labor has long demanded uniform federal standards, and what amounts to a virtual federal takeover of the unemployment program. Industry, on the other hand, seeks correction mainly by restraint on benefits.

In the 1970s several economists raised serious questions about the structure of the unemployment compensation system which, they found, entailed very strong adverse incentives. Particularly the analytical studies of Harvard economist Martin Feldstein concluded that the system often motivates workers against employment and causes employers to resort to layoffs more frequently and extensively. Official statistics that place average weekly benefits at about 37% of gross wages are misleading. Unemployment and benefits claimants are far more heavily represented in the low-skill, low-wage brackets where benefits equal more than 60% of lost net income, and in some states 80% and more. Feldstein concluded that the unemployment program "does impose efficiency loss by distorting the behavior of firms to lay off too many workers when demand falls rather than cutting prices or building inventories." He estimated that the unemployment benefit formula accounts for about half of temporary layoffs.[58]

An incisive report by the Comptroller General of the United States to the Congress in 1979 concluded that unemployment benefits have become so generous that many recipients lack financial incentive to get a job:[59]

> . . . compensation, either alone or combined with other income, replaced an average of 64 percent of a recipient's net income before unemployment. About 25 percent of these persons replaced over 75 percent of their net income, and about 7 percent replaced over 100 percent.
>
> Persons who replaced over 75 percent of their net income before unemployment
>
> —collected compensation over 2 weeks longer than those who replaced 75 percent or less,
>
> —were more apt to exhaust compensation
>
> —were nearly twice as likely to have quit their most recent jobs,

and

—generally had held jobs similar to ones listed by the Employment Service and local newspapers.

Further, nearly 30 percent of those who replaced over 75 percent of their net income told the General Accounting Office they had only a limited financial need to work. These factors indicate that some persons receiving compensation are not financially motivated to work . . .

. . . Retirement income such as social security, private and military pensions, when combined with unemployment compensation minimizes some recipients' financial incentive to work.

In an article "Let's Stop the Unemployment Compensation Rip-Off" Kenneth Y. Tomlinson cited numerous examples of workers who shifted from jobs to unemployment for economically sound reasons. He quoted one worker: "Why go to work when you can stay home and collect 90 or 100 tax-free bucks a week in unemployment checks?" and summarized: "Loose standards and open-ended benefits threaten to turn this once sound program into a dole for those who choose not to work."[60]

Unemployment compensation has come to subsidize much seasonal employment—and long seasonal vacations and usually is also paid, with a slight delay, to workers who quit their jobs or were fired for misconduct, and, in some states even to strikers. Sometimes a key group of workers goes on strike, bringing about the layoff of a large number of other workers who are then entitled to compensatory benefits. Workers in industries which are hurt by foreign imports are eligible for additional benefits. This lowers or removes incentives to bring output and wages into better balance, which would enable domestic producers to meet foreign competition in the marketplace. It also exerts an upward push on consumer prices.

Many unemployed workers are also eligible for other welfare benefits such as food stamps, or Aid to Families with Dependent Children in about half of all states (those that operate AFDC-UF programs). Some qualify for general assistance, housing subsidies, medical benefits, supplemental security income and other social welfare programs. Most states pay unemployment benefits for 26 weeks, the federal government subsidizes another 13 weeks of "extended unemployment benefits" and at times pays for an additional 26 weeks, for a total of 65 weeks.

These and other programs may be triggered by a rise in the unemployment rate beyond a preset level. The unemployment rate, that is the percentage of unemployed persons in the civilian labor force, has long been regarded the most important indicator of current economic trends, up or down. It plays a dominant role in considerations and decisions on economic policy, fiscal and monetary. Only at the end of the 1970s, when the CPI began to grow at two-digit levels, did the inflation rate attract public attention comparable to that given the unemployment rate. Even so, it is inconceivable that the president and Congress would have watched the unemployment rate rise from 5% to 10% and then to 18% with as little effective counteraction as they observed the inflation rate soar to those levels in 1979 and 1980. Somehow, unemployment seems to imply or express human misery more strongly and to touch politically sensitive nerves more painfully than comparable movements in the inflation rate. A 6% unemployment rate conjures up the image of 2-1/2 years of unemployment over an average 40-year working life, a terrifying waste and period of economic suffering.

The unemployment rate not only can automatically trigger several major federal programs, it is also used as a base on which to distribute close to $20 billion in federal funds among states and local communities. Rising unemployment rates, more than any other single factor, led to the expansion and extension of unemployment compensation and to an increasing liberalization of benefits.

The unemployment rate is widely understood as expressing the percentage of persons who have lost their livelihood (or of households whose breadwinners have lost their jobs) involuntarily and are unable, despite diligent efforts, to find other employment. Common wisdom interprets the existence of several million unemployed as meaning that due to insufficient aggregate demand the economy—especially the private economy—is not generating enough jobs for all persons who want them. Actually, employment grew at a respectable rate, more rapidly than population. But unemployment grew even faster.

In 1978 the unemployment rate averaged 6.0% of the civilian labor force, twice the 3.0% rate in 1952. But the number of gainfully employed persons, as a percentage of the U.S. population, 16 years and over, meanwhile grew from 58.7% to 59.9%. In other words, the number of jobs increased at a faster rate than the working-age population, but seemingly the number of persons who want a job and cannot get one increased even more rapidly. Between 1952 and 1978 U.S. population increased by 39%, population 16 years and over, by 48% and the number of persons in civilian employment by 57%. But the number of unemployed meanwhile jumped by 221%. What happened in between is, of course, that the labor force participation rate increased from 59.0% to 63.2%—despite a trend toward earlier retirement and a 2-year increase in the average number of years of school attendance. Which means that there was a strong drive toward joining the labor force in the "in-between" time, the prime working years.

The question is: does all of that mean that people really want a type of job they have a realistic chance of getting or does the total include sizable numbers of people who are just as willing to settle for the status of unemployment and its benefits? Such benefits are not available to persons who do not register as members of the labor force looking for a job.

One particular year such as 1952 or 1978 may not be a reliable mark in a field in which developments are volatile and trends fluctuate substantially up or down. A five-year average may give us a more reliable base. If we compare the 1952/56 period with 1974/78 we find that working population (16 and over) increased by 40%, employment by 44%, unemployment by 158%. In other words, the trends are still what they showed in a comparison of 1952 with 1978.

In absolute numbers, between 1952/56 and 1974/78: the civilian labor force grew by 31 million of which 27 million swelled the ranks of the employed and 4 million those of the unemployed.

It may help our understanding of the nature and cause of the growth in joblessness to analyze unemployment by various characteristics. As of January 1981[61] there were 7.8 million persons reported unemployed (seasonally adjusted), equal to 7.4% of the civilian labor force.

The most significant fact is that only about one-third of the unemployed had actually *lost* their jobs:

24% were new entrants or re-entrants to the labor force. It takes most new entrants considerable time to decide what type of work they really are fit for and what job they want, to explore the labor market, to identify and find the right job and finally to decide which of several potential openings may be the best. Many go through several job changes before they find their proper niche. This may again involve time "in between."

11% had quit their jobs

21% were on temporary layoff, waiting to be called back.

Only 34% had lost their jobs. Many of them, undoubtedly were let go because of lack of work to be done. But many others were dismissed because of poor performance, misconduct—or had arranged to be fired rather than quit.

Seven out of ten unemployed had been jobless for less than 15 weeks:

42% had been unemployed for less than 5 weeks—a very modest time span to look for and land a desirable job in a highly specialized labor market with widely varying demands, wage rates and side benefits. 28% had been unemployed for between 5 and 14 weeks, still a reasonable time, considering the many factors to be weighed—distance from home, hours, skills and promotional possibilities, not to mention the desire of many to take some time off—whether for taking it easy or going fishing, or fixing up the house or doing something else he or she had long wanted to do.

Thirty percent of the unemployed had been jobless for 15 weeks or more, half of them for over 26 weeks. The latter group formed the hard core who either wanted to get the most out of unemployment compensation, weren't willing to settle for the kind of job they *could* get or really weren't too keen on working anyway.

An unemployment rate of 7.4% leads many observers to conclude that the economy just does not generate enough work, due to lack of aggregate demand. But the fact is that overtime hours have consistently totaled more than hours lost by unemployment. Here is the picture for manufacturing, the only industry for which such records are available:

Average Overtime Hours

	As a Percentage of Total Hours	Unemployment Rate Average
1950s (1956–59)	6.1%	5.2%
1960s	7.8%	4.8%
1970s	8.1%	6.2%

Source: *Handbook of Labor Statistics 1978*, 1980 Bureau of Labor Statistics, Department of Labor.

Since 1973 the Census Bureau has taken an annual survey every May of the hours worked on premium pay among full-time workers in all industries. In the 6 years between 1973 and 1978, the number of hours at premium pay averaged 10% of all hours worked; the unemployment rate meanwhile averaged only 6.6%.[62]

Why would companies regularly and routinely pay 50% overtime instead of hiring more workers? Because they discovered that they get more value for paying 50% more to highly skilled workers, than lower rates to others who produce less. In other words, the choice is probably based on the personal qualifications of workers, on the relation between individual productivity and wage rates they have to be paid. The output of some workers may make even a regularly scheduled 50% premium pay economically justifiable and result in a lower cost per unit. They will seldom be unemployed for long. Others produce less value than the wages they will accept or must be paid under labor-management contracts or minimum wage laws. Therefore they will be hired only if more competent workers are unavailable or for temporary or casual employment at times of extraordinary work loads. In other words, the length and frequency of unemployment largely expresses the ratio between an individual's productivity and wages.

The hardship resulting from unemployment is somewhat mitigated for families by the fact that nearly half the unemployed husbands have employed wives, and 80% of the unemployed wives have employed husbands.

There is a strong and consistent correlation between occupational level and unemployment: the higher the skill, the less unemployment.

Unemployment rates were as follows:

	March 1980	January 1981
professional and technical	1.9%	2.7%
clerical	4.6	5.9
craftsmen	7.0	8.5
operatives (factory workers)	10.3	13.7
construction laborers	26.8	30.0
other laborers	12.8	16.3

This seems to suggest that there is a shortage of jobs in the low skill categories and ample openings in high-skill occupations. Therefore occupational training was proposed as the proper answer and over a dozen huge federal manpower programs were undertaken to upgrade skills of unemployed persons. Many billions were spent and are still being spent on such undertakings. But their results have been disappointing (see p. 227).

It now appears that there is no shortage of jobs at lower skill levels but rather a shortage of persons willing to take them. A U.S. Labor Department report indicated that the number of jobs in the lowest category (Group V) declined from 10.9% of all jobs in 1970 to 9.5% in 1980 and is projected to fall to 8.7% by 1985. A parallel trend is evident in the second lowest group (IV) from 20.7% down to 17.9%, while the highest occupational group (Group I) is projected to expand its share from 13.2% to 18.1%.

Here are the report's conclusions:

At the lower extreme of the job structure, the growth in potential requirements for Group IV and Group V occupations is expected to exceed the projected growth of available workers by 6.4 and 2.6 percent respectively. . . . The disparity between a projected "surplus" of workers in high-level jobs and a "shortage" in lower level jobs, is more clearly evident in the comparisons for the 1980–85 period. Both the groups I and II occupations are expected to experience a more rapid growth in labor supply than in jobs; while groups III, IV and V would all experience deficits in labor force growth compared with projected job needs. . . . These projections indicated that, in contrast to sharp projected increases in availability of workers for higher status, predominantly white-collar jobs, we can expect substantial reductions in the proportion of workers who will be available for the lower level groups IV and V jobs. . . . In some occupations, such as domestics, we can expect a further employment decline. An increasing number of families will be obliged to seek substitutes for the services of paid domestics, either through "product" substitution, such as increased use of commercial services, or by simply doing more of their own household chores. . . .[63]

The U.S. Employment Service lists more than 150,000 openings that remain unfilled at the end of every month. The number of private household workers dropped from two million to one million between 1960 and 1979—not for lack of jobs but of people to take them. For years the American public and the Congress have been told that there are not enough job openings at lower levels and that millions of persons with little skill are unable to find employment and must be sustained through more generous and extended unemployment compensation and other welfare programs. The fact is that there are ample jobs but many of them inevitably are "menial" or "dirty" or "stoop" labor. Low-skill workers are paid low wages because their productivity (value of output or service) is not high enough to make higher wages economically possible. Therefore many opt for workless income that compares favorably with what they could earn by their own labor, doing work within their capabilities. Higher-skilled persons must do their own "dirty" work and pay taxes to support unskilled persons in the style to which they have become accustomed by governmental generosity.

The above mentioned report of the Department of Labor commented:

The point of departure of the present study was the premise that workers in our society have a collective occupational preference schedule, in which jobs tend to be ranked in terms of desirability, based on the nature of the work performed, the rewards for this work, the conditions of work, and the prestige associated with the occupation [p. 105].

This clarifies the situation. Low-skill persons usually have little education—though most of them probably attended a public school for 10 to 12 years—and many may be of low intelligence. But they are not stupid. Why should they do cumbersome and unpleasant work at low pay as long as society is willing to sustain them at leisure?

Still, somebody has to perform the lowly jobs. In many societies young people with no skills would do them. But our unskilled young people show no more eagerness to take such jobs than their elders.

Unemployment rates by age groups in January 1981 were:

	male	female
16 to 21 years	20.1	15.5
20 to 24 years	15.1	11.2
25 to 54 years	6.2	6.6
55 to 64	4.0	4.1
65 and over	3.4	3.5

Many unskilled young persons who are listed as unemployed simply are not worth the wages they demand or have to be paid under minimum wage provisions. Organized labor strongly objects to making exceptions from the minimum wage law and has so far prevailed. Whether because of aptitude or attitude, many youngsters simply do not produce a service which justifies paying them a minimum wage. Even exceptions from the law would solve only part of the problem. Most of those youngsters may not be willing to take jobs with little pay as long as various public programs and other alternatives are available. Many young people are not just unemployed but unemployable, by attitude more than by aptitude.

Who then performs the jobs which Americans disdain? Immigrants, most of them "undocumented," that is illegal and most of them from Mexico. The Immigration and Naturalization Act of 1965 authorized a worldwide ceiling of 290,000 admissions, in addition to which 150,000 relatives and 234,000 refugees arrived in 1979 for a total of 674,000. But most of the one million Mexicans (*mas o menos*) who stream across the border annually come here illegally, to add to the estimated 6 to 8 million (or more) already here. The President and the Congress are overtly unwilling to enforce the laws that at one time they swore to uphold. Nor is the Immigration and Naturalization Service given the means and manpower required to stem the flood, let alone deport the millions of "undocumented workers" already here. Amnesty has been suggested for illegal immigrants already here but a stop to the steady stream coming in. Early in 1981 the U.S. Select Commission on Immigration called on Congress to impose sanctions on employers of illegal immigrants.

Large numbers of American employers strongly object to cutting off the flow— because they could not find Americans willing to work as hard at those wages. Some of the illegals do stoop labor, hand planting and harvesting on farms. But most of them work in factories and construction, garment manufacturing, laundries, restaurants, cleaning and maintenance throughout the country with heavy concentrations in the Southeast and Southwest.

U.S. Labor Secretary Ray Marshall said in an interview in the *Los Angeles Times* (December 2, 1979) that if only two million of the illegal workers were in jobs that otherwise would be held by American workers, "eliminating this displacement would bring unemployment down to 3.7%." He added that he did not advocate deporting illegal immigrants to solve the problem, understandably so, since President Carter had recommended granting amnesty and permanent status here for most of them. Mr. Marshall warned of the possible consequences of inaction in "sowing the seeds of a serious future civil rights struggle." Mexicans, as Hispanics generally, have extraordinarily high birthrates and could within not too many years become the country's largest minority group. The Miami riots in May 1980 were brought about, at least in part, by the reaction of the black community to the sudden influx of large numbers of Cubans. Confrontations between ethnic groups are a distinct possibility unless something is done soon to control the magnitude of the immigration. The importation of 10 million black slaves into the Western Hemisphere between the 16th and early 19th centuries generated problems of yet unfathomed dimensions. We may now be in the process of piling up huge amounts of dynamite that could blow up in our faces some day.

Several years ago industrial countries of Central, Western and Northern Europe began to reverse the flow of "guest workers" when unemployment among their own citizens became uncomfortable and frictions developed with local residents, bordering on riots. Their governments granted few new permits to foreign workers in recent years, strictly enforced labor laws and forced about two million workers to return to their Mediterranean homelands.

At this time it appears that this immigration wave, possibly the largest in United States history and its current and long-term potential dangers are being ignored. There is no end in sight to the influx across our southern border unless it is stopped, which the U.S. government currently seems unwilling to do. We may well be creating a problem of devastating proportions for decades and generations to come.

In his timely warning Mr. Marshall did not mention where and how he would find Americans to replace the illegal immigrants. It is unlikely that those low-level jobs could be filled locally as long as social programs enable millions of unskilled Americans to remain idle or casually and sporadically employed—just long enough to give them credit for another period of unemployment compensation.

What evidence is there of a shortage of job openings in America for persons willing to work, except the official unemployment rate? If millions of illegal Mexican immigrants with few skills and several strikes against them, are able to land jobs on farms, in factories, in stores, in households, why can't Americans?

The unemployment rate increased by 50% from the late 1960s to the late 1970s (from between 3.6% and 3.8% to between 5.8% and 6.2%). During the same period the Help-Wanted Advertising Index—which takes 1967 as its base—also rose by 50% (from 100 in 1967 to 149 in 1978 and 151 in 1980.) Why would employers boost their help-wanted advertising by 50% if they were swamped with applications from eager job hunters?

Men who live alone—divorced, separated, widowed, single (never married)—have consistently had 2.5 to 3 times as high an unemployment rate as married men who live with their wives. Unemployment rates for males 20 to 64 years old were:

	January 1979	January 1981
Married men living with spouse	3.2%	5.1%
Men living alone (single, divorced, etc.)	9.7	13.0

There is no indication that employers discriminate against unmarried men. But there are obvious reasons why a man with family responsibility is less likely to be out of a job than a single man. He may not quit a job before he has another one, he is almost certain to search harder and more likely to take an available job even if it is not exactly what he would like to have. A single man is more apt to quit in a huff, take time off, look around at leisure while he takes a vacation sweetened by unemployment compensation and be more choosy in what he takes on. In other words, whether a person is unemployed depends more on the individual and his motivations and actions than on the job market.

During congressional Joint Economic Committee hearings in June 1977 Commissioner of Labor Statistics Julius Shiskin mentioned that the growth of multiearner families tends to increase the unemployment rate because it gives the unemployed more freedom of choice in accepting or rejecting job offers. More than half of the unemployed are in families with one or more full-time workers. The intriguing fact however is that husbands with an employed wife have an unemployment rate of 3.6%, with an unemployed wife of 12.4%. Wives with an employed husband have an unemployment rate of 4.9%, with an unemployed husband of 15.1%. This suggests that unemployment of one spouse begets unemployment of the other. Often it is not the employed husband or wife who supports the unemployed spouse who is searching for a job but both spouses are unemployed simultaneously because two benefits are better than one. At the same hearings Mr. Shiskin admitted that the liberalization of unemployment insurance benefits—in terms of amount, coverage, and duration—has probably itself contributed to some increase in unemployment by enabling the unemployed to be more selective in the job search process.

The commissioner further conceded that "the employment-to-population ratio provides a better measure of labor-market conditions than the unemployment rate." If this be true—and I believe it is—why does the Bureau of Labor Statistics not publish the employment-to-population ratio? Why does it place all its emphasis on the unemployment rate?

The employment-to-population ratio can easily be computed from data in published labor force statistics. It has a record of astounding stability, varying only between 56.3% and 59.0% (ratio 1.00 to 1.05) between 1952 and 1977, while the unemployment rate (annual) fluctuated at a rate of nearly 1:3 (2.9% to 8.5%).

The employment-to-population ratio stood at 58.7% in 1952 and at 58.5% in 1977 while the unemployment rate registered 3.0% and 7.0% respectively. In 1978 the employment-to-population ratio advanced to 59.9% and hit a new record of 60.5% in 1979 which suggests that the labor market is receptive and able to absorb additional applicants *if* they are worth their wages. The unemployment rate jumped 22.4% between 1979 and 1980 (5.8% to 7.1%); the employment-to-population ratio dropped a mere 1.2% (from 60.5% to 59.8%).

The unemployment rate is not simply an oversensitive and hypertonic measure of labor market conditions but is outright misleading. This would not be so injurious if the rate were not used as the weather vane which triggers multibillion-dollar programs, allocates huge amounts of federal funds and were not the most powerful factor in influencing major economic policy decisions. The unemployment rate is widely viewed as the politically most sensitive indicator of economic health and used as if it were a reliable and precise measure, while, in fact, it is quite subjective and depends on the self-classification of persons with a direct economic interest.[64]

While European countries generally compute the unemployment rate on the basis of registration at employment offices, the U.S. rate is determined by a monthly survey among 56,000 households which is then blown up to represent all persons in the United States. The person who is present when the interviewer calls, is asked whether he or she, and other members of the household, are now working and, in the case of a negative answer, whether the person has been "looking for a job" in the preceding 4 weeks. If the reply is affirmative, the person is classified as unemployed.

That procedure does not produce valid results. Some persons may answer in the affirmative because they would feel embarrassed admitting that they have not been looking for a job because they prefer taking it easy for a while. Many register for work in order to become and remain eligible for unemployment compensation and various other social benefits. There is no attempt to ascertain whether a person is genuinely job hunting or only pretends to be, above all, for the type of job he or she can reasonably qualify for.

Many and maybe most people have an exaggerated notion of what type of job they should hold at what wage rate, because few are good judges of their own qualifications, limitations and economic value in the labor market. Many people would like a job—if it is well paid, at convenient hours, is closely located, offers pleasant work, and numerous other desirable conditions. Most people who really need a job know that they must be flexible and make concessions. But a person who can get along without that job—and would just as soon draw the most in welfare benefits—is less likely to compromise.

Even the fact that a person has looked for a job is therefore no proof that he or she is truly unemployed—with all the implications of hardship. Many low-skilled persons refuse "menial", cumbersome, "dirty" jobs if there is an available alternative—although they could by no means qualify for a position calling for higher skills. He or she may set the wage they demand much higher than the value of the services they have to offer and can perform.

Unemployment program rules refer to a "suitable" job. That is a very flexible term. Any job that is not at the desired level of dignity, title or compensation or at the level a person once had or would like to have, may be labeled unsuitable. By declaring available jobs unsuitable, a person gains and keeps access to the compensation rolls and several ancillary benefits. He or she is officially labeled "unemployed." There is only limited hope that unemployment costs can be restrained and unemployment rates be brought to a more reasonable level as long as current definitions and practices are allowed to continue. Huge amounts are paid out each year on fraudulent claims and for purposes for which unemployment compensation was never intended.[65]

Other industrial countries measure unemployment by different methods and their figures are not directly comparable with ours. The U.S. Bureau of Labor Statistics has attempted to adjust foreign statistics to U.S. concepts for comparative purposes. According to those statistics the United States has had a higher unemployment rate than any of the countries listed except Canada, consistently every year shown (1960 to 1977).[66] Some of the reasons could possibly be statistical. But the American tax system, which favors consumption over capital formation, and our generous unemployment compensation and related programs may have a distinct bearing on our unemployment rates.

The Soviet Union has no program of unemployment compensation, having "abolished" unemployment half a century ago. Every able-bodied person who is unable to find a job can go to a labor exchange and will be assigned to some work—at a minimum pay which since 1970 has been set at 70 rubles a month, equivalent to about $100 (compared with our $581). Any person who really needs it can get it by doing simple work for 6 to 8 hours a day. Which means of course that everybody who has any skill or qualification tries to get a job at better pay. It also means that everybody who takes a job at a low rate has thereby proven that he or she really needs it.

Whether it is desirable that such a system—establishment of an employer of last resort at low wages—could or should be tried in the United States is a subject that would require more detailed discussion than this framework permits. But there is a way to control unemployment and unemployment compensation costs. Current law has cutoff points: 26 weeks, 39 weeks, even 65 weeks. Cutoff of benefits is a crude and in some cases a cruel measure which decision makers understandably try to avoid. As an alternative, increasing economic pressure could be applied on recipients to find and accept a job even if the work, location, conditions or pay are not what he or she would like. If beyond a certain point, say, 20 or 26 weeks, benefits were cut 10% each month (or at some other rate) the claimant would be on notice, and under growing pressure to take, a job he can get rather than insist on getting what he wants.

Medical Services and Health

Among the three major functions in the social welfare field that dominate government's domestic activities—health, education and welfare—health in many ways stands by itself. Most persons have direct contact with education mostly in the early part of their lives, with welfare or income support in their later years. But availability of medical services is essential throughout life, though they may be used with greater frequency and intensity at the beginning and toward the end. They also are, in a literal sense, more vital to survival and well-being than any other service. Also, in contrast to education and welfare more than half the funds are derived from private, nongovernmental sources, with substantial leeway left for personal decision making.

Public expenditures in all three fields have expanded at an extremely rapid rate over the past quarter century, several times faster than outlays for other government activities or personal spending, in toto or in major categories (see Table 23). Spokesmen and organizations for the various services, have consistently battled for higher public appropriations and expanded programs, quite successfully so. They hold that the added funds were well spent, have returned rich dividends and need to be kept growing at a fast pace. With overall amounts of government spending and taxing reaching excessive levels however, tangible results of outlays must be and are being viewed with an increasingly critical eye.

In education, as unfortunately is only too evident, multiplied outlays were not accompanied by improved quality; in fact, educational performance is down by every known yardstick. In income support, some programs such as social security have undoubtedly brought wholesome results while others such as public assistance and unemployment compensation seem to have produced mixed, questionable or adverse returns. Medical services have on the whole, and with exceptions, brought positive and desirable results, though sometimes at too high a price.

Costs are virtually out of control and have become the central problem of medical care. Their growth over the past quarter century is shown in three tables on the succeeding page: in *constant* (1978) dollars, in percent of Gross National Product (GNP) and in a percentage breakdown by major categories. The table on p. 262 shows that between 1952 and 1978 medical expenditures multiplied in *constant* dollars (adjusted by the Consumer Price Index) more than five times; GNP meanwhile only slightly better than doubled. As a percentage of GNP, health costs jumped from 4.3% in 1952 to 9.0%. This means that we are now working more than one month each year just to pay our medical bills.

The public is barely aware of the enormous cost boosts that have taken place because *direct* payment of medical costs remained steady for two decades—at 2.6% of GNP in 1960 and still the same in 1978. Direct payments declined from over one-half of total costs in 1952 to less than one-third in 1978. Government and private insurers footed more than two-thirds of the medical bills in 1978. The public did not feel the sting because most of the governmental costs were raised by withholding from wages, while insurance premiums, paid by employers, were generally passed on to consumers through higher prices. It has been calculated that the health insurance provided by the Ford Motor Company to its employees adds about $130 to the price of every car made.[67]

The biggest jump in medical outlays occurred in the 1960s when public medical spending which had equaled 1.3% of GNP in 1952 and in 1960, went to 2.8% in 1970; it registered at 3.7% in 1978. The main cause

National Health Expenditures, 1952–1978

IN CONSTANT (1978) DOLLARS	1952	1960	1970	1978
		billions of 1978 dollars		
Total	$36.9	$59.2	$125.5	$192.4
Public expenditures	10.9	14.6	45.9	78.1
Medicare	0.0	0.0	12.6	25.9
Medicaid and other public assistance	0.3	1.1	10.4	20.6
General hospital medical care*	3.0	5.2	6.9	8.6
Department of Defense and veterans	4.2	4.0	6.1	8.6
Medical research	0.3	1.2	2.8	4.0
Medical facilities	1.4	1.1	1.8	1.9
Workmen's compensation	0.6	1.0	1.8	3.1
Other	1.1	1.0	3.5	5.4
Private expenditures	26.0	44.6	79.8	114.3
Direct payments	18.9	28.6	44.6	55.3
Insurance premiums	3.9	11.0	29.4	53.0
Other (construction, research, etc.)	3.1	5.0	6.2	6.0

IN PERCENT OF GROSS NATIONAL PRODUCT	1952	1960	1970	1978
Total	4.3%	5.3%	7.6%	9.0%
Public expenditures	1.3	1.3	2.8	3.7
Private expenditures				
Direct payments	2.2	2.6	2.7	2.6
Insurance premiums	0.5	1.0	1.7	2.5
Other	0.4	0.4	0.4	0.3

PUBLIC AND PRIVATE SHARES	1952	1960	1970	1978
Total	100.0%	100.0%	100.0%	100.0%
Public expenditures	29.6	24.7	36.5	40.6
Private expenditures				
Direct payments	51.3	48.3	35.5	28.7
Insurance premiums	10.7	18.6	23.0	27.6
Other	8.4	8.5	5.0	3.1

SOURCES: *Historical Statistics of the United States,* U.S. Bureau of the Census, 1975; and *Statistical Abstract of the United States,* 1979, U.S. Bureau of the Census. These tables, derived from data compiled by the Health Care Financing Administration, Department of HEW, include medical expenditures of the Department of Defense, Veterans Administration, for workmen's compensation, etc., which the Bureau of Economic Analysis, U.S. Department of Commerce classifies with their respective departments and not under health. These tables therefore differ somewhat from amounts in Table 23.

*Primarily state and local psychiatric hospitals and school health was the enactment in 1965 and the beginning in 1966 of the *Medicare* and *Medicaid* programs, whose outlays equaled 1.4% of GNP in 1970 and 2.2% in 1978. The two programs accounted for two-thirds of all public medical spending in 1978. All other public medical spending rose only slightly— from 1.2% in the early 1950s to 1.4% in 1970 and to 1.5% in 1978. Premiums for private medical insurance climbed from 0.5% of GNP in 1952, to 1.0% in 1960, to 1.7% in 1970 and to 2.5% in 1978.

With nearly 70 percent of medical bills met by *third-party payments*, whether by government or an insurer, the general public is effectively insulated from skyrocketing medical expenses and quite unconcerned about bills it never sees. Sometimes, what the public can't see *can* hurt it because it inevitably foots the bill, one way or another.

Overall, the United States is not out of line with other industrial countries with regard to medical outlays. A compilation by the Social Security Administration shows that in 1975 the United States spent 8.4% of GNP for medical purposes, compared with an 8.1% median of nine industrial nations. Most major European countries have had comprehensive and mandatory health insurance, usually through government, for several decades, while similar proposals in the United States failed of passage. However, the United States has ranked *above* the median in health expenditures for industrial countries for at least two decades, though it is slightly *below* Sweden, West Germany and the Netherlands.[68]

Do the American people get their money's worth from their huge medical outlays? Did they, at the end of the 1970s, get services that were sufficiently improved to justify the doubling of medicine's income share over the preceding quarter century? Is today's product really so much superior to yesterday's?

These questions cannot be answered with certainty. Medical services undoubtedly have improved, as has, in many respects, the health of the American people. But—does that necessarily prove a cause and effect relationship?

Life expectancy at birth lengthened by five years between 1950 and 1977. At age 65, males extended their life expectancy by 1.1 to 1.2 years between 1949/51 and 1977, females by 3.3 to 3.4 years. The annual death rate shrank from 9.5 per thousand in the early 1950s to 8.8 in 1977 (see p. 24). Infant mortality dropped from 29.2 per 1000 in 1950 to 14.1 in 1977. But much of this was not due to wider access to medical care nor to more effective therapeutical methods. Research has shown that infant mortality rates are more closely related to the quality of maternal care, to social class, education and intelligence of the mother, to diet and income than to the availability of doctors. Increase in abortions also helped lower infant mortality.

The incidence of major illnesses has been sharply cut and some centuries-old scourges of mankind have been almost wiped out. But much of this is due to the results of medical research which gets only two cents of the medical dollar. There is a limit to how much can be allocated to medical research at any one time and produce worthwhile results, although Congress for years—particularly after some members died—threw so much money at the National Institutes of Health that they soon were locally referred to as the National Institutes of Wealth.

Cleaner sanitary conditions, which minimized infectious diseases, improved dietary habits, and other nonmedical factors also helped. So did the increasing popularity of regular physical exercise. The number of persons who play tennis, bicycle, jog, swim or engage in dozens of other physical activities has multiplied—though exact figures are hard to come by. Cigarette smoking decreased 26% for males and 8% for females between 1964 and 1975, per capita consumption of tobacco fell by 22%.[69] There is an increased awareness of the need to restrict caloric intake although obesity continues to be a problem from middle age on, especially among low-income women.

On the other hand, the per capita consumption of alcohol has increased. That the share of alcoholic beverages in the total food and beverage bill (personal consumption expenditures) shrank from 13.6% in 1950 to 10.8% in 1977 may be a weak reed to derive much comfort from.

Motor vehicle fatalities, the third or fourth largest cause of death (behind cardiovascular diseases, malignancies and about even with pneumonia) declined from a range up to 30 (per 100,000 population) in the 1930s to 26.5 in 1973 and to 22.9 in 1977 (fatality rates related to mileage showed much sharper decreases). This was due mostly to nonmedical factors such as the construction of modernized (limited-access) roads, safer vehicles, stricter traffic law enforcement and, in the later 1970s, the imposition of a 55-mile-per-hour speed limit.

Much of the growth in extending the life expectancy of women over men from 2 years in the early twentieth century to 8 years in the later 1970s is probably due to medical progress in overcoming the risks of childbirth and related conditions. On the other hand, much research has found that a person's life-style and habits may have a stronger impact on his or her state of health and on life expectancy than the frequency of physician visits. Still, the growing utilization of medical services suggests that at least the *belief* in the efficacy of medical treatment is high among the general public although much of it may be based on faith more than on scientific evidence. Enough is known to justify the assumption that more extensive and intensive medical services have materially contributed to a better state of health which the average American now enjoys.

It has become customary to talk about health care, health services, and departments of health rather than about medical services or, what they really are, treatment of diseases and care of the sick. What used to be called the "old and sick" have become the "health-impaired elderly," as Eric J. Cassell of Cornell University Medical College well pointed out.[70] This semantic manipulation is intended to merchandise the services of doctors and hospitals and has done an effective job of it. We have become too maudlin to call things by their proper name and have to find euphemisms to make them more salable—as undertakers ("funeral directors") have long been doing in merchandising the American Way of Death. Insurers have been eminently successful in selling "health insurance" though no one really can insure health. They can insure us only against having to bear directly the full cost of medical services for the diagnosis and treatment of diseases. But by advertising as health care what really is medical services we have been sold billions of dollars more of them at vastly inflated prices.

The major concern at this point arises from the faster rise in the cost of medical services compared to everything else. Medical care is consuming a growing share of our income. The questions are *why* this has taken place, whether it really is necessary for the general availability of good medical treatment and what can be done about it.

Here is the record of medical prices according to the Consumer Price Index (CPI):

CONSUMER PRICE INDEX FOR MEDICAL CARE AND OTHER ITEMS

	All items	Food	Medical care
1952	100.0	100.0	100.0
1960	111.6	104.4	133.4
1970	146.3	136.3	203.4
1978	245.8	250.8	370.0
1980	310.4	302.0	448.4

SOURCE: *Economic Report of the President*, January 1981; *Social Security Bulletin*, April 1981.

About 40% of medical outlays goes to hospitals, close to 20% to physicians, the remaining 40% to nursing homes, drugs, dentists, etc. Hospitals experienced a veritable cost explosion: expenditure per patient day soared from $8 in 1950 to $164 in 1977.[71] This means that per patient cost multiplied eightfold in *constant* dollars. Hospital daily *charges* quintupled between 1966 and 1978 (from $44 to $225) while the general price level (CPI) doubled. Why did costs rise so exorbitantly?

As I showed in Chapter 1 (p. 23), full-time personnel in hospitals tripled between 1952 and 1978 (from 1.1 to 3.3 million) while the number of patient days *declined* by one fifth (from 1.3 to 1.1 million average patient days). This means that in relation to patients, full-time staff multiplied 3.6-fold.

Staffing patterns in other fields of public service have also become much "richer." In public education, for example, staff increased more than twice as fast as students (see p. 182). But the rate of expansion in hospital staffs is unique and set a new record. While productivity (output related to manpower) in medical and educational services dropped precipitously, it nearly doubled (+85%) in the private business economy between 1952 and 1978. This enabled American consumers to nearly double their general living standards and made it possible for certain services such as hospitals and public education to vastly expand their "life-styles." The ballooning of hospital staffs expresses many things: auxiliary staff (nurses, technicians, lab employees) now perform jobs doctors used to do themselves; a great deal of work is being done that just wasn't done a few decades ago; floor coverage and intensity of patient services have expanded; personnel hours have been shortened.

An enormous number of tests are now being conducted, and verified, examinations by other physicians repeated, partially to be armed against potential malpractice suits which have multiplied with jury awards and insurance premiums reaching levels that were unimaginable but a few years ago. While few grew rich from huge awards the added cost was in the end not borne by physicians and hospitals; it was passed on to the consuming public in higher charges.

Despite the disproportionate staff expansion, payrolls have been accounting for a declining share of total hospital expenditures, shrinking from about two-thirds of the total in the 1950s and early 1960s to one-half in the later 1970s. Humans have been overtaken by technology. Competition among hospitals—often largely to raise the prestige and satisfy the pride of their heads and top medical staffs—led to a mad race for possession of the latest and most expensive medical gadgetry in every local unit that managed to find an avenue (or sponsor) to finance their purchase. Some thought that the way to keep from going broke was to be able to boast of the flashiest body scanners and widest array of medical equipment which most closely resembles science fiction monsters on popular television programs.

The hospital industry has long been characterized by an edifice complex which was translated into reality with the help of the federal Hill-Burton hospital construction program. When after 28 years Hill-Burton was left to expire in 1974 it did not mean the end of hospital construction nor of federal funding. But building declined—for good reasons. The occupancy rate of hospital beds shrank from 86.0% in 1950 to 75.8% in

1978 and the U.S. Surgeon General estimated in October 1979 that there were 130,000 excess hospital beds in the United States.[72] Low occupancy rates are of course very expensive in hospital operation. But the drive for more construction is still on. The Stanford University Hospital, built in 1959 with the help of Hill-Burton funds, announced in April 1980 a $97 million modernization program that will not add a single bed. This amounts to an average modernization cost of $145,200 for each of the 668 current beds!

New and enormously expensive procedures such as renal dialysis, cobalt therapy, open-heart surgery and dozens of others have become matters of routine, often with little thought to the remaining life expectancy of the patient. The use of intensive care units may have become *too* intensive and, according to some calculations, add 10% to the nation's annual hospital bill.[73] Better than 90% of hospital bills are now paid by third parties. Small wonder that resources are being treated—by the patient and by physicians and hospitals which are assured of reimbursement—as if their cost were zero.

Hospitals are now being used by millions of patients for services which could be performed more simply and inexpensively in doctors' offices. Many insurance plans reimburse patients only if they are treated in a hospital. Most hospitals, faced with financial problems, are not averse to raising their utilization rate in every possible way.

A doubling of the number of newly licensed physicians between 1960 and 1975—stimulated by a 1963 federal aid to medical education program—helped to double the number of active M.D.s between 1950 and 1978. There was in 1950 one physician for every 700 persons in the population, in 1978 for every 500 people, estimated to rise to one for every 410 by 1990. This could be too many and lead to a healthy competition among them. Medical doctors are the highest earning profession in the country, averaging in 1977 $78,300, if incorporated, and $52,500 if not incorporated. Changes in the profession helped economically: three-fourths of M.D.s in 1940 were general practitioners; by 1977 five out of every six listed themselves as specialists. That may have been the only way to cope with the enormous multiplication of necessary knowledge. But neither did it hurt doctors' incomes.

The disproportionate and seemingly unstoppable rise in medical costs has long been a matter of serious concern to responsible public officials. But there was and is wide disagreement on what can or should be done about it. In 1977 President Carter proposed a "hospital cost containment plan" which tried to solve the problem by strict government regulation. It would have limited hospital revenue and costs, adjusted by patient population, to annual increases of 9 percent (later revised to 9.7 percent), plus a few minor allowances. After lengthy hearings and debates, the House of Representatives turned thumbs down, in November 1979, with a vote of 234 to 166. The plan's direct control approach was judged ineffective, yet capable of adversely affecting the quality of medical care besides bankrupting some hospitals.

Germany, wrestling with similar problems, had tried a medical cost containment law in 1977 which imposed a 5.5% ceiling on year-to-year fee increases. It seemed to succeed, for a few months, then fell flat on its face, with costs heading up steeply again.[74] Comparable experiences in several other countries suggest that this type of "cost containment" simply does not work because it treats symptoms not causes.

Nor do "voluntary" controls work which the House voted for—in addition to authorizing another study—while defeating the mandatory controls that the president had recommended. The term "voluntary controls" is a classical *contradictio in adjecto* to serve as an alibi for congressional rejection of Mr. Carter's plan.

The skyrocketing of medical costs over the past few decades was the result of a congressional drive at a high objective, without thought given to economic motivations and inevitable economic results. The drive achieved its aim—nearly universal protection against having to bear a material share of the cost of one's medical care. But by placing perverse incentives in the medical programs and in the tax laws, it produced a cost explosion. This cannot be corrected by presidential oratory ("jawboning"), nor by statutory patchwork, nor by playing around with the levers, with cost controls whether they be called mandatory or voluntary.

It can be corrected only by restoring the natural incentives of the market and letting immutable economic laws work their way. As long as decisionmakers, whether they be physicians, hospital managers or patients, are insulated from the economic consequences of their actions, they will tend to come up with the most expensive choice. Our desires, our wishes, our dreams are unlimited—until we have to foot the bill, or at least a sufficiently big share of the bill to make extravagant decisions painful.

Assurance to hospitals and physicians that they will be reimbursed for whatever costs they incur, leads to the most expensive choice, which in our minds we tend to identify with "the best." As my colleague Rita Ricardo-Campbell wrote: "If medical care is viewed as a right, different from all other goods and services, and that by some magic everyone is entitled to unlimited quantities of the best, costs cannot be controlled."[75]

Even a schedule of "reasonable" or "customary" fees cannot adequately prevent exorbitant costs. As long as the patient is reimbursed for most of the bill, the excess is, for most of them, too small an item to quibble. For persons in lower brackets it will routinely be waived. Moreover, the issue usually is not the size of the fee but whether a particular service is necessary and justifiable. If cost considerations are nonexistent for the patient—but positive for the physician and the hospital (usually both)—even a very remote chance that an attempted therapy might just conceivably do some good, may suffice for an affirmative decision. Some would—and do—go to any length to slightly prolong an ebbing life, just to demonstrate the triumph of technology over nature. Some would embark on projects as promising as a crusade fighting Tay-Sachs disease among blacks or sickle-cell anemia among Jews.

In 1976 a congressional committee reported that there were about 2.4 million unnecessary surgeries performed in 1974 at a cost to the American public of almost $4 billion and that unnecessary surgeries led to approximately 11,900 deaths.[76] When the American Medical Association protested the findings, the congressional committee re-examined the facts and reported in 1978:

> Unnecessary surgery remains a national problem which requires urgent and accelerated attention. The Subcommittee believes that contentions by organized medicine that unnecessary surgery cannot be defined are diversions and obfuscations which serve to be counterproductive.
>
> The Subcommittee finds that the public remains at risk and unnecessary surgery continues to waste lives and dollars. The Subcommittee believes that there were approximately two million unnecessary procedures costing over $4 billion and over 10,000 lives in 1977.[77]

About 25 million surgical operations are now performed each year. Few patients, except for cosmetic surgery cases, pay much of the cost, if any. Most of those bills are paid largely by the government or by insurers.

Main responsibility for the cost explosion rests on the three ways in which the major part of medical care is now financed: Medicare, Medicaid and private insurance.

Medicare and Medicaid

Medicare and Medicaid were authorized in 1965 and began operating in 1966. Medicare provides hospital insurance for persons 65 years or over (some under 65 if disabled). It is supposed to be financed—and partially still is—from social security contributions. A supplemental program covers physicians services, outpatient and related care and calls for a monthly premium by the insured which has been slowly increasing, was raised to $9.60 a month in July 1980, and to $10.60 in July 1981. But social security taxes and premiums fall short of outlays so that the federal government makes contributions from general revenue funds which now approach $10 billion a year.

As all medical programs, Medicare proved far more expensive than had been predicted. The only surprising thing about this is that anybody should be surprised, considering experience with such programs around the world. Medicare reimburses patients (or suppliers directly) for 80% of cost with a deductible, currently $204 for hospital service and $60 for the supplemental program. The option of buying a dollar's worth of medical services (hopefully so) for 20 cents, has proven a major stimulant among a population which by reason of its age has a high incidence of minor ills and inevitably, sooner or later, some major afflictions. Though most would like to postpone the evil day as long as possible, we all must die, some time.

A $60 deductible for physicians' (accounting for one-fourth of Medicare) and related services is far less than what any normal person—and especially one at an advanced age—should expect to incur routinely within a year. The deductible appears too low. Automobiles usually are insured with deductibles of $250, $500 or more, because owners know that a lower deductible would be too expensive. Of course, automobiles are not as sensitive as humans, nor do they vote.

Aged persons are understandably more concerned about the state of their health than are younger people and commonly have more time to devote to the subject. An opportunity to buy a medical dollar—and professional attention and concern—for 20 cents may offer a stronger temptation than many can resist. Hence the enormous cost of Medicare.

Medicaid was intended to provide needed medical services to persons who are uninsured and cannot afford to pay the cost themselves. Public assistance recipients (AFDC) are automatically eligible, as are most persons on SSI and the so-called "medically indigent," people who are able to take care of their daily needs but cannot cope with health costs. Slightly over 10% of the American people obtain Medicaid benefits each year, 64% of them are from AFDC families, 16% are age 65 or over.

Medicaid provides "first-dollar coverage," with no deductible, no coinsurance, no fees, with many in-kind benefits provided by state welfare agencies. Expenditures rose from $2.3 billion in 1967 to $20 billion in 1978 and are estimated at 28 billion in 1981. On last count, 32% of the total went for hospital inpatient care, 9% for physicians, 22% for intermediate care, 17% for nursing homes.

The purpose of Medicare and Medicaid was to provide equal access to medical care to all persons, regardless of their financial means. A comprehensive HEW report commented in 1979: "The development of Medicare and Medicaid programs during the late 1960s has affected this trend toward more equal utilization of health care services by income groups."[78]

"More equal utilization"? The same report revealed that families earning less than $5000 averaged 5.8 physician visits (the highest rate) in 1977, families with an income of $25,000 and over, 4.8 visits.[79] Low-income people receive three times more days of hospital care than the high-income group. The poor may, on the average, be sick more frequently than the nonpoor; there could be a circular effect. But are they really sick more often or are they just less well informed on conditions that call for medical attention or can be taken care of by their own actions? Is there a parallel between a person's ability to cope with economic and health requirements?

Medicaid uses the most expensive method of delivering medical care: "fee for service"—which does not discourage physicians or hospitals—and "first-dollar coverage" which does not discourage patients. Some countries ration service by limiting personnel and facilities and having people wait, sometimes for weeks or months. There is no answer that is satisfactory to everyone. Small service charges—adjusted to income level—might be one possible avenue.

This could reduce the widespread fraud and the operation of Medicaid mills which "ping-pong" patients among a multiplicity of services.

Insurance

It has long been the hope and goal of public policy that medical insurance would become near universal and include all persons who are not protected by a government program. We have come close to that goal—with over 90% of the population now covered by one or the other—but we seem to have employed the most costly methods to achieve our aims.

Insurance companies have long learned in several fields of coverage that coinsurance is a necessary safeguard against overuse wherever some discretion by the insured cannot be avoided. In most of our medical insurance, coinsurance is now underused, with costly results.

In prepaid health care, on the other hand, the provider has an interest in keeping the service from exceeding necessary and unavoidable procedures. He must, for his own protection, ration access. Some do so just by having people wait. That imposes a cost on the user in time and inconvenience while greater emphasis on coinsurance exacts a cost in money. Both methods are therefore unpopular with workers who regard employer-paid coverage an important—and untaxed—part of their compensation and like to get it all for "free." Health maintenance organizations (HMOs) which often supply prepaid medical care have been growing slowly because employees prefer fee for service—which tends to make the physician and the hospital more "cooperative." Their first choice is "first-dollar coverage" which makes it unnecessary to consider frequency, cost or extent of service.

Brookings Institution senior fellow Louise B. Russell described the dead end to which the current approach must lead, which makes economic considerations irrelevant to decisions about alternative therapies:

> For all practical purposes, there is no end to the amount of resources that can be absorbed by medical care when the economic restraints are removed. . . .
>
> Under complete third party payment, investment would proceed until the marginal benefit of any further investment equalled the marginal cost, zero.[80]

She pointed out that the evident ineffectiveness of technical controls—such as certificate-of-need laws and professional standard review committees—narrows the choice of methods by which the exorbitant growth rate of medical expenditures in recent decades can be slowed down:

> The two possibilities most often put forward are an aggregate limit on total resources (as through a national budget for medical care) or the partial reintroduction of prices in the form of coinsurance for all medical care (under coinsurance, the patient pays some fraction of all the costs he or she incurs; the fraction can be related to income). The choice between these two possibilities depends on such matters as whether it is considered more desirable to ration by queuing or by price or to discourage or encourage the patient's participation in the decisions about his medical care.[81]

Russell added that if cost to the patient is restricted by an upper limit, he will have no interest in savings beyond that point and that therefore an additional method of rationing will have to be applied.

Some would move in the other direction—toward comprehensive national health insurance. Such proposals have been debated in Congress for over 40 years. Their protagonists are undaunted by repeated defeats and continue to battle for eventual victory. They are encouraged by the undeniable popularity of comprehensive medical insurance, as evidenced in numerous public opinion polls. Most people like to get medical care for free—no strings attached—with the cost so well hidden that they can't see or feel it. Withholding from wages makes taxes nearly invisible—at least less painful than having to write a check—and, as long as the employer pays the insurance premium—who cares how much he pays? That it adds points to the inflation rate is regarded as just one of those esoteric and confused economic theories. Even so, it appears likely that comprehensive national health insurance has a great future behind it. Attention seems to be shifting toward other solutions of the problem of medical care costs.

It is becoming increasingly evident that we have gone overboard on the wrong kind of medical insurance by placing perverse incentives in our tax laws, as Harvard economist Martin Feldstein and Heritage Foundation economist Stuart M. Butler well pointed out.[82] Half of all individual medical insurance premiums up to $150 is deductible even if medical expenses do not exceed 3% of the taxpayer's adjusted gross income, with the other half deductible like other medical bills. Employer-paid premiums are viewed by the worker as tax-free compensation—and are so treated in collective bargaining negotiations. Individual deductibility as well as group insurance deductibility by the employer favor fee-for-service and first-dollar coverage, the most expensive form of coverage. In August 1980 the chairman of the U.S. House Ways and Means Committee, Al Ullman, was quoted as saying "Our federal tax system invites almost limitless health care spending."[83]

Among individual income taxpayers 72% have no "excess itemized deductions" and therefore derive no tax benefit from paying medical insurance premiums (nor other medical bills). But their employers can deduct the medical group premium they paid. Individuals and employers would tend to shift to more economical forms of medical insurance coverage if tax benefits were made contingent on the form of insurance they choose.

Insurance is not intended to protect an individual and his family against having to bear their normal, foreseeable and recurring living expenses. It must be designed to shield them against major, unexpected and unpreventable costs which they could bear only at the cost of severe deprivation or not at all.

Medical care is as necessary and as much part of the ordinary cost of living as are food, shelter and clothing. The question is only: where does the routine end and the emergency begin?

Medical care expenses totaled $192 billion nationally in 1978 which equals 14% of all personal income, 16% of adjusted gross income reported on income tax returns. Some would draw the line between "normal" and "extraordinary" at half of that, some at less. This is a question of judgment. The income tax law used to treat medical expenses exceeding 5% of gross income as unusual and deductible. This was reduced to 3%—which is surely too low.

The most economical and effective form of medical insurance is what used to be called "major medical," but is now more commonly referred to as "catastrophic" and probably most appropriately termed "major risk insurance" (MRI). If emphasis in the Internal Revenue Code were shifted to MRI, the federal subsidy to private health insurance plans, currently estimated at $11–13 billion could be substantially cut.

Initiative and drive for a shift toward MRI do not come from health professionals but from economists. Among leading advocates are Martin Feldstein of Harvard, Alain C. Enthoven of Stanford, Rita Ricardo-Campbell of Stanford, Clark C. Havighurst of Duke, Mark V. Pauly of Northwestern University.[84]

What may be significant: in 1980 the chairmen of the two tax-writing committees of Congress—Senator Russell B. Long and Rep. Al Ullman—expressed preference for the "catastrophic health insurance" approach and both sponsored appropriate legislative action to carry it into practice.

Some of the plans would superimpose catastrophic health insurance on existing programs, requiring employers to offer it to their workers. Others would go farther and create tax incentives *for* catastrophic insurance and *against* some of the currently popular coverages. Still others would turn catastrophic insurance into an all-encompassing umbrella with which, to the extent necessary, Medicare and even Medicaid could be integrated. Some would tie catastrophic insurance in with measures to reintroduce competition into the medical care market.

The health care industry is, at best, lukewarm about catastrophic insurance replacing, at least in part, existing coverages. A massive shift could mean that the picnic is over. But there is far stronger opposition from those who prefer a federal universal mandatory and comprehensive national health program which comes as close as possible to "free health care for all." There is no doubt about the wide popularity which such proposals enjoy. The spirit of the welfare state has permeated and enveloped the United States for many years and it favors governmental services for all major needs while frowning on the exercise of individual responsibility. Organized labor, and liberal forces in general, fight attempts such as catastrophic insurance to reverse the shift toward greater societal assumption of responsibility for, and direction of, major human activities. This is largely an ideological-philosophical issue, but not entirely. Assumption and discharge of individual responsibility for one's state of health play a much larger role in the final outcome than is widely believed. Rita Ricardo-Campbell pointed out that "80% of all medical intervention does not alter the course of disease" and "the highest life expectancies are found among people who exercise, eat sparingly, and consume far less medical care than the average American."[85]

Crime Without Punishment

There is one function, one major public duty in the domestic field which government was always expected to perform and which only government can properly and adequately carry out in a modern society: crime detection and prevention. It has turned this into the worst failure among its domestic activities.

No reliable statistics exist that would permit an accurate comparison of the incidence of crime in the United States and in other countries. But what we can piece together from available Interpol data and observations makes it certain that we have become the most crime-ridden of the world's major nations. In no other country could the leading newspaper of its largest city say, as the *New York Times* did: "This city's 8 million people live in daily fear of mugging, robbery and other violent crimes."[86] Nowhere else would a country's highest judge talk about "the reign of terror" in its cities.

The American public is increasingly frightened by the jungle-like conditions in our cities and anxious to restore civilized conditions. On June 30, 1972, *Life* published the results of a readers' survey on crime to which 45,000 responded. Eighty percent of the readers stated that they were afraid to walk their streets at night; nearly as many said they sometimes feel unsafe in their own homes. Since then the FBI's Crime Index has worsened by almost one-third.

For some years now respondents in national public opinion surveys have rated a lowering of the crime rate second only to controlling inflation as the most important and most urgent task of government (E. G. Roper surveys, May 1978 and May 1979). A Gallup poll in January 1973 showed that more than one of every five people across the nation has been victimized by crime in the preceding year—one in three in central cities. Respondents listed crime as the worst problem in their community.

In other world cities in capitalist, socialist, communist nations, in Paris, Moscow, Peking or Vienna, residents or tourists can freely promenade in daytime or evenings—which they would not dare in New York, Chicago, Atlanta, Detroit, or Washington. It is doubtful that a government could survive elsewhere that permitted such unsafe conditions in its major cities to exist as Americans have come to tolerate and suffer for the past few decades.

Nor is this simply a "crime wave" as it is often called. Waves crest and ebb, but the crime rate has been soaring upward, with no sign of cresting or ebbing. According to the FBI's *Uniform Crime Reports* the number of serious crimes leaped from 1.4 million in 1957 to 11.1 million in 1978. Preliminary estimates place the 1980 total at 13.3 million. Because of procedural changes the two figures may not be fully comparable. If we relate the 1957 to 1970 increase in crimes known to police of 292% and the 1970 to 1978 increase in "index crimes" of 38%, we get a 1957 to 1978 increase in the number of crimes of 441% in a period during which the U.S. population grew 28%. "Index crimes" are defined as seven major offenses: murder and nonnegligent manslaughter, forcible rape, robbery, aggravated assault, burglary, larceny-theft, motor vehicle theft. The *crime rate* (per 100,000 population) meanwhile grew by 321% which means that crimes in relation to population multiplied well over fourfold, with violent crimes and property crimes showing nearly identical rates of increase. The most rapid increase during the 1970s occurred in aggravated assault and rape, followed by burglary and larceny-theft, with robbery and murder somewhat behind.[87] Some reports have suggested that two to three times as many crimes are committed each year in the United States as appear in official police statistics.[88] According to preliminary reports, crimes increased by another 22% between 1978 and 1980.

Much of the literature through the 1960s and even into the 1970s blamed soaring crime on deficiencies of society and on shortcomings in its major institutions. Neglect of the poor, unemployed, disadvantaged, inadequate funds for public assistance, unemployment compensation and other social welfare programs, a tightfisted policy on Medicare, food stamps, public housing, a starving of school budgets, especially in central cities and ghetto areas were called the root causes of skyrocketing violent and property crime. Dozens of articles, books and media programs recommended a doubling or tripling of government spending for social purposes as the most effective strategy for fighting the "crime wave."

In February 1967 President Lyndon Johnson's Commission on Law Enforcement and the Administration of Justice, devised *A National Strategy* which focused on a war against social injustice such as poverty, discrimination and ignorance through forceful action in education, welfare, employment, health and civil rights:

> AMERICA CAN CONTROL CRIME. This report has tried to say how. It has shown that crime flourishes where the conditions of life are the worst, and that therefore the foundation of a national strategy against crime is an unremitting national effort for social justice. Reducing poverty, discrimination, ignorance, disease and urban blight, and the anger, cynicism or despair those conditions can inspire, is one great step toward reducing crime. It is not the task, indeed it is not within the competence, of a Commission on Law Enforcement and Administration of Justice to make detailed proposals about housing or education or civil rights, unemployment or welfare or health. However, it is the Commission's clear and urgent duty to stress that forceful action in these fields is essential to crime prevention, and to adjure the officials of every agency of criminal justice—policemen, prosecutors, judges, correctional authorities—to associate themselves with and labor for the success of programs that will improve the quality of American life.[89]

A year after the publication of this report President Johnson appointed a *National Commission on the Causes and Prevention of Violence* which submitted its final report in December 1969. It concluded that "if our future is to be more just, less violent, less crime-ridden, and free of fear, we obviously must do much better than we are now doing to speed social reform. . . ." The Commission found that "the time is upon us for a re-ordering of national priorities" and recommended cutting military expenditures and "increasing annual general welfare expenditures by about 20 billion dollars" (stated in 1968 dollars) and that those outlays "should continue to increase until essential social goals are achieved."[90]

Within two years the *National Advisory Commission on Criminal Justice Standards and Goals* was formed by the federal Law Enforcement Assistance Administration. It followed its predecessors in advocating expanded social programs and large appropriations for law enforcement, as well as schools. It set a goal of reducing the incidence of crime by at least 25% to 50% by the year 1983.[91] As it turned out, crimes were up 62% in 1980 (from 1972), with the trend still pointing up.

These national commissions were actually among the more moderate critics. Ramsey Clark, who served as assistant attorney general and attorney general in the Kennedy and Johnson administrations, pictured the criminal as a victim of society because of "the dehumanizing effect on the individual of slums, racism, ignorance and violence, of corruption and impotence to fulfill rights, of poverty and unemployment and idleness, of generations of malnutrition, of congenital brain damage, and prenatal neglect, of sickness and disease, of pollution, of decrepit, dirty, ugly, unsafe, overcrowded housing, of alcoholism and narcotics addiction, of avarice, anxiety, fear, hatred, hopelessness, and injustice. These are the fountainheads of crime. They can be controlled."[92]

Similarly shrill voices charged that stinginess in programs for the "deprived and oppressed" had generated a natural reaction among them and that the nation and its ruling class had only themselves to blame for the predictable consequences of their despicable policies.

Some observers of the crime scene learned from the experience of the 1970s and modified their position. Not so the senior judge of the country's secondmost important court in the field of public policy, the federal appeals court for the District of Columbia. In the *New York Times* of October 19, 1980, Judge David L. Bazelon identified the causes of crime as social injustice, grinding oppression, "overcrowded housing, lacking adequate nutrition and medicine, subjected to prejudice and educated in unresponsive schools . . . the real roots of crime are associated with a constellation of suffering so hideous that, as a society, we cannot bear to look it in the face."

Where does Judge Bazelon see a solution? "Assuring every family an income sufficient to provide the kind of home all children need." With many judges still confusing the criminal with his victims, it is small wonder that the rate of violent crime continues to soar.

The fact is that the past quarter century which witnessed crime multiplying to previously unimaginable dimensions also was the period during which public spending for social programs soared at an unprecedented rate, doubling its share of GNP from 10% to 20%. As shown in the earlier parts of this chapter (and in Table 23) public expenditures multiplied between 1952 and 1978 in *constant* dollars: for income support (public assistance, unemployment compensation, etc.) 10 times, for public education 6 times, for Medicaid and other health programs 9 times—while gross national income and product slightly better than doubled.

According to an HEW compilation social welfare expenditures on public programs multiplied between 1960 and 1978 3.5-fold in *constant* dollars. This was paralleled by a simultaneous growth in crime: 3.8-fold in the number of crimes committed, 3.1-fold in the crime rate (per 100,000 population).[93]

This suggests, by the rules of mathematics, a positive correlation between public spending for social purposes and the incidence of crime. It does not seem to give much comfort to the advocates of conventional wisdom about the social program–crime relationship nor add much strength to their pleas for expanding social funds as a means of reducing the incidence of crime.

It would take far more intensive research than can be presented in this framework to investigate whether there exists a causative relationship between lavish social spending and crime frequency. But I strongly suspect that the same mental attitude, the same "spirit of the welfare state" that is conducive to bringing about enormous social welfare programs also produced a system of law enforcement that resulted in a veritable crime explosion.

Some have attempted to relate high crime rates to the existence of poverty in America. But the number of persons below the official poverty level dropped from 22.4% in 1959 to 11.6% in 1977.[94] These statistics include only cash income (incompletely) and no in-kind income such as food stamps, rent subsidies, or school lunches. A more proper figure would *at most* be half of the 11.6% shown for 1977 (see p. 213).

The number of families with an income below $3000 (*constant* 1978 dollars) dropped from 11.2% in 1952 to 3.3% in 1978, of those with an income under $5000 from 19.9% to 8.2%. The number of families below the official poverty level dropped from 18.5% in 1959 (earliest year available) to 9.1% in 1978.[95] This does not prove nor suggest that poverty has been completely wiped out in the United States. But how can it be claimed that poverty is a factor, let alone a major causative factor, in the recent crime explosion, when the incidence of poverty drops to a fraction of its former size while crime multiplies? The facts which many carefully try to ignore is that crime expanded most spectacularly during the same time poverty diminished, that this has been occurring steadily and persistently for at least two decades, and that the assumption that these two developments may be merely coincidental is too farfetched to be believable. Supposing the trends of poverty and crime had been parallel—would not those who assert a positive and causative relation offer that fact as proof of their theory? Why then should an inverse trend be regarded as irrelevant to an explanation of the phenomenon?

Another explanation has been offered repeatedly for the growth of crime: inadequate appropriations for law enforcement. Said President Johnson's Commission on Law Enforcement and the Administration of Justice in 1967:

> This report has pointed out that legislatures and, by extension, the public despite their well-founded alarm about crime, have not provided the wherewithal for the criminal justice system to do what it could and should do . . . [p. 279].

The 1969 commission recommended that "we double our national investment in the criminal justice process" (p. 272). The doubling of expenditures to overcome the failure of programs to produce promised and expected results has been standard operating procedure among national study committees in many fields of inquiry for several decades. It is the most convenient alibi yet devised to explain the absence of positive results and to quiet widespread public dissatisfaction with governmental ineffectiveness. It may also be profitable to the members of those commissions who tend to be professionals deriving their livelihood within the field under review. "There is nothing wrong with the *xyz* program that couldn't be corrected by doubling the appropriation" (and salaries for an enlarged staff) has been a routine answer. It may sound plausible to somebody who does not know the record. But the record, usually, is devastating.

Expenditures for police protection (federal-state-local) multiplied five times (in *constant* dollars) between 1952 and 1978. They doubled as a percentage of GNP (Gross National Product).

This record does not indicate stinginess to be the most precise description of the treatment which police departments have been receiving from their respective governments. Between 1954 and 1977 (earliest and latest year now available) outlays for the entire criminal justice system

Expenditures for Police Protection (Federal, State, Local), 1952 to 1978

Year	Current dollars	1978 dollars	Percent of GNP
		millions	
1952	$1,080	$2,575	0.32%
1960	2,030	4,328	.41
1965	2,792	5,595	.43
1970	4,903	8,134	.51
1978	12,877	12,877	.64
1952–78 increase in percent	+ 1092%	+ 400%	

Sources: *Historical Statistics on Governmental Finances and Employment,* 1977 Census of Governments, and *Governmental Finances in 1977-78,* both: Bureau of the Census, U.S. Department of Commerce, 1980.

(police, judicial, public defense, corrections) increased 360% in *constant* dollars, with the share of police shrinking from 60% to 55%. It is discouraging that crime has been growing at about the same rate (in *constant* dollars) as outlays for the police. Hopefully, this will not suggest to some governments a shortcut to reducing the crime rate. Conceivably, crime might have proliferated even faster if police appropriations had not been boosted as much as they were, other circumstances being equal.

Personnel inadequacy is one of the most frequently used explanations—or, more properly, excuses—for the growth of crime. Employment in police departments nearly tripled between 1952 and 1978 and the ratio between police employment and population was cut in half.

	1952	1978	Increase percent
Police employment	254,000	689,000	+171%
U.S. population (million)	157.0	218.6	+ 39%
Police-population ratio	1:618	1:317	− 49%

Sources: *Historical Statistics on Governmental Finances and Employment,* 1967 Census of Governments, 1969, and *Public Employment in 1978,* both: Bureau of the Census, U.S. Department of Commerce.

Comparable statistics for the entire criminal justice system have become available only in recent years. During the 1970s, police departments expanded their employment only at half the rate or less of judicial, and legal services and correction.[96]

Data from New York City, Washington, D.C., and other major cities show a comparable picture: as the number of policemen and the size of police appropriations multiply, so do crimes, often at surprisingly similar rates.

One of the country's most eminent experts on police science, James Q. Wilson, professor of government at Harvard University, concluded in a survey of police attempts to prevent crime: "And yet to close observers of police at work there is also some reason to believe that the number and deployment of the police have little or nothing to do with the crime rate."[97] He pointed out that the size of the New York City Police Department was increased by 54% between 1954 and 1974, after a 1954 experiment in Manhattan's 25th Precinct with doubling police strength seemed to suggest positive results. But while New York City's population remained about constant between 1954 and 1974, crime increased even more rapidly than police manpower. A Kansas City experiment in the 1970s (sponsored by the Ford Foundation through the Police Foundation), which sharply increased police patrols in one part of the city, left them unchanged in another, and abolished them in a third, found no difference in the rate of reported crime or level of citizen fear among those city sections. The former general counsel to President Johnson's National Commission on the Causes and Prevention of Violence reportedly stated: "To the extent we tried dealing with the crime problem by increasing the number of police, we were doing something that everyone knew wasn't going to work. It was superficial relief from some symptoms. It is not a case of getting at the overall causes."[98]

What really does cause the continuing growth in crime? Liberal pundits have always had a ready explanation: poverty and inadequate social welfare programs. Police department heads advanced an equally convenient justification: Insufficient appropriations and staffs. But, as I have shown, neither of these propositions will "wash." They may sound convincing to true believers but are refuted by the record. Where can we turn for an explanation?

Congress established a National Institute of Law Enforcement and Criminal Justice as research arm of the Law Enforcement Assistance Administration, U.S. Department of Justice. Eight years later the U.S. House Judiciary Committee (Subcommittee on Crime) heard testimony on the institute's activities from its director:

> The National Institute was created in 1968 amid great expectations about what could be done to reduce crime. Time has tempered that vision. . . .

What can be said about our crime reduction capacity? Not much that is encouraging. We have learned little about reducing the incidence of crime, and have no reason to believe that significant reductions will be secured in the near future. . . .

The fact that little has been discovered, despite much effort, about either the "causes" of crime or how to reduce it is nevertheless significant. . . . The reason we don't do better in curing crime is that we don't know how.[99]

This, in my opinion confirms an old saying: There are none so blind as those who do not *want* to see.

In this book's predecessor, written in 1974, I offered this explanation for crime (p. 25): "There really is no mystery about the cause of the soaring crime rate: would-be criminals did their homework, they checked the record and came up with a simple fact: *crime pays.*" Thomas Plate chose *Crime Pays!* as the title of his excellent book in which he demonstrated just how well crime rewards its practitioners.[100] In a table of *Criminal Salaries* he listed various specialties that pay a successful criminal between $15,000 and $165,000 tax free on "office hours" that do not seem too demanding, with a risk that seems well worth taking.

James Q. Wilson argued that crime pays better now than it used to. Which suggests that crime does not grow with poverty but with affluence. It is the affluent society and the welfare state and the philosophy that created it that are at the root of the crime explosion.

In earlier chapters I pointed out that many persons on public assistance or unemployment compensation have made a rational and from an economic viewpoint justifiable choice among available alternatives. So have many criminals. The potential reward often compares favorably with the option of working long hours, at cumbersome menial and humdrum jobs for small rewards. A career in crime may bring higher returns at lower cost.

In the case of crime, cost includes a risk—the risk of being apprehended and incarcerated, being deprived of liberty, subjected to inconvenience and humiliation. How great is that risk?

As mentioned earlier, the FBI's annual reports placed the total of the seven "index" crimes at between 10 and 11 million a year in the later 1970s. During those years the courts turned over to state and federal prisons an average of 129,000 persons for terms of various length. This means that the risk of going to prison was about 1.1 to 1.2 in a hundred. The chance of *not* going to prison for committing a crime thus equals about 98.8%. Considering that some convicts may be in county jails—for "lighter" offenses and sentences—we may estimate that about 98% of those who commit crimes do *not* go behind bars. According to statistics compiled by the New York City police, the chance of a given felony arrest ending in a prison sentence in 1979 was about one in 108. Inevitably, the risk grows with the frequency of exposure and an industrious professional may occasionally get caught and even have to serve time. Also some ventures may not turn out to be as profitable as hoped. Thus crime may not always prove to be a lucrative career choice. Still, getting away with a criminal offense is a safer bet than most of us will ever have a chance of making in critical decisions of life.

The number of reported crimes increased by 429% between 1957 and 1977, the number of persons sent to prison by 60%, the size of the prison population by 42%. This means that the likelihood of a criminal's going to prison was cut to one-fifth (from 5.7% to 1.2%) within twenty years. Do we need to look further for the cause of skyrocketing crime?

How did it come about? In 1961, 26 percent of the offenses known to police were cleared by arrests, in the national average; this gradually shrank to 20.8% in 1978. In other words, a criminal now has four chances in five never to be arrested. If arrested he has better than five chances out of six *not* to serve time, although only 5 percent of those tried are acquitted. And the one in about 80, unlucky enough to wind up behind bars, served in 1978 on the average only 50% of the time to which he was sentenced—down from 61% in 1965. Is there any other money-making, ego-satisfying enterprise in which the chances are nearly as good?

Most noncriminals do not know this. After watching hundreds of all types of crime being committed on television screens, with the offenders unfailingly being caught and brought to justice, they do not realize that this represents but a tiny fraction of the crime outcome. So, they believe that all is right with the world—until they are hit themselves. Efrem Zimbalist—TV's FBI inspector Erskine in the popular program—never told them that the national average gross from a single truck highjacking is $47,000 and that few of the principals wind up in a cell.

Samuel Yochelson, a psychiatrist, and Stanton Samenow, a clinical psychologist, studied 252 male hard-core criminals and concluded:

> The criminal can and does choose his way of life freely in his quest for power, control and excitement. Moreover he can choose to change if he musters courage or will to endure the consequences of responsible choices.[101]

It was largely cold and dispassionate calculation, seasoned with some resentment against society, that caused crimes to climb to about 11 million a year in the late 1970s: only about 130,000 persons annually were being sent to prisons, and the prison population in the United States totaled

301,000 at the end of 1979. *Putting criminals behind bars has gone out of style.* It seems an anachronism in the age of the welfare state, which directed compassion at the criminal more than at the victim. Jessica Mitford, who regards law enforcement an instrument of oppression by the ruling class, has proposed to abolish prisons altogether.[102]

Why *do* we keep persons shut up behind walls for months or years? The practice of sentencing offenders to terms became widespread only about two centuries ago, replacing, for humanitarian reasons, various types of "cruel and unusual punishment." Prison was intended as punishment for transgressing upon the law of God and man and for doing harm to fellow man. Only in the 1870s did the idea take hold that time in jail should result in rehabilitation, a return to a virtuous life. Rehabilitation dominated the *theory* of criminology for most of the succeeding century, though not necessarily the *practice* of correctional institutions—more in some, less in others. Many of its believers hung on to it long after its abject failure had become obvious and practically uncontestable.

Incarceration now serves partially to isolate criminals and to incapacitate them for a limited time. But the main purposes still are punishment and deterrence. To believe in punishment requires a belief in free will and those of a determinist persuasion obviously cannot accept it.

That leaves deterrence which a growing number of scholars regard as the key to crime control. To its breakdown they attribute the crime explosion we have experienced.

Why has deterrence broken down? Some crimes of violence are cleared by an arrest: in 1977, 76% of murders, 62% of aggravated assaults, 50% of rape known to police. But only 26% of robberies were cleared. Only one out of six burglaries led to an arrest, one in seven motor vehicle thefts, and one in five cases of larceny-theft. Property crime is a low-risk occupation though it sometimes leads to violence and even homicide. Most street crimes go unpunished.

This does not suggest that police departments have been lying down on the job. Eleven hundred twenty-three policemen murdered in the line of duty between 1969 and 1978 testify to that. But it does suggest that something is terribly wrong with our methods, with the procedures under which police are forced to operate, and with the absurd rules imposed by federal courts whose concern seems to have shifted largely from the victim—and potential victims—of crime to the criminal who committed the offense. Our courts have gone to ridiculous ends to protect the "rights" of criminals and thereby create hundreds of thousands of additional victims, as Judge Macklin Fleming of the California Court of Appeals has shown in his book *The Price of Perfect Justice* (New York: Basic Books, 1975).

Judge Fleming captioned one of his chapters, "The Irrelevance of

Guilt," borrowing a phrase from Lord Diplock who thus referred in the British House of Lords to the so-called "exclusionary" rule of the U.S. Supreme Court, which requires the suppression of evidence obtained by means the court does not approve of. Many criminals, proven guilty beyond a shadow of a doubt, have been acquitted and were let loose on a peaceful citizenry because police, or a lower court, did not fully comply with some of the preposterous rules imposed by the highest court in the land.

On June 16, 1980, the U.S. Supreme Court in *U.S.* v. *Henry* (No. 79–121) overturned a Virginia man's bank robbery conviction because an FBI informer was, by coincidence, serving a sentence in the same cellblock. The informer had been told not to initiate conversations or ask direct questions. In the case of *Massiah* v. *U.S.* 377 US 201 (1964) the court held that by instructing an informer to elicit statements the government had violated the accused man's right to counsel. Although in the 1980 case the admission was not "deliberately elicited," the court vacated the conviction by a vote of 6:3. In Baltimore a convicted murderer was released on February 6, 1981 because his confession had been signed 24 hours and 12 minutes after his arrest—12 minutes later than the law allowed and therefore inadmissible in court.

If a tennis player commits a "foul" his opponent gains a point. That may be pedagogically sound—in a tennis game. But it is nothing short of madness in the deadly business of law enforcement and crime control. It is proper for a court to find that a police or court officer acted incorrectly and should be disciplined. But to let a guilty man go free because of it is obscene. No other country in the world would think of doing it. The number of criminals guilty but acquitted for purely procedural reasons may be small. But the practice has cast a pall over law enforcement and prevented in many thousands of cases the accumulation and presentation of evidence without which a successful prosecution appeared doubtful or hopeless.

The U.S. Supreme Court has blindfolded and handcuffed our law enforcement agencies, making police officers jump through rings by rules known by the names of *Miranda, Mallory, Wade*, and others. Congress attempted in the *Omnibus Crime and Safe Streets Act of 1968* to reverse the mentioned court decisions but the courts sublimely ignored this attempt to restore justice and common sense. Unfortunately, Congress did not have the courage to impeach the judges who inflicted those perverse rules nor passed a constitutional amendment to overrule the courts. Small wonder that four out of five crimes go without even an arrest, with many of the remaining one-fifth never being brought to justice.

Most attorneys and elected public officials are reluctant to confront the

High Court which, in this case—and in several others—has painted itself into a corner. Still, the final responsibility, under the Constitution, rests with the Congress which so far has responded only with mirror fighting—such as the mentioned and ineffective 1968 law. As a result, we are engaged in a crime war which we are losing. A Roman maxim of law was *Inter arma silent leges* (the laws are silent in war). It could conceivably prove necessary in some locations to impose temporarily some features of "martial law" if we are to have any hope of winning the war on crime.

There is, in my opinion, no chance that we can make progress in the "war on crime" until some of the nonsensical rules of the U.S. Supreme Court are overturned and our law enforcement agencies—from police to local prosecutors and courts—are vested with powers that their counterparts throughout the world outside the United States possess and wield.

This may involve some restrictions and inconvenience. We have for years been subjecting ourselves to much inconvenience in having our persons and belongings searched by airport security to forestall highjacking of aircraft. Privacy rules do not protect us when dealing with the IRS. Some otherwise undesirable tactics may have to be employed until we can gain an upper hand in the war on crime.

Handguns are used not only in most homicides, but also in many bank or street holdups, robberies, and numerous other violent and property crimes. Yet there is strong resistance to proposals to forbid the carrying of guns, especially when loaded (as most countries do), and even to making gun possession subject to police license or registration. Americans know that though a majority of law-abiding citizens might comply with such a law, if passed, the underworld would not. "If guns are outlawed, only outlaws will have guns." They feel that they need guns for self-protection and have no confidence in the ability of the police to enforce gun control laws. Thus the major result of gun control would be the disarming of lawful citizens. If our system of law enforcement were adequately tightened and violations certain to be severely punished—to the point where even outlaws would feel sufficiently threatened to give up their guns—the use of guns in the commission of crimes would substantially decline.

Growing intricacy of court procedures and willingness of courts to condone procrastinating maneuvers ad infinitum have lengthened American criminal trials to months and years while British (and other) trials seldom take more than a few days or, at most, weeks. Calendars have become so crowded by the courts' own and the U.S. Supreme Court's rules. The periodic appointment of additional judges is as effective in catching up as a dog's attempt to catch his own tail. The idea of "speedy justice" has become a mockery—only releases are speedy. It takes barely a few hours to "spring" an arrested person and let him loose to conduct his criminal pursuits for months or years without interference. Long-drawn-out trials help to keep thousands of lawyers in bread and butter.

At frequent intervals the American public is being told by Ralph Nader, Morris Udall and their confederates that there is a big problem in the country with white-collar crime—embezzlement, antitrust violations and the like. The *Wall Street Journal* (November 11, 1975) editorially called this "another variation of the currently popular sport of corporation baiting." It commented, "Any society concerned about self-preservation must necessarily pay greater attention to crimes of violence than to non-violent crime." James Q. Wilson declared predatory street crime to be a far more serious matter than consumer fraud because it "makes difficult or impossible the maintenance of meaningful human communities."

Most of today's criminals are not thieves like Victor Hugo's Jean Valjean, driven by need to steal bread to feed his family. Nor are they sick personalities who have attended an underfinanced school or are waiting to be trained in a simple manual occupation under a government program. Rather, they are career professionals in a large highly profitable industry that carries certain risks. That is why they employ astute, well-paid lawyers to keep them if not out of trouble then at least out of jail.

Crime can be reduced only by meting out certain and severe punishment and thereby making crime unprofitable, as Ernest van den Haag has argued effectively.[103] *Deterrence* is the key word. If repeaters are taken out of circulation and incapacitated for long enough periods and if the consequences of pursuing a criminal career are made intolerable, more would-be criminals will learn early enough in their lives from the experience of others, and if necessary their own, that crime doesn't pay.

In a series of penetrating articles in the early 1970s, subsequently published in book form, James Q. Wilson demonstrated most convincingly that effective deterrence is the only means by which the frightful growth of crime can be halted and reversed.[104] He called for certainty and greater severity of punishment. Ernest van den Haag concluded likewise in a simultaneous volume and numerous articles. Both authors ranked certainty of punishment ahead of severity. Gordon Tullock in "Does Punishment Deter Crime?" thought that their *relative* importance is insignificant: both are essential elements in a program that hopes to bring crime under control.[105]

The *Center for Econometric Studies of the Justice System* established at the Hoover Institution in 1975 in cooperation with the National Institute of Law Enforcement and Criminal Justice has conducted intensive research on the effectiveness of deterrence in the past few years. Results so far confirm that adherence to the law could be increased by making punishment for crime more certain and/or more severe.[106]

What needs to be done and can be done? The judiciary committees of both Houses of Congress played for nearly fifteen years with revision and codification of federal criminal laws and produced a 753-page plan, known at some time as S1. I used the verb "played" because the proposed code suggested only minor changes of a cosmetic nature and did not even come near to dealing with the vital and urgent problem of halting the growth of crime and reducing it. It died with the adjournment of the 96th Congress in 1980.

Real reform would above all require a restitution to law enforcement agencies of the powers they need to cope with the crime flood that has engulfed us. Congress destroyed—in the pursuit of its Watergate escapades—much of the FBI's (and the CIA's) ability to protect the American people against subversive movements, terrorism, conspiracies and more common types of crime, besides abolishing the Senate Internal Security Subcommittee and the House Committee on Un-American Activities. The FBI was ordered to abandon the job of monitoring "subversives." The results of these and related actions were well expressed in the title of an article by James Grant: "Missing Security: The U.S. Has Robbed Itself of Defense Against Terror."[107]

Laws currently on the books impose long sentences—longer than in most other countries—but they are being flouted. They must be made mandatory. In fact, as indicated earlier, most of the action to control crime needs to concentrate on the courts. Only Congress has the power to do so, if necessary by constitutional amendment. Various public opinion polls indicate beyond doubt that Americans would enthusiastically support more effective measures to identify and apprehend offenders (even at some inconvenience to the general public) and harsher treatment of criminals. Legislatures would probably approve such amendments with "all deliberate speed."

Yet, there will be strong and loud objections from those who believe that offenders are not responsible for their actions, that crime is the fault of society and not of the person who perpetrates it and that to impose tougher sentences and long imprisonment amounts to committing *The Crime of Punishment*. That, in fact, was the title of a book by a psychiatrist.[108]

This is the spirit that spawned the runaway welfare state. We are not only paying a high price for yielding to it but in the end may have to pay a far higher price than we are willing to pay. A society which holds its members less and less responsible for their actions and their own condition, which finds and accepts ever more sophisticated alibis and excuses for actions which are injurious to others and detrimental to society as a whole, cannot be surprised when rules of civilized behavior which are essential to the survival of society are increasingly disregarded. Unless individuals are held strictly accountable for what they do—or don't do—and know that they face certain punishment for transgressing upon the rules and upon the rights of others, a growing number will not exercise the self-discipline to resist ever present temptations and follow the primitive instincts of our jungle ancestors. We all are at times subjected to impulses which if carried out would violate the rights of others. Some of us overcome them by our own sense of proper action—Kant's categorical imperative—while others will be deterred only if the consequences of violation are certain and severe beyond the individual's willingness to suffer them.

Not only professional criminals will consider other careers when the cost of crime becomes prohibitive. Even some of the impulse crimes may decline when the known consequences of yielding to a sudden urge produce sober second thoughts before rash action, rather than after.

Housing Blight, City Plight and the Evanescence of Urban Revitalization

With his superb flair for dramatic locution, Franklin Delano Roosevelt illustrated the deprivations that the Great Depression had visited upon the American people in the 1930s in his *Second Inaugural Address* with the famous phrase of seeing one-third of a nation "ill-housed, ill-clad, ill-nourished." He visualized salvation for this "third of a nation" primarily through several types of income support programs which, on his recommendations, Congress had authorized in 1935, some related programs, and by the economic recovery he confidently predicted.

Economic growth during the war and in succeeding decades tripled *real* per capita personal income and ended genuine poverty as a mass phenomenon in the United States. It did not end poverty, as currently defined, because poverty is a *relative* term, which labels some persons poor because their income and living standards are lower than those of the majority of their fellow citizens or the national average. It does not necessarily mean a lack of the necessities of life though it implies absence of amenities which more productive people are able to enjoy.

There is no starvation in the United States though there is malnutrition, caused by a variety of factors among which the inability to obtain essential nourishment ranks relatively low. To be ill-clad can nowadays hardly be regarded as a widespread characteristic in this country save among people who so choose as an expression of their preferred life-style.

But there still are large numbers of "ill-housed" families and of abhorrent slums in some of our large cities. Such conditions are not confined to the United States; they have been a matter of concern to many European nations which experienced large rural-to-urban migrations. International comparisons in this field, as in most, are tenuous, because of differences in concepts and definitions. But it is comforting to note that the latest United Nations compilation shows the U.S. with the least crowded housing conditions among 20 listed countries, including the Soviet Union: we have the lowest average number of persons per room.[109] Our residential plant also ranks at or near the top by all available criteria of installed equipment, plumbing, etc., though there remain, here and elsewhere, wide discrepancies among socioeconomic classes.

Yet, there is a significant difference between the U.S. and other countries. Pierre de Vise observed: "North American cities are unique among the world's cities in having poor people living in the central city and rich people living in suburbs."[110] This gradual takeover and "corrosive erosion" of urban cores has led to a flight from the cities and threatens their economic base, their proper functioning and, in the long run, their very existence.

Several dozen governmental programs, large and small, have attempted over the past four decades to improve housing conditions of the poor and to wipe out decaying sections of many cities. But decrepit dwellings and slums seem like the Hydra which grew two new heads whenever Hercules chopped one off. Can something be done about urban blight?

Myres McDougal and Addison Mueller of the Yale Law School wrote in 1942 of

> the well-documented fact that slum clearance and the provision of sanitary low-rent housing decrease danger of epidemics, raise general public health, reduce crime, cut juvenile delinquency, reduce immorality, lower economic waste by reducing health, police and fire protection costs, make better citizens, eliminate fire hazards, increase general land values in the vicinity, cut the accident rate, and prevent the cancerous spread of slums to uninfected areas.[111]

Twenty years later in May 1962, New York City's Mayor Robert F. Wagner, a leading liberal of long standing, told the National Conference on Social Welfare:

> Once upon a time we thought that if we could just bulldoze the slums and build shiny new public housing for low-income people, all social problems involving these people would virtually disappear. This has turned out to be not so.
>
> Once we thought that if we built enough playgrounds and other recreational facilities, juvenile delinquency would disappear. This turned out to be not so.

Once we thought that having discovered a magic bullet to kill the microorganisms that cause venereal disease, we had conquered venereal diseases. That turned out to be not so.[112]

In the nearly twenty years since Mayor Wagner confessed disillusionment with his earlier ideas, similar experiences have caused many others to have second thoughts about proposed or attempted governmental solutions to intricate social problems. Certainly many of our social engineers and politicians have turned less exuberant, less sure of their favorite multi-billion-dollar wonder drugs. They seem to have become sadder—have they also become wiser?

Looking at their proposals, we may doubt it. With admirable ingenuity they have produced a kaleidoscopic variety of housing and urban renewal programs, some of them ephemeral, some persisting despite mediocre or adverse results. What housing expert Anthony Downs called the "law of compulsive innovation" was largely the wizards' response to failure of miracle cures which they or their brethren had prescribed and administered but a few years earlier and which had gone sour beyond responsible officials' ability to cover up.[113] But our planners and decision makers were and still are unwilling to learn from the lessons of their ventures in recent decades that huge schemes of income redistribution though they may please their direct beneficiaries will, far from resolving the underlying social conflicts, multiply them and make them virtually incurable.

Mayor Wagner was trying to tell his audience that when slums were bulldozed out of existence in one location they sprung up in another. Even newly built or restored housing turned into instant slums. It is a hard lesson to learn: *slums are not decaying buildings, slums are people.* It is far easier to construct gleaming edifices and to move people to another section of town than to change their behavior. Moses learned that though he could take the Jews out of Egypt, he could not take Egypt out of the Jews. It took a generation of tough desert living to produce a nation worthy and able to conquer the Promised Land.

Most proposals and actions in recent decades were and are based on the naive assumption—or philosophical conviction—that bad housing and poverty *cause* occupational incompetence, welfare dependency, family break-up, illiteracy, delinquency, crime and vandalism. But these are only the symptoms, manifestations of a far deeper malaise that cannot be cured by pouring hundreds of billion dollars' worth of concrete and modern plumbing. No more so than a century of attempted rehabilitation reformed many criminals or fifteen years of "compensatory education" turned illiterates into scholars. Much social pathology does not respond to what the doctor ordered, especially when his diagnosis was wrong. Some social pathology, unfortunately, is incurable.

The range of government programs for low-income housing is stupendous. It started out with low-rent public housing, intended as temporary aid for low-paid workers, became more ambitious when urban renewal undertook to rehabilitate whole sections of town, then turned to rent supplements, subsidized scaled rents, grants, loans, guarantees for developers, builders, lenders and other entrepreneurs, renters and homeowners; it shaped tax shelters, tax incentives, accelerated depreciation, shuttled emphasis from new construction to restoration and back, undertook emergency and rescue actions to bail out programs in trouble, encouraged homesteading, self-help, and dozens of other presumptive cures.

Each of these programs was attacked, at some time or other, as being ill-designed, ineffective, wasteful, counterproductive. But each was, in turn, defended by its protagonists as essential and being the best-known method of dealing with a major public calamity and human suffering which could be left untreated only at dire peril to the common good.

Somehow it seems that as the size of the programs grew, so did the estimates of "need," of the number of people to be helped, of the federal appropriations required. We appear to move farther from the goal, the more we strive to reach it. In all that confusion it is difficult to find out just what is being done, at what cost to the public treasury and what it accomplishes. But I shall try.

How Much Government Assistance to Housing?

No one really knows how much money the government devotes to housing purposes. Nor are the amounts shown in annual budgets or expenditure reports of much help. This is so not only because the promotion of housing is partially carried out through numerous tax concessions and guarantees and some of the activities are "off-budget" financed. Above all—much of the current spending is being done by private entrepreneurs and housing authorities at federal behest with the government footing the final bill by committing itself to pay off their outlays plus interest over the ensuing 15 to 40 years.

Expenditures for "housing and community development" or for "housing and urban renewal" are reported annually by the Bureau of Economic Analysis and by the Bureau of the Census, the main sources of public finance data; both are divisions of the Department of Commerce. They showed outlays of $4.7 billion and $6.0 billion respectively for 1978, equal to less than one percent of total government spending and about one-fourth of one percent of GNP. But this far understates the true magnitude of activities.

The U.S. Budget's functional classification of "housing" excludes the huge amounts for subsidized housing which are included in the totals for "income maintenance," properly so. Housing subsidy programs are not aimed at or trying to remedy a housing shortage. There is no *housing* shortage. There is a shortage of *money* among people who are trying to be housed beyond their means. Those means include their own earnings and income (if any) and benefits from various social programs. Most housing subsidies for low-income persons are therefore correctly classified as income maintenance (or income support) programs.

This still leaves us with the question unanswered: how much does the government spend on housing for low-income families? The Department of Housing and Urban Development (HUD) reported $4.1 billion outlays for low-cost or subsidized housing for FY 1978, which is barely the tip of the iceberg. The department's budgetary authority (BA) for 1978, the amount it is empowered to commit the federal government for, totaled $33.5 billion, with most of it contracted and obligated to be paid off in installments over up to 40 years. That is what the government actually *spends* but does not necessarily lay out in cash. What is included in reports on governmental spending, e.g., in the U.S. Budget, is only the $4.1 billion cash.

That may seem a reasonable procedure. After all, when a family buys a home it commits itself to a large amount through a mortgage which it promises to pay off in 20 or 30 or more annual installments. But there is a significant difference between a family and the government: a family buys and owns only one residence and usually has only one home at a time. Federal low-income housing is an annual and continuing program, with no end in sight. Therefore it ought to be financed and paid on an annual basis. By piling up each year's unpaid balance—$29.4 billion in FY 1978—it accumulates a debt which at an annual clip of nearly $30 billion will in time soar to astronomical proportions. It already totals a quarter of a trillion dollars, after only a few years operation of the rent subsidy (Section 8) program. When discounted to current value, those future commitments would of course be worth far less at the present time. Annual outlays are estimated to rise from $4.1 billion in 1978 to $7.1 billion in FY 1981 in the president's budget for FY 1981. At that rate of progression they will exceed $200 billion by the end of this century. In the four fiscal years 1978 to 1981 outlays are estimated at an aggregate $22 billion, budget authority (commitments) at $122.4 billion. Debt under Section 8 could reach $1 trillion or more by the year 2000.

But that is only part of the story. The Congressional Budget Office (CBO) suggested that the $26.7 billion that HUD requested to finance 300,000 subsidized housing units in FY 1980 will not cover the actual spending which could run two to three times higher over the 15 to 40 year period of the contracts. CBO found in a March 1979 report that "the long-term direct subsidy costs of the public housing program consistently exceed the amount of the budget authority reserved" and that "current budget documents do not consider many indirect costs." It estimated that the total direct and indirect cost of an average public housing unit could run between $268,400 and $491,000 instead of the $141,600 budget authority reserved, of a 40-year new construction/substantial rehabilitation unit between $272,800 and $756,800 instead of $203,900. HUD replied that it was too early to judge its long-range assumptions.[114] At the present time the differing assumptions and projections of HUD and CBO cannot be proved or disproved. Should CBO turn out to be right, the additional commitments that HUD is making each year for low-cost housing could grow to several trillion dollars by the turn of the century.

But this still is not all. At congressional hearings on FY 1980 appropriations HUD Secretary Patricia R. Harris testified that the department would be subsidizing housing for 3.2 million families in 1980 but nearly five times as many households—14.8 million—needed and were eligible for subsidization if they were to be provided with "adequate housing": there were 4.8 million units with "deficiencies" (3.4 million rented, 1.4 million owner-occupied), 1.2 million units "overcrowded" (half rented, half owner-occupied) and 8.7 million households with an "excessive cost burden" (6 million renters, 2.7 million owners).[115]

These 14.8 million households are eligible for aid but cannot now be served because of HUD's financial limitations. In contrast to most other welfare programs, which are "open-ended" and therefore paid in full to all persons *entitled* to benefits, housing assistance is limited by the magnitude of congressional appropriations. Organized groups have been pressing Congress to recognize "entitlements" in housing as fully as they are in public assistance, social security, and Medicaid. So far they have not succeeded. If Congress were to yield, annual costs of low-income housing subsidies would soon start to soar far above totals estimated earlier.

Questions can be raised about the validity of the claimed needs. The incidence of housing inadequacies has declined sharply over the years. Census surveys found that plumbing deficiencies dropped from 35.4% (of all housing units) in 1950 to 3.4% in 1976; dwellings needing other major repairs dropped from 9.8% in 1950 to 4.6% in 1970 (latest year available), "substandard" units dropped from 36.9% in 1950 to 9.0% in 1970 (latest year).[116] Annual Census surveys reported a substantial decline between 1973 and 1976 in all types of housing defects except "signs of mice or rats"; they are not as structural as behavioral—on the part of the occupants.

HUD's standard of "overcrowding" is: more than *one* person per room. The standard of overcrowding used in Scandinavian countries is more than *two* persons per room. *The 1976 Housing Survey* reported that only 1.0% of occupied housing units had more than 1.5 persons per room, down from 6.2% in 1950. This does not suggest an urgent need that government should spend billions of dollars to remedy.

The "excessive cost burden" is computed on the assumption that a family should not have to pay more than 15% to 25% of its total income (earned, welfare, etc.) for housing purposes.

Should 25% of income be accepted as an upper limit which its housing should cost a family? The 1976 annual Census housing survey reported 24 million renters of whom nearly half paid more than a fourth of their income for rent, over a fourth paid more than 35%. But those percentages were far higher in the lowest income quartile: nearly three-fourths of the low-income families paid 35% or more. Most renters in the upper quartiles paid less than 25% of their incomes for rent. That should not be surprising. Families at the lower end of the income scale normally spend all of their resources on essentials while high-income families are able to allocate a sizable share of their income to discretionary purposes. Households on public assistance and/or at poverty levels receive food stamps and have their medical needs taken care of by Medicaid; this leaves a larger share—though small in amount—for housing. Congress recognized this and in December 1979 authorized HUD to require a contribution between 20% and 30% of income. At this point it is doubtful whether and to what extent HUD will use this authorization.

The figures cited above cover only subsidized housing and include neither urban development and renewal programs—which run at about $5 billion annually—nor tax concessions and ancillary benefits which would add a few more billions. The question may be asked why a country in which the incidence of poverty has been declining and now is at a very low level (see p. 213), should have to lay out several hundred billion dollars in public funds for housing subsidies within a decade. Are there really so many families which cannot provide for their own housing?

It is not widely enough recognized that living standards have in recent decades been increasingly shaped by and identified with the income level of multiearner families. In 1978 there were 31.7 million families with two or more earners, only 18.3 million families with one earner. Median money income of multiple-earner families was $22,174, of one-earner families $14,239. Therefore, one-earner families whose head does not possess very high and lucrative occupational skills, can no longer enjoy *average* living standards because their income is *below average* in contemporary America. They can be enabled to do so only if the government redistributes income from multiearner families and other high-income recipients to below-average single-earner families.

Family composition has been changing. Households consisting of a married couple with children—thought to be the typical American family—now account for less than one-third of all households. Between 1960 and 1977 the number of married couples living together increased by 20%, of families headed by a male-alone by 25%, of families headed by a female-alone by 83%. That is where much of the problem lies because families headed by women often are in an economically precarious position. Unless a woman possesses a good marketable skill or a strong drive she may find welfare preferable to working. This limits household income and often makes housing costs a problem, although welfare departments usually consider them in public assistance budgets. Some elderly couples who do not own a paid-up home also may have a problem in paying for housing.

Early on, housing subsidies were granted only to households at the very bottom of the income scale. But income limits tended to move up. There simply are not enough votes at the lowest income levels for effective political power. Irving Welfeld mentioned another reason: "The aversion of Congress to exclusively low-income housing was based on its discovery, made during the 1950's and 1960's, that public housing for only the lowest-income families soon became public slums."[117] Workers with income just barely above the lowest (or subsidy-eligible) brackets may become jealous when they see families with a lower income (possibly coming from social welfare) moving into subsidized housing units, public or not, which may be better or newer than their own. The average U.S. household size dropped from 3.11 persons in 1970 to 2.75 persons in 1980 because large numbers of young people, as well as adults and elderly people, choose to live alone, whether they can afford it or not, and to try to get subventions in one form or another from public and private sources.

Political realities caused income limits to creet upwards until "low-income housing" programs became "low- and moderate-income housing" programs. Families with an income below 80% of the local median are now eligible for housing aid, which in 1980 typically meant an upper income limit of about $16,000. In practice, HUD subsidizes only a small number of families with income over $10,000 because of appropriation restraints. In October 1980 Congress authorized the subsidation of mortgage rates for families earning up to 130% of an area's median income—after shelving a White House proposal to include families earning up to 150% of average local income. Even at the 130% level, some families with an income up to about $36,000 may be eligible for housing subsidies. With far more households just above the lowest brackets than at the bottom itself, the extension to "moderate income" could become enormously expensive if Congress were to approve sufficiently large or "open-ended" appropriations.

Prices seem to have been rising faster for housing than for most other goods and services. This not only raised the amount of housing subsidies but made many moderate-income earners "housing-poor" (just as some became "medically indigent," [see p. 270]). "Housing costs" is a broad and intricate subject that needs to be discussed to understand the trends in government housing programs.

Runaway Cost of Housing?

The high cost of housing is now a major problem for millions of American families. Costs of acquiring or occupying decent housing have increased dramatically in recent years. . . . the high cost of shelter is not merely serious, it is too often an insurmountable crisis.

Thus opens the final report of HUD's *Task Force on Housing Costs*, dated May 25, 1978. It well expresses the opinion of most Americans. Page 3 of the report presents statistics, derived from the Bureau of the Census and the Bureau of Labor Statistics, to document the task force's findings. They show the following *annual* rates of increase:

	1963 to 1972	1972 to 1976
Cost of Homeownership*	5.17%	8.15%
Residential rent	2.55	4.97
Consumer Price Index	3.53	8.00
Median family income	6.60	7.05

*This index does not consider the effect of appreciation in market value or capital gain associated with homeownership.

Residential rents thus consistently advanced more slowly than the Consumer Price Index (CPI), the cost of homeownership rose slightly faster than the CPI, and average family incomes grew faster than home-owning or renting costs between 1963 and 1972 and more slowly than homeowning—but faster than renting costs—between 1972 and 1976. This seems to suggest that the problem developed in the 1970s and exists only in homeowning, not in renting.

Several analysts have been contending for several years that widely held concepts on housing costs are contrary to the facts. B. Bruce-Briggs of the Hudson Institute presented a broad array of statistics on the cost of housing and its components, comparing them with various economic yardsticks, and concluded "that American housing is *not* getting more expensive, except for the minority whose income is not keeping pace with natural gains."[118] John C. Weicher arrived at similarly optimistic conclusions in "The Affordability of New Homes."[119] HUD's *1978 Statistical Yearbook* (p. 306) showed that the ratio of median family income to the median sales price of homes has remained stable; it stood at 2.8 in 1949, at 2.9 in 1954, fluctuated little, and at 3.0 in 1976 and 1977.

Stanford economist Richard F. Muth demonstrated that "the rental cost of tenant-occupied dwellings has fallen relative to consumer prices generally over the twelve-year period 1965–1977" and that this is true also of owned homes. ". . . the real cost of occupying any given-size dwelling has probably fallen over the past fifteen years or so . . ." Muth concluded: "We have, in my view, probably made housing too cheap relative to other things that we as Americans buy and consume . . . It is too cheap in the sense that an additional dollar invested in the corporate sector earns over twice as much as an additional dollar invested in owner-occupied housing."[120] A bias in favor of consumption and against productive capital formation has been a characteristic of American public policy for many years.

International comparisons show that the United States ranks quite low among industrialized countries with regard to the rise in housing costs. When housing costs are related to the general price level or to per capita income, we did in the 1970s slightly better than most other countries.[121]

This may be a good point at which to review what the U.S. Bureau of Labor Statistics, the agency which monitors prices at the national level, reported about housing and other prices over the period generally examined in this book, the years 1952 to 1978:

The Consumer Price Index (CPI) for all goods and services increased by 146%.
Its housing component increased by 158%.

This means that over the entire 26-year period the price of housing (expressed in *constant* dollars) increased by 4.9% which averages out to less than 0.2% per year. That certainly is a somewhat less than spectacular rise.

But the share which expenditures for housing are of total consumer expenditures meanwhile increased by better than one-fourth—from 12.4% of personal consumption expenditures to 15.7%. Thus—assuming the price index to be correct—we substantially increased our consumption of housing, relative to other goods and services. This manifested itself not so much in the number of houses built—housing starts increased 35%, U.S. population 39%—but more in what could be called the quality of housing.

The average space in single-family homes grew from about 1100 square feet at the mid-century to over 1600 square feet in the late 1970s. This equals about a 50% increase in space during a period when the number of persons per household declined by over 16% (3.3 to 2.8). It means that in single-family homes a person now has about 70% more space than around 1950. The three-bedroom house replaced the two-bedroom house.[122] We have no comparable measurements for apartments but both apartments and owner-occupied residences now are on the average far more lavishly equipped in terms of plumbing, wiring, and other built-in appliances than they were a quarter century earlier. These changes largely account for our spending on housing a one-fourth larger share of our total consumption outlays and getting greater comfort and amenities in return. In other words: *what really boosted the cost of housing is not so much the high cost of living as the cost of high living.*

A few other factors are involved. Costs rose faster in construction than in other areas:

Between 1952 and 1978:

Cost of living index	increased by 146%
The composite construction cost index	increased by 195%
Residential construction costs (Boekh index)	increased by 238%

These figures may not necessarily be precise because they cannot measure quality as accurately as prices (though they try). But they give us a good idea of trends and relative movements.[123]

Why did construction prices rise faster than other costs? Because both wages and materials increased more steeply in construction than elsewhere.

Hourly wage rates increased between 1952 and 1978 (in *constant* dollars):

in construction	65%
in the total nonagricultural private economy	52%

Weekly wages increased between 1952 and 1978

in construction	56%
in the total nonagricultural private economy	37%

I should mention here that the unemployment rate has consistently been higher in construction than in any other major industry and that this holds true even in the main construction season.

The index for construction materials increased	228%
The general producers price index increased	195%

However, the "hard" costs of housing, meaning construction, have actually been declining relative to the "soft" costs—land and financing. HUD estimated that hard costs dropped from 62% of total costs in 1968 to 45% in 1978.[124] Land costs have risen from about one-eighth of housing costs to one-fourth. This is only partially due to higher prices and scarcity of suitable land. The United States still is among the most sparsely settled major countries; two-thirds of our population live on one percent of the land, despite the fact that our favored single-family housing consumes more space. Multistory housing—which dominates in most industrial nations outside the United States—cuts land cost per housing unit to a fraction, though it raises construction costs. But it also facilitates mass transportation between home and work place which is far more economical than expensive (and fuel-wasteful) individual driving.

Financing has become the most expensive part of housing. Interest now usually totals more, over the life of the mortgage, than the original cost of the house. Interest rates soared from between 5% and 6% in the 1960s to 9.5% in 1978, nearly 12% by the end of 1979, and exceeded 13% in 1980 and 1981. Much of the interest cost however may be offset by a decline in the real value of the mortgage in inflationary times.

High interest rates and tight money are widely being blamed for the difficulty of low- and middle-income earners in acquiring a home. But interest rates are barely ahead of inflation—which means that lenders get only a very small *net* return. If money were made more easily available as housing interest groups request, effective housing demand would expand and push house prices up even faster. Thus additional millions of marginal income families would be driven out of the housing market.

Perpetual inflation has made homes more than a shelter. A home has become the best form of investment for most families. While most other types of investment, such as bonds, savings accounts and even common stocks lost about half their value (in *constant* dollars) between 1965 and 1978, house prices have slightly risen (in *constant* dollars).

Tax policy subsidizes homeownership generously. The Treasury estimated that deductibility of mortgage interest, real estate taxes, and other items amounted to a savings to homeowners of $15.7 billion in 1978. This does not include the nontaxability of imputed income from owner-occupied homes which may amount to $10 billion nor accelerated depreciation. It has long been a policy of the U.S. government to encourage and promote homeownership. Certain civic virtues are widely held to be developed or strengthened with the change from renting to owning. Liberal tax benefits have helped substantially to boost homeownership to nearly two-thirds of American families. In the process they have also helped to drive up the demand and prices for single-family homes.

I pointed out earlier that the price of housing did not rise much faster than other prices between 1952 and 1978. But there is a difference between renting and owning. Between 1953 (earliest year available) and 1978, residential rents increased 104 percent, homeownership costs 203 percent.[125]

This means that residential rents were in 1978, on the average 16% lower in *constant* dollars than they had been 25 years earlier, while homeownership was 24% more costly. But homeowners have no cause for complaint: they get valuable tax benefits from government which renters are not getting and the value of their investment is going up, while the value of their mortgage debt is shrinking with inflation. "Would-be" owners of moderate means face a difficult problem and sometimes an insurmountable obstacle. But if government made more money available on "easy" terms, the added demand for houses would drive up prices even faster, thus generating more claims for increased government aid.

It actually is the tenants who have been complaining most loudly: rents are sky-high and keep going up fast. To be sure, rents have been increasing—as have all other prices—as the dollar's value shrank to 50 cents between 1965 and 1978. Expressed in *constant* dollars residential rents have actually been declining, as I showed earlier. They may be beyond the reach of some low-income families but they are too low to make the construction of apartment buildings an economically feasible proposition. That is why few are being built and 70 % of apartments constructed in 1979 had to be government-subsidized. Consequently, we have a serious apartment shortage which promises to stay with us for a long time. Twelve to fifteen years ago we had an excess of vacant apartments. But those days won't return for as far ahead as we can see.

Landlords, never popular with the media or the public, are under great pressure to keep rents lower than what costs and economic calculations call for, or what the market would bear, especially on units for low-income persons. Owners are now threatened with rent control which an increasing number of communities have been imposing. Rent control is a surefire method to kill any chance of apartment construction and make the shortage permanent. Local housing regulations for social goals also discourage the building of rental units. Only higher rents or huge government subsidies could restart apartment construction.

What is Government Doing in Housing for Low-Income Families?

The president's budget for FY 1981 proposed adding 300,000 housing units for low-income families, a 25% increase over the level authorized for FY 1980.

ADDITIONAL HOUSING UNITS FOR LOW-INCOME FAMILIES, U.S. BUDGET FY 1981

Number of Units	Type	Construction Cost	Annual Federal Cost Per Unit	Time Span (years)	Total Cost Per Unit
Subsidized (leased) housing (Section 8)					
114,700	New units		$5,235	20–30	$104,000–157,050
23,300	Substantially rehabilitated units		$6,125	20–30	$112,500–183,750
40,000	Moderately rehabilitated units		$4,200	15	$63,000
80,000	Existing units		$3,000	15	$45,000
Public housing					
38,000	traditional	$57,368	$5,340	30	$160,200*
4,000	Indian housing	$71,698	$6,790	30	$203,700*

*Construction and financing, not including operation.

The cost of the program is estimated at $34.4 billion, including operation and "modernization" (largely damage repair and improvements) of public housing projects, subsidies to "troubled projects," mortgage purchases, etc. It preempts most of the Department of HUD's budgetary authority with one major exception, $5 billion designated for community and urban development grants (successor to "urban renewal," a label discarded in 1974 after the program had acquired a reputation of being the very epitome of well-intentioned but counterproductive governmental escapades). HUD's 1981 low-income housing program provides for:
180,000 new or substantially rehabilitated units, of which:

>   42,000 are new public housing
>   114,700 are new subsidized, leased housing
>   <u>23,300</u> are substantially rehabilitated, leased housing
>   40,000 moderately rehabilitated, leased units
>   <u>80,000</u> existing, leased units

for a total of 300,000 additional units of which about half are new.

Subsidized housing (Section 8, authorized in 1974) "is proving to be vastly more expensive than anyone anticipated" commented Henry Aaron, of HEW and the Brookings Institution.[126] The reason is not hard to find. HUD relies for three fifths of the additional units on new construction and substantial rehabilitation, both of which are far more expensive than utilization of existing dwellings. The Office of Management and Budget attempted to reverse that emphasis but HUD prevailed in the end. Government housing programs have always been production oriented, even after the shift in the later 1960s and the 1970s to rent supplements. As a result, numerous poverty families are moving into tax-supported housing that is newer and better equipped than the housing which many taxpaying nonpoor can find and afford. One observer called this "analogous to a program providing new Buicks to families who are inadequately served by public transportation."[127]

Impecunious persons when buying an automobile look for an old car that has seen its best years, may not work quite as well as it once did, but can be bought for a fraction of its cost when new. There is—so far—no government program for low-income automobile renting or ownership. There is such a program in housing and we have the perverse situation in which the government provides poor families with new dwellings that sport conveniences which financially better-off working families go without in their decades-old residences.

Poor people usually take care of their old car's upkeep because they know that there may be no program to help or provide them with another car when old lizzy quits working. But if they don't maintain their apartment or house and let it deteriorate, aid will be forthcoming for neglect, repairs, damage and vandalism. They may, in time, if they raise enough fuss, even be given new housing, to restart the cycle. Therefore new apartments in government-subsidized housing have a record of aging at a record pace. After a while, they may no longer be better than the older residences of moderate-income earners who know that they are responsible for their home's condition and must live with it.

The High Cost of Low-Income Housing

The major components of the cost of housing are: land, construction and financing, and, during occupancy, maintenance. Land costs have risen both absolutely and as a share of total housing cost, as was pointed out earlier. They could be cut to a fraction if instead of building on one level we constructed 5 or 10 more levels on top of each other although this inevitably boosts the cost of construction. That is why most of the housing—and especially all public housing—in European countries where land prices are high is multistoried. So it is in some of the older parts of eastern American cities. All urban housing in the Soviet Union—which is decades ahead of us in its efficiency of residential construction—is multistoried.

In the early days of urban renewal, public housing projects were also built multistoried and high-rise—with devastating results. Eleven-storied Pruitt-Igoe was built in St. Louis at a cost of $52 million—equivalent to between $150 and $200 million today. Intended to be a showpiece of what public housing could be at its best—it won an award of the American Insitute of Architects—it demonstrated what public housing could be at its worst. Within a few years it turned into a nightmare of vandalism, filth, stench, and crime. Washington University sociologist Lee Rainwater wrote in 1967 after a 5-year study: "The words Pruitt-Igoe have become a household term . . . for the worst in ghetto living."[128] Five years later, 23 of the projects's 33 structures stood vacant and sealed. Having been raised with much hope and pride in 1954, the buildings were razed with dynamite in 1972 by their owner, the St. Louis Housing Authority. Thus the tenants, who had nearly bankrupted the housing authority by a nine-months rent strike—against a rent boost intended to pay for repairs and improvements the renters had demanded—got their revenge.

Nor is this an isolated case, though it may be the worst and best known. Boston's Columbia Point, Chicago's Robert Taylor and Cabrini-Green, Newark's Columbus Houses, Fort Greene Houses in New York are other examples out of many. Some public housing projects turned into instant slums because many of their tenants simply do not know how to live in clean and decent surroundings. Many are not prepared to accept responsibility and do the chores, let alone repairs, that maintaining sound housing requires. Projects occupied largely by working people or by elderly couples may long remain in an acceptable state. Those with a predominant welfare population quickly transform into urban jungles.

Most of the wretched conditons are the work of the tenants and often deliberately so. It was not only lack of discipline among children and adolescents—and many not so adolescents—and failure of parents to control them to keep them from dirtying, defacing, breaking everything in sight and make life in the projects living hell. The most pervasive characteristic among many slum dwellers is resentment and hatred of the outside world which they blame for their misery and which to many of them is personified by the landlord, the "bloodsucker," whether he be an individual or a public housing authority. In absence of a better outlet, they vent their wrath on their "oppressors" through destruction of property as a form of revenge for the "deprived," "inhuman" conditions to which they are subjected.

Crime and vandalism are rampant in slum areas. In single-family homes and small buildings damage can be wrought just to one unit or a few at a time. High rises for a hundred families can be made uninhabitable with but little additional effort. This may seem a "serves mother right if I get my fingers burned" type of attitude. But it is not necessarily so. If conditions become sufficiently obnoxious and repulsive, the city may condemn the building, possibly restore it, putting in the improvements the tenants wanted, or find other housing for them.

Because of their experience in the 1950s and 1960s, public housing authorities no longer place low-income families in high-rise structures. Tenants may neglect and damage smaller buildings too but at a slower pace and a lower cost to the owners.

Public housing authorities may be driven to the edge of bankruptcy by tenants' neglect and destruction and nonpayment of rent. But they are eventually rescued by Uncle Sam, and carry on. Private landlords are not. If they do not take in enough in rent to pay for current operations and repair of damage, they will sooner or later be forced to give up and "walk away." Abandonment of residential structures in central cities has reached epidemic proportions in the past two decades. It is an expression of hopelessness, a gesture of despair on the part of owners who are reluctantly accepting the fact that losing their investment is preferable to throwing more good money after bad.

Between 1978 and 1980 New York City took over, by *in rem* proceedings, more than 10,000 tax-delinquent buildings most of which proved unsalable because rents could not cover the cost of repairs and operations. Although the city spent over $300 million on rehabilitating some of the buildings, only 2% of the buildings could be sold and about two-thirds of the structures will have to be destroyed. The remaining 3,000 buildings still house 22,000 tenants who typically pay between $35 to $55 a month per room with the city footing the deficit.

There are no statistics on the extent of housing abandonment. One estimate in 1973 by J. S. Fuerst, assistant director of the Graduate Program in Urban Studies at Loyola University, estimated the national total at perhaps 700,000 units.[129] It could be higher now. The Comptroller General of the United States conducted a survey of housing abandonment in 1978 to which 149 cities responded.[130] He gathered much material and suggested that "new ideas should be tried to combat neighborhood decay" but offered no recommendations with a realistic chance for effective counteraction. The crux of the problem is: What do you do about the individuals and families who cause most of the trouble in public housing? No one has yet come up with a satisfactory answer. With multistory structures being shunned for the housing of poor families and current attempts to locate public and subsidized housing in sections where families of higher socioeconomic standing live, prospects of lowering the cost of land for low-income housing do not appear bright.

Lower Construction Costs?

In the early years of the Nixon administration, when George Romney served as secretary of HUD, interest focused on operation *Breakthrough*, an attempt to develop and use less expensive methods of housing construction, especially for low-income housing. If automobiles were built by methods used in traditional housing, largely manual labor, car prices would be beyond the reach of all but wealthy persons. Industrialized methods, it was hoped could replace much of the costly on-site labor by factory mass production and preassembly of modular parts. The use of precast sections dominates the huge Soviet housing industry, which at considerable speed and low cost has rebuilt most of their cities' residential plant—though not to space and other specifications which most Americans prefer.

HUD's efforts of the early 1970s failed for lack of acceptance. The construction industry—contractors and unions, as so often in a united front—opposed advanced factory methods which might reduce and partially eliminate the use of local labor and entrepreneurs. Political and lobbying organizations pressing Congress for expansion of public and subsidized housing thoroughly disliked the idea of "cheap" housing for the poor. They saw no reason why disadvantaged people should not be given the same standard type of housing that other Americans enjoy. So we continue building houses the way carriages were built before the assembly line came in.

The only large type of factory-produced housing now is what we generally call "mobile homes" though few of them ever move; "manufactured housing" is a more appropriate term. Their parts are prefabricated and preassembled, requiring little local labor for permanent placement. The average mobile home sold in 1978 for $15,900, which is less than one-third of the average $55,700 selling price of a standard one-family house. It does not take as much abuse nor will normally last as long as a traditionally built house. About one new home in five during the years 1970–74 was a mobile home; only one new home in 7.5 between 1975 and 1979 was mobile. Americans want a "traditional" house whether they can afford it or not. Elderly couples live in mobile homes very satisfactorily. They know how to take care of them and do keep them up. Poverty families capable of destroying solid structures in an amazingly short time would not last long in mobile homes unless they alter their behavior, which does not seem likely. Many local building codes and zoning regulations raise obstacles to the placement of mobile homes and make cost savings in home construction more difficult or impossible.

This adds up to the conclusion that the growth rate of construction costs for low-income housing will continue to rise rapidly as long as that type of housing is built to standards similar to those used for middle-class residences. The cost of housing low-income families is bound to be excessive as long as most of them are placed in new rather than "used" homes. This is part of a policy that insists on giving, at taxpayers' expense, *average* housing standards to families which are *subaverage* in terms of their contribution to society and consequently in income, and, often also in their ability to maintain the housing they are given, in sound condition.

Financing—Out of Control?

New home buyers now pay more for mortgage interest than for the house itself. As long as borrowers can pay principal and interest in dollars that are cheaper every succeeding year, this may not seem to be a bad deal—except for the lender. But the lender—usually a bank or savings and loan institution—pays its own lenders (savers) back in depreciated dollars. Who comes out ahead or behind in this game of musical chairs is a fascinating question.

Uncle Sam comes out way ahead in the debt game. He now owes close to a trillion dollars on the public debt whose total increases but is worth less every year. This is equally true of the U.S. housing debt under Section 8 which now amounts to a quarter of a trillion dollars, growing by another $25 to 30 billion every year. Why worry about or fool around with a deal where we are on the winning side? Really no reason to—if we are willing to settle for the prospect of an ever-rising inflation rate from the current teens to multiples of teens or hundreds. Many countries have traveled that road within the past thousand years and many more will. The question is: do we want the United States to become one of them? If we don't, then the fast growing housing debt is as good a place as any to start—next to the U.S. budget and the public debt. The current system of financing low-cost housing is easier—for the time being. A $6 or $7 billion item has far less of an impact on the budget than a $30 billion-plus item and, above all, it attracts much less attention. The American public might worry more about low-income housing if it knew that it now costs not $7 billion a year but $34 billion. And—it would be concerned if subsidized housing caused the budget deficit to be $27 billion bigger.

There is no reason for financing low income housing differently from, say, public works which are paid for when completed, but one: hiding the cost and making it appear smaller makes it easier to get big programs authorized. There would be a much tougher battle in Congress—and a livelier public debate—over $34 billion in the budget than over $7 billion. The program might wind up being not as big as it now is, if it had to be currently financed. Without financing, the cost of an average public housing unit would be $57,368 instead of $160,200 or more (see p. 302). The cost of subsidized housing would be out in the open—and might soon be much less. Many of the steps to tighten up which now seem politically unacceptable might be seriously considered if the alternative would look even less acceptable.

Revitalizing Our Cities?

For over thirty years the U.S. government has been trying to halt and reverse the downward slide of our major cities. Once the nation's joy and pride, a manifestation of its eminence in technology, commercial crafts-manship and financial power, a product as well as a symbol of American ingenuity and leadership in many fields of human endeavor, many cities have been deteriorating to a point where some view their ability to survive as viable entities with doubt. They have been losing in both essential components of an urban community, population and business enterprise, and with them, employment. A shrinking economic base has eroded their financial soundness, making them increasingly dependent on subsidies and aid from superior levels of government. Thereby their autonomy as well as their ability and claim to govern themselves have diminished. From being a subject of envy to much of the rest of the world, our cities have become a problem and even an embarrassment for whose shortcomings we some-times feel we ought to apologize.

Successive administrations have loosened on the cities a steady stream of imaginative programs, costing *in toto* hundreds of billions of dollars, intended to cure their most painful and perilous ills. I call the programs imaginative not only because they cover and try to deal with such a wide array of the multifarious aspects and troubles of urban life but also because it took a great deal of imagination—meaning unrealistic assumptions—to expect that they would produce what their sponsors hoped and promised. Some of the programs had counterproductive results.

So, as the number and size of public programs multiplied and their spending soared to stratospheric heights, the cities' downward slide became steeper and faster. In the 1960s 3.4 million persons migrated from central cities; between 1970 and 1978 11.6 million did.[131] Preliminary data from the 1980 Census disclose that three-fifths of our large cities lost population in the 1970s. The number of residents declined in New York City by 11%, in Chicago by 12%, in Philadelphia by 14%, in Baltimore by 13%, in

Washington D.C. by 16%. The flight from the cities is accelerating. To be sure, some people migrated *to* the cities—and that is where the problem lies. HUD Secretary Patricia Roberts Harris noted in March 1978 that 150,000 people had moved out of Chicago during the preceding 15 years while 140,000 had moved in. "But those who left were the best-educated, the higher-tax-paying people. And those who came in tended to be the more dependent population. So the loss is really a great deal more than just the numbers."[132]

Simultaneously, Rep. William S. Moorehead stated at hearings of the Subcommittee on Fiscal and Intergovernmental Policy of the Joint Economic Committee of Congress, which he chaired, that of the 75 cities with 20,000 or more manufacturing jobs between 1970–1976, jobs declined by 800,000 and in those same cities total employment decreased 17% between 1970 and 1975. He also noted that according to a Dun & Bradstreet study over one third of all business failings in 1976 had occurred in 25 central cities.[133]

Alarming as this is, it is not surprising. Dependent persons have been doing relatively well at the hands of cities through new and inexpensive housing and dozens of social programs and amenities while businesses are being treated to higher taxes and tighter regulations, their employees and managers (among the "best-educated" mentioned by Mrs. Harris) to rampant crime and bad schools. Small wonder that the "dependent" have been moving *into* the cities and the productive have been moving *out*. Of course, city policies were not designed for the purpose of attracting the hard-core poor and driving out the middle and upper classes. But they could not be much different if they had been drawn up with that goal in mind. The cities have but one excuse: many or most of those policies were imposed and/or financed by the national government, sometimes against desires and over the objections of city authorities, which, when they could not influence federal action tried, at least, to make the best of it. ("If you can't lick them, join them.")

University of Chicago sociologist James S. Coleman concluded "that the problem of metropolitan areas is not a failure to know what to do to strengthen these areas. It is the use of policies that are harmful to metropolitan areas, despite knowledge that they are harmful. The policies are implemented anyway, because they pursue other values that are collectively held to be more important than those of strengthening metropolitan areas." Coleman summarized "we simply do not, as a collective body, wish to vitalize the cities. If we did, we would do so."[134]

The basic truth of Coleman's thesis was confirmed when a few months after his article "Can We Revitalize Our Cities?" appeared, Secretary of HUD Patricia Roberts Harris stated that the "single most important decision we've made is to study the impact that new federal activities will have on urban areas. At the very least, we hope we can avoid the negative impact *from now on*" (emphasis supplied).[135] This amounts to an admission that up to that point federal programs (at least some of them) have had a negative impact on cities. Nor has there been much change since March 1978.

Coleman discussed four areas in which government action is motivating people to move away from cities and identified two common properties they have: policy initiation at higher levels of government and egalitarianism. Actually, egalitarianism governs most of the relevant government policies and underlies their failure: the view that the main difference among human beings is that some have more money than others, that their characteristics would not differ much from each other if it were not for the monetary gap and that government's principal job is to reduce monetary differences to a minimum, with equality the final goal. Coleman identified the four policy areas as housing, highways, crime and schools. Highways seem to me to be part of the urban housing complex because the provision of convenient and underpriced transportation (whether by road or public transit) enables many people to live in suburbs distant from their place of work downtown. But taxes do play a role in the flight of business and the middle and upper classes from the cities. Or, at least it so seems to an economist, as distinguished from Mr. Coleman, a sociologist.

I shall now review the four policy areas: housing (and transportation), taxation, crime and schools.

Four Reasons Why City Revitalization Is Not Working

Congress set lofty goals in the *National Housing Act of 1949*: "The realization as soon as feasible of the goal of a decent home and a suitable environment for every American family." The government proceeded to accomplish this through a huge urban renewal program to wipe out slums and replace them with solid modern structures. So it did, in many locations, after selling the land to developers for one third or less of its cost. Magnificent commercial high rises were erected in downtown areas, cleared of festering and decaying slums: San Francisco's Embarcadero Center, Philadelphia's Penn Center, Pittsburgh's Golden Triangle, Denver's Mile High Center, and many others. They drew many businesses, mostly of the service and shop type and arts centers, to the splendid new facilities. Suburbanites just love to drive in on the new superhighway, shop in the cute boutiques, visit their broker or attend an evening's performance. But they would not live there. Only few of the people who worked in the new offices moved to nearby luxury apartments which formed part of the same projects.

Most of the areas' former inhabitants, probably two million or more, moved elsewhere in town where they proceeded, with all deliberate speed, to recreate the slums they had been forced to evacuate. Urban renewal did not do much for them, nor, as it turned out, for revitalizing the cities.

Martin Anderson in his devastating critique of the program in *The Federal Bulldozer* concluded that "the federal urban renewal program is very costly, destructive of personal liberty, and is not capable of achieving the goals put forth by Congress."[136] He called for repeal. Urban renewal destroyed at least three times as many dwellings in the affected areas as it built and most of those it built were beyond the reach and means of the former occupants. Martin Meyer summarized the results succinctly: "In terms of housing and overall livability of the cities, urban renewal was a disaster."[137]

Beginning in the mid-1960s, the emphasis of federal housing activity shifted to rent subsidies, spawning new programs with such fancy names as demonstration cities, model cities, and new towns. They worked no better.[138] The urban renewal program became so discredited that it was left to expire in 1974, ending a disgraceful 25-year record. But as so often in well-intentioned but ill-conceived activities, the federal cash flow had to be maintained lest political machines grind to a halt. Urban renewal was replaced by programs named community development grants, urban development action grants, comprehensive planning grants, which, at a $5 billion annual clip are allocated by intricate formulas and channeled directly to cities. This pleases mayors and city councils and offers HUD a better alibi for negative results which sooner or later are bound to find their way into the media.

The flight of the middle and upper classes from the cities continues unabated, reconfirming Gresham's law that bad money drives out good money. When millions of former rural residents were made comfortable in the cities by inexpensive housing and numerous income support and welfare programs—most of them federally sponsored and/or financed—the movement to escape across city boundaries turned into mass migration.

States had tried by residency requirements to protect themselves and their cities against migrants who came to avail themselves of the more generous welfare benefit levels in major northern cities. Federal law, in fact, authorized such residency requirements up to one year. But in 1969 the U.S. Supreme Court declared state residency requirements for welfare applicants to be unconstitutional, because they interfered with the right to uninhibited travel. They "could not be justified as a permissible state attempt to discourage such indigents who would enter state solely to obtain larger benefits" nor because they "encourage earlier entry of new residents into labor force" (*Shapiro* v. *Thompson*, 394 U.S. 618). That left cities defenseless against invasion by hordes of rural poor, unaccustomed to urban living and unable to fend for themselves in a competitive surrounding. But the poor gradually took over.

The middle class surrendered with but little resistance when the national government helped with easy-term mortgages in sprouting suburbs and facilitated commuting to their jobs on 90% federally financed superhighways. Driving cars with just one or two occupants is an enormously expensive form of transportation on roads whose construction in urban areas may cost from $20 million to nearly $100 million a mile. But the individual does not figure it that way. He counts only his out-of-pocket expense which even at current gasoline prices accounts for a small fraction of the total economic cost. The average American derives a great feeling of satisfaction from driving his own car besides possibly greater convenience and saving time at a high cost; he is said to have a love affair with his automobile which some call auto-erotic. That kept a huge automobile industry and its satellites going at a high pace and seemed tolerable until growing energy consumption made the country too dependent on uncertain and extravagantly priced foreign crude oil. At that point the huge waste of precious energy sources and air pollution became intolerable.

But attempts to lure drivers to mass transportation by subsidizing it—though they helped to make suburban living an attractive proposition—failed abysmally, because freeway driving is just as underpriced, if not more so. The number of mass transport passengers, which had dropped from 23 billion in 1946 to below 10 billion by 1958, fell below 7 million in 1972. Subsequent cuts in transit fares—when expressed in *constant* dollars—boosted the number of riders by about 1.5 billion. But even tripled gasoline prices are not able to cause a sufficient number of drivers to switch to mass transit. Urban transit systems have long sustained chronic operating deficits and the aggregate operation of all mass transportation has been increasingly in the red since 1963. The annual deficits now exceed $3 billion of which one-third is covered by federal subsidies, the rest by state and local subventions.

Riders now pay for less than half the actual cost of running the major transit systems whose outlays have disproportionately risen. Between 70% and 80% of their expenses go for wages which have been excessively raised to a point where average transit workers are now paid between $25,000 and $35,000 annually. Local subsidies pushed several city treasuries against the wall and threaten bankruptcies and closedowns. The 94% of the population who are nonriders put up growing resistance to having their taxes boosted so the remaining 6% of the people can ride at half the cost or less. Transit systems put heavy pressure on property and other local taxes and contribute heavily to several cities' financial distress. It is unlikely that transit subsidies—federal, state, local—which now pay more than half the operating costs of transit systems, not to mention capital investment, can be maintained much longer at current levels.

Only two cities built transit systems within the past 60 years: Washington, D.C., where Congress appropriated construction and operating funds, and San Francisco. A bond issue to finance the Bay Area Rapid Transit System (BART) was voted in almost 2 decades ago not by residents who intended to use it but by drivers who hoped that others would get off the freeways so they would have an easier time commuting. It cost over $1.5 billion to build—more than twice the original estimate—though an outlay of $40 million could have bought enough buses to carry all passengers using BART.[139] In July 1980 the California Department of Transportation concluded an agreement with the Southern Pacific Railroad to operate San Francisco to San Jose commuter trains at an annual subsidy of $1500 per rider. Most American passenger rail systems went broke when they were run by private companies and now, operated by Amtrak, raise only 40% of their costs through fares with an average loss per passenger in 1980 estimated at $34. Evidence is overwhelming that railroad transportation generally is not energy efficient and is economically wasteful. The federal government has been providing capital grants to finance new equipment and facilities for urban transit systems since the early 1970s and huge demands are now being made to upgrade and expand systems in New York, Chicago, Houston, Los Angeles, and Indianapolis. Under the National Mass Transportation Act of 1974 the federal treasury has also been helping to cover ever-growing operating deficits. Can such a shift of the burden from the rider to the taxpayer be justified?

Early in 1981 a GAO report on transit operating subsidies concluded that the systems had not boosted productivity to offset rapidly rising wages and other operating costs and kept their fares at too low a level.

Transit systems are reluctant to boost fares faster than they have, for fear that this would cause more passengers to shift to their cars. There simply is no solution except pricing individual driving as well as transit fares closer to cost, with full-cost pricing the final goal. This will relieve the pressure on local (as well as state and federal) budgets and could motivate some people to start living closer to their places of work. American families now move, on the average, every five years.

Mass transportation as such is more energy- and cost-efficient than individual driving. That is why driving must be made more expensive than it is even though this is politically a very tough proposition. We must catch the commuter "on the run or on the roost." There is no way to operate mass transit in urban areas without large and growing public subsidies unless we can get the driver out of his car by imposing heavy levies on commuter driving or rationing gasoline. Higher transit subsidies mean higher general taxes—which are no more popular than increased highway user charges. Gasoline taxes have risen less than other taxes because their rates are related to volume, not to the price or amount as virtually all other taxes are.

Rapid transit systems on rails cannot be operated on a self-sustaining basis in most of our metropolitan areas where population density is below a 20,000 per square mile minimum.[140] American and European settlement patterns differ and call for different solutions. We must accept the fact that BART turned out to be an enormously expensive white elephant. But our current and prospective energy situation imperatively calls for a major shift from individual driving to mass transportation. The bus offers, for as far as we can see ahead, the most economical commuting in our urban areas. It is more flexible in scheduling and all aspects of operation than rail transit. Also, bus drivers are easier to find, train, and replace than operators of highly sophisticated electronic equipment. The bus is slower than rail transit but it could be substantially accelerated if individual driving were sharply reduced by higher levies and freeway congestion thereby alleviated. Settlement patterns change slowly and gradually. Proper policies could make transportation a positive rather than a negative factor for urban areas and development.

Transit deficits are big claimants for city taxes. So are a disproportionately large dependent population demanding expanded services and public employee unions growing stronger and insisting on higher compensation for their members (see Chapter 1). Generous pension programs, enacted many years ago, and large old debts also are coming home to roost. It all adds up to pressure for higher taxes.

That city taxes tended to be higher than rural taxes did not play a significant role in locational decisions as long as cities offered compensatory advantages to middle-class families and to businesses. But in many critical fields they no longer do. Moreover, as the average socioeconomic level of city populations declined, it became popular and rewarding in urban politics to shift the tax burden increasingly to business and to higher-income individuals.

Business has few votes at the ballot box, but many types of businesses can move. And move they did—taking the jobs with them. New York City lost nearly 600,000 jobs between 1969 and 1978, reflecting an estimated tax loss of almost $500 million. Some large city employment losses, 1970 to 1977 were estimated as follows:

New York	−14.0%	Detroit	−26.9%
Chicago	−18.7	St. Louis	−20.2
Philadelphia	−19.5	Cleveland	−18.1[141]

New Orleans Mayor Moon Landrieu suggested a remedy at congressional hearings on *Keeping Business in the City* in March 1978: give all cities the right that only few now enjoy—to annex adjoining areas without a vote by their residents.[142] That might frustrate the attempt of some firms and individuals to escape from city tyranny. It could also cause them to move a longer distance, beyond the reach of the city's claws.

In an April 1977 report on *The Long-Term Fiscal Outlook for New York City* the Comptroller General of the United States traced the city's financial problems to its persistent loss of business and economically productive population. "The fiscal and economic base of New York City continued to deteriorate, and this deterioration is at the root of the city's problems." Speaking in somber terms, the report sounded pessimistic about the general outlook on recovery, not only in New York but in major cities generally and found that "governmental policies (at any level) have generally not been effective in revitalizing the fiscal base of a city or a region." It did mention that "more than one-fifth of the new housing units completed in the city since 1927, have been public or publicly aided." This aggravated the city's problems—by strengthening the centripetal tendencies of dependent people, it promoted centrifugal trends among the productive population. As social services and their personnel ballooned, the city saw itself forced to boost its taxes which, in turn, motivated more businesses and upper- to middle-class families to move out.

Some of our cities may have crossed the point of no return. The majority of their voting population now favors more generous benefits for themselves and higher taxes on the "rich." Though city officials are aware of their need to hold the outflow and, if possible attract business, they are unable to carry such programs through. Office-holders could not be re-elected by the remaining residents of the city if they did not cater to their constituents' wishes.

That New York City, the world's financial capital and the largest city in the world's richest nation could come to the brink of bankruptcy from which it was barely rescued by federal intervention, was widely attributed to reckless and irresponsible spending policies of successive city administrations, justifiably so. Yet mayors and other city officials had for years sincerely tried to pursue a sound course but were unable to withstand the power of the organizations insisting on expanded services and the pressure of its employee unions for more and better paid jobs. Whether current attempts to return to a sound management by staff reductions, constraint on wage boosts, debt deferral and higher consumption taxes and user charges will succeed remains to be seen. New York's—and other cities'—ability to motivate commercial and industrial firms and middle- to upper-class families to return to the urban fold is doubtful. And without a stronger economic base, the cities' future looks dim.

Big-city mayors have for many years concentrated their energies and strongest efforts on getting more money from the federal government, and, to a lesser degree, from their states. They succeeded in multiplying categorical grants and loans for their major functions and added revenue sharing in the early 1970s. But none of this was enough—there just is no limit to demands on and by the cities. There is a limit however on congressional willingness to underwrite municipal profligacy.

In March 1978 President Carter proposed an enormous package of federal programs for cities that, according to one estimate, would have upped federal spending on metropolitan areas to $58 billion in 1979. Congress, conscious of the harvest of past and existing urban programs—as well as of the need to narrow the budgetary gap—rejected most of it. But federal funds for cities kept going up anyway.

In March 1980 HUD secretary, former New Orleans Mayor, Moon Landrieu told an interviewer that the "back to the cities movement" is a reality and that "there often tends to be growth among the middle and upper-income segments."[143] This is sheer fantasy, supported by no solid evidence. It would take a course of actions which, under federal restraints, are beyond their power, for cities to become again, as they once were, attractive to the nation's elite—not just to maintain a headquarters office but to live in and become part of. What the cities need if they are to be "revitalized" is, besides an enlarged economic and middle-class population base and a civic leadership group with talents and dedication that without major and currently unforseeable changes cannot be brought back.

A congressional study of the cities' current and prospective fiscal condition concluded that "one can expect a growing number of cities to experience severe fiscal stress" in the 1980s.[144] While housing and taxation are undoubtedly negative factors in considering the cities' prospects they may not be the most potent ones. The enormous growth in the incidence of crime and the precipitous fall in the quality of schools probably are the toughest obstacles—and the most difficult to overcome—in the cities' attempts to attract the caliber and number of people they need to regain the eminent position they maintained in American life throughout history, until not so many years ago.

What happened in crime and in school quality was described in earlier sections of this chapter. For thousands of years men have sought the protection of cities to obtain greater safety for their persons, families and property. They found it there and established a civilized society. This still is true, more or less, in many or most countries around the globe, but not in the United States whose central cities have become the most unsafe places to live in. That is why millions of families put a distance between themselves and the cities, why millions of others would dearly love to do so if they could afford it. Not that the suburbs and rural areas had not also been affected, uncontrolled crime being a festering sore that spreads. But in relative terms it still is far less risky to walk home in the evening through suburban streets than through many downtown sections.

I need not repeat here what I identified earlier as the cause of this sad turn of events. It was not the police or local officials who neglected their duty to protect lives and property. It was the courts, more specifically the U.S. Supreme Court, that hamstrung the police and lower courts and made adequate law enforcement in the United States impossible.

City school systems which ever since their founding had been at the apex of academic excellence, have abandoned all pretense of aiming at or maintaining educational standards and become breeding grounds for delinquency. They are more expensive than ever and endowed with lavish resources compared with most other schools. But children do not learn there and many leave after 10 or 12 years residence, unable to read their diploma and incompetent to fill an average job in today's economy.

The basic determinant of a school's quality is not the number of dollars spent per pupil nor the number of pupils per teacher. Rather, it is the learning ability and aspiration of the pupils. The teacher, regardless of personal likes, must primarily address the level of the children who lag behind the rest. This may or may not help them much but it keeps the level and progress of the class behind the capacity of more able children and causes them to goldbrick.

This was brought about by a range of factors, especially the egalitarian view and policies which came to prevail from about the mid-century on. But it was decisions of the U.S. Supreme Court, well-intentioned but without understanding—that have ruined most city school systems throughout the United States. The flight of white and black middle-class parents is basically not racially motivated. Most parents, white or black, nowadays do not care about the skin complexion of their children's classmates. But they do care about their children's learning and educational progress, about their behavior and attitudes, about their honesty, discipline, sexual mores, personal safety and exposure to physical violence. They are concerned less about who else enrolls in their children's schools or classes than about the impact that other children attending the same school have on their children. They make their decision not on prejudice but on "postjudice"—after watching what happened to and became of their children under conditions beyond their and the school authorities' control—under court orders which can best be summarized under the collective designation *the bus blunder.* That is why so many well-known liberals who have long led the fight for school integration, send their own children to private and suburban schools. They are not ready to sacrifice their own children to ideology. Other people's children might be worth risking.

Numerous national opinion polls have shown that an overwhelming majority of Americans are opposed to forced busing and to kid-glove treatment of criminal offenders. Congress has passed no laws and given no signs that it supports the policies imposed by those court orders. Nor would it dare to. But neither has it, so far, shown the strength and courage to assert its proper role in policymaking against an "imperial judiciary."

No "magnet schools," regardless of how lavishly equipped or how low their pupil-teacher ratio, will lure parents back to the city which they fled to escape the downgrading and abandonment of educational standards. Nor will an increase in the number and pay of police do so as long as the probability of being attacked or robbed—and the improbability of the offenders being caught and imprisoned—remains as high as they are—and keep going up.

Unless steps are taken to make city streets safer and turn city schools again into *educational* institutions, will middle-class families consider living in urban centers—as long as they can afford to live in more congenial surroundings? Then, and *only then* could changes in tax, housing, transportation policy have a chance of becoming effective in revitalizing cities. Most of this is beyond the power of local officials. Not until the courts will turn around—or are turned around by the Congress—can revitalization of American cities become a practical possibility, worth devoting efforts to and investing money in. But unless this is done, the downhill slide of American cities will continue, regardless of the billions spent, with no end in sight. We may indeed see the death of the American city.

Civil Rights and Civil Wrongs: The Minorities Problem

The minorities problem is probably the gravest and most difficult domestic issue the American people face and are trying to deal with. By all appearances it is the problem with the strongest destructive potential to national unity. Burning anger leading to street eruptions in the 1960s and 1970s and widespread manifestations of unrelieved tensions in the early 1980s—which may be ready to blow up at the slightest provocation or excuse—bear ominous witness to the seriousness and delicacy of the situation.

Congress sought solutions through civil rights legislation. It mandated in impeccable and seemingly unequivocal language that actions by government agencies as well as by nongovernment organizations and individuals be taken "without regard to race, color, religion or national origin." This has helped substantially to improve practices and attitudes and led to more equal treatment and fairness than prevailed only a few years or decades earlier. Some social programs, administrative policies and judicial orders, aimed to strengthen and accelerate progress by applying different rules to certain minorities, however, have generated fierce opposition, created sharp controversies and inflicted severe and widespread damage. They threaten, unless restrained, to intensify rather than ease existing discord and lead to severe and possibly violent clashes. They make consensus virtually unattainable, aggravate some of our toughest social, economic, and political problems, and tend to complicate or prevent reasonable compromise solutions. Initiated with the best of intentions, those actions failed to deliver on the accompanying hopes and promises and some turned out to be counterproductive. In no other field of domestic policy do opinions and deeply held convictions differ as widely as with regard to minority problems. Nor has any other subject of public policy been as devastatingly mishandled by the federal government as the minorities problem.

Even to define the problem satisfactorily seems almost impossible, because each observer considers it from his own angle and in his own terms. It reminds me of the Japanese play *Rashomon* in which four witnesses to a crime describe to the court in disparate and strongly contradictory terms their concept and recollection of what took place. An even closer parallel may be the story of the five blind men from Hindustan who were trying to describe an elephant from the tangible contact each had by touching the part of the animal's body closest to him—trunk, tusk, tail, legs or ears. Small wonder that they could not agree on what an elephant looks like, let alone how it should be dealt with.

The minorities problem is generally viewed as a problem of millions of Americans not sharing fully in the nation's life and abundance, economically, socially, intellectually. That, unquestionably, is its core. Twenty, thirty, maybe forty million, appear to be disadvantaged, handicapped in some way or other, deprived of crucial aspects of full citizenship in this most prosperous country on earth. Because certain ethnic minorities are disproportionately represented in this "underclass" this is widely held to be a minority problem although well over half of the "disadvantaged" belong, by ethnic background, to the majority. Only if the designation "minority" is defined in socioeconomic rather than racial terms are those disadvantaged persons, whether white or nonwhite, minorities.

Until not so many years ago, the adverse conditions of some of the ethnic minorities were attributed largely to widely practiced—and in some states until a quarter century ago statutory—racial discrimination, and to prejudice in everyday affairs, by individuals, businesses, educational institutions and government. A decisive change in attitude among the American public, as well as the passage of civil rights laws and regulations and court decisions, has altered those practices in recent decades. But racism has not quite disappeared and may not be fully wiped out for some time. Some governmental mandates intended to promote equality have resulted in employment and admissions preferences. Compulsory busing of children to achieve racial balance in schools has produced a backlash of rekindled racist sentiments and movements, which could assume serious proportions if the objectionable practices are expanded, as some demand, rather than alleviated.

Racial discrimination is now illegal, generally condemned, and to the extent to which it still exists, practiced in a clandestine manner. Racism no longer dares to function openly. Certainly its practice and incidence are now but a fraction of what they were until a few decades ago. Moreover, huge public programs have been enacted and expanded to combat and overcome aftereffects of past discriminatory procedures. Minorities have been making substantial progress, absolute and relative: statistical disparities of economic, social and other characteristics have been shrinking. In recent years, however, these disparities have diminished more slowly—and in some instances not at all. Progress has been slower than hoped despite enormous equalization efforts by governmental and nongovernmental forces.

Continuing sharp discontent among minorities is partly due to irresponsible promises of ambitious politicians, black or white, which had raised hopes beyond any possibility of fulfillment. It was the progress actually achieved, which had propelled many minority persons to positions of high prestige, power or affluence and about half of the minority population to middle-class status which added to the frustrations and inflamed violent attitudes among some of the "disadvantaged." Harvard sociologist David Riesman remarked that "the awareness that many blacks have been successful means that the underclass is more resentful and more defiant because its alibi isn't there."[145]

The number of those who believe that majority-minority differences can all be traced to racial discrimination—and could be eliminated by ending such discrimination once and for all—is declining and not many continue to persist in that view. Increasingly, the persistence of the minorities problem despite sincere efforts to solve it, is prompting a search for causes other than plain racism for the remaining majority-minority disparities and for means to reduce them. Some believe that governmental programs have become the strongest single factor in perpetuating discrepancies that would now be much smaller if federal social engineering had not inadvisedly and perversely intervened.

Still others regard as the most urgent problem the disproportionate share for which minorities account in the huge social programs which we discussed earlier in this chapter. Some of the programs of the 1960s and 1970s might conceivably not have been enacted, at least in their present form, and many other programs, old or new, might not have expanded to the point of creating a financial problem. Governmental spending might not have grown as rapidly and our fiscal situation—the squeeze between taxes which repress economic expansion and budgetary deficits which are inflationary—might not be as tight as it is. Some of our most painful social problems might not be as severe and potentially destructive.

To be sure, about half or more of the unemployed, poor, welfare-dependent, arrested offenders and prisoners are *not* members of minorities: they come from a wide variety of ethnic backgrounds but largely belong to the "majority," i.e., they are white. Even so, minorities tend to wind up at the bottom of the statistical scale: members of minorities are about four times as likely to be functionally illiterate as members of the "majority." They are twice as likely to be unemployed, four times as likely to be in poverty status, four times as likely to be welfare dependent, three times as likely to belong to a female-headed family, six times as likely to have been born out of wedlock, more than twice as likely to be arrested for a criminal offense, three times as likely to be in prison . . . The list could be continued. Let us have a closer look at these disparities.

The Minority-Majority Statistical Gap

The Census of Population reported the composition of the U.S. resident population as follows:

	1970	1980
White	87.5%	83.2%
Black	11.1	11.7
American Indian, Eskimo and Aleut	0.4	0.6
Asian and Pacific Islander	0.8	1.5
Other	0.3	3.0*

*86% of "all other" in 1980 were Hispanic, generally included among white in 1970.

Many Census statistics report ethnic data under "white" and "black," with the latter sometimes "black and other" (= nonwhite). The "black and other" category includes American Indians as well as Chinese and Japanese. Most Hispanics were included as white before 1980, a separate category was listed as "Spanish origin" ("may be of any race") and shown at 4.5% of the population in 1970, at 6.4% in 1980.

This grouping slightly narrowed the statistical gap: the inclusion of Hispanics lowered some white averages while the inclusion of Chinese and Japanese raised some "black and other" or "nonwhite" data. In other words, the disparity between white (without Hispanics) and black (which does not include Chinese and Japanese) tends to be somewhat larger than the commonly used "white" and "nonwhite" categories.

Data from the 1980 Census of Population are provisional at this writing. They are also controversial because of alleged undercounting of blacks and Hispanics, some of whom deliberately avoided being listed and counted.[146]

Income is probably the most widely used and significant economic yardstick. The succeeding table shows cash income—*not* including food stamps, housing subsidies or other "income in kind":

MEDIAN MONEY INCOME OF FAMILIES BY ETHNIC CATEGORIES
IN SELECTED YEARS 1947 TO 1978
IN CONSTANT (1978) DOLLARS

Year	White	Nonwhite (Black and other races)	Difference	Income of Nonwhite as Percentage of White
1978	$ 18,368	$ 11,754	$ 6,614	64.0%
1970	17,189	10,942	6,247	63.7
1960	12,848	7,113	5,735	55.4
1952	10,107	5,744	4,363	56.8
1947	9,217	4,711	4,506	57.1
Percentage increase 1947–78	+99.3%	+149.5%	+47%	

SOURCE: U.S. Bureau of the Census, *Current Population Reports*, P-60, #123.

The table above shows that the difference between white and nonwhite family income grew, in constant dollars, but that on a percentage basis nonwhite income increased at a faster rate. Data for black or Spanish-origin families are available only for a few years back but show that those families advanced more slowly than whites: between 1970 and 1978 black family income declined from 61.4% of white to 59.2%; Spanish family income declined from 74% of white in 1972 (earliest year available) to 68.4% in 1978.

Income changes at both ends of the scale may be even more significant. Families with an income under $3,000 (*1978* dollars) declined: whites from 9.5% (of all families) in 1947 to 2.6% in 1978; nonwhite from 30.1% in 1947 to 8.3% in 1978. Though the *relative* improvement among non-whites was substantial there still remains a sizable disparity regarding the frequency of low-income families. Families with an income of $25,000 and over (*1978* dollars) increased from 4% in 1952 to 29.5% in 1978 if white, from 0.6% in 1952 (earliest year available) to 16.0% in 1978 if nonwhite.

So there has been a narrowing of the gap. But the incidence of utter poverty (under $3,000 income) still is three times higher among blacks than whites, twice as high among Hispanics as whites. High income ($25,000 or more) occurs more than twice as frequently among whites as among blacks or Hispanics.

The most significant fact may well be that nearly half of all nonwhite families had an income above two-thirds of the national median in 1978 and thus can be called members of the middle class, with more than one-fourth of nonwhite families ranking above the national median. However, the "gap" grows as we move down the income scale. Seven percent of white families were reported as being below the official poverty level, 28% of black families. Two-thirds of white families reported themselves to be homeowners, less than one-half (44%) of the black families did. Some of the worst slums are occupied by minorities.

Additional data may help to explain *some* of those discrepancies: Eighty-six percent of white families are husband-wife families, but only 56% of black families. Twelve percent of white families are *female-headed*, 39% of black families. Female-headed families report less than half the income (44%) of male-headed families. Also, nearly half of all births to black mothers (46%) were out of wedlock; only 8% of all white births were to unmarried women. *Labor force participation* is higher among white males than among black (78% vs. 70%), though equal among women. The number of *earners* per family is about 11% higher among white families than black but there are 50% more black families with five or more *members*—usually dependents—than white, 72% more "Spanish origin" families. The nonwhite birthrate is about 50% higher than the white.

Overall income comparisons of averages inevitably wash out many significant facts. Andrew Hacker pointed out in a sophisticated analysis of 1978 Census income surveys that for husband-wife families where both spouses are employed, the white median is $24,627, and the black $22,125, down to a ten-percentage-point gap. And to this may be added that black women who put in a full year of work had a median income of $9,020, only seven points behind the $9,732 for comparable white women. Finally, black working women who had college degrees earned a higher median income than did their white counterparts. . . .

However, the real obstacle to black income progress is that the proportion of black households having a working husband present declined sharply between 1970 and 1978. Put the other way around, the number of black single-parent families headed by women rose from 1.4 million to 2.3 million—65 percent—in this eight-year period. (For whites the comparable rise was 40 percent.) It was the addition of almost a million such households that cancelled out such gains as were made by black two-spouse families. And that is why black income as a whole has remained a fixed percentage of whites.[147]

The *unemployment rate* has consistently been running twice as high among nonwhite men than among white, almost twice as high among nonwhite women than among white, and more than twice as high among nonwhite teenagers.[148]

Occupational levels of nonwhite workers have significantly improved but are on average below those of white workers. The percentage of nonwhite males in professional, technical, managerial and administrative fields jumped from 6% in 1958 to 17% in 1980 (below white males with 31% in 1980), of craftsmen from 9% to 17%. Nonfarm laborers and farm workers dropped from 39% of all employed nonwhite males to 15%—still above the 10% for whites. Occupational trends among women also point upwards.

The black-white gap in the *number of school years* completed which was still quite large at the mid-century has since dropped to almost zero. Persons 25 years and over had completed the following number of school years:

	White	Nonwhite	Difference
	School Years		
1950	9.7	6.9	2.8
1960	10.9	8.2	2.7
1978	12.5	12.0	.5

This of course includes many persons who completed their schooling 30 or more years ago.

If we consider only persons 25 to 29 years old we find that the number of school years completed was in 1978 for all persons 12.9, for nonwhites 12.7 years—virtually identical.[149] At ages 7 through 15 about 99% of all children were enrolled, black or white, with only small differences above and below those ages. Taking all ages from 3 to 34 years we find the surprising fact that in 1979 55.0% of blacks, but only 49.6% of whites and 48.6% of those of Spanish origin were enrolled in school.[150]

Preschool children, age 3 or 4, are now more likely to be enrolled in school if they are black. Dropout rates in the high school grades—particularly in states whose compulsory education ends at age 16—used to be consistently higher for black pupils than for white. But the difference shrank until by the end of the 1970s, dropout rates at ages 16 and 17 were lower for black students than for white.

What this adds up to is the fact that nonwhites have reached equality of educational attainment with whites—in professional parlance in which attainment means years of school completed. But are schools attended by nonwhites of the same quality as schools attended by whites? Until the 1960s it was generally believed that schools attended by white children were financially better supported, enjoyed smaller class sizes, employed more highly qualified teachers, used better school facilities, etc. The HEW-sponsored national school survey in 1966 conducted by James Coleman came as a shock to many when in *Equality of Educational Opportunity* it reported that there is virtually no difference in input factors between schools attended by white and by black children (see also p. 186).

Number of pupils per classroom, teachers' salaries, highest degree, years of experience and tenure, age of school building and dozens of other criteria were found to be approximately equal at white and black schools. In subsequent years, particularly under the influence of Title I of the Elementary and Secondary Education Act of 1965, large additional funds were concentrated in predominantly black schools. Reports indicate that per pupil spending now often is higher in schools which are predominantly black. As it turns out, this seems to have little impact on the students' learning. As was pointed out in the education section, the magnitude of resources appears to have little, if any, influence on student achievement. What counts in the end, of course, is acquisition of skills and knowledge and not just years of attendance.

Until a few decades ago public schools used to hold back, for one or several years, a student who did not perform at grade level. That practice was largely abandoned as automatic promotion grew popular. But many schools still retain a student in grade for a year or two if his skills and knowledge lag substantially. The percentage of students who are enrolled below their *modal* grade—that is the grade which is normal for their age—may give us some indication of the extent of such retardation. A Census Bureau study in 1976 (P-20 #337) showed that at age 5 to 13, 4.1% of the white pupils and 7.1% of the black were one or more grades below "modal."

Interestingly enough, white children from families below poverty level had a higher degree of retardation (9.3%) than all black children and even black children with a poverty background. This suggests that a student's inability to perform at a level that is normal for his age may be a socio-economic phenomenon rather than a racial characteristic. Between ages 14 and 17, when 8.9% of the white children and 16.6% of the black children are below their *modal* grade, 19.7% of white children from poverty families lag which is not too different from the black poverty lag of 22.6%.

The most significant data on student achievement have been produced by the National Assessment of Educational Progress (NAEP).[151]

Here are some of the 1973–77 scores (plus or minus signs indicate points *above* or *below* the national mean):

	Reading		Career and Occupational Development	
	White	Black	White	Black
Age 9	+2.5	−10.7	+2.5	−10.8
13	+2.8	−14.4	+2.5	−12.9
17	+2.8	−16.6	+1.8	−12.1

NAEP also tested educational levels of young adults (26 to 35 years old). They scored:

	Reading	Mathematics	Writing
White	+2.4	+3.9	+3.2
Black	−18.7	−24.5	−18.9
Other	−5.4	−12.4	−16.1

In every subject white children are ahead of the national norm or average, black children are behind. This is not always fully expressed at age 17 because some lagging students drop out after reaching the upper age limit of compulsory attendance.

Students' scores correlate well with their parents' education and, even more significantly, with their parents' income. The higher the income, the higher are educational scores. Forty-two percent of black seventeen-year-olds were found to be functionally illiterate compared to 9% of whites.[152]

Educational lag of black children correlates with and has generally been attributed to their parents' low educational level and low income. If children see no books at home nor other intellectual activities, if they have no role models, are not motivated to read and study, they are likely to tend in the same direction. That children are influenced by their home surroundings offers a persuasive explanation for their own attributes and inadequate progress.

But there is a disturbing fact: if poor home conditions were the main causative factor, we would expect them to be strongest when home is the *only* influence—that is up to the time a child begins to attend school. Then as the child spends the greater part of his weekday daylight hours in school and the school makes an impact, the impairment or retardation would gradually decline with the number of years the child attends.

The evidence, surprisingly, is to the contrary. A child who is 6 months behind at age 6, may be two years behind at the age of 11 or 12, and three to four years behind at age 17 or 18—unless he has already dropped out, as many pupils with the greatest lag do. There is no logical explanation for the educational lag to be *increasing*, the longer the child stays in school—and this casts considerable doubt on the home environment hypothesis. Unfortunately there are no comparable data available for nonminority children from low socioeconomic backgrounds, which could help to shed light on the puzzling phenomenon.

The Armed Services, between July 1950 and December 1972, examined 16.3 million youths and found that whites have consistently a higher medical failure rate than blacks—a 19.5% disqualification rate for blacks, 27.9% for whites—which held true throughout the 22-year period in all sections of the United States—although blacks were, on the whole, not getting better medical services than whites. In fact, the failure rate on "medical only" was more than twice as high for whites than for blacks (26.0% whites, 11.6% blacks). While whites had a 43% higher failure rate on medical examinations, blacks fell short of mental requirements more than four times as often—a mental disqualification rate of 10.9% for whites, of 48.0% for blacks.[153] No attempt has been made to correlate the results of Armed Forces Qualification Tests with socioeconomic background—which leaves us in the dark regarding the social or ethnic nature of the disparities.

There has, in fact, been an extraordinary reluctance to conduct extensive and intensive research in this area, for fear of dividing the academic community along ideological lines. The nation's leading scientific organizations appear afraid of research in greater depth which could produce results that might prove highly controversial. That may well be the main reason why this Pandora's Box has been left unopened and may remain so for a long time.

What conclusions can we draw from all of these figures? That a WASP majority suppresses and exploits some ethnic minorities and denies them their rightful share in the nation's abundance? Thomas Sowell, my colleague at the Hoover Institution, has stated well that "there is thus no ethnic majority to be contrasted with minorities, but a mosaic of many groups, and a large number of people who are mixtures of various groups."[154] Sowell pointed out that Anglo-Saxons are only 14 percent of the population, are "not pacesetters in income, occupations, or education" and that "Americans of Jewish, Japanese, Polish, Chinese, or Italian ancestry make more money." He added that "the presence of Jews and Japanese at the top of the income ladder among American ethnic groups is strong evidence that prejudice or discrimination alone is hardly a sufficient explanation. . . . two of the five highest income groups—Chinese and Japanese—are nonwhite. . . . West Indians are black, but their incomes differ little from the national average. The supposedly overwhelming effect of color on economic well-being is less apparent in census data than it is in media rhetoric." He added, "As for 'white racism' as the root cause of black crime, it has produced no such effect on other nonwhites such as West Indians or Japanese Americans." He concluded: "Nothing is easier to find in American history than ethnic or racial discrimination—in jobs, schooling, housing, and many other basic areas of all intergroup differences. But the presence of other large differences—in age, geographic distribution, and cultural orientation—means that discrimination cannot automatically be presumed to be the only factor, or necessarily even the major factor." Elsewhere Sowell made the significant observation that in many cases "the economic advancement of ethnic groups came first, toleration in practice next, and acceptance of the principle of tolerance or equality last, if at all."[155] This seemed to be more effective than the reverse sequence now attempted by the U.S. Government.

The Rev. Andrew M. Greeley, a few years ago, described the amazing progress of the Poles, "this most despised of all the white immigrant groups," and wondered about the reason for what he called "the ethnic miracle."[156] "It is no exaggeration to say that no one really knows, and that the success of the southern and eastern European immigrant groups who frantically crowded into the United States before the First World War is as unexplained as it is astonishing. . . . They were ignorant, illiterate, and dirty; they spoke little English, if any at all; their families, the sociologists of the time assured us, were chronically 'disorganized' . . . ." Father Greeley added that "there were no quotas, no affirmative action, no elaborate system of social services, and, heaven knows, no ethnic militancy. . . . If contemporary welfare, urban renewal, and public housing legislation had existed a half century ago, the Poles might still be poor, and sociologists might still be writing books about how the Polish family structure—one of the strongest in America—is 'disorganized.'"

The Poles and most of the other ethnic minorities which compose the American nation were fortunate that the government left them to their own resources, for better or worse, did not get them used to and make them dependent on welfare programs, did not weaken or kill their motivation for pulling themselves up by their own bootstraps.

Historically, ethnic minorities always formed much of the American "underclass," usually recent immigrants such as the Irish, Poles, Italians or Greeks, the Chinese and Japanese. Within a few generations a majority of the newcomers' descendants worked their way up to a middle-class status or better, while a minority remained at the bottom—distinguished from the rest not by ethnic but socioeconomic characteristics. Most of the immigrants came from a different environment but were used and adjusted to a competitive society. Most of the mass migration of the blacks from a rural plantation background to the cities occurred but a few decades ago. No effort could adequately adjust them to an urban society within a short period. But ill-conceived government programs could and did adversely affect the adjustment process.

Hispanics and American Indians also came from a primitive rural background and could not be expected to be adjusted to an impersonal, competitive, urban society environment, to a job hustle they had never experienced nor been prepared for.

Hispanics offer a problem different from that of blacks, even in definition. Blacks generally can be defined as persons of at least partial African (sub-Saharan) descent. Hispanics are usually defined as persons of Spanish origin or Spanish descent, with a Spanish surname the principal criterion. This raises the question: why should someone with a Spanish surname be classified or treated differently by government, or anybody else, from someone with a French, German, Italian or Polish surname? Does that not violate the equal rights clause of the Fourteenth Amendment? Why should someone who speaks—or whose parents spoke—Spanish be subjected to rules different from those applied to someone who speaks Turkish or Greek?

Fact is that the term "Spanish surname" is but a ruse. In 1971 Marco De Funis was refused admission to the University of Washington Law School (on its preferred list) despite his Spanish surname because he happened to be a Sephardic Jew. He was a member of an ethnic minority, but apparently not of the type of minority which the administrators of affirmative action and of preferred admissions had in mind in drawing up and interpreting their rules. De Funis probably would not have been eligible even if he had been a genuine Spaniard straight from the University of Madrid.

Of late, the designation Hispanics has come into wider use, apparently in an attempt to indicate that a person is somewhat—but not quite—Spanish. The categories "Hispanics" or "Spanish surname" or "Spanish origin" are intended for and applied mostly to immigrants from Mexico and Puerto Rico, who, coming from a primitive peasant background—and because of their huge number—encountered difficulties in adjusting to and settling in U.S. metropolitan areas. However, the 400,000 Cubans who came to the Miami area prior to 1980 caused little commotion and are reported to have revitalized the region as the Hispanic community rose from 6% of the population to 41 percent. The number of Cuban-owned businesses grew from less than 1,000 ten years ago to nearly 10,000 now. A recent survey found that "more than half a million Cuban refugees have transformed a declining resort town into a bustling bicultural city . . ." and "the successful marriage of Cuban hustle and Anglo finance has created the aura of an economic honeymoon over Miami."[157] How was this possible? Because most of the Cubans who came in the 1960s and 1970s had a middle-class background and commensurate skills, adjusted to their new surroundings and "melted in," economically and socially. The critical difference between those Cubans and most of the current Chicanos is not ethnic but cultural. The problem is primarily economic because of the low productivity of the newcomers. Mexican peasants cannot be culturally and economically quickly assimilated into our urban surroundings—no more so than other immigrants from rural backgrounds. It takes time and, because of the huge numbers of Mexicans in recent years, is bound to cause problems. Neither did earlier ethnic immigrants to the United States fail to cause problems—and often violent objections and hostility, which it took a long time to overcome.

To put this in a broader frame: the critical fact is not that Hispanics and blacks are ethnic minorities. So are all the other groups which came to the United States from many lands, the Greeks, Poles, Italians, Germans, Irish and Anglo-Saxons. Discrimination, poverty, and malnutrition which those earlier immigrants suffered seem to have left no "indelible scars" on their offspring, although many were treated worse in many respects than any ethnic groups have been in more recent decades. Nor is the critical fact that Hispanics and blacks are nonwhites: many Hispanics are Caucasian, at least in part. On the other hand, Japanese, Chinese, and West Indians are nonwhite but show none of the characteristics which were called "minority problems" when referring to blacks or Hispanics.

The term "minorities" as now used to identify "disadvantaged" groups which constitute an underclass is based on socioeconomic rather than racial criteria. More than half the population with the characteristics of an underclass are Caucasians. And most members of ethnic minorities are in no way members of the socioeconomic underclass.

Harvard sociologist Edward C. Banfield warned of "serious dangers in widespread overemphasis on prejudice as a cause of the Negro's trouble . . . it may lead to the adoption of futile and even destructive policies and to the nonadoption of others that might do great good."[158] That is exactly what did happen.

I stated my conclusions in a summary talk at the 1966 conference of the Philadelphia Society:

> It seems to me that there is no solution to the ethnic minority, or race, or color, or Negro problem in the United States until we quit looking at it and treating it as an ethnic or race or color or Negro problem. . . .
>
> The challenge this country faces is not of a racial nature—though fierce attempts are being made here—as they were and are being made in many foreign lands—to turn it into a race conflict. The challenge is of people who are poor, ignorant, without jobs, who behave badly or criminally toward themselves, their families, their neighbors or others and toward society.
>
> To know that some of them are white, black, red or yellow does not help us; it only confuses the issue and may make a peaceful solution well-nigh unattainable. Opportunity to avoid increasing violence, strife, and maybe chaos and rebellion, is offered by a public policy that is color-blind. It may be our only chance.[159]

The term "color-blind" is taken from Mr. Justice Harlan's dissent in the Supreme Court's 1896 decision in *Plessy* v. *Ferguson* (at 559): "Our Constitution is color-blind, and neither knows nor tolerates classes among citizens. In respect to civil rights, all citizens are equal before the law."

Mr. Justice Lewis F. Powell seemed to feel likewise when in July 1980, after agreeing with his colleagues in favor of a racial remedy, he remarked almost apologetically in his concurrent opinion, apparently looking forward to a future in which he would not feel constrained to make a decision not quite consonant with his conscience:

> The time cannot come too soon when no governmental decision will be based upon immutable characteristics of pigmentation or origin.[160]

Many governmental decisions within the past two decades, however, were based upon color of skin—despite the Constitution's "equal rights" clause and the Civil Rights Law's injunction against consideration of race, color or national origin. Some of them are discussed in the succeeding sections.

Affirmative Discrimination
(with apologies to Nathan Glazer)[161]

Blacks, Hispanics, American Indians and a few other, smaller, ethnic groups average in economic status below national totals in most statistics. They are, to use a term which has become widely used, "economically disadvantaged." Though they are not the only Americans in the lowest bracket, and account for only a fraction of the economically disadvantaged, the minority poor have attracted greater publicity than nonminority poor and have been a significant factor in bringing about government action. Societal concern and action to help improve the employment situation of minorities are justified, desirable and necessary. Viewing what has been and is being done, however, we must ask government, as we must in a number of other areas: Are you helping to solve the problem or are you part of the problem?

Minorities have long had a higher incidence of unemployment—at least twice the average of all persons in the labor force—they rank substantially below the "majority" on the occupational scale and, consequently, earn lower incomes. A disproportionate number of minority members are in financial distress and many suffer from related ills. To be sure, some of the measurable differences between "majority" and "minorities," illustrated in the preceding section, have been declining in recent decades. In fact, many members of the minorities succeeded in advancing to high ranks on the occupational ladder and to large incomes, some to wealth and prestige. But such progress has been painfully slow. Prospects that statistical majority-minority differences will disappear within the visible future are dim, to say the least.

Low socioeconomic status among ethnic minorities has long been a well-known phenomenon on the American scene. At one time it was true of the Poles, the Irish, the Italians and many other groups. This was accepted matter-of-factly as long as those groups gave tangible signs of moving up and egalitarianism had not yet become a dominant public philosophy and major motivator of public policy. The slow advance of some minorities has widely been attributed to continuing antagonism toward them and to racial discrimination in employment, education and other fields. Racial discrimination was also practiced in several sports and arts for a long time, but no noticeable effects of it remain today.

The end of racist attitudes and actions in the fields in which unfortunately they still exist seems most urgently needed. Many hold it to be the principal way to accelerate the assimilation of lagging minorities.

Governmental moves to eliminate racial discrimination in the United States originated about four decades ago, much later than in many other advanced nations. In 1833 the British Parliament, moved by one of Thomas Babington Macaulay's most powerful speeches, prohibited racial and religious discrimination in the Indian public service. This was done in the same year in which Parliament abolished slavery in the colonies but refused to remove the civil disabilities of Jews in England. Nor was nondiscrimination in the Indian service fully implemented until well over a century later. Europe's leading countries had established equal rights for all citizens several generations before the United States proceeded to do so. Of course, none of those countries experienced the presence of a sizable population of heterogenous origin. None of them ever had or has now a problem even remotely comparable to the minority problem in the United States.

President Franklin Roosevelt's Executive Order 8802 in 1941, aimed at defense contractors (i.e., most major industrial firms), established the ground rules of nondiscrimination which were also made applicable to the federal civil and military services and were expanded and strengthened in the Truman, Eisenhower and Kennedy administrations. Passage of the Civil Rights Act of 1964 promised to open a new era of equal treatment throughout the country. It mandated in unequivocal language, repeated several times in the law, that decisions regarding employment and other subjects must be made "without regard to race, color, religion, sex, or national origin." A congressional debate spreading over 13,000 pages of the *Congressional Record* made it amply clear that the new law and its sponsors intended to establish a *color-blind* policy in the United States—to carry out what Mr. Justice Harlan had envisaged 70 years earlier as the spirit of the Constitution.

Several members of Congress, aware of the growing pressure for preferential treatment of certain minorities expressed their concern about possible misinterpretations and loopholes. They were assured by the bill's sponsors that consideration of race in employment decisions would be illegal and strictly prohibited under the act's strong language. At the questioners' insistence a section (703 [j]), known as the Mansfield-Dirksen compromise, was inserted which specified that no employer could be required "to grant preferential treatment to any individual or group because of race, color, religion, sex or national origin."

To carry out the provisions of the Civil Rights Act of 1964, President Johnson issued in September 1965 Executive Order 11246, which still is the *Magna Carta* of "affirmative action" (AA). AA rules repeat the mandate of the Civil Rights Act that "all qualified applicants will receive consideration for employment without regard to race, creed, color, or national origin." It specifies:

> The contractor will not discriminate against any employee or applicant for employment because of race, color, religion, sex, or national origin. The contractor will take affirmative action to ensure that applicants are employed, and that employees are treated during employment, without regard to their race, color, religion, sex, or national origin. Such action shall include, but not be limited to the following: employment, upgrading, demotion, or transfer; recruitment or recruitment advertising; layoff or termination; rates of pay or other forms of compensation; and selection for training, including apprenticeship.

Nothing could be more unequivocal and clear. How then was it possible that under the pressure of the federal agencies enforcing AA, race, color and national origin became the governing and overriding considerations in "employment, upgrading, . . . recruiting . . . layoff . . . and selection for training, including apprenticeship"? How was it possible that, far from "without regard," color, race and national origin became principal criteria for recruitment, hiring, and promotion? How could the U.S. Supreme Court (in the *Weber* case) approve selection of trainees on the basis of race, and generally leave undisturbed federal orders to set hiring goals by race, color and national origin?

This parallels the experience in education where the Supreme Court 15 years after ordering the schools (in *Brown II*) "to achieve a system of determining admission to the public schools on a nonracial basis" decided that children must be assigned to public schools on a racial basis and that this should be carried out by compulsory busing. This was followed by the Court's rule in *Bakke* that educational institutions may take race into account in admitting students.

Racial criteria were approved by the Court, that had earlier outlawed them, because a policy of "without regard to" had not produced a hoped-for statistical parity or even a close approximation. Fifteen years of AA have not resulted in anything like equal employment status and black unemployment still is twice as high as white; after 25 years of school integration, the *New York Times* found "virtually all of the nation's largest school districts more racially imbalanced than ever."[162]

Anthony Lewis wrote in the *New York Times* in 1974:

> When the Supreme Court held racial segregation in the public schools unconstitutional, in 1954, many believed that the ideal of the first Justice

Harlan [a color-blind policy] had at last triumphed. From now on, they thought, the law would have to deal with Americans as individuals, not on such a group base as their race. Twenty years later Americans are wiser and sadder.[163]

I said in 1966:

Until not so long ago it was the "Equal Opportunity" banner under which the civil rights forces gathered and which all who believe in freedom and justice had no difficulty joining. Now that some of the earlier goals have largely been achieved, it has become painfully obvious that equal opportunity means unequal results. So, demands are being raised for more than equal rights—and since nothing can be more than equal, this means unequal rights, or, if you please, discrimination in reverse. The battle cry now is for preferential treatment for one ethnic group out of the many that have come to this country. (Elaborate rationalizations are being advanced for translating this form of racism into public policy.)[164]

AA and school integration repeated the experience of several programs discussed in earlier sections of this chapter: the failure of attempts at social engineering, even if they evidently are counterproductive, does not cause their sponsors to have second thoughts about the appropriateness and effectiveness of such methods. Quite the contrary: it causes them to demand expansion, further tightening and multiplied efforts to carry their practices to the extreme.

No reasonable person will deny that past racial discrimination, extending over generations, bears part of the responsibility for some of the existing discrepancies. Experience in recent years, however, has suggested that other factors may also be at work which do not respond to such attempted therapies as AA or compulsory busing. Some assert that while most overt racism may have been eliminated, there is a *"systemic discrimination"* at work.[165] AA then proceeded to offset systemic discrimination by *systematic discrimination*. However, two wrongs don't make one right. If we deviate from the principle of color blindness, of racial neutrality, there is no amount of injustice and foolishness we may not commit, no amount of damage we may not inflict upon society.

But not everyone agrees. If one assumes as a rock-hewn axiom that, absent racial discrimination, distribution at all levels would be absolutely random, then one must assume that only continued and persistent discrimination can produce the racial disparities that exist. Decision makers in all organizations, business, education, etc. must thus be ordered, under sanctions of law, to bring about the random distribution which, according to this theory, would exist if employers did not continue to engage in discrimination against minorities.

Therefore, a governmental agency enforcing AA does not need to prove that a business firm or a university has been practicing racial discrimination. If the firm does not employ the same percentage of specified minorities, in toto or by hierarchical and pay grade, as exists in the general population (or in some other total), it admits to a prima facie case of discrimination. There is no burden of proof on the government to document a specific violation. The burden is on the company or institution to hire and promote a sufficient number of members of minorities. AA rules state that it is "result-oriented": it hardly matters what method the employer uses to achieve the desired results, even if it violates the equal rights principle of the Constitution and the equal treatment mandate of the statute: the end justifies the means.

To be sure, the government does not order the presumed violator to give preference to minorities and hire or promote a sufficient number of them. That would too obviously run counter to the "without regard" rule of the law. The company is ordered to submit a plan establishing numerical "goals" of the number of minorities it will have in toto and at various levels, by departments, at specified dates, one or several years later. That it may be unable to achieve those goals *without* giving preference to minorities is deemed irrelevant, despite the statutory prohibition against it. A business or institution which does not set its minority goals high enough to satisfy the governmental agency, or fails to attain its goals, will be declared "out of compliance." It is then subject to cancellation of existing grants and contracts and exclusion from future participation. It also may have to pay sizable fines as well as back wages to complaining employees or would-be employees, compensation which in some cases has totaled dozens of millions of dollars. The government has been tough about suspending or cancelling grants to educational institutions which did not comply with AA orders. But it has taken no action to deny federal benefits to institutions which manifest their hostile attitude toward the national defense of the United States by driving ROTC from their campuses or refusing such studies the proper credit, thereby denying students who would like to serve their country an opportunity to do so.

To force employers to treat race, color, national origin, etc. as a determinant in employment decisions through the use of a law which clearly demands such decisions to be taken "without regard to race, color, national origin, etc." is possibly the most outrageous perversion of justice and of the English language ever committed. For the highest court in the land to approve such actions is, as University of Michigan philosophy professor Carl Cohen expressed it, "Justice Debased."[166]

During the Senate debate on the Civil Rights Act of 1964, Senator Hubert Humphrey expressed the congressional intent and general understanding of its mandate:

> Contrary to the allegations of some opponents of this title, there is nothing in it that will give any power to the [Equal Employment Opportunity] Commission or to any courts to require hiring, firing, or promotion of employees in order to meet a racial "quota" or to achieve a certain racial balance.
>
> That bugaboo has been brought up a dozen times; but it is nonexistent. In fact, the very opposite is true. Title VII prohibits discrimination. In effect, it says that race, religion, and national origin are not to be used as the basis for hiring and firing. Title VII is designed to encourage hiring on the basis of ability and qualifications, not race or religion.[167]

The U.S. Supreme Court seemed to agree with that interpretation in some of its decisions:

> Discriminatory preference for any group, minority or majority, is precisely and only what Congress has proscribed. . . . Congress has not commanded that the less qualified be preferred over the better qualified simply because of minority origin. Far from disparaging job qualifications, Congress has made such qualifications the controlling factor, so that race, religion, nationality, and sex become irrelevant. [*Griggs* v. *Duke*, 401 U.S. 424 (1971).]
>
> It is clear beyond cavil that the obligation imposed by Title VII is to provide an equal opportunity for each applicant regardless of race, without regard to whether members of the applicant's race are already proportionately represented in the work force. [*Furnco* v. *Waters*, 438 U.S. 567 (1978).]

In his dissent with the Court's avoidance to decide the merits of the *DeFunis* case in 1974, Mr. Justice Douglas stated:

> There is no constitutional right for any race to be preferred. . . . [A] white is entitled to no advantage by reason of that fact, nor is he subject to any disability. Whatever his race, he [has] a constitutional right to [be] considered on his individual merits.

Several decisions of the Court in the 1970s and in 1980, however, made it abundantly clear that, contrary to what it had said in *Griggs*, "irrelevant" was exactly what race did *not* become. The Court upheld several racial remedies to issues brought before it, usually with a less than impressive majority—five justices, or sometimes six, approving a color-conscious solution. In the *Weber* case the Court denied the plaintiff the right to participate in his employer's training program for no reason other than that he was white and the program had a 50:50 black-white quota. It avoided ruling on AA itself by finding that the plan (and quota) were *voluntary* on the employer's part, despite the fact that Kaiser Steel had adopted the plan under severe governmental pressure.

In his scathing dissent to the *Weber* decision, Mr. Justice Rehnquist said:

> Thus by a *tour de force* reminiscent not of jurists such as Hale, Holmes and Hughes, but of escape artists such as Houdini, the Court eludes clear statutory language, uncontradicted legislative history, and uniform precedent in concluding that employers are, after all, permitted to consider race in making employment decisions.

In *Bakke* the Court disallowed quotas but permitted race to be considered in decisions on admissions. In other cases, federal courts, following the Supreme Court's leadership, have not only permitted but ordered quotas. They have declared biased and unconstitutional long-established examinations and tests for employment, promotion, and admission because minorities failed those tests at a higher rate than others.

In 1970 the U.S. Civil Service Commission largely eliminated arithmetic and algebraic components of civil service entrance examinations—not because computational ability was found to be irrelevant to the performance of the jobs in question, but because blacks tended to fail at a higher rate than whites. The Supreme Court ruled in *Griggs* v. *Duke* (1971) that tests that blacks fail more frequently than whites are suspect. Earlier it had declared literacy requirements for voting eligibility to be unconstitutional. Illiterates must be assumed to possess as much knowledge and judgment as literates and must be given the same power to influence governmental decisions.

To invalidate tests because they do not show the desired results stands logic on its head. Would we declare medical tests biased because they indicate a higher incidence of certain illnesses among some ethnic groups? Would we apply the principle to basketball, boxing, brass music? Would we apply it to prisons? I tried to illustrate this point in a letter to the editor of the *Wall Street Journal* (March 31, 1975) in which I described what application of the principles of AA would do in prisons.

> In the editorial "Thinking the Unthinkable" (Mar. 14) you refer again, as you have on prior occasions, to "affirmative action" which aims to correct discrepancies in representation of women and ethnic minorities on campuses. It is often overlooked that representational discrepancies are much worse in prisons than on campuses. Women constitute 51% of the U.S. population but only 3% of the prison population. Blacks constitute 12% of the U.S. population but 42% of the prison population. That clearly proves the existence of discrimination which needs to be corrected by the adoption of proper policies. Goals need to be established by which affirmative action ought to be attained within a reasonable time. Progress toward reaching them should be closely monitored and strictly enforced.
>
> The mathematical goals are obvious: Women ought to constitute 51% of the prison population, blacks 12%. No group should be admitted to nor kept in prisons at a rate different from their percentage in the general population.
>
> The discrepancy is so great that action must be started at both ends: i.e., dismissal of men from prisons and accommodation of women—with specific numerical time goals until a 51:49 ratio is reached. This is equally true of blacks, whose share of the prison population must be reduced to 12%, by releasing those who are there now and the incarceration of more whites until they account for about 88% of the prison population.
>
> Income classes are also unequally represented. Persons with a pre-arrest income of $7,500 or more account for 33% of the general population but only 11% of the prison population. Effective steps must promptly be taken to raise their share to 33% among prison inmates. The Watergate trials, sensational though they were, were numerically inadequate to correct the imbalance. Moreover, in compliance with affirmative action goals, prison sentences will have to be allocated on a balanced basis between political parties.

Female arrests did rise faster than male after 1975. The assertion by some media that this might represent "the dark side of the women's liberation" was sharply rejected in a 1977 report of the Law Enforcement Assistance Administration which said that "it is virtually impossible to single out the women's liberation movement as the cause of the rise in female crime." Could it be that some authorities heeded my 1975 appeal for AA in law enforcement?

Some might conclude from the differential rate of imprisonment that minorities are more likely than whites to be sent to prison by racist judges. But a 1976 report of the Center for Econometric Studies of Crime and the Criminal Justice System at the Hoover Institution found that "minority defendants were less likely to be sentenced to prison than white defendants" and that "the results obtained are inconsistent with the conventional hypothesis that the criminal justice system discriminated against minority race defendants."[168] Because a larger percentage of minorities (than of "majority") are arrested and convicted of criminal offenses, employers are now forbidden to consider an arrest record in making employment decisions. This inevitably increases the likelihood that persons with criminal tendencies and records (minority or majority) will be hired and promoted to responsible positions—and thereby offered an opportunity to engage in criminal activities. This may help to explain the growing incidence of "inside jobs."

In consequence of several Supreme Court decisions during the 1970s, we now have two sets of law in the United States: one law for a few ethnic minorities and one law applied to all others. No longer is a university or a business firm permitted to hire or promote the best qualified candidate—unless he happens to be of the desired race, color, or national origin—the equal rights clause of the Fourteenth Amendment and the "without regard" clauses of the Civil Rights Act of 1964 to the contrary notwithstanding. To maintain a pretense of complying with constitutional and statutory mandates, the meaning of words is being perverted. A principal federal agency enforcing differential treatment for minority and majority members is labeled *Equal Employment Opportunity Commission* and an employer who gives preference to minorities is called an *equal opportunity employer*.

To be sure, racial quotas are nothing new or unique. For example, the government of Malaysia (despite a nondiscrimination clause in its constitution) has long maintained a rule of hiring three Malays for every Chinese in the civil service, of pressuring commercial and industrial enterprises to hire more Malays instead of Chinese and to increase the number of Malays who enter and graduate from the university.[169] Until two generations ago (or less) many European and American universities maintained a *numerus clausus*, limiting the number of Jewish applicants they would admit. Similar arrangements, usually less formal, existed in numerous industrial and financial institutions. Some such practices may still exist, though they are carefully disguised and their existence is strictly denied.

Such numerical limitations, exclusions, discrimination—whether regarding Jews or Chinese as mentioned, or Indians and Pakistanis throughout Eastern and Central Africa—are intended to protect the politically dominant *majority* of the local population against the advance of *minority* groups which are striving harder and are economically more successful. There is no charge of earlier discrimination against a majority which is occupationally and economically "disadvantaged," and which must be compensated for.

Nowhere outside the United States are racially discriminatory policies used to advance an economically less successful ethnic minority to equal a more effective majority. It is almost always the other way around. Nowhere else are ethnic minorities which are economically less successful regarded or treated as a problem that warrants government intervention to provide preferential treatment.

While federal agencies pressure business firms and universities to achieve proportionate representation of minorities, disparities in federal employment continue to be no less distinct. After four decades of nondiscrimination rules, nearly half the federal civilian employment in the lowest grade (GS 1) consists of minorities and one-third in the second lowest grade (GS 2) while only about 4 percent in the top grades are minorities. Such disparities exist in the federal courts, the White House, the Department of Justice and throughout the federal establishment. In 1980 21.6% of the enlisted men in the Armed Services were black, but only 4.8% of the officers. Congress wisely exempted itself from AA although representational differences are no less strong there than elsewhere. It is unlikely that much of the current ethnic disparities in the federal service, civilian or military, are the result of deliberate racial discrimination in hiring and promotion. But federal civil rights agencies act as if minority underrepresentation in business or educational institutions were due to such practices.

The U.S. Constitution and American tradition establish *individual* rights but never envisaged or sanctioned proportional representation of population segments by "race, color, national origin, or religion." If color of skin is to be made the basis of proportional representation in employment by administrative fiat—although it is prohibited by law—why should not other physical traits such as color of hair or eyes or length and weight of body be used to assure "equal representation"? They probably are just as relevant.

Public opinion polls (Gallup and other) have shown for years that Americans are overwhelmingly—eight out of ten questioned—opposed to preferential treatment to achieve statistical parity in racial or ethnic representation. This is why Congress never authorized preferential treatment and legislated against it in the *Civil Rights Act of 1964* (Sec. 703[j], cited earlier)—just as it has voted repeatedly against mandatory busing.

It is a paradoxical fact that in a system that supposedly is a "government by the people" the people's wishes are disregarded and overruled by a small group of men appointed for life, who are not elected by or answerable to the people. Even among them, most of the decisions upholding racial preferences were made with only five—or, at the most, six—votes among the nine members of the Supreme Court. Once before, when the Supreme Court ruled contrary to the nation's conscience, it took a civil war to restore justice. In the current controversy a less violent remedy through legislation or a constitutional amendment will hopefully be adopted before a frustrated majority despairs of a peaceful solution.

The results of basing hiring and promotional decisions not on individual merit and, on merit alone, of selecting not the best qualified candidate but the one whose skin is of the desired color, are becoming increasingly apparent. After an interview with Council of Economic Advisers Chairman Charles L. Schultze, *New York Times* reporter Jerry Flint wrote that equal opportunity rules that mean the hiring of the less efficient, the less educated, and the less skilled to promote equality among the races, is among the reasons for low—and of late declining—productivity.[170] Nor should the impact on employee morale be underrated of letting racial goals or quotas—which, as Sidney Hook has pointed out mean the same—overrule individual qualification, whether in business, education, or in the competitive, merit-based civil service or in the Armed Forces.

Colleges and universities historically have aimed for academic excellence by hiring for their faculty the most highly qualified individuals they were able to attract. The principle of hiring the "most qualified" is now being replaced, under severe governmental pressure, by selecting among persons who meet minimal qualifications those who help reach AA goals, i.e., specified minorities. Minimum requirements are usually set by educational attainment—the number of years spent in academic study, credit hours accumulated and degrees earned. At a time when high schools promote and graduate students by age and years of residence, when colleges and universities lower their admission and graduation requirements for minorities, when test results are disregarded or tests discarded if there is a significant disparity in the performance of minorities and non-minorities on them, and when references have become virtually meaningless because of governmental privacy rules, a gradual decline in the quality of education is inevitable.

Affirmative action as currently enforced by governmental agencies is gravely damaging American society and the economy. It is not producing the results which its protagonists had hoped for and promised. George A. McAlmon, a director of the Fund for the Republic, opened his emotional article "A Critical Look at Affirmative Action" with the observation: "After fifteen years, affirmative action as practiced to date has failed to achieve significant integration or improvement in living standards of ethnic minorities."[171] McAlmon proposed expansion and stricter enforcement of AA as the appropriate remedy. This repeats a frequent response by enthusiasts of social engineering to evident failure of their favorite projects: let us double or triple appropriations and efforts, but not re-examine the premise on which the action was based.

McAlmon was correct in observing that AA had not lived up to the expectations of its sponsors. It has not accomplished much for the black underclass. But it greatly advanced the fortunes of a black intelligentsia which, by spearheading demands for special government benefits and preferences, built for itself a devoted constituency, a political power base and economic affluence. Congressman Parren J. Mitchell, chairman of the Black Caucus, was quoted as commenting on efforts to move blacks from urban ghettos, "Will not the relocation of blacks—moving them out of the cities—destroy the political base that we blacks have begun to develop in this country?"[172]

Unemployment still is twice as high among minorities as among non-minorities; it is nearly three times as high among black teenagers as among white. But three decades ago, the unemployment rate was higher among white teenagers than among black, as Walter Williams has repeatedly pointed out. Would anybody conclude therefrom that racial discrimination has grown so much worse in the meantime? If not, why should we attribute the current high unemployment rate among nonwhite youths to racial discrimination? If for good reason we don't, why should we believe that AA, no matter how tightly enforced, could reduce the unemployment rate among minorities?

The nearly 40% unemployment rate among young minorities is the result of factors which cannot be corrected by AA: 1) Minimum wages which exceed the productive capacity (market value of service or work output) of low-skilled or unskilled people, 2) Relatively easy availability of alternative means of getting an income through workless pay, 3) Presence of millions of illegal immigrants who fill most of the unskilled, low-paid, menial job openings, 4) Failure of the common schools to teach pupils fundamentals and marketable skills at the level of their capacity, and 5) The holding out of unrealistic promises which creates counterproductive attitudes among less endowed young people.

All evidence points to the conclusion that affirmative action amounts to barking up the wrong tree, that it is doing so at a high cost without reaching its objectives, and that it is contrary to the word and spirit of our Constitution and laws. It is high time that AA be replaced by a truly impartial, racially neutral, color-blind policy.

Integration and Disintegration of the Public Schools:
The Bus Blunder

By outlawing segregation in the public schools in 1954, the Supreme Court took an action that had long been overdue. To be sure, the derivation of the new rule from the Fourteenth Amendment was farfetched and artificial, with no proof or even likelihood that it expressed the intent of its authors. The Court did in 1954 what it felt needed to be done, and what Congress should have done by constitutional amendment decades or generations earlier: repeal the "separate but equal" doctrine of *Plessy* v. *Ferguson* (1896).

In *Brown II* (1955) the Court defined the intent and purpose of its momentous step: ". . . to achieve a system of determining admission to the public schools on a nonracial basis. . . ."

The Court did not in its decision *interpret* the Constitution; it *amended* the Constitution to make up for the failure of Congress to do so. Maybe there were not enough votes in Congress to pass the needed amendment and, maybe there were not enough state legislatures to approve it with the required three-fourths majority. It is a national tragedy that a quarter century later there still appear to be not enough votes in the Congress to adopt a constitutional amendment prohibiting denial of a child's admission to a public school on account of race, creed, color or national origin.

Congress did, however, pass the *Civil Rights Act of 1964* which said (Title IV, Section 2000c[b]):

> "Desegregation" means the assignment of students to public schools and within such schools without regard to their race, color, religion, or national origin, but "desegregation" shall not mean the assignment of students to public schools in order to overcome racial imbalance.

Section 2000c-6 provided that:

> . . . nothing herein shall empower any official or court of the United States to issue any order seeking to achieve a racial balance in any school by requiring the transportation of pupils or students from one school to another or one school district to another in order to achieve such racial balance, or otherwise enlarge the existing power of the court to insure compliance with constitutional standards.

What caused federal courts and administrative agencies within a few years of *Brown* to order school systems to assign children to schools according to their race? How could they assign children to schools distant from their homes, contrary to federal law? Congress had proscribed such action in the *Equal Educational Opportunities Act of 1974* (Section 215):

> No court, department or agency of the United States shall . . . order the implementation of a plan that would require the transportation of any student to a school other than the school closest or next closest to his place of residence which provides the appropriate grade level and type of education for such student.

In the 1976 Labor-HEW appropriations bill Congress inserted a prohibition (Section 209):

> None of the funds contained in this act shall be used to require, directly or indirectly, the transportation of any student to any school other than the school which is nearest the student's home, and which offers the courses of study pursued by such student.

What motivated the Supreme Court to uphold the busing orders of lower courts which seemingly it had proscribed in *Brown II* and which Congress appeared to have forbidden? Before trying to answer that question I should clarify the significant difference between the situation *before* and *after* the *Brown* decisions.

Until 1954, black children, in Southern states, were forbidden to attend white schools and white children to attend black schools. Under rules enunciated by the courts in the 1960s and 1970s, many white children must be refused admission if the school of their choice is predominantly white; many black children must be refused admission if the school they choose is predominantly black.

Why did the Supreme Court reverse its nonracial admission rule and disregard congressional mandate? By what strange logic and legal technique did it do so?

In *Swann* v. *Charlotte-Mecklenburg* 401 U.S.1 (1971) the Court explained that "the objective today remains to eliminate from the public schools all vestiges of state-imposed segregation." But though state-imposed segregation never existed outside the South, federal courts soon began to issue, and the High Court sanctioned decrees that children in dozens of cities from Los Angeles to Minneapolis, Milwaukee, Chicago, Cleveland and Boston should be refused admission to neighborhood schools of their choice *because* of their race. They would have to be bused to distant schools against their parents' wishes, for the sole purpose of creating a racial balance in the affected schools.

Racial concentration in schools, black in some, white in others, is not necessarily due to state-imposed segregation. Sometime in the 1960s the Supreme Court found out—evidently to its surprise—that most parents when given freedom of choice, continue to send their children to neighborhood schools and that because of settlement patterns and personal preference these are, more often than not, schools attended predominantly by children of the same ethnic and socioeconomic background. That families of a similar background, ethnic or socioeconomic, tend to settle in contiguous areas is not exactly a new phenomenon. In fact, it has long been the prevailing pattern in the United States—and almost everywhere else on the globe—among mankind and most animal species. It seems to make them feel more comfortable.

That is why we find that in areas which never knew "state-imposed segregation," schools tend to be ethnically homogeneous—or close to it—more often than not—from Soviet Central Asia to the Fiji Islands, from India to East Africa. The belief that, absent state-imposed segregation, each school in the United States or anywhere else would be attended by the same ethnic percentage mix that exists in the country as a whole, or in the state or city, has no basis in fact. It was concocted in an ivory tower and then propagated for political purposes.

"Freedom of choice" plans which Southern school districts adopted after the 1954 decision, resulted in some black children—up to 15% or 20%—transferring to white schools, but few white children shifting to black schools. Some black middle-class parents, ambitious for their children to be taught at higher educational standards than were common in schools which had to adjust to a generally low learning level of their pupils, used the newly opened opportunity. Whites were not anxious to have their children go to schools where low educational standards were likely to prevail—even if their own children lacked the ability to live up to higher academic demands.

By the late 1960s the Supreme Court was disappointed when "freedom of choice" had produced little *de facto* integration. It struck out in *Green* v. *New Kent County*, 391 U.S. 430 (1968) and declared "freedom of choice" insufficient to satisfy its demand for desegregation. It had expected that black children would be streaming to formerly all-white schools when the 1954 decision opened the door by declaring state-imposed segregation to be unconstitutional. But many or most black parents did not seem eager to avail themselves of the opportunity to have their children bused to distant white schools. In *Green* the Court clarified that it had intended not only to grant black parents the *right* to send their children to a school attended by whites, but to impose the *duty* on an adequate number of them to do so—and to impose the duty on some white parents to send their children to formerly all black schools. Racial mixing turned from a civil right to a civil duty whether the children's parents wanted it or not.

More than four decades earlier, in *Pierce* v. *Society*, 268 U.S 510 (1925) the Court had declared that "the child is not the mere creature of the state," and that the right of parents to direct the education of their children was paramount. Subsequently, the United Nations added its voice in the *Declaration on Human Rights* which, in Article 26 (3) said, "Parents have a prior right to choose the kind of education that shall be given to their children."

But the Court held human rights or civil rights or freedom of choice to rank a lower priority than the need for racial mixing in schools. Why? Some regard it desirable that children destined to live in a multiracial society, experience daily contact with youngsters of other ethnic backgrounds during their formative and learning years. That seems a valid reason for *advocating* racial mixing but is by itself hardly sufficient to justify mandating *compulsion* and the drastic steps required to carry it into practice.

The main impetus for desegregation came from the awareness that something had to be done to raise the educational level of black children, who lag one to several years behind white children in basic skills and knowledge as measured on standard achievement tests. Only about 15% of black children perform at a level which 50% of white children attain. This is why the Supreme Court in *Brown* declared that "separate educational facilities are inherently unequal." Kenneth Clark—on whose expertise the Court drew while it was deliberating on *Brown*—referred to black children as "victims of tragically inferior public education."

Why and in what way is public education inferior for blacks? For generations state legislatures and communities gave black schools smaller appropriations than white schools. That often meant fewer and poorly paid teachers and austere or old buildings. But that changed substantially around the mid-century. The national school survey, mandated by the *Civil Rights Act of 1964* and conducted in 1965 by James Coleman, found to the researchers' and everybody else's surprise that there was no significant difference in terms of material resources—teacher qualifications, teacher-pupil ratios, teacher salaries, physical facilities, etc.—between schools attended by black or white children (see p. 186). This was amply confirmed by follow-up studies.

Moreover, the *Elementary and Secondary Education Act of 1965* shifted additional federal funds—now totaling $4 billion annually—to schools largely attended by "disadvantaged" children. That made it possible to hire more teachers and reduce class sizes substantially for disadvantaged children—about half of whom are minorities—run special remedial classes, start black children at earlier ages (on the average earlier than white children) and try out a wide variety of "compensatory" programs. But test results showed little progress, if any. An analysis of data in the *New York City School Fact Book*[173] shows substantially smaller class sizes and one-third higher per pupil expenditures in predominantly black schools than in white schools. But reading and math scores are two years behind in black schools.

When neither equalization of resources nor compensatory education and other attempted reforms (see pp. 200–209) succeeded in raising performance levels of black children, that failure was widely attributed to indifference, malice and incompetence among white (and possibly racist) administrators, school boards, and teachers who could not relate to black children, did not believe that they *could* learn and did not teach them properly. Therefore, a demand arose that "the black community must control its own schools if black children are to get a decent education."

Sponsored by New York Mayor John Lindsay and the Ford Foundation and strongly supported by black leaders such as Kenneth Clark, community control of neighborhood schools became a civil rights goal of the late 1960s. But the results of black-staffed and community-controlled schools such as Ocean Hill–Brownsville, Central Harlem and Twin Bridges in New York City and similar projects elsewhere were so devastating that its sponsors abandoned them within a few years. Kenneth Clark wrote recently: "It is now clear that the 'black power' and 'community control' movement, while having some temporary cathartic value, did not improve by one iota the educational and economic status of ghetto-entrapped underclass blacks."[174]

One reason for the black underclass being "ghetto-entrapped" was mentioned earlier in a quotation from Congressman Parren J. Mitchell: that relocating blacks from urban ghettos would destroy the political base that black leaders have developed (p. 343).

Failure of all attempts so far to raise the educational level of black children to something closer to the level of white children led to a desperate search for alternatives. One method, widely used, was to de-emphasize and discredit national achievement tests in the public schools by attacking them as biased, unfair, misleading. Some schools kept test results secret or abandoned tests altogether which is like the husband who after finding his wife with her lover on the sofa sold the sofa. Of course, tests are not an end in themselves. They only try to measure what in other ways will manifest itself sooner or later anyway. But reports of achievement tests which show predominantly black schools averaging substantially below white schools are embarrassing and hard to explain at a time when there no longer is a significant difference in material resources in favor of white schools.

There seemed to be only one way to abolish such disturbing comparisons once and for all: assign children on a racial basis so as to establish a uniform mix at each school, at least within each city. In *Swann* the Supreme Court pointed at the critical item: the feasibility "to identify a 'white school' or a 'Negro school' simply by reference to the racial composition of teachers and staff." If a condition were created where no one could identify a school as white or black, the evidence of an achievement gap between white and black would be wiped out. *Quod non est in actis, non est in mundo* (what is not on the record does not exist).

Because most of the predominantly black schools are in black neighborhoods and courts could not very well order large numbers of black families forthwith to move to white neighborhoods—nor white families to move to black neighborhoods—other means had to be found to bring about school integration. With all alternatives having proven ineffective, mandatory busing seemed the only way to produce the desired results. There would be no more "black" schools or "white" schools; no one would be able to complain that public education for blacks was "tragically inferior" and no comparisons would be published showing disparities between white and black educational achievements.

As it turned out, the buses shuttled children from one end of the city to the other but integration by racial assignment did not succeed except in parts of the South where segregation had previously been state-imposed.

Some of the advocates of desegregation by mandatory busing had expected—and predicted—that educational achievements of black children would quickly rise in an integrated environment and soon equal or at least approach the scores of white children. That seemed logical: if inadequate skills and knowledge of black children were caused by their schools' inferior education, transfer to institutions with presumably superior instruction and standards would undo the damage inflicted on them. Little attention was paid to two of the Coleman survey's most important findings: achievement differentials are far wider *within* schools than *among* schools; school characteristics account for very little of test score disparities.

In a re-examination of the Coleman survey, Christopher Jencks commented:

> The implications of this are in many ways more revolutionary than anything else in the Equal Educational Opportunity Survey. In the short run it remains true that our most pressing political problem is the achievement gap between Harlem and Scarsdale. But in the long run it seems that our primary problem is not the disparity between Harlem and Scarsdale but the disparity between the top and the bottom of the class in both Harlem and Scarsdale. Anyone who doubts this ought to spend some time talking to children in the bottom half of a "good" middle-class suburban school.[175]

This suggests that the educational outcome for each pupil is governed much less by what he *finds at* the school than what he *brings to* the school. James Coleman reported that the closest correlation exists between a child's test scores and the educational and socioeconomic status of his parents. He concluded that race itself is not a factor in academic achievements. We would, therefore, hardly expect that racial integration will significantly affect the learning of children, white or black, that it can materially raise or lower their educational level. Which is exactly what many subsequent studies found to be true.

The Coleman survey had found that black children attending school with whites tend to score slightly higher on standard achievement tests than black children enrolled in all or predominantly black schools. Some concluded from this that racial integration improves the learning of black children. Other researchers, such as Henry Levin and Samuel Bowles, pointed out that in the 1960s black children in integrated schools were not representative of the average of all black children. Black children in integrated schools were likely to come from parents of a higher socioeconomic status who had chosen to live in an integrated neighborhood or had managed to send their offspring to a school with higher academic standards. Coleman himself wrote in 1972 that his findings "have been used inappropriately by the courts to support the premise that equal protection for black children is not provided unless racial balance is achieved in the schools."

The Charlotte-Mecklenburg (N.C.) schools have long been integrated by extensive busing; schools of Charlotte City and Mecklenburg county were consolidated in 1960 which made white flight virtually impossible for most residents. In 1979 reading and math tests, 43% of the black 11th graders failed, but only 5% of their white classmates. In San Francisco, the first large city to integrate by court-ordered busing, Stanford's Sanford Dornbusch reported in 1979 that he found 62% of black male students four years behind whites in reading ability by the tenth grade.

Harvard sociologist David J. Armor summarized:

> None of the studies have been able to demonstrate conclusively that integration has had an effect on academic achievement as measured by standard tests.[176]

To be sure, average scores in formerly all-black schools went up after integration, just as scores in formerly all-white schools went down. That was largely the result of a different mix of pupils in each school. Most black children did not do better than they had before, nor did most white children do worse, though some studies did report black improvement. The educational level in public schools generally continued its downward slide, as schools, faced with the influx of children one or more years behind grade level in skills and knowledge, found it necessary to adjust their demands and standards and their curriculum.

Outside the South, courts had to devise a legal technique that could be used to justify desegregation orders. The U.S. Supreme Court had repeatedly based its desegregation decrees on the need to overcome the effects of state-imposed segregation. But Northern states had never known state-imposed segregation; it would have been contrary to their state constitutions and the prevailing public sentiment. Courts eventually found a subterfuge that enabled them to circumvent this obstacle in states that had never operated a dual school system: they declared that state and local legislatures, administrators (and communities voting on consolidation, annexation and related ballot issues) had "gerrymandered" the size and shape of the school districts and attendance areas and located school buildings so as to segregate students by race.

Available evidence suggests that attendance area and construction decisions sometimes are influenced by considerations of socioeconomic settlement patterns but basically governed by the wishes of the people in the affected communities for convenient access. Though large numbers of whites live in poverty areas and a growing number of blacks in more affluent neighborhoods, there exists a concentration of minorities in poor urban sections. Thus school attendance area decisions may result in ethnic concentrations. This does not prove that they were so intended. But some courts chose so to interpret them as a means of justifying busing orders.

Results of desegregation under pressure from federal agencies or in obedience to court decrees, however, were far from what busing protagonists had intended and expected. They led to what has been called *white flight* which left schools in many areas more segregated than ever.

The term white flight is a misnomer. Middle- and upper-class parents, white or black, enrolled their children in private schools or moved to suburbs (mostly white but some black), neither of which *poor* whites were able to do. The movement, especially in the North, succeeded in integrating the children of poor and lower middle-class parents who could not afford to pay private tuitions nor move to the suburbs. Families in high earning brackets are able to escape busing, which helps them to accept the integration of lower-class children with manifest equanimity. Some of the leaders in the drive for school integration—black or white—and some of the judges who had ordered compulsory busing send their own children to private schools.

School integration became increasingly a matter of class more than of race. University of Wisconsin demographer William H. Frey concluded from extensive studies that the "white flight can be explained much more fully by nonracial, economic and environmental factors than by those directly related to race."[177] Rand Corporation researcher David J. Armor testified before a Los Angeles Superior Court in November 1979 that "whites shunned schools that had low reading and math scores."[178]

Most parents opposed mandatory busing, not because they objected to the skin color of their offsprings' prospective classmates but because they were afraid of the impact which dismal inner city reading and math scores would have on their own children's learning. They also feared that in schools which manifestly are unable to enforce discipline, their children were likely to acquire offensive or detrimental attitudes, manners, behavior, mores, language, from children with a different cultural background. That issue is socioeconomic far more than racial. When families were unable to beat mandatory busing in the courts, they began voting with their feet.

The migration of middle- and upper-class families from central cities to the suburbs began long before the desegregation controversy. It was motivated by such factors as heavy city taxes, high crime rates, amenities of suburban living, growing affluence and others. But it gained momentum and turned into a mass flight of the middle class—white or black—when busing was forced upon cities all over the country. As might be expected according to Gresham's law, middle- and upper-class families left and the underclass took over the schools, and gradually the central cities.

It began, as most important changes nowadays do, in Washington. Shortly after the *Brown* decision in May 1954, President Eisenhower issued orders that the nation's capital should set an example of instant compliance to the rest of the country.

District of Columbia schools had long been operating a dual school system with more white pupils than black. In September 1954 Washington schools opened on an integrated basis. The school superintendent's attempt to cope with instructional problems by installing a four-track system was declared unconstitutional by the federal district court because the slow tracks were mostly black. This set in motion a middle-class family exodus to Virginia and Maryland which left Washington schools more than 96% black within a few years.

That pattern repeated itself in city after city from coast to coast. Atlanta's schools went from 43% black in 1959 to 90% by the end of the 1970s. New York City schools, 68% white in 1957, were 71% nonwhite by 1977, with an 86% nonwhite rate predicted within another ten years.

White children now account for less than one-fourth the enrollment in the public schools of Chicago, Baltimore, Detroit, Cleveland, St. Louis, New Orleans, San Antonio and numerous other cities. There is, in fact, just a handful of large cities left in whose public schools minorities do not constitute a majority of the student body. In many urban systems there simply are "not enough white children" left to make meaningful desegregation feasible.[179] Diane Ravitch, History and Education Professor at Teachers College, Columbia University, well described in 1978 the impact of court-ordered busing on racial changes in the public schools—a dramatic shift from white to black majorities.[180]

Judges are continuing to hand down busing orders, many of which soon prove to be self-defeating. Minorities account for one-fourth of total public school enrollment but, after a quarter century of attempted desegregation, three-fifths of them attend schools that are at least half minority. School boards, under duress and threatened with fines and jail for criminal contempt of court, operate large fleets of buses at multimillion dollar costs to carry on a Sisyphean task. It is an irony that as the pro-busing forces prevail in the courts, their litigative triumphs turn into Pyrrhic victories in pursuit of an evanescent goal.

There is a close parallel between compulsory busing and prohibition, the "noble experiment." Both were undertaken with splendid intentions and for the most appealing reasons. Both failed because they were based on a fundamental misunderstanding of human nature. Thus, the cure turned out to be worse than the disease.

Yet, there is a significant difference. Prohibition was voted in by constitutional amendment, adopted by proper methods. Busing was imposed by a group of public officials who were not elected by nor responsible to the people, but appointed for life. Relying on the enormous respect which the nation's highest court had acquired over nearly two centuries, they proceeded to demean and exhaust the court's eminent standing by displaying utter disdain for the concepts of fairness and equal justice held by an overwhelming majority of the American people. Through an outrageous perversion of language they twisted the words and meaning of the Constitution and laws. Forced busing which the Supreme Court imposed was never recommended by any president and would and could never have been voted in by the Congress, state legislatures or the people themselves. It is without parallel in the history of the United States or the rest of the world.

Repeated public opinion polls have shown consistently over the years a three to one majority *against* mandatory busing—and a similarly impressive vote *against* school segregation. They reported a majority of blacks as opposing forced busing.

What the people believe and what some of our highest judges do not seem to understand is that what matters is not whether a black student sits next to a white student, but that every student has an inalienable right to decide which school for which he is qualified he wishes to attend and that no government agency has the right to deny him admission to the school of his choice and assign him to another school because of his race. To treat individuals differently, according to race, is a flagrant violation of the equal rights clause of the Fourteenth Amendment—in whose name by a contorted logic the racial assignments were made.

Congress, aware of the public sentiment, has inserted several provisions in civil rights laws and appropriation bills intended to discourage, slow down or halt mandatory busing. But it never had the courage to take a decisive step to remove the subject from the Supreme Court's jurisdiction.

Article III, Section 2, of the U.S. Constitution provides that the "Supreme Court shall have appellate jurisdiction both as to law and fact, with such exceptions, and under such regulations as the Congress shall make." The last time Congress exempted a subject matter from Supreme Court jurisdiction was over a century ago. In *Ex parte McCardle*, 7 Wall 506 (1869), Congress removed a case which the Court then had under active consideration and which the legislators suspected might judicially be decided against their intentions.

Should the Supreme Court now refuse to bow to Congress—as Justice Douglas once indicated it might—a resulting constitutional crisis could be conclusively settled by a constitutional amendment which under those circumstances probably could be speedily adopted.

Congress has so far not decisively acted on compulsory busing, for political reasons. In many elections, presidential and congressional, the two major parties are almost evenly divided, with often shifting majorities. That gives a small but well-organized group a clout far beyond the size of its membership. The 1976 presidential race was decided by 90% of the black votes going to Mr. Carter. Presidential and congressional candidates are aware of this situation and many of them feel that they cannot afford to antagonize beyond redemption a small but possibly decisive segment of their constituency. The black vote is strongly guided, almost controlled by a black political leadership which, as distinct from their constituents, favors mandatory busing.

To succeed, the antibusing drive may need more momentum than it presently has. The Supreme Court could conceivably provide that momentum in the 1980s by going one step too far.

Many or most judicial and administrative desegregation orders failed to produce the desired results when large numbers of middle- and upper-class families moved from the city to its periphery to escape the jurisdiction of the central school district. A consolidation of city and suburban school districts—completely or just for integration purposes—would make such "white flight" ineffective and useless: children could then be bused between inner city and suburb.

NAACP and allied groups have long demanded "metropolitan area busing" and the U.S. Civil Rights Commission so recommended in 1977. Several federal district courts so ordered but the U.S. Supreme Court, in the Detroit case of *Milliken* v. *Bradley*, 418 U.S. 717 (1974), decided 5 to 4 against it and has maintained that position subsequently, right down to the Atlanta case in May 1980. It left the door slightly ajar, however, and could some day, with a close majority, approve metropolitan busing.

That would probably not, as did the *Dred Scott* decision in 1857, lead to a civil war though civil disorders and extensive violence cannot be ruled out. The most likely sequel to court ordered metropolitan busing would be a nationwide uprising leading to speedy passage of a constitutional amendment to end compulsory busing once and for all.

Compulsory busing has succeeded over the past two decades in bringing a substantial degree of racial mixing to Southern schools which had never known it. It has done so also, to a limited extent, in some Northern areas. But in city after city, court-ordered desegregation was soon followed by resegregation.

In more precise terms, integration led to dis-integration. Many would regard this as of no great consequence if color mix were the only thing that changed in the public schools.

In the process, unfortunately, major city school systems, once shining examples of academic excellence to Americans and foreign nations, were ruined—as were some of the cities themselves. The appalling decline in educational quality of public school systems throughout the country—discussed in this book's education section—was brought about by several factors. But compulsory busing and attempted integration contributed substantially to the disintegration of educational quality in the schools.

Public school leaders know that if the economic penalty for enrolling children in private schools were not so high, beyond the reach of most families, millions would shift from public to private schools. That is why public school forces so adamantly oppose a reduction in that penalty through vouchers or tax credits. Only economic necessity, the lack of feasible alternatives, keeps many or most American children in the public schools—not because those schools also enroll nonwhite students, but because the quality of learning and discipline in them is so low.

The flight of the upper and middle classes is the main cause of what is generally called "city plight." Cities are in a financial squeeze because the citizens on whom they must depend for support—economic, civic, cultural, social, educational—are deserting them in growing numbers to escape from oppressive rule. Net migration from central cities to the suburbs during the 1970s totaled 8.3 million persons of whom 856,000 were black. The fact that the black share was almost proportionate to the black share in the general population indicates that this cannot be called a white flight; the above-average educational attainment of the migrants, and the much higher income of those who moved *from* central cities than those who moved *to* them, clearly reveal that the distinguishing characteristic of the out-migrants was socioeconomic, not racial.[181]

No amount of federal funds can adequately make up for the absence of a productive citizenry. An underclass is increasingly taking over not only city schools but the cities themselves. America is the only country which is in the process of handing over its central cities to its lowest income group. It also is the only country in which children are transported, against the will of their parents, to distant schools for the purpose of producing a racial balance in those schools.

Evidence is now conclusive that compulsory busing offers no solution to the agonizing problem of the achievement gap between white and black students. Is there no answer to it?

Daniel Patrick Moynihan once wrote: "No one knows how to make a ghetto school work." He could be right. But after a quarter century or more of trying, we know—or at least ought to know—what does *not* work: smaller classes, compensatory education, starting children in school at an earlier age, community control, performance contracting, desegregation by mandatory busing. Nor has any of the 6,000 to 8,000 projects which over the past 15 years have been annually undertaken on local initiative, financed under Title I of the Elementary and Secondary Education Act of 1965 turned out to be the long-sought answer to the secret of how to raise the skills and knowledge of "disadvantaged" children.

I once compared this to the quest of the alchemists who for nearly 2,000 years tried to produce gold from base metals in the laboratory.[182] Despite the infusion of many billions of additional dollars into the schools, black children upon reaching the upper grades still are two to four years behind the average of white children—although that average has been dropping steadily for the past fifteen years or more. One reason for the general decline probably is the fact that public schools, in an effort to cope with less gifted children, have dropped their demands and standards to the lowest common denominator.

A Rockefeller Foundation–sponsored study by the National Commission on the Humanities concluded in October 1980 that "a dramatic improvement in the quality" of elementary and secondary schools needs to be the nation's top priority. There seems to be a consensus among many educators that educational standards have been permitted to deteriorate and that they need to be raised. But if standards were universally raised—how would less gifted children fare? Intellectually endowed students might be challenged by a tighter curriculum, greater demands, tougher standards and perform better. But others would fail—and those are the young people we are concerned with here.

One way to qualify applicants who might not make the grade under uniform standards has been to apply lower demands on certain ethnic minorities. But why should the line be drawn by race? Some blacks are able to meet high standards and some are not. So are whites. Would it not be preferable—and more effective—to draw the line by manifest and proven ability levels rather than by race? Would it not seem more appropriate to develop several sets of curricula, standards of grade promotion and graduation for various levels of learning capacity?

This is what schools in Europe and virtually every country outside the United States do. There are some inconspicuous, little publicized and often hidden approaches to that method in some American schools which use several parallel tracks.

Some educators appear embarrassed by ability grouping—they believe it to run counter to egalitarian ideals and practices which have dominated the American scene in recent decades. Some teachers and administrators regard assignment to one of several parallel tracks an invidious distinction and an admission of failure. They dislike the prospect of having to inform a mother or father that Mary or John will have to be in the "D" track. Actually, it is simply a recognition of a patent fact of life which can be ignored only at a heavy cost. "Late bloomers" could be protected by keeping open the option of lateral transfer. There is no reason for all children to enter school at the same age; we know that some are ready to learn earlier than others.

If the principle of parallel tracking were institutionalized and made central to school education, gifted children could advance faster. They could absorb an elementary-secondary curriculum in ten years or less instead of twelve, enter and graduate sooner from higher education and begin their chosen profession and earning career several years earlier.

Slow learners could be offered a curriculum that concentrates on the essentials they need to cope with the demands of everyday life. They could be trained in marketable skills which would enable them to qualify for entry-level jobs upon graduation from high school. European countries have long combined part-time school attendance in the higher grades with apprenticeship that leads to a full-time job.

Federal programs, now costing $7 billion annually, are trying to teach dropouts and other young people basic skills they could have acquired in regular schools, *if* they had been guided to an appropriate curriculum.

Will it work? Will it help to reduce the nearly 40% unemployment rate among minority youngsters? No one knows for sure. But there is at least a good chance that it may—*if* certain other measures are simultaneously taken such as adjustments in minimum wage rates for teenagers, reduction in the number of illegal aliens who now preempt many of the low-skilled jobs, etc.

In conclusion:

Forced busing provides a telling illustration of Tom Sowell's statement that "the ability of courts to supersede the authority of other institutions is not the same as the ability to achieve the social results aimed at." [183] Often, over the past quarter century, social engineers managed, through the power of government, to activate large programs at huge costs, despite strong objections to the utter futility of their ill-conceived and counterproductive ventures. In the case of busing, as in many others, the sponsors proved unable to deliver the results they had expected and promised.

High hopes that busing would be a temporary expedient to bring about racial integration and improved educational achievements of minority youth have proven to be a mirage. In fourteen years of operation, court-ordered busing turned out to be self-destructive, inflicting grave damage on the public schools and on the cities, severely aggravating social tensions into widespread violence. As a last irony, racial separation is now as pronounced in many of the affected cities as it was before busing, if not more so. But the busing enthusiasts—and our highest judges—seem to have learned nothing. *There are none so blind as those who do not want to see.*

The federal government could have helped to lower stress, strain and friction by de-emphasizing race and shifting attention to improvement of individual capacity, performance, productivity. By easing economic distress this could have aided in alleviating social problems. When courts and political leaders blamed the difficulties of minorities on continuing racial prejudice and discrimination they not only offered a convenient alibi for lack of personal effort and for individual failure, they aroused resentment, hatred against other segments of society and inflamed urban mobs against the "system" to the point of violence.

In his concurrent opinion in *Fullilove* v. *Klutznik* (July 1980) Justice Powell expressed hope that governmental decisions would soon no longer be based on "pigmentation." But this will not come about unless the Supreme Court changes its course or is overruled by appropriate action of Congress and the legislatures, responding to overwhelming popular demand.

It took fourteen years for the Eighteenth Amendment (prohibition) to be repealed. About the same time has gone by since federal courts and agencies began to order large-scale busing. On last count, about 1500 school districts with an enrollment of over 12 million students, nearly one-fourth of the total national enrollment, are now operating under desegregation orders of federal courts or agencies. It is high time that compulsory busing be ended.

The Supreme Court may not find it easy to escape from the corner into which it has painted itself. But it has seldom been at a loss to devise a formula for doing what it wanted to do, even if this required twisting the Constitution and laws, to mean the opposite of what their clear language commands. The Court might recall the Latin proverb: *Ducunt fata volentem, nolentem trahunt* (Fate guides the willing, it forces the unwilling).

Congress, in 1978, came within the narrowest of margins to restrict the authority of the Supreme Court to impose busing. It has considered several constitutional amendments to the same end. But a provision forbidding mandatory busing somehow does not seem to be a proper part of the Constitution. It is in negative terms and too limited. It would be far preferable to clothe the amendment into positive and more appropriate civil rights language such as this:

> No person shall be denied admission to a public educational institution, by the United States or by any state, on account of race, creed, color, or national origin, any provision in the constitution of the United States or of any state notwithstanding.

This would carry out what the Supreme Court announced in 1955 as the purpose of its decision in *Brown II*: ". . . to achieve a system of determining admission to the public schools on a nonracial basis."

The proposed amendment, possibly expanded to establish racial impartiality also in employment, would carry out the word and spirit of the U.S. Constitution: equal protection of law. If we continue to deviate from the principle of racial neutrality—of color blindness—there is no amount of injustice we may not commit, no amount of damage we may not inflict on our society. It seems high time to return to common sense.

5 ★★★★★★★★★★★★★★★★★★★★★★★★

Issues and Prospects

★ Viewing the record of governmental finances (federal-state-local) between 1952 and 1978, the most striking fact appears to be the exponential growth of expenditures for domestic purposes, primarily for social programs—income maintenance, education, health, housing, and community development. Those outlays jumped from $35 billion to $520 billion, a sixfold increase in *constant* dollars over a quarter century while the nation's output of goods and services only slightly better than doubled (Table 23).

The enormity of this change is even more clearly apparent in the federal picture. After a gradual growth over a century and a half, federal expenditures for domestic purposes reached a level of $12 billion in 1952; they then jumped to $287 billion within the succeeding twenty-six years (Table 21). To bring recent trends into sharp focus: federal spending for domestic purposes soared from $72 billion in 1969 to $364 billion in the President's Budget for 1981. This means that over the past dozen years it increased, in *constant* dollars, every two years by as much as the total it had reached as the result of a 163-year growth, from 1789 to 1952.

This amounts to nothing less than a revolution in the nature of government in the United States during the third quarter of the twentieth century. Domestic programs accounted for one-sixth of all federal spending in 1952; by 1971 they claimed more than one-half of the total and by 1978 three-fifths. To be sure, the significant change in recent years has not been the growth of government as such. In terms of the size of its revenues and expenditures governmental growth has expanded only slightly faster than the nation's economy. The overpowering fact is the sudden and unprecedented explosion of governmental and particularly federal activities in the broad field of social welfare.

Such an enormous jump in spending could not have been financed by raising taxes. The American people would have become aware of an added burden of that size loaded onto their shoulders and would not have tolerated it. That is why Congress did not even try. State and local taxes, to be sure, did rise steeply and the taxpayers were conscious of the impact and felt it. However, federal tax rates were *reduced* several times which helped to soften state-local increases and gave taxpayers the impression that the growing federal largesse was coming for free.

The primary method of financing the vast expansion of social benefits, to the extent to which it exceeded revenue from simultaneous economic growth, were twofold: (a) budgetary deficits climbing from a total of $7 billion over the first presidential term (1953–56) in the past three decades to $181 billion over the latest presidential term (1977–80). That was a major—though not the only—force that pushed our inflation rate from an annual average of 0.6% in the first-named presidential term to an average of 10% per annum in the latest four years; (b) a reduction in the share of U.S. resources allocated to national defense from two-thirds of the budget to less than one-fourth. That cut the nation's military strength from superiority to inferiority—to or below an acute danger point.

To many individuals and organizations in all walks of life—in government and politics, in academe, in labor and business—the expansion of social services to meet emerging needs was a point of pride. It seemed to prove that the United States was finally entering the twentieth century, later than most of Europe's industrial nations, but deliberately, purposely, and forcefully. If the American public was so selfish and backward that it would not willingly increase its taxes sufficiently for the less fortunate in its midst, then this had to be done by indirection, when an opportunity arose through an emergency such as the depression of the 1930s or after the end of a war when taxpayers had become accustomed to bearing a heavy load. To its protagonists and supporters the new programs were and are only the harbingers of greater things to come, down payments on a fair and just and therefore Great Society.

Opponents watched those trends with apprehension as part of an age-old struggle between the citizen and his government. They viewed the line between public and private spending as the dividing line between the areas of coercion and freedom and tried, without much success, to keep the decision makers from expanding the former at the expense of the latter.

There is no necessary difference in the nature or objective of public and private activities. Both may be operating a similar program as, for example, medical or old age insurance. The distinction is that in the private sphere the individual makes the decision for himself while in the public sphere the decision is made *for* him by governmental power, and he must comply. Gerhard Colm expressed it clearly: "The public realm is distinguished by the fact that it rests on authority, and if necessary, even on compulsion, while private relations rest on contract."[1]

William Henry Chamberlain once stated the issue well: "The level of government spending is perhaps the most clear-cut battlefield between American conservatives and liberals." Mr. Chamberlain then recounted a statement by Senator Robert Taft in the 1952 election campaign: "General Eisenhower emphatically agrees with me in the proposal to reduce drastically over-all expenses. Our goal is about $70 billion in fiscal '54 and $60 billion in fiscal '55."[2] As it turned out, administrative budget expenditures hit a low of $64.6 billion in FY 1955—with *all* of a $10 billion reduction since FY 1953 taken in national defense; they then resumed their inexorable steep climb to new heights.

To be sure, the dividing line between public and private activities and expenditures is not always clear-cut. Irving Kristol offered a useful definition:

> The terms "public sector" and "private sector," as commonly used, are summary answers to the question: Who spends the nation's money? Not: For what purpose? Not: With what consequences? Merely: Who?— government or private association and individuals?[3]

Concepts and practices differ on what should or should not be included in public, that is, governmental, expenditures. But by and large, all of the leading statistical data on governmental outlays—whether by the Bureau of the Census, or according to national income accounts, or from the federal unified budget, or even the now abandoned consolidated cash budget—are valid and helpful means of identifying magnitude and trends in public spending. The most widely used measure of the magnitude of governmental action is the percentage which governmental spending is of a national economic total—Gross National Product, net national product, national income, or personal income (Table 14). All of these, if employed consistently, are useful.

Some regard that percentage as an inverse measure of the extent of freedom that exists in a country. It expresses the share of an individual's income that is directly or indirectly taken and controlled by government so that he can control only the remainder. That is probably an oversimplification. Sidney Hook has pointed out that restrictions on economic freedom are not always followed by restraints on political freedom such as freedom of speech or the press.[4] He cited Great Britain, Sweden and Holland as examples of countries which levy heavy taxes, spend large amounts for social purposes but have maintained a good degree of political freedom. However, if citizens are deprived of the control of a substantial and growing share of their earnings, they are restricted in the exercise of personal freedom—in the making and carrying out of important decisions about their life and life-style. Such vital decisions as housing (where? how?), schooling for one's children (private or public?), how to secure one's retirement income, recreation, on starting and succeeding in one's own business, etc. are to a large part controlled by a) the amount of taxes taken from earnings, b) free or subsidized public services which make the right to exercise a choice often hypothetical. Moreover, a population which over the course of years has come to accept government protection against the economic risks of life, which has not made its own decisions and submitted to having its life regulated and ruled, may gradually change in its concepts of liberty, become unaccustomed to exercising responsibility for itself and prefer the comfort of easily available public services over the option preserving its right to choose among alternatives.

The percentage which taxes or public expenditures are of income may be a crude measure, but it is at this time still the best way to quantify the division of power between the citizen and his government, at least on a historical basis. Its use for comparisons among countries may be subject to question. In many less developed and poorer countries such as India, government extracts a smaller share of the GNP than it does in industrial nations, yet it controls economic and other activities more tightly by regulation.

Bigger government, expressed in terms of employee numbers or dollars spent or as a percentage of the GNP, is not in itself the ultimate goal of many or most of those who argue and work for it. Nor are bigger domestic public programs. Nor is the size of government and its programs the true and final reason for the opposition of those who fight them.

Michael Harrington, a liberal opinion leader, made it clear that he demanded a larger role for the public sector not for its own sake but as a means to an end. He believes that only government can raise the resources and enforce the correct priorities to wipe out slums, find jobs for the underemployed, provide efficient mass transportation, and reconstruct large cities as livable communities.[5]

Proponents do not really aim at big government as such, nor do opponents fight it. They aim at the *results* of big government, at what greatly enlarged public domestic programs will produce:

1. *a redistribution of income* from those who have more to those who have less in order to reduce or eliminate economic differences and

to approach, if not necessarily attain, an egalitarian status among all Americans and among all mankind. This is to be accomplished by a progressive tax structure and by expenditures that allocate benefits and services inverse to incomes.

2. *a shift of power* in decision making from the individual to organized society, that is, government, and from smaller units of government to larger ones, thence to the central government, and eventually to an international body encompassing all countries.

In other words, big government is largely a means to the ends of money and power, to a more equal distribution of the former, to a concentration of the latter. Resistance to big government basically attempts to retain claim to what one earns and possesses and to personal freedom.

A Built-in Growth Trend?

There is something in the American tradition that views big government with suspicion. The Jeffersonian saying that "the government that governs the least governs the best" may be obsolete but has left some indelible marks. To a Gallup poll in August 1968 asking "which of the following do you think will be the biggest threat to the country in the future—big business, big labor or big government?", 54 percent of those voicing an opinion answered by pointing at government, 31 percent at labor and 14 percent at business. The sentiment among all major groups, both political parties, and independents was clearly on the side that big government was the chief threat; there were two exceptions: blacks and persons with an annual family income under $3,000.[6] In other words, except for those two widely overlapping groups, which are the intended main beneficiaries of public social programs, most Americans fear big government, they do not favor it.

A 1978 survey by the National Opinion Research Center, which asked whether respondents had a great deal of confidence in various types of institutions, showed none as high as 50 percent. Banks and major companies rated 33% and 23% respectively, the executive branch of government and the Congress at 13% each, organized labor at 12%.[7]

Gunnar Myrdal observed that "it is fairly generally recognized by those who have studied the problem that there is a serious and irrational bias against public investment and consumption in America."[8] Yet he predicted that:

At the same time there is bound to be a bigger government in the sense that the government will have to take increased responsibility for organizing public consumption in the fields of education and health. It will have to redistribute incomes on a large scale by its taxation, social security schemes and agricultural policies. It will have to invest much more in slum clearance and low-rent housing and, indeed, in the complete renewal of the cities and their transport systems, as well as more generally in resource development. It will generally have to increase its responsibilities for a larger part of consumption and investment and, consequently, for employment and production.[9]

That Americans generally dislike big government is most clearly apparent from the fact that many presidents promised to reduce federal expenditures and tried to point with pride at isolated actual or claimed temporary successes, even though spending soared during their administrations.

It is now seldom remembered that Franklin D. Roosevelt campaigned in 1932 by denouncing President Hoover for his "reckless and extravagant" deficit spending and socialistic schemes and for pouring out relief. Roosevelt asserted that federal expenditures could be cut 20 percent.[10] As it turned out, federal expenditures more than doubled between 1932 and 1940.

One of President Eisenhower's main themes before and after assuming office was frugality in government. He promised in his budget message in January 1954: "We will reduce the share of the national income which is spent by the Government."[11]

He kept that promise. Federal expenditures, as a percentage of national income, dropped from 25.2% in 1953 to 22.4% in 1960, his last year in office (see Table 24). That reduction of 2.8 percentage points consisted of a 5.2 percent point *decline* in national defense and a 2.5 percent point *increase* in domestic expenditures (domestic expenditures doubled while national income rose only 36 percent). In this case, as so often, a rise in social expenditures was offset by a reduction in defense.

A first indication of the price to be paid was not long in coming. The Russians beat us in space by sending up Sputnik in 1957. That was not because our schools did not get enough money—as some were quick to claim—they were and still are far outspending Russian schools. America was then still technologically superior and could have been first in space IF the government had allocated sufficient money to it. But funds for space research and technology did not reach $100 million a year until 1959 and hit the first billion in 1962. "Scientific Investigation in Space" first appeared in the budget in 1959, two years after Sputnik, with $25 million.

American response to Sputnik was to pour additional billions into the schools, through the misnamed *National Defense Education Act of 1958*, which Lyndon Johnson's political skill maneuvered through Congress, in the nick of time before adjournment. It was the first step in a policy which eventually led to federal control of educational institutions and, ironically, to the most dismal deterioration and degeneration of quality in education in the succeeding two decades. Senator Daniel Patrick Moynihan correctly referred to the congressional response to Sputnik as "bailing out an administration that found itself in embarrassing political circumstances" (in a speech to the Yale alumni in Fall 1980). To Lyndon Johnson it was a first installment on what later became his Great Society.

Representative Adam Clayton Powell, a liberal leader and sponsor of much progressive legislation as chairman of the House Education and Labor Committee, commented in 1957 on President Eisenhower's policies: "Mr. Eisenhower's middle of the road today is left of Mr. Roosevelt's left of 25 years ago."[12] Now, nearly another quarter century later, "Mr. Eisenhower's middle of the road" appears way out on the right, considering subsequent developments.

John F. Kennedy, as a young congressman from Massachusetts wrote in 1950:

> Every time that we try to lift a problem from our own shoulders, and shift that problem to the hands of the government, to the same extent we are sacrificing the liberties of our people.[13]

After he had been in the White House for over two years, President Kennedy boasted at a news conference on April 24, 1963, that "in nearly every case, the percentage of expenditures and employment have gone down" and that "federal expenditures in relation to the population, nondefense expenditures, are declining."[14] Budget Director Kermit Gordon remarked simultaneously that federal civilian expenditures had increased proportionately *less* than the GNP. After correcting for the omission of $28 billion in expenditures excluded from the administrative budget, the record shows that federal nondefense spending, on a per capita basis, increased faster than the GNP, not more slowly. But what is important here is that the president and his budget director found it advisable to claim that they had been successful in cutting federal expenditures. This suggests that they believed the general public to be in favor of such policy which, by all appearances, probably was a correct assessment.

President Johnson pursued the same line. In a speech on November 19, 1964, he said: "I believe that, barring massive changes in defense spending, your federal government does not have to grow in size relative to the size of the economy. . . . Federal spending in 1965 will be the lowest in fourteen years in terms of our Gross National Product. Non-defense spending will be lower than it was thirty years ago in terms of our Gross National Product."[15] In his budget message in January 1965 President Johnson said that "We have good reason to expect that government expenditures in the years ahead will grow more slowly than the gross national product, so that the ratio of federal spending to our total output will continue to decline." The fact is, however, that during the eight years of the Kennedy-Johnson administrations, between 1960 and 1968, federal domestic spending increased 134 percent, the GNP only 72 percent (defense outlays meanwhile went up 76 percent) (see Table 24).

Both before and while holding office, one of President Nixon's favorite themes was economy in government spending. Listening to the large number of those who criticized his policies as miserly, starving vital public services, and reversing the trend toward social progress, one would think that President Nixon succeeded in drastically cutting federal non-defense spending. He did recommend in his budgets—as other presidents had—smaller amounts for some programs than their protagonists had demanded; he impounded, or at least tried to impound, some appropriated funds and vetoed a few appropriations. But he also proposed extremely expensive programs, some of which were not adopted by the Congress.

The record of actual spending trends for domestic functions by presidential terms shows a rather surprising picture. The table on p. 368 compares federal domestic outlays in the last year of each presidential term, converted to *constant* (1967) dollars, with the corresponding figure four years earlier, and reports the percentage increase.

Judging by the general image of recent presidents we might expect expansion during Mr. Eisenhower's regime to have been slow, under the Kennedy-Johnson administrations rapid, under Messrs. Nixon and Ford slow again and under Mr. Carter moderate. After all, Democrats are widely held to favor government growth more than Republicans do. But the record of actual spending, in the tables below, certainly does not bear this out.

The first table on p. 368 is based on data from the Bureau of Economic Analysis, Department of Commerce, which are available for years 1952 through 1978—but not yet for 1979 and 1980. Figures from the U.S. Budget are available for 1979 and 1980 but not, on a *unified budget* basis, farther back than 1958. The second table uses U.S. Budget figures for the last year of each presidential term from 1960 through 1980.

The two tables differ somewhat, because they are based on two sources which use different definitions. But they show roughly comparable trends: high rates of increase from term to term regardless of the incumbent president, a sharply reduced rate during the 1976-80 period.

Several possible explanations suggest themselves. One may be that

GROWTH OF FEDERAL OUTLAYS FOR DOMESTIC FUNCTIONS
DURING PRESIDENTIAL TERMS, 1952–78

Last Year of Term	President	Expenditures for Domestic Functions		Percent Increase in *constant* dollars
		Current $	1967$	
		millions		
1952	Truman	$ 12,658	$ 15,922	—
1956	Eisenhower I	18,669	22,935	44%
1960	Eisenhower II	32,508	36,649	60
1964	Kennedy	46,240	49,774	36
1968	Johnson	75,065	72,039	45
1972	Nixon	133,283	106,371	48
1976	Nixon-Ford	236,429	138,668	30
(1978)	(Carter)	(286,926)	(146,840)	(6)

SOURCE: For expenditure data, Table 24. The 1976–78 trend suggests a 12% growth rate on a 4–year basis.

GROWTH OF FEDERAL NONDEFENSE EXPENDITURES DURING PRESIDENTIAL TERMS
1960 TO 1980

Last Year of Term	President	Expenditures for Nondefense Purposes		Percent Increase in *constant* dollars
		current $	1980$	
		billions		
1960	Eisenhower	$ 47.1	$131.6	—
1964	Kennedy	67.1	178.9	36.0%
1968	Johnson	100.1	237.9	33.0
1972	Nixon	155.5	307.4	29.0
1976	Nixon-Ford	277.0	402.5	30.9
1980	Carter	443.4	443.5	10.2

SOURCE: *The Budget of the United States Government, Fiscal Year 1981* and subsequent release on FY 1980 results.

Congress sets the pace, regardless of the temporary occupant of the Oval Office. Imposing as the institutional presidency looks, and as axe-swinging as the media depict its budgetary arm, the office of Management and Budget, they may in the end not wield as much power over expenditure policies as appears from the outside. Both Houses of Congress had Democratic majorities throughout the period. Another possible explanation relates to the time lapse between a presidential recommendation and the point at which a new program reaches maturity. For example: Mr. Kennedy's domestic proposals were not enacted until after he was succeeded by Mr. Johnson; Mr. Johnson's vast programs attained their full potential not until the 1970s.

What explains the sharp drop-off in Mr. Carter's term? Again, there are several possibilities. Few expansionary initiatives were taken between 1970 and 1976 and presidential influence then was clearly aimed at restraining Congress and minimizing spending growth. Also, Mr. Carter ran for and won office on the basis of his expressed opposition to big government. By the mid-1970s the negative results of the 1960s social program expansion were known to Congress and the public, which may have exerted a dampening influence. Or, possibly, the trend toward an ever-expanding government had simply run its course.

Many would trace the growth trend in domestic spending to the New Deal of the 1930s but Solomon Fabricant has shown that it dates back at least to the beginning of the century and M. Slade Kendrick ran it back to the early days of the republic.[16]

The German socialist economist Adolf Wagner nearly a century ago first pronounced the "law of the increase of state activities," which has since been known as "Wagner's law":

> Comprehensive comparisons of different countries and different times show that, among progressive peoples, with which alone we are concerned, an increase regularly takes place in the activity of both the central and the local governments. This increase is both extensive and intensive: the central and local governments constantly undertake new functions, while they perform both old and new functions more efficiently and completely. In this way the economic needs of the people to an increasing extent and in a more satisfactory fashion, are satisfied by the central and local governments. The clear proof of this is found in the statistics which show the increased needs of central governments and local political units.[17]

Wagner's law did not attract much attention at the time—and even less support. But the record of recent decades certainly proved him to be correct. The trend goes back much farther in history and we find criticism of growing fiscal spending in ancient Egypt, Rome, and in Greek city-states. *Panem et circenses*, the pyramids and the Acropolis may have been WPA or Great Society projects of their day. Aristotle warned:

Where there are revenues the demagogues should not be allowed after
their manner to distribute the surplus: the poor are always receiving and
always wanting more and more, for such help is like water poured into a
leaky cask.[18]

Few politicians would nowadays dare write so bluntly.

We might assume that with incomes rising and the extent of poverty
shrinking, the need for government intervention on behalf of the poor or
low- to middle-income population might gradually decline. It would seem
that in countries in which most people are comparatively well off—as they
are in the United States—and few truly poor, individuals and families could
take care of their own requirements more adequately and would have to
depend less on support by the government. But it has not worked that way.
As prosperity grew so did the demands on government and the action of
politicians to meet them, with leaps forward during periods of actual or
claimed economic stagnation or decline. There is always a recession for
those who produce little or nothing. Also, government support programs
never satisfy an appetite. They only whet it for more.

The foundation for the spectacular expansion in expenditures for social
purposes in the United States was laid in the days of the Great Depression
and the New Deal. Yet federal spending for domestic purposes never ran
above $7 billion a year during the 1930s and barely exceeded $12 billion
in 1952.

Public spending was small during the 1930s when considered in terms
of today's magnitudes. New Deal policies aimed more at restoring prede-
pression prosperity than at remaking society, at least according to their
authors' pronouncements. Thus we might have expected the force of the
drive to diminish when economic conditions improved. But it was between
1952 and 1978 when GNP in *constant* dollars expanded 134%, when
disposable per capita income in *constant* dollars increased 85% (from $3612
to $6672 in *1978* dollars), and when the percentage of families with a cash
income under $3000 (in 1978 dollars) fell from 11.2% to 3.3%, and of those
with an income from $3000 to $4999 from 8.7% to 4.9% of the U.S.
population, that the big jump occurred in federal spending for domestic
purposes—from $12.7 billion in 1952 to $287 billion in 1978, an 822%
increase in *constant* dollars. That suggests that it was not greater need that
caused the spectacular expansion in social programs.

To a considerable extent it was of course some of the expanded welfare
programs that helped raise the income of persons at the low end of the
income scale and to shrink the number of those below the poverty threshold. But the amounts are far in excess of what would have been required
to lift only the poorest of the poor to more acceptable levels. In other words,

attempts to relieve the most disadvantaged do not account for the magnitude of social spending increases. To make transfer programs—that is, government income support and subsidy schemes—politically more acceptable and popular, the upper income limits of eligibility were raised and benefits made more attractive. Upward extension, to include the lower—and not-so-low—middle class multiplied the number of eligible persons and political supporters and skyrocketed costs. We don't have so many poor people but we do have a big middle class. It was an essential feature of such plans to make benefits highly visible and alluring while disguising or hiding a major part of the costs through indirect taxes, deficits, deferrals and various intricate financial and accounting tricks which diminished the cost to the current budget or turned it into an off-budget item.

Exorbitant income tax rates to which the public had become accustomed during World War II were subsequently only slightly reduced (instead of being cut sharply). Lower tax rates gave the public the impression that the new or expanded benefits and programs came cheap or for free. Intergovernmental arrangements effectively screened true costs from the taxpayers.

In a sophisticated analysis of postwar governmental growth David Cameron of Yale University offered several explanations which relate to pressures generated within a modern democracy by social and economic forces.[19] Allan H. Meltzer of the Carnegie-Mellon University explained the trend toward bigger government as an inherent and built-in characteristic of representative government, because the costs of government are diffused and the benefits concentrated.[20] Opposition to big government is widespread but insistent demand for specific programs concentrated and effectively organized. When threatened by an austerity plan, a tax- and budget-cutting drive, associations representing a whole range of social activities, and normally competing with each other for a bigger slice, combine to defeat the "common enemy." James Q. Wilson of Harvard expressed a similar thought in saying that "the risk of democracy is that elected officials will try to buy votes" by offering expanded benefits to various claimant groups.[21]

As mentioned earlier, the foundation for the big government trend was laid in the 1930s. It was the minds of the young intellectuals whose ideologies were formed during the depression days, who later became the shapers of public opinion, the makers of public policy decisions, the educators of the next generation. The seeds of the 1930s bore a rich harvest in the 1950s, 1960s, and 1970s for some—at a heavy cost to others.

This policy shift to the left does not seem to have been paralleled by the great mass of the American people, a majority of whom have expressed a conservative preference in repeated polls from the 1930s to the 1970s. In a

1980 Harris poll twice as many respondents labeled themselves conservative as liberal.

Successful politicians are usually cognizant of the ideological leanings of the majority of the voters and it is probably because they intuitively knew of the conservative persuasion of their constituents that the presidents whom I quoted earlier (as well as other officeholders) promised to economize in their expenditures policies or prided themselves on having held down spending. The decisive issue that divides liberals and conservatives is the magnitude of governmental activity in the domestic field.

In 1972 Charles Kadushin of Teachers' College, Columbia University, conducted an opinion poll among what he called the country's intellectual elite, the eight thousand or so persons who had contributed to the top twenty-two intellectual journals during the five-year period 1964–1968.[22] Here are his findings:

> Given their background and position where do elite intellectuals stand politically in comparison to everyone else? To the left. The American intellectual elite is more liberal on any issue of public policy than the American public at large, more liberal than any other segment of the American elite, and generally more liberal than the elite university professors surveyed in the Carnegie study.[23]

Most of those listed among the top group as the most prestigious intellectuals are known to be strongly on the left, though usually not members of the radical ("new") left.

Intellectuals may be small in numbers but their influence on public policy is enormous and sometimes decisive. The students and instructors of the 1930s became the professors, heads of departments, and textbook writers of the 1950s and 1960s, the editors, authors, reporters, commentators, the members and staffs of legislative bodies, the technical and policy officials in executive departments, the leaders of professional associations, presidents, board members and staffs of grant-giving foundations, top attorneys in public affairs cases, protagonists and organizers of civic causes and, last but not least, the law clerks and judges of our courts. Many of them worked with a dedication rarely equaled elsewhere and their efforts produced tangible results in due time.

What became of the intellectually gifted with conservative leanings, those who did not absorb and assimilate the anticapitalist, egalitarian spirit of the 1930s? Most entered business careers and independent professions to become financially more successful but politically less interested or effective. Many of the rest who chose academe soon learned on which side the bread was buttered.

The majority of intellectuals were attracted to ever-growing government because it affords an opportunity to exercise power over the affairs of state in planning, influencing, and directing the fate of people, the action and fortunes of the nation. To wield such power is a most basic instinct and desire of ambitious individuals. The average academician as one of hundreds or thousands on a campus is but a tiny wheel with little direct authority, often frustrated beyond endurance in his ideas and aims. He can become the governing force of immense power while working in or advising government—if he develops or promotes plans to expand and exercise that power and participates in it. And the greater the authority concentrated in government, whether expressed in percentage of the GNP channeled through it or in regulation or other legal power, the greater the academician's satisfaction in money and stature.

Moreover, while men in leading industrial, commercial, and financial positions possess greater economic power than the academician, the latter finds that his best chance to overrule them, to reduce their strength and add to his own, is to increase the size and force of government. He can thus prove that the pen is mightier than the dollar. Joseph Schumpeter long ago, in his *Capitalism, Socialism and Democracy*, attributed the intellectuals' alienation to the success of capitalism.

It is the intellectuals whose ideas germinated in the spiritual climate of the 1930s, who became the pacesetters and formed the "establishment" of the 1950s and 1960s. The small group of intellectuals in academe who differed, who warned of the dangers of big government and opposed it— such men as Friedrich A. Hayek, Wilhelm Roepke, Ludwig von Mises— were ignored, ridiculed, or viewed and treated as hopelessly antiquated or outsiders who could not grasp the spirit of the times.

It was only when some of the gargantuan programs failed to produce the hoped-for and promised socially wholesome results that keener observers among the liberal intellectuals began to have second thoughts and to voice doubts about the effectiveness of the tools chosen or even about the attainability though not necessarily the desirability of the announced goals. Some began to ask government: are you helping to solve the problem or are you part of the problem? Opponents to the new social programs, formerly but voices crying in the wilderness, grew in number and their publications now match, or possibly exceed, those of the enthusiasts of governmental growth who had dominated the scene for so long.

The Protagonists of Governmental Expansion

The drive for the expansion of domestic public activities was largely suspended during World War II and resumed soon afterwards in President Truman's Fair Deal, in the form of campaigns for specific social programs such as national health insurance, public housing and urban renewal, fed-

eral aid to education, etc. The issue of big government as such came to the
forefront with the publication in 1958 of John Kenneth Galbraith's *The
Affluent Society*.

In his brilliant writing style, Galbraith advanced the thesis that government is too small and private consumption too big, that public services
are being starved while the consumer luxuriates.

> The community is affluent in privately produced goods. It is poor in
> public services. The obvious solution is to tax the former to provide the
> latter. . . . By making private goods more expensive, public goods are
> made more abundant. . . .
>
> The line which divides our area of wealth from our area of poverty is
> roughly that which divides privately produced and marketed goods from
> publicly rendered services.[24]

That *The Affluent Society* was able to gain such wide popularity is truly
amazing. Its proposition that taxes are too low and that the average man has
too much money left to spend according to his own whims is out of step
with generally held beliefs and is, if understood, not likely to attract much
following among the American people. Which politician would want to
run on a platform that proposes a boost in taxes because consumers have
more money than they know what to do with and that "excess" money
should therefore be taken from them?

But Galbraith's thesis that public goods are scarce while private goods
are abundant, has a ring of truth to it and merits further study. Why
is it that public facilities and services always appear to be inadequate or
scarce—space for driving and parking, hospitals and medical care, schools
and teachers, public parks and sanitation, police, and dozens of others,
while there is no shortage of automobiles, television sets, houses, clothing,
power boats, cosmetics, or camping equipment?

The answer is simple: because there is no limit to human wants or
desires for things that are free. Our appetite for private goods is disciplined
by the necessity of paying for them. There can be no shortage of goods in a
free market for people willing to pay a fair price except under war or
emergency conditions or when the government interferes with the market
by price control or other regulations. When an effective demand rises in a
free market, supply will soon catch up with it, with price acting as a
balancer.

But most public services are not paid for by the user directly. They
seem to come "for free," with the cost borne by someone else or by that
distant abstraction, "the government." If the cost of public services is

defrayed from business taxes that are supposedly borne by the corporation and its stockholders (though they are actually included in the price to consumers), or paid from state or federal "grants-in-aid," users are given the illusion that the services cost nothing. So, they like them and want more. As long as goods and services can be had gratis or at a fraction of their cost, demand will exceed supply. That is why public goods will always be scarce.

Balance between demand and supply will be achieved only if the would-be purchaser foots the bill. In public services this is possible only in direct-charge services, for earmarked revenues such as those in programs for old age, medical care or disability, in road construction financed from highway-user charges, or in various local programs financed by a tax levy for a specific and identified purpose. The balance between supply and demand is disturbed when large sections of the population are freed from tax liability—as has been the case increasingly in the federal income tax—though they can enjoy public benefits at someone else's expense and retain the right to vote for candidates who promise to support greater benefits for them. Unless those who make the decision must weigh the pleasure of getting the service against the pain of having to pay the cost, decisions will be unbalanced with a perpetual bias to increase public spending. It was H. L. Mencken who once called an election an advance auction of stolen goods.

When Galbraith talked about the consumer luxuriating while government is being starved and about the imbalance between public and private spending, he conveniently ignored the fact that government spending for nondefense purposes had been rising twice as fast as personal consumption spending.

The table on p. 376 shows that government consumption rose substantially faster than private both before and after the compilation of *The Affluent Society*. In the 1929–52 period, whose statistics were available when Galbraith wrote his book (but was careful not to mention them) personal consumption multiplied 1.8-fold (in *constant* dollars), government nondefense spending 3.7-fold. Those trends continued through the 1950s, 1960s, and 1970s. Over the past half century—1929 to 1978—personal consumption expenditures in *constant* dollars multiplied 4.6-fold, government nondefense expenditures 16.8-fold.

Consumers spent 8.6 times as much as government (nondefense) in 1929, 4.2 times as much in 1952, 2.3 times as much in 1978. It is hard to see how anyone can claim that government services are being "scandalously starved" while the consumer luxuriates when public consumption multiplied nearly four times faster than private over the past half century.

GOVERNMENTAL NONDEFENSE EXPENDITURES
AND PERSONAL CONSUMPTION EXPENDITURES
1929, 1952 AND 1978

	Governmental Nondefense Expenditures	Personal Consumption Expenditures	Ratio between Public and Private Consumption
		billions	
1929	$ 9.0	$ 77.2	1:8.6
1952	51.8	217.1	1:4.2
1978	576.7	1350.8	1:2.3

Multiplier of expenditures in *constant* dollars

1929 to 1952	3.7	1.8	
1952 to 1978	4.5	2.5	
1929 to 1978	16.8	4.6	

SOURCES: *Survey of Current Business*, July 1979; and 1967 Supplement to *Economic Indicators*. P.S. 1929 is the earliest year for which these data are available, 1978 the latest year for which they are available at this writing.

But some still do. Robert Lekachman wrote in 1979: "Galbraith's 1968 contrast between private affluence and public squalor—in *The Affluent Society*—is not less relevant now than it was in the Eisenhower era."[25]

Consumer spending for food, clothing, housing and household operations increased 115% between 1952 and 1978, for transportation and recreation 208%; simultaneously government spending for education went up 487%, for income support 919%, for medical care 838% (all in *constant* dollars) (see Table 26).

This record does suggest a spending bias or imbalance. But it certainly is not in the direction of private consumption, as Galbraith asserted, while he scorned the vulgar manner in which the consumer spends his earnings on trivia. Some of Galbraith's disciples and followers such as Seymour Melman, Kenneth Boulding, Robert Heilbronner and others aimed their criticism more at the imbalance between spending for defense and for nondefense purposes. They seem to have had a decisive impact on public policy: national defense dropped from 49% of all government expenditures in 1952 to 16% in 1978 (see Table 23). The consequences of our unilateral disarmament are now becoming more evident with every passing year.

The publication of *The Affluent Society* in the late 1950s made a deep impact in intellectual and political circles and spawned many other books and articles advocating a similar approach and voicing hope that those ideas would be put into practice. As Henry Steele Commager predicted in 1959:

> It is inevitable that there will be an immense growth of the welfare state. Government, and particularly the national government, will necessarily take on ever larger responsibilities in the realm of conservation, education, science, public health, urban rehabilitation, hydroelectric power, communication and so forth. The dividing line between "private" and "public" and between "local" and "general," already blurred, will become all but meaningless.
>
> Finally, an affluent society, universal education, the welfare state, and a growing awareness of and respect for world opinion should go far to bring about a truly classless society in the United States. That has always been an American ideal, and in the nineteenth century the Western world looked to the United States as exemplar and model of equalitarianism.
>
> But our progress toward true equality has been slower than anticipated, and today some Old World societies are more truly equalitarian than is the American.[26]

Michael Harrington's *The Other America: Poverty in the United States* in 1962 which was followed by several dozens of similar books, not to mention streams of articles in magazines and newspapers and television programs, strongly influenced President Kennedy and his successor, and can claim part of the credit for the New Frontier and Great Society programs. When multibillion dollar spending did not bring the promised results, Harrington blamed failure on niggardly and restricted benefits and budgetary austerity.

In *Decade of Decision: The Crisis of the American System*, eighteen years after *The Other America*, Mr. Harrington, repeated his demands for more generous and more easily available welfare benefits. "Moreover, for these women, heads of large families who are able to work, the pay which they can obtain is, in some cases, less than the payments they receive from Aid to Families of Dependent Children. If they act according to the approved profit calculus of the society, these women will not work. And a good number do not for precisely that reason."[27]

Harrington is correct. Many welfare recipients refuse "menial jobs" and the only type of work their aptitude and attitude qualify them for, precisely because the value of their services and, therefore, their potential wages are lower than the workless pay the government offers them. Whether that justifies even more generous benefits, at the expense of millions of working people is, to say the least, highly questionable.

Efforts toward more restrictive fiscal policies are widely met with an outcry that cuts would be taken out of the hides of the poor and the minorities, that they would primarily hurt the disadvantaged, unfortunate, oppressed, most vulnerable.[28] This emphasizes the fact that more than half of total federal spending now consists of income support payments which have been the fastest growing item in the federal budget. Social security accounts for a sizable share of transfer payments and is in a different category from public assistance and other forms of public welfare. Recipients of social security or their deceased spouses or parents made contributions toward the annuities during their working life. But most social security beneficiaries so far have been getting far more than they paid in, especially those in the lower earnings brackets. Congress almost always raised benefits more than taxes which accounts for the periodic financial squeeze on the social security trust funds. The majority of federal outlays now redistribute earnings from the productive to the nonproductive part of the population—with a predictable detrimental impact on the productivity of the American economy.

Some of the protagonists of big government, undeterred by failures, continue to defend their "belief that the 1960s programs and policies and their continuation had a massive, overwhelmingly beneficial, impact and that the weight of evidence convincingly supports this view" as Sar Levitan and Robert Taggart wrote in the *Promise of Greatness.*[29]

Arthur Schlesinger, Jr., criticized President Carter for saying in his 1978 State of the Union Message:

> Government cannot solve our problems. It can't set our goals. It cannot define our vision, Government cannot eliminate poverty or provide a bountiful economy, or reduce inflation, or save our cities, or cure illiteracy, or provide energy.

Schlesinger expressed his feelings that the "conservative panic about 'Big Government' seems exaggerated" and his confidence is unshaken that the republic will "gird itself up once again to confront the urgent problems of the domestic community. For that time is bound to come and soon. Sometime in the 1980s the dam will break, as it broke at the turn of the century, in the 1930s and in the 1960s."[30]

Henry Fairlie wrote "In Defense of Big Government"[31] "that the question is not whether there should be a strong central government, but whose interests that government should serve."

Some of the front-ranking liberal social scientists, however, were haunted by doubts if not about their goals then about their methods. They seemed sadder, if not necessarily wiser, and voiced a disillusionment with the ideas they had so forcefully, convincingly and effectively broadcast to the American public and its policymakers in the 1960s. Henry J. Aaron of the Brookings Institution who served as assistant secretary for planning and evaluation of the Department of HEW under the Carter administration did so in a thoughtful volume *Politics & the Professors: The Great Society in Perspective.*[32] Aaron contrasted "a country that in 1965 had seemed confident of its military strength and purposeful in its missions abroad, that was embarked on a series of efforts to solve problems that had long troubled a newly ascendant majority of the American people" with the situation in 1976: "Americans, divided and uncertain about what to do abroad and fearful of military inferiority [who] had become equally despairing of their capacity to deal affirmatively with domestic problems." A Rip van Winkle, asleep from 1965 to 1976, "would encounter lamentations about the failure of all national efforts to reduce inequality and eliminate poverty, to improve schools, to reduce unemployment and its hardships; he would also find a sense that not only had past efforts failed, but future ones were also doomed by the incapacity of the government to act effectively."

Aaron appeared far less certain of the wholesome impact on society of the new programs than he had seemed years earlier. Still he was not ready to switch sides. But many other liberal scholars were.

The Failure of the Great Society and the Rise of the Neoconservatives

The ineffectiveness of some of the programs initiated or enlarged over the past quarter century became increasingly apparent toward the end of the 1960s and made an impact on scholars in the social sciences, many of whom had been in the forefront of reform movements not so many years earlier. Columbia University sociologist Amitai Etzioni offered an agonizing reappraisal:

> We have come of late to the realization that the pace of achievement in domestic programs ranges chiefly from the slow to the crablike—two steps backward for every one forward—and the suspicion is growing that there is something basically wrong with most of these programs. A nagging feeling persists that maybe something even more basic than the lack of funds or will is at stake. Consequently, social scientists like myself have begun to reexamine our core assumption that man can be taught almost anything and quite readily. We are now confronting the uncomfortable possibility that human beings are not very easily changed after all.[33]

In a *Fortune* article entitled "The Social Engineers Retreat Under Fire," Tom Alexander concluded that "the disappointing results of government ventures into social reform have cast doubt on some widely held theories and thrown the social sciences into an uproar."[34] He summarized:

> Like good empiricists faced with unexpected results many (sociologists, psychologists and anthropologists whose theories provided designs for so many ill-fated attempts at "social engineering") have come to question their previous assumptions. The orthodox view of environment as the all-important influence on people's behavior is yielding to a new awareness of the role of hereditary factors; enthusiasm for schemes to reform society by remolding men is giving way to a healthy appreciation of the basic intractability of human nature.

Even some of the architects and sponsors of the new programs in health, education and welfare have bared their self-doubt. Alice Rivlin, former assistant secretary for planning and evaluation in the Department of Health, Education and Welfare, and now director of the congressional budget staff, wrote:

> ... the liberals have lost their innocence. By the end of the 1960s it was evident that merely spending more federal money was not necessarily going to produce results. Money for education would not automatically teach children to read. . . . More money for health might only escalate the price of health care, or put more people in hospitals who need not be there. . . . More money for welfare would only perpetuate a badly constructed system. . . .[35]

A reading of the Brookings Institution's annual reviews of the U.S. Budget reveals a gradual shift from hope and enthusiasm about new or expanded social programs to comments that are more qualified, or reserved, then to ambivalence and later to careful skepticism. In their introduction to *Setting National Priorities: The Next Ten Years* (Brookings, 1976), Henry Owen and Charles L. Schultze wrote:

> There is also rising public skepticism about the federal government's ability to perform effectively. During most of the 1960s, the prevalent belief was that some kind of federal budgetary program could be designed to deal with almost any social problem—deteriorating central cities, juvenile delinquency, low reading scores of poorer children, rat infestation, or inefficient local police departments. Scores of programs were enacted, usually in the form of federal grants-in-aid to state and local governments,

to deal with those problems. This conventional wisdom of a few years ago seems now to have been replaced by its polar opposite: most federal programs do not work well and consist principally in "throwing money at problems."

That tone differs significantly from evaluation in similar Brookings reports about a decade earlier.

A growing number of eminent social scientists who had long been leaders of liberal thought began to take positions and use arguments which had previously been used by dyed-in-the-wool conservatives. Writings by such well-known scholars as Nathan Glazer, Sidney Hook, Daniel Patrick Moynihan, Daniel Bell, Irving Kristol, Seymour Martin Lipset, Edward C. Banfield, James Q. Wilson, Bayard Rustin and dozens of others in the decade of the 1970s give living proof that ideas which until the mid-1960s would have been ignored or ridiculed as reactionary and hopelessly out of date had acquired a new respectability. What is more, they exerted an increasing influence on public opinion, on the oratory of public officials and even, to a more limited extent, on public policy.

As Robert Cassidy wrote: "What is more striking, however, is that many so-called conservative arguments regarding social welfare programs are being taken seriously by the government and even by die-hard liberals."[36]

The campus revolt of the later 1960s and the *at oculos* demonstration of the utter disregard left-leaning leaders show for the rights of others when given a chance to suppress opponents, gave many lifelong liberals second thoughts about their political direction and associations. But the negative and often counterproductive results of welfare state programs were the major cause of the strong rightward shift among intellectuals, on and off campus.

Some of the more radical liberals persisted. Michael Harrington wrote in 1974 that "the failures of the welfare state in recent years are the results of its conservatism, not of its excessive liberalism, or more preposterously, of its radicalism."[37] He denied the egalitarian trends of the welfare state in the 1960s and, not surprisingly, blamed the ineffectiveness of most of its programs on "penny pinching." He recognized, however, that the "failures of the welfare state in the sixties have served as stimulus for, and rationale of, the rise of neoconservative thought in the seventies."[38]

Robert Lekachman wrote in 1979: "A lesson of the Great Society experience indeed seems to be that many of its failures, complete or partial, stemmed from too little rather than too much intervention into the operations of private and public markets."[39]

There is as yet little evidence that the social profitability of existing or

proposed programs, the tested and proven effectiveness—or lack thereof—
of small-scale experiments, and the relationship between the social cost of
resources and the social value of the product play a significant role in the
deliberations of Congress and in its decisions to authorize and fund domestic services. Several large evidently unproductive programs have been
repeatedly extended and their allocations multiplied. The overriding theme
in the congressional debates leading to adoption was: "How much federal
money can I get for my congressional district?"

The proponents of social spending schemes seem to say, as Ben Wattenberg and Richard Scammon expressed it: "the liberal battle-cry has
become, 'We have failed; let us continue!'"[40] This suggests that the underlying thought and overriding goal in much of the tax and spending
decisions is not so much social reform *per se* as redistribution of income,
from those who have more to those who have less. That meets a deep-
seated desire which is widespread, if not universal, and is at the core of
almost all conflict in this world: the yen or appetite of some people for what
other people possess. Historically much of the redistribution of property
between nations or within nations, has been accomplished by violence—
robbery, revolution, or war. Progressive taxation and social spending
through cash transfers and public programs appear now to have become a
more popular and more widely used method of accomplishing by the
legislative process what previously could be obtained only by individual
productive effort, stealth or dispossession by force.

Redistribution of income and property is increasingly viewed as the
prime purpose and task of government and this, more than anything else,
explains the spectacular growth in domestic public expenditures over the
past two decades. To redistribute through the political process the rewards
and punishments of the market has become the foremost goal of those who
do not believe that a man is entitled to the value of his product, who feel that
the allocation of natural talent—of intelligence, inventiveness, judgment,
drive, aspiration, persistence—is basically unfair to those less endowed and
must be overruled and revised in a more egalitarian direction. Since talent
as such cannot be redistributed among persons, at least the product of such
talent and effort should be. The record of the past few decades suggests that
those who so feel were having their way.

Redistributing Income

Keynesian theory which dominated economic policy for close to half a
century, holds that slow growth is the result of inadequate demand. It
concludes therefrom that economic activity can be stimulated and made to
expand by shifting income from upper to lower income classes. The latter

and particularly the poor are almost certain to spend promptly whatever they get while the former save and invest a goodly share of their income. Thus the solution to stagnant or slow economic growth is for the government, besides just printing more money, to tax high-income recipients heavily and spread the funds among low-bracket individuals. It also seems to be a politically profitable approach to advocate loading additional burdens on the rich and granting relief to persons at lower income levels: there are greater numbers—and potential *votes*—among the latter than the former.

This is why Keynesian and neo-Keynesian policies have been placing major emphasis on income redistribution through taxing and spending. In recent decades it became increasingly apparent that such policies, despite sophisticated "fine tuning," were not as effective as hoped in generating high and stable economic growth. But they proved eminently effective in the U.S. and in other nontotalitarian countries in creating and multiplying inflationary pressures which stubbornly resisted governmental attempts to control, arrest or reverse.

When inflation rates reached two-digit levels, the popularity of demand-side policies seemed to pale and supply-side economics attracted wider attention and more supporters. Discussion of remedies for unsatisfactory economic performance shifted from boosting consumer income and credit to stressing the need for greater capital formation and industrial investment.

Both before and after entering office, President Carter generally followed a standard populist line of recommending heavier burdens on the rich while freeing lower-income persons from tax liability altogether or, at least, reducing their load. The latest example was the $227 billion boost (over 10 years) in social security taxes, effective from 1979 on, almost all of which was placed on persons in high brackets and on business. A slight change in attitude seems to have taken place in 1980 when Mr. Carter recommended some easing of the business tax burden in order to revitalize the economy.

Greater redistribution is being advocated by those who, as Edgar K. Browning expressed it in a perspicacious article "How Much More Equality Can We Afford?" "believe the economy is going to continue churning out more and more goods and services, regardless of the incentives confronting the producers."[41] A tax system that increases its burden sharply the harder a person works, the more he produces, raises the penalty for effort to a point where the cost of working becomes too high for the most productive and the price of leisure negligible or negative. A welfare and tax system that does not keep a sizable distance between a person's earning potential and available workless benefits diminishes the attraction of working to zero. Redistribution of income by government, by reducing motivation for toil, exertion and risk-taking slows down economic growth to stagnation.

It is ironic that, in contrast to the United States and many other capitalist countries, the Soviet Union has long recognized the importance of material motivation for economic progress. Its constitution (Article 14) pronounces the "principle of socialism": "From each according to his abilities, to each according to his work" (not "to his need" as many people believe the Soviet principle to be). It adds: "The state, combining material and moral incentives, *and encouraging inventiveness and a creative attitude to work,* furthers the transformation of labor into the prime necessity of life of every Soviet man and woman." For about half a century now, the Soviet system has provided strong financial incentives for increased productivity, and reinforced them in 1963–64 by tying them to enterprise profits. It keeps income tax rates low and relies for government revenues mostly on what we would call consumption taxes.[42]

Some American economists discount the need for economic motivation. Unreconstructed neo-Keynesians still believe that income redistribution promotes economic growth. Lester C. Thurow of MIT wrote in *The Zero-Sum Society* (1980):

> Since government must alter the distribution of income if it is to solve our economic problems, we have to have a government that is capable of making equity decisions. Whose income ought to go up and whose income ought to go down? To do this, however, we need to know what is equitable. What is a fair or just distribution of income resources.

In 1972 Thurow told the Joint Economic Committee of Congress:

> One of the prime functions of government is continually to redistribute market incomes so that incomes are in accordance with our social or collective judgments as to what constitutes a just distribution of economic resources.[43]

This sounds as if all income belonged by right to the government which then, in its generosity and wisdom, decides how to distribute it among its citizens. The thought that the individual who *earns* an income thereby acquires a legitimate claim to it, does not seem to occur to our contemporary egalitarians. Their attempts to justify redistribution on economic grounds are largely rationalizations which need not be taken seriously. But their drive to redistribute income and wealth toward an egalitarian ideal is deadly serious, being powered by one of the strongest and most pervasive human emotions: *envy.*

Most advocates of greater redistribution base their case not on economic arguments but on what they call equity, which in their dictionary is synonymous with equality.

"Many people regard inequalities of income as a clear cas · of the tyranny of the strong and fortunate over the weak and poorly en owed," wrote University of Wisconsin economist Harold Groves a doze n years before the appearance of *The Affluent Society*.[44] Demands for e onomic equality, or at least a narrowing of differentials in income and wealth, are of course age-old and have been at the core of many political move nents—socialism, communism, populism. Progressive taxation and public expenditures to or for the benefit of low-income persons have been tl e main instruments of carrying out those aims, at least in countries that did not resort to outright expropriation.

University of Chicago economist Henry C. Simons wrote four decades ago: "The case for drastic progression in taxation must be rested on the case against inequality—on the ethical or aesthetic judgment that the prevailing distribution of wealth and income reveals a degree (and/or kind) of inequality which is distinctly evil or unlovely."[45] The case for reducing or eliminating income inequality rests in Simons' words on another ethical precept: "At any rate it may be best to start by denying any justification for prevailing inequality in terms of personal desert."[46]

A widely acclaimed work by Harvard social philosopher John Rawls, *A Theory of Justice*, presents other current trends in egalitarian thought. Rawls asserts that a social order is just and legitimate *only* to the degree that it is directed to the redress of inequality:

> There is no more reason to permit the distribution of income and wealth to be settled by the distribution of natural assets than by historical and social fortunes. . . . No one deserves his greater natural capacity, nor merits a more favorable starting place in society. . . . All social primary goods—liberty and opportunity, income and wealth and the basis of self-respect—are to be distributed equally unless an unequal distribution of any or all these goods is to the advantage of the least favored.[47]

Reviewing Rawls's theory, Daniel Bell called it "the most comprehensive effort in modern philosophy to justify a socialistic ethic" and added: "It is striking that Rawls, like Jencks, does not discuss either 'work' or 'effort'—as if those who had succeeded, in the University, or in business or government, had done so largely by contingent circumstances or fortune or social background."[48]

Rawls's central point is what he calls the "principle of redress": "Since the inequalities of birth and natural endowment are undeserved, these inequalities are to be somehow compensated for. . . ." In other words,

Rawls does not recognize the natural right of every person to his innate attributes, to his body, his mental capacity and other characteristics. A person is not entitled to his strength, health, intelligence, drive, beauty and other traits. Government obviously cannot take these qualities from him and bestow them on someone less endowed. But it can, does—and according to Rawls should—take from him the fruits of his talents and labor and give them to someone else, so as to more nearly equalize, if not the gifts of nature, then at least the product of those gifts.

Rawls admits that "none of these remarks is intended to deny that appeal to justice is often a mask for envy. What is said to be resentment may really be rancor."[49] His philosophy, in other words, could be called an attempt to provide a respectable and attractive shield and euphemism for the age-old human feelings of envy and jealousy, when one individual detects in another superior qualities he would like to possess and would, if he could, appropriate to himself.

Less successful persons have a psychological need to attribute the advance of others either to socially detrimental or undesirable activities (profiteering, ruthless scheming) or to sheer luck ("If you don't believe in luck—how do you explain the success of your enemies?"). To admit an element of genuine merit in the accomplishments of others would impose a heavy mental burden on a person, might force him to assume at least part of the blame for his failure. ("You can always get a lot of votes by telling people that their troubles are not their own fault.") The best way to rationalize personal limitations is to deny the owners of greater endowment a legitimate claim to them, and to act upon their illegitimacy by taking part of the products of those endowments and efforts.

If we carried Rawls's principles to their logical conclusion, we would wind up with a system that deliberately penalizes natural talent and success and thereby discourages industriousness and effort while rewarding low capacity and even sloth. Such a system of punishing merit would be suicidal and lead to the ruin of a society that adopted and practiced it.

Some regard redistribution of income from the top down as a clear case of the tyranny and exploitation of a productive but vote-weak minority by a greedy and vote-strong majority, and feel that rewards for effort are still necessary. University of Chicago law professors Walter J. Blum and Harry Kalven, Jr., have argued: "Whatever we may think in moments of tranquility, we do not live from day to day without the help of the assumption that those around us and we ourselves deserve in some way the praise and blame, the rewards and the punishments, we all dispense and receive."[50] Blum and Kalven referred to the ever-present danger that tax legislation may be turned into (or is) "class legislation in its most naked form."[51]

Income used to be distributed in the shape of a pyramid: a mass of low-income people at the bottom, sidelines narrowing to a peaked top. In much of the world it still is. But in the United States and some other industrial countries it has changed to the shape of a diamond or a pear: the great bulk is in the middle with a narrower base and top. (See table below.)

DISTRIBUTION OF FAMILIES, ACCORDING TO MONEY INCOME
1955 and 1979, in *Constant* 1979 Dollars

	1955 percent	1979 percent
Families with money income:		
under $5,000	16.2%	6.9%
$5,000 to under $10,000	22.7	13.5
$10,000 to under $25,000	53.1	45.0
$25,000 and up	8.0	34.7
	100.0%	100.0%

SOURCES: *Money Income and Poverty Status of Families and Persons in the United States: 1979 (Advance Report)*; and U.S. Bureau of the Census, *Current Population Reports*, Series P-60, No. 125, October 1980.

The shift in income distribution among American families over the past quarter century is truly spectacular. The percentage of families with a money income under $10,000 was cut into half, the percentage of families with an income of $25,000 or over multiplied more than four times. The center ($10,000 to $25,000) accounted then and now for close to one-half of all families. If income in kind and subsidies such as food stamps, housing subventions, Medicaid, etc. were included, the percentage of families in the two lowest brackets would be cut substantially below the figures shown above. The saying that "the rich get richer and the poor get poorer" is contrary to fact. The poor certainly do not get poorer; they just become fewer.

The demand for redistribution of income has converted the historic American principle of equality of opportunity to a claim for equality of results. It equates equity with equality and basically denies a person's right to the fruits of his labor, aiming to take from those who are productive and give to those who are unproductive or nearly so. It regards such action not as charity but as a basic precept of social justice regardless of whether lack of productivity is the result of voluntary action and personal attitude or brought about by insuperable forces and misfortune.

H. L. Mencken once wrote:

All government, in its essence, is a conspiracy against the superior man: its one permanent object is to oppress him and cripple him. If it be aristocratic in organization, then it seeks to protect the man who is superior only in law against the man who is superior in fact; if it be democratic, then it seeks to protect the man who is inferior in every way against both. One of its primary functions is to regiment men by force, to make them as much alike as possible and as dependent upon one another as possible, to search out and combat originality among them.[52]

Irving Kristol suggested a historic parallel:

For over two thousand years, the consensus among political philosophers was that democracy—the rule of the majority—was an inherently unstable and therefore undesirable form of government. The reason they came to this conclusion was not because they were snobs or disliked the common people, or because ordinary people then were inferior to the people of today. It was because they believed, on the basis of experience (in the ancient Greek city-states especially), that in a democracy the majority, being poor, would always use its power to expropriate the wealth of the more affluent minority, and that this would lead (as it always had) to economic chaos, followed by political chaos, followed by the restoration of order by a dictator.[53]

Kristol added that these are not *necessarily* the consequences of democracy as long as economic growth remains a credible reality. "It is the expectation of tomorrow's bigger pie, from which everyone will receive a larger slice, that prevents people from fighting to the bitter end over the division of today's pie." Insistent demand for greater redistribution, however, amounts exactly to "fighting . . . over the division of today's pie."

In *The Zero-Sum Society* Lester Thurow advanced the proposition that there is only a limited amount of goods and services to go around and that if some have more, others have less: The winners' gains equal the losers' losses. This, to be sure, is not a novel theory. Some have long contended that the basic issue in political economics is how to divide the wealth. Thurow holds, as egalitarians generally do, that as a matter of justice, as well as for social and political tranquility, government should distribute income and wealth more evenly so as to restore or at least approach a presumed original status of equality. It is one way to interpret the declaration that "all men are created equal," but in my opinion an incorrect way. The egalitarian creed does not recognize that goods and services are not a natural right, free gifts of nature, or society's to give, that they must be earned and that wealth is *created* as George Gilder so brilliantly demonstrated in *Wealth and Poverty*. A policy of punishing the creators of wealth by taking from them a goodly share of the fruit of their toil to give it to others, diminishes the creation of wealth. It has been said that a free market (capitalism) generates prosperity unevenly shared, while redistribution (socialism) produces misery more evenly shared.

The falsity of the hypothesis that there is a fixed sum of wealth to be allocated among claimants either evenly or unevenly by the forces that control government, becomes even more manifest when we compare various countries with each other rather than individuals and groups within a country. What the residents of an area or a country do with available resources usually is far more decisive in making them affluent or poor than the magnitude of existing local resources. This amply documented fact, however, has only a very limited appeal for the poor. Tanzania's president, Julius Nyerere, once asserted: "In one world as in one state, when I am rich because you are poor and I am poor because you are rich, the transfer of wealth from the rich to the poor is a matter of right."

A transfer from the rich to the poor as a matter of right has been the prime theme and goal of the countries generally referred to as less developed (LDCs) or third world, more recently sometimes as the fourth world. In 1974 the Sixth Special Assembly of the United Nations pronounced a New International Economic Order: financial and technical aid from the "haves" to the "have-nots" should be multiplied and the latter ought to be guaranteed purchase of their export products at "fair," that is, far higher prices.

Early in 1980 the Brandt Commission—officially, the Independent Commission on International Development, chaired by former West German Chancellor Willy Brandt—likewise prescribed a massive transfer of wealth to the third world by a quick tripling of the approximately $20 billion in annual development funds. Soon after, the United Nations Industrial Development Organization voted that the richer nations should accumulate a $300 billion fund for the benefit of "developing nations." The 4:1 majority included the Eastern Bloc (communist) countries which intended the capitalist countries to be the fund's principal contributors. They also made it clear that they had no intention of sharing their own technology or skills with the have-nots.

Such soak-the-rich schemes should come as no great surprise. The United Nations has long been viewed as a global community chest. But community chests usually talk in terms of requests and charity. The mentioned plans are phrased in terms of rights, entitlements and obligations. In other words, the United Nations aspires to create a worldwide welfare state, redistributing wealth from producers to non- (or low-)producers. For many years the United Nations has been dominated by the approximately hundred countries, most of them new, that joined subsequent to the organization's founding. Less than ten percent of the world's population is now able to cast a two-thirds vote in the General Assembly, a discrepancy that has made that body for all practical purposes irrelevant. But neither has the Security Council been able to do much about its intended purpose: to end multiple aggressions across national borders which have been taking place in many parts of the world.

Conceived and founded nearly half a century ago in the hope that it would bring peace to a troubled world, the United Nations has proven unable to prevent, intervene in, or settle crises among major and often even among minor countries. Now spending $2.5 billion a year, it maintains the world's most extravagant bureaucracy of 44,000—with 78 staff members who in 1979 made from $75,000 on up, more than any U.S. official except the president and the chief justice. The United States has been paying 25% of U.N. assessments, more than the combined total of 142 of the 151 member nations, in return for which, besides getting about 0.6% of the vote in the General Assembly, it has been on the receiving end of undisguised hostility from most of those countries. In a vain attempt to buy friendship among a multitude of voting members, the United States has been turning against some of its genuine friends and living up to a foreign policy principle of punishing its friends and rewarding its enemies.

Since the end of World War II, the United States has allocated over $200 billion in financial and technical aid to foreign governments, with additional sums contributed by a few other countries. The results have been mixed. Europe's war-devastated nations and Japan were helped to recover quickly and become prosperous once again; in some developing countries that pursue free market policies, such as Taiwan, South Korea, Brazil, Malaysia and Ivory Coast, economies expanded and continued on an upward course; a majority of the recipient countries failed to show genuine economic progress and gave no signs of self-sustaining growth. Although huge amounts of financial and technical aid to LDCs were provided over the past three decades by the United States and other countries, the gap between the "haves" and the "have-nots" appears to have been widening. Tanzania is a good example of a country which insisted on pursuing egalitarian, counterproductive policies, herding millions of its people into communized villages. Despite large aid from the United States, China and other sources, Tanzania still totters from one crisis to the next. In many countries foreign aid was dissipated and helped temporarily to boost consumption without creating an economic base for the future. In others, the infusion of funds from abroad largely benefited a reigning political elite, and left most of the country's people as poor as before, if not poorer.

Lack of natural resources or former colonial status is seldom a plausible explanation for failure of an economy to expand. Some of the world's most prosperous countries, such as Switzerland and Japan, have few industrially useful resources, Singapore and Hong Kong have none, while some resource-rich nations, despite frequent and large financial transfusions, seem unable to rise above poverty. Some of the richest countries such as Canada, Australia and the United States were once colonies—but do not seem to have been damaged by it. Many former colonies would be in as primitive and poor a status as they were for centuries before being colonized, were it not for the investments, technical and medical advances made by their former masters. Ethiopia was never colonized, but has remained close to the bottom of the economic ladder.

Nearly a hundred countries have gained political independence since World War II. Some of them have used it to engage in economically counterproductive policies and were enabled to do so by foreign aid. Is foreign aid really indispensable to poor countries which aim to rise, as is widely claimed? Who helped the Western countries at a time when foreign aid was unheard of, when there were no examples to follow, no advanced technologies to copy and when world conditions were far more difficult? The people of the Western countries went through the toil and agony of an agricultural revolution from which they derived the means to finance a no less painful industrial revolution. Many of today's LDCs are trying to skip the agricultural revolution and to reap the harvest of an industrial revolution before having sown its seeds. The third world people's impatience is humanly understandable. But it seems that a long time span must pass between inventing the wheel—which the inhabitants of some of the third world countries never did—and the ability to build and run a steel mill or an airline. That could be the mysterious "missing ingredient" which Gunnar Myrdal in his massive *Asian Drama* held responsible for the failure of so many poor countries to respond to heavy infusions of financial and technical aid with economic growth. Foreign aid may help to accelerate the process slightly but seems to be no substitute for the blood, sweat and tears, intelligently spent, with which Western people earned their affluence.

Much of whatever economic advance third world countries have been making is partially or wholly devoured by their exorbitant population growth. Median annual population growth in the 15 richest countries runs at less than 0.8%, among the 15 poorest countries at 2.5% or more. Could inherent traits for expanding reproduction and economic production be inversely related? At 3% per annum, population doubles within a quarter century, a rate which can be exceeded in economic growth only by very efficient methods. World population which stood at 2 billion in 1930, at over 4 billion in 1980, is estimated to exceed 6 billion by the year 2000. This has ominous implications. For aeons nature maintained a balance between births, deaths and the resource base. When Western medical advances and technology disturbed that balance and extended the average life span, the people of many countries commensurately adjusted their reproduction rate. But residents of parts of the third world did not. Thus we have recurring reports of famines and growing desertification of formerly fertile lands. Western food shipments may ease some of those famines but could thereby cause famines affecting two to four times as many people one or two generations later.

A few of the third world countries grew enormously rich within the past few decades when oil was found in their territory. Those countries' inhabitants had been sitting on top of huge oil pools, hidden under sand and rock, without knowing about them. Nor would they have cared much, had they known. They were poor and might have been even poorer today and for a long time ahead, if Western nations had not created a use for the oil and a technology for finding it and getting it out. Westerners—prospectors, engineers, entrepreneurs, financiers—searched for, drilled for, and pumped the oil from the bowels of the earth, refined, transported it and put it to economic use—and eventually permitted it to be taken from them in disregard of contract or rights of discovery and development. This truly was redistribution of wealth from the producers, from those who had the know-how and drive to develop the resource but lacked the will and courage, the "guts," to hold on to it, to the drones. OPEC countries now exact about $300 billion a year from the rest of the world with a devastating impact on the global economy that is bound to grow worse.

The promise or hope held out by some that redistribution of wealth and income, within a country or among countries, will reduce social and international tensions and conflicts is erroneous. Redistribution has not done so nor is likely to do so, because often it only stirs cupidity and the demand for more. Most conflict in this world—strife among individuals, social struggles and wars among nations, as well as most crime—is caused by the desire of some people for what other people have. That desire is often clothed in a pseudoethical justification—reasons why other people are not entitled to what they possess and why those who have not, should have it.

As long as law and order, personal property rights, and inviolability of boundaries, among nations and among individuals, are maintained, the extent of violence is likely to remain small. But once those fences are broken, when official justifications are given and laws are imposed that take from some and give to others, action is encouraged and demands are raised beyond limit, because no amount of "remedy" will satisfy those who feel that they are entitled to what others have. The move toward egalitarianism may lie at the root of much violent upheaval. In all likelihood it was probably no coincidence that the wave of redistributive legislation in the 1960s was shortly followed by unprecedented outbursts of civil disturbances that rocked the country from end to end and left deep scars that may not heal for many years.

These considerations do not intend to question the justification for welfare programs to aid persons who due to circumstances beyond their control are unable to earn their livelihood. In the past two decades, however, social programs have gone far beyond necessity and too often created, multiplied, perpetuated the miserable conditions which they were intended to alleviate.

The War on Poverty and Other Great Society Escapades

The American people have long been engaged in the most successful war on poverty the world has ever known. A huge primeval territory in which several million natives had been eking out a bare and primitive existence for twenty millennia or more, was invaded and occupied by millions of immigrants—most of them utterly impoverished, many destitute—who created within less than two centuries the wealthiest and most powerful nation on earth.

The theory that underlay Great Society plans, however, was that poverty is a deficiency which is bound to perpetuate itself through generations unless eradicated by governmental action of the type instituted in the 1960s. If that hypothesis were true, most of America's 226 million inhabitants would still be as penniless, ignorant and unemployed as their ancestors were when they landed on these shores. It seems that the history of the United States, and its strong mobility upward—and downward—stand as living proof of the fundamental error in this theory. The American record suggests that the condition of poverty is not so much a cause but a result, and that it can best be remedied—to the extent and in the cases where it *can* be remedied—by the individual and his efforts.

Why then is there still poverty? Until such time as we learn how to abolish the lowest 10 or 20 percent on the income scale, there will be persons on the lower end of that scale who may be called poor—by comparison. That a money income of $7412 for a 4-person nonfarm family—not counting in-kind income and food, housing, medical subsidies—can be called poverty is due only to the high income levels prevailing in the United States which have lifted the average family income above

$20,000 a year. Our official poverty level would be regarded as a respectable middle-class income in most other lands and represents an envied status of affluence to the great majority of inhabitants of well over half of the world's 150 countries.

To abolish poverty is a noble idea but certainly not a new idea. By offering freedom and opportunities to those able and willing to work, the American people have conducted an effective antipoverty campaign which has changed the historical distribution of income from the shape of a pyramid to that of a diamond. Can the lower end be completely wiped out?

Upon signing the Economic Opportunity Act on August 20, 1964, President Johnson declared it to be "the policy of the United States to eliminate the paradox of poverty in the midst of plenty." Is "poverty in the midst of plenty" truly a paradox? It is, in the same sense that the presence of shadows is a paradox when the sun shines. If there were no sunshine, there would be no shadows.

The fact is that productivity, that is, the value of the output of goods and services, varies more widely among individuals in the United States than income. How far can government go in penalizing the productive and rewarding the unproductive in an effort to abolish poverty, without weakening or paralyzing the force that powers the economy's upward drive?

Few of President Kennedy's imaginative New Frontier proposals were enacted into law. It took Lyndon Johnson's political genius to conceive a War on Poverty as a road to the Great Society and thereby a means—as he hoped—to establish his role in history. With a power possessed by no president since and with rare skill, he maneuvered the program's major parts through Congress—the Economic Opportunity Act, Civil Rights Act, Elementary and Secondary Education Act, Medicare and Medicaid, and several others, as well as many changes in existing laws on minimum wages, housing, etc.

The new programs, it was expected, would revolutionize the United States. They did, or at least came close to it, considering the widespread rioting in many urban areas and on campuses during the late 1960s and 1970s.

To those who believe that "there are no great problems in the alleviation of poverty that the direct disbursement of money to the poor will not tolerably remedy"[54] the poverty war was an unquestioned if limited success. It multiplied and vastly expanded several forms of income support programs and thereby reduced the incidence of poverty. But it had been the prime idea of the war on poverty that much of the money distribution would need to be only a temporary expedient. By alleviating poverty and under the impact of a variety of new programs, major social problems would be eased and gradually resolved. Thus the need for income support would diminish. It did not work out that way because the ivory-tower-conceived schemes utterly misunderstood human nature: they refused to recognize unpleasant facts of life. Capacity, drive and aspirations vary widely among human beings and the work ethic is less than enthusiastically embraced or universally practiced.

Thus the vision that by spending *more* on education, as well as on general youth and manpower training, *less* would have to be spent later on for welfare, crime fighting, and to remedy the cost of various social ills, turned out to be a mirage. Public assistance, especially AFDC, was vastly expanded and the number of aided children multiplied threefold. But social evils such as teenage pregnancy and family abandonment soared simultaneously—and not just coincidentally—and the rates of violent and property crime, of drug peddling and abuse continued to establish new records each year.

"The answer for all of our national problems," President Lyndon Johnson was quoted as saying, "comes to a single word. That word is education." The infusion of many billions of dollars into public school systems, sharply reduced teacher-pupil ratios and doubling or tripling of per pupil expenditures succeeded in keeping more children in school for more years. But educational accomplishments, knowledge and skills of students and graduates, persisted in declining, year after year.

Little attention was paid to James Coleman's most important finding that for the groups studied "by far the largest part of variation in student achievement lies within schools and not between schools."[55] Christopher Jencks summarized his findings:

> There is no evidence that school reform can substantially reduce the extent of cognitive inequality, as measured by tests of verbal fluency, reading comprehension, or mathematical skill. . . .
>
> These findings imply that school reform is never likely to have any significant effect on the degree of inequality among adults. . . .
>
> Our research suggests, however, that the character of a school's output depends largely on a single input, the characteristics of the entering children. Everything else—the school budget, its policies, the characteristics of the teachers—is either secondary or completely irrelevant, at least so long as the range of variation among schools is as narrow as it seems to be in America.[56]

There is no need to retell the experiences with governmental programs in education, welfare, housing, crime fighting, etc, which are cited in the respective sections of Chapter 4. Nor does it seem necessary to repeat the alternative solutions which are advanced there.

In a review of seven books on related subjects the *New York Times'*
Elizabeth Drew well summarized government's failure:

> It is widely believed that we tried the items on our national agenda, and
> they did not work. We spent a lot of money on our problems, and we
> don't feel better. We entrusted the government to the brightest in our
> midst, and they appear to have fouled up.[57]

Not until we accept the fact that *Operation Procrustes*, attempts to shape
all to uniform length or in a uniform mold, is bound to fail, do we have a
reasonable chance of beginning to solve the burning social problems on
which we have wasted huge sums for meager or negative results over the
past quarter century.

But programs are continuing because there are millions of people with
a personal stake and vested interest, people who either receive various
forms of regular cash or in-kind benefits for free or were given and hold
jobs at a salary and with a power they never could have obtained otherwise.
Others serve as advisers or consultants to government or foundations and
hold fat contracts. But as far as members of Congress and the executive
branch are concerned, they have solved the problem by appropriating
billions of dollars; they feel that this is all that can be expected of them.

The expansion of federal activity to many hundreds of domestic benefit and service programs, however, had grave consequences beyond mere
cost. The blunder at the Bay of Pigs can be charged, at least in part, to the
fact that President Kennedy devoted only little time to an advance study of
the proposed action and had to rely mostly on others because he was
preoccupied with his New Frontier programs. President Johnson became
so deeply involved in Vietnam not because he had so planned. Quite the
contrary. His primary interest was focused on domestic affairs and he
aimed to devote his undivided attention to the pursuit of the Great Society.
In consequence he gave inadequate time to the study of the extremely
complicated situation in Southeast Asia, acted rashly—and it blew up in his
face with a vengeance. That ruined his chances to achieve what he had
wanted above everything else: another term in the White House, an
honored role during his incumbency and fame in the history books. President Carter repeated those experiences in his ill-considered actions on
foreign emergencies such as in Iran and Afghanistan which, to all appearances, contributed substantially to his rejection by the voters at the 1980
elections. When, after the invasion of Afghanistan, he stated that he "had
learned more about the Russians in the last week than in the preceding two
and a half years," he admitted that he had not sufficiently studied what

should have been his first priority: the problems the Soviet Union poses to the United States and the world.

Domestic matters now consume most of the time of the president and Congress and leave insufficient hours for the study of national security and foreign affairs, which only our highest national officials can properly weigh and decide. Governors, state legislatures, mayors, city councils, county commissioners, and school boards could resolve domestic service problems, with some fiscal aid from the national government, if necessary. This would leave the president and Congress free to concentrate on matters that inevitably are their responsibility.

Senator James L. Buckley complained in 1978:

> The simple fact of the matter is that the Congress has involved itself (and therefore the national government) in so vast an array of concerns that no one member can any longer concentrate on and master more than a small fraction of the legislative business that comes before it. Members of Congress have become so embroiled in the myriad details once thought to be the sole province of state and local authorities (e.g., employee safety standards in the corner drugstore) that they haven't the time to truly study or understand such uniquely national concerns as the need for a comprehensive energy policy or the consequences of the growing imbalance between Soviet and American arms.
>
> Demands on the time and attention of the members have grown to the point where they exceed the Congress' collective capacity to operate with any degree of deliberative thought. . . .[58]

The issue was clearly presented fifteen years earlier, in 1963, by W. Glenn Campbell, director of the Hoover Institution on War, Revolution and Peace at Stanford University:

> The core of the problem is that the President who is called upon to make decisions on which hang the very existence of the nation and lives of many millions, decisions which require more study than there are hours in the day, must cut short his consideration of foreign policy and national security to deal with aid for sewage treatment plants, to round up an extra five or ten votes for a Department of Urban Affairs or for public works acceleration, to worry in whose district he should place some of the added public works projects, or to figure out how to make some discredited and unpopular aid-to-education bills acceptable to a Congress which has concluded after examining the evidence on innumerable occasions that they are unnecessary, and has rejected them time and again.

A review of the *Congressional Record* shows that most of the time of Congress is spent on approving numerous types of local benefits and not on the most vital and urgent business at hand—national security. There may not have been too much harm in engaging in politically more rewarding pursuits than national security in a simpler world, when the nation was not so gravely threatened. But today it is intolerable to have the President and Congress devote so much of their time to domestic affairs which can as well or better be handled by others.

There are no objective yardsticks, no scientific criteria, and no hard and fast formulae by which anybody can measure the needs of defense and of a hundred other services in order to assign relative priorities. Former Budget Director Bell testified, "It is plain that considering the national security in this broad sense requires the President—and the Congress—to make a difficult series of choices for which we do not have a satisfactory set of criteria." Nor is it possible to solve such choices with an automatic calculus. They require wisdom, and human wisdom of the highest order. If the President and Congress are to concentrate on them we must devise a better division of labor in regard to governmental functions than we have at the present time.

It would seem, therefore, that the first and foremost priority for national security rests, not on money, but rather on the brains of our top officials—on their adequate time for study, for deliberation, for decision. They should not be called upon to deal with hundreds of local services and benefits which can be adequately judged by officials who are closer to the scene and can devote their whole time and talents to these tasks.[59]

The need for a reversal of the centralizing trend was even more drastically demonstrated in the years that have passed since the statement above was written. Federal direction of domestic functions, national involvement in state and local affairs have sharply intensified since 1963. By infinitely detailed federal grants, by regulation—and by judicial actions—Washington has tightened its control and supervision of virtually all public functions in states and cities. The results of federal preoccupation with domestic matters has now become obvious: The strength of the United States and its position in the world have diminished and the country has blundered from one foreign "emergency" to another, in each case manifesting its impotence, its inability to face tough problems and deal with them effectively.

One essential step on the way to freeing the national government from unnecessary involvement is to reverse the trend of decision making. We are told that federal grants to state and local governments are needed because only the superior fiscal capacity of the national treasury is able to meet the vast financial requirements. Fact is, that federal revenues fell ten percent short of meeting expenditures in the 1970s. This means that three-fifths of the $525 billion federal grants between 1970 and 1979 were not financed from tax receipts but through budgetary deficits. If the national government had not shared its alleged "affluence" with state and local governments, it could, other circumstances even, have had a $200 billion surplus instead of a $315 billion deficit during the decade of the 1970s. Inflation rates would most certainly have been more moderate if the federal budget had produced surpluses rather than deficits between 1970 and 1980.

No one would suggest that federal aid to state and local governments which now approaches $100 billion a year can or should be cut off. But it can be gradually reduced. Above all, it should not be divided among some 500 conditional grant systems, each with its own controls, but be consolidated into a purely fiscal grant.

A shift from categorical to fiscal grants was repeatedly suggested in the 1950s and 1960s. But when revenue sharing on a modest scale was established in the early 1970s, it was not used to *replace* categorical programs but *put on top* of them. When Congress in 1980 attempted to restrain federal spending, its victim was not categorical grants but revenue sharing to the states. That was an act of political vengeance on the governors who had implored Congress to balance the federal budget. Congress said, in so many words: "If you want a spending cut—we'll give you a taste of it."

A gradual cutback of *categorical* grants—with some bunching into block or fiscal grants and federal tax relief—a reduction of the range and intensity of federal regulatory activity—and restraint by, or if necessary on, the expansionist tendencies of the federal judiciary—could free Congress and the executive branch of having to devote most of their time to subjects which need not, and should not—be theirs to decide.

Concentration of Power and Loss of Freedom

By its massive entry into the field of domestic services since the end of World War II, the national government drastically altered the nature of the American system of government. Two centuries ago, when the Founding Fathers established a federal structure, with an intricate system of checks and balances, they aimed to disperse authority so widely, that no one branch of government—no one man or group of men—could prevail over all others. The document's authors had learned from history that concentration of power corrupts and sooner or later leads to abuse and eventual ruin. Whenever a nation disregards that age-old lesson, its truth is brought home, sooner or later, with a brutal shock.

Growing loss of confidence of the American people in their government, a steady decline of faith in its ability to cope with its primary tasks, has become manifest in recent decades. Annual opinion polls by the University of Michigan's Institute for Social Research show that the percentage of the citizenry that believes that it can trust the government to "do what is right" fell from a high of 77% in 1964 to 34% in 1976.[60]

Congress appears aware of its shortcomings. "An overwhelming majority of the senators and house members answering a survey conducted by *U.S. News and World Report* (in 1980) concedes that Congress is doing either poor or only fair in responding to the nation's needs. Fewer than 1 in 4 think Congress is doing a good job."[61] But Congress seems unwilling or unable to take the necessary corrective action.

MIT political scientist Walter Dean Burnham characterized sentiment in the early 1970s as "the pervasive belief of millions of Americans that they had lost control over their lives, that they had no leverage over the political process, and that they were the victims of the illegitimate exercise of raw power."[62] Events of the later 1970s revealed a deep-seated alienation among the general public, based on a feeling that something had gone terribly wrong. Most could not define just what the root of the trouble was. But basically it seemed to be the inability and incompetence of the government to live up to the enormous breadth of responsibilities it had blithely assumed. That is why it failed, both in its established and in its newly acquired functions.

As it turned out, the upward shift in responsibility and decision-making power from the 50 states and thousands of cities and smaller communities, had not strengthened the top of the pyramid, but weakened it. Within not too many years after Richard Neustadt had extolled *Presidential Power* and Arthur Schlesinger, Jr., eulogized *The Imperial Presidency*, Joseph Kraft described its decline to *The Post-Imperial Presidency*.[63] The piling up of authority at the top manifested that the limit of the presidency's load-bearing capacity had been reached and finally exceeded. The machinery's command center was no longer able to perform adequately.

Attempts to cope with the volume of work by multiplying staff helped but eventually could not hide failure at the apex. The Executive Office listed 37 positions in 1939, to which administrative reform in the succeeding year added six presidential assistants ("men with a passion for anonymity") and a few clericals, upping the total to 55. By 1979 the Executive Office of the President, not counting the Office of Management and Budget, nor the sizable number of temporary ("invisible") White House aides, carried on the payroll of other departments, boasted of 1043 positions.

The decisions to be made by the president were too many, and too important or crucial to be delegated. In consequence, policy decisions tended to vacillate and, in too many cases, were plainly wrong, sometimes with disastrous results. This was not so much because the United States—as the only major nation—requires its head of government also to serve as chief of state. It was the multiplicity of subject matters which, in a governmental system that depends on the consent of the governed—in a country of enormous size, complexity and worldwide obligations—is beyond the reach or span of a single person.

The Constitution, as designed by its authors and approved by the states, assigned to the national government only certain specified and delegated functions ("powers") such as national security, foreign affairs, money coinage, the postal service and a few others. Most of the domestic public services were left within the realm of the states and their local subdivisions. (In more precise language, the states *retained* those powers.) That was not only a reasonable and manageable division of labor. It also aimed to assure the citizens of the various states that they could make their own decisions on the nature and extent of governmental services they desired. What the residents of one or several areas wanted—and were willing to pay for—did not necessarily have to be forced on all others. There is a legitimate case for maintaining diversity, particularly in a country that spans a continent and was settled by people from many lands and of many descents.

Local autonomy and home rule are essential to the preservation of individual liberty. It has well been said that *freedom is indivisible*. National uniformity may or may not be efficient though it sometimes provides good government. But good government is no substitute for self-government. National uniformity, appealing as it is in many ways, also is a milestone on the *Road to Serfdom*.

When special interest groups petitioned Congress to establish, and pay nationally for programs they were unable to persuade the people's elected representatives in their own states to approve or impose, Congress yielded, at first slowly and reluctantly, and later at an accelerating rate. Several provisions in the Constitution were used, or reinterpreted, to legitimize action on subject matters which the states had not delegated to the United States. It was, at first, mainly the interstate commerce clause, later the general welfare clause (spending power), the supremacy clause and, eventually, with increasing frequency, the equal rights clause of the 14th Amendment. Total disregard by the Supreme Court of the 10th Amendment—"powers not delegated to the United States nor prohibited by it to the states are reserved to the states respectively or to the people" enabled the national government to acquire and exercise authority which the Founders had never intended to confer upon the "government of limited powers" they established.

The most effective, and for many years most widely employed, means of expanding the federal reach was use of the spending power. The national government could not, or preferred not to, act *directly* in education, housing, public assistance and dozens of other fields. But it could offer the states incentives through financial grants, to operate programs it wanted, on terms and conditions set by Congress and federal administrators.

When the number of grant-in-aids proliferated in the post–World War II period and grew to over 60 programs for a total of $2.6 billion in the early 1950s, concern arose about their broader implications and unintended, cumulative effects. On Senator Robert Taft's suggestion, President Eisenhower recommended to Congress and established in 1953 a temporary *Commission on Intergovernmental Relations* which, it was hoped, would be instrumental in reversing the trend of governmental concentration. The commission and its successors tried, in a moderate way, to carry out their mandates but soon found out that political forces of overwhelming strength were arrayed in the opposite direction. The number of federal grant programs to state and local governments, covering virtually all of their activities, grew to 498 by 1980 and their amount to $89 billion, estimated in President Carter's FY 1981 Budget to increase to $112 billion by 1983.

From a small beginning in the late XIX century, national regulatory action was for many decades operating in just a few subject matter fields. But it was enormously expanded and intensified in the 1970s. By the end of the decade there was virtually no public activity that was not controlled from Washington and there were very few private transactions left which, in one way or another, had not come under federal rules. Life in the United States had become thoroughly regulated.

Organizations of a great variety of special interests succeeded in persuading Congress that enactment of programs for their benefit was in the national interest. Those groups concluded, correctly, that they could get far larger amounts for their purposes with the help of federal grants, matchable by the states.

Grants-in-aid, as the executive director of the Advisory Commission on Intergovernmental Relations William G. Colman told a congressional committee in 1962, "are an impenetrable jungle of legal, financial, and political and professional interlacings." Such intergovernmental arrangements often make it virtually impossible to know just how much is being spent on a particular program or project and to relate outcome to the costs.

Congress, in 1976, directed the Advisory Commission on Intergovernmental Relations to prepare a comprehensive report on the problems of the fiscal intergovernmental system. Three of ten planned volumes were published in the Fall of 1980. An introductory report, captioned *A Crisis of Confidence and Competence* listed the four major problems:

> *administrative failures*, red tape, and tension between the levels of government—the problem of "implementation";
> *poor performance* and inadequate results—the question of impact of "evaluation";
> *excessive cost and waste*—the matter of fiscal "efficiency"; and
> *lack of adequate control* and responsiveness through the political process—the issue of "accountability."

The commission concluded:

> The root problem, then, is that, in intergovernmental programs no level bears the full administrative responsibility for the use of public funds. Fiscal accountability is divided and confused.[64]

Attempts to reverse the process have been singularly unsuccessful. The recipients of the benefits and their organizations know that any attempt to revert services to the states would result in substantial cutbacks. If citizens knew the total cost of each program and were able to relate it to its positive achievements, they would soon reduce or abolish many of them. Only by hiding costs through intergovernmental arrangements—such as categorical federal grants—can the programs be preserved and steadily enlarged.

But the worst result of many of those programs is not just the enormous waste of taxpayers' money but the restrictions they impose on individual freedom.

When the right of citizens is restricted to run public services in their communities and states according to their own concepts—which may and do differ widely—the freedom of those citizens is adversely affected. A central government that holds sway over local governments thereby also controls the individuals who live in those jurisdictions. Most residents of the United States are increasingly dependent upon the national government in some form—for wages, promotions, grants, subsidies, orders, or pensions, or are subject to favors or harassment by regulatory or tax enforcement agencies.

Few can afford to oppose policies of the federal bureaucracy; few have a chance to succeed if they do by standing up for their rights. Enforced consensus and conformity have become the rule because the penalty for deviation is too severe. Extension of federal grants into every nook and cranny of local services smoothed the road and conditioned public attitude toward increasing federal regulation and interference by new laws, administrative rules, practices of dedicated and power-hungry bureaucrats, and orders of ambitious judges who shifted from interpreting the law to policymaking and amending the meaning of the constitution. There are few if any activities or practices left to local governments, business firms, associations or individuals that are not governed or can be governed and often drastically changed by federal authorities under sanction of law.

While ample lip service is being lavished on the precept of home rule, particularly by those who are busy digging its grave, and a facade of local autonomy is being maintained—because the architects of centralization "wisely refrained from tampering with the Ark of the Covenant," preserved the symbols, and respected the rituals—the substance of self-government has been drained.

As long as local diversity is maintained, citizens who find themselves in the minority in their home areas can move to jurisdictions whose policies or governments are more appealing to them. When national uniformity is imposed, by federal law or regulation or by federal courts, the individual's choice and the right of communities to exercise home rule and local autonomy come to an end.

The multiplication of federal grants for domestic services has led to the formation of a *vertical functional autocracy* which supersedes the self-government of local communities that used to characterize the American scene. If grants were intended to aid states and local governments, as is often asserted, they could be given without conditions, to be spent at the discretion of local authorities.

Revenue sharing was recommended in 1967 by a study group which I chaired, under the direction of the Republican National Committee. The committee's final report *The Restoration of Federalism in America* favored grant consolidation as a means of shifting decision-making power back to states and communities. When revenue sharing was enacted in 1972, it was put on top of the categorical grants rather than replace them and subjected to various federal conditions and controls. It is those less restricted grants to the states which Congress undertook to eliminate in 1980.

Until just a few years ago, most political scientists—and particularly those who were inclined toward bigger government—favored a stronger shift of power from state and local governments to the national government. Events of recent years have caused some of the former enthusiasts of greater concentration of authority to have second thoughts.

Charles L. Schultze of the Brookings Institution, who served as director of the Bureau of the Budget under President Johnson and as chairman of President Carter's Council of Economic Advisers, suggested that federal grants ought not to be so closely controlled from Washington:

> But there seems little reason not to leave this kind of judgment to state and local officials, who are much closer to the people being served, and much merit in consolidating these numerous grants into a few broad groups supporting the delivery of educational and social services at the state and local level, with discretion for the precise allocation of funds left to the recipient government.[65]

The expansion and intensification of domestic public services have had a direct and negative impact on personal freedom. Again, if we define freedom as the ability of the individual to make meaningful choices among known alternatives, then it follows that the extent of his freedom depends on the range of decisions which he can make for himself and his family as opposed to those being made for him. The larger a share of an individual's product or resources government takes *from* him and spends *for* him, the less an individual can allocate to his manifold needs and wants—for housing, education, health, recreation—according to his own judgment, desire or preference. The heavier his taxes are for public schools, the less able is he to send his children to a private school of his choice.

When a government expands and intensifies its activities and tightens the rules under which its residents must live, it always does so in the name of the people and for their presumed benefit. It may retain established rituals and honored traditions by which it hides the change and stakes out a seemingly respectable claim to legitimacy. Hitler, Mussolini, and Stalin claimed to be governing in the long-range interest and for the good of their citizens, many of whom (and at times a majority of whom) believed, at least temporarily, that it was all done for their own "liberty and pursuit of happiness." Half a century ago, Mr. Justice Brandeis, one of the leading liberals of his day, warned that

> experience should teach us to be most on our guard to protect liberty when the government's purposes are beneficent. Men born to freedom are naturally alert to repel invasion of their liberty by evil-minded rulers. *The greatest dangers to liberty lurk in insidious encroachment by men of zeal, well-meaning but without understanding.*[66]

It is the nature of government to continually try to extend the range and intensity of its functions and to penetrate deeply into affairs which used to be regarded as being in the private sphere, thereby narrowing and endangering individual freedom. "Liberty has never come from the government," Woodrow Wilson wrote, reminding us that "a history of liberty is the history of limitations of governmental powers, not the increase of it."

It is for good reason that a recognized leader in behavioral sciences, B. F. Skinner—who has been called "the most influential of living American psychologists"—came to the conclusion in his book, *Beyond Freedom and Dignity*, that we can no longer afford freedom, and that it must be replaced with control over man, his conduct, and his culture.

Is there an alternative? Can the trend toward growing control by the central government be reversed? Action to oppose and defeat hundreds of proposals to establish or enlarge categorical federal grant programs has proven utterly ineffective over the past three decades: the number of such grants meanwhile jumped from five dozen to five hundred. Single-interest lobbyists "ganged up" on moves intended to enhance the decision-making power of the states, knowing that they would not be able to sell their favorite programs to state legislatures as easily as they could to Congress. Congress pays little attention to whether the programs it approved produce the promised results. Its members focus attention mainly on how much in federal funds they can secure for local projects in their own constituencies. Thus attempts to stem the spending tide by fighting proposals one by one proved a futile exercise.

If there is to be restraint it will have to come from the top, by imposing spending limits. Congress, of course, is not anxious to put fetters on its own power and no Congress can bind its successors. Only a constitutional amendment could keep the spending urge in line, either by an expenditure ceiling expressed as a percentage of GNP, or by forcing the balancing of the budget. Though committee hearings on such plans were held, neither house was willing to restrict its freedom of action.

That left only one possible strategy: adoption by two-thirds of the states of a resolution demanding the calling of a constitutional convention which could draft an amendment to be submitted to the states for ratification. That procedure, authorized by Article V of the U.S. Constitution is cumbersome but apparently the only avenue that could lead to the desired goal. A movement arose in the late 1970s which succeeded by 1979 in getting approvals from about thirty state legislatures. Somehow the drive then slowed down. Whether attempts to rekindle it in the early 1980s will be successful remains to be seen. Whether Congress will take commensurate action *without* being forced appears uncertain at this point.

Judicial Supremacy vs. Government by the People

Distrustful of government, the Founding Fathers carefully fragmented its powers. As a safeguard against the possible rise of a tyranny in the United States, they employed the idea of a separation of powers in Montesquieu's *L'Esprit des Lois*, and divided authority among three *coequal* branches of government. Each branch could be expected to jealously protect its privileges against transgressions by the others and thereby prevent concentration of control in a single place.

The Constitution's authors knew from history and experience that wielders of power always thirst for more, that no "limitations on parchment" will long restrain ambitious men unless a countervailing force exists, eager to guard its own prerogatives and strong enough to keep others from exceeding their boundaries. Above all, officeholders are not very likely to invade the domains of others as long as the people themselves can watch and judge their servants' actions and have the unrestricted right and power to dismiss—or re-elect—incumbents at specified regular intervals. "The people themselves," Jefferson said, "are the only safe depositories of government."

That did not keep Congress—nor state legislatures which are similarly constituted—from occasionally trying to act on matters and in ways that were reserved to the Executive or to the Judiciary. Nor did it prevent eager executives from attempting to cross boundaries into the legislative or judicial realm. But executives and legislators knew that the propriety of their actions would be adjudicated by their voters soon or, at the most, within a few years and that they could not afford to stray far beyond their assigned authority without dire consequences. That left one, seemingly small, loophole: federal judges are not subject to periodic review of their performance in office; they are independent of, and not responsible to, the people who hold sway over legislators and executives. Federal judges are appointed for life, and can only in the most extreme circumstances—and for the most flagrant derelictions of duty—be removed from office, by impeachment.

But judges are as ambitious for greater decision-making authority over the nation's affairs as everybody else. Thus they have gradually pushed their boundaries outward, at first tentatively, later more daringly, until they felt bold enough to assert supremacy over the other branches and levels of government.

Chief Justice John Marshall in 1803 first claimed the right to override a decision of a "coequal" branch of government. But knowing that President Jefferson would blandly ignore such pretension, he wisely chose to waive his claim in the case under review, confident in his belief that *Marbury* v. *Madison* would establish a lasting precedent of judicial supremacy for the future—as indeed it did.

In only a few later cases were the judges beaten back by legislators, through statutory or constitutional revision—or by shrewd executives through well-selected appointments when vacancies occurred. Franklin Roosevelt's attempt to pack the Supreme Court failed—but he succeeded soon after, when a benign Providence allowed him to appoint four loyal followers within the succeeding two years. Only one of the Court's decisions, *Dred Scott* v. *Sanford* in 1857, had to be overruled by recourse to arms.

The Founders had intended for the Congress to *pass* the laws, for the President to *carry them out* and for the courts to *apply* the general rules of Constitution and statutes—and regulations adopted thereunder—to individual cases. Judges were expected to *interpret* the law from its language and, when necessary, by ascertaining the intent of its authors.

For a long time now the Supreme Court has gone beyond interpreting the Constitution and laws. By pushing its power far beyond any conceivable meaning of the term interpretation, it has, for all practical purposes, been sitting as a legislature but even beyond that, as a continuing constitutional convention. Chief Justice Charles Evans Hughes expressed the Court's attitude succinctly in his famous dictum that "the constitution is what the Supreme Court says it is" although he tried in his later years to explain this away.[67]

Chief Justice Harlan F. Stone wrote in a 1936 dissent that "the only check upon our own exercise of power is our own sense of self-restraint."[68]

More often than not, it was a judge disagreeing with a majority of his brethren, who would criticize their failure to exercise judicial restraint. Justice Hugo L. Black wrote in a dissent in 1966, ". . . there is no constitutional support whatsoever for this court to use the Due Process Clause as though it provided a blank check to alter the meaning of the Constitution as written so as to add substantive constitutional changes which a majority of the Court at any given time believes are needed to meet present day problems."[69]

In his dissent with the Court's famous—or as some feel, infamous—decision in *Adkins* v. *Children's Hospital* (1923)[70] (which declared unconstitutional an Act of Congress establishing minimum wages and maximum hours for women and minors in the District of Columbia), Chief Justice William Howard Taft wrote:

> . . . it is not the function of this Court to hold congressional acts invalid because they are passed to carry out economic views which the Court believes to be unwise or unsound.

Justice William O. Douglas wrote in 1965: "We do not sit as a super legislature to determine the wisdom, need and propriety of laws that touch economic problems . . . or social conditions."[71]

But the same judges and a majority of the court on numerous occasions ignored and perverted the meaning of constitutional and statutory provisions; they invented artificial and farfetched constructions and interpretations, to suit their own concepts of justice, fairness, desirable social order, wisdom or need. *Judges take an oath of office to support the Constitution, not an oath to dispense justice—as each may see it. But the Supreme Court has taken us a long ways from a government of laws to a government of men.*

Criticism of the Supreme Court's deviation from its proper role has been mounting for years. Raoul Berger of the Harvard Law School captioned a scholarly volume, the result of four years of painstaking research, *Government by Judiciary*, Nathan Glazer and Ernest Van Den Haag wrote about the *Imperial Judiciary*, Martin Shapiro about *Judicial Activism*, and Marvin Stone about *Dictatorship by Judiciary*.[72]

Berger opened his opus: "The Fourteenth Amendment is the case study par excellence of what Justice Harlan described as the Supreme Court's 'exercise of the amending power,' its continuing revision of the Constitution under the guise of interpretation." The Founders had manifestly excluded the judiciary from policymaking and reserved to the legislative branch the right and duty to judge the wisdom and fairness of a rule and the need for it. But the court arrogated to itself authority to close whatever "gaps" Congress had left. The judges felt they were entitled to fill those gaps according to their political ideology—which until about 1937 outraged the political left and ever since the political right.

The "separate but equal" rule of *Plessy* v. *Ferguson*[73] was clearly irreconcilable with the moral beliefs of the twentieth century and intolerable to its concepts of civil rights. But to remedy the rule was a responsibility and prerogative of Congress, not of the Court. It was Congress, not the Court, to which the Fourteenth Amendment gave the "power to enforce, by appropriate legislation, the provisions of this article." Nor did the Court *interpret* the Fourteenth Amendment in 1954. It *amended* it. To outlaw school segregation was far from the mind of the authors of the Fourteenth Amendment. The Court had to twist language and logic to mandate in *Brown II* "a system of determining admission to the public schools on a nonracial basis." It had to use even more contorted arguments sixteen years later when in *Swann* v. *Charlotte-Mecklenburg*[74] it ordered the assignment of students to public schools on a racial basis.

Chief Justice Charles Evans Hughes explained the Supreme Court's working principles most succinctly to freshman William O. Douglas: "At the constitutional level at which we work, ninety percent of any decision is emotional. The rational part of us supplies the reasons for supporting our predilections." Unwilling to leave some solutions to the gradual working of the political system, the judges opted for court intervention when a pending case gave them that opportunity.

The Supreme Court expanded its authority and usurped legislative power largely through the use of what is commonly called "substantive due process." Article V of the Constitution specifies that "[no person shall be] deprived of life, liberty, or property, without due process of law"—a concept of Anglo-Saxon law dating back at least to the fourteenth century. The Fourteenth Amendment extended the clause to apply to the states.

Unequivocally, this was a requirement to observe prescribed procedures and intended to apply to the courts. But when the judges were dissatisfied with the results of "due process" in the legislative branch, if they disliked the substance of a congressional decision, they concluded that something must have been wrong with the procedure if it did not produce a solution that was, to their mind, *substantively* correct. Hence the term "substantive due process" which clearly is a *contradictio in adjecto*. Something is either procedural *or* substantive, but not both. It was a dialectical device to open the door to the Court's jurisdiction over the wisdom of a decision, not to its conformance, or lack thereof, with the language and intent of the Constitution.

By using *substantive due process*, the Supreme Court has for a century or more rationalized decisions which a dispassionate interpretation of the law would not have permitted. In earlier times, substantive due process was used to thwart legislative or executive attempts at protecting workers, women, minors. Such acts were struck down as restricting the *liberty of contract*. After 1937, when the Court's majority changed from a *laissez-faire* philosophy to a preoccupation with what it regarded as *social justice*, it changed its direction though not its methods.

In recent decades, several Court decisions perverted the meaning of "equal protection of the laws," "without regard to race, color, creed, sex or national origin" or "equal treatment" and interpreted them as authorizing and even requiring preference for members of some groups over others. The Court attempted to carry out the 1964 Civil Rights Act's declaration that "'desegregation' shall not mean the assignment of students to public schools in order to overcome racial imbalance" by approving compulsory busing orders of lower courts precisely to overcome racial imbalance.

Chief Justice Harlan F. Stone in 1945 first noted a change in direction:

> My more conservative brethren in the old days [read their preference] into the Constitution. . . . history is repeating itself. The Court is now as much in danger of becoming a legislative and Constitution-making body, enacting into law its own predilections, as it was then.[75]

Archibald Cox commented that the Warren Court "behaved more like a Council of Wise Men and less like a Court than the *laissez faire* Justices"[76] and Alexander Bickel suggested that "a broadly-conceived egalitarianism was the main theme to which the Warren Court marched."[77]

Egalitarianism (through redistribution) and concentration of power are of course the main goals and characteristics of the welfare state, as discussed earlier in this chapter (pp. 382-93). This is why Bickel in *The Supreme Court and the Idea of Progress* (p. 8) and many other observers thought that the resignation of Chief Justice Warren signaled the end of an era. As it turned out, it did not; the Burger Court carried on with but few changes.

Cox phrased the crucial issue well:

> The real question, which Chief Justice Marshall never discussed, is whether a few judges, appointed for life or the elected representatives of the people will better exercise the ultimate, uncontrollable power of determining what rules shall prevail in the areas arguably governed by the original charter.[78]

Ignoring the old maxim that no one can be a judge in his own case, the U.S. Supreme Court made itself the ultimate judge in conflicts in which it was one of the contending parties. It adjudicated disagreements between itself and the executive or legislative branches of the federal government as well as controversies between the federal government (of which the Court is a branch) and state governments. Not surprisingly, the other parties to the argument usually lost out. That is how supremacy works among "coequals."

Conflicts between the federal government and state governments must of course, if irreconcilable by negotiation, be settled by a superior tribunal. But, must that tribunal necessarily be an integral part of one of the parties involved? Would it not be preferable to bring intergovernmental disputes to an authority representative of both sides rather than of one? Alternatively, since most of the controversies are over substantive policy issues rather than mere procedural questions, should the decisions not be made by the representatives of the people in Congress?

Suffrage had always been regarded a matter of state legislation. Raoul Berger wrote that "the proof is all but incontrovertible that the framers meant to leave control of suffrage with the states, which had always exercised such control and to exclude federal intrusion."[79]

But in *Baker* v. *Carr* the Supreme Court ordered reapportionment of both houses of state legislatures on a one-man one-vote basis.[80] Allocation by geographical representation of political jurisdictions may suffice for the United States Senate but was declared just not good enough for state

senates. Representation in federal, state and local legislatures was no longer
a matter for those legislative bodies themselves to decide, when the Court
assumed control in 1962.

After ruling on several voting rights cases, winding up in *South Carolina* v. *Katzenbach*[81] the Supreme Court in 1965 outlawed the use of
literacy tests which a number of states had required for the exercise of the
right to vote. Literacy tests had unquestionably been abused in some
locations to deny Negroes access to the ballot box. But the remedy for
abuse is a proper procedural safeguard, not abolition of the rule itself. The
Court apparently held that ability to read and be informed on the issues and
persons to be voted on is irrelevant to the purpose of an election and
discriminates against illiterates. In the following year, in *Katzenbach* v.
Morgan[82] the Court further enlarged the provisions of the Fourteenth
Amendment and, contrary to state laws, enfranchised persons who do not
know the English language.

In nearly fifty decisions relating to the opening clause of the First
Amendment—nonestablishment of religion—the Court has over the past
thirty years zigzagged, usually with the narrowest of majorities, leaving the
field and the affected matters a shambles.

The clause itself is, as Daniel Patrick Moynihan well pointed out,
"simplicity itself. The clause states 'Congress shall make no law respecting
an establishment of religion. . . .' The term establishment referred to a state
church, such as the Church of England, an altogether familiar concept at
the time, and rather a familiar institution."[83]

Most of the states, while they still were British colonies, had established churches—Anglican, Dutch Reformed, Congregational. The states'
representatives, in drafting and approving the Bill of Rights, wanted to
eliminate any possibility that the U.S. Congress at some time might want to
establish a church of its own. Hence the "nonestablishment" clause, whose
meaning remained clear for more than a century and a half. But starting
with an outrageous misinterpretation in *Everson* (1947) which it revised
five years later in *Zorach*[84] the Court shuttled back and forth at rapid speed.

The Supreme Court approved public funds for the transportation
of parochial school children (*Everson*, 1947), loans of publicly owned
schoolbooks to them (*Allen*, 1968), various other special activities in
parochial schools, federal grants for construction at church-connected colleges (*Tilton*, 1971), but in *Niquist* (1973) it declared state tax deductions
for tuition payments to religiously connected schools to be violative of the
establishment clause.[85]

Only three years prior to *Niquist* the Court had, in *Walz*, upheld, in
strong and unequivocal language, religious exemptions from taxation.[86]
The deductibility for tax purposes of donations to churches is firmly

established—why then should tax deduction of payments to schools sponsored by those churches be repugnant to the Constitution? Are churches less engaged in "religious activities" than church schools?

The daily prayers at the opening of congressional sessions, the employment of chaplains in the Armed Forces, divine invocation at the opening of Supreme Court sessions, the words "In God We Trust" on U.S. coins, are unquestioned—but voluntary prayers in schools, and even the posting of the Ten Commandments in a school building, are forbidden. How confused—and confusing—can a court get?

In dozens of cases the Supreme Court routinely overruled policy, administrative and judicial decisions of state governments, usually without knowledge or care of the burdens it imposed on taxpayers nor giving much thought to other consequences. In June 1980, in *Maine* v. *Thiboutot* the Court allowed welfare recipients dissatisfied with the size of their benefits to sue the states, a decision that may prove as expensive to taxpayers as earlier decisions on residency, confidentiality, home suitability, etc. of welfare claimants.

In their eagerness to establish national uniformity rather than help preserve a vestige of local autonomy, our highest judges have created a situation in which, in the words of Senator Everett McKinley Dirksen in the mid-1960s, the time is not far distant when "the only people interested in state boundaries will be Rand McNally."

Lacking expertise in fields beyond their competence, courts have done untold damage by marching into sensitive areas like elephants trampling through a China shop. They did so in the secure knowledge that they bore no responsibility for providing the financial means to implement their decisions nor for cleaning up the wreckage. They set as the prime goal of their actions *fiat justitia, ruat coelum* (Let there be justice, even if the heavens fall)—*that is, justice as each judge happens to see it.*

In many ways the Court more than opened the doors to easy litigation. It virtually invited a multiplication of lawsuits which for a growing number of persons involve no expense or risk to them but hold out the prospect of potentially high awards or attractive settlements from defendants threatened with huge legal costs. The number of private civil cases in federal courts of appeal multiplied seven times between 1950 and 1978 and the number of judges and lawyers in the United States almost tripled (+174%).

The Supreme Court is patently unable to cope with the over 4,000 appeals and petitions filed with it every year and accepts only four to five percent of those cases. The Court's vacillation, its inability to lay down clear rules, its tendency to send out blurred signals and follow a zigzag course, its narrow majorities which arouse hopes among petitioners, in a doubtful case, that they might succeed, encourages litigation which is swamping the lower courts. Addition of 152 judicial positions in 1978 may have helped to shorten waiting times temporarily but does not offer a long-run solution. One-fourth of the 130 cases the Supreme Court decided with written opinions in its 1979–80 term (34 cases) were settled by a 5:4 vote or with disagreement on the reasons among the majority.

Federal judges are supposed to be appointed on the basis of merit only and without regard to political affiliation. President Carter promised in his 1976 campaign that he would do so. During his term he appointed more judges than any president before him—202 to district benches, 56 to the appeals bench—well over one-third of all federal judges in office. According to one survey, only 97.8 percent of his nominees identified themselves as Democrats—which makes us wonder what a *political* selection would have looked like.[87] Many of the appointees were identified as liberal activists of an antibusiness, progovernment bent.

The situation on the Supreme Court is not quite the same as on the lower courts because Mr. Carter had no opportunity to nominate even one member. With five of the justices in their seventies, and some of them ailing, several new appointments may be forthcoming in the next few years which, conceivably, could change the Court's attitude and direction. But it might be futile to expect drastic changes such as occurred after 1937. Only a major reform of the U.S. judicial system could effectively restrain the Court's long-standing ambition to be the final arbiter, to wield the final power in policy issues brought before it.

Respect for our highest court has been shrinking. According to annual surveys by the National Opinion Research Center of the University of Michigan, the percentage of people who have "a great deal of confidence" in the U.S. Supreme Court which had been above 30% during much of the 1970s dropped to 20.5% in May 1980. In a *Los Angeles Times* poll in December 1979, the judicial system was rated lower than business and industry, the nominating process or the political system:

	Basically sound	Not too sound
Business, industry	71%	23%
Nominating process	70	27
Political system	62	35
Judicial system	49	48

Pending school busing orders may have helped to lower confidence in the judicial system.

Philip Kurland, a constitutional expert at the University of Chicago Law School, charged that frequently the courts, including the U.S. Supreme Court, "no longer look for anything patently unconstitutional. Instead they rewrite the Constitution every time they hand down a decision." Professor Kurland warned: "At some point a decision will be rendered where both the Congress and President simply say 'No.'"[88]

A situation of outright revolt against the Court could arise and lead to a reduction of its role to what it was intended to be by the framers of the Constitution. Such an outburst could be triggered, for example, by a decision to extend compulsory busing across jurisdictional lines, from cities to suburbs—as some organized groups have long demanded and a few lower courts have ordered, only to be narrowly overruled by the High Court. Some Court decisions in criminal cases have outraged concepts of justice among wide sectors of the citizenry which some day might express themselves in more than street demonstrations. It is not without reason that Supreme Court rulings which appear to be more protective of offenders than of victims are widely held responsible for a goodly share of the enormous increase in crime.

Some of the busing decisions have wrought havoc in major urban school systems, making a shambles of standards, reducing educational quality and causing a flight of much of the middle class, thereby pushing some of the cities to the brink of ruin. By upholding rules on racial preference in employment, euphemistically labeled affirmative action, the Court has been lowering competence and morale in governmental, business and educational institutions throughout the country, depressing performance and productivity.

One of the Court's recent capers which has so far attracted little attention was its March 31, 1980 decision, with a 6:3 vote, in *Branti* v. *Finkel*: it denies public officials, after a change in the governing party, the right to replace non-civil service employees, serving at their pleasure, unless the officials can prove that the employees are incompetent. Political appointees can no longer be dismissed because they belong to the "wrong" party. Justice Powell remarked in his dissent that the decision "decreases the accountability and denigrates the role of our national parties . . . . The Court's decision today thus limits the ability of the voters . . . to structure their democratic government in the way that they please."

Numerous public opinion polls over the years manifest the overwhelming opposition of the American people—often at ratios of 3:1 or better—to such rules as compulsory busing to attain racial balance in schools, racial preference in employment, and "soft" treatment of criminals. A majority of respondents in national polls favor permission for voluntary school prayer and stricter discipline by school authorities which courts have hampered; voters resent the protection given to promoters of obscenity. Most of those Court rules could not have been adopted by

Congress or state legislatures which are responsible to the people and as responsive to their wishes as the High Court appears contemptuous.

Sidney Hook lucidly defined the crucial point in *The Paradoxes of Freedom*.[89]

> The basic issue we are considering is whether the practice of judicial supremacy can be reconciled in principle with the philosophy of a democratic government. Those who defend the theory of judicial supremacy cannot easily square their position with any reasonable interpretation of the theory of democracy. . . .

Hook concluded that even if the judges "are always and completely correct, their power is patently incompatible with the assumptions of a democratic, self-governing community."

How can this vexing problem be resolved? It has been said that the Supreme Court reads the election results. Its change of direction in the late 1930s so suggests. But there is no indication that the Court was listening closely in the 1970s nor an assurance that it will do so in the 1980s. A gradual change in membership by well-chosen replacements, as vacancies occur, could help. But we have moved so far from the framers' intent of a separation of powers among three *coequal* branches and a government of limited and designated powers that a gentle fumbling with the levers cannot undo the damage wrought over more than a century. The Court has not proven adept at learning the virtue of humility.

A major study should be undertaken for the purpose of restoring the balance in our federal system of government by clearly defining the areas of decision making of the branches and levels of government and of means to effectively restrict their activities within designated boundaries. It should be staffed by the elected representatives of the people in Congress, the presidency, and the states—which also happen to be the "aggrieved" parties. The Court should of course be heard, as a *de facto* defendant, but as such not be a member of the panel. The commission should be directed to draft whatever constitutional amendments or statutes it deems necessary to attain the desired end—to assure the supremacy of the will of the people over the arrogated powers of nonelected officials.

Even the most carefully drafted definition of the roles and powers of the branches and levels of government cannot prevent disagreements to arise in the course of time on what a particular rule or prohibition means or how it is to be applied in a specific case. Who is then to decide? The courts have demonstrated that as long as they wield the exclusive and ultimate power to interpret the law, they will decide according to what they believe the law *ought* to be.

Some countries have established a constitutional court to have the final word. But who keeps the constitutional court within its boundaries? Austria found that its Supreme Court and Constitutional Court disagreed on a vital matter and this led to a constitutional crisis. One possible solution might be the establishment of a tribunal composed of representatives of both sides *directly* involved, with the chair selected by the uninvolved power or powers.

Alternatively, we could borrow a leaf from the parliamentary system. If a parliamentary government no longer controls a majority of its legislative assembly and loses on a major question of "confidence," it will call an election. We would not need to elect another Congress or president. But the choice among competing heads of a tribunal to decide a particular conflict could be made by the people themselves in a special election.

Judges could be kept within bounds by subjecting them to a periodic test at the polls. Experience in states where judges are elected for specified terms manifest that judges fail of re-election only on rare occasions. But the knowledge that he can act against the conscience and the wishes of the people only at his peril, is likely to keep a judge responsible and responsive. That—reviewing the history of the Supreme Court—may well be the most important and urgent step in restoring a balance among the three branches of the federal government.

Two Decades to the Millennium? Prophecies, Projects and Prospects

Forecasting the future is an ancient art, eagerly sought and pursued, whose practitioners for centuries were widely held in genuine awe. But it is a hazardous undertaking. The Delphian and Sibylline oracles guarded their eminent repute by clothing prophecies in arcane language, unclear in meaning to the uninitiated, open to interpretations sufficiently broad to fit any course subsequent events might take. Contemporary augurs in economic, political and related fields still master the skill of speaking in terms incomprehensible to the common man—their ability to do so often being proportionate to the number of credit hours they accumulated during years of study and apprenticeship—in words sufficiently qualified and flexible to accommodate untoward turns with which fate might attempt to trip them up. A wise statistics professors advised his students never to make a prediction for less than fifteen years, so they could keep their jobs for fourteen.

The target in this chapter, the turn of the century, lies at this writing more closely ahead than the mid-century lies behind. That does not seem to make projections more reliable but widens the freedom to interpret, reinterpret or misinterpret events of the past three decades.

There is a seemingly irresistible attraction to pin our dreams and hopes and expectations on a millennial year which, over the course of history, so many have visualized as the realization of the romantic notion of *the millennium*. It was so a thousand years ago when huge masses waited and prepared themselves for the Second Coming or the Thousand Year Reich and it is so again when there is much speculation about the year 2000. Of course, most of the scholarly studies that have been undertaken are more down to earth and some are somewhat disappointing to those who harbor great hopes. Herman Kahn and Anthony Wiener wrote in 1967: "We would be willing to wager small sums, at even odds, that the next third of a century will contain fewer surprises than either of the preceding thirds (i.e., that in this respect the world is more like 1815 than 1914)."[90] Nor did the comprehensive study of the *Commission on the Year 2000*, sponsored by the Carnegie Foundation, foresee many fundamental or spectacular changes or developments.[91]

Barely a dozen years later Herman Kahn seemed less eager to make the wager he had offered in 1967. He wrote that "in the 1980s . . . we will be a bit more disaster-prone than we have been in recent history," and referred to the "sobering '80s" because the United States and the developed world had "entered a period that I describe as an *epoque of malaise*."[92]

The 1980 report *Global 2000* prepared for President Carter by the State Department and the Council on Environmental Quality described the future in somber tones and "reads like something out of *The Empire Strikes Back*."[93]

As we move closer to the magical year, utopian expectations of the millennium seem to be increasingly transformed into an attitude that can more properly be termed *fin de siècle*, a sense of decline or doom. It is what Lance Liebman called "the negativist reaction to the Promethean fallacy . . . the new pessimism that exists concerning the human capacity to achieve social ends" because of "the failure of domestic reform in the 1960s."[94]

It is what Herbert Gans in 1972 diagnosed as "The American Malaise," as the consequence of a recent "widening of the gap between these expectations and their achievement."[95]

The term malaise came into broader use after President Carter employed it in an address on July 15, 1979, to describe a "crisis of the American spirit," a "crisis of confidence." It reflected a widespread sense of an economic, social and political decline as evidenced by the growing weakness and impotence of the United States abroad, by roaring inflation, tightening energy supplies, multiplying crime and increasing governmental interference with traditions and individual freedom.

In the introduction to his *History of the Idea of Progress*,[96] Robert Nisbet wrote: "No single idea has been more important than, perhaps as important as, the idea of progress in Western civilization for nearly three thousand years." Later in the book he complains "that Western faith in the dogma of progress is waning rapidly in all levels and spheres in this final part of the twentieth century." He blames this less on wars and economic afflictions than on the "fateful if less dramatic erosion of all the fundamental intellectual and spiritual premises upon which the idea of progress has rested throughout its long history."

In the book's last chapter Nisbet refers to negative implications. "It is not simply a matter of growing disillusionment with government and bureaucracy; fundamentally, it is declining faith in politics as a way of mind and life."

Calling the signal decline in America and Europe of faith in the value and promise of Western civilization "most devastating" he wrote:

> What has succeeded faith is, on the vivid and continually enlarging record, guilt, alienation and indifference. An attitude—that we as a nation and as a Western civilization can in retrospect see ourselves as having contaminated, corrupted, and despoiled other peoples in the world, and that for having done this we should feel guilty, ashamed, and remorseful—grows and widens among Americans especially, and even more expecially among young Americans of the middle class. For good reasons or bad, the lay clerisy of the West—the intelligentsia that began in the eighteenth century to succeed the clergy as the dominant class so far as citizen's beliefs are concerned—devotes a great deal of its time to lament, self-flagellation and harsh judgment upon an entire history: Western history.

James Burham in 1968 called the attitudes and policies of Europeans and Americans *Suicide of the West* and Andrew Hacker predicted in his book *The End of the American Era* that "only a few decades remain to complete the era America will have known as a nation."[97]

Former President Nixon, whose foreign policy initiatives stand in favorable contrast to those of some of his predecessors and successors warned in his latest book *The Real War*:

> The central thesis of this book is that the West, today, has crossed the threshold of a period of acute crisis in which its survival into the twenty-first century is directly at stake. We have the material capacity, the economic and technological strength, to prevail—which means to main-

tain our freedom and to avert a major war. But the capacity alone is not enough. Sir Robert Thompson, the British expert on guerrilla warfare, has trenchantly defined national power as manpower plus applied resources, *times* will. We have the resources and the manpower. Have we the will to use them?[98]

Reviewing the book, Aram Bakshian, Jr., remarked, "The tragedy of Richard Nixon is that, thanks both to his own failings as a domestic leader and the hysteria of his foes, his valid warning of coming peril is likely to fall on deaf ears."[99]

The gradual decline in general confidence, in optimism, during the 1970s can be traced year by year in the annual budget reviews prepared by the Brookings Institution, leading to the dire prediction in the opening of its symposium volume *Setting National Priorities: Agenda for the 1980s* that "the prospects for achieving a healthy economy and maintaining peace are not good" (p. 1).

While the book's authors attribute the crisis largely to incompetence in government, to failures of incumbents, it is likely that the whole thrust of governmental policy more than management and procedure are at the root of the problem. Government, as William Kristol well pointed out in a review of the mentioned Brookings volume[100] needs more than competent managers, it requires "a fundamental redirection of our politics down a different road."

It is, of course, possible that the recent pessimistic projections for the "sobering eighties" and beyond turn out to be as far "off" as the more optimistic expectations in the "soaring sixties" were. Or—could they just be more realistic?

Projections during the early 1960s tended to overestimate the size of the future U.S. population, slightly overrated economic growth, and were overly optimistic regarding the tranquility that would pervade the nation and the rest of the globe. Most foresaw correctly that there would be no worldwide conflagration but some minor wars, though none expected the deep involvement of the United States in the decade's most troublesome armed conflict in Southeast Asia, nor our severe setbacks in other parts of the world. They did not predict the crime explosion, the youth and drug revolt, the campus, urban and racial riots, and few, save those with a special interest, expected the tidal wave of social legislation. Where they went wrong the farthest: none predicted inflation to be as steep, persistent, and worldwide as it has been and still is and few thought that domestic government spending would grow as fast or as much as it did. None expected the precipitous decline in American strength and standing as manifested in a sequence of debacles from the Bay of Pigs to Vietnam and to the Iran-Afghanistan events.

No economist predicted in the early 1970s the global wave of high-rate inflation beginning in 1973, the doubling to quintupling of the prices of oil and other major commodities on the world's markets. That experience with a clouded crystal ball, not the first of its kind, should caution us on numerical forecasts for the years ahead.

Most forecasts are prepared by projecting historical trends into the future, with some adjustments, up or down, according to the author's intuition. Trends are of course powerfully influenced by public policies, not necessarily by the goals and intentions of the policymakers, but by their effects. The prophets of the welfare state a few decades ago foresaw a glowing future ahead in consequence of their programs. Those programs' failure to produce the promised results has inevitably dampened popular expectations for the future. The question is: Will those policies be sufficiently changed and if so, can such changes undo the damage already done? Unforeseen—and perhaps unforeseeable—events in the rest of the world inevitably have an impact on American fortunes. Until not so long ago the United States, by its strength and demonstrated intentions, was able to influence and even shape world events, to act powerfully to produce desired results. It did not, as it recently seems to, largely react to initiatives taken by others.

The United States, and possibly the Western world, may have passed a turning point in their history, where the road no longer leads up, but down. This makes it even more hazardous to predict what the future may bring. We can only project discernible trends, qualifying them by their dependence on the policies that may be pursued by the United States and by other nations. Here are some likely developments in terms of population and the economy.

Trends and Prospects:

a) Zero Population Growth?[101]

From a high of 25 births per 1000 population in 1955 the birthrate dropped to about 15 where it remained for over a decade, with only faint recent signs of a slight upturn. More significantly, the total fertility rate, that is, the number of children an average woman bears during her lifetime, slid from 3.8 in 1957 to 2.5 in 1970 and stabilized at about 1.8 in 1975. The replacement level, the fertility rate at which the population would replace itself within a lifetime, is 2.1 children per woman. In other words, the United States population would in due time, at current rates, become stationary—*zero population growth*—and then start to decline, if it had no net immigration.

That the U.S. population currently shows a *natural* increase of about 1.5 million a year—the difference between 3.4 million live births and 1.9 million deaths—is mainly the result of an unusual and temporary age distribution, due to the baby boom of the early postwar years. The fifteen- to thirty-four-year-old population group jumped from 60 million in 1970 to 80 million in 1980, a growth of one-third while population above and below those ages grew only 3%. This passing concentration in the reproductive ages postpones zero population growth.

Lowered fertility is related to the growing labor force participation of women, and especially of married women. Above all, it manifests changed attitudes among the American people and less than exuberant—not to say pessimistic—expectations about the future.

The figures above exclude immigration. Net immigration has been averaging 400,000 a year for over a decade, and the Census Bureau uses that figure for projections. Political and economic refugees from Southeast Asia, Cuba, Haiti and other parts of the world raised immigration to nearly 800,000 in 1980. Those totals do not include illegal immigration, mostly from Mexico, which has been estimated at half a million a year or more. Illegal Mexican immigrants now in the United States may number more than 5 million. The Census Bureau has difficulty counting them because many prefer not to be identified. If that influx is permitted to continue, it will have a distinct impact on the United States, not merely on the size of its population.

The 1980 Census counted 226.5 million, an 11.4% increase over 1970. It is conceivable that up to 3 million, largely illegal immigrants may have been missed.

The latest long-range projections place the population in the year 2000 at 260 million (*Current Population Reports*, Series P-25, No. 796).

U.S. population could be far higher than 260 million by the turn of the century if immigration from Mexico, legal and illegal, continues at its level of recent years, considering the Chicanos' high fecundity. To be sure, most of the newcomers work hard for their keep—as immigrants have done throughout American history—which is why they are being hired and often sought after by employers. They contribute substantially to the economy by their labor and even through taxes and fill many types of jobs which Americans often are reluctant to take. But they reduce the number of openings available for unskilled or low-skilled labor which makes our un-employment rates run higher than they otherwise would. Nor is the cost of schools, medical services, welfare inconsequential, because of the large and uncontrolled numbers. European countries prevent illegal "guest workers" from coming and remaining by imposing fines on employers for hiring those without work permits. That has been suggested in the United States but is a controversial proposition.

U.S. Department of Education rules which direct public schools to instruct children with a foreign language background in their native language—rather than attempt to accelerate their acquisition of fluency in English—will delay and partially obstruct attempts to assimilate and absorb the newcomers and their children. Their concentration in a few areas will pave the way from so-called bilingual education to bilingual states and bilingual regions of the United States. Hispanics may, within a few decades, become our largest ethnic minority with a growing likelihood of serious clashes with the currently largest minority, the blacks, and with other ethnic groups. The Miami riots in the summer of 1980 may turn out to have been only a gentle warning.

Government policy itself influences birthrates, particularly among the lowest income groups, through various types of welfare and social services, in which the approval and size of benefits are contingent on the presence and number of children in the household. Low-income families have more children than middle-class and high-income families, a fact which may have distinct long-range economic and social consequences.

Population does not grow at uniform rates throughout the country, largely because of internal migration. Almost all of the population increase in the 1970s took place in the sunbelt, and this is likely to continue for a long time. In itself, that may not constitute a serious problem but the urban-rural movement will.

In 1960, the U.S. population was almost evenly divided between central cities, suburbs, and rural areas (including small cities), with a third of the total in each. Subsequent shifts reduced the share of the central cities by 1980 to 27 percent and raised the suburbs to 40 percent. The number of whites in central cities shrank by 11 percent, the number of blacks increased 9 percent. If welfare benefits and social services continue to expand, cities will become increasingly attractive to persons and families with low-income capacity and low ambition. Furthermore, if compulsory school busing continues under current rules, the flight from the cities is likely to accelerate further. Should busing be extended to cover entire metropolitan areas, that flight may sharply decline. While the number of whites in the suburbs grew by 13% between 1960 and 1980, the number of blacks rose 47%. In other words, not only whites flee the cities, but also the black middle-class. American cities are likely to face growing difficulties of all types, and some cities eventual ruin, unless current governmental policies undergo a decisive change.

We may, therefore, conclude that while population growth and population shifts can be plotted on a chart by extending past trends, they will be significantly affected by governmental policies which no one can predict with any degree of certainty for decades ahead. This is even more significant with regard to economic trends.

b) Sustained Economic Growth?[102]

Attempts at estimating future economic growth commonly begin with the fundamentals: working-age population, labor force participation, productivity.

Total population will continue to increase by approximately one percent per annum over the next two decades and beyond but will expand faster if the influx from Mexico remains unrestrained. The percentage which persons in their main productive years, 20 to 64 years, constitutes of the whole population, stood at 58% in 1950, gradually declined to 52% by 1960, due to the baby boom, and subsequently recovered to 57% in 1979. It is expected to remain stable for at least the next two decades.

Labor force participation—which the Bureau of Labor Statistics computes as a percentage of the population 16 years and over—has increased from 59.9% in 1950 to 64.3% in 1980. This is the composite of two divergent trends. Labor force participation of men declined from 86.4% to 78.0% while the rate for women jumped from 33.9% to 51.7%. Within the short span of 30 years the ratio in labor force participation rates between men and women fell from 1:2.5 to 1:1.5, a drastic change. Male labor force attachment declined largely because of earlier withdrawal in response to more generous public and private retirement benefits as well as a result of growing affluence in general. Some might say that men could afford to work less as women worked more and increased their contribution to household income.

Women have increasingly been seeking gainful employment and are able to hold full-time or part-time jobs because of an easing of household chores—more appliances, shopping conveniences, prepared foods, etc., lower rates of childbearing, a widening of occupational and promotional opportunities and, last but not least, changed cultural and family attitudes and patterns. The female share of the labor force grew from 27 percent in the immediate postwar period to 42 percent in 1980. The upward trend will in all likelihood continue, possibly at a slower rate. Women could conceivably constitute nearly half the labor force by the end of the century. Whether male labor force participation rates will stabilize—or even turn upward—may depend on the fate of proposals to raise the age at which public retirement benefits become available and on the severity of the penalties for concurrent earnings and for early retirement.

The aggregate labor force participation rate, which in 1980 stood at 64.3% of the population 16 years and over, may well keep inching up, but is not likely to reach or even approach 70% in the foreseeable future. Weekly working hours in private nonagricultural industries have been sliding from an average of 39.8 in 1950 to 35.2 in 1980, a shrinkage of 1.5 hours per decade. This partially reflects a shortening of the workweek. More important is a shift from goods-producing to service-producing industries—retail and wholesale trade, finance, state and local government—whose employees typically labor fewer hours. Those trends are likely to continue.

To predict the unemployment rate for a year or even six months ahead is a rash undertaking. A comparison of predictions in the President's annual Economic Report and in its review by the congressional Joint Economic Committee with subsequent actual results inspires only limited confidence in our computers' economic sophistication. To project unemployment rates for a decade or two would be an idle undertaking. But it may be worthwhile to consider some of the major factors that will influence the rate.

The unemployment rate has shown an upward trend. It averaged 4.5% and 4.8% in the 1950s and 1960s respectively, 6.2% in the 1970s, and stood at 7.4% in December 1980. These figures are not directly comparable with much lower rates reported by many European countries because of a different—and loose—definition of unemployment in United States practice.

Numerous factors are responsible for our seemingly high unemployment which because of its human, economic and political implications is given wide publicity by our media and is a focal subject in public discussions of economic conditions and policies. Leading among influential factors are our tax and spending policies which generally are egalitarian, antibusiness and anti-capital formation, burdensome regulations, minimum wage laws, contractual wage scales which adversely affect the competitive position of U.S. industries, ever-increasingly generous unemployment and welfare benefits that make gainful employment a second-best choice for many low-productive persons, nonenforcement of immigration laws. It is hard to see why, without drastic changes in public policy, unemployment rates would move to and remain below a 6% to 7% level.

It should be said, however, that involuntary unemployment is not as high as Bureau of Labor Statistics reports make it appear, nor are resulting hardships as severe as is often asserted. Much or most of the reported unemployment is not due to inadequate demand (spending) by consumers and government, as is widely claimed. Overtime hours have almost consistently been running at a greater percentage of total working hours than the simultaneous unemployment rate. Besides the 7% and up addition to normal hours by overtime, close to five percent of hours worked are accounted for by "moonlighting" of persons holding second jobs. Metropolitan daily newspapers regularly carry many pages of "vacant positions" advertising, and state employment offices list hundreds of thousands of openings for janitors, dishwashers, maids and similar low-skilled jobs which go begging because they are menial and do not pay enough to attract applicants.

Much or most of our reported unemployment is not due to lack of work to be done. Some of it is frictional—temporary, during job changes. More of it relates to an imbalance between a worker's productivity—the value of his output—and the wages he demands or would have to be paid. (This is discussed in greater detail on pp. 245–60.)

In one respect the employment picture looks brighter than it has for some time. Based on the number of births, 42 million Americans, a record total, turned 18 in the 1970s and competed for jobs. In the 1980s only 38 million and in the 1990s 33 million will reach an age at which they are likely to enter the labor market. That should relieve pressure for jobs substantially and help reduce unemployment, especially among new entrants to the labor force.

The most serious and complex problem, however, contributing heavily to unemployment and inflation, is the precipitous fall in productivity growth which began in the late 1960s and has haunted our economy ever since. Productivity growth rates have declined in other industrial nations also, but they were and are running higher there than in America.

Between 1947 (earliest year for which data are available) and 1967, output per man-hour in the private business sector increased at an annual average of 3%. The rate declined and averaged only about half that in the succeeding ten years. Productivity improved a mere 0.6% in 1978, turned negative in 1979 and so remained in 1980. The seriousness and implications of this unprecedented development were quickly recognized. For the first time in twenty years, the annual report of the congressional Joint Economic Committee in 1979 was endorsed by the members of both political parties when it focused on the need to improve productivity. The committee's 1980 report was no less emphatic about the imperative need to restore growth to productivity.

There is no general agreement on the causes and possible cures of the ill. Some blame workers, some management and others government. Deteriorating work habits, inadequate education by the schools, indolence, lack of industriousness or union rules are sometimes cited, usually with evidence more anecdotal than statistical. Some blame management for lack of enterprise and efficiency, for inadequate or wrongheaded planning, failure to modernize plants and methods. There may be something to all of these charges. But most of the responsibility lies with counterproductive government policies.

Productivity growth rates began to deteriorate in the late 1960s and early 1970s. This coincided with a major expansion in government spending, the start of huge back-to-back budgetary deficits, initiation or maturation of large social programs, and a multiplication of regulatory activities. By all appearances, this was no mere coincidence. It was a matter of cause and effect.

An avalanche of regulations in the 1970s placed exorbitant additional burdens on business enterprises, large and small. Many of the new rules were intended to help improve environment, health or safety; several were experiments in social engineering. Some turned out to be effective, many proved futile. Few were based on impartial cost-analyses. Completion of the $120 million Tellico dam in Tennessee was stopped when it was claimed that it might jeopardize a small local species of fish.

The aggregate cost of the new regulations had a devastating impact on productivity. Established methods of hiring the most competent applicants and promoting the most efficient workers to supervisory positions had to take a backseat when government superimposed higher priorities for employment actions. This not only affected staff capacity and productivity negatively but had an adverse impact on employee morale generally because qualification and performance were no longer the final criteria for career advancement. Numerous disincentives built into our tax laws act against improved productivity. The growing incidence of property crime, a result of government's failure to fight it effectively and prevent it, imposes heavy costs on business which reduce productivity. It is estimated that the likelihood of a criminal's going to prison was cut from 5.7% to 1.2% within the past twenty years (see p. 283).

Inadequate productivity growth is a potent factor in accelerating inflation. Rapid inflation, in turn, reduces productivity. Under our tax system, depreciation is computed on historical costs which, in inflationary times, make insufficient allowance for the higher cost of replacement items. This delays and may prevent the installation of modern and more efficient plants and equipment. The crucial factor may well be inadequate attractiveness of industrial investment because *aftertax* profits are too low.

Stagnation of productivity could be overcome in the next few years and a modest growth resumed. A return to 3% annual growth rates, however, appears doubtful. Major changes in some government policies will be required if annual improvements of as much as 2% are to be reached. It will also depend on the extent to which inflation will be controlled in the next few years and reduced to more tolerable levels.

For many years, inflation has been our most serious domestic problem. Numerous statements by national leaders across a broad political spectrum and dozens of opinion polls confirm this as a national consensus. It is equally obvious that though the American people want to end or at least sharply cut the inflation rate, they want other things more. No broad popular movement has arisen or drawn much support with a program that would effectively reduce the inflation rate to anything approaching its level of fifteen or twenty years ago.

Every president since World War II has denounced inflation in scathing language. Eisenhower called it "a robber and thief" when it stood at a mere 1.4% per annum and some of his successors designated fighting inflation as their "top economic priority." But within the past three decades the rate has been higher in every succeeding presidential term except one.

INFLATION RATE BY PRESIDENTIAL TERMS, 1952 TO 1980

President	Years	Increase in Consumer Price Index
Eisenhower I	1952–56	+ 2.4%
Eisenhower II	1956–60	9.0
Kennedy (Johnson)	1960–64	4.7
Johnson	1964–68	12.2
Nixon	1968–72	20.3
Nixon-Ford	1972–76	36.1
Carter	1976–80	45.3

To call the object of our national dislike *inflation* is a misnomer. What most people call inflation, is a general rise in prices. It actually is a shrinkage in the value of the dollar, measured by the Consumer Price Index.

At the 1980 annual rate of 12.4%, a dollar would be worth a nickel in 25 years, and about 1.6 cents in 35 years, the length of an average working life. Which does not make saving over one's lifetime, at least in dollars, seem to be a profitable proposition.

Most people regard the idea preposterous that the current or even higher inflation rates could continue for years and decades. But far worse has happened in many countries over the past 1200 years, ever since paper money was first used by the Tang dynasty in China's *Golden Age* and soon abused. There is no reason to ridicule the idea that long-lasting runaway inflation could occur here. It could happen unless a great deal is done to prevent this from happening.

Inflation is not an economic illness. It is the symptom of an illness, of an imbalance between our desires and our willingness to pay for the cost of what we want. So we create artificial money, a poisonous drug, and feed it to the body economic. Inflation is an expansion of the money supply which has been at the core of every lasting inflation in history. To avoid semantic confusion, we may as well use the word inflation to mean what nowadays is generally meant by it: a general price rise.

Disproportionate expansion of money supply is at the root of every major inflation. Many leading economists conclude therefrom that every inflation can be reduced and ended by controlling the money supply. That is undoubtedly true—in theory. Whether that theory can be carried out in a country with a freely elected government—without other types of simultaneous action—is another question.

After high-rate inflation has lasted for a considerable time, large sectors of the economy and millions of people have at least partially adjusted to it in current actions and in preparations for the future. If at that point money were suddenly tightly controlled, it might arrest further price rises. But hardships to wide sections of the population by plant closings and layoffs would be so severe that public pressure would become irresistible to "relax" controls. Monetary authorities in many countries, including our Federal Reserve Board, have repeatedly attempted to get "tough," hold money tight and let interest rates rise. But when large budgetary deficits had to be covered and "inflated" payrolls financed, when complaints about excessive interest rates became deafening, they yielded, sooner or later, to what seemed to be the political reality at the time.

To be sure, inflation cannot be lastingly cured without a consistent control of the money supply. But such action is not very likely to succeed unless several other economic steps are taken which may be politically difficult. Is there an easier alternative?

Many times in history, powerful rulers have attempted to prevent prices from rising by imposing price controls, usually with draconic penalties. Unless they also restricted the quantity of money—whether paper or, prior to its invention, debased metal coins—it never worked for long. Government price control is like putting a tight lid on a boiling pot while keeping it on a hot stove. It will do nicely for a while, then blow up.

Americans have yet to learn that lesson. Well over half the respondents to public opinion polls have consistently expressed support for price controls. It is a very appealing idea and at an age when every problem is expected to be solved by government edict, the popularity of price controls is understandable. But price controls, when kept on for more than a short period, inevitably lead to growing scarcities, black markets and eventual breakdown of the controls—and of much of the economy.

Over the past decade or two we have been trying to learn to live with inflation instead of doing what is needed to end it. "If you can't lick 'em, join 'em." About half of the American people now get some form of automatic income adjustment by an escalator clause. Two-thirds of American families own homes and most of them enjoy seeing their equity rapidly multiply as the remaining mortgage debt becomes worth less and less and monthly payments absorb a shrinking share of their paychecks. That is why so many people are buying real estate with small down payments or are acquiring other tangible values—which is precisely what is disproportionately driving up the prices of homes, antiques, coins and other "tangible" items. It is a game at which everybody is trying to beat everybody else—and many of the losers don't find out until much later that they have been had.

What then offers a possible solution to the inflation problem and what are the prospects for it? It is now widely recognized that there is no realistic chance of bringing inflation under control as long as the government incurs huge budgetary deficits, year after year. Until not so long ago a belief was widespread that deficit spending and money creation would not produce inflation at a time of sizable unemployment. There was supposed to be a trade-off between inflation and unemployment. We could have lower unemployment if we tolerated higher inflation.

We have since learned a few things—that in a highly structured and rigid society, with wages and most other payments flexible only in one direction—up—we can enjoy—more or less—high-rate inflation and unemployment at the same time. We call it stagflation. We also learned—though some may yet have to learn it—that trying to cure structural unemployment by easing money supply and inflating demand will not, in the long run, reduce unemployment but drive up prices.

The simple truth is now widely accepted that our chances for controlling inflation are slim unless the government budget is balanced. Monetary authorities cannot simply tell the government to find other sources of financing or declare itself bankrupt. This is politically impossible. Moreover, if the government absorbed all or most savings available in the money market, how would business and private needs be financed?

Balancing the budget is easier promised than accomplished—as several presidents have found out. How conceivably it can be done will be discussed in the next and last section of this book.

A major share of all payrolls is now automatically escalated by the CPI and most other payrolls are similarly raised. The demand for such adjustments is understandable because everybody wants at least to maintain his standard of living, and, if possible, improve it. Hence the push of labor unions to "catch up" with inflation. But living standards can be raised only if productivity rises at a respectable rate throughout the economy. Otherwise the recipients just get more dollars that buy less.

A general wage rise boosts the cost base for the goods and services turned out and is inevitably reflected in higher prices—absent a sufficiently higher productivity. Big steel companies in 1980 approved a contract giving steelworkers average pay increases of 30% to 37% over three years. First-year wage increases of construction workers negotiated during the first nine months of 1980 averaged 13.9% and similar outcomes are expected in 1981. How can we expect prices not to keep going up at a rapid rate?[103]

Why don't the corporations just take the higher wage cost out of their profits? Because profits have already been at too low a level to attract sufficient investment for expanding and modernizing industrial plants—to improve productivity and create more jobs. Figure 14 shows that between 1952 and 1978 the corporation profits dropped from 12.4% to 9.7% of national income while employee compensation increased from 68.5% to 75.6% of national income. The share of proprietors fell even more sharply. There is no way we can have a vibrant and growing economy when enterprise profits are inadequate to attract capital.

By trying to isolate major segments of the U.S. population from the impact of inflation, we reduce their motivation and thereby their effort to fight inflation. We cannot hope to muster the political strength to end inflation if we make people more comfortable with it. Only if people are sufficiently uncomfortable will they be willing to forgo some of the government spending that is a major cause of deficits and inflation. Only if industries do not have to face a payroll next year that is, say, 10% higher than last year's can they forgo boosting their prices to make up for higher costs. Inflation will continue as long as wage rates rise faster than productivity.

It is of course impossible to eliminate wage and benefit indexing at one blow or even a large part of it. It would have to be a slow adjustment over a period of years just as the ending of inflation will have to come gradually—with a balanced budget and tight monetary control coming first.

This is a difficult course because organized labor will demand that prices be stabilized before we can begin to stabilize wage rates. The political problem seems unsurmountable. But the economic problem must somehow be resolved. Unless we break the spiral somewhere, it will continue up indefinitely.

The United States which historically was a major steel and automobile exporter has in recent years become a large net importer of steel products and automobiles. One-fourth of the new cars now sold in the U.S. are of foreign manufacture. We import four times as much in iron and steel mill products as we export. With labor accounting for 84% of corporate income (see p. 97), the cause of our competitive disadvantage is not hard to identify: auto- and steelworkers are overpaid in relation to their productivity. A sizable segment of American labor has priced itself out of the market.

Nearly a century ago, the United States adopted antitrust legislation prohibiting "conspiracy in restraint of trade." To protect the public against overcharges by business cartels, Congress and the Department of Justice have been tightening antitrust enforcement against big corporations ever since. But they have not acted against "conspiracy in restraint of trade" committed by organized labor. Quite the contrary, they have encouraged and aided unionization by labor laws and executive intervention although employee compensation accounts for from three-fourths to four-fifths of production costs and therefore inevitably is a more powerful determinant of prices than corporate profits.

In much of the rest of the industrial world both, business and labor, are organized and cartelized. They negotiate on a par level. In some of the economically most successful countries such as Germany, Japan and Austria, labor and management accept the fact that they must "either hang together or will hang separately" and find a common meeting ground. Their trade unions make more moderate demands and settle for wage rates that keep the prices of their products internationally competitive. This commonsense approach, more than any other single factor, explains the "*wirtschaftswunder*," the *economic miracle* of economic growth, low unemployment and low inflation in those countries.

The U.S. government has interfered with market forces and thrown its weight in the scales of labor for half a century. That does not make for balanced economic forces—and we are paying a high price for it. I do not argue for imposing antitrust rules on organized labor. But I do suggest that a better balance could be found between the two forces, despite an obvious imbalance in the number of votes they can deliver.

Steel- and autoworkers' unions, the third and fourth largest unions in the country—exceeded in size only by teamsters and teachers—succeeded, at least in part. They cannot force foreign consumers to buy overpriced American products. But they have been trying their best to prevent American consumers from being able to buy the less expensive cars and steel products of other countries.

The United States, the world's leading industrial country, is also, now more than ever, its largest grain exporter. American agriculture is recognized as the most productive on the globe. One reason that it has remained so highly competitive is that there are only weak organizations of fieldworkers in the United States and no large or national labor unions in agriculture. Were it otherwise, American consumers who now devote a smaller share of their income to food than the residents of any other country, would be paying higher prices for their nutrition. Also, we probably would not be exporting so much grain to the four corners of the world.

What does all of this imply for the future course of inflation? That depends on forces which no one can predict with certainty or a high degree of probability.

Unless progress is made in at least some of the directions which I have suggested, high-rate inflation may be with us for a long time. Rates might even increase, as they have for the past two decades. There is at least a good chance at this time that self-restraint on the part of government and major sectors of the economy may within a reasonable time bring inflation rates below a two-digit level where they might stabilize. A return to the inflation rates of the 1950s or early 1960s does not seem to be in the cards without action which at the present time has only an outside chance.

What does this mean for future economic growth?

Over the past half century, going back to 1929 the starting year of our economic statistics, Gross National Product (GNP) has *in constant dollars* multiplied over 4.5-fold, for an average 20-year growth rate of 84%, barely above a 3% annual rate:

GROSS NATIONAL PRODUCT IN CONSTANT (1972) DOLLARS,
Selected Years, 1929–1979

	Billions	Percent Increase at 20-year rate
1929	$ 314.6	
1949	490.7	+ 56%
1969	1,078.8	120
1979	1,431.6	76

With GNP in 1980 at $2,626 billion, a 3% annual growth would place GNP in the year 2000 at 4.7 trillion (1980 $).

That could be achieved *if*

the federal budget is in approximate balance for most of the next twenty years, monetary supply rises at a constant moderate level between 3% and 4% p.a., no unforeseeable world events occur that threaten or upset the balance of power or peace, and at least some of the options on taxes and spending I advanced in this book are carried out.

With our tax, spending, budget and other economic policies that prevailed in 1980 the rate of economic growth will be much lower than 3% and the GNP in the millennial year substantially below $4.7 trillion (1980 $).

Twilight of the Welfare State?

Six years ago I described developments in the public sphere between 1952 and 1972 in *The Growth of American Government.* I tried to present, as clearly and as forcefully as I could, the enormous increase in governmental expenditures and employment, the multiplication of activities and concentration of power in Washington during the two decades, and their consequences. Projecting trends into the future, I predicted that the growth of public spending for domestic purposes and the related expansion of the bureaucracy could not possibly go on much longer at their 1952–1972 rates, certainly not for the rest of the century. I did not expect an actual cutback in money or personnel but foresaw a gradual and increasing decline in their rates of growth.

With regard to the precipitous drop in the share of resources for national security in the preceding two decades and a widespread mentality which supported it, I thought in 1974 that I detected "a few signs that attitude may be changing."

In this volume the period under review was extended by six years and covers the span from 1952 to 1978. The data indicate that domestic public programs continued to expand, at a substantially slower rate, in the second half of the 1970s. Attitudes toward the defense establishment changed among the American public and in Congress (in that order) and now favor substantial increases to strengthen the preparedness of our Armed Forces.

The November 1980 elections for Congress and the presidency manifested a belief among the American people that government had gone too far in expanding and multiplying its myriad of social programs, that it had excessively tightened interference with or control over the activities and lives of Americans, and that national attention and priorities should revert to where they had been for most of the country's history: the nation's security and its protection against potential threats to our vital interests.

Opinion surveys indicate that while the public wants relief from heavy taxes and demands an end to high-rate inflation, it does not necessarily favor a wholesale dismantling of the welfare state nor sharp cutbacks in some of its major programs to whose benefits it has become accustomed. It appears evident that people expect a contemporary state to perform many or most of the services which the several levels of government now provide. But some programs can be and must be slimmed. Restraint on public spending is the most important and focal part of an effective anti-inflation program.

Many governmental activities have gone beyond necessity or justification and need to be trimmed back or eliminated. Numerous programs fell far short of what their protagonists had promised and produced few positive results that would justify their costs. They offer little hope of ever being able to "earn their keep." Some programs—too many among those initiated in recent decades—have proven counterproductive, wasted enormous amounts of taxpayers' money and aggravated rather than alleviated existing social and economic problems.

There is no reason why many or most programs providing domestic services should be designed, mandated, supervised by the federal government. Its officials are already overburdened with other duties which by nature or necessity require national direction. The states, cities and other local governments can more properly and efficiently establish and manage programs providing local services in keeping with the widely varying wishes of their citizens, under appropriate financial arrangements among levels of government.

Experience has shown that programs, good or bad, once established, soon create vested interests which seem virtually impossible to dislodge. This is particularly true of activities which are largely or wholly financed from federal funds and seem to the local taxpayer and public official to come for free.

Frontal attacks on programs which distribute money or provide services to large sections of the public, even if costs are excessive and general benefits minimal or nonexistent, are almost always defeated by the determined resistance of special interest groups. Nor is Congress eager to "shoot Santa Claus." This explains much of the enormous expansion in domestic federal expenditures, creating huge deficits which fuel inflation.

If restraint is our goal, then it seems logical and proper to reduce expenditures first and then, as a reward, lower taxes. That strategy has been tried time and again and seems to run into stone walls. Political realities suggest different approaches: cut taxes first—which is always popular—and tie this in with an ironclad requirement to balance the federal budget. Since no Congress can bind a succeeding Congress, this would have to be done by a constitutional amendment which Congress cannot override except under specified emergency conditions.

Congress itself is not anxious to tie its own hands. It has turned a deaf ear to proposals of a constitutional amendment to balance the budget. Therefore, another approach may have to be used: the calling of a constitutional convention by a vote of two-thirds (34) of the states. The convention could then draft an amendment and submit it for ratification by three-fourths (38) of the states. About thirty state legislatures have approved the call for a constitutional convention in recent years. Only a few more states are needed to make the request mandatory upon Congress.

A constitutional amendment could require not only the balancing of the federal budget but also limit federal taxes or federal expenditures to a fixed percentage of the Gross National Product (GNP). Federal revenues increased from 18.6% of GNP in 1960 to 20.6% in 1980, federal expenditures from 18.5% of GNP to 23.0%. A lid on spending rather than on taxes would thus appear to be a more effective means of restraining further growth though a limit on taxes would probably be more popular.

The addition of such an amendment to the Constitution would be a move toward reducing inflation to a tolerable level. It might have only a limited impact on the inflation rate—at a time when the coal industry grants its workers a 38% boost in wages and benefits over the life of a 40-month contract. But it would limit the financial ability of the federal government to expand its activities and to exert a tightening control over the country and its citizens. It would not by itself dismantle the *welfare state*. It could dismantle the *wayward* welfare state, the excessive and wasteful extension of the federal government into areas that should be left to state and local governments and to individual initiative and responsibility.

A constitutional amendment restraining further fiscal growth at the national level would leave citizens free to expand services in their states or communities if they are willing to pay their cost. State and local taxation is limited only by whatever restrictions citizens imposed on their own governments. It can be loosened or tightened by local decisions.

Congress would still have discretion to allocate its huge revenues as it sees fit—unless initiative and referendum, now used only at the state level, were also authorized at the federal level.

Passage of a constitutional amendment to limit federal spending could stabilize expenditures at their current percentage of GNP. But even without such an amendment the growth rate of federal expenditures is likely to decline gradually barring international or political developments which cannot now be foreseen.

As it is, the magnitude and nature of governmental activities in the decades to come will be decided by the American people and by their representatives in the Congress on their philosophical attitudes on three major issues:

1) *Strong or Weak National Defense*

Over the past quarter century the strength of our national defense has been declining as the share of resources allocated to it was reduced to a fraction. Our defense establishment is now, according to the judgment of many military experts, inferior to the military forces of the Soviet Union and inadequate to meet the challenges it may be faced with at any time. The strength of an army is not necessarily determined by the amount of money spent on it. But it is evident that without a major increase in the percentage of GNP and the federal budget allocated to the Armed Forces, the security of the United States will remain inadequate and in dire peril.

2) *Rewards by a Free Market vs. Redistribution of Income*

Redistribution of income through taxes and governmental spending to create a more egalitarian society has characterized public policy in recent decades. It has reduced incentives and motivation for individual initiative and prevented maximum economic expansion. Those who view rewards and punishments by the market to be purely fortuitous, devoid of personal merit, and grossly unjust, will continue to push for stronger redistribution through tax, transfer and social service programs. Choice between the alternative goals will decide whether Americans will in years to come grow richer—though economic differences will remain—or whether they will more equally share far lower resources.

3) *Freedom vs. Government*

If governmental activity continues to expand, as it has for decades, aiming to deal with and resolve most major social ills by appropriation of funds, intensification of service programs and regulation, the freedom of the individual to make his own decisions and to rise or fall by his own actions will gradually diminish. Judging by experience in the 1960s and 1970s, the tangible benefits that may be derived from expanded government programs are unlikely to exceed the resulting diminution of personal freedom and responsibility.

★★★★★★★★★★★★

Appendix

TABLE 1

Governmental Revenues in the United States, 1902–1978
(by Level of Government)

Fiscal Year	All Government (in millions)	Federal Government (in millions)	State and Local Government (in millions)	All Government (in percent of GNP)	Federal Government (in percent of GNP)	State and Local Government (in percent of GNP)
1902	$ 1,694	$ 653	$ 1,041	8.2%	3.2%	5.0%
1913	2,980	962	2,018	8.1	2.6	5.5
1922	9,322	4,261	5,061	12.8	5.9	7.0
1932	10,289	2,634	7,655	15.4	3.9	11.4
1942	28,352	16,062	12,290	20.4	11.5	8.8
1952	100,245	71,798	28,447	29.6	21.2	8.4
1962	168,062	106,441	61,621	30.8	19.5	11.3
1972	382,835	223,378	159,456	34.4	20.1	14.3
1978	731,736	429,722	302,015	36.5	21.4	15.1
Multiplier						
1902–1952	59.2	110.0	27.3			
1952–1978	7.3	6.0	10.6			
1902–1978	432.0	658.1	290.1			
Multiplier in *constant* dollars						
1902–1952	18.5	34.4	8.5			
1952–1978	3.0	2.5	4.4			
1902–1978	56.6	86.3	38.0			

Sources: U.S. Bureau of the Census, *Historical Statistics on Governmental Finances and Employment*, 1967 Census of Governments, 1969; idem, 1977 Census of Governments, 1979; *Governmental Finances in 1977–78*, 1980. 1902–1922 GNP from Raymond W. Goldsmith, *A Study of Savings in the United States*, vol. 2 (Princeton, N.J.: Princeton University Press, 1956). 1932–1978 GNP for *fiscal years* from U.S. Department of Commerce, Bureau of Economic Analysis, *National Income and Product Accounts of the United States, 1929–1974, Supplement to the Survey of Current Business*, 1977; *Survey of Current Business*, July 1979.

TABLE 2

GOVERNMENT EMPLOYMENT AND POPULATION, 1870–1978

	Government Employees[a] (all governments) (in thousands)	U.S. Population (in thousands)	Ratio of Government Workers to Persons in Population
1870	265	39,818	1:150
1900	1,401	75,994	1: 54
1920	2,920	105,710	1: 36.2
1940	4,902	132,122	1: 27.0
1949	7,559	149,188	1: 19.7
1952	10,697	156,954	1: 14.7
1972	16,208	208,846	1: 12.9
1978	17,748	218,594	1: 12.3

SOURCES: 1870: Fabricant, *The Trend of Government Activity*, table B1, p. 168 (this figure is not strictly comparable with later data). 1900, 1920, 1940, 1949: Ibid., table B14, p. 198 (the figure for 1940 does not include government emergency workers. If they are included, the total is 7,794,000 and the ratio 1:17.0). 1952, 1972, 1978: *Economic Report of the President*, January 1980; U.S. Bureau of the Census, *Historical Statistics on Governmental Finances and Employment*, 1967 Census of Governments, 1969; idem, 1977 Census of Governments, 1979; and idem, *Public Employment in 1978*, 1979.

[a] Includes armed forces.

TABLE 3

GOVERNMENTAL EMPLOYMENT, PRIVATE EMPLOYMENT, AND POPULATION,
1952 AND 1978

	1952 (in thousands)	1978 (in thousands)	Percent Increase and Decrease 1952 to 1978
Governmental employment[a]			
Total	10,697	17,748	+ 66%
National defense and international relations	4,934	3,104	− 37
All other (domestic services)	5,763	14,644	+154
Employment in private industry	53,642	78,897	+ 47
U.S. population	156,954	218,594	+ 39
Ratios to population			
Total	1:14.7	1:12.3	
National defense and international relations	1:31.8	1:70.4	
All other (domestic services)	1:27.2	1:14.9	
Ratios to private employment			
Total	1: 5.0	1: 4.5	
National defense and international relations	1:10.9	1:25.4	
All other (domestic services)	1: 9.3	1: 5.4	

SOURCES: Population, private employment and armed forces: *Economic Report of the President*, January 1980. All other governmental employment: U.S. Bureau of the Census, *Historical Statistics on Governmental Finances and Employment*, 1967 Census of Governments, 1969; and idem, *Public Employment in 1978*, 1979.

[a]including Armed Forces.

TABLE 4

GOVERNMENTAL EXPENDITURES IN THE UNITED STATES, 1902–1978

Fiscal Year	Total Governmental Expenditures	National Defense and International Relations	All Other
	In Millions of Dollars		
1902	$ 1,660	$ 165	$ 1,495
1913	3,215	250	2,965
1922	9,297	875	8,422
1932	12,437	721	11,716
1942	45,576	26,555	19,021
1952	99,847	48,187	51,660
1962	176,240	55,172	121,068
1972	399,098	79,258	319,840
1978	745,438	114,811	630,627
Multiplier			
1902–1952	60.1	292.0	34.6
1952–1978	7.5	2.4	12.2
1902–1978	449.1	695.8	421.8
Multiplier in *constant* dollars			
1902–1952	18.8	91.3	10.8
1952–1978	3.1	1.0	5.1
1902–1978	58.9	91.2	55.3
	In Percent of Gross National Product		
1902	8.0%	0.8%	7.2%
1913	8.8	0.7	8.1
1922	12.8	1.2	11.6
1932	18.5	1.1	17.4
1942	32.2	18.8	13.4
1952	29.5	14.2	15.2
1962	32.3	10.1	22.2
1972	35.9	7.1	28.8
1978	37.2	5.7	31.5

SOURCES: U.S. Bureau of the Census, *Historical Statistics on Governmental Finances and Employment*, 1977 Census of Governments, 1979; and idem, *Governmental Finances in 1977–78*, 1980, GNP figures for 1902, 1913, and 1922 from Raymond W. Goldsmith, *A Study of Savings in the United States* (Princeton, N.J.: Princeton University Press, 1956), 2: 427.

TABLE 5

FEDERAL EXPENDITURES, 1902–1978

Fiscal Year	Total Federal Expenditures	National Defense and International Relations	All Other
	In Millions of Dollars		
1902	$ 572	$ 165	$ 407
1913	970	250	720
1922	3,763	875	2,888
1932	4,266	721	3,545
1942	35,549	26,555	8,994
1952	71,568	48,187	23,381
1962	113,428	55,172	58,256
1972	242,186	79,258	162,928
1978	479,297	114,811	364,486
Multiplier			
1902–1952	125.1	292.0	57.4
1952–1978	6.7	2.4	15.6
1902–1978	837.9	695.8	895.5
Multiplier in *constant* dollars			
1902–1952	39.1	91.3	18.0
1952–1978	2.8	1.0	6.5
1902–1978	109.9	91.2	117.4
	In Percent of Gross National Product		
1902	2.8%	0.8%	2.0%
1913	2.6	0.7	2.0
1922	5.2	1.2	4.0
1932	6.4	1.1	5.3
1942	25.1	18.8	6.4
1952	21.1	14.2	6.9
1962	20.8	10.1	10.7
1972	21.8	7.1	14.7
1978	23.9	5.7	18.2

SOURCES: U.S. Bureau of the Census, *Historical Statistics on Governmental Finances and Employment*, 1977 Census of Governments, 1979; and idem, *Governmental Finances in 1977–78*, 1980, GNP figures for 1902, 1913, and 1922 from Raymond W. Goldsmith, *A Study of Savings in the United States* (Princeton, N.J.: Princeton University Press, 1956), 2: 427.

TABLE 6

	1952		1978	Percent Increase (Current Dollars)	Percent Increase (Constant Dollars)
	1952 Dollars	1978 Dollars	Dollars		
Total: all government and government enterprises	$3,296	$8,102	$13,758	317%	70%
Federal	3,373	8,291	15,361	355	85
Civilian	4,202	10,329	18,948	351	83
Military	2,891	7,106	11,588	301	63
Government enterprises	3,789	9,313	16,701	341	79
State and local	3,177	7,809	13,008	309	67
School	3,169	7,789	13,392	323	72
Nonschool	3,116	7,659	12,512	302	63
Government enterprises	3,655	8,984	13,640	273	52
Total: all private industries	3,490	8,578	13,263	280	55
Manufacturing	3,895	9,574	14,918	283	56
Wholesale and retail trade	3,269	8,035	11,178	241	39
Services	2,553	6,275	11,216	339	79
Finance, insurance, and real estate	3,557	8,743	13,337	275	53
Contract construction	4,093	10,061	15,371	276	53
Agriculture	1,696	4,169	7,099	319	70

Sources: U.S. Department of Commerce, Bureau of Economic Analysis, *National Income and Product Accounts of the United States, 1929–1974*, Supplement to the *Survey of Current Business*, 1977. U.S. Department of Commerce, Bureau of Economic Analysis, *Survey of Current Business, National Income Issue*, July 1979. Consumer price index from *Economic Report of the President*, 1980.

Note: The consumer price index was 79.5 in 1952 and 195.4 in 1978, an increase of 145.8 percent.

TABLE 7a

Governmental Employment by Level of Government, 1952–1978

	Total (in thousands)	Federal			State and Local		
		Total (in thousands)	Civilian (in thousands)	Armed Forces (in thousands)	Total (in thousands)	State (in thousands)	Local (in thousands)
1952	10,697	6,175	2,583	3,592	4,522	1,060	3,461
1953	10,593	5,930	2,385	3,545	4,663	1,082	3,580
1954	10,582	5,723	2,373	3,350	4,859	1,149	3,710
1955	10,481	5,427	2,378	3,049	5,054	1,199	3,855
1956	10,542	5,267	2,410	2,857	5,275	1,268	4,007
1957	10,847	5,239	2,439	2,800	5,608	1,300	4,307
1958	10,933	5,041	2,405	2,636	5,892	1,408	4,484
1959	11,039	4,951	2,399	2,552	6,088	1,454	4,634
1960	11,322	4,935	2,421	2,514	6,387	1,527	4,860
1961	11,672	5,056	2,484	2,572	6,616	1,625	4,992
1962	12,216	5,367	2,539	2,828	6,849	1,680	5,169
1963	12,474	5,286	2,548	2,738	7,188	1,775	5,413
1964	12,803	5,267	2,528	2,739	7,536	1,873	5,663
1965	13,312	5,311	2,588	2,723	8,001	2,028	5,973
1966	14,511	5,984	2,861	3,123	8,527	2,211	6,316
1967	15,313	6,439	2,993	3,446	8,874	2,335	6,539
1968	15,877	6,519	2,984	3,535	9,358	2,495	6,864
1969	16,197	6,481	2,975	3,506	9,716	2,614	7,102
1970	16,216	6,069	2,881	3,188	10,147	2,755	7,392
1971	16,132	5,688	2,872	2,816	10,444	2,832	7,612
1972	16,208	5,244	2,795	2,449	10,964	2,957	8,007

1973	16,464	5,112	2,786	2,326	11,352	3,013	8,339
1974	16,857	5,103	2,874	2,229	11,754	3,155	8,599
1975	17,154	5,070	2,890	2,180	12,084	3,271	8,813
1976	17,156	4,987	2,843	2,144	12,169	3,343	8,826
1977	17,746	4,981	2,848	2,133	12,765	3,491	9,274
1978	17,748	5,005	2,888	2,117	12,743	3,539	9,204

Percent increase and decrease 1952–1978

	+65.9%	−19.0%	+11.8%	−41.1%	+181.8%	+233.9%	+165.9%

SOURCES: 1952–1977: U.S. Bureau of the Census, *Historical Statistics on Governmental Finances and Employment*, 1967 Census of Governments, 1969; idem, 1977 Census of Governments, 1979. 1978: U.S. Bureau of the Census, *Public Employment in 1978*, 1979. Armed forces: *Economic Report of the President*, January 1980, table B-27.
NOTE: Data are as of October, except for 1957 figures, which are for April.

TABLE 7b

GOVERNMENTAL EMPLOYMENT BY LEVEL OF GOVERNMENT, 1952–1978
(per 1000 Population)

	Total	Federal			State and Local		
		Total	Civilian	Armed Forces	Total	State	Local
1952	67.9	39.2	16.4	22.8	28.7	6.7	22.0
1953	66.1	37.0	14.9	22.1	29.1	6.8	22.3
1954	64.9	35.1	14.6	20.5	29.8	7.0	22.8
1955	63.2	32.7	14.3	18.4	30.5	7.2	23.2
1956	62.4	31.2	14.3	16.9	31.2	7.5	23.7
1957	63.1	30.5	14.2	16.3	32.6	7.6	25.0
1958	62.5	28.8	13.7	15.1	33.7	8.1	25.6
1959	62.1	27.9	13.5	14.4	34.2	8.2	26.0
1960	62.7	27.3	13.4	13.9	35.4	8.5	26.9
1961	63.5	27.5	13.5	14.0	36.0	8.8	27.2
1962	64.8	28.5	13.5	15.0	36.3	8.9	27.4
1963	65.9	27.9	13.5	14.4	38.0	9.4	28.6
1964	66.7	27.4	13.2	14.2	39.3	9.8	29.5
1965	68.5	27.3	13.3	14.0	41.2	10.4	30.8
1966	73.8	30.4	14.6	15.8	43.4	11.3	32.1
1967	77.0	32.3	15.0	17.3	44.7	11.8	32.9
1968	79.1	32.5	14.9	17.6	46.6	12.4	34.2
1969	79.9	32.0	14.7	17.3	47.9	12.9	35.0
1970	79.1	29.6	14.1	15.5	49.5	13.4	36.1
1971	77.9	27.5	13.9	13.6	50.4	13.7	36.7
1972	77.6	25.1	13.4	11.7	52.5	14.2	38.3
1973	78.2	24.3	13.2	11.1	53.9	14.3	39.6
1974	79.6	24.1	13.6	10.5	55.5	14.9	40.6
1975	80.3	23.7	13.5	10.2	56.6	15.3	41.3
1976	79.7	23.2	13.2	10.0	56.5	15.5	41.0
1977	81.8	22.9	13.1	9.8	58.9	16.1	42.8
1978	81.2	22.9	13.2	9.7	58.3	16.2	42.1

SOURCES: 1952–1977: U.S. Bureau of the Census, *Historical Statistics on Governmental Finances and Employment*, 1967 Census of Governments, 1969; idem, 1977 Census of Governments, 1979. 1978: U.S. Bureau of the Census, *Public Employment in 1978*, 1979. Armed forces: *Economic Report of the President*, January 1980, table B-27. U.S. population: idem, January 1980, table B-22.

TABLE 8a

GOVERNMENTAL EMPLOYMENT BY FUNCTION, 1952–1978

	Total	National Defense (in thousands)			Nondefense (in thousands)							
		Total	Armed Forces	Department of Defense and International Relations	Total	Education	Postal Service	Highways	Health and Hospitals	Police Protection	Natural Resources	All Other
1952	10,697	4,934	3,592	1,342	5,763	1,884	525	460	589	254	292	1,759
1953	10,593	4,752	3,545	1,207	5,841	1,960	500	467	626	263	282	1,743
1954	10,582	4,539	3,350	1,189	6,043	2,059	504	482	662	281	279	1,776
1955	10,481	4,250	3,049	1,201	6,231	2,181	509	478	690	295	287	1,791
1956	10,542	4,064	2,857	1,207	6,478	2,286	516	496	723	309	297	1,851
1957	10,846	4,022	2,800	1,222	6,824	2,470	524	479	750	316	289	1,996
1958	10,993	3,757	2,636	1,121	7,176	2,600	541	530	795	337	309	2,064
1959	11,039	3,673	2,552	1,121	7,366	2,756	554	522	821	347	308	2,058
1960	11,323	3,611	2,514	1,097	7,712	2,930	568	537	850	363	322	2,142
1961	11,672	3,694	2,572	1,122	7,978	3,062	580	545	879	367	334	2,211
1962	12,216	3,963	2,828	1,135	8,253	3,236	585	562	907	380	342	2,241
1963	12,475	3,853	2,738	1,115	8,622	3,448	590	568	939	390	365	2,322
1964	12,804	3,833	2,739	1,094	8,971	3,687	593	568	975	401	355	2,392
1965	13,312	3,843	2,723	1,120	9,469	3,974	610	582	1,002	420	372	2,509
1966	14,511	4,393	3,123	1,270	10,118	4,331	692	594	1,049	437	379	2,636
1967	15,311	4,797	3,446	1,351	10,514	4,568	705	600	1,089	458	386	2,708
1968	15,879	4,888	3,535	1,353	10,991	4,847	714	604	1,130	489	394	2,813
1969	16,190	4,828	3,506	1,322	11,362	5,079	728	602	1,162	514	393	2,884
1970	16,216	4,388	3,188	1,200	11,828	5,316	731	612	1,202	538	404	3,025
1971	16,128	3,981	2,816	1,165	12,147	5,501	716	613	1,231	557	417	3,112

TABLE 8a (continued)

	Total	National Defense (in thousands)			Nondefense (in thousands)							
		Total	Armed Forces	Department of Defense and International Relations	Total	Education	Postal Service	Highways	Health and Hospitals	Police Protection	Natural Resources	All Other
1972	16,217	3,561	2,449	1,112	12,656	5,753	666	601	1,324	583	421	3,308
1973	16,467	3,379	2,326	1,053	13,088	5,922	692	604	1,375	616	413	3,466
1974	16,858	3,296	2,229	1,067	13,562	6,188	699	602	1,419	652	438	3,564
1975	17,152	3,231	2,180	1,051	13,921	6,294	692	609	1,449	664	454	3,759
1976	17,157	3,158	2,144	1,014	13,999	6,330	661	587	1,466	670	467	3,818
1977	17,756	3,122	2,133	989	14,634	6,725	662	568	1,571	678	491	3,939
1978	17,748	3,104	2,117	987	14,644	6,586	650	588	1,579	689	515	4,037

Percent increase and decrease 1952–1978

| +65.9 | −37.1 | −41.1 | −26.1 | +154.1 | +249.6 | +23.8 | +27.8 | +168.1 | +171.3 | +76.4 | +129.5 |

SOURCES: 1952–1977: U.S. Bureau of the Census, *Historical Statistics on Governmental Finances and Employment*, 1967 Census of Governments, 1969; idem, 1977 Census of Governments, 1979. 1978: U.S. Bureau of the Census, *Public Employment in 1978*, 1979. Armed forces: *Economic Report of the President*, January 1980, table B-27.

NOTE: Data are as of October, except for 1957 figures, which are for April.

TABLE 8b

GOVERNMENTAL EMPLOYMENT BY FUNCTION, 1952–1978

(per 1000 Population)

	Total	National Defense			Nondefense							
		Total	Armed Forces	Department of Defense and International Relations	Total	Education	Postal Service	Highways	Health and Hospitals	Police Protection	Natural Resources	All Other
1952	67.9	31.3	22.8	8.5	36.6	12.0	3.3	2.9	3.7	1.6	1.9	11.2
1953	66.1	29.7	22.1	7.6	36.4	12.2	3.1	2.9	3.9	1.6	1.8	10.9
1954	64.9	27.8	20.5	7.3	37.1	12.6	3.0	3.0	4.1	1.7	1.7	10.9
1955	63.2	25.6	18.4	7.2	37.6	13.1	3.1	2.9	4.2	1.8	1.7	10.8
1956	62.4	24.1	16.9	7.2	38.3	13.5	3.1	2.9	4.3	1.8	1.8	10.9
1957	63.2	23.4	16.3	7.1	39.8	14.4	3.0	2.8	4.4	1.8	1.7	11.7
1958	62.5	21.5	15.1	6.4	41.0	14.9	3.1	3.0	4.5	1.9	1.8	11.8
1959	62.1	20.7	14.4	6.3	41.4	15.5	3.1	2.9	4.6	2.0	1.7	11.6
1960	62.7	20.0	13.9	6.1	42.7	16.2	3.1	3.0	4.7	2.0	1.8	11.9
1961	63.5	20.1	14.0	6.1	43.4	16.6	3.2	3.0	4.8	2.0	1.8	12.0
1962	64.8	21.0	15.0	6.0	43.8	17.2	3.1	3.0	4.8	2.0	1.8	11.9
1963	65.9	20.3	14.4	5.9	45.6	18.2	3.1	3.0	5.0	2.1	1.9	12.3
1964	66.7	20.0	14.3	5.7	46.7	19.2	3.1	2.9	5.1	2.1	1.8	12.5
1965	68.5	19.8	14.0	5.8	48.7	20.4	3.1	3.0	5.2	2.2	1.9	12.9
1966	73.8	22.3	15.9	6.5	51.5	22.0	3.5	3.0	5.4	2.2	2.0	13.4
1967	77.1	24.1	17.3	6.8	52.9	23.0	3.5	3.0	5.5	2.3	1.9	13.6
1968	79.1	24.3	17.6	6.7	54.8	24.2	3.6	3.0	5.6	2.4	2.0	14.0
1969	79.9	23.8	17.3	6.5	56.1	25.1	3.6	3.0	5.7	2.5	2.0	14.2
1970	79.1	21.4	15.6	5.8	57.7	25.9	3.6	3.0	5.9	2.6	2.0	14.7
1971	77.9	19.2	13.6	5.6	58.7	26.6	3.5	3.0	5.9	2.7	2.0	15.0

TABLE 8b (continued)

	Total	National Defense			Nondefense							
		Total	Armed Forces	Department of Defense and International Relations	Total	Education	Postal Service	Highways	Health and Hospitals	Police Protection	Natural Resources	All Other
1972	77.7	17.1	11.7	5.4	60.6	27.5	3.2	2.9	6.3	2.8	2.0	15.8
1973	78.3	16.1	11.1	5.0	62.2	28.1	3.3	2.9	6.5	2.9	2.0	16.5
1974	79.5	15.6	10.5	5.0	64.0	29.2	3.3	2.8	6.7	3.1	2.1	16.8
1975	80.3	15.1	10.2	4.9	65.2	29.5	3.2	2.9	6.8	3.1	2.1	17.6
1976	79.7	14.7	10.0	4.7	65.1	29.4	3.1	2.7	6.8	3.1	2.2	17.7
1977	81.9	14.4	9.8	4.6	67.5	31.0	3.1	2.6	7.2	3.1	2.3	18.2
1978	81.2	14.2	9.7	4.5	67.0	30.1	3.0	2.7	7.2	3.2	2.4	18.5

SOURCES: 1952–77: U.S. Bureau of the Census, *Historical Statistics on Governmental Finances and Employment*, 1967 Census of Governments, 1969; idem, 1977 Census of Governments, 1979. 1978: U.S. Bureau of the Census, *Public Employment in 1978*, 1979. Armed forces: *Economic Report of the President*, January 1980, table B-27. U.S. population: idem, January 1980, table B-22.

TABLE 9

Average Number of Full-time and Part-time Employees by Industry, 1952 and 1978

	1952 (in thousands)	1978 (in thousands)	Percent Increase or Decrease
Total all private industries	46,510	74,754	+ 61%
Agriculture, forestry, fisheries	2,333	1,702	− 27
Mining	915	874	− 4
Contract construction	2,707	4,276	+ 58
Manufacturing	16,743	20,569	+ 23
Transportation	2,920	2,887	− 1
Communication	788	1,240	+ 57
Electric, gas, and sanitary services	566	778	+ 37
Wholesale and retail trade	10,106	19,646	+ 94
Finance, insurance, and real estate	2,085	4,779	+ 129
Services	7,415	18,003	+ 143
Government and government enterprises	11,190	18,698	+ 67
Federal	6,737	5,836	− 13
State and local governments	4,453	12,862	+ 189
National defense[a]	5,508	3,835	− 30
Domestic services	5,682	14,863	+ 161

SOURCES: U.S. Department of Commerce, Bureau of Economic Analysis, *National Income and Product Accounts of the United States, 1929–1974*, Supplement to the Survey of Current Business, 1977; idem, *Survey of Current Business, National Income Issue*, July 1979; and U.S. Civil Service Commission, *Annual Reports*, 1952 and 1978 (for civilian employment in the Department of Defense).

NOTE: Data in this table differ from the data in Tables 3, 7, and 8 because they were taken from a different source with a different definition of employment. They show similar trends, however.

[a]Armed forces and civilian employment in the Department of Defense.

TABLE 10

COMPARISON OF FEDERAL SALARY RANGES UNDER THE GENERAL SCHEDULE, 1952 AND 1978

General Schedule Grade	1952 Minimum	1952 Maximum	1978[a] Minimum	1978[a] Maximum	Current Dollars Minimum	Current Dollars Maximum	Constant Dollars Minimum	Constant Dollars Maximum
1	$ 2,500	$ 2,980	$ 6,561	$ 8,532	162	186	7	16
2	2,750	3,230	7,422	9,645	170	199	10	21
3	2,950	3,430	8,366	10,877	184	217	15	29
4	3,175	3,655	9,391	12,208	196	234	20	36
5	3,410	4,160	10,507	13,657	208	228	25	34
6	3,795	4,545	11,712	15,222	209	235	26	36
7	4,205	4,955	13,014	16,920	209	241	26	39
8	4,620	5,370	14,414	18,734	212	249	27	42
9	5,060	5,810	15,920	20,699	215	256	28	45
10	5,500	6,250	17,532	22,788	219	265	30	48
11	5,940	6,940	19,263	25,041	224	261	32	47
12	7,040	8,040	23,087	30,017	228	273	33	52
13	8,360	9,360	27,453	35,688	228	281	34	55
14	9,600	10,600	32,442	42,171	238	298	37	62
15	10,800	11,800	38,160	47,500[b]	253	303	44	64
16	12,000	12,800	44,756	47,500[b]	273	271	52	51
17	13,000	13,800	47,500[b]	47,500[b]	265	244	49	40
18	14,800	14,800	47,500[b]	47,500[b]	221	221	31	31

With header spanning: **Percent Increase** spans Current Dollars (Minimum, Maximum) and Constant Dollars (Minimum, Maximum).

SOURCES: U.S. Department of Labor, Bureau of Labor Statistics, *Monthly Labor Review*, vol. 81, no. 12, December 1958; *The Budget of the United States Government*, FY 1980, Appendix.

[a]Salary ranges pursuant to Executive Order 12087, effective October 1978.

[b]The rate of basic pay for employees at these rates is limited by section 5308 of title 5 of the United States Code to the rate for level V of the Executive Schedule (as of February 20, 1977, $47,500).

TABLE 11

COMPARISON OF FEDERAL EMPLOYEE AVERAGE SALARIES
BY GENERAL-SCHEDULE GRADES, 1952 AND 1978

General Schedule Grade	1952	1978	Percent Increase Current Dollars	Constant Dollars
Total All Grades	$ 4,149	$17,578	324	72
1	2,600	6,404	146	0
2	2,886	7,249	151	2
3	3,126	8,524	173	11
4	3,401	9,917	192	19
5	3,703	11,319	206	24
6	4,123	12,779	210	26
7	4,503	13,944	210	26
8	4,949	15,843	220	30
9	5,349	16,921	216	29
10	5,769	18,869	227	33
11	6,220	20,560	231	35
12	7,344	24,757	237	37
13	8,634	29,752	245	40
14	9,855	35,081	256	45
15	11,180	41,790	274	52
16	12,130	46,618	284	56
17	13,089	47,500	263	48
18	14,800	47,500	221	31

SOURCES: U.S. Civil Service Commission, *Pay Structure of the Federal Civil Service, June 1952*, 1953; idem, *Fiscal 1978 Annual Report*, 1979.

TABLE 12

GRADE DISTRIBUTION BY MAJOR GROUPS OF FEDERAL GENERAL-SCHEDULE EMPLOYEES,
1952 AND 1978

	1952	1978	Percent Increase	Percentage of Total 1952	1978
Total all grades	917,173	1,396,265	+ 52%	100.0%	100.0%
GS 1–3	337,507	119,014	− 65	36.8	8.5
GS 4–10	467,405	776,870	+ 66	50.9	55.6
GS 11–12	79,836	304,154	+281	8.7	21.8
GS 13–15	31,844	191,267	+501	3.5	13.7
GS 16–18	581	4,960	+754	0.1	0.4

SOURCES: U.S. Civil Service Commission, *Pay Structure of the Federal Civil Service, June 1952*, 1953; idem, *Fiscal 1978 Annual Report*, 1979.

TABLE 13
PUBLIC EMPLOYEE COMPENSATION AND RETIREMENT BENEFITS IN 1952, 1968 AND 1978

	1952		1968		1978	
	millions	percent	millions	percent	millions	percent
Federal Civil Service						
Salaries	$ 7,744		$ 18,230		$ 38,351	
Retirement pay	300		2,150		11,004	
Retirement pay as % of salaries		3.9%		11.8%		28.7%
Federal Military Service						
Salaries	10,730		18,845		25,656	
Retirement pay	331		2,095		9,171	
Retirement pay as % of salaries		3.1		11.1		35.7
Federal Civil & Military Service						
Salaries	18,474		37,075		64,007	
Retirement pay	631		4,245		20,175	
Retirement pay as % of salaries		3.4		11.4		31.5
State and Local Governments						
Salaries	12,045		48,996		137,703	
Retirement pay	530		2,829		10,774	
Retirement pay as % of salaries		4.4		5.8		7.8
Federal Civil & Military Service and State and Local Governments						
Salaries	30,519		86,071		201,710	
Retirement pay	1,161		7,074		30,949	
Retirement pay as % of salaries		3.8		8.2		15.3

NB: Statistics of the U.S. Bureau of the Census show only retirement outlays from trust funds, thereby omitting military retirement and several other small federal retirement systems. Adjustment required the use of several other sources such as the U.S. Budget and the use of the national income and product accounts. The table above shows 98–99% of relevant governmental operations.

Sources: Federal Employee Compensation: *The National Income and Product Accounts of the United States, 1929–74. Supplement to the Survey of Current Business,* 1977, *Survey of Current Business,* July 1979. Civil Service Retirement: U.S. Bureau of the Census, *Historial Statistics on Governmental Finances and Employment,* 1977 Census of Governments, 1979; *Governmental Finances in 1977–78,* 1980. Military Retirement Pay: *The Budget of the United States Government,* FYs 1954, 1970, 1980, Appendix. State and Local Employee Compensation and Retirement: U.S. Bureau of the Census, *Historical Statistics on Governmental Finances and Employment,* 1977 Census of Governments, 1979; *Governmental Finances in 1977–78,* 1980.

TABLE 14

Governmental Revenues and Expenditures as a
Percentage of Gross National Product, Net National Product,
National Income, and Personal Income, 1952 and 1978

	FY 1952		FY 1978	
Measured by:	Total Governmental Revenues	Total Governmental Expenditures	Total Governmental Revenues	Total Governmental Expenditures
Gross national product	29.6%	29.5%	36.5%	37.2%
Net national product	32.3	32.2	40.7	41.5
National income	35.9	35.8	45.3	46.1
Personal income	38.2	38.1	45.2	46.1

Sources: Revenue and expenditure data: U.S. Bureau of the Census, *Historical Statistics on Governmental Finances and Employment*, 1977 Census of Governments, 1979; idem, *Governmental Finances in 1977–78*, 1980.

Gross national product, net national product, national income, personal income for *fiscal* year: U.S. Department of Commerce, Bureau of Economic Analysis, *National Income and Product Accounts of the United States, 1929–74, Supplement to the Survey of Current Business*, 1977; *Survey of Current Business, National Income Issue*, July 1979.

TABLE 15

CURRENT GOVERNMENT RECEIPTS IN OECD MEMBER COUNTRIES IN 1978
(AS A PERCENTAGE OF GROSS DOMESTIC PRODUCT)
AVERAGE (MEAN) 39.3%
AVERAGE (MEDIAN) 39.0%

	Percentage of GDP
1. Sweden	60.9
2. Netherlands	54.0
3. Luxembourg	52.8[a]
4. Norway	51.2
5. Denmark	46.5[a]
6. Finland	43.5
7. Germany	43.5
8. Austria	43.0
9. France	42.2
10. Belgium	41.8
11. United Kingdom	40.6[a]
12. Italy	37.4
13. Ireland	36.8[b]
14. Canada	36.4
15. Switzerland	34.3
16. Australia	32.0[c]
17. United States	32.0
18. Greece	29.4
19. Portugal	28.3[a]
20. Turkey	27.1[d]
21. Spain	26.7
22. Japan	24.5

SOURCE : *The OECD Observer*, March 1979.

[a]1976
[b]1975
[c]1976–1977
[d]1972

TABLE 16

GOVERNMENTAL REVENUE FROM OWN SOURCES,[a] 1952 AND 1978

FY 1952

	Total	Federal	State (in millions)	Local	Percentage of GNP	Percentage of all Taxes	Percentage of all Revenue
Total revenues	$100,245	$71,798	$14,330	$14,117	29.6%		100.0%
Income taxes	50,983	49,147	1,751	85	15.0	64.5	50.9
Consumption taxes	15,689	9,332	5,730	627	4.6	19.8	15.7
Property taxes	8,652	—	370	8,282	2.6	11.0	8.6
Other taxes	3,743	1,264	2,006	473	1.1	4.7	3.7
All taxes	79,067	59,743	9,857	9,467	23.3	100.0	78.9
Social Security taxes	3,547	3,547	0	0	1.1		3.5
Other revenues	17,631	8,507	4,473	4,651	5.2		17.6
Percent of GNP	29.6%	21.2%	4.2%	4.2%			
Percent of Total	100.0%	71.6%	14.3%	14.1%			
Exhibit:							
Individual income taxes	28,919	27,921	913	85[b]	8.6	36.6	
Corporation income taxes	22,064	21,226	838	—	6.5	27.9	

459

Table 16   (continued)

FY 1978

	Total	Federal	State (in millions)	Local	Percentage of GNP	Percentage of all Taxes	Percentage of all Revenue
Total revenues	$731,736	$429,722	$171,550	$130,464	36.5%		100.0%
Income taxes	284,854	240,940	39,843	4,071	14.2	60.8%	38.9
Consumption taxes	93,049	25,453	58,270	9,326	4.6	19.9	12.7
Property taxes	66,422	0	2,364	64,058	3.3	14.2	9.1
Other taxes	23,836	8,126	12,784	2,926	1.2	5.1	3.3
All taxes	468,161	274,519	113,261	80,381	23.4	100.0	64.0
Social Security taxes	104,502	104,502	0	0	5.2		14.3
Other revenues	159,073	50,701	58,289	50,083	7.9		21.7
Percent of GNP	36.5%	21.4%	8.6%	6.5%			
Percent of Total	100.0%	58.7%	23.4%	17.8%			
Exhibit:							
Individual income taxes	214,164	180,988	29,105	4,071	10.7	45.7	
Corporation income taxes	70,690	59,952	10,738	0	3.5	15.1	

SOURCES: *U.S. Bureau of the Census, Historical Statistics on Governmental Finances and Employment, 1967 Census of Governments,* 1969; idem, *Governmental Finances in 1977–78,* 1980.

NOTE: Because of rounding details may not add to totals.

aEXCLUDING intergovernmental revenues.

bIncludes minor amounts of corporation income tax.

TABLE 17

Individual Taxes as a Percentage of GDP at Market Prices in OECD Member Countries (Average 1975–1977)

	Taxes on Goods and Services	Taxes on Personal Income	Taxes on Corporate Income	Total Taxes on Income and Profits	Taxes for Social Security	Property Taxes	Other Taxes
Average (median)	9.7%	11.1%	2.0%	13.4%	8.3%	1.6%	0.9%
Average (mean)	9.9	10.8	2.5	13.4	9.2	1.9	1.2
Australia	7.4	13.2	3.6	16.8	—	2.8	2.8
Austria	13.1	8.5	1.4	9.9	11.0	1.1	3.7
Belgium	10.8	13.5	2.8	16.4	13.2	1.1	0.4
Canada	8.4	10.9	4.0	15.1	3.5	3.1	2.4
Denmark	13.9	22.2	1.4	23.6	0.5	2.4	1.0
Finland	13.4	19.5	1.7	21.2	4.4	1.0	0.2
France	12.1	4.9	2.2	7.1	15.9	1.4	2.3
Germany	9.0	11.2	1.8	13.0	12.6	1.2	1.1
Greece	10.9	2.6	1.0	4.2	7.3	2.8	1.3
Ireland	15.6	9.0	1.6	10.6	4.7	3.0	0.8
Italy	9.5	5.9	2.2	8.8	15.7	1.2	-0.4
Japan	3.3	5.0	3.4	8.4	6.5	1.9	1.6
Luxembourg	9.0	12.4	8.1	20.5	14.5	2.5	0.7
Netherlands	10.7	12.3	3.3	15.6	17.4	1.5	0.8
Norway	17.5	17.0	1.8	18.9	8.3	0.9	0.6
Portugal	9.9	2.6	n.a.	5.6	8.0	0.5	2.4
Spain	5.0	3.3	1.5	4.8	10.0	1.2	-0.1
Sweden	11.5	21.8	1.8	23.5	11.4	0.5	3.3
Switzerland	5.6	11.3	2.3	13.6	9.0	2.2	0.4
Turkey	8.5	7.5	1.0	9.4	4.8	1.7	0.2
United Kingdom	8.7	13.6	2.1	15.6	7.0	4.5	0.9
United States	4.7	9.9	3.3	13.2	7.4	4.1	0.5

Source: Organization for Economic Cooperation and Development, *Revenue Statistics of OECD Member Countries, 1965–1978*, 1979.

TABLE 18

INDIVIDUAL TAXES AS A PERCENTAGE OF TOTAL TAXATION IN OECD MEMBER COUNTRIES (AVERAGE 1975–1977)

	Taxes on Goods and Services		Taxes on Income and Profits Paid By: Personal Income		Corporate Income		Total Income and Profits Taxes	
	Average (median)	26.0%	Average (median)	30.5%	Average (median)	5.6%	Average (median)	39.0%
	Average (mean)	28.1	Average (mean)	29.5	Average (mean)	7.1	Average (mean)	37.1
1.	Ireland	45.1	Denmark	53.6	Luxembourg	17.1	Denmark	57.0
2.	Greece	41.0	Finland	48.5	Japan	15.9	Australia	56.5
3.	Norway	37.9	Australia	44.5	Canada	12.3	Finland	52.8
4.	Portugal	37.7	Sweden	43.5	Australia	12.0	Sweden	47.1
5.	Turkey	34.4	United Kingdom	37.0	United States	10.8	Canada	46.5
6.	Austria	33.6	Norway	36.9	Switzerland	7.5	Switzerland	44.1
7.	Denmark	33.6	Switzerland	36.6	Netherlands	7.2	United States	44.0
8.	Finland	33.5	Canada	33.5	Spain	7.0	Luxembourg	43.5
9.	France	31.1	United States	33.2	Belgium	6.8	United Kingdom	42.6
10.	Italy	27.2	Belgium	32.2	Italy	6.3	Norway	40.9
11.	Canada	26.0	Turkey	30.6	United Kingdom	5.6	Belgium	39.1
12.	Belgium	25.9	Germany	30.4	France	5.5	Japan	38.9
13.	Australia	24.8	Netherlands	26.8	Germany	4.8	Turkey	38.4
14.	Germany	24.4	Luxembourg	26.4	Ireland	4.6	Germany	35.3
15.	United Kingdom	23.7	Ireland	26.0	Finland	4.3	Netherlands	34.0
16.	Spain	23.7	Japan	23.0	Turkey	4.2	Ireland	30.7
17.	Netherlands	23.2	Austria	21.9	Norway	4.0	Austria	25.5
18.	Sweden	22.9	Italy	16.8	Austria	3.6	Italy	23.1
19.	Luxembourg	19.0	Spain	15.7	Greece	3.6	Spain	22.7
20.	Switzerland	18.1	France	12.7	Sweden	3.6	Portugal	20.4
21.	United States	15.7	Portugal	9.8	Denmark	3.4	France	18.3
22.	Japan	15.2	Greece	9.7	Portugal	n.a.	Greece	15.6

Social Security		Property Taxes		Other Taxes	
Average (median)	27.8	Average (median)	5.5	Average (median)	2.2
Average (mean)	26.3	Average (mean)	5.9	Average (mean)	3.8
Spain	47.6	United States	13.6	Austria	9.8
Italy	45.1	United Kingdom	12.2	Portugal	9.8
France	41.0	Greece	10.6	Australia	9.5
Netherlands	37.8	Canada	9.6	Canada	7.2
Germany	34.2	Australia	9.3	Japan	7.1
Belgium	31.5	Japan	8.9	Sweden	6.3
Luxembourg	30.8	Ireland	8.7	France	6.1
Portugal	30.2	Switzerland	7.0	Greece	5.4
Japan	29.9	Turkey	6.7	Germany	2.9
Switzerland	29.3	Denmark	5.8	United Kingdom	2.5
Austria	28.2	Spain	5.8	Denmark	2.3
Greece	27.4	Luxembourg	5.2	United States	2.1
United States	24.6	France	3.5	Ireland	2.0
Sweden	22.7	Italy	3.5	Netherlands	1.7
Turkey	19.5	Netherlands	3.3	Luxembourg	1.5
United Kingdom	19.0	Germany	3.2	Switzerland	1.5
Norway	18.0	Austria	2.9	Norway	1.2
Ireland	13.5	Belgium	2.6	Italy	1.1
Finland	10.8	Finland	2.5	Turkey	1.0
Canada	10.7	Norway	2.0	Belgium	0.9
Denmark	1.3	Portugal	1.9	Finland	0.4
Australia	—	Sweden	1.0	Spain	0.2

Source: Organization for Economic Cooperation and Development, *Revenue Statistics of OECD Member Countries, 1965–1978,* 1979.

463

TABLE 19a

Adjusted Gross Income, Taxable Income, and Effective Tax Rates on Federal Income Tax Returns, 1977

Adjusted Gross Income Class	Adjusted Gross Income (in billions)	Taxable[a] Income (in billions)	Untaxed Income[b]		Tax Liability (in billions)	Effective Tax Rate on	
			(in billions)	As Percent of Adjusted Gross Income		AGI	TI
Total	$1,155.7	$731.4	$424.3	36.7%	$163.5	14.1%	22.4%
Under $5,000	51.1	6.2	44.9	88.0	.9	1.8	14.5
$5,000 to under $10,000	142.7	61.0	81.6	57.2	9.0	6.3	14.8
$10,000 to under $15,000	176.8	104.6	72.2	40.8	17.5	9.9	16.7
$15,000 to under $20,000	197.7	129.6	68.1	34.4	23.6	11.9	18.2
$20,000 to under $30,000	291.3	204.6	86.7	29.8	41.6	14.3	20.3
$30,000 to under $50,000	173.5	129.0	44.6	25.7	32.1	18.5	24.9
$50,000 and over	122.7	96.3	26.3	21.4	38.8	31.6	40.3

Sources: U.S. Internal Revenue Service, *Statistics of Income, 1977, Individual Income Tax Returns* (Preliminary), 1979.

[a]Taxable income computed according to Internal Revenue Code prior to 1977 *Tax Reduction and Simplification Act.*

[b]Difference between AGI and TI.

TABLE 19b

SHARES OF INCOME AND OF INCOME TAX BY INCOME BRACKET
ON FEDERAL INCOME TAX RETURNS, 1977

AGI Class	Number of Returns	AGI	TI	Untaxed Income	Tax Liability
Total	100.0%	100.0%	100.0%	100.0%	100.0%
Under $5,000	26.8	4.4	0.8	10.6	0.6
$5,000 to under $10,000	22.4	12.3	8.3	19.2	5.5
$10,000 to under $15,000	16.5	15.3	14.3	17.0	10.7
$15,000 to under $20,000	13.2	17.1	17.7	16.0	14.4
$20,000 to under $30,000	14.0	25.2	28.0	20.4	25.4
$30,000 to under $50,000	5.5	15.0	17.6	10.5	19.6
$50,000 and over	1.6	10.6	13.2	6.2	23.7

SOURCES: U.S. Internal Revenue Service, *Statistics of Income*, 1977; *Individual Income Tax Returns* (Preliminary), 1979.

TABLE 20

CURRENT GOVERNMENT EXPENDITURES IN OECD MEMBER COUNTRIES, 1978
(AS A PERCENTAGE OF GROSS DOMESTIC PRODUCT)
AVERAGE (MEAN) 37.4%;— AVERAGE (MEDIAN) 40.1%

	Percentage of GDP
1. Sweden	55.6
2. Netherlands	52.3
3. Norway	46.2
4. Luxembourg	44.4[a]
5. Belgium	43.5
6. Ireland	43.3[b]
7. Denmark	42.8[a]
8. Italy	42.5
9. United Kingdom	41.5
10. Germany	41.3
11. France	40.4
12. Austria	39.8
13. Canada	37.0
14. Finland	35.6
15. United States	32.6
16. Portugal	31.1[a]
17. Switzerland	30.4
18. Greece	29.0
19. Australia	28.9[c]
20. Spain	23.4
21. Japan	22.3
22. Turkey	18.0[d]

SOURCE: *The OECD Observer*, March 1979.   [a]1976   [b]1975   [c]1976–1977   [d]1972

TABLE 21

FEDERAL EXPENDITURES, 1952 AND 1978

	Expenditures (in millions)		Percent Increase 1952–1978		Expenditures as a Percentage of GNP		Percentage of Total Expenditures	
	1952	1978	Current $	Constant $	1952	1978	1952	1978
Total Expenditures	$71,052[a]	$459,751[a]	547%	+ 163%	20.5%	21.6%	100.0%	100.0%
National security and cost of past wars	53,969	138,055	156	+ 4	15.5	6.5	76.0	30.0
National defense	46,138	108,798	136	– 4	13.3	5.1	64.9	23.7
International affairs	2,380	5,381	126	– 8	0.7	0.3	3.3	1.2
Space research and technology	—	3,997	—	—	—	0.2	—	0.9
Veterans benefits and services	5,451	19,879	265	+ 48	1.6	0.9	7.7	4.3
Interest on debt	4,457	34,816	681	+ 218	1.3	1.6	6.3	7.6
Domestic Services	12,658	286,926	2,167	+ 822	3.6	13.5	17.8	62.4
Social welfare[b]	5,687	212,035	3,628	+ 1,417	1.6	10.0	8.0	46.1
All other	6,971	74,891	974	+ 337	2.0	3.5	9.8	16.3
Exhibit: Education	326	12,574	3,757	+ 1,470	0.1	0.6	0.5	2.7
Income support (social security, unemployment compensation, and public welfare)	4,759	140,240	2,847	+ 1,100	1.4	6.6	6.7	30.5
Health, hospitals and medical insurance	432	34,927	7,985	+ 3,189	0.1	1.6	0.6	7.6
Population of the U.S. (July 1) (in thousands)	156,954	218,594	39	—	—	—	—	—

GNP (in billions)	$347.2	$2,127.6	513	+ 135^c	—	—	—	—
Consumer price index (1967 = 100)	79.5	195.4	146	—	—	—	—	—
Implicit price deflator (GNP) (1972 = 100)	58.0	152.05	162	—	—	—	—	—

SOURCES: 1952: U.S. Department of Commerce, Bureau of Economic Analysis, *The National Income and Product Accounts of the United States, 1929–1974*, a Supplement to the *Survey of Current Business*, 1977. 1978: U.S. Department of Commerce, Bureau of Economic Analysis, *Survey of Current Business, National Income Issue, July 1967–July 1979.*

[a] Functional amounts on accrual basis, totals on disbursement basis. Difference in 1952, $32 million; 1978, $46 million.

[b] Includes education; health and hospitals; social security and public welfare; labor; housing and community development.

[c] Using implicit price deflator GNP.

TABLE 22

STATE AND LOCAL EXPENDITURES, 1952 AND 1978

	Expenditures (in millions)		Percent Increase 1952–1978		Expenditures as a Percentage of GNP		Percentage of Total Expenditures	
	1952	1978	Current $	Constant $	1952	1978	1952	1978
Total expenditures	$25,481	$303,576	1,091%	385%	7.3%	14.3%	100.0%	100.0%[a]
Social welfare[b]	14,252	192,673	1,252	450	4.1	9.1	55.9	63.5
General government	2,579	46,818	1,715	639	.7	2.2	10.1	15.4
Other domestic services	8,339	70,313	743	243	2.4	3.3	32.7	23.2
Net interest paid	13	−7,072[a]	—	—	.004	−0.3	.0005	−2.3
All other	298	1,019	241	39	.09	.05	.01	0.3
Exhibit:								
Education	8,247	116,120	1,308	473	2.4	5.5	32.4	38.3
Income support (social security, unemployment compensation, and public welfare)	2,841	41,301	1,354	491	0.8	1.9	11.1	13.6
Health, hospital, and medical insurance	2,267	28,030	1,136	403	0.7	1.3	8.9	9.2
Population of the U.S. (July 1) (in thousands)	156,954	218,594	39	—	—	—	—	—
Consumer price index (1967 = 100)	79.5	195.4	146	—	—	—	—	—
GNP (in billions)	$ 347.2	$2,127.6	513	135[c]	—	—	—	—
Personal consumption (in billions)	$ 217.1	$1,350.8	522	153	—	—	—	—
Implicit price deflator (GNP) (1972 = 100)	58.0	152.05	162	—	—	—	—	—

Functional amounts on accrual basis, totals on disbursement basis. Difference in 1978: $175 million.

SOURCES: 1952: U.S. Department of Commerce, Bureau of Economic Analysis, *The National Income and Product Accounts of the United States, 1929–74*, a Supplement to the *Survey of Current Business*, 1977. 1978: U.S. Department of Commerce, Bureau of Economic Analysis, *Survey of Current Business, National Income Issue*, July 1979.

ªState and local governments paid out $15 billion in interest in 1978 but received $22.1 billion interest or securities they hold, for a net *negative* expenditure of $7.1 billion. Their debts totaled $280 billion, their cash and security holdings $319 billion.

ᵇIncludes education; health and hospitals; social security and public welfare; labor; housing and community development. Includes expenditures from federal grants. Therefore, Table 22 (state and local expenditures) and Table 21 (federal expenditures) aggregate more than Table 23 (governmental expenditures). Federal grants to state and local governments must be netted out to equal total governmental expenditures. (Table 23)ʼ

ᶜUsing the implicit price deflator GNP.

TABLE 23

Governmental Expenditures in the United States, 1952 and 1978

	Expenditures (in millions)		Percent Increase 1952–1978		Expenditures as a Percentage of GNP		Percentage of Total Expenditures	
	1952	1978	Current $	Constant $	1952	1978	1952	1978
Total expenditures (federal, state, local)	$93,887ᵃ	$685,985ᵃ	631%	+197%	27.0%	32.2%	100.0%	100.0%
National security and cost of past wars	54,082	138,215	156	+ 4	15.6	6.5	57.6	20.1
National defense	46,205	108,998	136	– 4	13.3	5.1	49.2	15.9
International affairs	2,380	5,381	126	– 8	.7	.3	2.5	.8
Space research and technology	–	3,997	–	–	–	.2	–	.6
Veterans benefits and services	5,497	19,839	261	+ 47	1.6	.9	5.9	2.9
Net interest paid	4,470	27,744	521	+ 153	1.3	1.3	4.8	4.0
Domestic services	35,367	520,247	1,371	+ 498	10.2	24.5	37.7	75.8
Social welfareᵇ	18,087	351,145	1,841	+ 690	5.2	16.5	19.3	51.2
All other	17,280	169,102	879	+ 298	5.0	7.9	18.4	24.7
Exhibit: Education	8,374	120,823	1,343	+ 487	2.4	5.7	8.9	17.6
Income support (social security, unemployment compensation, and public welfare)	6,262	156,803	2,404	+ 919	1.8	7.4	6.7	22.9
Health, hospitals and medical insurance	2,584	59,590	2,206	+ 838	.7	2.8	2.8	8.7
Population of the U.S. (July 1) (in thousands)	156,954	218,594	39	–	–	–	–	–

GNP (in billions)	$347.2	$2,127.6	513	+135[c]	—	—	—	—
Consumer price index (1967 = 100)	79.5	195.4	146	—	—	—	—	—
Personal consumption (in billions)	$217.1	$1,350.8	522	+153	—	—	—	—
Implicit price deflator (GNP) (1972 = 100)	58.0	152.05	162	—	—	—	—	—

SOURCES: 1952: U.S. Department of Commerce, Bureau of Economic Analysis, *The National Income and Product Accounts of the United States, 1929–1974*, a Supplement to the *Survey of Current Business, 1977*. 1978: U.S. Department of Commerce, Bureau of Economic Analysis, *Survey of Current Business, National Income Issue, July 1967–July 1979*.

[a]Functional amounts on accrual basis, totals on disbursement basis; difference in 1952: $32 million; 1978: $221 million.

[b]Includes education; health and hospitals; social security and public welfare; labor; housing and community development.

[c]Using the implicit price deflator for GNP.

TABLE 24

Federal Expenditures, 1952–1978

	Total Expenditures[a] (in millions)	National Defense (in millions)	Domestic Services (in millions)	All Other (in millions)				
				Total	Space Research and Technology	International Affairs and Finance	Veterans Benefits and Services	Net Interest on Debt
1952	$ 71,052	$ 46,138	$ 12,658	$12,288	$ —	$2,380	$ 5,451	$ 4,457
1953	77,108	48,945	16,220	11,867	—	2,216	5,097	4,554
1954	69,772	41,511	16,514	11,747	—	1,989	5,114	4,644
1955	68,142	38,898	17,058	12,186	—	2,264	5,324	4,598
1956	71,918	40,686	18,669	12,563	—	2,147	5,345	5,071
1957	79,624	44,614	21,930	13,080	—	2,076	5,466	5,538
1958	88,933	46,240	29,621	13,072	30	2,153	5,681	5,208
1959	90,964	46,354	30,328	14,282	262	2,201	5,654	6,165
1960	93,106	45,314	32,508	15,284	574	2,223	5,681	6,806
1961	101,944	47,985	38,168	15,791	893	2,513	6,137	6,248
1962	110,434	52,166	41,168	17,100	1,796	2,588	5,958	6,758
1963	114,159	51,581	43,085	19,493	3,370	2,611	6,203	7,309
1964	118,182	50,523	46,240	21,419	4,629	2,660	6,147	7,983
1965	123,807	51,071	49,778	22,958	5,591	2,629	6,358	8,380
1966	143,632	62,146	57,197	24,289	5,947	2,796	6,386	9,160
1967	163,676	73,514	65,634	24,528	4,857	2,697	7,134	9,840
1968	180,563	79,256	75,065	26,242	4,548	2,560	7,637	11,497
1969	188,443	79,064	81,451	27,928	3,898	2,664	8,513	12,853
1970	204,194	76,809	96,828	30,557	3,641	2,875	9,785	14,256

Year								
1971	220,607	74,051	114,598	31,997	3,464	3,351	11,208	13,974
1972	244,734	77,853	133,283	34,081	3,353	3,595	12,581	14,552
1973	264,997	78,425	148,179	38,401	3,044	3,515	13,640	18,202
1974	299,727	83,114	172,203	43,880	3,353	4,290	15,324	20,913
1975	356,825	90,688	216,163	49,974	3,802	4,328	18,645	23,199
1976	385,016	94,298	236,429	54,289	3,741	4,472	19,322	26,754
1977	421,715	102,603	262,257	56,855	3,841	4,826	19,205	28,983
1978	459,751	108,798	286,926	64,073	3,997	5,381	19,879	34,816
Percent increase 1952–1978								
Current dollars	+547%	+136%	+2167%	+421%	—	+126%	+265%	+681%
Constant dollars	+163%	−4%	+822%	+112%	—	−8%	+48%	+218%

SOURCES: U.S. Department of Commerce, Bureau of Economic Analysis, *National Income and Product Accounts of the United States, 1929–1974, Supplement to the Survey of Current Business*, 1977; idem, *Survey of Current Business, National Income Issue, July 1967–July 1979*.

aFunctional amounts on accrual basis, totals on disbursement basis. Difference in 1952: $32 million; 1978: $46 million.

TABLE 25

Governmental Expenditures in the United States, 1952–1978
(Federal, State, Local)

	Total Expenditures (in millions)	National Defense (in millions)	Domestic Services (in millions)		All Other (in millions)			
				Total	Space Research and Technology	International Affairs and Finance	Veterans Benefits and Services	Net Interest on Debt
1952	$ 93,887	$ 46,205	$ 35,367	$12,347	$ —	$2,380	$ 5,497	$ 4,470
1953	101,552	49,015	40,540	11,921	—	2,216	5,144	4,561
1954	97,020	41,585	43,628	11,807	—	1,989	5,114	4,704
1955	97,958	38,965	46,629	12,364	—	2,264	5,408	4,692
1956	104,458	40,763	51,023	12,672	—	2,147	5,371	5,154
1957	115,250	44,702	57,311	13,237	—	2,076	5,545	5,616
1958	127,598	46,337	67,970	13,291	30	2,153	5,772	5,336
1959	131,005	46,458	70,065	14,482	262	2,201	5,728	6,291
1960	136,402	45,416	75,546	15,440	574	2,223	5,774	6,869
1961	149,072	48,078	84,961	16,033	893	2,513	6,266	6,361
1962	160,483	52,273	90,910	17,300	1,796	2,588	6,012	6,904
1963	167,785	51,697	96,482	19,606	3,370	2,611	6,233	7,392
1964	176,289	50,633	104,309	21,347	4,629	2,660	6,179	7,879
1965	187,823	51,185	114,301	22,337	5,591	2,269	6,393	8,084
1966	213,566	62,266	127,636	23,664	5,947	2,796	6,421	8,500
1967	242,419	73,641	145,133	23,645	4,857	2,697	7,183	8,908
1968	268,885	79,375	164,541	24,969	4,548	2,560	7,692	10,169
1969	285,648	79,181	180,088	26,379	3,898	2,664	8,592	11,225

1970	311,919	76,934	206,355	28,630	3,641	2,875	9,870	12,244
1971	340,520	74,184	236,302	30,243	3,464	3,346	11,279	12,154
1972	370,889	77,995	261,224	32,003	3,353	3,590	12,653	12,407
1973	404,904	78,576	290,628	35,688	3,044	3,508	13,785	15,351
1974	458,817	83,273	335,457	39,557	3,353	4,290	15,594	16,320
1975	532,842	90,850	396,634	45,358	3,802	4,328	18,804	18,424
1976	573,960	94,461	429,313	50,186	3,741	4,472	19,317	22,656
1977	626,136	102,775	471,515	51,846	3,841	4,826	19,183	23,996
1978	685,985	108,998	520,247	56,961	3,997	5,381	19,839	27,744

Percent increase 1952–1978

Current dollars	+631%	+136%	+1371%	+361%	—	+126%	+261%	+521%
Constant dollars	+197%	+ 4%	+ 498%	+ 88%	—	– 8%	+ 47%	+153%

Functional amounts on accrual basis, totals on disbursement basis. Difference in 1952: $32 million; in 1978: $221 million.

SOURCES: U.S. Department of Commerce, Bureau of Economic Analysis, *National Income and Product Accounts of the United States, 1929–1974*, Supplement to the *Survey of Current Business*, 1977; idem, *Survey of Current Business, National Income Issue, July 1967–July 1979*.

TABLE 26

PUBLIC AND PRIVATE CONSUMPTION, 1952 AND 1978

	1952 (in millions)	1978 (in millions)	Percent Increase Current Dollars	Percent Increase Constant Dollars
Personal Consumption				
Expenditures	$217,093	$1,350,762	522%	153%
Food	68,357	289,578	324	72
Clothing and personal care	29,198	126,211	332	76
Housing and household operation	58,272	407,175	599	184
Medical care	10,638	131,026	1,132	401
Transportation (includes automobiles)	25,202	191,327	659	209
Recreation	12,102	91,244	654	207
Private education and research	1,957	20,770	961	332
All other	11,367	93,431	722	234
Government Expenditures for				
Domestic Services	35,367	520,247	1,371	498
Education	8,374	120,823	1,343	487
Social security, unemployment compensation, and public welfare	6,262	156,803	2,404	919
Health, hospitals and medical insurance	2,584	59,590	2,206	838
All other	18,147	183,031	909	310

SOURCES: U.S. Department of Commerce, Bureau of Economic Analysis, *National Income and Product Accounts of the United States, 1929–1974,* Supplement to the *Survey of Current Business,* 1977; idem, *Survey of Current Business, National Income Issue,* July 1979.

★★★★★★★

Notes

Preface

1. Roger A. Freeman, "The Wayward Welfare State," *Congressional Record*, October 5, 1970; *Vital Speeches of the Day*, October 15, 1970, *Modern Age*, Fall 1971.

2. Solomon Fabricant, *The Trend of Government Activity in the United States Since 1900* (New York: National Bureau of Economic Research, 1952).

3. M. Slade Kendrick, *A Century and a Half of Federal Expenditures* (New York: National Bureau of Economic Research, 1955).

Technical Notes on Statistics

1. However, release of 1979 data was indefinitely postponed, pending computation of revised benchmarks for national economic statistics.

Chapter 1: *The Public Payroll*

1. Sources: *The National Income and Product Accounts of the United States, 1929–74* Statistical Tables, A Supplement to the *Survey of Current Business*, U.S. Department of Commerce, 1977; and idem, *Survey of Current Business*, July 1979.

Employment is measured in various ways by federal agencies. The Bureau of Economic Analysis, Department of Commerce, presents several series such as Full-time and Part-time Employees, Full-time Equivalent Employees, Persons Engaged in Production, etc. The Bureau of Labor Statistics, Department of Labor, uses different standards in its statistics and the Bureau of the Census, Department of Commerce, uses still other definitions. Some details or breakdowns are available in one series but not in others. This may be very confusing. But the general trends over time in all series are similar or identical. The important thing is to use for time comparisons only data from the *same* series, no matter which of the several series is being used. Data shown above are for full-time equivalent employees.

2. For many years the U.S. budget has annually shown a table and a graph which emphasizes the *relative* decline of federal employment.

3. *Congressional Record*, October 27, 1971, pp. E11330, E11345 et seq.

4. Barbara Cottman Jon, "More Public Services Spur Growth in Government Employment," *Monthly Labor Review*, September 1978.

5. See: Herbert Kaufman, *Are Government Organizations Immortal?* (Washington, D.C.: Brookings Institution, 1976).

6. Donald Lambro, "In and Out at HEW: Doing Well by Doing Good Through Consulting," *Policy Review*, Winter 1979.

7. Source of data: U.S. Bureau of the Census, *Public Employment in 1978* (Washington, D.C., 1979). The annual growth was 83,000 at the state level and 191,000 at the local level. These are full-time equivalent data.

8. Rowland Egger, "Painless Economy and the Mythology of Administrative Reorganization," *Proceedings of the Forty-second Annual Conference on Taxation*, National Tax Association, 1949.

9. Jerome A. Mark, "Progress in Measuring Productivity in Government," *Monthly Labor Review*, December 1972.

10. "Symposium on Productivity in Government," *Public Administration Review*, November–December 1972.

11. Ibid.

12. "A Symposium: Productivity in Government," *Public Administration Review*, January–February 1978.

13. Ibid. "Productivity Analysis: A Search for Definition and Order."

14. U.S. Congress, Joint Economic Committee, *Measuring and Enhancing Productivity in the Federal Sector*, A Study Prepared for the Use of the Joint Economic Committee, Congress of the United States, by Representatives of the Civil Service Commission, General Accounting Office and the Office of Management and Budget, JEC Committee Print, 1972.

15. U.S. Congress, Joint Economic Committee, *Federal Productivity: Hearings before the Subcommittee on Priorities and Economy in Government of the Joint Economic Committee*, 93rd Cong., 1st sess., 1974, p. 21.

16. Charles Ardolini and Jeffrey Hohenstein, "Measuring Productivity in the Federal Government," *Monthly Labor Review*, November 1974.

17. *Public Administration Review*, January–February 1978.

18. *Productivity in the Federal Sector*, Hearings before a Task Force on Tax Expenditures, Government Organization and Regulation of the Committee on the Budget, H.R. 95th Cong., 2d sess., 1978.

19. When 12,000 post offices announced in 1978 the opening of exams to replenish hiring registers, 1.1 million persons applied, two-thirds of whom had other jobs they were willing to give up for a postal position.

20. *Estimates of Income Unreported on Individual Income Tax Returns*, Internal Revenue Service, September 1979.

21. For example: Raymond T. Olsen, "Productivity in State and Local Government," *Management Controls*, July 1975; and Committee for Economic Development, *Improving Productivity in State and Local Governments*, 1976.

22. "A Conversation with Victor Gotbaum (American Federation of State, County and Municipal Employees, AFL–CIO)," *Public Administration Review*, January/February 1978.

23. Data on instructional staff and enrollment from U.S. Office of Education, *Statistics of State School Systems, 1951–52*, 1955; and *The Condition of Education*, National Center for Education Statistics, 1979 edition.

24. *Economic Report of the President, January 1980*, p. 296.

25. Coleman et al., *Equality of Educational Opportunity*.

26. *New York City School Fact Book*, Marilyn Gittel, ed. Institute for Community Studies, Queens College of the City University of New York, 1968.

27. Lawrence J. Lau, "Educational Production Function," in *Economic Dimensions of Education*, Report of a Committee of the National Academy of Education, 1979, p. 41.

28. 1957: U.S. Bureau of the Census, *Historical Statistics of the United States, Colonial Times to 1970*, 1975.

1978: *Crime in the United States 1978, FBI Uniform Crime Reports*, U.S. Department of Justice, 1979.

29. *Special Analyses, Budget of the United States Government, F.Y. 1975*.

30. Frederick C. Mosher, *Democracy and the Public Service* (New York: Oxford University Press, 1968).

31. "Is Bureaucracy Out of Control?," *U.S. News & World Report*, May 17, 1971.

32. "Civil Servants Pull Ahead in the Pay Race," *U.S. News & World Report*, February 20, 1978.

33. In a highly critical review of the white-collar comparability process in 1974, the U.S. Comptroller General concluded that "federal pay adjustments were not based on well-founded, logical premises that reflect the legislative pay

principles" and the methods used "resulted in significant deviations from comparability for Federal employees and in inequitable pay distribution among employees" (Comptroller General to the Director of the Office of Management and Budget, and the Chairman of the Civil Service Commission, July 12, 1974).

34. President Carter proposed in 1979 that they be included.

35. *Federal White Collar Employees—Their Pay and Fringe Benefits*, Congressional Budget Office, January 1979, p. xi.

36. *New York Times*, April 20, 1980, p. 6E.

37. Robert Tilove, *Public Employee Pension Funds* (New York: Columbia University Press, 1976), p. 339.

38. *Pension Task Force Report on Public Employee Retirement Systems*, Committee on Education and Labor, 1978, p. 3. An excellent summary of this report was prepared by Ronald F. Hancberg, "Public Pension Plans: Are They Really as Bad Off as They Seem?" *Pension World*, March 1979.

39. William R. Keech, "Public Issues in Providing Retirement Income," *Public Administration Review*, March/April 1978.

40. Frank P. Zeidler, "New Roles for Public Officials in Labor Relations," Public Relations Library no. 23 (Chicago: Public Personnel Association).

41. For an excellent survey of federal pensions see: *Federal Employee Retirement Systems* (New York: Tax Foundation, 1978).

42. U.S. Civil Service Commission *Fiscal 1978 Annual Report*, p. 34. See also: U.S. Civil Service Commission, *Union Recognition in the Federal Government*, 1977. Other union membership data are from U.S. Bureau of the Census, *Statistical Abstract of the United States, 1979*, and earlier years.

43. *Labor Management Relations in State and Local Government, 1976*. U.S. Department of Commerce and U.S. Department of Labor, 1978.

44. *Labor-Management Relations in State and Local Governments*, 1977 Census of Governments, U.S. Bureau of the Census, 1979.

45. The NEA was saved $281,984 in taxes in 1979 on its $15 million headquarters building in Washington by being labeled a nonprofit organization that "fosters education" rather than a labor union, which, for all practical purposes, it is.

46. The District of Columbia Education Board president was quoted as commenting: "The teachers' contract was running the school system," *Economist*, April 7, 1979.

47. *NEA Research Bulletin*, October 1970.

48. "Public Workers Take to the Warpath," *U.S. News & World Report*, March 17, 1980.

49. Edwin Vieira in *Compulsory Unionism in the Public Sector*, National Right to Work Committee, 1979. The *New York Times* reported on September 22, 1974: "The nation's teachers organizations have vastly increased the amount of money they are giving to political candidates this year and have become one of the best financed groups in the nation."

50. The activities of organized labor in influencing elections were well described and documented in Douglas Caddy, *The Hundred Million Dollar Payoff* (New Rochelle, N.Y.: Arlington House, 1974). In an article entitled "Unions Jump Into Campaign," *U.S. News & World Report*, October 7, 1974, reported: "Now taking shape among American labor unions is the most strenuous campaign they have ever conducted in a congressional election. The goal of organized labor: Elect enough sympathetic lawmakers—mostly Democrats—to insure passage of favored legislation. The tactics: Raise a record amount of money and manpower to do the job."

51. Only eight states have granted their public employees the right to strike.

52. Quoted in A. H. Raskin, "The Revolt of the Civil Servants," *Saturday Review*, December 7, 1968.

53. The fine against the union was reduced to $700,000.

54. When lower courts imposed jail sentences and fines on Philadelphia union chiefs for leading an illegal teachers' strike, the Pennsylvania Supreme Court canceled sentences and fines in October 1974.

55. *National Labor Relations Board* v. *Mackay Radio and Telegraph Co.*, 304 U.S. 333 (1938).

56. Cases and arguments are cited in: John M. Capozzola, "Public Employee Strikes: Myths and Realities," *National Civic Review*, April 1979; and Leroy H. Schramm, "The Job Rights of Strikers in the Public Sector," *Industrial and Labor Relations Review*, April 1978.

57. Theodore W. Kheel in: *Public Employee Unions* (San Francisco, Institute for Contemporary Studies, 1976), p. 9.

58. *Improving Management of the Public Work Force*, Committee for Economic Development, 1978, pp. 126–28.

59. D. S. Chauhan, "The Political and Legal Issues of Binding Arbitration in Government," *Monthly Labor Review*, September 1979.

60. *Comparative Growth in Compensation for Postal and Other Federal Employees Since 1970*, Report to the Congress by the Comptroller General of the United States, February 1979, pp. i–ii.

61. Raymond D. Horton, "Economics, Politics and Collective Bargaining: The Case of New York City" in *Public Employee Unions* (San Francisco: Institute for Contemporary Studies, 1976), p. 186.

Chapter 2: *Public Revenues*

1. "Spenders State to Take in Some Sail," *U.S. News & World Report*, March 17, 1980; *Economic Indicators*, February 1981.

2. "Is Heavy Taxation of Capital Socially Desirable?" *Tax Review*, Tax Foundation, October 1978.

3. "Next Tax Cuts—What to Expect," *U.S. News & World Report*, February 12, 1979.

4. "Chances for a Tax Cut: Views of a Key Senator," *U.S. News & World Report*, March 17, 1980.

5. *Blueprints for Basic Tax Reform*, Department of the Treasury, January 1977.

6. Roy Blough, *The Federal Taxing Process* (New York: Prentice-Hall, 1952), p. 464.

7. Source for data in this and subsequent tables: *Statistics of Income 1977, Preliminary, Individual Income Tax Returns*, Internal Revenue Service (6–79).

8. *Money Income in 1977 of Households in the United States*, U.S. Bureau of the Census, Current Population Series P-60, no. 117, December 1978.

9. For a more detailed discussion: Roger A. Freeman, *Tax Loopholes: The Legend and the Reality* (Washington, D.C.: American Enterprise Institute; Stanford: Hoover Institution, 1973).

10. "Federal Personal Income Taxes: Liabilities and Payments," *Survey of Current Business*, May 1978.

11. Computed according to the Internal Revenue Code *prior* to the *1977 Tax Reduction and Simplification Act*.

12. Raised to $1,000 for 1979 and subsequent years.

13. Raised to $2,300 and $3,400 respectively for 1979 and subsequent years.

14. Recent studies suggest that income fraudulently unreported may be far larger than had been assumed. If unreported income is bigger than had been believed, the total for personal income will also be higher.

15. Some authors have asserted: "In summary, the U.S. tax system is essentially proportional for the vast majority of families and therefore has little effect on the distribution of income." Joseph A. Pechman and Benjamin A. Okner, *Who Bears the Tax Burden* (Washington, D.C.: Brookings Institution, 1974), p. 10. Also, idem, "Who Paid Taxes in 1966?" *American Economic Review*, May 1974.

Pechman and Okner were able to produce such results by extensively "adjusting" family income from concepts of personal income used in national income accounting. For example, they treated not only realized capital gains as current income but also unrealized capital gains such as those resulting from the impact of inflation on inventories, they attributed retained earnings of corporations to their stockholders' family income, and they excluded income which resulted from employer contributions—treating such benefits as income in the year in which the employer contributions were made rather than when the benefits were received.

The authors admitted that "high effective tax rates at the lower end of the income scale are probably due primarily to the use of a one-year accounting period for measuring income. When the accounting period is limited to a single year, there is a heavy concentration of retired-person families and of individuals with temporarily low income in these income classes. . . . Thus the annual tax burdens shown . . . for the lowest income classes are probably not representative of the tax burdens of families whose incomes are low when measured over longer periods" (Pechman and Okner, *Who Bears the Tax Burden*, p. 8).

16. *Statistics of Income, 1978, Preliminary, Individual Income Tax Returns*, Internal Revenue Service (4–80).

17. *Estimates of Income Unreported on Individual Income Tax Returns*, Internal Revenue Service (9–79).

18. "The Underground Economy: How 20 Million Americans Cheat Uncle Sam out of Billions in Taxes," *U.S. News & World Report*, October 22, 1979; and Terri Schultz, "The Untaxed Millions," *New York Times Magazine*, March 16, 1980.

19. *Economic Indicators*, February 1980.

20. Edward T. Thompson and Charles E. Silberman, "Can Anything be Done About Corporate Taxes?" *Fortune*, March 1959.

21. Corporate profits data from: First National City Bank of New York, *Monthly Economic Letter*, April 1979 and earlier issues.

22. GATT rules permit reimbursement of value-added tax for exports but not of a corporate profits tax. Also, the value-added tax is imposed on imports.

23. For a more friendly and balanced view, see: Robert Hessen, *In Defense of the Corporation* (Stanford: Hoover Institution Press, 1979).

24. *Statistics of Income 1975; Corporation Income Tax Returns*, Internal Revenue Service, February 1980; and idem, *Preliminary 1976*, July 1979.

25. Norman R. Ture, *The Value Added Tax: Facts and Fancies* (Washington: Heritage Foundation, 1979), pp. 70–71.

26. FICA = Federal Insurance Contributions Act.

27. See: Martin Anderson, "The Roller-Coaster Income Tax," *Public Interest*, Winter 1978. A December 1977 amendment made the impact of the earned income credit even more erratic.

28. This might not have altered the eventual burden. Most economists now believe that the employer's share of the social security tax is shifted to the employee in the form of lower wages than would otherwise prevail. The employer's tax is treated as a cost of labor just as direct wages are.

29. Rita Ricardo Campbell, *Social Security: Promise and Reality* (Stanford: Hoover Institution Press, 1969), p. 252.

30. *Social Security Bulletin*, August 1979.

31. This paragraph is quoted from my book *Taxes for the Schools*, Financing the Public Schools, Vol. II (Washington: Institute for Social Science Research, 1960), p. xxvi. It is, I believe, as timely and fitting today as it was when it was written twenty years ago.

32. Jens Peter Jensen, *Property Taxation in the United States* (Chicago: University of Chicago Press, 1931), p. 478.

33. George W. Mitchell (then economist for the Federal Reserve Bank of Chicago, later a member of the board of governors of the Federal Reserve System), "Is This Where We Came In?" *Proceedings of the Forty-ninth Annual Conference on Taxation* (National Tax Association, 1956), p. 492.

34. Robert Cassidy in *New Republic*, May 15, 1971.

35. *Changing Times*, May 1974.

36. For an extensive discussion of this question: "Proceedings of a Conference on Tax and Expenditure Limitations," *National Tax Journal*, June 1979, Supplement.

37. Property tax relief was enacted prior to the vote, contingent on failure of proposition 13.

38. Computed from: U.S. Department of Commerce, *Construction Statistics, 1915–1964*, A Supplement to *Construction Review*, 1966; and *Construction Review*, December 1978, July 1979. The totals do not include large amounts for additions, restorations and remodeling, which are generally considered in property tax appraisals and reassessments.

39. Construction costs have been rising faster than other price indexes, consumers or wholesale, for as long as those indexes have been in existence. Between 1915 (earliest year available) and 1978 the Consumers Price Index (CPI) increased 543%, while the composite construction cost index went up 1252 percent, or more than twice as much. Source: see footnote 38. See also U.S. Bureau of the Census, *Historical Statistics of the United States Colonial Times to 1970*, 1973; *Economic Report of the President*, January 1980.

40. Henry Aaron, "The Property Tax: Progressive or Regressive? A New View of Property Tax Incidence," *American Economic Review*, May 1974; and Richard A. Musgrave, "Is a Property Tax on Housing Regressive?" *American Economic Review*, May 1974.

41. *Newsweek*, June 19, 1978.

42. *Changing Public Attitudes on Governments and Taxes*, Advisory Commission on Intergovernmental Relations, 1979.

43. *Taxable Property Values and Assessment/Sales Price Ratios*, U.S. Bureau of the Census, 1977 Census of Governments, Vol. 2.

44. *Annual Housing Survey, 1977: Financial Characteristics of the Housing Inventory*, U.S. Departments of Commerce and of Housing and Urban Development, Part C.

45. It is also conceivable that the property tax is regressive at the low end of the income scale. Richard Netzer, *The Economics of the Property Tax* (Washington, D.C.: Brookings Institution, 1966).

Chapter 3: *Public Expenditures*

1. These data are from Bureau of the Census statistics for *fiscal* years (FY). Some of the succeeding tables are, for technical reasons, from the U.S. Budget which uses different definitions; still others from National Income and Product Accounts (Bureau of Economic Analysis, Department of Commerce), which uses *calendar* years. While absolute figures may slightly differ, trends in the three series are identical.

2. Source of expenditure and GNP data 1900 to 1948: *Historical Statistics of the United States, Colonial Times to 1970*, U.S. Bureau of the Census, 1975.

3. Data according to the Office of Management and Budget, using the consolidated cash budget in 1952, the unified budget in 1978. By definitions of the Bureau of the Census, the 1952 surplus amounted to $230 million, the 1978 deficit $48 billion.

4. Cynthia Cates Colella, "The Creation, Care and Feeding of Leviathan: Who and What Makes Government Grow," *Intergovernmental Perspective*, U.S. Advisory Commission on Intergovernmental Relations, Fall 1979.

5. *Counterbudget: A Blueprint for Changing National Priorities 1971–1976*, Robert S. Benson and Harold Wolman, eds. (New York: Praeger, 1971).

6. *First Concurrent Resolution on the Budget F.Y. 1980*, Hearings before the Committee on the Budget, U.S. Senate, 96th Cong., 1st sess., April 1979.

7. "The New Negativism," *Newsweek*, August 14, 1978.

8. William T. Poole, *The Anti-Defense Lobby*, The Heritage Foundation (3 parts), April–December 1979 (proc.).

9. Philip Morrison and Paul Walker, "A New Strategy for Military Spending," *Scientific American*, October 1978.

10. Clayton Fritchey, "Inflation's Roots Are in the Military Budget," *Washington Post*, September 9, 1978.

11. "A Fat Budget for Defense," *New York Times*, January 24, 1979.

12. Charles L. Schultze et al., *Setting National Priorities: The 1973 Budget* (Washington, D.C.: Brookings Institution, 1972), p. 38.

13. Ibid.

14. *Agenda for the Nation*, Kermit Gordon, ed. (Washington, D.C.: Brookings Institution, 1968), p. 9.

15. Samuel Huntington, *The Common Defense: Strategic Programs in National Politics* (New York: Columbia University Press, 1961), p. 221. See also: Warner R. Schilling, Paul Y. Hammond and Glenn H. Snyder, *Strategy, Politics and Defense Budgets* (New York: Columbia University Press, 1962); and Maxwell D. Taylor, *The Uncertain Trumpet* (New York: Harper, 1960).

16. *Wall Street Journal*, January 28, 1980.

17. Ibid., February 11, 1980.

18. *Congressional Record*, October 11, 1979, p. S14411.

19. Somerset Maugham, *Strictly Personal* (Garden City, N.Y.: Doubleday, 1941), p. 216.

20. *First Concurrent Resolution on the Budget*, Fiscal Year 1980, Senate, p. 114.

21. Huntington, *The Common Defense*, p. 221.

22. Roger A. Freeman, "National Security and Competing Costs," in *National Security: Political, Military, and Economic Strategies in the Decade Ahead*, David M. Abshire and Richard V. Allen, eds. (New York: Praeger, 1963), p. 823.

23. Lawrence J. Korb, "The Budget Process in the Department of Defense, 1947–77; The Strengths and Weaknesses of Three Systems," *Public Administration Review*, July/August 1977.

24. Hanson Baldwin, "The McNamara Monarchy," *Saturday Evening Post*, March 9, 1963.

25. See "Can the Budget be Controlled?" (p. 151).

26. Roger A. Freeman, "The Armed Services and the Charmed Services," *National Review*, September 21, 1965.

27. "The FY 1980–1984 Defense Program: Issues and Trends," *AEI Foreign Policy and Defense Review*, Vol. 1, No. 4, 1979.

28. *World Military Expenditures and Arms Transfers 1968–1977*, U.S. Arms Control and Disarmament Agency, 1979.

29. *A Dollar Cost Comparison of Soviet and U.S. Defense Activities, 1968–78*, Central Intelligence Agency, 1979.

30. (Washington D.C.: American Enterprise Institute, 1980); also: Ralph Kinney Bennett, "Our Army is Unprepared," *Readers Digest*, March 1981.

31. Fred Charles Iklé, "Arms Control and National Defense," and Edward Teller, "Technology: The Imbalance of Power" in *The United States in the 1980s*, Peter Duignan and Alvin Rabushka, eds. (Stanford: Hoover Institution Press,

1980.) Several other recent publications discuss in factual and impressive ways contemporary military developments and means to cope with the crises. Among the *concise* presentations are: Lawrence J. Korb, "The 1980–1984 Defense Program: Issues and Prospects," *AEI Foreign Policy and Defense Review*, Vol. 1 No. 4 (American Enterprise Institute), 1981–1985 volume forthcoming; "Defense Program Alternatives: FY 1981 and Beyond," *National Security Record*, The Heritage Foundation, March 1980; Francis P. Hoeber, Norman Polmar, and William Schneider, Jr., *Arms, Men, and Military Budgets: Issues for Fiscal Year 1981* (New York: National Strategy Information Center, 1980). Forthcoming (= updating a volume on FY 1979); and Wayne A. Schroeder, "Assessing Defense Spending," *Backgrounder*, No. 106, The Heritage Foundation, December 10, 1979.

32. Wayne A. Schroeder, "Assessing Defense Spending," *Backgrounder*, The Heritage Foundation, December 10, 1979. See also: Donald H. Rumsfeld in *Congressional Record*, October 11, 1979, p. S14407.

33. Maxwell D. Taylor, "National Policy Too Lightly Armed," in *Grand Strategy for the 1980s*, Bruce Palmer, Jr., ed. (Washington, D.C.: American Enterprise Institute, 1978), p. 15.

34. Sar A. Levitan and Robert Taggart, *The Promise of Greatness* (Cambridge: Harvard University Press, 1976), p. 26.

35. Samuel M. Cohn, "Needed Discipline in Federal Budget Policy," *Tax Review*, Tax Foundation, January 1977.

36. *Public Opinion*, American Enterprise Institute, February/March 1980.

37. David Novick, ed., *Program Budgeting: Program Analysis and the Federal Budget* (Washington, D.C.: Government Printing Office, 1965), p. iii.

38. Allen Schick, "The Road from ZBB," *Public Administration Review*, March/April 1978.

39. Sunset Laws: One More Idea Gone Awry?" *U.S. News & World Report*, May 29, 1978.

40. Robert D. Behn, "The False Dawn of the Sunset Laws," *The Public Interest*, Fall 1977. See also: Maynard H. Waterfield, "Rethinking the Sunset Concept," *Tax Review*, Tax Foundation, September 1979; and Tom Ascik, "Sunset Proposals: Can They Reform the Bureaucracy?" *Backgrounder*, The Heritage Foundation, October 1977.

41. *Congressional Record*, September 20, 1972, p. S15414.

42. Joel Haveman, "A Casualty of the Budget Process," *National Journal*, September 8, 1979.

43. Eugene J. McAllister, *Congress and the Budget, Evaluating the Process* (Washington, D.C.: The Heritage Foundation, 1979) pp. 25–26.

44. *Congressional Record*, December 5, 1979, p. S17833–34. Also: "Preserving Budgetary Indiscipline," *Wall Street Journal*, December 12, 1979.

Chapter 4:   The Promise and the Harvest of the Welfare State

1. *Federal Expenditure Policy for Economic Growth and Stability*, 85th Cong., 1st sess., papers submitted by panelists, pp. 1100 ff, hearings, pp. 587 ff. Also: Roger A. Freeman, "Grants Without Strings," *National Civic Review*, June 1959; *Congressional Record*, June 25, 1959, p. A5506.

2. *The Restoration of Federalism in America*, Final Report of the Study Group on Revenue Sharing, Republican National Committee, December 1967.

3. Will Myers and John Shannon, "Revenue Sharing for States: An Endangered Species," *Intergovernmental Perspective*, Advisory Commission on Intergovernmental Relations, Summer 1979.

4. *1965 Proceedings of the 58th Annual Conference on Taxation*, National Tax Association, 1966; *Congressional Record*, July 12, 1966, pp. 14673 ff.

5. *Public Papers of the Presidents of the United States*, Lyndon B. Johnson, 1963–64, no. 431, p. 819.

6. *First Concurrent Resolution on the Budget*, Fiscal Year 1980, Hearings before the Committee on the Budget, 96th Cong., 1st sess., vol. II, pp. 760, 768.

7. Roger A. Freeman, *School Needs in the Decade Ahead* (Washington, D.C.: Institute for Social Science Research, 1958), p. 77.

8. James S. Coleman, "Toward Open Schools," *Public Interest*, Fall 1967.

9. "A Reappraisal of the Most Controversial Educational Document of Our Time," *New York Times Magazine*, August 10, 1969. The report itself: Christopher Jencks et al., *Inequality: A Reassessment of the Effect of Family and Schooling in America* (New York: Basic Books, 1972).

10. Lawrence J. Lau, "Educational Production Functions," in *Economic Dimensions of Education*, Report of a Committee of the National Academy of Education, Douglas M. Windham, ed., May 1979, p. 41.

11. Paul R. Mort, "Cost-Quality Relationships in Education," in *Problems and Issues in Public School Finance*, R. L. Johns and E. L. Morphet, eds. (New York: Teachers College, Columbia University, 1952), pp. 9–10.

12. *A Time for Priorities: Financing the Schools for the 1970s*, NEA Committee on Educational Finance, 1970.

13. *New York Times*, June 6, 1969.

14. Enrollment and staff data from reports of the U.S. Office of Education, achievement scores from reports of the New York City schools.

15. Examples from recent years: "On Opening Day America's Schools Ponder Some Sobering Lessons," *U.S. News & World Report*, September 12, 1977; "Quest for Better Schools," *U.S. News & World Report*, September 11,

1978; "Kids, Teachers and Parents: Give us Better Schools," *U.S. News & World Report*, September 10, 1979; "Why Johnny Can't Write," *Newsweek*, December 8, 1975; "City Schools in Crisis," *Newsweek*, September 12, 1977; "The Collapse of Public Schools," *Saturday Review*, August 1979 (John C. Sawhill); "Why Our Public Schools Don't Work," *Readers Digest*, August 1979; and "Why Our Schools Went Wrong," *Changing Times*, May 1978. This list could easily continue for pages.

16. *National College-Bound Seniors, 1979*, College Entrance Examination Board.

17. *The Condition of Education*, National Center for Education Statistics, 1979, p. 204. Data are for year-round full-time workers, 25 years old and over. *Money Income of Families and Persons in the United States: 1978*, Current Population Reports, Series P-60, No. 123, U.S. Bureau of the Census.

18. *The Condition of Education*, 1979 ed., pp. 60, 62.

19. Ibid., p. 62.

20. For a more extensive treatment, see my paper under the same title: *Congressional Record*, April 24, 1969, pp. 3374–80.

21. Washington, D.C.: Brookings Institution, 1978.

22. *Aid to Elementary and Secondary Education*, Hearings before the General Subcommittee on Education of the Committee on Education and Labor, House of Representatives, 89th Cong. 1st sess. (1965), pp. 1383–427; *Elementary and Secondary Education Act of 1965*, Hearings before the Subcommittee on Education, Committee on Labor and Public Welfare, U.S. Senate (1965), pp. 2757–782. Also: Roger A. Freeman, "How to Railroad a School Bill," *National Review*, May 18, 1965. An excellent history of the 1965 education act is: Julie Roy Jeffries, *Education for Children of the Poor* (Columbus: Ohio State University Press, 1978).

23. *Education of the Disadvantaged*, An Evaluative Report on Title I, ESEA of 1965, HEW, 1968, p. 8.

24. *Congressional Record*, September 26, 1968, p. E8820.

25. *Title I ESEA: A Review and a Forward Look, 1969*, 4th Annual Report of the National Advisory Council on the Education of Disadvantaged Children, HEW, September.

26. Data from: *New York City School Fact Book*, Marilyn Gittel, ed., Institute for Community Studies, Queens College of the City University of New York, 1968; *Achievement Test Results, 1970–71*, Research Department, Oakland Public Schools, 1971.

27. *Assessment of Reading Activities Funded under the Federal Program of Aid for Educationally Deprived Children*, Comptroller General of the U.S., MWD-76-54, p. 15.

28. *Improving Compensatory Education Through Changes in ESEA Title I, Patterns in ESEA Title I Reading Achievements* (Menlo Park, CA: SRI, 1976).

29. U.S. Office of Economic Opportunity, *Performance Contracting: An Experiment in Accountability*, 1971, p. 3.

30. Ellis B. Page, "How We All Failed in Performance Contracting," *Educational Psychologist*, May 1972.

31. U.S. Office of Economic Opportunity, *An Experiment in Performance Contracting: Summary of Preliminary Results*, February 1972, p. 17.

32. Henry J. Aaron, *Politics and the Professors: The Great Society in Perspective* (Washington, D.C.: Brookings Institution, 1978), p. 84.

33. See: David Bresnick, "The Federal Educational Policy System: Enacting and Revising Title I," *Western Political Quarterly*, June 1979; Harrison H. Donelly, "Bill Tilts Education Funds away from South," *Congressional Quarterly*, June 10, 1978.

34. *The Budget of the United States Government, Fiscal Year 1981*, p. 223–24.

35. Martin Anderson, *Welfare: The Political Economy of Welfare Reform in the United States* (Stanford: Hoover Institution Press, 1978), p. 15.

36. Morton Paglin, *Poverty and Transfers In-kind* (Stanford: Hoover Institution Press, 1980).

37. *Social Security Amendments of 1971*, Hearings before the Committee on Finance, U.S. Senate, 92nd Cong., part 3, pp. 1511–619.

38. E. Uhr, "Child Support: the Avoided Obligation," *Focus*, Institute for Poverty Research, Madison, Wisconsin, Fall 1979.

39. Subcommittee on Fiscal Policy of the Joint Economic Committee (Staff Study), *Welfare in the 70's: A National Study of Benefits Available in 100 Local Areas*, Studies in Public Welfare, Paper no. 15, 93d Cong., 2d sess., July 22, 1974, pp. 6–8.

40. Daniel P. Moynihan, "The Crisis in Welfare," *Public Interest*, Winter 1968.

41. Alvin L. Schorr, "ADC–What Direction?" *Child Welfare*, Department of HEW, February 1962.

42. Roger A. Freeman, "Aid to Dependent Children," *Vital Speeches of the Day*, November 1, 1962.

43. *Social Security Amendments of 1971*, Hearings before the Committee on Finance, United States Senate, 92d Cong., 1st sess., part 3, pp. 1511–619.

44. Martin Anderson, "Welfare Reform," in *The United States in the 1980s*, Peter Duignan and Alvin Rabushka, eds. (Stanford: Hoover Institution Press, 1980), p. 162.

45. *Studies in Public Welfare*, Paper No. 3, *The Effectiveness of Manpower*

Training Programs: A Review of Research on the Impact on the Poor. A Staff Study prepared for the Subcommittee on Fiscal Policy of the Joint Economic Committee, 92d Cong., 2d sess., 1972, pp. 1–14.

46. Charles D. Hobbs, *The Welfare Industry*, (Washington, D.C.: Heritage Foundation, 1978).

47. Robert M. Hutchins, "Welfare, Remarriage and Marital Search," *American Economic Review*, June 1979.

48. Beverley L. Johnson, "Marital and Family Characteristics of the Labor Force, March, 1979," *Monthly Labor Review*, April 1980.

49. Jane Bryant Quinn, "Divorce Economic Style," *Newsweek*, June 9, 1980.

50. Michael J. Boskin, "Social Security and the Economy," in *The United States in the 1980s*, Peter Duignan and Alvin Rabushka, eds. (Stanford: Hoover Institution Press, 1980).

51. James M. Buchanan, "Social Insurance in a Growing Economy: A Proposal for Radical Reform," *National Tax Journal*, December 1968.

52. New York: Free Press, 1980.

53. *Social Security Bulletin, Annual Statistical Supplement*, 1976, 1979, p. 22. Most social security data in this section were derived from the cited publication and from other issues of the *Social Security Bulletin*.

54. Most labor force data in this section are derived from: *Handbook of Labor Statistics 1978, 1980*, Bureau of Labor Statistics, Department of Labor; and *Employment and Earnings*, Bureau of Labor Statistics, Department of Labor, December 1980.

55. Richard Burkhauser and Roberta Kimmel, "Why Older Americans Don't Work," *Focus*, Institute for Research on Poverty, University of Wisconsin, Winter 1978–79.

56. Rita Ricardo Campbell, *Social Security: Promise and Reality* (Stanford: Hoover Institution Press, 1977), p. 306; and idem, "The Problems of Fairness" in *The Crisis in Social Security: Problems and Prospects*, Michael J. Boskin, ed. (San Francisco, Institute for Contemporary Studies), 1977.

57. Mordechai E. Lando et al., "Disability Benefit Applications and the Economy," *Social Security Bulletin*, October 1979.

58. Martin Feldstein, "Unemployment Compensation: Adverse Incentives and Distributional Anomalies," *National Tax Journal*, June 1974; idem, *The Importance of Temporary Layoffs: An Empirical Analysis*, Brookings Papers on Economic Activity, 1975; idem, "Temporary Layoffs in the Theory of Unemployment," *Journal of Political Economy*, October 1976; and idem, "The Effect of Unemployment Insurance on Temporary Layoff Unemployment," *American Economic Review*, December 1978.

59. *Unemployment Insurance—Inequities and Work Disincentives in the Current System*, U.S. General Accounting Office, August 28, 1979.

60. *Reader's Digest*, December 1975.

61. *Employment and Earnings*, Bureau of Labor Statistics, Department of Labor, February 1981.

62. George D. Stamas, "Long Hours and Premium Pay, May 1978," *Monthly Labor Review*, May 1979.

63. *The Labor Supply for Lower Level Occupations*, prepared by Harold Wool, U.S. Department of Labor, 1976, pp. 69, 73, 106.

64. See: Kenneth W. Clarkson and Roger E. Meiners, *Distortions in Official Unemployment Statistics: Implications for Public Policy Making* (College Station: Center for Education and Research in Free Enterprise, Texas A & M University, 1979).

65. "Crackdown on Cheaters Who Draw Jobless Pay," *U.S. News & World Report*, May 15, 1978.

66. *Handbook of Labor Statistics, 1978*, U.S. Department of Labor, p. 581.

67. *Time*, May 28, 1979, p. 60.

68. Joseph G. Simanis and John R. Coleman, "Health Care Expenditures in Nine Industrialized Countries, 1960–76," *Social Security Bulletin*, January 1980.

69. *Healthy People, The Surgeon General's Report on Health Promotion and Disease Prevention*, 1979, p. 120.

70. Eric J. Cassell, "Our Sickness System," *Wall Street Journal*, March 3, 1980.

71. These and other data in this section derived from: *Historical Statistics of the United States*, U.S. Bureau of the Census, 1975; and *Statistical Abstract of the United States, 1979*, U.S. Bureau of the Census. Some data are from: *Health, United States, 1979*, Public Health Service, U.S. Department of HEW.

72. "Why Americans are Healthiest Ever: A New Size-Up," *U.S. News & World Report*, October 29, 1979.

73. "Is Intensive Care Too Intensive?" *Newsweek*, May 5, 1980.

74. Jonathan Spivak, "Health Cost Controls in Germany," *Wall Street Journal*, December 19, 1979.

75. Rita Ricardo Campbell, "Your Health and the Government" in *The United States in the 1980s*, Peter Duignan and Alvin Rabushka, eds. (Stanford: Hoover Institution Press, 1980), p. 329.

76. *Cost and Quality of Health Care: Unnecessary Surgery*, report by the Subcommittee on Oversight and Investigations, Committee on Interstate and Foreign Commerce, U.S. House of Representatives, 94th Cong, 2d sess., January 1976, p. 5–9.

77. *Surgical Performance: Necessity and Quality*, 95th Cong., 2d sess., De-

cember 1978, p. 2.

78. *Health United States, 1979*, Public Health Service, Department of HEW, p. 213.

79. Ibid., p. 177. See also: Harry Schwartz, "Health Care and the Poor," *Wall Street Journal*, February 15, 1980.

80. Louise B. Russell, *Technology in Hospitals: Medical Advances and Their Diffusion*, (Washington, D.C.: Brookings Institution, 1979), pp. 156–57.

81. Ibid., p. 164.

82. Martin Feldstein, "The High Cost of Hospitals and What To Do About It," *Public Interest*, Summer 1977; and Stuart M. Butler, "The Competitive Prescription for Health Cost Inflation," *Backgrounder*, Heritage Foundation, February 25, 1980.

83. *Congressional Quarterly*, August 4, 1979, p. 1588.

84. Elizabeth Wehr, "Competition in Health Care: Would it Bring Costs Down?" *Congressional Quarterly*, August 4, 1979.

85. In a speech reported in the *Peninsula Times Tribune*, Palo Alto, Calif., January 17, 1980.

86. *New York Times*, June 3, 1969.

87. *Crime in the United States, 1978*, FBI Uniform Crime Report, U.S. Department of Justice, 1979; *Historical Statistics of the United States, Colonial Times to 1970*, Bureau of the Census, 1975, p. 413.

88. President Johnson's Commission on Law Enforcement and Administration of Justice in 1967 estimated that there were twice as many crimes committed as reported; a Bureau of the Census survey in 1973 thought that it might be three times as many. Subsequent research confirmed those conclusions.

89. *The Challenge of Crime in a Free Society*, President's Commission on Law Enforcement and Administration of Justice, p. 279.

90. *To Establish Justice, To Insure Domestic Tranquility*, Final Report of the National Commission on The Causes and Prevention of Violence, December 1960, pp. 16, 27.

91. *A National Strategy To Reduce Crime*, National Advisory Commission on Criminal Justice Standards and Goals, 1973, pp. 7, 57, etc.

92. Ramsey Clark, *Crime in America* (New York: Simon & Schuster 1970), pp. 17–18.

93. Alma McMillan and Ann Kallman Bixby, "Social Welfare Expenditures under Public Programs, Fiscal Year 1978" *Social Security Bulletin*, U.S. Department of HEW, May 1980.

94. *Characteristics of the Population Below Poverty Level: 1977*, Current Population Reports, Series P-60, No. 119, U.S. Bureau of the Census.

95. *Money Income of Families and Persons in the United States: 1978*, Current

Population Reports, Series P-60, No. 123, U.S. Bureau of the Census; *Character-istics of the Population Below the Poverty Level: 1978,* Current Population Reports, Series P-60, No. 124, U.S. Bureau of the Census.

96. *Trends in Expenditure and Employment Data for the Criminal Justice System 1971–1977,* U.S. Departments of Justice and Commerce, 1980. Data for earlier years may be found in the *Statistical Abstract of the United States, 1979* and in the *Historical Statistics of the United States Colonial Times to 1970,* 1975, both by the Bureau of the Census.

97. James Q. Wilson, "Do the Police Prevent Crime?" *New York Times Magazine,* October 6, 1974. Subsequently Professor Wilson wrote: "Nearly ten years ago I wrote that the billions of dollars the federal government was then preparing to spend on crime control would be wasted and indeed might even make matters worse if they were merely pumped into the existing criminal justice system. They were and they have" (James Q. Wilson, "Lock 'em Up and Other Thoughts on Crime," *New York Times Magazine,* March 9, 1975.)

98. Orde Coombs, "The Three Faces of Harlem," *New York Times Magazine,* November 3, 1974.

99. Gerald M. Caplan at hearings on *Law Enforcement Assistance Administration,* Subcommittee on Crime, Committee on the Judiciary, U.S. House, 94th Cong., 2d sess., 1976, serial no. 42, part I, pp. 549, 551.

100. Thomas Plate, *Crime Pays!* (New York: Simon & Schuster, 1975), pp. 92, 96.

101. As paraphrased by Eugene H. Methvin, "The Criminal Mind: A Startling New Look," *Readers Digest,* May 1978, from the 3-volume study by Yochelson and Samenow, *The Criminal Personality* (New York: Jason Aronson, 1976).

102. Jessica Mitford, *Kind and Usual Punishment: The Prison Business* (New York: Knopf, 1973).

103. Ernest van den Haag, *Punishing Criminals* (New York: Basic Books, 1975).

104. James Q. Wilson, *Thinking About Crime* (New York: Basic Books, 1975).

105. *Public Interest,* Summer 1974.

106. Center for Econometrics Studies of the Justice System, *Research Developments* (Stanford: Hoover Institution, 1979).

107. *Barron's,* December 10, 1979.

108. Karl Menninger, *The Crime of Punishment* (New York: Viking Press, 1966).

109. *Compendium of Housing Statistics*, United Nations, 1976.

110. Pierre de Vise, "The Wasting of Chicago," in *Crisis in Urban Housing*, Grant S. McClellan, ed. (New York: H. W. Wilson, 1974), p. 41.

111. Quoted from: Martin Mayer, *The Builders: Houses, People, Neighborhoods, Government, Money* (New York: W. W. Norton, 1978), p. 184.

112. "The Social Welfare Forum," *Proceedings of the Eighty-ninth Annual Forum*, National Conference on Social Welfare, May 27–June 1, 1962, New York City, pp. xv–xvi.

113. Anthony Downs, "The Successes and Failures of Federal Housing Policy," *Public Interest*, Winter 1974.

114. *Department of HUD etc. Appropriations for 1980*, Hearings before the Subcommittee of the Committee on Appropriations, House, 96th Cong., 1st sess., part 7, pp. 215 ff.

115. Ibid, pp. 17–23.

116. *The Tenth Annual Report on Housing Goals*, U.S. Department of HUD, September 1, 1979, pp. 53, 57.

117. Irving Welfeld, "American Housing Policy: Perverse Programs by Prudent People," *Public Interest*, Summer 1977.

118. B. Bruce-Briggs "The Cost of Housing," *Public Interest*, Summer 1973. The term "minority" does not refer to ethnic minorities but to individuals who advanced economically at a slower pace than the great majority or the "average" of Americans.

119. *Journal of the American Real Estate and Urban Economics Association*, Summer 1977.

120. Richard F. Muth, "National Housing Policy," in *The United States in the 1980s*, Alvin Rabushka and Peter Duignan, eds. (Stanford: Hoover Institution Press, 1980), pp. 346–348, 364. Muth's calculations include gains from the homeowner's equity.

121. E. Jay Howenstine, "Housing Costs in the United States and Other Industrialized Countries, 1970–1977," *Construction Review*, January 1980.

122. George Sternlieb and James W. Hughes described this "enormous escalation of housing standards" in "The Post-Shelter Society," *Public Interest*, Fall 1979.

123. Most economic data are derived from the *Economic Report of the President*, January 1980, and *Economic Indicators* (monthly). Construction data are from *Construction Review* (monthly), U.S. Department of Commerce.

124. *HUD Appropriations, 1980, etc.*, pp. 39–40.

125. Derived from: *Economic Report of the President*, January 1980, p. 259.

126. Henry Aaron, "The Domestic Budget" in *Setting National Priorities, The 1980 Budget,* Joseph A. Pechman, ed. (Washington, D.C.: Brookings Institution, 1979), p. 119.

127. Welfeld, "American Housing Policy," p. 133.

128. Lee Rainwater, "The Lessons of Pruitt-Igoe," *Public Interest,* Summer 1967.

129. J. S. Fuerst, "Survival Kit for Public Housing," *Commonweal,* September 7, 1973.

130. *Housing Abandonment: A National Problem Needing New Approaches,* Report to the Congress by the Comptroller General of the United States, August 1978. Abandonment of section 235 housing (aid to low-income homeowning) is caused by the fact that beneficiaries have no investment and virtually no equity in the house. When major repairs become necessary or other trouble develops the "owners" simply walk away because they paid no more—and possibly less—than rent would have been.

131. *Is The Urban Crisis Over?* Hearings before the Subcommittee on Fiscal and Intergovernmental Policy of the Joint Economic Committee, 96th Cong., 1st sess., March 20, 1979, p. 90.

132. Quoted by Susanna McBee in the *Washington Post,* March 29, 1978.

133. *Keeping Business in the City,* Hearings before the Subcommittee on Fiscal and Intergovernmental Policy, Joint Economic Committee, 95th Cong., 2d sess., March 1978, p. 2.

134. James S. Coleman, "Can We Revitalize Our Cities?" *Challenge,* November-December 1977.

135. "Cities May Need More Than Carter Plan," *Washington Post,* March 29, 1978. At congressional hearings cited earlier, Rep. William S. Moorehead, the committee's chairman, suggested to "examine all of our federal policies for unintended antiurban bias."

136. Cambridge, Mass.: MIT Press, 1964, p. x.

137. Martin Meyer, *The Builders* (New York: W.W. Norton, 1978), p. 119.

138. Christopher C. Demuth, "Deregulating the Cities," *Public Interest,* Summer 1976; and Charles Longstreet Weltner, "The Model Cities Program: A Sobering Scorecard," *Policy Review,* Fall 1977.

139. Melvin M. Webber, "The BART Experience—What Have We Learned?" *Public Interest,* Fall 1976.

140. B. Bruce-Briggs, "Mass Transportation and Minority Transportation," *Public Interest,* Summer 1975. An excellent summary of the problems and dilemmas.

141. *Is the Urban Crisis Over?*, pp. 7, 12.

142. Joint Economic Committee, 95th Cong., 2d sess., March 1978, pp. 178–181. Mayor Landrieu subsequently was appointed Secretary of HUD by President Carter.

143. "How Cities Are Luring People Back," *U.S. News & World Report*, March 24, 1980.

144. *Trends in the Fiscal Condition of Cities: 1978-1980*, Subcommittee on Fiscal and Intergovernmental Policy, Joint Economic Committee, 96th Cong., 2d sess., April 1980, p. 5.

145. *Time*, August 29, 1977, cover story.

146. Most data in this section are derived from bulletins of the U.S. Bureau of the Census, *Current Population Reports*, Series P-20 and P-60, unless otherwise noted.

147. Andrew Hacker, "Creating American Inequality," *New York Review*, March 20, 1980.

148. Labor force data from: *Handbook of Labor Statistics*, 1978, and *Employment and Earnings*, May 1980, both by Bureau of Labor Statistics, U.S. Department of Labor.

149. *Digest of Education Statistics 1979*, National Center for Education Statistics, Department of HEW, p. 16.

150. *School Enrollment—Social and Economic Characteristics of Students: October 1979*, U.S. Bureau of the Census, Current Population Report, Series P-20, No. 355, August 1980.

151. *Digest of Education Statistics 1979*, National Center for Education Statistics, Department of HEW, pp. 29–33.

152. From the National Assessment for Educational Literacy; Robert I. Lerman, *The Nature of the Youth Employment Problem: A Review Paper*, prepared for the Vice-President's Task Force on Youth Employment, November 1979, p. 55.

153. "Results of the Examination of Youths for Military Service, 1972," Supplement to *Health of the Army*, Department of the Army, Office of the Surgeon General, September 1973.

154. Thomas Sowell, "Myths about Minorities," *Commentary*, August 1979.

155. Thomas Sowell, *Race and Economics* (New York, David McKay, 1975), p. 207.

156. Andrew M. Greeley, "The Ethnic Miracle," *Public Interest*, Fall 1976.

157. Herbert Burkholz, "The Latinization of Miami," *New York Times Magazine*, September 21, 1980.

158. Edward C. Banfield, *The Unheavenly City Revisited* (Boston: Little, Brown, 1974), p. 98.

159. *Congressional Record*, September 13, 1966, p. 21547.

160. *Fullilove* v. *Klutznik*, No. 78–1007, U.S. Supreme Court, decided July 2, 1980.

161. Nathan Glazer, *Affirmative Discrimination: Ethnic Inequality and Public Policy* (New York: Basic Books, 1975).

162. Robert Lindsay, "School Integration Looks More Than Ever Like a Lost Horizon," *New York Times*, August 24, 1980.

163. Anthony Lewis, "The Legality of Racial Quotas," *New York Times*, March 3, 1974.

164. *Congressional Record*, September 13, 1966, p. 21545.

165. *Affirmative Action: Its Legal Mandate and Organizational Implications*, Center for the Study of Higher Education, School of Education, University of Michigan, 1974, p. 11.

166. Carl Cohen, "Justice Debased: The Weber Decision," *Commentary*, September 1979. By the same author: "Why Racial Preference is Illegal and Immoral," *Commentary*, June 1979.

167. *Congressional Record*, March 30, 1964, p. 6549.

168. David A. Lombardo, Frederick C. Nold, and Michael K. Block, *Burglary and Robbery Cases in California, 1973: A Statistical Analysis of the Relationship Between the Disposition of Criminal Cases and Selected Social, Economic and Criminal Characteristics of Defendants*, Center for the Econometric Studies of Crime and the Criminal Justice System, Hoover Institution, April 1976 (proc.), pp. 15, 16, 24, 26, 29.

169. Roger A. Freeman, *Socialism and Private Enterprise in Equatorial Asia: The Case of Malaysia and Indonesia* (Stanford: Hoover Institution, 1968), pp. 45ff.

170. *New York Times*, January 27, 1979.

171. *Center Magazine*, March/April 1979.

172. "The Black Plight: Race or Class," *New York Times Magazine*, October 5, 1980.

173. Marilyn Gittel, ed., Institute for Community Studies, Queens College of the City University of New York, 1969.

174. "The Black Plight: Race or Class," *New York Times Magazine*, October 5, 1980.

175. *On Equal Educational Opportunity*, Frederick Mosteller and Daniel P. Moynihan, eds. (New York: Random House, 1972), p. 86.

176. David J. Armor, "The Evidence on Busing," *Public Interest*, Summer 1972.

177. Jan Blakeslee, "White Flight to the Suburbs: A Demographic Approach," *Focus*, Institute for Research on Poverty Newsletter, University of Wisconsin, Winter 1978–79; and William H. Frey, "Central City White Flight: Racial and Nonracial Causes," *American Sociological Review*, June 1979.

178. "Researcher Discounts Race as 'White Flight' Factor," *Los Angeles Times*, November 7, 1979. See also Armor's comments in "Busing and 'White Flight,'" *Public Interest*, Fall 1978.

179. "Not Enough White Children," *Newsweek*, September 15, 1980. Also: "24 Years of Integration: Has Busing Really Worked?", *U.S. News & World Report*, May 8, 1980; and "Lots of School Buses, Not Enough Whites," *U.S. News & World Report*, October 13, 1980.

180. Diane Ravitch, "Social Science and Social Policy: The 'White Flight' Controversy,'" *Public Interest*, Spring 1978; also "A Bifurcated Vision of Urban Education," in *Future Trends in Education Policy*, Jane Newii, ed. (Lexington, Mass.: Lexington Books, 1979).

181. *Geographic Mobility: March 1975 to March 1979*, Current Population Reports, Series P-20, No. 353, U.S. Bureau of the Census, August 1980.

182. *Congressional Record*, April 24, 1969, p. E3374.

183. Thomas Sowell, *Knowledge and Decisions* (New York: Basic Books, 1980), p. 263.

Chapter 5: *Issues and Prospects*

1. Gerhard Colm, "Theory of Public Expenditures," *Annals of the American Academy of Political and Social Science*, 183 (January, 1936).

2. William Henry Chamberlain, "State vs. Individual," *Wall Street Journal*, March 11, 1960.

3. Irving Kristol, "Is the Welfare State Obsolete?" *Harper's*, June 1963.

4. Sidney Hook, *Philosophy and Public Policy* (Carbondale: Southern Illinois University Press, 1980), p. 113.

5. Michael Harrington, *Toward a Democratic Left: A Radical Program for a New Majority* (New York: Macmillan, 1968).

6. "Big Government Is Feared in Poll," *New York Times*, August 18, 1968.

7. *Public Opinion*, October/November 1979. Medicine rated highest at 46%, the science community 40%, organized religion 32%, the military 31%, the Supreme Court 29%, the press 21%, television 14%.

8. Gunnar Myrdal, *Challenge to Affluence* (New York: Pantheon, 1968), p. 64.

9. Ibid., p. 93.

10. See Frank Freidel, *Franklin D. Roosevelt: The Triumph* (Boston: Little, Brown, 1956).

11. Eisenhower added: "We are convinced that more progress and sounder progress will be made over the years as the largest possible share of our national

income is left with individual citizens to make their own countless decisions as to what they will spend, what they will buy, and what they will save and invest."

12. U.S. Congress, House, Committee on Education and Labor, *Federal Aid to States for School Construction*, 85th Cong., 1st sess., 1957, p. 395.

13. *Boston Post*, April 23, 1950.

14. *Wall Street Journal*, April 22, 25, 1963. See also a reply, "Putting a Myth to Rest," *Wall Street Journal*, May 29, 1963.

15. *Saturday Review*, January 9, 1965, pp. 28–29.

16. Fabricant, *The Trend of Government Activity in the United States*; Kendrick, *A Century and a Half of Federal Expenditures*.

17. Adolf Wagner, *Grundlagen der Politischen Oekonomie* (1893), as cited by Charles J. Bullock, *Selected Readings in Public Finance*, 3d ed. (Boston: Ginn, 1924), p.32.

18. Benjamin Jowett, trans., and W. D. Ross ed., *The Works of Aristotle* (Oxford: Clarendon Press, 1921), vol. 10, *Politics*, 6. 5. 1320a.

19. David R. Cameron, The Expansion of the Public Economy: A Comparative Analysis," *American Political Science Review*, Vol. 72, No. 4 (December 1978).

20. Allan H. Meltzer, *Why Government Grows* (Los Angeles: International Institute for Economic Research, 1976).

21. "Buying the Vote," *Commentary*, December 1978.

22. The list of those journals, to be sure, was biased on the left and did not include *National Review* or any other journal that could be called even moderately conservative. Few of the journals listed would carry an article by a conservative or with a conservative bent. It is, however, a fact that there are more intellectual journals on the left than on the right. Individuals who are conservatively inclined have not done as much writing—and apparently not as much intellectual reading—as liberals. Conservative journals therefore could not and did not develop to the extent to which liberal journals did, at least not before the late 1970s.

23. Charles Kadushin, "Who Are the Elite Intellectuals?" *Public Interest*, Fall 1972.

24. Galbraith, *The Affluent Society* (Boston: Houghton Mifflin), 1958, pp. 315, 251.

25. Robert Lekachman, "Troubles of the Welfare State," *Dissent*, Fall 1979.

26. Henry Steele Commager, "Brave World of the Year 2000," *New York Times Magazine*, November 1, 1959.

27. Michael Harrington, *Decade of Decision: The Crisis of the American System* (New York: Simon & Schuster, 1980), p. 223.

28. "Who Could Get Hurt by Federal Budget Cuts," *U.S. News & World Report*, September 29, 1980.

29. Cambridge: Harvard University Press, 1976, p. viii.

30. Arthur Schlesinger, Jr., "Is Liberalism Dead?" *New York Times Magazine*, March 30, 1980.

31. *New Republic*, March 13, 1976.

32. Washington, D.C.: Brookings Institution, 1978, p.1.

33. Amitai Etzioni, "Human Beings Are Not Very Easy To Change After All," *Saturday Review*, June 3, 1972.

34. *Fortune*, October 1972.

35. "Why Can't We Get Things Done?" *Brookings Bulletin*, Spring 1972.

36. Cassidy, "How We Got from 'Equal Opportunity' to 'Equal Results,'" *Planning*, American Society of Planning Officials, February 1974.

37. Michael Harrington, "The Welfare State and its Neoconservative Critics," in *The New Conservatives: A Critique from the Left*, Lewis A. Coser and Irving Howe, eds. (New York: Quadrangle, 1974), p. 53.

38. Ibid., pp. 29, 39, 46, 57, 108.

39. Robert Lekachman, "Troubles of the Welfare State," *Dissent*, Fall 1979.

40. Ben J. Wattenberg and Richard J. Scammon, "Black Progress and Liberal Rhetoric," *Commentary*, April 1973.

41. *Public Interest*, Spring 1976.

42. Roger A. Freeman, "What Makes Ivan Run?" *National Review*, March 7, 1967.

43. U.S. Joint Economic Committee, *The American Distribution of Income: A Structural Problem*, 92d Cong., 2d sess., March 17, 1972, p. 1.

44. Harold C. Groves, *Financing Government* (New York: Henry Holt, 1946), p. 31.

45. Henry C. Simons, *Personal Income Taxation* (Chicago: University of Chicago Press, 1938), p. 18.

46. Ibid.

47. John Rawls, *A Theory of Justice* (Cambridge, Mass.: Harvard University Press, 1971), pp. 74, 102, 303.

48. Daniel Bell, "On Meritocracy and Equality," *Public Interest*, Fall 1972.

Christopher Jencks also attributes economic success to luck or fortuitous circumstances and therefore not a matter of personal merit that would justify a reward in the form of higher income or status. "Economic success seems to depend on varieties of luck and on-the-job competence that are only moderately related to family background, schooling, or scores on standard tests" (Christopher Jencks et al., *Inequality*, p. 8).

49. Rawls, *A Theory of Justice*, p. 540.

50. Walter J. Blum and Harry Kalven, Jr., *The Uneasy Case for Progressive Taxation* (Chicago: University of Chicago Press, 1953), p. 82.

51. Ibid., p. 20.

52. H. L. Mencken, *A Mencken Chrestomathy* (New York: Alfred A. Knopf, 1949), p. 145.

53. Irving Kristol, "On the Necessity of Economic Growth," *Wall Street Journal*, November 26, 1979.

54. Robert L. Heilbronner, "Priorities for the Seventies," *Saturday Review*, January 3, 1970.

55. James S. Coleman et al., *Equality of Educational Opportunity*, p. 297.

56. Mary Jo Bane and Christopher Jencks, "The Schools and Equal Opportunity," *Saturday Review of Education*, October 1972.

57. Elizabeth Drew, "Contemplating the National Navel," *New York Times Book Review*, June 4, 1972.

58. James L. Buckley, "The Trouble With Federalism: It Isn't Being Tried," *Commonsense: A Republican Journal of Thought and Opinion*, 1, Summer 1978.

59. W. Glenn Campbell, "Assuring the Primacy of National Security," in *National Security: Political, Military, and Economic Strategies in the Decade Ahead*, David M. Abshire and Richard V. Allen, eds. (Stanford: Hoover Institution on War, Revolution and Peace; New York: Praeger, 1963), pp. 976–77.

60. *Public Opinion*, American Enterprise Institute, July–August 1978.

61. "What Congress Really Thinks of Itself," *U.S. News & World Report*, January 14, 1980.

62. Walter Dean Burnham, "Jimmy Carter and the Democratic Crisis," *New Republic*, July 3 and 10, 1976.

63. Richard E. Neustadt, *Presidential Power* (New York, John Wiley & Son, 1960); Arthur M. Schlesinger, Jr., *The Imperial Presidency* (Boston, Houghton Mifflin Co., 1973); and Joseph Kraft, "The Post-Imperial Presidency," *New York Times Magazine*, November 2, 1980.

64. *The Federal Role in the Federal System: The Dynamics of Growth*, Vol. I, *A Crisis of Confidence and Competence*, Advisory Commission on Intergovernmental Relations, 1980, pp. 5, 17.

65. "Federal Spending: Past, Present, and Future" in *Setting National Priorities: The Next Ten Years*, Henry Owen and Charles L. Schultze, eds. (Washington, D.C.: Brookings Institution, 1976), p. 367.

66. *Olmstead* v. *United States*, 277 U.S. 438 (1927), at 477. Emphasis added.

67. *The Autobiographical Notes of Charles Evans Hughes*, D. J. Danielski and J. S. Tulchin, eds. (Cambridge: Harvard University Press, 1973), p. 143.

68. *United States* v. *Butler*, 297 U.S. 1.

69. *Harper* v. *VA. Board of Elections*, 383 U.S. 663.

70. 261 U.S. 525.

71. *Griswold* v. *Connecticut*, 381 U.S. 479.

72. Raoul Berger, *Government by Judiciary: The Transformation of the Fourteenth Amendment* (Cambridge: Harvard University Press, 1977). The title *Government by Judiciary* was used nearly a half century earlier by Louis B. Boudin for a 2-volume scathing criticism of the Supreme Court for arrogating to itself power it did not, under the Constitution, possess (New York: William Goodin, 1932); Nathan Glazer, "Toward an Imperial Judiciary?" *Public Interest*, Fall 1975; Ernest Van Den Haag, "The Growth of the Imperial Judiciary," *Policy Review*, Spring 1978; Martin Shapiro, "Judicial Activism" in *The Third Century: America as a Post-Industrial Society*, Seymour Martin Lipset, ed. (Chicago: University of Chicago Press, 1979); Marvin Stone, "Dictatorship by Judiciary?" *U.S. News & World Report*, February 27, 1978.

73. 163 U.S. 537 (1896).

74. 402 U.S. 1 (1971).

75. Alpheus Thomas Mason, *Security Through Freedom: American Political Thought and Practice* (Ithaca: Cornell University Press, 1955), pp. 145–46.

76. Archibald Cox, *The Role of the Supreme Court in American Government* (New York, Oxford University Press, 1976), p. 50.

77. Alexander M. Bickel, *The Supreme Court and the Idea of Progress* (New Haven, Yale University Press, 1978), p. 103.

78. Cox, *Role of the Supreme Court*, pp. 13–14.

79. Berger, *Government by Judiciary*, p. 7.

80. 369 U.S. 186.

81. 383 U.S. 301 (1965).

82. 384 U.S. 641 (1966).

83. "What Do You Do When the Supreme Court Is Wrong?", *Public Interest*, Fall 1979.

84. *Everson* v. *Board of Education*, 330 U.S. 1 (1947); *Zorach* v. *Clauson*, 343 U.S. 306 (1952).

85. *Board* v. *Allen*, 392 U.S. 236 (1968); *Tilton* v. *Richardson*, 403 U.S. 672 (1971); *Committee* v. *Niquist*, 413 U.S. 756 (1973).

86. *Walz* v. *Tax Commission*, 307 U.S. 664 (1970).

87. "How Carter Put His Stamp on Federal Courts," *U.S. News & World Report*, October 20, 1980; also, "The Judges Carter Picks—Activist and Liberal," *U.S. News & World Report*, June 18, 1978.

88. "Are Judges Getting Too Powerful?" *U.S. News & World Report*, January 16, 1978.

89. Berkeley: University of California Press, 1964, pp. 95–96.

90. Herman Kahn and Anthony J. Wiener, *The Year 2000: A Framework for Speculation on the Next Thirty-Three Years* (New York: Macmillan, 1967), p. 38.

91. Daniel Bell, ed., *Toward the Year 2000: Work in Progress* (Boston: Houghton Mifflin, 1967).

92. "Next Decade Will Be the 'Sobering '80's,'" *U.S. News & World Report*, August 20, 1979.

93. "A Grim Year 2000," *Newsweek*, August 4, 1980.

94. Lance Liebman, "Social Intervention in a Democracy," *Public Interest*, Winter 1974.

95. Herbert J. Gans, "The American Malaise," *New York Times Magazine*, February 6, 1972.

96. New York: Basic Books, 1980, pp. 4, 9, 331, 356.

97. New York: Atheneum, 1970, p. 3.

98. New York: Warner Books, 1980, p. 6.

99. "A Cassandra's Valid Warning of Coming Peril," *Wall Street Journal*, May 7, 1980.

100. "Brookings Evades the Debate on Government," *Wall Street Journal*, June 20, 1980.

101. Most data from *Current Population Reports*, Series P-25 and P-20 of the Bureau of the Census, and *Vital Statistics Reports* (monthly), U.S. Department of Health and Human Resources.

102. Statistics from *Handbook of Labor Statistics, 1978, 1980, Monthly Labor Review*, October 1980, and *Employment and Earnings*, October 1980, all by the Bureau of Labor Statistics, U.S. Department of Labor.

103. Joann S. Lubin, "Unions Push to 'Catch' Inflation Will be Big Issue in 1981 Bargaining," *Wall Street Journal*, December 5, 1981.

Index

★★★★★★★

A

Aaron, Henry J., 201–2, 206, 379
Adjusted gross income (AGI), 86, 87
Advisory Commission on Intergovernmental Relations (ACIR), 59, 76, 105–6
Advisory Council on the Education of Disadvantaged Children, 203–4
Advisory Council on Social Security, 110, 242
Affirmative action, 32, 39–40, 333–45
AFL-CIO, 19–20, 21, 48
Aid to dependent children, 215–32
American Federation of Teachers, 21
American Nurses Association, 48
Aspin, Les, 138, 148

B

Baker v. *Carr*, 411
Bakke case, 334, 338
Bazelon, David L., 277–78
Big government, 363–64, 373–79

Binding arbitration, 52–53
Black, Hugo L., 408
Brandeis, Louis, 405
Brown II case, 334, 344, 345, 347, 359, 409
Buckley, James L., 397
Budget, xxiii, 151–57, 160–62
Budget and Accounting Act of 1974, 92
Budget reform, 157–66
Bureau of the Budget, 13
Bureau of the Census, 47, 118, 121, 213, 252, 292
Bureau of Economic Analysis, 292
Bureau of Labor Statistics, 33, 34
Burns, Arthur F., 71, 159
Busing, 344–59, 415

C

Califano, Joseph, 7
Campbell, W. Glenn, 397–98
Capital gains, 93–94
Carter, James, 2–6 *passim*, 28–29,

Carter, cont.
  71–75 *passim,* 129–40 *passim,*
  159–60, 256, 369, 383, 396,
  416–18 *passim*
Categorical grants, 399
Central Intelligence Agency, 146
Cities, revitalization of, 308–18
Civil rights, 318–59
Civil Rights Act of 1964, 31, 32, 333,
  344, 347
Civil Service Commission, 5, 32,
  33–34, 47
Clark, Ramsey, 277
Coleman, James S., 21, 185–86, 309,
  310, 350
Coleman report, 203
Collective bargaining contracts,
  48–49
Commission on Intergovernmental
  Relations, 64, 174, 402, 403
Comptroller General, 14, 15, 20, 53,
  205, 248–49, 305, 315
Congressional Budget Office (CBO),
  36, 163–68 *passim,* 213, 293, 294
Consumer Price Index (CPI), 16, 55,
  116, 136, 232, 237, 265, 297
Consumption, private and public, 476
  (table)
Consumption tax, 94–95, 102–6
Corporate income, 96
Corporation profits tax, 95–102
Council of Economic Advisers, 70,
  140
Crime, 274–89, 316–17

D

Department of Agriculture, 16–17
Department of Commerce, 47, 100
Department of Defense, 4, 5, 47, 145

Department of Education, 5, 203
Department of Housing and Urban
  Development (HUD), 293–97
  passim, 303, 306
Department of Labor, 253–54
Disability insurance, 244–45
Discrimination, 31, 319–20, 333–45
Douglas, William O., 337
Dred Scott case, 355

E

Economic growth, 424–34
Economic Opportunity Act of 1964,
  223, 394
Education, 20–23, 46, 128, 129, 167,
  180, 181–200, 261, 317–18; employment in, 9; federal aid to,
  183–85; declining quality of,
  188–91, 191–200; as solution to
  poverty, 200–209; for blacks,
  324–27; and affirmative action,
  344–58
Egalitarianism, 363–64, 382–93, 411
Eisenhower, Dwight D., 3, 64, 144,
  152, 173, 174, 365, 366
*Elementary and Secondary Education
  Act of 1965* (ESEA), 203, 205,
  208, 347
Employment and affirmative action,
  336–37
Employment in industry, 442 (table)
  445 (table), 453 (table)
Employment-to-population ratio, 258
Expenditures; federal, 360, 444 (table), 466–67 (table), 472–73 (table);
  government, 360, 443 (table), 457
  (table), 465 (table), 470–71 (table), 474–75 (table); state and local,
  468–69 (table)

F

Family Assistance Plan, 129, 225
Federal aid, 6, 30, 169–77, 183–85,
  398–99
Federal authority, expansion of,
  399–406
Federal bureaucracy, 3, 6–7, 10, 28
Federal employment, 4–5, 19
Federal Salary Reform Act of 1962,
  33, 37
Federal spending, 130–31
Financial Accounting Standards
  Board, xxvi, 100
Fiscal capacity, 64–65
Fiscal grants, 170–71, 399
Ford, Gerald, 2, 8, 48, 108, 139, 153
Foreign affairs, 396–97
Foreign aid, 390–92
Fullilove v. *Klutznik,* 358
Furnco v. *Waters,* 337

G

Galbraith, John Kenneth, 60, 374
Gallup poll, 58, 117, 151–52, 275, 364
General Schedule (GS) pay scale,
  36–40
GNP, *see* Gross national product
Government employment, 1–2, 8–9,
  441 (table), 442 (table), 446 (ta-
  ble), 448 (table), 449–50 (table),
  451–52 (table)
Government, growth of, 364–73
Government pensions, 41–46
Government spending, 368 (table)
Green v. *New Kent County,* 346
Griggs v. *Duke,* 337, 338
Gross National Product (GNP),
  55–56, 74–76 *passim,* 100–107

passim, 122–33 *passim,* 139–44
passim, 167, 210, 261, 362, 433

H

Harrington, Michael, 377, 381
Harris, Patricia Roberts, 294, 309
Harris poll, 58, 139
Health, 20, 128, 129, 167, 180; em-
  ployment in, 9, 23–26; and welfare,
  260–74; major risk insurance,
  273–74
Heller, Walter, 70, 170
HEW, 203; *see also* Department of
  Education
Hoover, Herbert, 152, 365
Housing, 180, 289–308; low-income,
  292–306; government subsidy of,
  301–3; cost of low-income, 303–6;
  construction costs, 306–7; financ-
  ing of, 307–8; and urban renewal,
  310–12
HUD, *see* Department of Housing
  and Urban Development
Hughes, Charles Evans, 409
Humphrey, Hubert, 337
Huntington, Samuel P., 138, 143

I

Illegal aliens, 255–57
Immigration, 422–23
*Immigration and Naturalization Act of
  1965,* 255
Imprisonment, and minorities,
  339–40
Income redistribution, 123, 124, 131,
  210, 363–64, 382–93
Income support, 128, 129, 378
Income tax, 68–70, 74–95, 464 (ta-

Income tax, cont.
  ble), 465 (table); changes in, 73,
  76; graduated, 75–76; state, 95
Industry, 431–32
Inflation, 383, 420, 427–31, 433
Insurance, medical, 271–74
Intellectual elite, political leanings of,
  372–73
Internal Revenue Code, 77, 84, 86,
  89, 90, 100, 121
Internal Revenue Service, 17–19,
  29–30, 91

J

Jefferson, Thomas, 364
Jencks, Christopher, 186, 349, 395
Johnson, Lyndon, 4, 145, 152–53,
  178–79, 184–85, 276, 366–67,
  394–96 *passim*
Joint Economic Committee, 13,
  218–20
Judicial supremacy, 407–17

K

Katzenbach v. *Morgan*, 412
Kennedy, John F., 33, 70–75 *passim*,
  144–45 *passim*, 152, 183, 222–23,
  366, 377, 396
King, Martin Luther, 52
Korb, Lawrence J., 144, 145
Korean War, 73, 96, 127, 143
Kristol, Irving, 362, 388

L

Labor Department, 253–54
Life expectancy, 263–64
Lindsay, John, 51, 187, 348

M

Mackay Doctrine, 51
McNamara, Robert, 144, 145, 158
Medical insurance, 271–74
Medicaid, 263, 269–71
Medicare, 111, 263, 269–71
Milliken v. *Bradley*, 355
Mink, Patsy, 135–36
Minorities, 32, 321–23, 329–30
Money supply, 429
Moynihan, Daniel Patrick, 220–21,
  225, 356, 366, 412
Municipal employees, 40

N

National Academy of Education, 21,
  189, 195
National Assessment of Educational
  Progress (NAEP), 22, 189, 326
National defense, 2, 126–27, 130,
  131, 141–49, 361, 436–37; vs.
  domestic services, 134–41; man-
  power in, 148–49; balance of
  power, 149–51
National Education Association, 21,
  48, 49, 183, 184, 202
National health insurance, 129,
  272–73
National Housing Act of 1949, 310
National income, 96
National Institute of Law Enforce-
  ment and Criminal Justice, 281–82
National Opinion Research Center,
  364, 414
National Urban Coalition, 135
National Urban League, 136
Neoconservatives, rise of, 379–82
New Deal, 69, 123
Nixon, Richard M., 5–8 *passim*,
  46–51 *passim*, 88, 129, 153, 163,
  204, 223–25 *passim*, 367, 419–20

O

Office of Administration, 7
Office of Economic Opportunity (OEO), 205–6
Oil, 104–5
OPEC, 104
Opinion Research poll, 117
Organization for Economic Development and Cooperation (OECD), 60, 125

P

Paperwork Reduction Act, 29
Parkinson's Law, 7
Pay, in government, 33–46
Personal income (PI), 86, 96
Pierce v. *Society*, 347
Planning, Programming, Budgeting System (PPBS), 13, 157–59
Plessy v. *Ferguson*, 344, 409
Police, 9, 20, 26–27
Population distribution, 423–24
Postal Reorganization Act, 15
Postal Service, xxiv, 14–16, 47, 51, 53
Poverty, war on, 209–15
Powell, Adam Clayton, 366
Private consumption, 374–76, 376 (table)
Productivity growth rate, 426–27
Productivity indexes, 13, 14
Productivity in government, 12–33
Profits, 98–99, 102
Property tax, 112–21
Prophecies, 417–21
Proposition 13, 59, 113–15
Public consumption, 374–76, 376 (table)
Public services, 12, 123
Public spending, 122–24; upward trends in, 124–26; for national defense, 126–27; shift in, 127–28; for domestic purposes, 128–32; in late 1970s, 132–34; national defense vs. social services, 134–41

R

Ramspeck Act of 1940, 31
Reagan, Ronald, 229
Rehnquist, William H., 338
Rent subsidy (Section 8) program, 293–94
Retirement, employees: payment toward, 42–43
Revenues, 440 (table), 459–60 (table)
Revenue Act of 1978, 84
Revenue sharing, 404
Rivlin, Alice, 203, 380
Rockefeller, John, 51
Roosevelt, Franklin D., 49–50, 102, 152, 222, 246, 289, 365
Roper poll, 58, 189, 275
Ross, Stanford G., 111–12, 235

S

Savings, 71–72
Schlesinger, Arthur Jr., 378
Scholastic Aptitude Tests (SATs), 22, 189, 193, 199
Schultze, Charles L., 158, 380–81, 405
Senate Armed Services Committee, 139
Social security, xvii, 41–45 *passim*, 214–15, 232–45, 261, 378
Social Security Act of 1935, 214, 215, 222
Social Security Administration, 263
Social security tax, 74, 106–12, 383
Social services, xvii–xviii, 6, 57, 131, 360; for health, 260–74; financing

Social security, cont.
   of, 361; vs. national defense,
   134–41; and personal freedom, 363
South Carolina v. *Katzenback*, 412
Soviet Union, 142, 145, 146–47, 260,
   384
Sowell, Thomas, 328, 358
Space race, 365–66
State-local revenues, 62–65
States' rights, 401
Steiger Amendment, 94
Stock market, 99–100
Stone, Harlan F., 410
Strikes, 46–47, 48–49, 51–52
Sunset laws, 160–62
Supplemental security income (SSI),
   215, 217, 245
Supply and demand, 374–75
Supreme Court, *see* U.S. Supreme
   Court
Surrey, Stanley, 88, 93
Swann v. *Charlotte-Mecklenburg*, 345,
   349, 409
Symposium on Productivity in Gov-
   ernment, 12, 14

T

Taft, Robert, 64, 362
Taft, William Howard, 408
Task Force on Housing Costs, 297
Tax, consumption, 94–95, 102–6
Taxable income, 84, 86, 87
Taxation in federal government,
   62–67
Taxes, 461 (table), 462–63 (table);
   rising, 55–57; public opinion of,
   58–60; state and local, 58, 59; compared to other countries, 60; allocation of, 65–67; consumption, 66;
   city, 314–16

Tax Reform Act of 1969, 84, 89
Tax structure, composition of, 60, 62
Tax system, American, 67–74
Taylor Act, 51
Truman, Harry S., 144, 373
Twain, Mark, 55

U

Unemployment insurance, 245–60
Unemployment rate, 324, 425–26
Uniform Crime Reports, 275
Unionization, 46–54
United Mine Workers Union, 50
United Nations, 389–90
U.S. Arms Control and Disarmament
   Agency, 147–48
U.S. Civil Rights Commission, 203
U.S. Congress, 6, 29–38 *passim*, 84,
   107–11 *passim*, 129–32 *passim*,
   154, 207, 359, 406, 435; and budget
   reform, 162–66; and crime, 285–86
U.S. Supreme Court, 32, 50, 131,
   285–86, 311, 317, 334–46 *passim*,
   351–59 *passim*, 408–17
Urban blight, 308–18
Urban renewal, 310–18
Urban transit, 312–14

V

Veterans Administration, 16
Vietnam War, 136, 138, 144
Voluntary conscription, 148–49

W

Wagner Act, 49
Wagner, Robert F., 290–91

Wagner's Law, 369
War on poverty, 393–99
Weber case, 334
Welfare, 167, 169, 215–32
Welfare state, xvii, xix–xx, 124,
 177–81, 381–82, 434–37
White House, 7, 32
Wilson, James Q., 281, 282, 287
Windfall profits tax, 59
Work ethic, 76
World War I, 56, 124, 127

World War II, 56, 69, 102, 115,
 124–36 *passim*, 143, 371, 373

Y

Yochelson, Samuel, 283

Z

Zeidler, Frank P., 44
Zero population growth, 421–24